# TELE -

# 1998

### COMPILED BY
### MIKE PRESTON

## THE REFERENCE BOOK OF MUSIC FOR TELEVISION COMMERCIALS, PROGRAMMES FILMS AND SHOWS

# MIKE PRESTON MUSIC 1998

T E L E - T U N E S   1 9 9 8

The Reference Book Of Music For
Television Commercials, Programmes
Films and Shows

16th Edition Completely Revised 1998
First Edition Published 1979

Compiled and Edited by Mike Preston
Assisted by Pru and Robb Preston
With Cathy and Dale Wattam

Published in Great Britain 1998

ISBN 0 906655 15 3

Published 1998 by
Mike Preston Music
The Glengarry
Thornton Grove
Morecambe
Lancashire
LA4 5PU
England
UK

Orig Copyright Regs. Stationers Hall
London England 1979, 1986 and 1994
Registration Number B9 / 1187 / 37068

Printed and Bound in England by
Redwood Books, Trowbridge,
Wiltshire BA14 8RN

T E L E - T U N E S   1 9 9 8

# CONTENTS

TELE-TUNES: Updated Quarterly Supplements
Published in April July and October under
ISSN 0266-6944 Subscription Details p.351

TELE-TUNES 1998 : THE REFERENCE BOOK OF MUSIC FOR TV
COMMERCIALS, TV PROGRAMMES, FILMS AND SHOWS

THE 16TH COMPLETELY REVISED EDITION OF TELE-TUNES

---

*TELEVISION COMMERCIALS*
ALPHABETICAL PRODUCT-MUSIC TITLE-(COMPOSER if Known)-
ARTIST-LABEL-(DISTRIBUTOR)-CATALOGUE NUMBER-(FORMAT)
*Note: The Artist Listed Is Not Always The Performer On
The Commercial. Ads With Specially Commissioned Music
Are usually marked unavailable or NA = NOT AVAILABLE*

---

*TELEVISION PROGRAMMES / FILMS AND SHOWS* Integrated A-Z
TELEVISION: PROGRAMME TITLE-PRODUCTION COMPANY-T/X DATE
            THEME TITLE-COMPOSER-ARTIST-LABEL (DISTRIB)
            CATALOGUE NUMBER (FORMAT) *NA= NOT AVAILABLE*
FILMS:      TITLE-YEAR-SCORE COMPOSER -S/T- OTHER INFO-
            LABEL (DISTRIB)-CATALOGUE NUMBER-(FORMAT)
SHOWS:      COMPOSER/LYRICIST-ORIG.CAST-YEAR-LEADING
            CAST-LABEL (DIST)-CATALOGUE NUMBER-(FORMAT)

NOTE: NEW CROSS REFERENCE LISTING OF TV THEMES etc.
STATES HOW MANY VERSIONS CAN BE FOUND IN COLLECTIONS

---

*COLLECTIONS*
OVER 400 COLLECTIONS NUMBERED FROM 1 UP AND BY TITLE
AND ARTIST ALPHABETICALLY.COLLECTION NUMBER-TITLE (OR)
ARTIST/COMPOSER SURNAME-RECORD LABEL-(DISTRIBUTOR)-CAT
ALOGUE NUMBER-(FORMAT)-YEAR + CROSS REFERENCED TRACKS

---

*WALT DISNEY / JAMES BOND / ELVIS PRESLEY*
ALPHABETICAL DISNEY AUDIO & VIDEO INDEX. JAMES BOND AND
ELVIS PRESLEY CHRONOLOGICAL FILM INDEX.

---

NB: MOST OF THE ITEMS LISTED IN THIS BOOK ARE CURRENTLY
AVAILABLE FROM RECORD SHOPS. RECENT DELETIONS ARE GIVEN
FOR REFERENCE ONLY, SOME ITEMS MAY ONLY BE AVAILABLE
FROM SPECIALIST IMPORT DISTRIBUTORS

---

TV ADS, PROGRAMMES, FILMS & SHOWS *NOT LISTED* PLUS ITEMS
*DELETED* FROM PREVIOUS EDITIONS ARE HELD FOR REFERENCE
IN THE MIKE PRESTON MUSIC INFORMATION DATABASE. THIS
DATABASE CONTAINS DETAILS OF TV AND FILM MUSIC COVERING
A FAR WIDER SPECTRUM THAN WE CAN HOPE TO PUBLISH IN THE
BOOK OR SUPPLEMENTS.     ACCESS TO THIS INFORMATION IS
AVAILABLE TO SUBSCRIBERS TO THE FULL TELE-TUNES 1998
SUBSCRIPTION SERVICE : FOR DETAILS SEE PAGE 351

---

7UP-3 "Runaway" (Del Shannon-Max Crook) by DEL SHANNON
  *DELTA-TARGET (BMG): CD 6011 (CD)*
7UP-2 "Rain Rain Beautiful Rain" (Joseph Shambalala)
  THE LADYSMITH BLACK MAMBAZO on 'Shaka Zulu'
  *W.BROS (WEA): WX 94C (MC) 925582-2 (CD)*
7UP-1 "Disco Inferno" (Leroy Green-Ron Kersey)
  *TV version unavailable* orig by TRAMMPS - featured
  on -S/T- to 'SATURDAY NIGHT FEVER' *(RSO-POLYDOR)*
ADDICTION (Faberge) "Gopher Tango" PEREZ PRADO & HIS
  ORCH 'Cha Cha Cha D'Amour' (Ultra Lounge Volume 9)
  *CAPITOL (EMI): CDEMS 1596 (CD)*
ADIDAS "Dive" by The PROPELLERHEADS *WALL OF SOUND
  (Vital): WALLT 034 (12"s limited edit of 5000)*
AEG "Morning" from 'Peer Gynt Suite No.1 op.46'(GRIEG)
AER LINGUS "Andante" - 'Piano Concerto No.21' (MOZART)
AIRTOURS "Let's Work Together" (Wilbert Harrison) by
  CANNED HEAT 'Best Of Canned Heat'
  *LIBERTY (EMI): CZ 226 (CD) TCGO 2026 (MC)*
ALBERTO PURE & CLEAR "Polegnala E Todata" p.Momentum
  BULGARIAN VOICES on 'Les Mystere Des Voix' Vol.1
  *4AD (Pinn):CAD 603CD(CD) CADC 603(MC)*
ALL GOLD (Terry's) "Will You" by HAZEL O'CONNOR feat
  WESLEY MacGOOGHAN (sax) 'Live In Berlin' on
  *START (DISC): SRH 804 (CD) see also COLLECT.274*
ALLIED DUNBAR-3 "Let's Face The Music And Dance" (Ir
  • ving Berlin) NAT KING COLE *EMI: CDEM 312 (CDs)*
ALLIED DUNBAR-2 "You Can't Always Get What You Want"
  (Jagger-Richards) ROLLING STONES 'Let It Bleed'
  *DECCA (Poly): 820 052-2 (CD)*
ALLIED DUNBAR-1 "Chanson De Matin No.2" Op.15 (ELGAR)
  London PO - *EMI EX 290617-3 (2LP) EX 290617-5 (MC)*
ALPEN-2 "Ocean Drive" LIGHTHOUSE FAMILY 'Ocean Drive'
  *POLYDOR (Poly): 523 787-2 (CD) -4 (MC)*
ALPEN-1 based on "Reasons To Be Cheerful Pt.3" (I.Dury)
  orig by IAN DURY & THE BLOCKHEADS on 'Sex Drugs and
  Rock'n'Roll' *DEMON (Pinn): FIENDCD 69 (CD)*
ALPEN MUESLI "Sun Rising" (Jon Marsh) from 'Happiness'
  BELOVED *WEA: WX 299(C)(CD) see also COLLECT.267*
ALTON TOWERS "In The Hall Of The Mountain King" from
  'Peer Gynt Suite' (GRIEG) *many recordings*
AMBRE SOLAIRE "Relax" FRANKIE GOES TO HOLLYWOOD *ZTT-
  ISLAND: ZTTIQ 1 (Dbl LP) ZCIQ 1 (C) ZCIDQ 101 (CD)*
AMBROSIA RICE (Art competition ad) "Left Bank Two" by
  NOVELTONES 'SOUND GALLERY 2' *EMI: CDTWO 2002 (CD)*
AMIGA GAMES "Sunshine On A Rainy Day" (Glover-Pollock)
  ZOE *M&G (Poly): MAGS(MAGX)(MAGCD) 14 (7"/12"/CDs)*
ANCHOR BUTTER-4 "Born Free" (John Barry-Don Black)
  *TV arrangement unavailable. see also 'BORN FREE'*
ANCHOR BUTTER-3 based on "My Girl" (William Robinson-
  Ronald White) orig TEMPTATIONS on *MOTOWN (Poly):
  530015-2(CD) -4(MC) -5(DCC)* OTIS REDDING 'Dock Of
  The Bay' *ATLANTIC (WEA): 9548 31708-2(CD) -4(MC)*
ANCHOR BUTTER-2 "In The Mood" (Andy Razaf-Joe Garland)
  GLENN MILLER ORCH *RCA (BMG): PD 89260 (CD)*

ANCHOR BUTTER-1 "Day Trip To Bangor" (Fiddlers Dram)
FIDDLERS DRAM *DINGLES: SID 211 (7"s)*
ANCHOR CREAM SWIRLS music based on "Open House" theme
(Brian Fahey)*(TV Vers.unavail)* original by BRIAN FA
HEY ORCH 'SOUND GALLERY 2' *EMI: CDTWO 2002 (CD)*
ANCHOR SLOW MATURE CHEDDAR "Canon In D" (PACHELBEL)
ANDREX "Lonely Pup" (A.Alexander) *TV vers.unavailable*
ADAM FAITH 60's version on *EMI: CDEM 1513 (2CD)*
ANTI DRINK DRIVING CAMPAIGN "In The Sumertime" (Ray Dor
set) *SARAJA (THE): MJCDS 1 (CD single)* also avail:
orig MUNGO JERRY *OLD GOLD (Pickwick): OG 3505 (CD)*
APPLETISE "Tempted" performed by SQUEEZE on 'Greatest
Hits' *A.& M. (Poly): 397 181-2 (CD)*
AQUA LIBRA "Cico Buff" from 'Bluebell Knoll' by COCTEAU
TWINS *4AD Records: CAD(CADC)CADT 807 (LP/CD/MC)*
ARGOS "Cryin' Mood" *TV arr.by* RONNIE PARIS *unavailable*
orig song by ELLA FITZGERALD on 'Early Years 1' on
*GRP (BMG): GRP 26182 (2CD)*
ARIEL FUTUR "Canon In D" (PACHELBEL) on 'Essential
Classics' *POLY: 431 541-2 (CD) -4 (MC)*
ARIEL ULTRA 'Overture to The Thieving Magpie' Opera 'La
Gazza Ladra' (ROSSINI) *many recordings available*
ARISTON (Electronic Stabilisers ad) "Shake Your Booty"
(Casey-Finch) orig by KC & The SUNSHINE BAND 'Best
Of KC & S.Band' *EMI ROULETTE (EMI): CDROU 5007 (CD)*
ARTHUR'S CAT FOOD-2 "Sexy Eyes" (Robert Mather-Keith
Stegall-Chris Waters) DR.HOOK "Completely Hooked:
est of" *CAPITOL (EMI): 799209-2 (CD) TCESTV 2 (MC)*
ARTHUR'S CAT FOOD-1 "What Do You Get" (Shelley-Devoto)
BUZZCOCKS *FAME-MFP (EMI): CDFA 3241 (CD)*
ASDA-2 (Bottom Patting ads) composed by Roger Greenaway
and arranged by Graham Preskett *unavailable*
ASDA-1 "Perfect" (Mark E.Nevin) FAIRGROUND ATTRACTION
'First Of A Million Kisses' *RCA: 74321 13439-2 (CD)*
AUDI MOON VEHICLE (AUDI A8)-2 "Moonlight Sonata"
(BEETHOVEN) *TV version unavailable*
AUDI MOON VEHICLE (AUDI A8)-1 "Mooncar" (Vince Pope)
Music Gallery *unavailable*
AUSTRALIA (Seen To Be Believed) "Epic" (JOHN ALTMAN)
p.Jeff Wayne Music *unavailable*
AUTO WINDSCREENS-2 "Toreador's Song" from 'Carmen'
(BIZET) *many recorded verions available*
AUTO WINDSCREENS-1 "My Guy" (William Robinson) orig:
MARY WELLS 'My Guy' *CHARLY CLASS: CDCD 1146 (CD)*
AVANTE GARDE - see 'IMPULSE AVANTE GARDE'
AXA EQUITY & LAW "Don't Worry Be Happy" BOBBY McFERRIN
'Walking On Sunshine' *KENWEST (THE):KNEWCD 742(CD)*
'Best Of B.M.' *BLUENOTE (EMI): CDP 853329-2 (CD)*
**B**ACARDI "Phone-In" by PETER LAWLOR *unavailable*
BACI CHOCOLATES (a) "Overture Cavalleria Rusticana"
(MASCAGNI) (b) "Nessun Dorma" (PUCCINI) *various*
BAILEYS IRISH CREAM-2 "Big Bamboozle" (B.Adamson)
BARRY ADAMSON from 'Oedipus Schmoedipus'
*MUTE-RTM (Disc): CDSTUMM 134 (CD)*

BAILEYS IRISH CREAM-1 "Barcarolle"(Tales Of Hoffmann)
(OFFENBACH) Elizabeth Schwarzkopft-Jeanine Collard
'CLASSIC EXP.' *EMI (CD)(TC)EMTVD 45 (2CD/MC) 94TV
vers.*(G.MacCormack-Simon Goldenberg) *unavailable*
BARBIE DOLL based on "She'd Rather Be With Me" (Gerry
Bonner-Alan Gordon) orig by TURTLES on 'Happy Toget
her Very Best' *MCI (THE): MCCD 046 (CD)*
BARCLAYCARD / VISA "If I Had A Hammer" (Pete Seeger-Les
Hayes) sung by TRINI LOPEZ *KOCH: 399531 (CD)* also:
*WOODFORD (THE-DISC): WMCD 5647 (CD) WMMC 4657 (MC)*
BARCLAY'S BANK Cashpoint "Ride On" by LITTLE AXE on
*WIRED (3MV-Sony): WIRED 27 (CD) WIRED 47 (MC)*
BEAMISH STOUT (Courage) "Karla With A K" by THE HOOTERS
on 'One Way Home' *SONY: 465564-2 (CD) 4 (MC)*
BEEFEATER RESTAURANTS "Moment Scale" SILENT POETS 'CAFE
DEL MAR IBIZA' VOL.2 *REACT (Vital): REACTCD 062(CD)*
BENDICKS MINTS (Bendicks Of Mayfair) "Missing You" (Rom
eo-Law-Mazelle) SOUL II SOUL feat KYM MAZELLE on
'New Dance Decade' *VIRGIN (EMI): DIXCD 90 (CD)*
BENYLIN "Nessun Dorma" 'Turandot' (Puccini) *TV version
by* ANTONIO NAGORE and R.P.O. *unavailable*
BHS (BRITISH HOME STORES) "Don't Worry Be Happy" BOBBY
McFERRIN 'Best Of' *BLUENOTE (EMI): CDP 853329-2 CD*
BIRDS CUSTARD based on "Bloop Bleep" (Frank Loesser)
*orig version by* DANNY KAYE *MCA deleted*
BIRDS-EYE CRISPY CHICKEN "Chicken Rhythm" (Slim Gaill
ard) SLIM GAILLARD on 'The Legendary McVouty" on
*HEP (New Note/Pinn): HEPCD 6 (CD)*
BIRDS-EYE MENU MASTER "Just The Two Of Us" (B.Withers-
W.Salter-R.McDonald) GROVER WASHINGTON with Bill
Withers on 'Winelight' *ELEKTRA: K2-52262 (CD)*
BIRDS-EYE VEGETABLE CUISINE "Bread And Butter" (Parks
Turnbow) NEWBEATS *SEQUEL/CASTLE (BMG) NEXTCD 231*
BISTO-2 "Black Eyes" or "Dark Eyes" Russian Folk melody
"Otschi Tchornyie" (Niklas Krotsch) ver: PALM COURT
THEATRE ORCH 'Picnic Party' *CHANDOS: CHAN 8437 (CD)*
BISTO-1 "Save The Best For Last" by VANESSA WILLIAMS
'The Comfort Zone' *POLYDOR: 511267-2 (CD) -4(MC)*
BLACK & DECKER-3 (WORKMATE PLUS) "Acroche Toi Caroline"
(from VISION ON) PARIS STUDIO GROUP *COLL* 'THIS IS
THE RETURN OF CULT FICTION' *VIRGIN: VTCD 112 (CD)*
BLACK & DECKER-2 (DUSTBUSTER) "Blockbuster" (M.Chapman-
Nicki Chinn) orig The SWEET *RCA (BMG): ND(NK) 74313*
BLACK & DECKER-1 (SNAKELIGHT) based "The Wanderer" (E.
Maresca) DION 'Runaround Sue' *ACE (Pinn): CDCHM 148*
BLACK MAGIC-2 "Love Is The Sweetest Thing" (Ray Noble)
AL BOWLLY & RAY NOBLE ORCHEST.*EMI:CDP 794341-2 (CD)*
BLACK MAGIC-1 (It's The Black Magic) 'Stranger Theme'
(Christopher Gunning) *unavailable*
BLOCKBUSTER VIDEO "Sound and Vision" (Bowie) by DAVID
BOWIE 'SINGLES COLL' *EMI: CD(TC)EM 1512 (CD/MC/LP))*
BLUE BAND MARGARINE "Pastoral-Shepherds Thanksgiving Af
ter The Storm" 'Symph No.6 in F.Major' (BEETHOVEN)
BODDINGTONS-5 "Athlete" by JOE GLASSMAN *unavailable*

BODDINGTONS-4 "Release Me" (Miller-Stevenson-Harris)
 *TV version* MIKE FLOWERS POPS *unavailable*
BODDINGTONS-3 (Beach ad) "Stay" (Maurice Williams)
 TV vers.not available / *version by* THE HOLLIES
 on 'Best Of' *EMI: CDEMTV 74 (CD)*
BODDINGTONS-2 (Gondola ad) "O Sole Mio" (Di Capua)
 sung by ENRICO CARUSO '18 Favourite Arias & Songs'
 on *Deja Vu Refer (THE): DCRECD(DVREMC) 61 (CD/MC)*
BODDINGTONS-1 (Smoke Rings ad) "Smoke Rings" (Roger
 Webb) *unavailable*
BOLD WASHING POWDER "Ebben-Ne Andro Lontana" Aria from
 'La Wally' (A.CATALINI) *see coll* 'ESSENTIAL OPERA'
BOOTS (Merry Christmas 96) "Make Someone Happy" (Styne-
 Green-Comden) sung by JIMMY DURANTE *film* 'SLEEPLESS
 IN SEATTLE' *EPIC (Sony): 473594-2 (CD) -4 (MC) also
 WB (WEA): W.0385CD (CDs) W.0835C (MCs)*
BOOTS CHEMISTS (Winter 96) "I'm Alive" (Clint Ballard)
 The HOLLIES on 'Best Of' *EMI: CD(TC)EMTV 74 (CD/MC)*
BOOTS NO.7 -2 'Red' "Cose Cose Cose" (Castro) by PEREZ
 PRADO ORCHESTRA *RCA (BMG): number unconfirmed*
BOOTS NO.7 -1a "La Cumparsita" (G.Matos Rodriguez) *TV
 vers.arr.by Jeff Wayne (unavailable)* orig recording
 by XAVIER CUGAT ORCHESTRA on 'Mundo Latino' collect
 on *SONY: SONYTV2CD (CD) SONYTV2MC (MC) also on*
 -S/T- of 'KIKA' *IMS (Polyg): E.51777-2 (CD) others:*
 STANLEY BLACK OR 'S'Wonderful' *PRESID: PLCD 527(CD)*
BOOTS NO.7 -1b "You Wear It Well" (Rod Stewart-Martin
 Quintetton) ROD STEWART Coll 'Best Of Rod Stewart'
 on *WEA: 926034-2 (CD) WX 314C (MC)*
BOOTS NO.7 -1c "I Say A Little Prayer" (Burt Bacharach-
 Hal David) TV instrumental version *not available
 orig* ARETHA FRANKLIN (1968) *ATLANTIC Records (WEA)*
BOUNTY BAR (a)"Try A Little Tenderness" (Woods-Campbell
 Connelly)*TV vers.unavailable* OTIS REDDING *ATLANTIC
 (WEA): K41118-2 (CD)* (b) (Island ad) orig music by
 Malcolm McLaren *unavailable*
BP-MOBIL "Sing Sing Sing" (Louis Prima) *TV Version not
 available.* orig. by BENNY GOODMAN & HIS ORCHESTRA
 feat.GENE KRUPA (drs) on '16 Most Requested Songs'
 *COLUMBIA (Sony Music): 474 396-2 (CD) -4 (MC)*
BRANSTON PICKLE "Left Bank 2" by WAYNE HILL on 'A-Z OF
 BR.TV THEMES V2' *PLAY IT AGAIN (BMG): PLAY 006 (CD)*
BRISTOL & WEST BUILDING SOC. "Adagietto" from Symphony
 5 in C.Sharp Minor (Gustav MAHLER) *many recordings*
BRITANNIA BUILDING SOCIETY "Ain't No Stopping Us Now"
 (Gene McFadden-John Whitehead-Jim Cohn) McFADDEN &
 WHITEHEAD 'Gr.Hits' *KENWEST (TBD): KWEST 5406 (CD)*
BRITISH AIRWAYS-4 (1997 ad) "Flower Duet" from 'Lakme'
 (DELIBES) sung by LESLEY GARRETT 'Diva' *Sil.Screen
 (Koch): SONGCD 903 (CD)* also available by the VARD
 SISTERS on 'HEAVENLY' *SONY: 488 092-2 (CD) -4 (MC)*
BRITISH AIRWAYS-3 (1996 ad) "Fashion Show No.2" from
 'Three Colors Red' ZBIGNIEUW PREISNER on 'Spirits
 of Nature' *VIRGIN (EMI): VTCD 87 (CD)*

BRITISH AIRWAYS-2 (Winking Eye ad 1993-96) "Aria" by
YANNI on 'Live At The Acropolis' on *PRIVATE MUSIC
(BMG): 01005 82122-2 (CD) see also COLLECTION 267*
BRITISH AIRWAYS-1 (ads 1993-96) "Flower Duet" from
'Lakme' (Delibes) / various recordings:-
1.MADY MESPLE-DANIELLE MILLET & PARIS OPERA ORCH
*EMI: 568 307-2 (CD)* 'Most Famous Movie Classics 2'
2.MALCOLM McLAREN "Aria On Air" *Virgin: VTCD 28
(CD)* 'NEW PURE MOODS' see *COLLECTION 267*
3.CRAZY FAN TUTTI African Mix "VIVA" *Oval (WEA):
OVAL 109CD (CD) OVAL 109T (12") OVAL 109C (MC)*
4.JENKINS-RATLEDGE PRODUCTS.(Space ad) *unavailable
other mus:* "Va Pensiero" (Chorus Of Hebrew Slaves)
from Act 3 'Nabucco' (Verdi) - *many versions*
5. "Fashion Show No.1" -S/T- 'THREE COLOURS (RED)'
ZBIGNIEW PREISNER *Virgin: CDVMM 14 / 839 784-2 (CD)*
BRITISH GAS-2 "The Universal" by BLUR from
'The Great Escape' *FOOD-EMI (EMI): FOOD(CD)(TC) 14*
BRITISH GAS-1"Dance A Cachucha Fandango Bolero"
from act 2 of 'The Gondoliers' (GILBERT & SULLIVAN)
*MFP (EMI): CDCFP 4609 (CD) TCCFP 4609 (MC)*
BRITISH HEART FOUNDATION-2 "Waiting For The Miracle" by
LEONARD COHEN from 'The Future' *SONY: 472 498-2
(CD) -4 (MC) -1 (LP) -3 (MD)*
BRITISH HEART FOUNDATION-1 "Stop In The Name Of Love"
(Holland-Dozier-Holland) DIANA ROSS AND SUPREMES
*MOTOWN (Poly): 530 013-2 (CD) 530 013-4 (MC)*
BRITISH MEAT-4 "I Got You Babe" (S.Bono) SONNY & CHER
*ATLANTIC (WEA): 9548 30152-2 (CD) -4 (MC)*
BRITISH MEAT-3 "Let There Be Love" (I.Grant-L.Rand)
NAT KING COLE '20 Golden Greats' *EMI: CD(TC)EMTV 9*
BRITISH MEAT-2 "Addicted To Love" (Robert Palmer) by
ROBERT PALMER on 'Addic tions' *ISLAND (Poly): CID
9944 (CD) ICT 9944 (MC) 842 301-5 (DCC)*
BRITISH MEAT-1 "Don't Tell Me Your Troubles" (Don Gib
son) by SHAKIN' STEVENS from 'Shaky' *EPIC (Sony):
450524-2* (CD) -4* (MC) EPC 10027* (LP) *deleted*
BRITISH RAIL INTERCITY - *see under* 'INTERCITY'
BRITISH TELECOM - see under BT
BRUT-2 "The Men Are Back" (Ray Gomez) *unavailable*
BRUT-1 "On The Road" from soundtrack of 'Rain Man'
-S/T- *CAPITOL (EMI): CZ 4567 (CD) TCATAK 180 (MC)*
BRYLCREEM-2 "Breakdown" (Tony Gibber) *unavailable*
BRYLCREEM-1 "Principles Of Lust" (Curly-Fairstein) by
ENIGMA *VIRGIN: DINSD 110 (CDs) DINSC 110 (MC)*
BT "Always On My Mind" sung by ELVIS PRESLEY *RCA (BMG)
74321 48541-2 (CDs) 74321 48541-4 (MC)* also on 'All
-Time Greatest Hits' *RCA (BMG): PD 90100-2 (2CD)*
BT **Pager Easy Reach** "I've Gotta Get A Message To You"
(Gibb Bros) BEE GEES 'Very Best' *POLY: 847 339-2 CD*
BT **Pay Phones** ad "Secret" (Dave A.Stewart) DAVE STEWART
on *EEAST WEST(WEA): EW 009CD (CDs) EW 009C (MC)*
BT **Weekend Rates** "Quintet For Strings (Violin,Cello,and
Viola) in C" (D.956) (SSHUBERT) *various recordings*

BUDWEISER-8 (poker game) "Dirt" by DEATH IN VEGAS on
    *CONCRETE (RTM/DISC): HARD 27CD (CDs)*
BUDWEISER-7 (money in suitcase/taxi) "Crawl" composed
    and produced by ROBERT WHITE *unavailable*
BUDWEISER-6 "St.James Infirmary Blues" (Irving Mills,
    adapt.from trad.folk song) sung by SNOOKS EAGLIN
    *cat.no.unconfirmed. version by* CAB CALLOWAY on 'Hi
    De Hi De Ho' *RCA (BMG): 74321 26729-2 + 18524-2 (CD)*
BUDWEISER-5 (Ants) "Get Down Tonight" KC & THE SUNSHINE
    BAND on 'Greatest Hits' *EMI GOLD: CDGOLD 1021 (CD)*
    *TCGOLD 1021 (MC)*
BUDWEISER-4 "Daydreamer" by MENSWEAR 'Shine Coll' *Polyg*
BUDWEISER-3 "Connection" by ELASTICA *DECEPTIVE (Vital)*
    *BLUFF 014(CD)(MC)(LPN)*
BUDWEISER-2 "The Passenger" (Iggy Pop-Ricky Gardiner)
    by MICHAEL HUTCHENCE on -S/T- 'Batman Forever' on
    *ATLANTIC (WEA): 7567 82759-2 (CD) -4 (MC)*
BUDWEISER-1 (Blues Train ad) "Smokestack Lightning"
    HOWLIN'WOLF "Smokestack Lightning" *INSTANT-CHARLY*
    *CDINS 5037 (CD) TCINS 5037 (MC) INSD 5037 (2LP)*
BURGER KING-4 "Who Do Ya Love" by GEORGE THOROGOOD &
    THE DESTROYERS from 'Move It On Over'
    *DEMON (Pinn): FIENDCD 58 (CD)*
BURGER KING-3 "Double Vision" by FOREIGNER on 'Best'
    *ATLANTIC-E.WEST (WEA): 7567 80805-2(CD) WX 469C(MC)*
BURGER KING-2 "I Don't Want To Set The World On Fire"
    (E.Dunham-E.Seiler-S.Marcus-B.Benjamin) *TV version*
    *unavailable.* orig by INK SPOTS on 'Best Of' *MFP EMI*
    *TCMFP 50529 (MC)* GERALDO & HIS Orch with DOROTHY
    CARLESS- 'Dance Band Hits' *MFP (EMI) CDDL 1885 (CD)*
BURGER KING-1 based on "That's The Way I Like It"
    (Harry Casey-Robert Finch) KC & SUNSHINE BAND (75)
    'Best Of' *EMI ROULETTE: CD(TC) ROU 5007 (CD/MC)*
BUSINESS PAGES "You're More Than A Number In My Little
    Red Book" (Tony Macaulay-Roger Greenaway) DRIFTERS
    on 'Kissin' In The Back Row' COLL *MCI (THE): MCCD*
    *100 (CD) MCTC 100 (MC)*
BUXTON SPRING WATER "Concerto For Cello & Orch In E.Min
    Op.85" (ELGAR) Royal Philh Orch (YEHUDI MENUHIN) &
    JULIAN LLOYD WEBBER - *PHILIPS (Poly): 416354-2 (CD)*
**C.**& A. "Ya Ho He" by NC TRIBE *WOLFEN (German import*
    *through ZYX dist): WOL 00308 (CDs)*
CADBURY (tastes like heaven) "Show Me Heaven" (M.McKee-
    J.Rifkin-E.Rackin) from film 'Days Of Thunder' orig
    MARIA McKEE on Coll 'Number One Movies Album' on
    *POLYGRAM TV: 525 962-2 (CD)*
CADBURY'S *see brand name:* 'Milk Tray'/'HighLights' etc.
CAFFREY'S ALES (a) "Jump Around" (Muggeraud-Shrody) by
    HOUSE OF PAIN on *XL (WEA): XLS 32 CD (CDs) XLT 32*
    *(12"s) XLC 32 (MC)* + 'HOUSE OF PAIN' *XLCD(MC) 111*
    (b) 'MILLER'S CROSSING' (Carter Burwell) -S/T- on
    *VARESE (Pinn): VSD 5288 (CD) VSC 5288 (MC) deleted*
CALLARD & BOWSER TOFFEES "River Kwai March" (Kenneth
    Alford) see BRIDGE ON THE RIVER KWAI *Film Section*

CANON PHOTO COPIERS-2 "T'ain't What You Do" (Sy Oliver-
J.Young) BANANARAMA WITH FUN BOY 3 on *LONDON (Poly)*
*828 146-2 (CD) KRAMR 5 (MC) RAMR 5 (LP)*
CANON PHOTO COPIERS-1 "Ndebele" (I.Cowley) *unavailable*
CAREX BODYWASH "Raindrops Keep Falling On My Head" from
'Butch Cassidy & The Sundance Kid'(Bacharach-David)
*TV vers.unavailable* orig -S/T- *POLY: 551 4330-2(CD)*
CARLING BLACK LABEL-3 "Dam Busters March" (Eric Coates)
*Coll (94 book)* 'SALUTE TO HEROES'/'BIG WAR THEMES'/
'GREAT BRITISH LIGHT ORCH' (S.Torch)/'MOVIE BRASS'
CARLING BLACK LABEL-2 (Synchro-Swimmers) "Excaliber"
(Rachel Portman) p.Jeff Wayne Music *unavailable*
CARLING BLACK LABEL-1 (squirrel) "Mission Impossible"
(Lalo Schifrin) *see TV Programme*
CARLING PREMIER-2 "California Dreamin'" (J.Phillips)
*MCA (BMG): MCSTD 48058 (CDs)* also on 'MAMAS & PAPAS
Golden Greats' *MCA (BMG): DMCM 5001 CD*
CARLING PREMIER-1 "Cars" (Gary Numan) by GARY NUMAN on
'Peel Sessions' *STRANGE FRUIT Rio (Poly): SFMCD
202 (CD) SFMAC 202 (MC)*
CARLSBERG (Guitars) "Duelling Guitars" (Dan Simmons-Joe
Glasman) *not available* note: similar to "Duelling
Banjos" from film 'Deliverance' *WB (WEA) K.16223 7"*
CARLSBERG EXPORT-2 *(Beach Cricket)* "An Ubhal As Airde"
(The Highest Apple) RUNRIG on "The Cutter And The
Clan" *CHRYSALIS (EMI): CCD(ZCHR) 1669 (CD/MC)* and
*CHRYSALIS (EMI): CD(TC)CHS 5021 or 5029 (CDs/MC)*
CARLSBERG EXPORT-1 *(Wedding Party)* "Cherry Pink Apple
Blossom White" (Jacques Lerue-M.David) PEREZ PRADO
ORCH on 'King Of Mambo' *RCA (BMG): ND 90424 (CD)* /
EDDIE CALVERT on 'EMI Years' *EMI:CD(TC)EMS 1461*
CARLSBERG LAGER "Make Me Smile (Come Up And See Me)"
(Steve Harley) *orig 1977 by* STEVE HARLEY & COCKNEY
REBEL on 'Best Years Of Our Lives' *EMI: CZ 385 (CD)*
CARTE NOIR Kenco "Try To Remember" fr.'The Fantasticks'
(Harvey Schmidt-Tom Jones) *TV vers.sung by* RICHARD
DARBYSHIRE *VIRGIN (EMI): VSCDT(VSC) 1584 (CDs/MC)*
CATHAY PACIFIC-2 Part of'Symph.No.4 in A Op.90 Italian'
(MENDELSSOHN) *various recordings available*
CATHAY PACIFIC-1 'Drums' "Drums" (Ryuichi Sakamoto)
(originating from Hong Kong) *unavailable*
CELEBRATION MINI BARS "Montok Point" (WILLIAM ORBIT) by
STRANGE CARGO 'Hinterland Strange Cargo Volume 4'
*WEA: 4509 99295-2 (CD)*
CELLNET "Busy Line" (Murray Semos-Frank Stanton) - ROSE
MURPHY with PETER SKELLERN *RCA (BMG): PD 44088(CDs)*
from 'A String of Pearls' *ARIOLA (BMG): 260342 (CD)*
CESAR DOG FOOD "If You Leave Me Now" (Peter Cetera) by
CHICAGO *COLUMBIA (Sony): CD 32391(CD) 40-32391 (MC)*
CHANEL ALLURE "Spiritual High" (Anderson-Vangelis) by
MOODSWINGS featuring CHRISSIE HYNDE on 'Moodfood'
*ARISTA BMG (BMG): 74321 III/0-2 (CD) -4 (MC) -1(LP)*
CHANEL "L'EGOISTE" "Dance Of The Knights" from Act.1 of
'Romeo & Juliet' Op.64 (PROKOFIEV) *many recordings*

CHANEL NO.5 (a) "Sea Of Love" (George Khoury-Phil Bapti
    ste) (1959) MARTY WILDE *POLYGRAM: 551 794-2 (CD)*
CHANEL NO.5 (b) "My Baby Just Cares For Me" (Donaldson-
    Kahn) NINA SIMONE on *CHARLY RECORDS*
CHANEL NO.5 (c) "I Wanna Be Loved By You" (Kalmar-Ruby-
    Stothart) from 'SOME LIKE IT HOT' *w:* MARILYN MONROE
CHANEL NO.19 (a) "Spring"'Four Seasons Suite No.1 in E'
    (VIVALDI) *many recordings available*
CHANEL NO.19 (b) "Arrival Of The Queen Of Sheba" 'Solom
    on' Oratorio (HANDEL) *many recordings available*
CHANNEL TUNNEL - see 'EUROTUNNEL'
CHEESESTRINGS "Bend Me Shape Me" (S.English-L.Weiss)
    *TV Version unavailable* original by AMEN CORNER
CHELTENHAM & GLOUCESTER B.SOC. (underwater 'diver' ad)
    "Song Of Tears" *Virgin Vent (EMI): CDVEX 932 (CDs)*
    *also on* 'ADIEMUS 2-CANTATA MUNDI' (extract only) by
    KARL JENKINS feat MIRIAM STOCKLEY & LONDON PHIL.ORCH
    *see COLLECTIONS 9, 267*
CHOCOLATE BREAK-2 "Kinderszenen" Op.15 No.7 Traumerei
    (SCHUMANN) *played by* HOWARD SHELLEY (piano) on
    *CHANDOS (Chandos): CHAN 8814 (CD) /also by* VLADIMIR
    HOROWITZ *RCA VICT (BMG): GD(GK) 87755 (CD/MC)*
CHOCOLATE BREAK-1 "It's In His Kiss" (Rudy Clark) by
    BETTY EVERETT on comp. "Women In Love" *STARDUST-WIS
    EPACK (TBD): STACD 050 (CD)  also recorded by* CHER
CHRISTIAN AID WEEK "First Time Ever I Saw Your Face"
    (Ewan MacColl) ROBERTA FLACK on 'Best Of Roberta
    Flack' *ATLANTIC (WEA): 250840 (CD) 450840 (MC)*
CITIZEN WATCHES "Kyrie" from 'Misa Criolla' Mass (Ariel
    RAMIREZ) JOSE CARRERAS + A.Ramirez, Laredo Choral
    Salve and Bilbao Choral Society on *PHILIPS (Polyg):
    420 955-2PH (CD) 420 955-4PH (MC) 420 955-1PH (LP)*
CITROEN AX-2 "Sleep" by MARION 'This World and Body'
    *LONDON: 828 695-2 (CD) -4(MC) -1(LP) LONCD 381(CDs)*
CITROEN AX-1 "Cupid" (Sam Cooke) JOHNNY NASH 'Gr.Hits'
    *EPIC: 465306-2 (CD) -4 (MC) Old Gold: OG 9196*
CITROEN SAXO "Counter Clockwise Circle Dance" (Ly-O-Lay
    Ale-Loya) from 'SACRED SPIRIT' Collection on
    *VIRGIN EMI: CDV 2753 (CD) TCV 2753 (MC)*
CITROEN XANTIA  "Somethin' Stupid" (C.Carson Parks)
    orig (67) by FRANK & NANCY SINATRA: 'Greatest Hits'
    *PARADISO-CNR (THE): PA 711-2 (CD)*
CITROEN XANTIA ESTATE  "Pit Stop" (Vince Pope) *unavail.*
CITROEN XSARA "Move On Up" by CURTIS MAYFIELD on 'Best
    Of Curtis Mayfield' *NECTAR (Pinn): NTMCD 538 (CD)*
CITROEN ZX-3 (Rallying) "Personality Crisis" (J.Hansen)
    NEW YORK DOLLS 'Rock'n'Roll' *Mercury 522 129-2 (CD)*
CITROEN ZX-2 16 Valve "Marriage Of Figaro" (MOZART)
CITROEN ZX-1 "You Can't Hurry Love" (Holland-Dozier-
    Holland) DIANA ROSS & SUPREMES on 'Anthology'
    *MOTOWN (Polyg): 560 196-2 (2CD)*
CLAIROL "I Got You (I Feel Good)"(James Brown) by JAMES
    BROWN on 'Sex Machine The Very Best' *POLYDOR (Poly)
    845 828-2 (CD) 845 828-4 (MC)*

CLAIROL NATURAL INSTINCTS "Flashdance (Oh What A
Feeling)" -S/T- *CASABLANCA (Poly): 811492-2 (CD)*
CLARK'S SHOES-2 "Happy Feet" (Jack Yellen-Milt Agar)
JACK HYLTON ORCH with PAT O'MALLEY (v) on 'Jack's
Back' *ASV LIVING ERA (Koch): AJAZC 5018 (MC)*
CLARK'S SHOES-1 "Overture" from 'Peter And The Wolf'
(PROKOFIEV) *many versions available*
CLASSIC BAR - see 'FOX'S CLASSIC BAR'
CLERICAL MEDICAL "Clerical Medical" (Rod Bowkett) Final
Touch Productions *unavailable*
CLOVER MARGARINE "Love Is In The Air (H.Vanda-G.Young)
*TV vers:* BOB SAKER *unavailable / original by* JOHN
PAUL YOUNG *LASERLIGHT (Target-BMG): 1221-2 (CD)*
CLUB MED "Everybody's Talking" (Fred Neil) by NILSSON
from -S/T- 'Midnight Cowboy' *EMI: CDP 748409-2 (CD)*
COCA COLA-5 (boys cricket) "Mustt Mustt" NUSRAT FATEH
ALI KHAN on 'Mustt Mustt' *REAL WORLD-VIRGIN (EMI):
CDRW 15 (CD) RWMC 15 (MC)*
COCA COLA-4 (olympics 96) "Temple Head" by TRANSGLOBAL
EXPRESS from 'Dream Of A Hundred Nations' on *Nation
RTM (Disc): NR 021CD (CD) NR 021C (MC) NR 021L (LP)*
COCA COLA-3 (soccer ad) "Eat My Goal" by COLLAPSED LUNG
*Deceptive (Vital): BLUFF 029CD (CDs) also on* Col1
'The Beautiful Game' (Official Album Of EURO 96)
*RCA (BMG): 74321 38208-2 (CD) -4 (MC)*
COCA COLA-2 "Always Coca-Cola" (Terry Coffey-John Net
tles) *not available (USA production)*
COCA COLA-1 "The First Time" (Spencer-Anthony-Boyle)
ROBIN BECK *Mercury: MER(X) 270 (7"/12") deleted*
COCA COLA early commercials collection (65 COCA-COLA co
mmercials feat various artists) including SEEKERS-
TOM JONES-ARETHA FRANKLIN-RAY CHARLES-PETULA CLARK-
SUPREMES-BEE GEES-DRIFTERS-JAN AND DEAN-MOODY BLUES
etc. *EAST ANGLIA PRODUCTIONS: CC1 (CD)*
COCA COLA - see also DIET COKE
COLGATE B.SODA TOOTHPASTE "One More Kiss Dear" (Don Per
cival) on -S/T- 'BLADERUNNER' *WEA: 4509 96574-2 /-4*
COLGATE TOOTHPASTE (Flashback ad) "I Could Be Happy" by
ALTERED IMAGES on 'Best Of Altered Images' *CONNOISS
EUR COLL (Pinn): VSOPCD 177 (CD) VSOPMC 177 (MC)*
COMFORT CONDITIONER-2 "Words Of Love" (Buddy Holly)
*TV ver.by Lisa Millett unavailable* orig BUDDY HOLLY
'20 Gold.Greats' *MCA (BMG): MCLD(MCLC) 19220(CD/MC)*
COMFORT CONDITIONER-1 "Air That I Breathe" (Hammond-Haz
lewood) by The HOLLIES *EMI: CDP 746 238-2 (CD)*
COMFORT SILK "Feeling Good" (Leslie Bricusse-Anthony
Newley) sung by NINA SIMONE on 'Feeling Good - The
Very Best Of' *VERVE (Poly): 522 669-2 (CD)*
CONCORDE WINE "(He Was) Really Saying Something" (Eddie
Holland-Norman Whitfield-William Steveson) sung by
BANANARAMA with FUN BOY 3 (1982) on 'Greatest Hits'
*LONDON (Poly): 828 106-2 (CD) -5 (DCC) KRAMC 005*
CO-OPERATIVE BANK "The Big Blue" (E.Serra) ERIC SERRA
'BIG BLUE' -S/T- *VIRGIN Fra.(Discov): 87790-2 (2CD)*

COW & GATE  BABY FOOD "Nothing Compared 2 U" (Prince)
  *TV version not available.* original by PRINCE *(WEA)*
  or SINEAD O'CONNOR *(Ensign)*
CREAM EGGS-2 "Float On" (W.Willis-A.Ingram-J.Mitchell)
  THE FLOATERS *OLD GOLD: OG 9218 (7"s)*
CREAM EGGS-1 "Intro & Outro" (Viv Stanshall) original
  by THE BONZO DOG BAND - *LIBERTY (EMI): CZ 499 (CD)*
CRISP N'DRY (based on)"Mama Don't Want No Peas An' Rice
  An'Coconut Oil" (L.Wolfe Gilbert-Charles Lofthouse)
  *TV Version by* BILL FREDERICKS *unavailable* ORIG by
  COUNT BASIE ORCHESTRA with Jimmy Rushing
CRUNCHIE (Cadbury) "I'm So Excited" (Pointer-Lawrence)
  *ORIG (82)* POINTER SISTERS on 'Break Out' *PLANET-RCA
  (BMG): FD 89450 (CD) FK 89450 (MC)*
CUSSONS-3 "Protecting The Fabric Of Life" by SACRAL
  CHAKRA *NEW WORLD MUSIC (-)*
CUSSONS-2 (PEARL) "One Fine Day" from 'Madam Butterfly"
  (PUCCINI) *many recordings available*
CUSSONS-1 (PEARL) "Venus" (Ed Marshall) FRANKIE AVALON
  1959 hit on Coll 'The Fabulous Frankie Avalon' on
  *ACE (Pinn): CDFAB 007 (CD) FABC 007 (MC)*

**D**AEWOO CAR INSURANCE "Adagietto" from 'Symphony No.5'
  (MAHLER) vers.on 'CINEMA CLASSICS 1' *NAXOS (Select)
  8551151 (CD) see listing in Collections*
DAILY TELEGRAPH "Adagio for Strings" (SAMUEL BARBER)
  *also used in 'ELEPHANT MAN' and 'PLATOON' etc.
  various recordings inc:* 'CLASSIC FM' *Collection*
DAIRY MILK-2 Cadbury "Thinkin' About Your Body" (Bobby
  McFerrin) B.McFERRIN *BLUENOTE (EMI):CDP 853329-2CD*
DAIRY MILK-1 Cadbury (Town Square) performed by THE
  LADYSMITH BLACK MAMBAZO GROUP *unavailable*
DAY NURSE "Mama Said" *TV vers.unavailable /* orig by The
  SHIRELLES on 'Best Of' *ACE (Pinn): CDCHD 356 (CD)*
DE BEERS - *see under* 'DIAMONDS'
DEEP FRESH based on "Deeply Dippy" (Fred & Richard Fair
  brass-Rob Manzoli) orig RIGHT SAID FRED (92) on *TUG
  (BMG): SNOGCD 1 (CD) SNOGMC 1 (MC) SNOGLP 1 (LP)*
DEL MONTE "Humming Chorus" from 'Madame Butterfly'
  (PUCCINI) *many recordings available*
DELIGHT-3 "Jelly's Blues" (Keith Nicholls) *unavailable*
DELIGHT-2 Spread "La Vie En Rose" (E.Piaf-R.Louiguy-F.
  Eyton) EDITH PIAF *EMI: CZ 132 (CD) TCEN 5008 (MC)*
DELIGHT-1 Cream (Pump Room Bath) "Annen Polka Op.117
  for Orch" (J.Strauss II) VIENNA P.O.(Karajan) on
  *DG (Poly): 413 432-2 (2CD) other versions available*
DELTA AIRLINES "Adiemus" (Karl Jenkins) by ADIEMUS *feat*
  MIRIAM STOCKLEY & LONDON PHILHARMONIC *VIRGIN (EMI):
  CD(TC)VE 925 (CD/MC) and VEND 4 (CDs) VENC 4 (MCs)
  also on* 'NEW PURE MOODS' *see COLLECTION 267*
DETTOL-2 "Clouds" sung by MAE McKENNA *unavailable*
DETTOL-1 "Smile" / 'Modern Times' (C.Chaplin-J.Turner-
  G.Parsons) *TV version unavailable /* NAT KING COLE
  '20 Golden Greats' *Capitol EMI: CD(TC)EMTV 9(CD/MC)*

DFS FURNITURE "Spring" from 'Four Seasons Suite'
    (VIVIALDI) *various versions available*
DHL WORLDWIDE EXPRESS "Ain't No Mountain High Enough"
    (Nick Ashford-Val Simpson) - DIANA ROSS 'Anthology'
    *MOTOWN (Pol): WD 72532 (2CD)* 'G.Hits' *WD 72478 (CD)*
DIAMOND WHITE CIDER "Moskowski Serenata" (MOSKOWSKI) by
    KREISLER-MCCORMACK on 'Kreisler-McCormack Duets' on
    *PEARL (Pavilion): GEMM CD 9315 (CD)*
DIAMONDS (A Diamond Is Forever) (De Beers) "Palladio"
    (Karl Jenkins) LONDON PHILHARMONIC ORCH (K.Jenkins)
    on 'Palladio' *SONY CLASSICAL: SK(ST) 62276 (CD/MC)*
DIET COKE-6 "I Put A Spell On You" (Hawkins) sung by
    NINA SIMONE on Coll 'Feeling Good-The Very Best Of
    Nina Simone' *VERVE (Poly): 522 669-2 (CD) -4 (MC)*
DIET COKE-5 "I Just Wanna Make Love To You" (W.Dixon)
    ETTA JAMES *MCA (BMG): MCSTD(MCSC) 48003 (CDs/MC)*
    also on COLL 'V.Best Of Blues Brother-Soul Sister'
    *DINO (Pinn): DINCD(MC) 115 (CD/MC)*
DIET COKE-4 ('Frankenstein' ad) "Passion Springs"
    (Peter Lawlor) p.Water Music *unavailable*
DIET COKE-3 "The Sabre Dance" (KHACHATURIAN) *various*
DIET COKE-2 "The Weight" (Jaime R.Robertson) THE BAND
    'Collect' *CASTLE (BMG): CCS(CD)(MC) 333 (CD/MC)*
DIET COKE-1 "I Just Wanna Make Love To You" (W.Dixon)
    ETTA JAMES on *CHESS-MCA (BMG): MCLD 19168 (CD)*
DISCOVERY - see LAND ROVER
DISNEYLAND PARIS-2 "When You Wish Upon A Star" (Leigh
    Harline-Ned Washington) sung by CLIFF EDWARDS
DISNEYLAND PARIS-1 "It's Magic" sung by DINAH WASHING
    TON on CD 'What A Difference A Day Makes' *MERCURY
    (Poly): 818 815-2 (CD)*
DORITOS - see WALKERS DORITOS
DRAMBUIE (Dinner Party) "45 Revolution" (Martin Swan)
    MOUTH MUSIC on 'Blue Door Green Sea' *TRIPLE EARTH
    (Sterns): TERRACDEP 209 (CD)*
DRIFTER BAR (Nestle) "Drift Away" (Dobie Gray) - DOBIE
    GRAY *COTTAGE (THE): CDCOT 106 (CD) TCCOT 106 (MC)*
DULUX-4 FINISHING TOUCHES "Dance Of The Sugar Plum
    Fairy' 'Nutcracker Suite' (TCHAIKOVSKY) *various*
DULUX-3 WEATHERSHIELD "Jupiter" ('The Planets Suite')
    (G.HOLST) *various versions available*
DULUX-2 VINYL SOFT SHEEN "Orinoco Flow" (Enya) 'Water
    mark' ENYA *WEA INT (WEA): 243875-2 (CD) -4 (MC)*
DULUX-1 VINYL SILK PAINTS "A Whiter Shade Of Pale"
    (Reid-Brooker) PROCUL HARUM 'Greatest Hits'
DULUX ONCE "The Moldau" from 'Ma Vlast' (My Country) by
    SMETANA *vers* 'CLASSIC ADS' *EMI CLASS: 7243 568116-2*
DUNLOP TYRES-4 "21st Century Schizoid Man" Robert Fripp
    by KING CRIMSON 'In The Court Of The Crimson King'
    *EG-VIRGIN (EMI): EGCD 1 (CD) EGMC 1 (MC)*
DUNLOP TYRES-3 "Venus In Furs" (Lou Reed) VELVET UNDERG
    ROUND on 'Velvet Underground With Nico' *POLYDOR
    (Poly): 823 290-2 (CD) 823 290-4 or SPEMC 20 (MC)
    SIRE (WEA): W0224CD (CDs) W0224C (MC) W0224 (7"s)*

DUNLOP TYRES-2 "He's Misstra Know It All" (S.Wonder)
STEVIE WONDER from 'Innervisions' *MOTOWN (Pol): WD
72606 (CD) ZK 72012 (MC) ZL 72012 (LP)*
DUNLOP TYRES-1 "You're So Vain" (C.Simon) CARLY SIMON
*ELEKTRA (WEA): EKR 123(CD)(T)(C) (7"/CD/12"/MC)*
and 'Best Of' *Elektra (WEA): 0548 30460-2 (CD)*
DUSTBUSTER *see* 'BLACK & DECKER DUSTBUSTER'

EAGLE STAR INS.-2 "You Spin Me Round (Like a Record)"
by DEAD OR ALIVE on 'Youthquake' *EPIC (Sony Music):
477 853-2 (CD)*
EAGLE STAR INS.-1 "Driving In My Car" by MADNESS from
'Divine Madness' *VIRGIN (EMI): (CD)(TC)(V) 2692*
EASY JEANS "Easy Snappin'"(Theopholus Beckford) by THEO
BECKFORD *METRONOME: MR 001 (7"s)*
EDWARDIAN HOTELS "O Mio Babbino Caro" (Oh My Beloved Fa
ther) from 'Gianni Schicchi' (PUCCINI) / on 'Opera
Without Words' - *EMI: CDP 746 931-2 (CD) deleted*
EGYPT HOLIDAYS "Triumphal March" from 'AIDA' (VERDI)
*special arrangement-not available*
ELECTRICITY COUNCIL-2 'Time On Your Hands' solo piano
"Gnossiennes" (Erik Satie) ANNE QUEFFELEC *Virg: VC
790754-2 (CD)* ANGELA BROWNRIDGE *EMI: CDEMX 9507(CD)*
ELECTRICITY COUNCIL-1 "You Can Do Magic" (S.Linzer)
(73) LIMMIE & FAMILY COOKING *OLD GOLD: OG 9477 (7")*
ELECTROLUX CLEANERS "Shake A Hand" (Joe Morris) LINDA
HOPKIN-JACKIE WILSON 'Hit Story Vol.2' *ROOTS PROV
OGUE (Pinn): RTS 33051 (CD)*
ELIZABETH SHAW CHOCOLATES "Crazy"(Nelson) WILLIE NELSON
'Very Best Of' *MFP (EMI): CD(TC)MFP 6110 (CD/MC)*
EMIRATES AIRLINES "Award Winners" (Adrian Sutton) by
NATURAL SOUNDS *unavailable*
ENERGY CENTRE - see BRITISH GAS
ENTENMANNS CAKES "Raccalto Harvest" from Days Of Heaven
by ENNIO MORRICONE -S/T- on *LEGEND (Silva Screen):
LEGEND CD16 (CD)* + -S/T-'TWO MULES FOR SISTER SARA'
ERICSSON MOBILE PHONES mus: CHRIS BLACKWELL *unavailable*
ERNEST AND JULIO GALLO WINE "Harp Concerto In C.Major"
(Adrien BOIELDIEU) - The Paris Chamber Orchestra on
*TURNABOUT (Conif): TV 334 148 (LP) KC 334 148 (MC)*
ESSO-5 (price watch) "Night Watch" (Tony and Gaynor
Sadler) p.Logorhythm Music *unavailable*
ESSO-4 'SIMPLE' Paint (94) "Iris" (Wim Mertens) WIM
MERTENS on 'Epic That Never Was'(Live In Lisbon)
*CREPESCULE (Vital): TWI 9832 (CD)*
ESSO-3 UNLEADED FUELS (tiger snow landscape ad) "Ice
Floe" (Raf Ravenscroft-John Phillips) *unavailable*
ESSO-2 UNLEADED FUELS "I Want To Break Free" (Brian
May-Freddie Mercury) QUEEN on 'Live Magic' *EMI:
CDP 746 413-2 (CD) TCEMC 3519 (MC) EMC 3519 (LP)*
ESSO-1 THE COLLECTION "Eye Of The Tiger" 'Rocky 3'
*see Coll* 'NUMBER ONE MOVIES ALBUM'
ESTEE LAUDER WHITE LINEN "Tristesse" Etude No.3 Op.10
(CHOPIN) *Many recordings available*

EURODISNEY - see 'DISNEYLAND PARIS'
EUROMILK "The Clog Dance" from ballet 'LA FILLE MAL
   GARDEE' (HEROLD) *EMI EMINENCE: CDEMX 2268 (CD)*
EUROTUNNEL (Le Shuttle) "Bean Fields" (Simon Jeffes) by
   The PENGUIN CAFE ORCHESTRA on 'Signs Of Life' on *EG
   (Poly): EEGCD 50 (CD) EGEDC 50 (MC)*

FELIX CAT FOOD-3 (RASCALS REWARD ad) "You've Been Away"
   by RUBIN from 'Wigan Casino Story Volume 1'
   *GOLDMINE (Vital): GSCD 051 (CD)*
FELIX CAT FOOD-2 "Mambo No.5" (P.Prado) PEREZ PRADO
   on 'King Of Mambo' *RCA (BMG): ND 90424 (CD)*
FELIX CAT FOOD-1 "The Entertainer" (Scott Joplin) 'The
   STING' *see FILMS & SHOWS* (2) "I'm The Leader Of The
   Gang (I Am)" (G.Glitter-Mike Leander) GARY GLITTER
   'Back Again' *PICKWICK (Carlton): PWKS(PWKMC) 4052*
FERRERO ROCHER "The Ambassador's Party" (dance version)
   ROBERT FERRERA *KRUNCHIE (Pinn): KCD1 (CDs) KT1(12")*
   orig music (Graham De Wilde) *not available*
FIAT BRAVO-2 / BRAVA   "2:1" (Matthews) by ELASTICA
   'Elastica' *DECEPTIVE (Vital): BLUFF 014(CD(MC)(LP)*
FIAT BRAVO-1 "Amami Se Vuoi" (Panzeri-Mascheroni) by
   MARISA FIORDALISA on Collection 'ITALY AFTER DARK'
   *EMI: CDP 780023-2 (CD) TCEMS 1458 (MC)*
FIAT CINQUENCENTO "But I Do" (Paul Gayten-R.Guidry)
   CLARENCE FROGMAN HENRY *MCA (BMG): MCSTD(MCSC) 1797
   (CDs/MC)* 'But I Do' *CHESS (Charly): CDRED 13 (CD)*
FIAT COUPE "Amami Se Vuoi" (Panzeri-Mascheroni) sung by
   TONINA TORRIELLI *UK rel.unconfirmed-see next item*
FIAT MAREA "Tanz" 6th movement from 'Carmina Burana'
   (CARL ORFF) *various recordings available*
FIAT PUNTO-2 "Amami Se Voui" sung by TANZIN DALLEY
   *TV version unavailable.* Coll (1) 'ITALY AFTER DARK'
   version by MARISA FIORDALISA *EMI: CDP 780023-2 (CD)*
   Coll (2) 'FESTIVAL DE SAN REMO VOLUME 1' version by
   TONINA TORRIELLI *Butterfly Music (Import CD)*
FIAT PUNTO-1 "Watermelon Woman" *lib.track unavailable*
FIAT TEMPRA "Only You" (Simon Goldenberg-Geoff McCo
   rmack) sung by PRAISE feat Miriam Stockley - *EPIC:
   469 048-2 (CD) 469 048-4 (MC)* 'COMMERCIAL BREAKS'
FIRST DIRECT-2 (Bob Mortimer ad) "Gurney Slade theme"
   MAX HARRIS (1960) *deleted*
FIRST DIRECT-1 (Midland Bank) "Atmosphere" JOY DIVISION
   on 'Substance' *LONDON (Poly):520 014-2(CD) -4(MC)*
FISHERMAN'S FRIEND "I Want You" by the UTAH SAINTS on
   *FFFR-LONDON (Poly): FCD 213 (CDs) 828 379-2 (CD)*
FLORA-3 "Everybody Needs Somebody To Love (S.Burke-B.
   Berns-J.Wexler) from 'The BLUES BROTHERS' *TV vers.
   unavailable* (BLUES BROTHERS -S/T) *(WEA) K.250715 CD*
FLORA-2 "You Make Me Feel So Young" (Mack Gordon-Joseph
   Myrow) *TV version by* TERESA JAMES *unavailable*
FLORA-1 "If I Love Ya Then I Need Ya" (Bob Merrill)
   EARTHA KITT on 'BEST OF EARTHA KITT' on *MCA (BMG):
   MCLD 19120 (CD) MCLC 19120 (MC)*

FLYMO SPRINTMASTER "Devil's Gallop" 'Dick Barton' theme
(Charles Williams) CHARLES WILLIAMS ORCHESTRA on
*GRASMERE: GRCD 10 (CD) GRTC 10 (MC)*
FORD  "Driven By You" (B.May) BRIAN MAY *PARLOPHONE EMI
CDPCSD 123 (CD) TCPCSD 123 (MC) PCSD 12D 123 (LP)*
FORD ESCORT-5 "Jeepers Creepers" *TV version unavailable*
LOUIS ARMSTRONG version on 'JEEPERS CREEPERS' on
*MILAN (BMG): CDCH 602 (CD)*
FORD ESCORT-4 SERENADE "Love Is Is The Air" (H.Vanda-
George Young) by JOHN PAUL JONES available on -S/T-
'STRICTLY BALLROOM' *COLUMBIA (SM): 472 300-2 (CD)*
FORD ESCORT-3 "Here It Comes Again" (B.Mason-L.Reed)
FORTUNES on 'World Of' *SPECTRUM-POLY: 552 023-2 CD*
FORD ESCORT-2 "I Love The Sound Of Breaking Glass" by
NICK LOWE 'Best Of' *DEMON (Pinn): FIENDCD 142 (CD)*
FORD ESCORT-1 "Lovely Day" (B.Withers)  BILL WITHERS
*COLUMBIA: 469048-2(CD) -4(MC)* 'Commercial Breaks'
FORD FIESTA-1 (AZURA) "Carnaby Street" (A.Hawshaw-Keith
Mansfield) *KPM MUSIC LIBRARY unavailable*
FORD FIESTA-2 (series of shorts)
  (a) "Thus Sprach Zarathustra" (Richard Strauss)from
      '2001 A SPACE ODYSSEY' *various recordings*
  (b) "The Rumble" (Link Wray) LINK WRAY on 'This is
      Cult Fiction' *VIRGIN (EMI): VTCD 59 (CD)*
  (c) "Joe 90" (Barry Gray) BARRY GRAY ORCHESTRA on
      'This Is Cult Fiction' *VIRGIN: VTCD 59 (CD)*
  (d) "Popcorn" (G.Kingsley) orig by HOT BUTTER on
      'Light Flight' *TRUE TRAX (THE): TRTCD 121 (CD)*
  (e) "Mr.Sandman"(Pat Ballard) CHORDETTES on 'Mainly
      Rock'n'Roll' *ACE (Pinn): CDCHD 934 (CD)*
  (f) "Wheels" (Norman Petty) orig STRING-A-LONGS on
      'Wheels' *ACE (Pinn): CDCHD 390 (CD)*
FORD GALAXY-2 "Mirror" (Boris Blank) *unavailable*
FORD GALAXY-1 "Flower Duet from Lakme" (DELIBES)
*special piano arrangement unavailable*
FORD KA "Bright Red" (Laurie Anderson) *TV version unava
ilable* original LAURIE ANDERSON version on "Bright
Red" *WB (WEA): 9362 45534-2 (CD) -4 (MC)*
FORD MONDEO-2 "Speaking Of Happiness" (Radcliffe-Scott)
by GLORIA LYNNE *ISLAND (Poly):CID(CIS) 659 (CDs/MC)*
*also on* -S/T- 'SEVEN' *EDEL (Pinn): 0022432CIN (CD)*
FORD MONDEO-1 "Whiter Shade Of Pale" (Reid-Brooker)
PROCUL HARUM 'Best' *BR-TARGET (BMG): BRCD 106 (CD)*
FORD PROBE-2 "Fly Me To The Moon" (Bart Howard) sung by
JULIE LONDON 'Best Of Liberty Years' *Liberty (EMI)
EMI CZ 150 (CD)* also on Coll 'THIS IS THE RETURN
OF CULT FICTION' *VIRGIN (EMI): VTCD 112 (CD)*
FORD PROBE-1 "You Can Go Your Own Way" (Chris Rea)
sung by CHRIS REA on 'Best Of Chris Rea' *EAST-WEST
(WEA): 4509 98040-2 (CD) -4 (MC)*
FORD PUMA "Bullitt" score from 1968 -S/T- LALO SCHIFRIN
*W.BROS (Fra.imp)(WEA/Discovery): 9362 45008-2 (CD)*
*also available* the Black Dog remix on *WEA:
WESP 002CD (CDs) WESP 002C (MC) WESP 002T (12"s)*

FORD SIERRA "Don't Worry 'bout A Thing" (Bob Marley)
'Exodus' BOB MARLEY AND THE WAILERS *ISLAND (Poly)*
*CID 9498 (CD) ILPM 9498 (LP) ICM 9498 (MC)*
FOREHEAD C. "The Water Mill" (RONALD BINGE) on *CD* Colls
'BRITISH LIGHT MUSIC CLASSICS' *HYPERION: CDA 66868*
'40 YEARS OF BBC TV THEMES' *EMPORIO: EMPRCD 633 CD*
FORTE (TRUSTHOUSE) "Le Lac De Come" (Galas) *(TV version
unavailable)* vers.on 'Classics' by FRANCK POURCEL &
HIS ORCHESTRA on *EMI: CZ 22(CD) TCEMS 1263 (MC)*
FOSTER'S LAGER "This Is Hip" (Hooker) JOHN LEE HOOKER
RY COODER on 'Mr.Lucky' *SILVERTONE (Pinn): ORECD
519 (CD) ORELC 519 (MC) ORELP 519 (LP)*
FOX'S CLASSIC BAR "Heaven On Earth" (Buck Ram) PLATTERS
on 'Sincerely' *SPECTRUM/KARUSSELL (Poly): 550 052-2
(CD) 550 052-4 (MC)*
FOX'S CLASSIC BISCUITS "Light Cavalry Overture" (Franz
VON SUPPE) NEW YORK P.O. (L.Bernstein) *-CBSCD 44719
(CD)* BERLIN P.O. (Karajan) *DG (Poly): 415377-2 (CD)*
FOX'S ROCKY BAR - *see under* 'ROCKY BAR'
FRIEND'S PROVIDENT "Chi Mai" (Ennio Morricone) by ENNIO
MORRICONE on 'Film Music Of Ennio Morricone' on
*VIRGIN VIP (EMI): CD(TC)VIP 123 (CD/MC) see also
Collection* 'PURE MOODS'
FRIZZELL INSURANCE-3 "My Special Angel" (Jimmy Duncan)
MALCOLM VAUGHAN on 'EMI Years' *EMI: TCEMS 1358 (MC)*
BOBBY HELMS 'Fraulien' *BEAR FAMILY: BCD 15594 (2CD)*
FRIZZELL INSURANCE-2 "Everything Is Beautiful" (Ray
Stevens) RAY STEVENS on 'Hit Singles Collectables'
on *DISKY (THE): DISK 4510 (CD)*
FRIZZELL INSURANCE-1 "I'll Never Find Another You" by
(Tom Springfield) JUDITH DURHAM & THE NEW SEEKERS
'Carnival Of Hits' *EMI:CDEMTV 83(CD) TCEMTV 83(MC)*
FRUIT & NUT (Cadbury) "Dance Of The Mirlitons" from The
'Nutcracker Suite' (TCHAIKOVSKY) *many versions incl*
'The Classic Experience' *EMI: CDEMTVD 45 (2 CD's)*
FRUIT-TELLA.2 "Let's Talk About Sex" by SALT'n' PEPA
feat PSYCHOTROPIC on 'Greatest Hits' on *FFFR LONDON
(Poly): 828 291-2 (CD) 828 291-4 (MC)*
FRUIT-TELLA.1 "I'm Too Sexy" (Fred/Richard Fairbrass-
Rob Manzoli) RIGHT SAID FRED *TUG (BMG): CDSNOG 1
(CDs) CASNOG 1 (MC) 12SNOG 1 (12"s) SNOG 1 (7"s)*
FRUITOPIA music (Robin Guthrie-Simon Raymonde) by The
COCTEAU TWINS *specially recorded and not available*
FUJICOLOR FILM "Sabre Dance" (KHACHATURIAN) *various rec
ordings all formats*

GAIO YOGHURT "Return To Innocence" (Michael Cretu) by
ENIGMA from 'Cross Of Changes' *VIRGIN: CD(TC)VIR 20
also on* 'PURE MOODS' *Virgin (EMI): VTCD 28 (CD)*
GALAXY-3 "You Do Something To Me" (Cole Porter) *TV
Version sung by* LUCE DRAYTON *unavailable*
GALAXY-2 "My Ship" (George & Ira Gershwin) sung by
SARAH VAUGHAN on 'Gershwin Songbook Volume 1' on
*PERSONALITY-Target (BMG): PRS 23021 (CD)*

**GALAXY-1** "Rhapsody In Blue" (Gershwin) LEONARD BERNST
   EIN 'Bernstein's America' *DG (Poly): 427 088-2 (CD)*
**GAS** - *see under heading BRITISH GAS*
**GENERAL ACCIDENT** "Storm In A Teacup" (Ron Roker-Lynsey
   De Paul) orig by The FORTUNES 'Greatest Hits'on
   *ROYAL COLLECT (Target): RC 83118 (CD) 82118 (MC)*
**GEORGE AT ASDA** "Get Ready For This" by 2 UNLIMITED on
   'Get Ready' *PWL (WEA): HFCD 47 (CD) HFC 47 (MC)*
**GILLETTE / GILLETTE CONTOUR PLUS** "Looking Sharp" (Jake
   Holmes) and "The Best A Man Can Do" *unavailable*
**GINSTERS CORNISH PASTIES** "The Watermill" (RONALD BINGE)
   *EMPORIO (DISC): EMPRCD 633 (CD)*
**GIVENCHY AMARIGE** "Mon Manege A Moi" (Constantin-Glanzbe
   rg) EDITH PIAF 'Piaf Album' *EMI: TCEMS 172789-4 Cas*
**GLADE CANDLES** "Rain Forest 2" (Andy Quinn) *unavailable*
**GLADE TOUCH AND FRESH** "Incredible" (Smith-Elms) Amber
   Productions *unavailable*
**GM VAUXHALL CREDIT CARD** "Fanfare For The Common Man"
   (Aaron COPLAND) on 'Great Concert Halls Of T.World'
   BOSTON POPS OR (J.Williams) *PHILIPS: 438 002-2 (CD)*
**GOLDEN WONDER CRISPS** "You Really Got Me" (Ray Davies)
   KINKS on 'Complete Collection' *CASTLE (BMG): CCSCD
   300 (CD) CCSMC 300 (MC)*
**GOLDEN WONDER POT NOODLES** (Star Jumps) "Fiesta De La Pr
   ima Vere" 'Salsa Mexico' *unavailable*
**GOLDEN WONDER POT TV** "Ace Of Spades" by MOTORHEAD on
   'Anthology' *RAW POWER/Castle (BMG): RAWCD 011 (CD)*
**GRAHAM & BROWN'S SUPER FRESCO** based on "Spinning Wheel"
   (David Clayton Thomas) orig 1969 by BLOOD SWEAT AND
   TEARS on *BGO (Pinn): BGOCD 28 (CD) BGOLP 28 (LP)*
**GRANT'S WHISKY** BABY BIRD track from the album 'Ugly
   Beautiful' *ECHO (Vital-EMI): ECHO(CD)(MC)(LP) 011*
**GREEN FLAG NATIONAL BREAKDOWN** "Rescue Me" (Carl Smith-
   R.Miner) FONTELLA BASS on 'Sisters Of Soul' with Su
   gar Pie DeSanto *ROOTS-PROVOG (Pinn): RTS 33024 (CD)*
**GUINNESS-7** (Strange But Untrue) "First Big Weekend' by
   ARAB STRAP *CHEMICAL UNDERGROUND (SRD):CHEM 007 (7")*
**GUINNESS-6** (Saint Patrick's Day) "I'm Sitting On Top Of
   The World'" (Young-Henderson-Lewis) by AL JOLSON
   *PRESIDENT (BMG): PLCD 542 (CD)*
**GUINNESS-5** (old man) "The Story Of My Life" (Burt Bacha
   rach-Hal David) sung by MICHAEL HOLLIDAY on 'The EP
   Collection' *SEE FOR MILES (Pinn): SEECD 311 (CD)*
**GUINNESS-4** (bicycle) "I'm Gonna Wash That Man Right
   Out Of My Hair" (R.Rodgers-O.Hammerstein II) sung
   by MITZI GAYNOR from -S/T- of 'South Pacific' *RCA
   (BMG): ND 83681 (CD) NK 83681 (MC)*
**GUINNESS-3** (Pure Genius) zoom "We Have All The Time In
   The World" (John Barry-Hal David) LOUIS ARMSTRONG
   from -S/T- 'On Her Majesty's Secret Service' *EMI:
   CDEM 357 (CDs) TCEM 357 (MC) also CDEMTV 89 (CD)
   TCEMTV 89 (MC) EMTV 89 (LP)* plus JAMES BOND 30TH
   ANN.ALBUM' *EMI: CD(TC)BOND 007 (CD/MC)* -S/T-
   *Liberty EMI: CDP 790 618-2 (CD) E4 90618-4 (MC)*

GUINNESS-2a (Pure Genius) "Laudate Dominum" / 'Vesperae
   Solennes De Confessore' (K.339) (Mozart) *vers:* KIRI
   TE KANAWA-ST.PAUL'S CATHEDRAL CHOIR *PHILIPS (Poly):*
   *412 629-2 (CD)*   (2b)"Party Time" (L.Smith-Gerry Th
   omas-Dave Gibson) FATBACK BAND on "Raising Hell' on
   *ACE-SOUTHBOUND (Pin): CDSEWM 028(CD) SEWC 028(MC)*
GUINNESS-1 (Pure Genius) mambo dance "Guaglione" PEREZ
   PRADO ORCH 'King Of Mambo' *RCA (BMG): ND 90424 (CD)*

H. SAMUEL "Bladerunner Love Theme" (Vangelis) VANGELIS
   'Bladerunner'-S/T-*EAST WEST (WEA):4509 96574-2 (CD)*
HAAGEN-DAZS ICE CREAM "Make Yourself Comfortable" (Bob
   Merrill) sung by SARAH VAUGHAN on 'Golden Hits'
   *Mercury (Poly): (CD/MC) number unconfirmed*
HAITI AMERICAN GUM "The Thunderer" (John Philip Sousa)
   *version* BAND OF HER MAJESTY'S ROYAL MARINES 'Hands
   Across The Sea' on *EMI: EL 270152-4 (MC)*
HALIFAX-9 "Consider Yourself" from 'Oliver' (Lionel
   Bart) *TV version unavailable* FOR OTHER RECORDINGS
   see under 'OLIVER'
HALIFAX-8 (Kaleidoscope) "Surfin'" by ERNEST RANGLIN
   from 'Below The Bassline' *ISLAND (Poly): IJCD4002*
   *(CD) IJMC 4002 (MC) IJLP 4002 (LP)* also CDsingle
HALIFAX-7 Week In The Life "The Gift" (Wisternoff-
   Warren-MacColl) by WAY OUT WEST and JOANNA LAW *De*
   *CONSTRUCTION (BMG):74321 40191-2(CD) -4(MC) -1(12")*
HALIFAX-6 Financial Services (figures skating ad)
   "Clock" (David A.Stewart) *unavailable*
HALIFAX-5 Financial Services "Moon River" (H.Mancini-
   Johnny Mercer) *TV vers.unavailable* / HENRY MANCINI
   Coll 'IN THE PINK' on *RCA (BMG): 74321 24283-2 (CD)*
HALIFAX-4 Financial Services "Sentinel" (M.Oldfield)
   from 'Tubular Bells II' MIKE OLDFIELD on *WEA (WEA)*
   *4509 90618-2 (CD) -5 (DCC) WX 2002(C) (LP/MC)*
HALIFAX-3 "Let's Do It (Let's Fall In Love)" (C.Porter)
   EARTHA KITT 'Best Of' *MCA (BMG): MCLD(MCLC 19120*
HALIFAX-2 "I Only Want To Be With You"(Hawker-Raymonde)
   DUSTY SPRINGFIELD 'Sounds Of 60s' *PICKWICK: PWK 104*
HALIFAX-1 "Our House" (Jenkins-Nash) CROSBY STILLS
   NASH & YOUNG on 'Deja Vu' *ATLANTIC: K.250001 (CD)*
HALL'S MENTHOLYPTUS "Air That I Breathe"(Albert Hammond
   -lee Hazlewood) The HOLLIES *EMI: (TC)EMIV 11 (Cass*
   *LP) CDP 746238-2 (CD)* also on *MFP: HR 8153 (MC)*
HALL'S SOOTHERS "Addicted To Love" (R.Palmer) ROBERT
   PALMER on 'Addictions' *ISLAND (Poly): CID 9944 (CD)*
   *ICT 9944 (MC) 842 301-5 (DCC)*
HAMLET CIGARS "Air On A G.String"Suite No.3 in D (BACH)
   JACQUES LOUSSIER TRIO *START (Koch): SMCD 19 (CD)*
HARROD'S (Sales) "Lascia Ch'io Pianga" from act 2 of
   'RINALDO' (HANDEL) *version* on *OPUS III (Harmonia*
   *Mundi): OPS 30174* also available on *DELOS (Pinn):*
   *CDC 3026 (CD)* feaf ARLEEN AUGER (sopr)
HARTLEY'S STRAWBERRY JAM "Fur Elise" (Bagatelle No.25)
   (BEETHOVEN) 'Clasic Ads 2' *EMI: CDM 656 721-2 (CD)*

HARVESTER INNS-2 "Good Times" by CHIC on 'MegaChic'
   *WEA Int (WEA): 2292 41750-2 (CD)*
HARVESTER INNS-1 "A Night To Remember" by SHALAMAR on
   'Very Best Of Shalamar' *SOLAR-CASTLE Comm.(BMG):*
   *CCSCD 803 (CD) CCSMC 803 (MC)*
HARVEY'S BRISTOL CREAM "The Clog Dance" from 'La Fille
   Mal Gardee' (Louis HEROLD) ROYAL OPERA HOUSE ORCH.
   (John Lanchbery) *DECCA (Poly): 436 658-2 (CD)*
HAZE "Dancing Flowers" (RACHEL PORTMAN) *unavailable*
HEINEKEN-8 "Intermezzo from Cavalleria Rusticana"
   (MASCAGNI) *versions on* 'OPERA AT THE MOVIES' on
   *NAXOS (Select): 8.551164(CD)* & 'CLASSIC EXPERIENCE'
   *EMI CLASS: CDCLEXP 1 (2CD) TCCLEXP 1 (2MC)*
HEINEKEN-7 (Russian ad) "Soyuz Nerumskimi Republik
   Svobodnikh" (USSR Nat.Anthem) (A.Aleksandrov)
   *version on* 'National Anthems' *CONIFER: TQ 306 (CD)*
HEINEKEN-6 "Non Je Ne Regrette Rien" (No Regrets)
   (Charles Dumont-Michel Vocaire-H.David) - EDITH
   PIAF 'Very Best Of' *EMI: CZ 84(CD) TCEMC 3142(MC)*
HEINEKEN-5 Yachts "Down The Hatch" (Simon Davison).. *NA*
HEINEKEN-4 "Alabatross" (Peter Green) by FLEETWOOD
   MAC on 'Albatross' *CBS (Sony):CD31569(CD) 40-(MC)*
HEINEKEN-3 (Nigel Short Chess) "William Tell Overture"
   (ROSSINI) *many recorded versions*
HEINEKEN-2 "Big Spender" ('Sweet Charity') (Cy Coleman-
   Dorothy Fields) SHIRLEY BASSEY *EMI:CDP 790469-2(CD)*
HEINEKEN-1 "The Blues" (Paul Hart) produced JOE & CO
   performed by LONNIE BROOKS *unavailable*
HEINZ (Baked Beans/Tomato Soup etc.) "Inkanyezi Nezazi"
   (Joseph Shambalala) by THE LADYSMITH BLACK MAMBAZO
   on 'Star and The Wiseman' (Inkanyezi Nezazi) on
   *FLAME TREE-TIMBUKTU (Pinn/Sterns): FLTRCD 502 (CD)*
   *also on A.& M. (Polyg): 582 389-2 (CDs) -4 (MCs)*
HEINZ BAKED BEANS (Heinz Builds Brits) "Diddle'um Song"
   by CHAS & DAVE 'All The Best' album *EMI deleted*
HEINZ SPAGHETTI (based on) "I Can't Do My Bally Bottom
   Button Up" (John P.Long) version by IAN WALLACE on
   'Best Of Ian Wallace' *EMI: CD(TC)GO 2056 (CD/MC)*
HEINZ WEIGHT WATCHERS "Ying Tong Song" (Spike Milligan)
   The GOONS on 'World Of The Goons' *DECCA (Polyg):*
   *820 646-2 (CD) 820 908-4 (MC) GOONCD 1 (CDsingle)*
HELLMANNS MAYONAISSE-3 "Waltz Of The Flowers" from
   'The Nutcracker Suite' (TCHAIKOVSKY) *var.records*
HERO AFTERSHAVE (Boots) "Holding Out For A Hero" (Jim
   Steinman) BONNIE TYLER from 'Footloose' -S/T- on
   *CBS 463000-2 (CD) CBS 463000-4 (MC) -1 (LP)* also
HIGHLIGHTS-2 (Cadbury's) "Sweet And Lovely" (G.Arnheim-
   -Harry Tobias-Jules Lemare) sung by AL BOWLLY on
   "Very Thought Of You" *EMI CEDAR (EMI): CZ 306 (CD)*
HIGHLIGHTS-1 "The Game Of Love" (Clint Ballard) *orig*
   WAYNE FONTANA & The MINDBENDERS on 'Hit Singles Ant
   hology' *FONTANA-MERCURY (Poly): 848 161-2 (CD)*
HOLSTEN PILS "Sugar Sugar" orig The ARCHIES (1969) on
   -S/T- 'NOW AND THEN' *COL (Sony): 481 606-2 (CD)*

HONDA ACCORD  "Flashdance What A Feeling" (G.Moroder-
-K.Forsey-I.Cara) *orig* 1983 by IRENE CARA on -S/T-
FLASHDANCE *CASABLANCA (Poly): 811 492-2 (CD)*
HONDA SOLAR POWERED CAR music taken from 'STABAT MATER'
by PERGOLESI *TV version unavailable.* Version on
*NAXOS (Select): 8.553433 (CD)*
HORIZON PERFUME (Guy Laroche) "Storms Over Africa"
ENYA 'Watermark' *WEA INT: 243 875-2 (CD) -4 (MC)*
HORLICKS "You Sexy Thing" (Tony Wilson-Errol Brown) by
HOT CHOCOLATE '20 Hottest Hits' *EMI: CZ 213 (CD)*
HORLICKS LOW-FAT INSTANT "Blue Danube Op.314" (STRAUSS)
Vienna Phil Or (C.Abbado) *DG-POLYG: 423662-2 (CD)*
HOTPOINT MISTRAL PLUS "Sweets For My Sweet" (Doc Pomus
Mort Shuman) *orig (63)* SEARCHERS on 'Complete Coll'
*CASTLE COMM (BMG): CCSCD 303 (CD) CCSMC 303 (MC)*
HOVIS BREAD "Largo" from Symph.9 in E.Min Op.95 DVORAK
HP SAUCE "That's The Way I Like It" (Casey-Finch) orig
by KC & SUNSHINE BAND 'Best Of' *EMI:CDROU 5007 (CD)*
HYUNDAI LANTRA "Jungle Jazz Room" STEVE GRAY *unavailab.*

IBM COMPUTERS  "Fur Elise" Bagatelle No.25 in A.Minor
(BEETHOVEN) *many recordings available*
ICELAND "Driving Home For Christmas" (C.Rea) CHRIS REA
'BEST OF CHRIS REA' *MAGNET (WEA): 243841-2 (CD)*
ICL COMPUTERS "Falls" from 'The Mission' (Ennio Morrico
ne) -S/T- on *VIRGIN: CDV 2402 (CD) TCV 2402 (MC)*
IMMAC-2 "I Get The Sweetest Feeling" (Van McCoy-Alicia
Evelyn) orig (68) JACKIE WILSON 'Very Best Of
Jackie Wilson on *ACE (Pinn): CDCH 913 (CD)*
IMMAC-1 Special lyrics and arrangement set to music
from ballet 'Coppelia' (DELIBES) *not available*
IMPERIAL LEATHER - *see under* CUSSONS IMPERIAL LEATHER
IMPULSE-7 (art class) "Pressure Drop" by The MAYTALS
*ISLAND Records (Poly):*
IMPULSE-6 "Cars" (DAVID ARCH-MARK CAMPBELL)*unavailable*
IMPULSE-5 VANILLAS "The Happening" (F.de Vol-Holland-
Dozier-Holland) *orig by* DIANA ROSS & THE SUPREMES
'Anthology' on *MOTOWN (Poly): 530 199-2 (2CD)*
IMPULSE-4 FREE SPIRIT "Fever" (J.Davenport-Edd Cooley)
PEGGY LEE 'The Capitol Years' *EMI:CZ 108 (CD)*
IMPULSE-3 DYNAMIQUE "Venus" (Robert De Leeuwen) orig
SHOCKING BLUE (1970) on 'Golden Years 1970 Vol.2'
*CONNOSSEUR COLLECT.(Pinn): RRT(CD)(MC) 70 (CD/MC)*
IMPULSE-2 AVANTE GARDE "Can't Get Enough" Mick Ralphs
orig (1974) by BAD COMPANY available on 'Best Of'
*ATCO (WEA): 756 792307-2 (CD) 756 792307-4 (MC)*
IMPULSE-1 "Hello Mary Lou" (Gene Pitney) RICK NELSON
'Best Of Rick Nelson V.2' *LIBERTY (EMI): CZ 420 CD*
INDEPENDENT The "Music For A Found Harmonium" PENGUIN
CAFE ORCH *EG (Poly): EEGCD 38 (CD) OVEDC 430 (MC)*
INSIGNIA BODY SPRAY "It's All Over Now"(Shirley & Bobby
Womack) *TV Vers.unavailable* ORIG - ROLLING STONES
INSPIRATIONS-3 (Cadbury)(Telescope Ad) music (Richard
G.Mitchell) *unavailable*

INSPIRATIONS-2 (Cadbury) "Sentimental Journey" (L.Brown
   B.Green-B.Homer) 'A Portrait Of DORIS DAY' on
   *STYLUS: SMD 984 (CD) SMR 984 (LP) SMC 984 (MC)*
INSPIRATIONS-1 (Cadbury) "Girl Talk" (Neal Hefti-Bob
   Troupe) 'Hits Of VINCE HILL' *MFP: HR 418106-4 (MC)*
INTEL PENTIUM-2 "Shake Your Groove Thing" by PEACHES &
   HERB on Collect 'Then That's What They Call Disco'
   *ELEVATE (3MV-SONY): CDELV 05 (CD)*
INTEL PENTIUM-1 "Play That Funky Music" by WILD CHERRY
   on 'Night Fever' *GLOBAL TV (Pinn): RADCD 24 (2CD)*
INTERCITY-2 (92) "Mishima" (Philip Glass) PHILIP GLASS
   *WEA ELEKTRA/NONESUCH: 979113-2 (CD) EKTC 23 (MC)*
INTERCITY-1 (89-91) "Relax" (L.Redbone) LEON REDBONE
   *PRIVATE (BMG): 662 885 (CD single\* also contains*
   *'Intercity' 90 Ad "Untwist"* ('Let's Twist Again')
   'Relax' on 'Sugar' *(BMG): 260555 (CD) 410555 (MC)*
IONICA "Something In The Air" (John Keene) *TV Version:*
   OCEAN COLOUR SCENE *unavailable.(orig.by* THUNDERCLAP
   NEWMAN)'Golden Hits 60s' *PICKWICK: BOXD 16P CDx3*
IRELAND (TOURISM) ('Live A Different Life' ad) "Dream"
   by The CRANBERRIES from 'Everyone Else Is Doing It
   So Why Can't We' *ISLAND (Poly): CID(ICT)(ILPS) 8003*
IRN BRU-2 'Different' "Dies Irae" from 'Requiem Mass'
   (VERDI) vers: 'CLASSIC ADS 2' *EMI: CDM 565721-2 CD*
   Complete Mass on *EMI Class: CDEMXD 2503 (2CD)*
IRN BRU-1 based on "You Don't Love Me Any More"(A.Yanko
   vich) Mick Mullans *unavailable* WEIRD AL YANKOVICH
   on 'Off The Deep End' *Polyd: 512 506-2(CD) -4(MC)*

JAMAICA (Tourist Board ad) "One Love" (Bob Marley) BOB
   MARLEY & WAILERS on 'Exodus' *TUFF GONG/ISL (Poly):*
   *TGLCD 6 (CD) TGLMC 6 (MC) TGLLP 6 (LP)*
JAMMIE DODGERS "Dance Of The Hours" from 'La Gioconda'
   (Amilcare PONCIELLI) *many available versions*
JERSEY HOLIDAYS "Bergerac" theme (George Fenton)
   GEORGE FENTON *see under TV theme*
JERSEY ROYAL POTATOES "Ma Vlast"'My Country' (SMETANA)
   Concertgebouw Orch (Antal Dorati) *PHILIPS (Poly):*
   *420 607-2 (CD) 420 607-1 (2LP) 420 607-4 (MC)*
JIF-2 "Flower Duet" from 'Lakme' Opera (DELIBES)
   'Opera Spectacular' *IMP (Pickwick): MCD 15 (CD)*
   complete 'Lakme' Opera - MADY MESPLE & PARIS OPERA
   COMIQUE ORCH (A.Lombard) *EMI: CDST 749430-2 (2CDs)*
JIF-1 "Dance Of The Hours" from Act 3 'La Gioconda'
   (Amilcare PONCHIELLI) *many recordings available*
JJB SPORTS "Everyone's A Winner" (Errol Brown) orig by
   HOT CHOCOLATE 'Greatest Hits' *EMI: CD(TC)EMTV 73*
JOHN SMITH'S BITTER (Ladybirds ad) "Je T'aime Moi Non
   Plus" (S.Gainsbourg) JANE BIRKIN-SERGE GAINSBOURG
   (69) on 'Amoreuse' coll *PICKWICK: PWKS 539 (CD)*
JOHN SMITH'S EXTRA STRONG (Penguins) "Help Yourself"
   (Gli Occhi Miel)(C.Donida-J.Fishman) *TV vers.not*
   *available* TOM JONES *DERAM (Poly): 820 559-2 (CD)*
JOHN SMITH'S MILLER LITE - see under MILLER LITE

**JOHNSONS BABY BATH** "Yes Sir That's My Baby" (Gus Kahn Walter Donaldson) *various recordings available*
**JOHNSON'S PH5** "P.H.5" by DAVID DUNDAS *unavailable*
**JOHNSON'S PLEDGE** "Humming Chorus" ('Madam Butterfly') (PUCCINI) *TV version unavailable*
**JOHNSON'S SPARKLE** "This Ole House" (Stuart Hamblen) vers: SHAKIN'STEVENS *EPIC: 466993-2 (CD) -4 (MC)* ROSEMARY CLOONEY *BRIDGE (Target): 100 006-2 (CD)*

**K**ATTOMEAT (Skateboard Cat Ad) "You Gotta Fight For Your Right To Party" BEASTIE BOYS (87) from 'Licenced To Ill' on *DEF JAM (Sony):450062-2(CD) -4(MC) -1(LP)*
**KELLOGG'S BRAN FLAKES** "Spirit In The Sky" (N.Greenbaum) *orig by* NORMAN GREENBAUM on 'Spirit In The Sky-Back Home Again' *EDSEL-DEMON (Pinn): ECDC 470 (CD) also*
**KELLOGG'S CORN FLAKES-2** "Brideshead Revisited" theme m. GEOFFREY BURGON *SILVA SCREEN (Koch): FILMCD 117 CD)*
**KELLOGG'S CORN FLAKES-1** "Oh What A Beautiful Mornin'" (Rodgers-Hammerstein) Glenn Miller Army Air Forces Training Command Or'CLASSIC THEMES FROM TV & RADIO' *HAPPY DAYS (Con-BMG): 75605 52283-2(CD) -4(MC) also on* '1943-44 Rare Broadcast Performances' *LASERLIGHT Target (BMG): 1571-2 (CD) 7971-2(MC)*
**KELLOGG'S CRUNCHIE NUT CEREAL** "Purple Electric Violin Concerto" by ED ALLEYNE-JOHNSON *EQUATION Records (RTM/Pinn): EQCD 001 (CD) EQTC 001 (MC)*
**KELLOGG'S FROSTIES** (92) "Eye Of The Tiger" from 'ROCKY 3'(1982) SURVIVOR *see Coll* NUMBER ONE MOVIES ALBUM
**KELLOGG'S SPECIAL K** "Turning Ground" CAROLINE LAVELLE from 'Spirit' *WEA (WEA): 4509 98137-2(CD) -4(MC)*
**KELLOGG'S START** "Let's Stick Together" Bryan Ferry *EG-POLY: 2302 045 (LP) 3100 345 (C) 821 561-2 (CD)*
**KENCO COFFEE** "Bailero" from 'Songs Of The Auvergne' by (CANTELOUBE) - ENGLISH CHAMBER ORCHESTRA on *VIRGIN: VC 7907-14-2 (CD) /* LAMOUREUX CONCERT ORCHEST with Victoria De Los Angeles - *EMI: CDC 747970-2 (CD)*
**KENTUCKY FRIED CHICKEN** - see KFC
**KFC-2** (Fire Station) "Disco Inferno" from) 'SATURDAY NIGHT FEVER' by TRAMMPS -S/T- *POLY: 825 389-2 (CD)*
**KFC-1** "Canteloupe (Island)" (Herbie Hancock) version US3 on Collection 'Jazz Moods' *TELSTAR (BMG): TCD 2722 (CD) STAC 2722 (MC) ALSO by* HERBIE HANCOCK on 'Best Of H.Hancock' *BLUENOTE (EMI): BNZ 143 (CD)*
**KILKENNY IRISH BEER-2** "She Moves Through The Fair" sung by SHANE McGOWAN *TV version unavailable. other recordings inc.* FEARGAL SHARKEY on 'CELTIC MOODS'
**KILKENNY IRISH BEER-1** "Need Your Love So Bad" (P.Green) FLEETWOOD MAC on 'Greatest Hits' *SONY Nice Price Collection: R.460704-2 (CD) -4 (MC)*
**KINGSMILL BREAD** "Big Spender" from 'Sweet Charity' (D. Fields-C.Coleman) *TV version unavailable* SHIRLEY BASSEY 'The Collection' *MFP (EMI): CDDL 1239 (CD)*
**KIT KAT-3** (Sheep Dog) Orig theme of 'One Man And His Dog' (Alan Benson) *unavailable*

KIT KAT-2 Andy Capp "Stand By Your Man" (Billy Sherrill
-Tammy Wynette) ORIG (68) by TAMMY WYNETTE- *EPIC*
KLEENEX-3 TISSUES "Overture to Cavalleria Rusticana"
(MASCAGNI) GHEORGHE ZAMFIR *PHILIPS: PHHC 5 (MC)
830627-2 (CD)* also on *EMI* 'The Classic Experience'
KLEENEX-2 Bathroom + other campaigns) "Comfort" origin
composition (Rachel PORTMAN) *unavailable*
KLEENEX-1 Tissues "1812 Overture" (TCHAIKOVSKY) *various*
KNORR PASTORIA "Overture from The Thieving Magpie" (La
Gazza Ladra) (ROSSINI) *various records available*
KODAK GOLD "They Can't Take That Away From Me" (G.& I.
Gershwin) TV version sung by SAM BROWN *unavailable*
from 'Shall We Dance' (37) with Fred Astaire
KOTEX SIMPLICITY "Eintritt" from 'Waldszenen' Opus 82
(Woodland Scene) (Robert Schumann) vers.by Vladimir
Ashkenazy on *DECCA (Poly): 421 290-2 (CD) -4 (MC)*
KP CRISPS "They're Coming To Take Me Away Aha" orig by
NAPOLEON XIV - *OLD GOLD (Pinn): OG 9551 (7"s)*
KP DISCOS-2 "Stayin' Alive" (Gibb Brothers) BEE GEES
83 Film -S/T- on *RSO Polydor: 813 269-2 (CD only)*
KP DISCOS-1 "Jealousy" (Jacob Gade-Winif.May-V.Bloom)
from 'Anchors Aweigh'/'Painting The Clouds With Sun
shine' *various verions available*
KP LOWER FAT CRISPS "It Started With A Kiss" (E.Brown)
HOT CHOCOLATE *RAK EMI:TCEMTV 42(MC) CDP 746375-2CD*
KP SALTED PEANUTS-2 "The Stripper" (David Rose) DAVID
ROSE & HIS ORCHESTRA *Emporio (THE): EMPRCD 501 (CD)*
KP SALTED PEANUTS-1 "Rebel Yell" (B.Idol) BILLY IDOL
*CHRYSALIS: IDOL 6 (7"s) IDOLX 6 (12"s)*
KRAFT MELLO "Mellow Yellow" (Donovan Leitch) by DONOVAN
*EMI: CZ 193 (CD) EMS 133 (LP) TC-EMS 133 (MC)*
KWIK-FIT song based on "The Thing" (Grean) original by
PHIL HARRIS *LIVING ERA-ASV (Koch): CDAJA 5191 (CD)*

L'EGOISTE AFTERSHAVE Chanel "Dance Of The Knights"
from Act.1 of 'Romeo And Juliet' Op.64 (PROKOFIEV)
LADYBIRD COLL-3 Woolworths "Into Each Life Some Rain
Must Fall" (Roberts-Fisher) by The INK SPOTS
*CONNOISSEUR (Pinn): XPOTTCD 201 (CD)*
LADYBIRD COLL-2 Woolworths "Q5 Theme"/"Ning Nang
Nong" (Spike Milligan) SPIKE MILLIGAN 'A Collect
ion Of Spikes' *EMI: CDECC 11 (CD) ECC 11 (MC)*
LADYBIRD COLL-1 Woolworths "We'll Meet Again" (Ross
Parker-H.Charles) sung by TOMMY COOPER *unavailable*
LAND ROVER DISCOVERY-4 "Mad Alice Lane (A Ghost Story)"
(Peter Lawlor) by LAWLOR *WATER (3MV-Sony) WAT 1CD
(CDs) WAT 1MC(MC) see Coll* 'SPIRITS OF NATURE'
LAND ROVER DISCOVERY-3 "Antarcticar" (Geoff McCormack-
Simon Goldenberg) *unavailable*
LAND ROVER DISCOVERY-2 "Dambusters March" (Eric COATES)
Coll 'WORLD WAR II THEMES *MFP (EMI): 832836-2 (CD)*
LAND ROVER DISCOVERY-1 "Hippopotamus Song" orig version
by FLANDERS & SWANN on *EMI: CDEM 1340 (CD)* also by
IAN WALLACE on 'All Aboard' *EMI: CDEMS 1479 (CD)*

LANSON CHAMPAGNE "Tipitina" PROFESSOR LONGHAIR 'Big Chi
   ef' *TOMATO/PLAY IT AGAIN SAM (Vital):598109320 (CD)*
LE SHUTTLE - see 'EUROTUNNEL'
LEA & PERRINS WORCESTER SAUCE-2 "Sorcerer's Apprentice"
   (Paul DUKAS) *many recordings available*
LEA & PERRINS WORCESTER SAUCE-1 "Shake Rattle & Roll"
   (Calhoun) BILL HALEY & COMETS *MCA*
LEE JEANS-8 (Hard To Be Parted From ad) music by
   JOHN ALTMAN (Jeff Wayne Productions) *unavailable*
LEE JEANS-7 "Legends" by SACRED SPIRIT *VIRGIN (EMI):*
   *VSCDT 1598 (CDs) VSC 1598 (MC)* from album 'SACRED
   SPIRIT 2' *VIRGIN (EMI): CDV(TCV) 2827 (CD/MC)*
LEE JEANS-6 "Baby Lee" (J.L.Hooker) JOHN LEE HOOKER
   with ROBERT CRAY on 'The Healer' *SILVERTONE (Pinn)*
   *ORE(CD)(MC) 508 (CD/MC) / ORE(CD)(C) 81 (CDs/MC)*
LEE JEANS-5 "Jailbird" by PRIMAL SCREAM 'Give Out But
   Don't Give In' *CREATION (Pinn): CRECD 146 (CD)*
LEE JEANS-4 "Bamboo" (Ronk-Cooder) DAVE VAN RONK and
   RY COODER *currently unavailable*
LEE JEANS-3 "Boom Boom" (J.L.Hooker) JOHN LEE HOOKER
   *POINTBLANK/VIRGIN: POBD3(CDs) POB3(MC) POB3(7"s)*
   'Boom Boom' *PB/VIRGIN: VPBCD12 (CD) VPBMC12 (MC)*
LEE JEANS-2 "Vedi! Le Fosche" (The Anvil Chorus) from
   'Il Trovatore' (VERDI) *many recordings available*
LEE JEANS-1 "Homely Girl" UB 40 on 'Labour Of Love 2'
   *DEP/VIRGIN (EMI): DEPCD 14 (CD) CADEP 14 (MC)*
LEEDS BUILDING SOCIETY (George Cole Ads) "Liquid Gold"
   (John Altman) p.Jeff Wayne Music *unavailable*
LEGAL & GENERAL-2 (Plant It With.) "Chanson Du Matin"
   Op.15/2 (ELGAR) Bournemouth Sinfonietta (Norman
   Del Mar) on *CHANDOS: CHAN 8371 (CD)*
LEGAL & GENERAL-1 "Bring Me Sunshine" (Sylvia Dee-
   Arthur Kent) vers: PHIL KELSALL 'At The Wurlitzer
   Blackpool' *EMI: CDIDL 111 (CD) TCIDL 111 (MC)*
LEMSIP-3 "And Always Care For Me" (Mike Connaris for
   Mcasso Productions) *unavailable*
LEMSIP-2 "Moon River" (Henry Mancini-Johnny Mercer)
   HENRY MANCINI *see 'Henry Mancini' Collections*
LEMSIP-1 "Goodnight Sweetheart Well It's Time To Go"
   (Calvin Carter-James Hudson) by The SPANIELS on
   'Play It Cool' *CHARLY R&B: CDCHARLY 222 (CD)*
LEVI 501 JEANS ADS (most recent ads first):-
         SEE ALSO COLLECTION 278
LEVI-26 (kung-fu) "Stepping Stones" (Johnny Harris)
   JOHNNY HARRIS ORCH *EMI: CD(TC)LIC 108 (CDs/MCs)*
LEVI-25 (mermaid) "Underwater Love" (Nina Miranda)
   by SMOKE CITY *JIVE (Pinn): JIVECD 422 (CDs) JIVEC
   422 (MC) JIVET 422 (12"s)*
LEVI-24 "The Art Of Self Destruction Part 1" by
   NINE INCH NAILS from 'Further Down The Spiral'
   *ISLAND (Poly): IMCD 8041 (CD)*
LEVI-23 (sci-fi) "Spaceman" (Jasbinder Mann) performed
   by BABYLON ZOO from 'Boy With The X-Ray Eyes"
   *EMI:CD(TC)EMC 3742 (CD/MC) / CD(TC)(12)EM 416*

LEVI-22 "Boombastic" (Shaggy-Robert Livingston) by
  SHAGGY on *VIRGIN (EMI): VSCDT 1536 (CDs) VST
  1536 (12"s) VSC 1536 (MC)* / album: *CD(TC)V 2782*
LEVI-21 "Novelty Ways" (Biosphere) BIOSPHERE on
  *APOLLO (Vital): APOLLO 020(CD)(MC) 020*
LEVI-20 "Turn On Tune In Cop Out" (Norman Cook) by
  FREAKPOWER on *4TH & BROADWAY (Isl-Poly): BRCD 606*
LEVI-19 (Accident/Hospital) "Fall" (Peter Lawlor)
  p.White Water Music *unavailable*
LEVI-18 (Swimming Creek) "Inside" (Peter Lawlor) by
  STILTSKIN on *WHITE WATER (3MV/Sony): LEV 1CD
  (CDs) LEV 1C (MC) LEV 1 (7"s) LEV 1T (12"s)*
LEVI-17 "Tackle" by CHRIS BLACKWELL *unavailable*
LEVI-16 "Ring Of Fire" (Merle Kilgore-June Carter) by
  JOHNNY CASH 'Biggest Hits' Coll *SONY MUSIC:
  CD 32304 (CD) 40.32304 (MC)*
LEVI-15 "Heart Attack And Vine" by SCREAMING JAY
  HAWKINS *EPIC (Sony): 659109-2(CDs) -4(MC) deleted*
  also on *DEMON (Pinn) FIENDCD(MC) 211 (CD/MC)*
LEVI-14 "Piece Of My Heart" (Bert Berns-Jerry Ragavoy)
  by ERMA FRANKLIN *EPIC (SM): 472413-2 (CD) -4 (MC)*
  JANIS JOPLIN *CBS: CBS 32190-2 (CD) 40-(MC)*
LEVI-13 "Mad About The Boy" from 'Words & Music' (Noel
  Coward) DINAH WASHINGTON 'Best Of' *MERCURY (Poly):
  512214-2(CD) -4(MC)* / KEN MACKINTOSH & HIS ORCH
  'Mac's Back' *PRESIDENT (Prism-Target): PLCD 532(CD)*
LEVI-12 "20th Century Boy" (Marc Bolan) by T.REX
  'Ultimate Collection' *TELSTAR (BMG): TCD(STAC) 2539*
LEVI-11 "Should I Stay Or Should I Go" The CLASH *CBS
  SONY M:'Story Of The Clash' 460244-2 (CD) -4 (MC)*
LEVI-10 "The Joker" (S.Miller) by the STEVE MILLER BAND
  on *'The Joker' FAME-MFP (EMI): CDFA 3250 (CD)*
LEVI-9 "Can't Get Enough" by BAD COMPANY on '10 From 6'
  *ATLANTIC (WEA): 781625-2 (CD)* also 'Bad Company'
  *ISLAND: ILPS(ICT) 9279 (LP/MC)*
LEVI-8 "Ain't Nobody Home" B.B.KING 'Best Of B.B.King'
  *MCA: MCLC 1612 (MC) CMCAD 31040 (CD)*
LEVI-7 "Be My Baby" (Phil Spector-E.Greenwich-Jeff
  Barry) The RONETTES on 'Dirty Dancing' -S/T-
  *RCA (BMG): BK 86408 (MC) BD 86408 (CD)*
LEVI-6 "Mannish Boy" (Morganfield-McDaniel-London) by
  MUDDY WATERS
LEVI-5 "C'mon Everybody" (Eddie Cochran-Jerry Capehart)
  EDDIE COCHRAN *LIBERTY (EMI): (CD)(TC)ECR 1*
LEVI-4 "When A Man Loves A Woman" (C.Lewis-A.Wright)
  PERCY SLEDGE *OLD GOLD (Pinn): OG 9496 (7"s)*
LEVI-3 "Stand By Me" (B.E.King-M.Stoller-Jerry Leiber)
  BEN E.KING *ATLANTIC: A.9361 (7"s)*
LEVI-2 "Wonderful World" (S.Cooke-L.Adler-Herb Alpert)
  SAM COOKE *RCA: PD 87127 (CD)*
LEVI-1 "I Heard It Through The Grapevine" (Norman Whit
  field-Barrett Strong) orig MARVIN GAYE *MOTOWN-POLY*
LEVI DOCKERS "I'm Sitting On Top Of The World" (Lewis-
  Young-Henderson) by BOBBY DARIN *CAPITOL (EMI)*

LEVINGTON EVERGREEN "Barwick Green" ('The Archers') (A.
   Wood) NEW CONCERT ORCH *CON-BMG: 75605 52271-2 (CD)*
LIBRA BODYFORM Music by Nick Glennie-Smith *unavailable*
LILT "Come Dig It" (Machel Montano) by MACHEL *LONDON*
   *(Poly): LONCD 386 (CDs) LONCS 386(MC) LONX 386(12")*
LINDT CHOCOLATE "Wild Is The Wind" (D.Tiomkin-N.Washing
   ton) sung by NINA SIMONE on 'COLPIX YEARS'
   *EMI ROULETTE: CDP 798584-2 (CD)*
LION BAR (Nestle) 'Beast Of A Bar' and 'Urban Jungle'
   ads orig music by (Nigel Corsbie) *unavailable*
LISTERINE MOUTHWASH "Kiss" (Prince) TOM JONES with Art
   Of Noise on 'At This Moment' *JIVE (BMG): TOMCD 1*
   *(CD) TOMTC 1 (MC) TOMTV 1 (LP)*
LITTLEWOODS (Berkertex Fashion Range) "Perdido" (Juan
   Tizol-H.Lenk-E.Drake) DUKE ELLINGTON ORCHESTRA on
   '16 Most Requested Songs' *COLUMBIA (Sony M):*
   *476 719-2 (CD) 476 719-4 (MC)*
LLOYDS BANK & TSB "Let's Work Together" by CANNED HEAT
   *LIBERTY (EMI): CZ 226 (CD) TCGO 2026 (MC)* 'Best Of'
LLOYDS BANK-2 music produced by JOE & CO and based on
   Symphony No.1 (Brahms) *TV vers.specially recorded*
LLOYDS BANK-1 "Zion Hears The Watchmen Singing" from
   'Wachet Auf,Ruft Uns Die Stimme'(Sleepers Awake The
   Voice Is Calling) "Cantata No.BWV 140" (J.S.BACH)
LOU-LOU "Pavane" (FAURE) *many recorded versions*
LUCOZADE-7 (NRG) "Leave You Far Behind" by LUNATIC CALM
   *MCA (BMG): MCSTD 40131 (CDs) deleted*
LUCOZADE-6 "EVA" (Prilly-Perrault-Badale) JEAN JACQUES
   PERREY *ACE (Pinn): EVA 001 (12"s)* from album 'MOOG
   INDIGO' *BGP-ACE (Pinn): CDBGPM 103 (CD)*
LUCOZADE-5 orig composition by Anthony Capel-Martin
   Green (Tomato Productions) *unavailable*
LUCOZADE-4 "She Sells Sanctuary" (Ian Astbury-William
   Duffy) sung by The CULT on 'Pure Cult-Very Best Of'
   *BEGGARS BANQUET (WEA): BEGA 130CD(CD) BEGC 130(MC)*
LUCOZADE-3 "Soul Power" (J.Brown) JAMES BROWN 'Sex
   Machine & Other Soul Classics' *POLY: 825 714-2 (CD)*
LUCOZADE-2 "I Believe" (J.Atkin-I.Dench-Zack Foley)
   EMF from 'Schubert Dip' *EMI-PARLOPHONE (EMI)*
   *CDPCS 7353 (CD) TCPCS 7353 (MC) PCS 7353 (LP)*
LUCOZADE-1 (Daley Thompson) "Phantom Of The Opera"
   Steve Harris Phil Maloney)'Iron Maiden' IRON MAIDEN
   *FAME-MFP (EMI): CDFA 3121 (CD) TCFA 3121 (MC)*
LURPAK-3 "Flight Of The Bumblebee" (Rimsky-Korsakov)
   and part of "Requiem" (FAURE) *many recordings avail*
LURPAK-2 "Spread A Little Happiness" from the Musical
   'Mr.Cinders' (V.Ellis-R.Myers-G.Newman) - STING on
   *A.& M.: AMS 8242 (7"s)* see also 'Mr.Cinders' SHOWS
LURPAK-1 "Leader Of The Pack" (E.Greenwich-J.Barry-G.
   Morton) SHANGRI-LAS on *OLD GOLD: OG 9085 (7"s)*
LUX BEAUTY SOAP "Pavane" Op.50 (FAURE) *many recordings*
LYNX AFTER SHAVE "Boom Shack-A-Lak" by APACHE INDIAN
   from 'Make Way For The Indian' on *ISLAND (Poly):*
   *CID 8016 (CD) ICT 8016 (MC) ILPSD 8016 (2LP)*

**M** & M.'s (FUN PACK ad) "Trip Your Trigger" by Stephen
Williams *unavaiable*
McCAINS HOME FRIES "I'm A Believer" (Neil Diamond) The
MONKEES on 'Greatest Hits' *WEA: 0630 12171-2 (CD)*
McCAINS MICRO CHIPS "Yakety Yak" (Jerry Leiber-Mike
Stoller) *originally by* COASTERS on 'Greatest Hits'
*ATLANTIC (WEA): 7567 90386-2 (CD)*
McCAIN'S SNACK ROLLA (music based on) "Charlie Brown"
(Jerry Leiber-Mike Stoller) orig The COASTERS on
*WEA RHINO (WEA): 7567 90386-2 (CD)*
McCAINS SOUTHERN FRIES based on "Yeh Yeh" (John Hendric
ks-Roger Grant-Pat Patrick)orig GEORGIE FAME on '20
Beat Classics' *POLYDOR: 847 810-2 (CD) -4 (MC)*
McCOYS CRACKER SNAPS "Two-Step Farouche" by JOHN DELAF
OSE and The Eunice Playboys from 'Per Et Garcon' on
*ROUNDER (Celtic Music): ROUNDER CD 2116 (CD)*
McDONALDS-2 "Singin' In The Rain" (N.H.Brown-A.Freed)
*TV version by* GAZEBO and DEE JACOBEE *EMI Records:*
*CDLIC 107 (CDs) TCLIC 107 (MC)*
(b) "Don't Fence Me In" (Porter) *TV version by*
*Jeff Wayne Music Productions unavailable*
McDONALD'S-1 (Hat TRICK (football ad) "Life Of Riley"
(I.Broudie) The LIGHTNING SEEDS from 'Sense' on
*VIRGIN (EMI): CDV 2690 (CD) TCV 2690 (MC)*
McEWANS LAGER ('Trainspotting' montage ad) "Do What You
Wanna Do" by EDDIE & THE HOT RODS on 'Best Of Eddie
and The Hot Rods *ISLAND (Poly): IMCD 156 (CD)*
McVITIES GOLD BAR "Working In The Coal Mine" (Allen
Toussaint) LEE DORSEY *OLD GOLD: OG 9108 (7")*
MALIBU "One Love"/"People Get Ready" (Bob Marley) BOB
MARLEY & THE WAILERS on 'Exodus' *ISLAND: CID 9498*
*(CD) ILPM/ICM 9498 (LP/MC)*
MALTESERS "Tease Me" by CHAKA DEMUS & PLIERS on 'Tease
Me" *MANGO-ISLAND (Poly): CIDMX(MCTX) 1102 (CD/MC)*
MANDATE AFTER SHAVE "Missing You" (J.Waite-M.Leonard-C.
Sandborn) JOHN WAITE on 'Missing You' (collect)
*EMI: CDEMTV 53 (CD) TCEMTV 53 (MC)*
MARMITE "Low Rider" (Jerry Goldstein and War) by WAR
*SONY MUSIC TV: SONYTV 30CD (CD) 30MC (MC)*
MARS BAR-2 "Crazy World" REDD KROSS on 'Phaseshifter'
*THIS WAY UP-ISLAND (Poly): 518 167-2 (CD) -4 (MC)*
MARS BAR-1 "Venus" (R.Van Leeuwen) *TV ver.not available*
orig by SHOCKING BLUE *OLD GOLD: OG 9736 (7")*
MASTERCARD-2 (Elvis Car) "Black Twist" by JACK TROMBEY
*unavailable*
MASTERCARD-1 "Angelina" (Allan Roberts-Doris Fisher-
Paolo Citarella-L.Prima) perf.by LOUIS PRIMA ORCH
*CAPITOL (EMI): CZ 423 (CDP 794072-2)(CD)*
MAXWELL HOUSE-2 "Going Home" (Mark Knopfler) from film
'Local Hero' -S/T- *VERTIGO (Poly): 811 038-2 (CD)*
*VERCD 81 (CDsigle)*
MAXWELL HOUSE-1 "The Mission" (Ennio Morricone) from
film -S/T- of the 1986 Robert De Niro-Jeremy Irons
movie *VIRGIN (Poly): CDV 2402 (CD) TCV 2402 (MC)*

MAYNARDS JUST FRUITS based on "Gimme Dat Ding" (Mike Ha
zlewood-Albert Hammond) orig The PIPKINS (1970)
MAYNARDS WINE GUMS "Hoots Mon" (Harry Robinson) by LORD
ROCKINGHAM'S XI (1959) on *DECCA (Poly): 882 098-2
(CDs) 882 098-4 (MC) 882 098-7 (7")* also 'BRITISH
'BEAT BEFORE THE BEATLES VOL.3' *EMI CDGO 2048 (CD)*
MAZDA CARS-2 "Double Concerto for Saxophone and Cello"
(Michael NYMAN) with JOHN HARLE-JULIAN LLOYD WEBBER
*EMI CLASSICS: CDC 556413-2 (CD)*
MAZDA CARS-1 'Shock Of The New' ad) 'Protection' by
MASSIVE ATTACK feat: TRACY *see COLLECTION 267*
MERCEDES BENZ-2 "Mercedes Benz" sung by JANIS JOPLIN
'Pearl' *COLUMBIA (Sony): CD 480 415-2 (CD)*
MERCEDES BENZ-1 from opera 'Cosi Fan Tutte' (MOZART)
MERCURY COMMUNICATIONS "Einstein A-Go-Go" (Burgess-Walt
ers-Heaton-Pask-Thomas) orig LANDSCAPE *RCA deleted*
MERCURY ONE-TO-ONE "Telephone and Rubber Band" (Simon
Jeffes) PENGUIN CAFE ORCHESTRA on 'Penguin Cafe Orc
hestra' *EG-VIRGIN (EMI): EEGCD 11(CD) OVEDC 429(MC)*
MFI "Just My Imagination" TEMPTATIONS (1971) 'Motowns
G.Hits' *MOTOWN (Poly):530105-2(CD) -4(MC) -5(DCC)*
MICHELOB LAGER-2 "Possente-Possente" (Act 1 'AIDA')
VERDI *(TV version unavailable)* also on Coll 'Relax
ing Opera' *CFP (EMI): CD(TC)CFP 4664 (CD/MC)*
MICHELOB LAGER-1 "Put A Little Love In Your Heart" (J.
De Shannon-Holiday-Myers) *sung by* JACKIE DE SHANNON
'Definitive Collection' *EMI LIBERTY: 829 786-2 (CD)*
MICROSOFT-4 "Heroes" (D.Bowie) sung by DAVID BOWIE
*EMI: CDP 797720-2 (CD)*
MICROSOFT-3 "Ring Of Fire" (Merle Kilgore-June Carter)
JOHNNY CASH 'Biggest Hits' *SONY:CD(40)32304 (CD/MC)*
MICROSOFT-2 "What A Wonderful World"(G.Weiss-G.Douglas)
*TV version: USA session vocalist (unavailable)*
MICROSOFT-1 "High Hopes" (Sammy Cahn-Jimmy Van Huesen)
JANET WEISS BAND (Holland) *unavailable*
MICROSOFT WINDOWS 95 "Start Me Up" (M-Jagger-K.Richard)
ROLLING STONES 'Tattoo You' *VIRGIN : CDV 2732 (CD)*
MIDLAND BANK-5 **Now I Need A Little Help (a)** based on
"Maggie May" (R.Stewart-M.Quittenton) *unavailable*
original recording by ROD STEWART *MERCURY Records*
MIDLAND BANK-4 **Now I Need A Little Help (b)** based on
"It Must Be Love" (Labi Siffre) *TV ver.unavailable*
orig recordings by MADNESS & LABI SIFFRE *available*
MIDLAND BANK-3 **Now I Need A Little Help** (c) based on "I
Say A Little Prayer" *not available* orig record. by
ARETHA FRANKLIN 'Best Of' *ATLANTIC:7567 81280-2 CD*
MIDLAND BANK-2 **Dough** / music based on "I Got You Babe"
(Sonny Bono) *TV version unavailable / orig vers
by* SONNY and CHER *ATLANTIC (WEA)* 'Greatest Hits'
MIDLAND BANK-1 "Sloop John B" *original by* BEACH BOYS
'20 Golden Greats' *EMI: CDP 746 738-2 (CD) TCEMTV 1*
MILK-2 *Dancing Bottles* "Grasshopper's Dance" (Ernest
BUCALOSSI) PALM COURT THEATRE ORCH. 'Picnic Party'
*CHANDOS: CHAN 8437 (CD) LBT 002 (MC)*

MILK-1 "Clog Dance" from ballet 'LA FILLE MAL GARDEE'
(Louis HEROLD) *EMI EMINENCE: CDEMX 2268 (CD)*
MILK - see also 'EURO MILK' and 'SCOTTISH DAIRIES'
MILK TRAY (Cadbury's)(orig ad)"The Night Rider" (Chris
Adams) by ALAN HAWKSHAW on Coll 'SOUND GALLERY' on
*EMI STUDIO TWO: CD(TC)TWO 2001 (CD/MC)*
MILK TRAY (Cadbury's) (White Pullover ad) "Man In Black
theme" (Chris Adams) arr.by Gary Bell *unavailable*
MILLER GENUINE DRAFT "Town Without Pity" (D.Tiomkin-Ned
Washington) *sung by* EDDI READER on *BLANCO Y NEGRO
(WEA): NEG 90CD (CDs) NEG 90MC (MC)*
MILLER LITE-2 "Somewhere Down The Crazy River" ROBBIE
ROBERTSON *GEFFEN-MCA (BMG): GFLD 19294 (CD)*
MILLER LITE-1 "He Ain't Heavy He's My Brother" (Russell
-Scott) The HOLLIES *EMI: CDP 746238-2 (CD)*
MINOLTA CAMERAS "You Are So Beautiful" (Billy Preston-
Bruce Fisher) by BONNIE TYLER *currently unavailable*
*orig* JOE COCKER *POLYDOR: 515 411-2 (CD) -4 (MC)*
MOBIL 1 "A Kind Of Magic" (Roger Taylor) *orig by* QUEEN
'A Kind Of Magic' *EMI: CDP 746 267-2 (CD) -4 (MC)*
MORRISSONS SUPERMARKETS "Mexican Hat Dance" (J.Tapatio)
JAMES LAST 'Trumpet A Go-Go' *POLYDOR 821 587-2 (CD)*
MULLER MULLERICE "Captain Of Your Ship" (Kenny Young-B.
Yardley) REPARATA & DELRONS *currently unavailable*
MULTI-CHEERIOS (Nestle) "Chinese Dance" from 'Nutcrack
er Suite' (TCHAIKOVSKY) *many versions available*
MURPHY'S IRISH STOUT (4) "The Wild Rover" (Trad.)....*NA*

**N.**P.I.PENSIONS "As Time Goes By" (Herman Hupfeld) from
'CASABLANCA' *see under Film title*
N.S.P.C.C. (a) "Sorry Seems To Be The Hardest Word" (El
lton John) ELTON JOHN 'G.Hits' *POLY: 846947-2 (2CD)*
(b) "Tell Me There's A Heaven"(Chris Rea) CHRIS REA
'Road To Hell' *WEA MAGNET: 246 285-2 (CD) WX 317(C)*
(c) "Turn Turn Turn" (Pete Seeger) BYRDS on Collect
'20 Essential Tracks' *COLUMBIA: 471665-2 (CD) -4*
NAPOLINA SAUCES "Luna Rossa" (De Crescenzo-Antonio Vian
Kermit Goell) by ANEMA ECORE on 'Neopolitan Songs
1945-58' *ENTERPRISE LIBRARY: OM 3305 (CD)*
NAT WEST "Crockett's Theme" (Jan Hammer) JAN HAMMER
'Escape From Television'*MCA (BMG): MCLD(MCLC)19133*
NATIONAL POWER "The Right Stuff" (Bill Conti) -S/T- on
*VARESE (Pinn): VCD 47250 (CD) with* 'NORTH & SOUTH'
NATIONAL SAVINGS OPTION BONDS-2 "Let's Twist Again"
(Kal Mann-Dave Appell) orig by CHUBBY CHECKER
NATIONAL SAVINGS OPTION BONDS-1 "Morning Mood" from
'Peer Gynt Suite No.1' Op.46 (GRIEG) BERLIN PHILHAR
MONIC ORCH (Von Karajan) *DG-POLYG: 423 208-2 (CD)*
NATIONWIDE B.SOC.5 "One Nation Under A Groove" original
FUNKADELIC on 'Best Of Funkadelic 1976-81' *CHARLY
GROOVE: CDGR 104 (CD) GRLPD 104 (2LP)*
NATIONWIDE B.SOC.4 "You Can Get It It You Really Want
It" (Jimmy Cliff) DESMOND DEKKER & ACES on 'Best Of
Desmond Dekker' *MCI (THE): MCCD(MCTC) 115 (CD/MC)*

NATIONWIDE B.SOC.3 (Alfred Hitchcock theme ad)
"Funeral March Of A Marionette" (Charles GOUNOD) on
Coll 'Chiller' TELARC (Con-BMG): CD 80189 (CD)
NATIONWIDE B.SOC.2 "Makin' Whoopee" (Walter Donaldson-
Gus Kahn) orig from 'Whoopee' and 'Show Business'
(EDDIE CANTOR films) TV vers.unavailable
NATIONWIDE B.SOC.1 (Letter / Special Dream)
"Dreams" (John Trivers-Stanley Myers) unavailable
NATREL PLUS (Flower Girl) "Read My Lips (Saturday Night
Party)" (A.Party) ALEX PARTY CLEVELAND CITY BLUE
(3MV Sony): CCICD 17000 (CDs) CCI 17000 (12"s)
NATREL PLUS (Willow ad) "Sex Sleep Eat And Drink" by
KING CRIMSON DISCIPLINE-VIRGIN (EMI): KCCDY 1 (CDs)
NESCAFE "Dawn" 'Peer Gynt Suite No.1" Op.46 (GRIEG)
NESCAFE CAPPUCCINO "Dock Of The Bay" (Steve Cropper-O.R
edding) OTIS REDDING ATLANTIC (WEA): A.4432CD (CDs)
A.4432C (MC)
NESTLE - see under brand name e.g. 'LION BAR'
NETWORK Q "Only You" (Buck Ram) TV vers.not available
orig by The PLATTERS 'Golden Hits' MERCURY-POLY:
826 447-2 (CD)
NIKE-5 (Eric Cantona ad) "Parklife" by BLUR
FOOD (EMI): FOOD(CD)(MC)(LP) 10
NIKE-4 ("Trail Running" ad)(ILS) by MO-WAX unavailable
NIKE-3 AIR MAX "Revolution" (Lennon-McCartney) JULIANA
HATFIELD arr.by SMASHING PUMPKINS curr.unavailable
NIKE-2 (Olympics 96) "Search and Destroy" (Iggy Pop)
IGGY & STOOGES 'Raw Power' SONY: 476 610-2 (CD)
NIKE-1 "My Way" (C.Francois-J.Revaux-P.Anka) by SHANE
MacGOWAN on ZTT-WEA: ZANG 79D (CDs) ZANG 79C (MC)
NIBLE BREAD (60's ad) "I Can't Let Maggie Go" (Pete
Dello) The HONEYBUS on 'At Their Best' on
See For Miles (Pinn): SEECD 264 (CD)
NISSAN (theme) "Astrea" by JOHN HARLE on 'SILENCIUM'
ARGO-DECCA (Poly): 458 356-02 (CD) see COLLECT 409
NISSAN ALMERA-2 "The Sweeney" by HARRY SOUTH
see COLLECTION 5
NISSAN ALMERA-1 "The Professionals" (Laurie Johnson)
see COLLECTION 5
NISSAN MICRA-5 "The Glory Of Love" (B.Hill) version by
JIMMY DURANTE WB (WEA): 9362 45456-2 (CD)
NISSAN MICRA-4 "I Dream Of Jeannie" theme (Hugo Monten
egro-Buddy Kaye) see COLLECTION 339
NISSAN MICRA-3 ('Hollywood') (Stuntman) "Beach Samba"
ASTRUD GILBERTO on 'Beach Samba' on VERVE-POLYDOR
(Polyg): 519 801-2 (CD)
NISSAN MICRA-2 "You Don't Love Me (No No No)" (Dawn
Penn) DAWN PENN see COLLECTION 10
NISSAN MICRA-1 "Don't Blame It On That Girl" by MATT
BIANCO on 'The Best Of Matt Bianco' on WEA INT:
9031 72590-2 (CD) WX 376C (MC)
NISSAN PRIMERA-3 "Aquarium" -'Carnival Of The Animals'
(SAINT-SAENS) I MUSICI DE MONTREAL (Turovsky)
CHANDOS: CHAN 9246 (CD)

NISSAN PRIMERA-2 "Wild Thing" (Chip Taylor) The TROGGS
'Greatest Hits' *POLYGRAM: 522 739-2 (CD)*
NISSAN PRIMERA-1 New Primera 1996 "Lifted" (Tucker-Baiy
ewu-Brammer) LIGHTHOUSE FAMILY from 'Ocean Drive'
*POLDOR: 523 787-2(CD) -4(MC) / 851 669-2 CD* s
NIVEA LOTIONS "Blue Velvet" (Bernie Wayne-Lee Morris)
by BOBBY VINTON (63) *EPIC (SM): 467570-2(CD) -4(MC)*
NO.7 - see BOOTS NO.7
NOKIA MOBILE PHONES "Gran Valse"(Francesco Parago) *KOKA
France Import: KLA 3008 UK availability unconfirmed*
NORTHERN IRELAND (Peace ad) "Brown Eyed Girl" VAN MORRI
SON on 'Best Of' *POLYDOR: 841 970-2 (CD) -4 (MC)
-1 (LP) -5 (DCC) also used* "Coney Island" VAN MORRI
SON *POLY: 839 262-2 (CD) -4 (MC) -1 (LP) -5 (DCC)*
NORTHERN ROCK BUILDING SOC.2 "Fields Of Gold" (Sting)
STING from 'Ten Summoners Tales' *(TV Vers: special
edit) A.& M.(Poly): 540 075-2 (CD) -4 (MC) -1 (LP)*
NORTHERN ROCK BUILDING SOC.1 "Nocturne No.19" Op.72 No.
1 (CHOPIN) *various recordings available*
NORWICH UNION (Space) (the choral ad) "Space" composed
and conducted by Robert LOCKHART..*unavailable*
NUROFEN-2 "Etude" (Francisco TARREGA) by MIKE OLDFIELD
from ' The Killing Fields' -S/T- *VIRGIN: OVED 283
(LP) OVEDC283(MC) CDV2328 (CD)* also 'Gakkaen' (Aki
ra Tamba) by ONO GAGAKU KAI SOCIETY ORCH on 'Japon'
*OCORA C.559018(CD)* BOTH TRACKS: *VIRGIN VS 1328 (7")*
NUROFEN-1 "The Great Gig In The Sky" (Pink Floyd) on
'The Dark Side Of The Moon' - PINK FLOYD *HARVEST
CDP 746001-2 (CD SHVL 804 (LP) TC-SHVL 804 (MC)*
NUROFEN PLUS orig music by Michael NYMAN *unavailable*
NUTCRACKER Terry's "Chinese Dance" from 'The Nutcracker
Suite' (TCHAIKOVSKY) *many recordings available*
ODDBINS "Cocktails For Two"(S.Coslow-A.Johnston) SPIKE
JONES & CITY SLICKERS *RCA (BMG): 74321 13576-2 CD*
OIL OF ULAY-2 "First Time Ever I Saw Your Face" (Ewan
MacColl) ROBERTA FLACK *OLD GOLD: OG 9524 (7"s)*
OIL OF ULAY-1 "Stay As Sweet As You Are" (Mack Gordon-
Harry Revel) *TV vers.not available* / NAT KING COLE
'Love Is The Thing' *CAPITOL (EMI):CDP 746 648-2(CD)*
OLD SPICE-2 "I Feel Good" (J.Brown) JAMES BROWN 'Very
Best of James Brown' *Poly: 845 828-2(CD) -4(MC)*
OLD SPICE-1 "Prima Vere" (Carmina Burana) (Carl ORFF)
OLYMPUS CAMERAS "Gala Performance" (This Is Your Life)
(L.Johnson) LAURIE JOHNSON ORCH Coll'A-Z Of British
TV Themes Vol.3' *PLAY IT AGAIN (BMG): PLAY 010 (CD)*
ONE-TO-ONE (Mercury) "Telephone and Rubber Band" (Simon
Jeffes) PENGUIN CAFE ORCHESTRA on 'Penguin Cafe Orc
hestra' *EG-VIRGIN (EMI): EEGCD 11(CD) OVEDC 429(MC)*
OPAL FRUITS "Oh Happy Day" (Edwin Hawkins) original by
EDWIN HAWKINS SINGERS *CASTLE (BMG): MAT(CD)(MC) 280*
ORANGE HUTCHINSON-4 "I Loves You Porgy" (from G.& I.Ger
shwin's Porgy & Bess) sung by NINA SIMONE on 'Lady
Blue' *CHARLY: CPCD 82402 (2CD) also on* 'Great Nina
Simone' *MCI (DISC): MCCD 312 (CD)*

ORANGE HUTCHINSON-3 "To Cure A Weakling Child" by The
APHEX TWIN from the album 'Richard D.James LP' on
*WARP (RTM-Disc):WARP(CD)(MC)43*
ORANGE HUTCHINSON-2 "Blow The Wind Southerly" arrang.
by JOCELYN POOK and featuring KATHLEEN FERRIER on
*VIRGIN (EMI): VTDCD 158 (2CD) see COLLECTION 267*
*origin* KATHLEEN FERRIER solo on 'World Of Kathleen
Ferrier' *DECCA (Poly): 430 096-2 (CD) -4 (MC)*
ORANGE HUTCHINSON-1 music by PHILIP GLASS *unavailable*
*but similar to* PHILIP GLASS opera "Einstein On The
Beach" *ELEKTRA NONESUCH (WEA): 7559 79323-2 (3CDs)*
ORANGINA "Pida Me La" (Michel Berger) GYPSY KINGS 'Grea
test Hits" *COLUMBIA: 477242-2 (CD) -4 (MC) -1(LP)*
ORGANICS SHAMPOO "Blossoming Women" (Karl Jenkins- Mike
Ratledge) Jenkins-Ratledge Productions *unavailable*
OVALTINE LIGHT "Hev Yew Gotta Loight, Boy?" by Alan
Smetherst (SINGING POSTMAN 1966) orig on 'Best Of'
*EMI: GEP 8956 (EP) Starline: SRS 5063 (LP) deleted*
OVALTINE OPTIONS "Mind Blowing Decisions" (John Wilder)
HEATWAVE on 'Powercuts' *EPIC (SM): 468921-2 (CD) -4*
**P.**& O.EUROPEAN CRUISES  "The Bell Song" from 'Lakme'
(DELIBES) arr.by MALCOLM McLAREN *unavailable*
P.& O.EUROPEAN FERRIES-2 "C'est Si Facile De Vous Aim
er"sung by JOSEPHINE BAKER Coll 'Great French Stars
Of 30's" *HAPPY DAYS (CON-BMG): CD(MC)HD 157 (CD/MC)*
P.& O.EUROPEAN FERRIES-1 "Stompin'At The Savoy"(B.Goo
dman-Andy Razaf-E.Sampson-Chick Webb) BENNY GOODMAN
*RCA BLUE BIRD (BMG): ND(NK) 90631 (CD/MC)*
PANADOL EXTRA "He Ain't Heavy He's My Brother" HOLLIES
*EMI: CDP 746238-2 (CD)*
PANASONIC NICAM TV "Rondo" Finale 'Eine Kleine Nachtmus
ik' Serenade No.13 in G.K525 (MOZART) *various vers.*
PAXO STUFFING "I'm In The Mood For ('Ska') Love" (Jimmy
McHugh-Dorothy Fields) by LORD TANAMO on *MOONCREST*
*(Total-BMG): MOON 1009 (7"s) 12MOON 1009 (12")*
also TECHNIQUES on 'BaBaBoom' *TROJAN: TRLS 265 (LP)*
PEARL INSURANCE (a) based on "Greased Lightning" (from
'Grease') *Orig on Polydor see under Film title*
"Lean On Me" (Withers) *ver:* BILL WITHERS: *SONY: RCD*
*(40)32343 (CD/MC)* (c) based on "Fame" *see FILM*
PEARL PENSIONS "As Time Goes By" (Herman Hupfeld) from
'Casablanca' (1943) *see under Film title*
PEARL SOAP - *see under* 'CUSSONS PEARL'
PEDIGREE CHUM-2 "The Best" (Knight-Chapman) TINA TURNER
'Foreign Affair' *CAPITOL (EMI): CD(TC)ESTU 2103*
PEDIGREE CHUM-1 1st m/m from 'New World Symphony' No.9
in E.Min.Op.95 (DVORAK) *many recordings available*
PENTIUM - see INTEL
PEOPLE'S PHONE (Mobile Phones) "Yes We Have No Bananas"
(Frank Silver-Irving Cohn) *TV version unavailable*
PEPSI-5 NEXT GENERERATION "Step To Me" by SPICE GIRLS
*available only through PEPSI promotions*
PEPSI-4 "Rhythm Of My Heart" (Jordan-Capek) ROD STEWART
*W.BROS (WEA): W0017(7")(T=12")(C=Cas)(CD)*

# 36      T . V .COMMERCIALS

PEPSI-3 "Seal Our Fate" (G.Estefan) GLORIA ESTEFAN
    *EPIC: 656773-7(7") -6(12") -4(MC) -2(CDs)*
PEPSI-2 "The Best" (Knight-Chapman)- TINA TURNER
    'Foreign Affair' *CAPITOL (EMI): CD(TC)ESTU 2103*
PEPSI-1 "It Takes Two" (William Stevenson-Sylvia
    Moy) ROD STEWART & TINA TURNER (1990) *W.BROS.(WEA):*
    *ROD 1(T)(C)(CD) (7"/12"/Cas/CD)* /orig (1966) MARVIN
    GAYE & KIM WESTON on *MOTOWN (Poly): ZD 72397 (CD)*
PERNOD "Free The Spirit" by DANNY CAMPBELL *unavailable*
PERRIER "Crossroads Blues" (Robert Johnson) on Collect
    'King Of The Delta Blues Singers' *COLUMBIA (Sony):*
    *4844102 (CD)* + *'Complete Rec.'Sony: 46222-2 (CD)* +
    'CROSSROADS' The BRIDGE *ILC (SONY): ILC 1CDS (CDs)*
PERSIL (Stain Release) (based on 'Prelude in C.Minor'
    (CHOPIN) TV ver:Paul Hart-Joe Campbell *unavailable*
PERSIL (Concentrated Liquid)(CHORAL AD) "Liquid Asset"
    (Ralph Allwood) prod.Joseph Glasman *unavailable*
PERSIL **New Generation** "Chariots Of Fire" (Vangelis)
    on 'Themes' *POLYDOR (Poly): 839 518-2 (CD) -4 (MC)*
PERSIL **NON BIO** "Teddy Bears Picnic" (Jimmy Kennedy-John
    Bratton) *TV version not available*
PEUGEOT 106-3 KEY WEST / KEY LARGO (spec.edit.) "Open
    Your Heart" (Madonna Ciccone-Gardner Cole-Peter Raf
    elson) by MADONNA from 'True Blue' (86) *SIRE (Wea):*
    *925 442-2 (CD) WX 54C (MC) WX 54 (LP)* & *on single*
PEUGEOT 106-2 "(We Want)The Same Thing" (Rich.Howells-
    Ellen Shipley) BELINDA CARLISLE on 'Best Of Belinda
    V.1' *VIRGIN (EMI): BELCD(MC)(MD)1 (CD/MC/mini-ds)*
PEUGEOT 106-1 MARDI GRAS (spec.edit) "My Blue Heaven"
    (Walter Donaldson-George Whiting) FATS DOMINO on
    'Best Of Fats Domino' *MFP (EMI): CDMFP 5026 (CD)*
PEUGEOT 306-6 "Can't Take My Eyes Off You" Crewe-Gaudio
    ANDY WILLIAMS on 'Can't Get Used To Losing You'
    *COLUMBIA (Sony): 477 591-2(CD)*
PEUGEOT 306-5 "Last Night" (Axton-Smith-Newman-Caple-
    Moman) orig by MAR-KEYS (1961) also used as theme
    for BBC series 'BOTTOM' on 'BEST OF BRITISH TELEVIS
    ION' *MCI (THE): MCCD 225 (CD)*
PEUGEOT 306-4 "Return To Innocence" (Enigma) ENIGMA
    on 'Cross Of Changes' *VIRGIN (EMI): CDVIR 20 (CD)*
    *MCVIR 20 (MC) VIR 20 (LP) DINSD 123 (CDsingle)*
PEUGEOT 306-3 "I Drove All Night" ROY ORBISON on 'King
    Of Hearts' *VIRGIN (EMI): CDVUS 58 (CD) VUSMC 58*
    *(MC)* and *Virgin: VUS(C)(CD) 79 (7"/CDs/MC)*
    'Very Best Of' *MOTOWN (Poly): 530292-2(CD) -4(MC)*
PEUGEOT 306-2 based on "It Must Be Love"(Labi Siffre)
    orig by MADNESS on 'Divine Madness' *VIRGIN:CDV 2692*
PEUGEOT 306-1 "Sexual Healing" (M.Gaye) - MARVIN GAYE
    *Various G.Hits compilations*
PEUGEOT 405 "Take My Breath Away"(Moroder-T.Whitlock)
    BERLIN from -S/T- 'Top Gun' *COLUMBIA (Sony)*
PEUGEOT 406-2 (Kim Basinger) "Dream A Little Dream Of
    Me" (Kahn-Schwandt-Andre) orig MAMAS AND PAPAS on
    '20 GOLDEN GREATS' *MCA (BMG): MCLD 19125 (CD)*

PEUGEOT 406-1 "Search For The Hero" (Mike Pickering)
M.PEOPLE from 'Bizarre Fruit II' De CONSTRUCTION
(BMG): 74321 32817-2 (CD) -4 (MC) / previously
74321 28796-2(CDs) -4(MC) -1(12") deleted
PHILIPS ELECTRICAL-2 "Natural Woman" (Carole King) by
RONNIE BOND Productions unavailable
PHILIPS ELECTRICAL-1 "Hold On I'm Comin'" (Isaac Hayes-
David Porter) SAM & DAVE on 'Best Of Sam and Dave'
ATLANTIC (WEA): 781 202-2 (CD) -4 (MC)
PHILIPS PHILISHAVE FOR MEN "The Man Inside" by JOHN
SILVERMAN unavailable
PHOSTROGEN (Dancing Hedgehogs ad) "Ma Belle Marguerita"
from 'Bless The Bride' (V.Ellis-A.P.Herbert)sung by
GEORGES GUETARY DRG (New Note-Pinn): CDXP 605 (CD)
+ ROSSENDALE MALE VOICE CHOIR CHANDOS: CHAN 6604 CD
PICNIC (Cadbury) "My Coo Ca Choo" (Peter Shelley) ALVIN
STARDUST on 'Greatest Hits' on CONNOISSEUR (Pinn):
CSALP 105 (LP) CSAPMC 105 (MC) CSACD 105 (CD)
PIMMS "Summertime" (George & Ira Gershwin) from 'Porgy
& Bess' KIRI TE KANAWA 'Kiri Sings Gershwin' EMI EL
270474-1/-4 / CDC747454-2 (CD) see Films & Shows
PIONEER IN-CAR CD SYSTEM "Driver's Seat" SNIFF 'N' THE
TEARS CHISWICK (Pinn): CDWIK 102(CD) WIKC 102(MC)
PIRELLI TYRES-6 (Running Girl) "Elektrobank" CHEMICAL
BROTHERS FREESTYLE DUST-VIRGIN (EMI):CHEMSD 6 (CDs)
PIRELLI TYRES-5 (Carl Lewis) music by Richard James
performed by The APHEX TWIN unavailable
PIRELLI TYRES-4 (Sharon Stone) "Symph.No.9' (BEETHOVEN)
+ "Worldly Woman" (Steve Parsons) unavailable
PIRELLI TYRES-3 "Riders On The Storm" (J.Densmore-Jim
Morrison-Robbie Krieger-Ray Manzarek) THE DOORS on
'L.A.Woman' ELEKTRA (WEA): K2-42090 (CD) K4 (MC)
PIRELLI TYRES-2 "Vesti La Giubba"'On With The Motley'
from 'Pagliacci' (LEONCAVALLO) versions inc: FRANCO
CORELLI EMI: CDC 747851-2(CD) JOSE CARRERAS HMV: EX
290811-3 (2LP) EX 290811-5 (2Cas) LUCIANO PAVAROTTI
DECCA:414590-2(2CD) JUSSI BJORLING EMI:CDC 749503-2
PIRELLI TYRES-1 "Nessun Dorma" (None Shall Sleep)from
'Turandot' (PUCCINI) GEOFF LOVE ORCH 'Opera Without
Words' EMI: CDP 746931-2 (CD) PLACIDO DOMINGO 'The
Essential Domingo' DG: 429305-2 (CD) PDTVC 1 (MC)
LUCIANO PAVAROTTI DECCA 417011-2 (2 CD's)
PIZZA HUT "Hot Hot Hot" by ARROW (84) on'Sound Of Soul'
BLATANT (CASTLE COMM/BMG): BLATCD 11 (CD)
PLAYTEX CHERISH "Oh Lori" originally by ALESSI (77) on
Coll 'Walking On Sunshine' KENWEST: KNEWCD 742 (CD)
POMAGNE "Pizzicato" from 'Sylvia' Ballet (DELIBES)
POT TV - see under 'GOLDEN WONDER POT TV'
POWERGEN - see under 'NATIONAL POWER'
PPP HEALTHCARE-2 "Boum!" by CHARLES TRENET on 'PARIS..
CAFE CONCERT' FLAPPER (Pavilion-Pinn): PASTCD 9797
also 'Extraordinary Garden Best Of CHARLES TRENET'
EMI: CDP 794 464-2 (CD) / also available on 'Boum'
MUSIDISQUE (Target-BMG): MDF 10264 (CD)

PPP HEALTHCARE-1 "Someone To Watch Over Me" (George &
   Ira Gershwin) *TV vers* DUSTY SPRINGFIELD *unavailable*
PRESTIGE OVENWARE "What Becomes Of The Broken Hearted"
   (Riser-Dean-Weatherspoon) - JIMMY RUFFIN - *MOTOWN*
   *(Poly):* 530 057-2 *(CD)* 530 057-4 *(MC)*
PRETTY POLLY-3 Legacy "All Day And All Of The Night"
   (Ray Davies) KINKS (64) 'Kinks Collection' *CASTLE*
   *COLLECTORS (BMG):* CCSCD 113 *(CD)* CCSMC 113 *(2MC)*
PRETTY POLLY-2 "Mario Mario" Love Duet Act 1 'Tosca'
   (PUCCINI) TV version: MARIO DEL MONACO with Renata
   Tebaldi on *DECCA:* 417 175-4DA *(MC)* OTHERS 'Great
   Love Duets' JOSE CARRERAS and Katia Ricciarelli on
   *DECCA 421308-2(CD)*  also GIACOMO ARAGALL & KIRI TE
   KANAWA and Nat.Philh.Orch *DECCA:* 414 597-2 *(2 CDs)*
PRETTY POLLY-1 "The Very Thought Of You" (Ray Noble)
   AL BOWLLY on 'Love Is The Sweetest Thing' *CHARLY*
   *CDCD 1136 (CD)*
PRUDENTIAL-2 "Moonglow" (Mills-DeLange-Hudson) *TV Vers*
   *unavailable* orig by BENNY GOODMAN ORCH *various CDs*
PRUDENTIAL-1 (Whatever You Want In Life) "Prudential"
   NICHOLAS DODD *unavailable*
PYRAMINTS Terry's 'Egyptian-Ella' (Walter Doyle) JACK
   HYLTON ORCH (1931) *available version:* TED WEEMS &
   HIS ORCH on 'Marvellous!' *LIVING ERA-ASV (Koch Int)*
   *CDAJA 5029 (CD) ZCAJA 5029 (MC)*
Q.C.SHERRY "Orchid Ella" (Pierre Arvay) published by
   De Wolfe Music *unavailable*
QUITLINE (Anti-Smoking Campaign) "Ain't Go No - I Got
   Life" (Ragni-Rado-McDermott from 'Hair') sung by
   NINA SIMONE on "Feeling Good" *POLY: 522669-2 (CD)*
QUALITY STREET "Magic Moments" (Burt Bacharach-H.David)
   *TV Version by* NEIL INNES *unavailable*
   PERRY COMO *Old Gold: OG 9606 (7")*
RAC 2 "Midnight Cowboy" (theme) (John Barry) on Colls
   'HITS FROM THE MOVIES' *MFP (EMI): CD(TC)* MFP 6138
   and also 'MOVIOLA' *EPIC Soundtrax:* 472 490-2 *(CD)*
RAC 1 (New Knights Of The Road) "Gimme Shelter" (M.
   Jagger-K.Richard) ROLLING STONES on 'Hot Rocks 64-
   71' *LONDON (Poly):* 820140-2 *(2CD)* -4 *(MC)* also on
   "Let It Bleed" *London:* 820052-2 *(CD) SKL(KSKC)* 5025
RADIO TIMES "Oriental Shuffle" by DJANGO REINHARDT and
   STEPHANE GRAPELLI Quintet Of The Hot Club Of France
   *FLAPPER (Pav/Pinn):* PASTCD 9738*(CD)* PAST 7738*(MC)*
RADION MICRO PLUS "In The Mood"(Andy Razaf-Joe Garland)
   GLENN MILLER ORCHESTRA *RCA Various compilations*
RADOX BATH SALTS "Sleepless in Sydney" composed and per
   formed by Chris Blackwell *unavailable*
RAGU PASTA SAUCE-5 "Funiculi-Funicula" (DENZA) version
   JOSE CARRERAS *POLY: 400015-2 (CD)* LUCIANO PAVAROTTI
   *DECCA: 410015-2 (CD) and 417011-2 (CD)*
RAGU PASTA SAUCE-4 "Vesto La Guibba" from 'I Pagliacci'
   (LEONCAVALLO) *various versions available)*
RAGU PASTA SAUCE-3 "La Donna E Mobile" from 'Rigoletto'
   (VERDI) *various versions available*

RAGU PASTA SAUCE-2 "Anvil Chorus" from 'Il Travatore'
(VERDI) *various versions available*
RAGU PASTA SAUCE-1 Aria "Largo Factotem" from 'Barber
Of Seville' (ROSSINI) *various versions available*
RAILTRACK SHARE OFFER "North By Northwest" (Bernard Her
rmann) -S/T- *EMI PREMIER: CDODEON 6 (CD)*
RANIERI - see WALLS RANIERI
RAPPORT AFTER SHAVE "Let's Stay Together" by AL GREEN
*HI-DEMON (Pinn): HIUKCCD 130(CD) HIUKCASS 130(MC)*
RED MOUNTAIN COFFEE-3 "Country Living" composed and
performed by JOHN CAMERON *unavailable*
RED MOUNTAIN COFFEE-2 "I'm The Leader Of The Gang"
(Gary Glitter-Mike Leander) GARY GLITTER & GLITTER
BAND 'Very Best' *PICKWICK CARLTON: PWKS 4052 (CD)*
RED MOUNTAIN COFFEE-1 "Ever Fallen In Love With Someone
You Shouldn't'ave" (P.Shelley) BUZZCOCKS on 'This
Is Not A Love Song' *CONNOISS.COLL: VSOPCD 193 (CD)*
REEBOK-5 (Raindrops ad) 2nd m/m Symphony No.7 in A.Maj
(BEETHOVEN) *TV ver: special arrangement unavailable*
REEBOK-4 "Let's Do One" (Lisa Inayoue) "Do What I Want"
(Dominic Jennings) "What Could It Be" (Ingrid Konup
ek) "Extreme" (Daniel Caccavo) *all unavailable*
REEBOK-3 "Meet The Flintstones" (Hoyt Curtin) 'Televi
sion's G.Hits V.1' *EDEL (Pinn):*
REEBOK-2 "Life Party" (2 Deep) 2 DEEP on *ATOMIC/A.& M
(Poly): WNR 821 (7") WNRT 821 (12") WNRCD 821 (CDs)*
REEBOK-1 "Epic" by CHRIS BLACKWELL *unavailable*
RENAULT (Nicole - Papa ads) "Johnny and Mary" (Robert
Palmer) MARTIN TAYLOR on '100% SUMMER JAZZ' Collect
*TELSTAR (BMG): TCD 2781 (CD) STAC 2781 (MC)*
RENAULT CLIO (new) "Keep On Movin'" by SOUL II SOUL on
'Classic Singles' *VIRGIN-EMI: CDV(TCV) 2724 (CD/MC)*
RENAULT LAGUNA "Paper Chase" (Colin Towns) *unavailable*
RIBENA "Absurd" by FLUKE *CIRCA-VIRGIN (EMI): YRCD 126
(CDs) YRT 126 (12"s)*
RIGHT GUARD-2 - based on "Working In The Coal Mine"
(Allen Toussaint) by LEE DORSEY 'Gold Mine' Coll
*CHARLY Classics: CDCD 1115 (CD) CDMC 1115 (MC)*
RIGHT GUARD-1 "Three Little Birds" (Don't Worry' bout
A Thing)(B.Marley) BOB MARLEY & WAILERS 'Legend'
*ISLAND: BMWCD 1 (CD) BMWCX 1 (MC) BMWX 1 (LP)*
RIMMELL COSMETICS 3 "Girl Like You" EDWYN COLLINS 'Gorg
eous George' *SETANTA (Vital): SET(CD)(MC)(LP) 014*
RIMMELL COSMETICS-2 "Allright" by SUPERGRASS from
'I Should Coco' *EMI PARLOPHONE: CD(TC)PCS 7373*
RIMMELL COSMETICS-1 "Silk" by PHIL SAWYER *unavailable*
ROAD SAFETY (Don't Look Now) "Mysteries Of Love" JULEE
CRUISE from 'Floating Into The Night' *W.BROS (WEA):
925 859-2 (CD) 925 859-4 (MC)*
ROCKY BAR (Fox's) based on "Rockin'Robin" *originally by*
BOBBY DAY (58) on 'Rockin'Robin' *ACE: CDCH 200 (CD)*
MICHAEL JACKSON (72) 'Best Of M.Jackson' *MOTOWN BMG*
ROVER 200 "Englishman In New York" (Sting) by STING
'Fields of Gold' *A.& M.(Poly): 540307-2(CD) -4(MC)*

ROVER 400-4 "Rupert Bear" from 'The ENGLISH PATIENT'
by GABRIEL YARED *FANTASY (Pinn): FCD 16001 (CD)*
ROVER 400-3 "God Moving Over The Face Of Waters" MOBY
from album 'Everything Is Wrong' *MUTE (RTM/Disc):*
*CDSTUMM 130 (CD) CSTUMM 130 (MC) STUMM 130 (LP)*
ROVER 400-2 "Unforgettable" (Irving Gordon) version
by NAT KING COLE on 'Unforgettable Nat King Cole'
*CAPITOL (EMI): CDEMTV 61 (CD) TCEMTV 61 (MC)*
ROVER 400-1 "Nevertheless" (Bert Kalmar-H.Ruby) from
'Three Little Words' (Film 36 with Fred Astaire) TV
version by NILSSON on 'A Little Touch Of Schmilsson
In The Night' *see ROVER 800*
ROVER 800 "Lullaby In Ragtime" (Harry Nilsson)- NILSSON
on 'A Little Touch Of Schmilsson In The Night' *RCA:*
*(BMG) NK 83761 (MC) NL 83761 (LP)*   *CD unconfirmed*
ROVER KENSINGTON 100  "Brass In Pocket" (Chrissie Hynde
James Honeyman Scott) The PRETENDERS 'The Singles'
on *Real (WEA): 242229-2 (CD) WX 135C (MC)*
ROVER METRO RIO "Rio" (Duran Duran) by DURAN DURAN on
'Rio' *PARLOPHONE (EMI): CD(TC)PRG 1004 (CD/MC)*
ROYAL AIR FORCE 2 (Boredom) "Adagietto" from Symphony
No.5 (G.MAHLER) *various recordings available*
ROYAL AIR FORCE 1 (Payload) "Crystal Method" (remix)
by 808 STATE *recording unconfirmed*
ROYAL BANK OF SCOTLAND-6 "Savings Symphony" CARL DAVIS
*unavailable*
ROYAL BANK OF SCOTLAND-5 "Cursum Perficio" (Enya) from
'Watermark' ENYA - *WEA: 243875-2 (CD) -4 (MC)*
ROYAL BANK OF SCOTLAND-4 "Playful Pizzicato" from 'A
Simple Symphony' Op.4 (B.BRITTEN) *many recordings*
ROYAL BANK OF SCOTLAND-3 "Pictures At An Exhibition"
(MUSSORGSKY) *many recordings available*
ROYAL BANK OF SCOTLAND-2 "Lieutenant Kije Suite" Op.60
(PROKOFEV) *EMI: EG 290298-1 (LP) -4 (MC)* (A.PREVIN)
ROYAL BANK OF SCOTLAND-1 "The Sorcerer's Apprentice"
(DUKAS) - *various versions available*
ROYAL LIVER ASSURANCE "Lean On Me" *TV vers unavailable*
BILL WITHERS *SONY: CD 32343 (CD) 40-32343 (MC)*
ROYAL MAIL "Patricia" (Prado) *original by* PEREZ PRADO
ORCH on 'KING OF MAMBO' *RCA (BMG): ND 90424 (CD)*
RSPCA CREDIT CARD "All Creatures Great and Small" by
JOHNNY PEARSON *PLAY IT AGAIN (BMG): PLAY 006 (CD)*
RYVITA Sarah Stockbridge ad "Black Velvet"*p.De Wolfe.*NA

SAAB (var.inc.'Beyond The Conventional') "Saab"/"Naked"
"Testing" Paul HART and Joe CAMPBELL) *unavailable*
SAINSBURY'S-2 "I'm Putting All My Eggs In One Basket"
(I.Berlin) LOUIS ARMSTRONG 'Rhythm Saved The World'
*GRP-MCA (BMG): GRP 16022 (CD)*
SAINSBURY'S-1 "Thirtysomething" (W.G.Snuffy Walden)
SALON SELECTIVES "Breakout" (M.Jackson-C.Drewery-A.Conn
ell) by SWING OUT SISTER on 'It's Better To Travel'
*FONTANA-MERCURY (Poly): 832 213-2 (CD) SWICD 9(CDs)*
SANATOGEN "Do You Feel Alright" Chris BLACKWELL *unavail*

SARSONS VINEGAR "Coronation Scott" (Vivian Ellis) *Coll*
   'FAMOUS THEMES' *GRASMERE (BMG): GRCD 10 (CD)*
SCHWEPPES MALVERN WATER "Symphony No.1-4th movement"
   (ELGAR) *many recordings available*
SCHWEPPES MIXERS "Celebration" by Mark CAMPBELL
                                        *unavailable*
SCHWEPPES SCHIZAN "Return To Innocence" (Michael Cretu)
   by ENIGMA on 'Cross Of Changes' *VIRGIN (EMI): CDVIR
   20 (CD) MCVIR 20 (MC)*
SCOTCH VIDEO TAPES "Not Fade Away" (B.Holly-N.Petty) by
   ROLLING STONES *(DECCA)* and BUDDY HOLLY *(MCA)*
SCOTTISH DAIRIES (MILK) "Don't You Forget About Me" (Ke
   ith Forsey-Steve Schiff) by SIMPLE MINDS on *VIRGIN
   SMTVD 1 (CD) SMTVC 1(MC) SMTVM 1(MD) 463168 (DCC)*
SCOTTISH TOURIST BOARD  "Wild Mountain Thyme" tradit.
   performed by THE SILENCERS on 'NEW PURE MOODS' on
   *VIRGIN (EMI): VTDCD 158 (2CD)*
SCOTTISH WIDOWS "Looking Good" (Tony & Gaynor Sadler)
   p.Logorythm Music *unavailable*
SCRUMPY JACK CIDER "The Moldau" 'Ma Vlast'(My Country)
   Smetana *vers.*'CLASSIC ADS' *EMI: 7243 568116-2 (CD)*
SEALY BEDS "In The Still Of The Night" (Cole Porter)
   FIVE SATINS from -S/T- 'Dirty Dancing' *RCA (BMG):
   BD 86408 (CD) BK 86408 (MC)*
SEAT IBIZA "Living Daylights" (John Barry-A Ha) *TV vers
   not available* / original (87) by A-Ha on 'Hits Of
   A-Ha' on *WB (WEA): 7599 26773-2 (CD) WX 450C (MC)*
SEAT TOLEDO "I Want It All" (Queen) QUEEN *Parlophone
   EMI:* 'The Miracle' *CDPCSD 107(CD) TCPCSD 107(MC)*
SEGA GAMES "Wonderman" performed by RIGHT SAID FRED on
   *TUG (BMG): (CD)(MC)(12)SNOG 9 (CDs/MC/12"s/7"s)*
SENSIQ COSMETICS "Strati Angelaki" (arr: Alex Yossifov)
   THE TRIO BULGARKA on 'Balkana: Music Of Bulgaria'
   *HANNIBAL (Pinn): HNCD 1335 (CD) HNBC 1335 (MC)*
SENSODYNE TOOTHPASTE "Cry" (Kevin Godley-Lol Creme) by
   JOE GLASMAN *unavailable* orig (1985) GODLEY AND
   CREME on "Changing Faces" on *POLYD: 816 355-2 (CD)*
SETTLERS TUMS "Love Story" theme (Francis Lai) Orig
   -S/T- *MCA (BMG): MCLD 19157 (CD)*
SEVEN SEAS SLUMBER CUP "Dream Baby" (Cindy Walker) *TV V
   ers.unavailable* / original by ROY ORBISON VIRGIN
SHAKE 'N' VAC  "Straight Down The Middle"(Jimmy Van Hue
   sen-Sammy Cahn) BING CROSBY on 'The Collection' on
   *CASTLE (BMG): CCSCD(CCSMC) 275*
SHAPE YOGHURT - see under ST.IVEL
SHEBA CAT FOOD-3 "There You Are" *unavailable*
SHEBA CAT FOOD-2 "When I Need You" (Albert Hammond-
   Carole B.Sager) LEO SAYER - *CHRYSALIS*
SHEBA CAT FOOD-1 "If" (David Gates) - BREAD 'Sound Of
   Bread' *ELEKTRA (WEA): K 252062 (CD) K 452062 (MC)*
SHLOER MINERALS-3 "Whatever You Want In Life" (Nicholas
   Dodd) *unavailable (also used for PRUDENTIAL ad)*
SHLOER MINERALS-2 "English Country Gardens" by Percy
   GRAINGER *various recordings available*

SHLOER MINERALS-1 "I Get A Kick Out Of You" (Anything
    Goes)(Cole Porter) GARY SHEARSTON *CHARISMA*
SIEMENS S10 (Mobile Phone) "Canon In D." (PACHELBEL) on
    'CLASSIC ADS' *EMI: 7243 568116-2 (CD)*
SILVIKRIN HAIR PRODUCTS  "Saltibanco" (Rene Dupere) by
    CIRQUE DU SOLEIL on 'Il Sogno Du Volare' *RCA (BMG):
    74321 25707-2 (CD) -4 (MC)*
SIMPLE SOAP "Simple Soap" (David Dundas)  *unavailable*
SINGAPORE AIRLINES-2 orig mus (Tim Everill) *unavailable*
SINGAPORE AIRLINES-1 "Singapore Serenade" You're A
    Great Way To Fly' ANDREW THOMAS *Arena RIA17 deleted*
SKITTLES "Supergrass" by JOHN ALTMAN *unavailable*
SKY FOOTBALL (Sean Bean ad) "Strings For Yasmin" by TIN
    TIN OUT *VIRGIN (EMI): VCRD 20 (CDs) VCRT 20 (12"s)*
SMIRNOFF BLACK "Conquest Of Paradise" (Vangelis) -S/T-
    '1492 CONQUEST OF PARADISE' by VANGELIS *EAST WEST
    (WEA): 4509 91014-2 (CD) WX 497C (MC)*
SMIRNOFF RED "Naked and Ashamed" by DYLAN RHYMES on
    'Attack Of The Killer DJ's' compilation on
    *JUNIOR BOYS OWN (RTM/Disc): JBOCD 6 (CD)*
SMIRNOFF VODKA (Reflections in Bottle Ad) "Midnight The
    Stars And You" (H.Woods-J.Campbell-R.Connelly) *TV
    version not available* orig: RAY NOBLE ORCHESTRA and
    AL BOWLLY *MONMOUTH EVERGREEN Impt: MES 6816 (LP)*
SNICKERS (Elephants ad) "Elephant Walk" composed and
    arrranged by LOWIS HOLLAND (USA) *unavailable*
SODA STREAM "Hippy Hippy Shake" (Chan Romero) by The
    SWINGING BLUE JEANS on 'The Best Of The EMI Years'
    *EMI:CDEMS 1446 (CD) TCEMS 1446 (MC)*
SOFT & GENTLE DEODORANT "Move Closer" (Phyllis Nelson)
    TV version: MASON JAMES *SOFT G* (Pinn): *SOFTGCD 001
    (CD) SOFTGMC 001 (MC) SOFTGT001 (12"s)*
SOLTAN (BOOTS) "Summer Breeze" by The ISLEY BROTHERS on
    'Greatest Hits *EPIC (SM): CD 487 996-2 (CD)*
SOLVITE "Let's Stick Together" (W.Harrison) BRYAN FERRY
    'Let's Stick Together' *EG-VIRGIN (EMI) EGCD 24 (CD)*
SONY CAMCORDER "Teddy Bears Picnic" (Jimmy Kennedy-John
    Bratton) Orig 1933 Recording HENRY HALL & HIS ORCH.
    on 'All Aboard' *EMI: CDEMS 1479 (CD) TCEMS 1479 Cas*
SONY HANDYCAM VISION "Days" (Ray Davies) sung by KIRSTY
    MacCOLL on 'Galore' *VIRGIN (EMI): CDV 2763 (CD)* and
    *TCV 2763 (MC)* also *VSCDT 1558 (CDs) VCS 1558 Cass*
SONY IN-CAR STEREO "I Want You" by The INSPIRAL CARPETS
    from the album 'Devil Hopping' *COW/MUTE (RTM-Pinn):
    DUNG 25CD (CD) DUNG 25C (MC)* also *DUNG 27CD (CDs)*
SONY MINI-DISC.2 "Chinese Burn" by CURVE on *ESTUPENDO
    Universal-MCA (BMG): UMD 80423 (CDs)*
SONY MINI-DISC.1 "Naked" by REEF on *SONY S2 (Sony M):
    662062-2 (CDs) 662062-7 (7"s) 662062-4 (Cass sing)*
SONY MOBILE PHONES "It's Not Unusual" (G.Mills) sung by
    TOM JONES *DECCA (Poly): 844 286-2(CD) -4(MC) -1(LP)*
SONY MUSIC SYSTEMS "Get Up I Feel Like Being A Sex Mach
    ine" (Brown-Byrd-Lenhoff) JAMES BROWN & HIS FAMOUS
    FLAMES *POLYDOR: COLE(X)(C)(CD) 15 (7"/12"/Cass/CD)*

SONY PLAYSTATION "Carrera Rapida" Rapid Racer theme by
    APOLLO 440 *Stealth Sonic-Epic (Sony): SSX8CDX (CDs)*
SONY PC7 DIGITAL HANDYCAM "White Wedding" by BILLY IDOL
    on 'Billy Idol' *CHRYSALIS (EMI): ACCD 1377 (CD)*
SOUTH WEST TRAINS *based on* "Biggie Wiggie" (Jools Holl
    and) *not available* / "Biggie Wiggie" by JOOLS HOLL
    AND & His R.& B.Orchestra on 'Live Performance' on
    *BEAUTIFUL (Vital): BT 002CD (CD) BT 002MC (MC)*
SPECSAVERS OPTICIANS-2 "Aquarium" from 'Carnival Of The
    Animals' (SAINT-SAENS) *version on CHANDOS Records*
    *CHAN 9246 (CD)*
SPECSAVERS OPTICIANS-1 "Blue Danube Waltz" (J.STRAUSS)
    *many versions available*
SPILLER'S ARTHUR'S  - *see under* 'ARTHUR'S CAT FOOD'
SPILLERS PRIME *see under* 'WINALOT-PRIME'
SPRITE (COCA-COLA) "Freeze The Atlantic" by CABLE on
    *INFECTIOUS (RTM-Disc): INFECT 38S (7"s)* from album
    'When Animals Attack' *INFECTIOUS (RTM-Disc):*
    *INFECT 35CD (CD) INFECT 35LP (ltd edit LP)*
ST.IVEL SHAPE based on "You're The One That I Want"
    (John Farrar) from 'Grease' *TV version unavailable*
ST.IVEL SHAPE TWINPOT "Think" by ARETHA FRANKLINA on
    'Best Of' *Atlantic (WEA): 7567 81280-2 (CD) -4 (MC)*
STANDARD LIFE ASSURANCE "Wonderful Life" (Colin Vearn
    combe) by BLACK (1987) from 'Wonderful Life' *A.& M.*
    *(Poly): CDMID 166 (CD) CMID 166 (MC)*
STELLA ARTOIS-2 'Jean De Florette'/'Manon Des Sources'
    (JEAN CLAUDE PETIT) TOOTS THIELMANS *see under Films*
STELLA ARTOIS-1 (Oil Painting) "La Forza Del Destino"
    (VERDI) as used in 'JEAN DE FLORETTE' *see FILM*
STENA LINE FERRIES music ANGELO BADALAMENTI *unavailable*
STREPSILS (Sword Swallower) "Waltz In Black" STRANGLERS
    on 'Meninblack' *FAME (EMI): CDFA 3208 (CD)*
STRONGBOW CIDER-2 "Toccata & Fugue in D.Min" (BWV 538)
    (BACH) *version* PETER HURFORD 'Great Organ Works'
    *DECCA (Poly): 436 225-2 (CD)*
STRONGBOW CIDER-1 "Smoke On The Water" (Ritch.Blackmore
    Ian Gillan-Roger Glover) by DEEP PURPLE on 'Machine
    Head' *FAME-MFP (EMI): CDFA 3158(CD) TCFA 3158(MC)*
SUN ALLIANCE-2 "Always The Sun" performed by STRANGLERS
    on 'Felline/Dreamtime' *EPIC (Sony): 466 835-2 (?CD)*
SUN ALLIANCE-1 (Fairground Ad) "Telstar" (Joe Meek)
    TORNADOS 'Greatest Hits' *MCI (THE): MCCD 161 (CD)*
SUNKIST Solar Power "Krupa"(Noko-Gray-Gray) APOLLO 440
    from album 'ELECTRO GLIDE IN BLUE' *STEALTH SONIC*
    *(Sony): SSX 2440CDR (CD) SSX2440CR (MC)*
SUPERDRUG "Y'a D'La Joie" (C.Trenet) by CHARLES TRENET
    on 'Very Best Of Charles Trenet' *EMI: CZ 314 (CD)*
SURE SENSIVE "Jeepers Creepers" (Harry Warren-Johnny Me
    rcer) LOUIS ARMSTRONG from film 'Going Places' (38)
    on 'Jeepers Creepers' *MILAN: CDCH 602 (CD) deleted*
SWATCH WATCHES a) "Dress In Black" (Ben Vaughn) b) "Car
    Wash" (Chris Bell) *both unavailable*
SYBARIS PERFUME "Adagio In G.Minor" (ALBINONI) *various*

**T.A.** 2 "Ride On Josephine"(Thorogood) GEORGE THOROGOOD
& THE DESTROYERS *DEMON (Pinn): FIENDCD 55 (CD)*
T.A. 1 "Saturday Night At The Movies" (Barry Mann-Cynt
hia Weill) DRIFTERS 'Best Of' *PICKWICK: PWKS 589 CD*
TABASCO SAUCES "Amazing" by DICK WALTER *unavailable*
TALKING CLASSICS "Enigma Variation No.9" (ELGAR)
TAMPAX "It's My Life" (Dr.Alban-Pop) DR.ALBAN *LOGIC AR
ISTA (BMG): 665330 (CDs) 115330 (7") 615330 (12"s)*
TANGO BLACKCURRANT "Don't You Want Me" (Fexix-Ware-Wash
ington-Richardson-Jenkins) sung by FELIX (96 Remix)
*DeCONSTRUCTION (BMG): 74321 41814-2 (CDs) -4 (MCs)*
TATE & LYLE (Gary Rhodes ad) "Won't You Get Off It, Ple
ase" by FATS WALLER on collection 'You Rascal You'
*ASV (Koch): CDAJA 5040 (CD) ZCAJA 5040 (MC)*
TCP **(Gargling Horse ad)** "White Horses" (Carr-Nisbet)
*TV ver.unavailable* / original by JACKY on 'THIS IS
THE RETURN OF CULT FICTION' *VIRGIN: VTCD 112 (CD)*
TEACHER'S HIGHLAND CREAM WHISKY "Cement Mixer" (Slim
Gaillard-L.Ricks) SLIM GAILLARD on 'Legendary McVou
ty' *HEP-N.NOTE (Pinn):HEPCD 6 (CD)* + 'CEMENT MIXER
PUTTI PUTTI' *PRESIDENT-DELTA (BMG): PLCD 558 (CD)*
TENNENT'S-7 (feminist ad) "The More I See You" (H.Warren
Mack Gordon) sung by CHRIS MONTEZ on Coll 'And The
Beat Goes On' (Vol.1) *DEBUTANTE (Poly): 535 693-2
(2CD) 535 693-4 (2MC)*
TENNENTS-6 (Romeo & Juliet)"Can't Take My Eyes Off You"
(Crewe-Gaudio) ANDY WILLIAMS on 'Can't Get Used To
Losing You' *COLUMBIA (Sony): 477 591-2(CD)*
TENNENTS-5 (Video Nasty) "Egyptian Reggae" by
JONATHAN RICHMAN & MODERN LOVERS on '23 Great Recor
dings' *ESSENTIAL-CASTLE (BMG): ESS(CD)(MC) 128*
TENNENTS-4 (Father/Son) "You Will Know When"
composed & performed by ALAN PRICE *unavailable*
TENNENTS-3 "Money's Too Tight (To Mention)" (Hucknall)
SIMPLY RED 'Picture Book' *WEA: 960 452-2 (CD)*
TENNENTS-2 (London Tube) "Caledonia" (Dougie MacLean)
DOUGIE MACLEAN on 'Craigie Dhu' *DUNKELD (Celtic
Music): DUN 001 (CD)* also by FRANKIE MILLER on
'PRIDE' *(Coll) RCA (BMG): 74321 28437-2 CD)*
TENNENTS-1 (Designer) "Nobody's Perfect" (Mike Ruther
ford) MIKE & THE MECHANICS from 'Livin' Years' on
*WEA: WX 203CD (CD) WX 203C (MC) WX 203 (LP)*
TERRITORIAL ARMY *see under* 'T.A.'
TERRY'S - *see under brand name e.g.* 'ALL GOLD'
TETLEY TEA-6 **(Drawstring)** "The Stripper" (David Rose)
DAVID ROSE ORCH on *EMPORIO (THE): EMPRCD 501 (CD)*
TETLEY TEA-5 "I've Got My Love To Keep Me Warm" (Irving
Berlin) *TV vers.sung by* JOAN VISKANT *unavailable*
TETLEY TEA-4 "Reach Out I'll Be There" (Holland-Dozier
ier-Holland) FOUR TOPS on 'Motown's Greatest Hits'
*MOTOWN-POLYDOR (Poly): 530 016-2 (CD) -4 (MC)*
TETLEY TEA-3 "I Won't Last A Day Without You" (Roger
Nichols-Paul Williams) *TV vers.unavailable* Orig by
CARPENTERS on 'Greatest Hits' *A.& M: CDA 1990 (CD)*

TETLEY TEA-2 "The Sorcerer's Apprentice" (Paul DUKAS)
The Ulster Orchestra (Vernon Handley) *CHANDOS
CHAN 8852 (CD) ABTD 1469 (MC)*
TETLEY TEA-1 "Lovely Day" (Bill Withers) BILL WITHERS
on 'Commercial Breaks' *COLUMBIA (SM) 469 048-2 (CD)*
TETLEY'S BITTER "Sabre Dance" (KHACHATURIAN) *various*
THRESHER WINES "Canon In D" (Pachelbel) *vers.on* "The Cl
assic Experience" *EMI: EMTVD 45 (2CD) TC-EMTVC 45
(MC) or* "Essential Classics" *Poly: 431541-2(2CD)*
TIMES NEWSPAPER "Labyrinth" by PHILIP GLASS from '1000
Airplanes On The Roof' *VIRGIN (EMI): CDVE 39 (CD)*
TIMEX INDIGLO "Dance Of The Hours" from 'La Gioconda'
(PONCHIELLI) *many versions available*
TIMOTEI MINERALS SHAMPOO (Waterfalls ad) orig composit
ion by JENKINS-RATLEDGE productions *unavaliable*
TIXYLIX MEDICINES "Dance Of The Sugar Plum Fairy" from
'The Nutcracker Suite' (TCHAIKOVSKY) *many versions*
TOFFEE CRISP "If I Were With Her Now" by SPIRITUALIZED
from 'Laser Guided Melodies' *DEDICATED (Vital):
DEDCD 004 (CD) DEDMC 004 (MC)*
TOYOTA-3 "Miserlou" (Barry Kirsch) DICK DALE & DELTONES
-S/T- of 'Pulp Fiction' *MCA (BMG): MCD 11103 (CD)*
TOYOTA-2 "Laura's theme from Twin Peaks" (Angelo Badala
menti) *special version unavailable.*
MOBY "Go" on *MUTE (RTM/Pinn): CD(C)(12)NOCAR 1*
TOYOTA-1 "Book Of Days" (Enya) by ENYA 'Shepherd Moons'
on *WEA: 9031 75572-2 (CD) WX 431C (MC)*
TOYOTA CARINA 94 "Leaner Meaner Cleaner" (Nick Whitecro
ss) arr.by John Hall & George Stewart *unavailable*
TOYOTA COROLLA 97 "Yo Yo" by VINCE POPE (SCRAMBLE
SOUND PRODUCTIONS) *unavailable*
TOYOTA PICNIC "Cape Fear" (BERNARD HERRMANN) CITY OF
PRAGUE P.ORCH *SILVA SCREEN (Koch): FILMCD 162 (CD)*
TOYS'R'US "Walking In The Air" (Howard Blake) sung by
PETER AUTY from 'The Snowman' *CBSCD 71116 (CD) 40-C*
TREBOR SOFT MINTS "Mister Soft" (S.Harley) STEVE HARLEY
& COCKNEY REBEL *EMI:EDP 154677-3 (2LP) CZ15 (CD)*
TRUSTHOUSE FORTE - *see under* 'FORTE'
TSB-2 (Cinema Vouchers) "Saturday Night At The Movies"
DRIFTERS 'Golden Hits' *ATL.(WEA): 7567 81440-2 (CD)*
TSB-1 "Morning Papers Waltz" Op.279 (Johan STRAUSS II)
TWEED PERFUME "Pastoral" from 'Symphony No.6 in F.Major
Op.68' (BEETHOVEN) *many recordings available*
TWIRL (Cadbury's) "Dizzy" (Tommy Roe-Fred Weller) TOMMY
ROE 'Best Of' *MCI (THE): MCCD 136(CD) MCTC 136(MC)*
TWIX-2 (Norman's grey car) "Beat Boutique" ALAN HAWSHAW
and KEITH MANSFIELD on 'GIRL IN A SPORTS CAR' on
*Coliseum (WEA): 0630 18071-2 (CD) or HF 53CD*
TWIX-1 "I Want It All" composed and performed by QUEEN
'Greatest Hits 2' *EMI: CDP 797971-2 (CD) -4 (MC)*
TWYNINGS TEA Excerpt from "Madam Butterfly" (PUCCINI)
TYCO TOYS "Thunderbirds" (Gray) BARRY GRAY ORCH 'A-Z OF
BRITISH TV THEMES' *PLAY IT AGAIN (BMG): PLAY 004 CD*
TYPHOO TEA "Nimrod"'Enigma Variations' (ELGAR) *various*

UNCLE BEN'S CLASSIC RECIPES "Fur Elise Bagatelle No.25"
  (BEETHOVEN) *many recordings available*
U.P.S. (UNITED PARCEL SERVICES) "Simple Task" (Geoffrey
  Vilinski) *unavailable*
UMBRO SPORTSWEAR "Beautiful Game" composed & performed
  by Steve Parsons *unavailable*
UNITED FRIENDLY INSURANCE "All Together Now" originally
  by The FARM on *PRODUCE (Vital): CDMILK 103 (MC)*
VAUXHALL "Layla" (Eric Clapton) DEREK AND THE DOMINOS
  DOMINOS *POLY: 800014-2 (CD)* + "Baker Street" from
  'City To City'GERRY RAFFERTY *FAME-MFP:CDFA 3119(CD)*
VAUXHALL ASTRA "Peter And The Wolf" (PROKOFIEV)
VAUXHALL ASTRA CDX "Lawrence Of Arabia theme" (Maurice
  Jarre) on 'Epic' *SILV.SCREEN (Koch) FILMCD 036 (CD)*
VAUXHALL CARLTON "Rondo from Horn Concerto No.4 in E.Fl
  at" KV 495 (MOZART) *many recordings available*
VAUXHALL CAVALIER "Sledgehammer" (Peter Gabriel) PETER
  GABRIEL on 'So' *VIRGIN: PGCD 5 (CD) PGMC 5 (MC)*
VAUXHALL SINTRA "Pure" by The LIGHTNING SEEDS from
  'Cloudcuckooland' *VIRGIN (EMI): CDOVD(OVDC) 436*
VAUXHALL TIGRA "Fiesta" (Pogues) The POGUES from 'If I
  Should Fall From Grace With God' on *WEA (WEA):
  244493-2 (CD) WX 2434C (MC)*
VAUXHALL VECTRA-2 "Peter Gunn theme" (Henry Mancini)
  *TV version unavailable* / HENRY MANCINI vers: 'Best
  Of HENRY MANCINI' *RCA (BMG): 74321 47676-2 (CD)*
VAUXHALL VECTRA-1 "The Next Millenium" (D.Arnold) DAVID
  ARNOLD on 'Senses' *POLYGRAM: 516 627-2 (CD)* / *vocal
  vers* BJORK *on* 'This Is Cult Fiction' *VIRGIN VTCD 59
  (CD)* and 'NEW PURE MOODS' *see COLLECTION 267*
VENEZIA PERFUME (Laura Biogitti) "Four Seasons Suite
  for Violin and Strings" Op.8 Numbers 1-4. (VIVALDI)
VENO'S COUGH MIXTURE "Little Does She Know" (Burch-Doug
  las-Shuttleworth) adapt.from KURSAAL FLYERS 77 hit.
  orig on 'In For A Spin-Best Of The Kursaal Flyers'
VIMTO "Ain't That A Shame" (Antione Domino-Dave Barthol
  omew) *TV version not available* / FATS DOMINO on
  'Best Of' on *MFP (EMI): CDMFP 5026 (CD)*
ViFIT YOGHURT "Get A Life" (Romeo-Brown) SOUL II SOUL
  on 'Classic Singles' *TEN-VIRGIN (EMI): CD(TC)V 2724*
  +'New Dance Decade' *TEN-VIRGIN (EMI): DISCD 90 (CD)*
VITALITE-2 "Oh What A Night (December 1963)' (Gaudio-
  Parker) orig FRANKIE VALLI & FOUR SEASONS Very Best
  Of' *FLYING (Poly): 513 119-2 (CD) 513 119-4 (MC)*
VITALITE-1 "The Israelites" (Desmond Dekker-Les Kong)
  DESMOND DEKKER & THE ACES *Mooncrest (Total-BMG):
  (12)MOON 1009 (7"/12"s)*
VODAPHONE-2 Nov/Dec 97 'words' ad (Roland Armstrong)
  performed by FAITHLESS *release to be confirmed*
VODAPHONE-1 "Busy Line" - details under CELLNET ad

VOLKSWAGEN-2 "Changes" (Alan Price)from 'O Lucky Man'
  Film) ALAN PRICE - *ARIOLA (BMG): 109911 (7") 609911
  (12"s)* 'Liberty' *4-10042(MC) 260042 (CD) DELETED*

VOLKSWAGEN-1 (93) "Call Me Irresponsible" (Sammy Cahn-
Jimmy Van Huesen) sung by DINAH WASHINGTON 'Best Of
Dinah Washington The Roulette Years' *EMI ROULETTE
CDROU 1054 (CD) TCROU 1054 (MC)*
VOLKSWAGEN GOLF-5 "Autumn Leaves" (Joseph Kosma-John
ny Mercer) *unavailable*
VOLKSWAGEN GOLF-4 ('Desert ad') "Amarillo Swing" from
'Country & Western Bluegrass' *KPM Lib. unavailable*
VOLKSWAGEN GOLF-3 'Match' Stranger On The Shore" by
(Acker Bilk-Robert Mellin) ACKER BILK 'Very Best Of
Acker Bilk' *PICKWICK: PWKM 4067 (CD) HSCM 262(MC)*
VOLKSWAGEN GOLF-2 "Brideshead Revisited" (Geoffrey
Burgon) *MFP (EMI): CD(TC) MFP 6172* also on 'BETWEEN
THE LINES' *S.SCREEN Koch: TVPMCD 805 (CD)* & 'BRIDE
SHEAD REVISITED' *S.Screen FILM(C)(CD) 117 (CD/MC)*
VOLKSWAGEN GOLF-1 "Feeling Good" (Leslie Bricusse-Anth
ony Newley) sung by NINA SIMONE on 'Feeling Good -
The Very Best Of' *VERVE (Poly): 522 669-2 (CD)*
VOLKSWAGEN GTI "Young At Heart" (Robert Hodgens-Siobahn
Fahey) BLUEBELLS *LONDON (Poly): LONCD 338 (CDs)*
VOLKSWAGEN PASSAT-4 "Summer Wind" (J.Mercer-H.Mayer)
*TV VERSION UNAVAILABLE* / FRANK SINATRA version on
'GREATEST HITS' *REPRISE (WEA): 244011 (CD)*
VOLKSWAGEN PASSAT-3 "I Talk To The Trees" (AJ.Lerner
F.Loewe) from 'Paint Your Wagon' TONY BAVAAR from
1951 Orig Broadway Cast *RCA (BMG): GD 60243 (CD)*
VOLKSWAGEN PASSAT-2 "Sorry But I'm Gonna Have To Pass"
The COASTERS *ATLANTIC (WEA): A4519(CD)(C) (CDs/MC)*
& 'Coasters G.Hits' *ATLANTIC (WEA):9548 32656-2(CD)*
VOLKSWAGEN PASSAT-1 "God Bless The Child" (Art.Herzog-
Billie Holiday) BILLIE HOLIDAY - 'Lady & The Legend
1952-56' *RHAPSODY (Presid): RHA(C) 6026 (LP/MC)*
BLOOD SWEAT & TEARS 'Greatest Hits' *CBS:CD 64803 CD*
VOLKSWAGEN POLO-2 "Agnus Dei" from 'Requiem' (G.FAURE)
*NAXOS (Select): 8.550765 (CD)*
VOLKSWAGEN POLO-1 "La Vie En Rose" (R.Louiguy-E.Piaf)
*version by* EDITH PIAF *EMI: CDEMC 3674 (CD)*
VOLVO S40 "One To One Religion" (White Knuckle Remix)
by BOMB THE BASE (orig track on 'Clear') *FOURTH &
BROADWAY-ISL.(Poly): BRCD 611 (CD) BRCA 611 (MC)*
VOLVO V40 "Butterfly 747" by MOLOKO from album 'Do You
Like My Tight Sweater' *ECHO (Pinn): ECH(CD)(LP) 7*
*also on* -S/T- 'TWIN TOWN' *A.& M. (Poly): 540 718-2*
VOLVO 850 (Tornado) by ANNE DUDLEY *unavailable*

WALKERS CRINKLES (Gary Lineker) "Catch Us If You Can"
(D.Clark-L.Davidson) DAVE CLARK 5 on Collect 'Glad
All Over Again' *EMI: CDEMTV 75 (CD)*
WALKERS CRISPS "Welcome Home" (Jan Dupre-Stanislas
Beldone-Bryan Blackburn) by PETERS & LEE on *MERCURY
MER(CD)(MC) 424 (CDs/MC)* also 'Through The Years'
*PICKWICK (Carlton): PWKS 4214(CD) PWKMC 4214(MC)*
WALKERS DORITOS-2 "Drip Drop" (Jerry Leiber-Mike Stoll
er) *originally by* The DRIFTERS *ATLANTIC deleted*

**WALKERS DORITOS-1** "Bread and Butter" (Larry Parks-Jay Turnbow) orig by NEWBEATS on 'Best Of The Newbeats' on *SEQUEL-CASTLE (BMG): NEXTCD 231 (CD)*

**WALKERS DORITOS (SCRATCH CARDS)** "In The Mood" (Andy Raz af-Joe Garland) *orig.version by* GLENN MILLER *(RCA)*

**WALKERS DOUBLE CRUNCH** "Walk Like A Man" (Bob Crewe-Bob Gaudio) FRANKIE VALLI & FOUR SEASONS on 'Very Best Of' *FLYING-POLYDOR (Polg): 513 119-2 (CD) -4 (MC)* also on *ACE (Pinn): CDCHD 507 (2CD Collection)*

**WALKERS QUAVERS-2** "Puffin' Billy" (Edward WHITE) on Coll 'Famous Themes' *GRASMERE (BMG): GRCD 10 (CD)*

**WALKERS QUAVERS-1** "Cape Fear" (Bernard HERRMANN) see *Film title*

**WALL'S CALIPPO** "My Generation" (Pete Townshend) The WHO 'The Singles' *POLYDOR: 815 965-2(CD) WHOHC 17(MC) 854 637-2 (CDs) 863 918-4 (MC) -7 (7"s)*

**WALLS CORNETTO** "O Sole Mio" (Di Capua) Neapolitan song 'It's Now Or Never' ELVIS PRESLEY based *RCA (BMG)*

**WALLS MAGNUM AFFAIR (a)** "Affair" (Jasper Winge-Leisner) **(b)** "Pearls" (Michael Storey) *unavailable*

**WALLS RANIERI ICE CREAM** "Harry's Game" (Paul Brennan) CLANNAD on 'Past Present' *RCA (BMG): PD(PK) 74074 (CD/MC)* or *74321 118122 (CDsingle)*

**WALL'S ROMANZA** "Come Back To Sorrento' (E. de Curtis-C. Aveling) FRANCO CORRELLI *EMI: CDC 747835-2 (CD) and* JOSEPH LOCKE 'Hear My Song' *MFP (EMI): (TC)DL 1033* ELVIS PRESLEY 'Surrender' *RCA (BMG) various compil*

**WALLS VIENETTA** "Love For Sale" performed by FINE YOUNG CANNIBALS on 'Red Hot And Blue' on *CHRYSALIS (EMI): CCD 1799 (CD) ZCHR 1799 (MC)*

**WEETABIX-6** ADVANTAGE "Lucas With The Lid Off" by LUCAS *WEA number unconfirmed*

**WEETABIX-5** "I Will Survive" (D.Fekaris-F.Perren) *TV Version unavailable* original by GLORIA GAYNOR on 'Greatest Hits' *POLYDOR (Poly): 833 433-2 (CD)*

**WEETABIX-4** "Shaft" theme (ISAAC HAYES) *TV version NA original version by* ISAAC HAYES *on* COLL 'THIS IS CULT FICTION' *VIRGIN (EMI) VTCD 59 (CD)*

**WEETABIX-3** "Born To Be Wild" (Mars Bonfire) *TV version unavailable* / original by STEPPENWOLF from 'EASY RIDER' *MCA (BMG): MCLD 19153 (CD) MCLC 19153 (MC)*

**WEETABIX-2** "Delilah" (Reed-Mason) ALEX HARVEY BAND on 'Delilah' *SPECTRUM (Poly): 550 663-2 (CD) -4 (MC)*

**WEETABIX-1** (Pirate Ship ad) "My Brudda Sylvest" (Mark Campbell-Dave Arch) *version by* HOUGHTON WEAVERS on 'Work Of The Weavers' *TARGET-BMG: KFS 040 (MC) others* FIVEPENNY PIECE/YETTIES/MIKE HARDING *deleted*

**WELLA COLOUR MOUSSE** "Great Balls Of Fire" (O.Blackwell-Jack Hammer) JERRY LEE LEWIS *CHARLY: CDCHARLY 185*

**WHISKAS-9** "Hold Tight (I Want Some Sea Food Mama)" sung by FATS WALLER *CLASSICS (Discov): CLASSICS 943 (CD)*

**WHISKAS-8** (Kittens) "Onions" (Sidney Bechet) *TV vers. unavailable* /HUMPHREY LYTTLETON BAND on 'Parlophone Years' *DOORMOUSE (N.Note-Pinn): DM21CD deleted*

WHISKAS-7 "Teach Me Tiger" sung by APRIL STEVENS on
  'Cocktail Capers-Ult.Lounge 8' *EMI:CDEMS 1595 (CD)*
WHISKAS-6 "Tico Tico" (Abreu) by The ANDREWS SISTERS
  on 'Tico Tico' *MAGIC (Hamonia Mundi): DAWE 49 (CD)*
WHISKAS-5 New Whiskas w.add.Catisfaction "Ghosts On
  Horseback" (Colin Frechter-Bob Barratt) *unavailable*
WHISKAS-4 New Whiskas w.add.Catisfaction "Tico Tico"
  (Abreu) ANDREWS SISTERS on 'Very Best Of' *PICKWICK
  (Carlton): PWK 4000 (CD) HSC 3234 (MC)*
WHISKAS-3 New Whiskas w.add.Catisfaction "Piano Conc
  erto No.21 in C.Maj.K467" ('Elvira Madigan theme')
  (MOZART) *see Col1* 'MOST FAMOUS MOVIE CLASSICS' *EMI*
WHISKAS-2 (Waltham Care ad) "The Cat's Back" instrume
  ntal by ALAN DARBY *library track unavailable*
WHISKAS-1 "Friends" by ARRIVAL - orig *DECCA F.12986
  (1970-7"s) F.13763 (1978-7"s) both now deleted*
WILDLIFE OF BRITAIN MAGAZINE "Victorian Kitchen Garden"
  PAUL READE-EMMA JOHNSON *BBCCD 705 deleted*
WILKINSON SWORD EDGE "Protector" (Olivier Bloch-Laine)
  specially recorded in Germany *unavailable*
WINALOT-PRIME "The Long March" (Chris Gunning)  Barking
  Light *KENNEL (BMG): WOOF 1 (7"s) DELETED*
WINDOWS 95 - see MICROSOFT
WOODPECKER CIDER (car in puddle) "Mr.Vain" CULTURE BEAT
  'Serenity' *EPIC (SM): 474 101-2 (CD)-4 (MC) -8 (MD)*
WOOL "Canon In D" (PACHELBEL) *Col1* 'CLASSIC EXPRIENCE'
WOOLMARK (LOVE FROM) "The Coldest Winter" (Roland Roman
  elli) p.Torpedo (France) *unavailable*
WOOLWORTHS (Alien ad) adapted fom "Aba Daba Honeymoon"
  (Fields-Donavan) (from film 'Two Weeks With Love')
  *unavailable*
WOOLWORTH'S LADYBIRD COLLECTION - see 'LADYBIRD'
WOTSITS "Wot" (C.Sensible) orig 1982 CAPTAIN SENSIBLE
  *A.& M.: PLACD(PLAMC) 6 (CDs/MC single) deleted*
WRANGLER JEANS-4 "Key To The Highway" (Monque'd) vers
  BIG BILL BROONZY on 'House Rent Stomp' on *BLUES
  ENCORE/TARGET (BMG): CD 52007 (CD)*
WRANGLER JEANS-3 'DJ Rap' (Ron-In) *unavailable*
WRANGLER JEANS-2 "You're Undecided" (J.& D.Burnette-P.
  Burlisson) by JOHNNY BURNETTE TRIO on 'Rock-A-Billy
  Boogie' *BEAR FAMILY (Rollercoaster): BCD 15474 (CD)*
WRANGLER JEANS-1 "Cross Town Traffic" (J.Hendrix) JIMI
  HENDRIX 'Singles Album' *POLYDOR: 827 369-2 (2xCD)*
WRIGLEY'S SPEARMINT-2 (Porsch in desert ad) "Shadows"
  (Karl Jenkins-Mike Ratledge) *unavailable*
WRIGLEY'S SPEARMINT-1 "All Right Now" (Andy Fraser-Paul
  Rodgers) by FREE on 'All Right Now' *ISLAND CITV 2
  (CD)  CID 486 (CDsingle) CIS 486 (MC single)*
XCESS (XS Perfume) "Time Of The Gipsies" (Goran Bregovi
  cch) -S/T- *Imp (S.Screen): 515 862-2(CD) -4(MC)*
YARDLEY BLACK VELVET "Love Theme" 'Romeo & Juliet' (68)
  (Nino ROTA) *deleted*
YARDLEY LACE PERFUME "Elvira Madigan Theme" from 'Piano
  Concerto No.21 in C' (MOZART) *various recordings*

YARDLEY WHITE SATIN PERFUME "Nights In White Satin" The
     MOODY BLUES *DECCA*
YELLOW PAGES-3 "Baby I Love You" (P.Spector-E.Greenwich
     J.Barry) The RAMONES from 'End Of The Century'
     *SIRE (WEA): 7599 27429-2 (CD) / original vers.by*
     *by* The RONETTES 'Best Of' *EMI: PSCD 1006 (CD)*
YELLOW PAGES-2 "Days" (Ray Davies) by The KINKS on
     'Best of Ballads' *ARISTA (BMG): 74321 13687-2 (CD)*
YELLOW PAGES-1 (J.R.Hartley book ad) (piano piece) by
     DICK WALTER *unavailable*
YOUNGS SEAFOODS "Symphony No.8 in B.minor" 'Unfinished'
     (SCHUBERT) *many recordings available*

ZURICH MUNICIPAL Ins. "You've Got What It Takes" (Gwen
     Gordy-Raquel Davis-Berry Gordy Jnr.) SHOWADDYWADDY
     *CHARLY: CDCD 1150 (CD)*

---

*TV COMMERCIALS (COLLECTIONS)*

*FOR FULL TRACK DETAILS SEE FOLLOWING COLLECTIONS*

---

AFTER THE BREAK *(COLLECTION NUMBER 10)*

CLASSICS ADS *(COLLECTION NUMBERS 83,84)*

CLASSICS EXPERIENCE *(COLLECTION NUMBERS 86,87,88,89)*

CLASSICS PAN PIPES *(COLLECTION NUMBER 94)*

INSTRUMENTAL MOODS *(COLLECTION NUMBER 213)*

NEW PURE MOODS *(COLLECTION NUMBER 267)*

ORIGINALS *(COLLECTION NUMBERS 278,279)*

SILENCE *(COLLECTION NUMBER 310)*

SPIRITS OF NATURE *(COLLECTION NUMBER 324)*

STAND BY ME *(COLLECTION NUMBER 328)*

TAKE A BREAK! *(COLLECTION NUMBER 334)*

2.4 CHILDREN (BBC1 3/9/91) theme music: HOWARD GOODALL
   see COLLECTION 229
6.5 SPECIAL (BBC 1950's) see COLLECTION 402
9 - see also NINE
9 MONTHS - see NINE MONTHS
9 TO 5 (Film-TV) Theme DOLLY PARTON (BMG) ND 84830 (CD)
   see COLLECTION 168
9½ WEEKS (1986) Music score: JACK NITZSCHE -S/T- reiss
   CAPITOL (EMI): CDP 746722-2 (CD)
21 JUMP STREET (USA) theme music: LIAM STERNBERG
   see COLLECTIONS 12,345
21st CENTURY (USA TV) see COLLECTION 342
26 MEN (USA TV) see COLLECTION 342
42nd STREET (1933 MUSICAL) feat DICK POWELL-RUBY KEELER
   WARNER BAXTER-BEBE DANIELS inc.songs 'SKY'S THE LIM
   IT'/'DUBARRY WAS A LADY' TARGET (BMG):CD 60010 (CD)
42nd STREET (REVIV.BROADWAY CAST 1982) Songs (Al Dubin-
   Harry Warren) feat DANNY CARROLL-JERRY ORBACH-TAMMY
   GRIMES-LEE ROY REAMES RCA: BD(BK) 83891 (CD/MC)
77 SUNSET STRIP (USA) see COLLECTION 339
99 TO 1 (Zenith/Carlton 5/1/94) original music by
   MICHAEL GIBBS unavailable
101 DALMATIONS (1996) Music score: MICHAEL KAMEN -S/T-
   DISNEY (B.Vista): WD 69940-2 (CD) WD 69940-4 (MC)
187 (1997) VARIOUS ARTISTS -S/T- on
   ATLANTIC (WEA): 7567 92760-2 (CD) -4 (MC)
200 MOTELS (1971) music by FRANK ZAPPA with The MOTHERS
   OF INVENTION and ROYAL PHILHARMONIC ORCH.AND CHORUS
   -S/T- reiss with additional items RYKODISC (Vital):
   RCD 10513/14 (2CD) RAC 10513/14 (2MC)
500 BUS STOPS (BBC2 24/6/97) original music by
   GRAHAM FELLOWS unavailable
633 SQUADRON (64) Mus sco: RON GOODWIN -S/T- deleted
   see COLLECTIONS 35,62,158,238,
999 (LIFESAVERS etc) (BBC1 25/6/92) see COLLECTION 402
1492 CONQUEST OF PARADISE (1992) Music score: VANGELIS
   S/T- EAST WEST (WEA): 4509 91014-2(CD) WX 497C(MC)
1914-18 (BBC2 10/11/96) Music score: MASON DARING -S/T-
   'The Great War and The Shaping Of The 20th Century'
   DARING (Direct Dist): DARINGCD 3029 (CD)
1941 (1979) Music score: JOHN WILLIAMS -S/T- reissue on
   VARESE (Pinn): VSD 5832 (CD)
1969 (1988) Music score: MICHAEL SMALL -S/T- reissue
   POLY (IMS-Poly): AA 837 362-2 (CD)
1984 (1984) Mus.comp/perform by EURYTHMICS -S/T- reiss:
   VIRGIN-MFP (EMI): CDVIP 135 (CD) TCVIP 135 (MC)
2001-A SPACE ODYSSEY (1968) Classical m -S/T- featuring
   "Blue Danube" (J.STRAUSS) "Also Sprach Zarathustra"
   (R.STRAUSS) etc. -S/T- EMI ODEON: CDODEON 28 (CD)
   see COLLECTIONS 62,68,97,109,140,160,171,258,273,
   284,292,301,320,322,329,
2001-A SPACE ODYSSEY (REJECTED SCORE by ALEX NORTH)
   National Philharmonic Orchestra (JERRY GOLDSMITH)
   VARESE (Pinn): VSD 5400 (CD)

A    *see under next word*
A.TEAM The (USA)ITV from 29/7/83) theme mus: MIKE POST
   PETE CARPENTER *see COLLECTIONS 12,100,168,341,361*
ABBOTT & COSTELLO SHOW The (USA TV) *see COLLECTION 342*
   *also available* 'WHO'S ON FIRST' (comedy routine) on
   *ON THE AIR-DELTA (Target-BMG): OTA 101913 (CD)*
ABOUT FACE (Central from 6/11/89) theme: DENIS KING
   *on Coll* 'LOVEJOY THE MUSIC OF DENIS KING' *deleted*
ABOUT LAST NIGHT (1986) Music sco: MILES GOODMAN -S/T-
   *EMI AMER (EMI): CDP 746560-2 (CD)*
ABOVE THE RIM (1993) M.sco: MARCUS MILLER -S/T- V.Arts
   *INTERSCOPE-MCA (BMG): IND 92359 (CD) also on*
   *WEA: 6544-92359-2 (CD) -4 (MC)*
ABSOLUTE BEGINNERS (Film Musical 86) Score: GIL EVANS
   -S/T- *VIP (EMI): CDVIP 112 (CD) TCVIP 112 (MC)*
   *also* Highlights on *VIRGIN: CDV 2386 (CD)*
ABSOLUTE POWER (1996) Music score: LENNIE NIEHAUS with
   CLINT EASTWOOD -S/T- *VARESE (Pinn): VSD 5808 (CD)*
ABSOLUTELY (C4 22/8/90) title music: PETE BAIKIE perf.
   by PETE BAIKIE-MORWENNA BANKS & CAST *unavailable*
ABSOLUTELY ANIMALS (ITV 20/9/95) music: MIKE NIELSEN
   and BEN STAPLES *unavailable*
ABSOLUTELY FABULOUS (BBC2 12/11/92) theme "This Wheel's
   On Fire" (Bob Dylan-Rick Danko) ABSOLUTELY FABULOUS
   (aka PET SHOP BOYS) *EMI: CDR(TCR)(12R) 6382 deleted*
   1968 version JULIE DRISCOLL-BRIAN AUGER TRINITY on
   'I WILL SURVIVE' *PICKWICK (Carlton): PWKS 4092 (CD)*
ABYSS The (Film 89) Music score: ALAN SILVESTRI -S/T-
   *VARESE (Pinn): VSD 5235 (CD)*
ACE OF CLUBS (Show 1950) *see under Coll* 'NOEL COWARD'
ACE VENTURA PET DETECTIVE (93) Music score: IRA NEWBORN
   V.Arts -S/T- *Polydor: 523 000-2 (CD) see COLLECT 79*
ACE VENTURA: WHEN NATURE CALLS (95) Music score: ROBERT
   FOLK -S/T- V.Art STING-PATO BANTON-WHITE ZOMBIE-GOO
   GOO DOLLS-NATIVE-MATTHEW SWEET-MONTELL JORDAN etc.
   -S/T- *MCA (BMG): MCD(MCC) 11374 (CD/MC) DELETED 97*
ACT The (1978) ORIG BROADWAY CAST *feat:* LIZA MINNELLI
   ORIG CAST RECORDING *DRG (Pinn): CDDRG 6101 (CD)*
ADAM 12 (USA) *see COLLECTION 339*
ADDAMS FAMILY The (USA 64) Music from orig TV ser.by
   VIC MIZZY *RCA IMP (S.Screen): 61057-2(CD) -4 (MC)*
   *see COLLECTIONS 110,339*
ADDAMS FAMILY The (1991) Music sco: MARC SHAIMAN -S/T-
   *CAPITOL (EMI): CDESTU 2161 (CD) TCESTU 2161 (MC)*
ADDAMS FAMILY VALUES (1993) Music score: MARC SHAIMAN
   SCORE -S/T- *VARESE (Pinn): VSD 5465 (CD)*
   SONGS -S/T- *POLY: 521 502-2 (CD) -4(MC) deleted 95*
ADIEMUS - *see COLLECTIONS 9,267*
ADJUSTER The (1991) Music score: MYCHAEL DANNA -S/T-
   *VARESE (Pinn): VSD 5674 (CD)*
ADVENTURES IN PARADISE  (USA TV) *see COLLECTION 342*
ADVENTURES OF AGGIE (ITV) theme music "High Stepper"
   RONALD BINGE *see COLLECTION 42*
ADVENTURES OF AN * - *see* 'JOURNEY TO NEXT'

ADVENTURES OF BLACK BEAUTY The (LWT 23/9/72 & C4 1986)
theme "Galloping Home" by DENIS KING  London String
Chorale *see COLLECTIONS 4,160 see also NEW ADV.OF..*
ADVENTURES OF DAWDLE The (ITVC 2/9/97) title theme song
composed and sung by CHRIS DE BURGH *unavailable*
ADVENTURES OF DON JUAN (1948) *see COLLECTION 332*
ADVENTURES OF HUCK FINN The (1993) Mus sco: BILL CONTI
-S/T- *VARESE: VSD 5418 (CD)*
ADVENTURES OF HUCKLEBERRY FINN (1960) Music score by
JEROME MOROSS *on COLLECTION 377*
*SILVA SCREEN (Koch): FILMCD 161 (CD)*
ADVENTURES OF MARCO POLO (1937) Music: HUGO FRIEDHOFER
Suite on Coll "HUGO FRIEDHOFER" *with* 'THE LODGER'/
'RAINS OF RANCHIPUR'/'SEVEN CITIES OF GOLD' perform
ed by The MOSCOW SYPHONY ORCH (cond: W.T.Stromberg)
*MARCO POLO (Select): 8.223857 (CD)*
ADVENTURES OF MARK TWAIN (1944) Music sc: MAX STEINER
score performed by BRANDENBURG PHILHARMONIC ORCHEST
(William T.Stromberg) *also feat* 'PRINCE AND THE PAU
PER' (E.W.KORNGOLD) *RCA (BMG): 09026 62660-2 (CD)*
ADVENTURES OF NICHOLAS NICKLEBY *See COLLECTION 6*
ADVENTURES OF OZZIE AND HARRIET (USA TV) *see COLL.342*
ADVENTURES OF PINOCCHIO (1996) Mus sco: RACHEL PORTMAN
*& songs by* STEVIE WONDER-JERRY HADLEY-SISSEL-BRIAN
MAY -S/T- *LONDON (Poly): 452 740-2 (CD)*
ADVENTURES OF PRISCILLA QUEEN OF THE DESERT (1994) Mus
sco: GUY CROSS -S/T- *MOTHER (Poly): 516937-2 (CD)*
*516937-4 (MC)*
ADVENTURES OF ROBIN HOOD The (ITV 17/2/56-1960) theme
mus (Carl Sigman) DICK JAMES *EMI:TCEM 1307 (MC)*
*CDS 791255-2 (CD)* GARRY MILLER *see COLLECT.340,372*
ADVENTURES OF ROBIN HOOD The (1938) Mus sco: ERICH WOLF
GANG KORNGOLD -S/T- *TER (Disc): (CD)(ZC)TER 1066 +
VARESE: VSD 47202 (CD) / see COLLECTION 332*
ADVENTURES OF ROBINSON CRUSOE The (BBC1 12/10/65) Music
score: ROBERT MELLIN-GIAN PIERO REVERBERI Original
TV S/TRACK *reissued w.ADDITIONAL unreleased music
S.SCREEN (Koch): FILMCD 705 (CD) also COLL.109,303*
ADVENTURES OF SHERLOCK HOLMES (Gra+7/10/96 or.ITV 1984)
title mus: PATRICK GOWERS on Coll 'SHERLOCK HOLMES-
CLASSIC THEMES' *VARESE (Pinn): VSD  5692 (CD)*
ADVENTURES OF WILLIAM TELL The (ITC 15/9/58-1959 )theme
sung by DAVID WHITFIELD 'Sings Stage & Screen Favou
rites' *PICKWICK CARLTON PWK 096 (CD) SDTO 2004 (MC)*
AFRICAN SANCTUS 1 (BBC2 29/7/95) Music: DAVID FANSHAWE
new digital rec.feat: WIILHELMENIA FERNANDEZ and
KATAMANTO with BOURNEMOUTH SYPHONY CHORUS + CHORIS
TERS FROM ST.GEORGE'S CHAPEL, WINDSOR.*SILVA SCREEN
(Koch): SILKD 6003 (CD) SILKC 6003 (MC)*
*see also* 'MISSA LUBA' in Films & Shows section
AFRICAN SANCTUS 2 (BBC1 1978) A Mass For Love and Peace
DAVID FANSHAWE *PHILIPS: 426 055-2 (CD) -4(MC)*
*also available* Allmanna Sangen cond. by ROBERT SUND
*PROPRIUS Records: PR(C)(CD) 9984 (LP/MC/CD)*

AGAINST ALL ODDS (1984) Music sco: MICHEL COLOMBIER
-S/T- *VIRGIN (MFP-EMI): CDVIP 112 (CD)*
AGAINST THE ODDS (BBC2 14/7/95) music "Cursum Perficio"
and "Watermark" (Enya) by ENYA on 'Watermark' on
*WEA INT (WEA): 243875-2 (CD) 243875-4 (MC)*
AGAINST THE WIND (Australian TV) *see COLLECTION 168*
AGATHA CHRISTIE'S POIROT (LWT from 8/1/89) Music: CHRIS
GUNNING *see COLLECTIONS 138,175,388*
AGE OF INNOCENCE (1992) *see COLLECTION 79*
AGONY AGAIN (BBC1 31/8/95) theme "Lean On Me" (Bill Wit
hers) sung by ELKIE BROOKS *unavailable* orig "Agony"
theme by Graham Field (BABS FLETCHER) *PRT79 deleted*
AGONY AND THE ECSTASY The (1965) Music sco: ALEX NORTH
*with* 'PRIDE & THE PASSION' (George Antheil) 75mins
*CLOUD NINE (Import, S.Screen): CNS 5001 (CD)*
AIN'T MISBEHAVIN' (ITV 28/7/97) orig mus: NIGEL WRIGHT
*songs* "Ain't Misbehavin'"/"The Kiss Polka"/"A Night
ingale Sang In Berkeley Square" on ROBSON & JEROME
album 'Take Two' *BMG: 74321 42625-2 (CD) -4 (MC)*
AIN'T MISBEHAVIN' (BBC1 20/3/94) music: CLEVER MUSIC
title song (Andy Razaff-Thomas Waller-Harry Brooks)
sung by PAUL JONES *unavailable*
AIN'T MISBEHAVIN' (ORIG LONDON CAST 1995)
*FIRST NIGHT (Pinn): CASTCD 53 (CD) CASTC 53 (MC)*
AIN'T MISBEHAVIN' (ORIG BROADWAY CAST 1979) Music: FATS
WALLER with Andre de Shields-Nell Carter-Ken Page
*RCA Import (S.Screen): 2965-2 (2CD) CBK2 2965 (MC)*
AIR FORCE ONE (1997) Music score: JERRY GOLDSMITH with
additional music by JOEL McNEELY -S/T- on
*VARESE (Pinn): VSD 5825 (CD)*
AIRPORT (1970) Music score: ALFRED NEWMAN -S/T- reissue
*VARESE (Pinn): VSD 5436 (CD)*
AIRPORT (BBC1 2/4/96) title mus: HAL LINDES *unavailable*
AIRWOLF (USA 84-ITV) Theme music: SYLVESTER LEVAY
*see COLLECTIONS 12,242,344*
AKIRA (Cartoon 1991) Music sco: YAMASHIRO SHOJI *VIDEO
Manga:IWCV 1001VHS* -S/T- *DEMON (Pinn): DSCD 6 (CD)*
AKIRA 2 (1994) Animated Manga Video / Music score
YAMASHIRO SHOJI -S/T- *DEMON (Pinn): DSCD 7 (CD)*
ALADDIN (1993) Music and songs: ALAN MENKEN-HOWARD ASHM
AN-TIM RICE -S/T- *feat* "A Whole New World" sung by
PEABO BRYSON-REGINA BELLE -S/T- *DISNEY (B.Vista):
WD 74260-2 (CD) WD 74260-4 (MC)*
see also WALT DISNEY INDEX p.343
ALADDIN (SHOW 1959) Songs: COLE PORTER Orig Cast Record
Cyril Richard-Sal Mineo-Dennis King-Basil Rathbone-
Anna Maria Alberghetti) *Sony Broadway: CD48205 (CD)*
ALAMO The (1960) Music sco: DIMITRI TIOMKIN title song
"Green Leaves Of Summer" (Tiomkin-Webster) sung by
BROTHERS FOUR -S/T- *COLUMBIA (S.Scre) CB 66138 (CD)*
ORCHESTRAL SUITE on 'HIGH NOON' (D.TIOMKIN Collect)
*RCA VICTOR (BMG): 09026 62658-2 (CD)*
ALAN CLARK'S HISTORY OF THE TORY PARTY (BBC2 14/9/97)
music by PETER SALEM *unavailable*

ALAS SMITH AND JONES (UKGold 6/11/92 orig BBC2 31/1/84)
   Music: PETE BREWIS *feat:* MEL SMITH-GRIFF RHYS JONES
   *BBC Video: BBCV 4674 (1) AND BBCV 4861 (2)*
ALCHEMIST The (1985) Music score: RICHARD BAND -S/T- on
   *INTRADA (S.Screen): MAF 7046D (CD)* also contains
   *-S/T-* to 'THE HOUSE ON SONORITY ROW' (Richard BAND)
ALEXANDER NEVSKY (1938 Eisenstein) Mus sco: S.PROKOFIEV
   ST.PETERSBURG PHILHAR.ORCH *RCA: 09026 61926-2 (CD)*
   also avail: Scottish National Orch (Neeme Jarvi) &
   Linda Finnie (mezzo-sopr) *CHANDOS: CHAN 8584 (CD)*
ALEXANDER THE GREAT (1956) Music sco: MARIO NASCIMBENE
   score WITH 'BARABBAS' *DRG (Pinn): DRGCD 32964 (CD)*
ALF (ALIEN LIFE FORCE) (USA TV) *see COLLECTION 344*
ALFIE (1966) Music sco: SONNY ROLLINS -S/T- score *reiss*
   *IMPULSE-MCA-GRP-New Note (BMG): IMP 12242 (CD)*
   Title song (Burt Bacharach-Hal David) *sung by* CHER
   *see also COLLECTIONS 38,280,*
ALFRED HITCHCOCK PRESENTS (USA 55) / ITV 60's) Theme
   "Funeral March Of A Marionette" (GOUNOD)
   *see COLLECTIONS 61,109,339*
ALIAS SMITH AND JONES (USA 71/BBC1 70s) title theme mus
   BILLY GOLDENBERG *see COLLECTIONS 2,168*
ALICE IN WONDERLAND (50) see WALT DISNEY INDEX p.343
ALICE IN WONDERLAND (1968 RECORDING reissued) *featuring*
   Karen Dotrice-Kenneth Connor-Beryl Reid-Dorothy Squ
   ires-Bruce Forsyth-Fenella Fielding-Tommy Cooper-Pe
   ggy Mount-Ian Wallace-Arthur Haynes-Frankie Howerd-
   *EMI: CDEMS 1471 (CD) TCEMS 1471 (MC)*
ALICE'S RESTAURANT (1969) Songs: ARLO GUTHRIE *feat* PETE
   SEEGER -S/T- *REPRISE (WEA): K244045(CD) K44045(LP)*
   30TH ANNIVERSARY EDITION *KOCH: 37959-2 (CD)*
ALIEN (1979) Music sco: JERRY GOLDSMITH -S/T- with The
   Nat.Phil.O *SILVA SCREEN (Koch): FILMCD 003 (CD)*
   *see also COLLECTIONS 11,109,156,258,268,273,322*
ALIEN (2) ALIENS (1986) Music score: JAMES HORNER -S/T-
   *VARESE USA (Pinn): VCD 47263 (CD)*
ALIEN 3 (92) Music score: ELLIOT GOLDENTHAL -S/T- on
   *MCA (BMG): MCD 10629 (CD)*
ALIEN 4 (97) Music score: JOHN FRIZZELL -S/T-
   *RCA (BMG): 09026 68955-2 (CD)*
ALIEN EMPIRE (BBC1 15/2/96) theme & mus.score composed
   by MARTIN KISZKO with The Munich Symphony Orchestra
   (cond: Harry Rabinowitz) 'The Ocellus Suite' -S/T-
   *SOUNDTRACK EMI: CD(TC)EMC 3730 deleted*
ALIEN NATION (USA/SKY1 13/6/94) mus: STEVE DORFF-LARRY
   HERBSTRITT-DAVID KURTZ -S/T- on *GNP (Silva Screen)*
   *GNPD 8024 (CD) GNP5 8024 (MC)*
ALIEN NATION (1988) Music sc: JOE HARNELL *see COLL.345*
ALL CREATURES GREAT AND SMALL (UKGO 17/9/93 orig BBC1
   8/1/78) Theme and incidental music: JOHNNY PEARSON
   *see COLLECTIONS 4,168,284,285*
ALL IN GOOD FAITH (Thames 11/4/88) Theme mus "Klavier
   stuck in F" K.33b (Mozart) by DANIEL BARENBOIM on
   *HMV (EMI): CDC 747384-2 (CD) EL 270382-4 (MC)*

ALL IN THE FAMILY (USA TV) see *COLLECTION 341*
ALL OVER ME (1996) Music score: MIKI NAVAZIO -S/T- Impt
*TVT (Cargo-Greyhound): 8110 (CD)*
ALL PASSION SPENT (BBC2 9/12/86) see *COLLECTION 192*
ALL QUIET ON THE PRESTON FRONT (BBC1 4/1/94) theme mus
"Here I Stand" by The MILLTOWN BROTHERS on 'Slinky'
*A.& M. (Poly): 395 346-2 (CD) 395 346-4 (MC)*
ALL THAT JAZZ (1979) Mus sco: RALPH BURNS "On Broadway"
GEORGE BENSON -S/T- *SPECTRUM (Poly):551 269-2 (CD)*
ALL THAT MONEY CAN BUY (aka 'The Devil And Daniel Webs
ter')(1941) Music score: BERNARD HERRMANN National
Philharmonic Orchestra (B.Herrmann) Film Suite on
*UNICORN-KANCHANA (Harmonia Mundi): UKCD 2065 (CD)*
ALL THE BROTHERS WERE VALIANT (1953) Music sco: MIKLOS
ROSZA *PROMETHEUS (Silva Screen): PCD 131 (CD)*
ALLAN QUATERMAIN AND THE LOST CITY OF GOLD (1986) Mus
score: MICHAEL LINN *also includes Suites from:*
'MANIFESTO' (88- Nicola Piovani) 'MAKING THE GRADE'
(84- Basil Poledouris) 'DOIN' TIME ON PLANET EARTH'
(87- Dana Kaproff) 'SEVEN MAGNIFICENT GLADIATORS'
(83- Dov Seltzer) *S.SCREEN: SIL 1528-2 (CD)*
ALVIN'S SHOW (USA TV) see *COLLECTION 341*
ALWAYS (1990) Music score: JOHN WILLIAMS
-S/T- *MCA USA (Silva Screen): MCAD 8036 (CD)*
AMADEUS (1984) Music (MOZART) Academy Of St.Martin-In
The Fields (Neville Marriner) -S/T- *LONDON (Poly):
825 126-2 (CD)* 'MORE AMADEUS' *827 267-2 (CD) and
LONDON 511 126-2 (CD Boxed Set) see also
COLLECTIONS 65,66,69,70,71,72,73,97,139,171*
AMATEUR The (1982) Music score: KEN WANNBERG -S/T-
select.with 'LATE SHOW'/'OF UNKNOWN ORIGIN' Imp
*PROMETHEUS (Silva Screen): PCD 137 (CD)*
AMERICA IS DYING SLOWLY (1995) RAP Music Various Arts
-S/T- *WEA (WEA): 7559 61963-2 (CD) 04(MC) 01(LP)*
AMERICAN BANDSTAND (USA TV) see *COLLECTION 341*
AMERICAN BUFFALO (1996) Music sco: THOMAS NEWMAN -S/T-
+ *from* 'THREESOME' *VARESE (Pinn): VSD 5751 (CD)*
AMERICAN GIGOLO (1980) Music sc: GIORGIO MORODER -S/T-
with V/Arts *reiss SPECTRUM (Poly) 551 103-2 (CD)*
"Seduction Love Theme" JAMES LAST *POLY:831786-2 CD*
AMERICAN GOTHIC (USA95/C4 5/6/96) mus: JOSEPH LoDUCA.*NA*
AMERICAN GRAFFITI (1973) Music by VARIOUS ORIG ARTISTS
*MCA (BMG): MCLDD 19150 (CDx2)*
AMOS 'N' ANDY (USA TV) see *COLLECTION 342*
AN AMERICAN IN PARIS (1951) Songs:GEORGE & IRA GERSHWIN
1.-S/T- including out-takes and featuring 47 tracks
*EMI-Soundtrack Music (EMI): CDODEON 20 (2CD)*
2.import score with -S/T- of 'SINGIN' IN THE RAIN'
*BLUE MOON (Discovery): BMCD 7008 (CD)*
3.new recording on *VIRGIN (EMI): VM 561247-2 (CD)*
AN AMERICAN TAIL (1987) Music score: JAMES HORNER song:
"Somewhere Out There" (J.Horner-Barry Mann-Cynthia
Weill) sung by LINDA RONSTADT & JAMES INGRAM -S/T-
*MCA (S.Screen): MCAD 39096 (CD) MCAC 39096 (MC)*

AN AMERICAN TAIL 2: Fieval Goes West (1991) Mus score:
JAMES HORNER -S/T- MCA: MCAD(MCAC) 10416 (CD/MC)
AN AMERICAN WEREWOLF IN PARIS (1996) Music sco: WILBERT
HIRSCH -S/T- Hollywood (Poly): 162 131-2 (CD)
AN ANGEL AT MY TABLE (1990) Music score: DON McGLASHAN
-S/T- DRG USA (Pinn): CDSBL 12603 (CD) also on
AN AWFULLY BIG ADVENTURE (1994) Music: RICHARD HARTLEY
-S/T- FILMTRACKS (S.Screen): TRAXCD 2001 (CD)
AN EVENING WITH ALAN JAY LERNER (ORIG LONDON CAST 1987)
Song lyrics:Alan Jay Lerner / Music:Frederick Loewe
L.Bernstein-B.Lane-C.Strouse) Feat: LIZ ROBERTSON-
MARTI WEBB-PLACINDO DOMINGO-ELAINE PAIGE and others
FIRST NIGHT (Pinn): OCRCD 6012 (CD)
AN INSPECTOR CALLS (C4 15/4/96) theme mus "Dance Of The
Knights" from 'Romeo & Juliet' (PROKOFIEV) other
music "After The Storm" from 'Pastoral Symphony'
(BEETHOVEN) various recordings available
AN OFFICER AND A GENTLEMAN (1982) Mus sc: JACK NITZSCHE
"Up Where We Belong" (Jack Nitzsche-Buffy Saint Ma
rie-Will Jennings) sung JOE COCKER-JENNIFER WARNES
-S/T- ISLAND (Polyg): IMCD 77 (CD) ICM 2041 (MC)
see also COLLECTIONS 262,274
AN UNSUITABLE JOB FOR A WOMAN (P.D.JAMES)(ITV 24/10/97)
music score by COLIN TOWNS unavailable
ANACONDA (1997) Music score: RANDY EDELMAN
-S/T- EDEL (Pinn): 002281-2CIN (CD)
ANASTASIA (1997) Music score: DAVID NEWMAN
-S/T- Atlantic (WEA): 7567 80753-2 (CD) -4 (MC)
ANASTASIA: THE MYSTERY OF ANNA Mus: LAURENCE ROSENTHAL
SOUTHERN CROSS (S.Screen): SCCD 1015 (CD)
ANCHORS AWEIGH (1945 MUSICAL) feat: FRANK SINATRA-GRACE
KELLY-KATHRYN GRAYSON TARGET (BMG): CD 60003 (CD)
also abailable -S/T- Import with 'ON THE TOWN'
BLUE MOON (Discovery): BMCD 7007 (CD)
AND THE BAND PLAYED ON (1993) Music sco: CARTER BURWELL
-S/T- VARESE (Pinn): VSD 5449 (CD)
AND THE WORLD GOES ROUND (Musical Tribute Show To compo
sers John Kander & Fred Ebb) Orig BROADWAY Cast on
BMG USA (Silva Screen): 60904-2 (CD) 60904-4 (MC)
ANDORRA (BBC 1967) music: RON GRAINER see COLLECTION 7
ANDY GRIFFITH SHOW (USA) see COLLECTION 339
ANDY WARHOL'S DRACULA and FRANKENSTEIN (1974) Music sc
CLAUDIO GIZZI -S/T- IMPT (S.Screen): OST 119 (CD)
ANGEL (USA 1983) Music sco: CRAIG SAFAN -S/T- INTRADA
USA Imprt (Silva Screen-Koch): MAF 7047D (CD)
ANGEL & THE SOLDIER BOY The (1989) BBC1 27/12/89
-S/T- reissue BMG Kidz (BMG): 74321 25081-2 (CD)
ANGEL BABY (1995) Music sco: JOHN CLIFFORD WHITE -S/T-
MILAN (BMG): 74321 44359-2 (CD) / also Imported on
ICON (Pinn.Imports): ICON 19951 (CD)
ANGEL HEART (1987) Music score: TREVOR JONES -S/T- on
ISLAND (Poly) IMCD 76 (CD) ICM(ILPM) 2025 (MC/LP)
ANGELIQUE (1964) Music score: MICHEL MAGNE -S/T-
MOVIE SELECT AUDIO (Direct): MSA 99011 (CD)

ANGELS (BBC1 1976-80) theme music "Motivation" by ALAN
    PARKER *see COLLECTIONS 2,4,*
ANGELS AND INSECTS (1994) Mus sco: ALEX BALANESCU perf
    BALANESCU QUART.-S/T- *MUTE-RTM (Disc) CDSTUMM 147*
ANGIE (1993) Music sco: JERRY GOLDSMITH -S/T- *VARESE
    (Pinn): VSD 5469 (CD)*
ANGST (1986) Electronic Music sco: KLAUS SCHULZE -S/T-
    *THUNDERBOLT-MAGNUM (MMG): CDTB 2.027 (CD)*
ANGUS (1995) -S/T- *WEA: 9362 45960-2 (CD) -4 (MC)*
ANIMAL HOSPITAL (BBC1 5/1/95) theme music composed
    and arranged by RONALD DE JONG *unavailable*
ANIMAL HOUSE - *see under* 'National Lampoon's...'
ANIMAL MAGIC (BBC1 to 84) "Las Vegas" by LAURIE JOHNSON
    *see COLLECTIONS 4,163,358,381*
ANIMAL SHELF (ITVC 25/6/97) mus: ERNIE WOOD *unavailable*
ANIMAL SQUAD UNDERCOVER (C4 5/10/92) original music by
    ROBERT HOWES and ROD ARGENT *unavailable*
ANIMALS OF FARTHING WOOD The (BBC1/EBU 6/1/93) music
    DETLEV KUHNE & WDR ORC *BBC (Pinn): YBBC 1452 (2MC)*
    *see COLLECTION 60*
ANIMANIACS (ITV 24/2/94) Songs from series *ATLANTIC
    (WEA): 8122 71570-2 (CD) -4 (MC)*
ANNA KARENINA (1997) TCHAIKOVSKY-RACHMANINOV-PROKOFIEV
    *w:* St.Petersburg Phil.Orch cond.by Sir GEORG SOLTI
    *with* GALINA GORCHAKOVA sopr; MAXIM VENGEROV violin
    -S/T- *LONDON (Poly): 455 360-2 (CD) 455 360-4 (MC)*
ANNA LEE (ITV 27/2/94) music score: ANNE DUDLEY / theme
    "Sister Sister" sung by LUCIANA *Chrysalis: CDCHS
    5008 (CDs) TCCHS 5008 (MC) 12CHS 5008 (12") delet*
ANNA OF THE FIVE TOWNS (BBC2 9/1/85) title music: NIGEL
    HESS London Film Orch *see COLLECTION 192*
ANNE OF GREEN GABLES (ORIG LONDON CAST 1969) Songs by
    NORMAN CAMPBELL-DONALD HARRON *featur* POLLY JAMES
    BARBARA HAMILTON on *SONY Broadway: SMK 53495 (CD)*
ANNIE - songs by Charles Strouse and Martin Charnin
    1.FILM MUSICAL 1982 *feat:* ALBERT FINNEY-AILEEN QUINN
      CAROL BURNETT -S/T- *Sony: 467 608-2 (CD) -4 (MC)*
    2.ORIG BROADWAY CAST 1977 *feat:* ANDREA McARDLE-REID
      SHELTON-DOROTHY LOUDEN-SANDY FAISON-ROBERT FITCH
      *COLUMBIA (S.Screen): CK 34712 (CD) JST 34712 (MC)*
      *see also COLLECTIONS 47,315*
ANNIE GET YOUR GUN - songs by Irving Berlin
    1.LINCOLN CENTER EDITION FIRST COMPLETE RECORDING *w:*
      JUDY KAYE-BARRY BOSTWICK *TER (DISC): CDTER2 12292*
    2.CARLTON SHOWS COLLECTION 1995 *feat:* GEMMA CRAVEN-
      with EDMUND HOCKRIDGE-STEVE BUTLER-ALISON COX
      *CARLTON Shows Collect: 30362 0022-2 (CD) -4 (MC)*
    3.NEW LONDON CAST 1986 *feat:* SUZI QUATRO & Company
      *FIRST NIGHT (Pinn): OCRCD 6024 (CD)*
    4.ORIG BROADWAY CAST 1946 *with* ETHEL MERMAN-BRUCE YAR
      NELL-BENAY VENUTA-JERRY ORBACH *BMG: RD 81124 (CD)*
    5.STUDIO 1990 *feat:* KIM CRISWELL-THOMAS HAMPSON-JASON
      GRAAE-REBECCA LUKER-Ambrosian Chor-London Sinfonia
      (J.McGlinn) *EMI: CDANNIE 1 (CD) TCANNIE 1 (MC)*

**ANNIE'S BAR** (C4 1/2/96) music: JOHN HARLE *unavailable*
**ANOTHER DAWN** (1937) Music sco: ERICH WOLFGANG KORNGOLD
   *new version:* MOSCOW S.ORCH (Stromberg) also featur:
   "Ballet Fantasy" from 'ESCAPE ME NEVER' *MARCO POLO*
   *(Select): 8.223871 (CD)*
**ANOTHER 48 HOURS** (1990) Music score: JAMES HORNER + V/A
   -S/T- POLYDOR IMS-Poly: E.846 872-2 (CD)
**ANT & DEC SHOW** (BBC1 6/4/95) m: STEVE BROWN *unavailable*
**ANTARCTICA** (HORIZON BBC2 30/10/97) o.score: PHILIP POPE
   *unavailable* "Musica Poetica" (Carl Orff-G.Keetman)
   TOLZ BOYS CHOIR *RCA (BMG): 09026 68031-2 (CD)*
**ANTARCTICA** (1983) Music score: VANGELIS -S/T- *POLYDOR*
   *815732-2 (CD) -4 (MC) and on* 'SYNTHESIZER MEGA-H'
**ANTHOLOGY - THE BEATLES** (ITV 26/11/95) music and songs
   TV S/T *EMI Parloph: CD(PC)PCSP 727 (2CD/2MC/3LPs)*
**ANTHONY ADVERSE** (1936) Mus sco: ERICH WOLFGANG KORNGOLD
   suite 'Hollywood Chronicle' *VARESE (Pinn): VSD 5351*
**ANTIQUES INSPECTORS** The (BBC1 7/9/97) theme music "Hot
   Club Swing" by JOHNNY HAWKESWORTH *De Wolfe library*
**ANTIQUES ROAD SHOW** (BBC1 18/2/79-1998)
   *1989-98 series theme:* PAUL READE *unavailable*
   *1985-89 series theme:* ROGER LIMB *unavailable*
   *orig theme* 'Brandenburg Concerto No.3 in G.Maj" and
   'Little Suite From Anna Magdalena Notebook' J.S.BACH
**ANTIQUES SHOW** The (BBC2 7/4/97) title mus: NIGEL BEAHAM
   POWELL and BELLA RUSSELL *unavailable*
**ANTONIA'S LINE** (1995) Music score: ILONA SEKACZ -S/T-
   *SILVA SCREEN (Koch): FILMCD 183 (CD)*
**ANTONIO CARLUCCI'S ITALIAN FEAST** (BBC2 17/9/96) music:
   CROCODILE MUSIC *see COLLECTION 337*
**ANTONY AND CLEOPATRA** (1972) Music score by JOHN SCOTT
   Royal Philharmonic Orch (Scott) Symphonic score on
   *JOHN SCOTT Records (Silva Screen): JSCDC 114 (CD)*
**ANYONE CAN WHISTLE** (ORIG BROADWAY CAST) Songs: STEPHEN
   SONDHEIM *with* Angela Lansbury-Lee Remick & Company
   *CBS USA (S.Screen): CK 02480 (CD) JST 02480 (MC)*
**ANYTHING GOES** - songs by Cole Porter
   1.**ORIG LONDON CAST 1989** *feat:* ELAINE PAIGE-HOWARD
     McGILLIN-BERNARD CRIBBINS and Comp *FIRST NIGHT*
     *(Pinn): OCRCD 6038 (CD)*
   2.**STUDIO RECORDING 1989** *feat:* FREDERICA VON STADE-KIM
     CRISWELL-CRIS GROENENDAAL-JACK GILFORD-LONDON SYMPH
     ONY ORCHESTRA and AMBROSIAN CHORUS (John McGlynn)
     *EMI: CDC 749848-2 (CD) EL 749848-4 (MC)*
**ANYWHERE I WANDER** (1993) Songs by FRANK LOESSER sung by
   LIZ CALLAWAY *VARESE (Pinn): VSD 5434 (CD)*
**APHRODITE INHERITANCE** The (UKGO 10/5/94 or.BBC1 3/1/79)
   music score: GEORGE KOTSONIS -S/T- *BBC deleted*
**APOCALYPSE NOW** (1979) Music: CARMINE & FRANCIS COPPOLA
   inc.'Die Walkure' (WAGNER) + V.Art -S/T- *reiss WEA:*
   *7559 60689-2 (2CD) see COLLECTIONS 65,384,*
**APPLE TREE** The (ORIG BROADWAY CAST 66) Songs JERRY BOCK
   SHELDON HARNICK *featuring* BARBARA HARRIS-LARRY BLYD
   DEN-ALAN ALDA *SONY MUSIC: CD 48209 (CD)*

APOLLO 13 (1994) Music score: JAMES HORNER -S/T- *with*
   JAMES BROWN-YOUG RASCALS-JEFFERSON AIRPLANE-WHO
   JIMI HENDRIX-NORMAN GREENBAUM-HANK WILLIAMS etc.
   *MCA (BMG): MCD 11241*
   *see COLL 34,82,273,300,322*
APRIL MORNING - see under 'IRONCLADS'
AQUA MARINA (ATV 60's) theme music by BARRY GRAY with
   vocal by GARRY MILLER *see COLLECTIONS 357,364,372*
ARCHIES The (USA TV) *see COLLECTION 341*
ARCTIC BLUE (1993) Music score: PETER MELNICK -S/T-
   *NARADA (New Note-Pinn): ND 63030 (CD)*
ARE YOU BEING SERVED? (BBC1 14/3/73) theme mus: RONNIE
   HAZLEHURST-D.CROFT) *new version by* GRACE BROTHERS
   *EMI Premier: 7243 82799-2 / PRESCD 1 (CDs mixes)*
ARE YOU LONESOME TONIGHT (ORIG LONDON CAST 1985) Play:
   Alan Bleasdale / *ELVIS PRESLEY songs sung by* MARTIN
   SHAW-SIMON BOWMAN *FIRST NIGHT (Pinn): OCRCD 6027*
ARENA (BBC2) Theme "Another Green World" by BRIAN ENO
   BRIAN ENO *EG (Poly): EGMC 21 (MC) EGCD 21 (CD)*
   *see also COLLECTION 267*
ARISTOCATS The (1970) Songs: RICHARD and ROBERT SHERMAN
   -S/T- *DISNEY (B.Vista): WD 74250-2 (CD) -4 (MC)*
   see WALT DISNEY INDEX p.343
ARMCHAIR THEATRE (ATV 50s-60s) music "Proscenium" by
   ROBERT FARNON *see COLLECTION 220*
ARMY OF DARKNESS (1992) Music sco: JOSEPH LoDUCA -S/T-
   *VARESE (Pinn): VSD 5411 (CD) VSC 5411 (MC)*
ARMY GAME The (ITV Granada 57-62) Theme feat ALFIE BASS
   MICHAEL MEDWIN-BERNARD BRESSLAW on 'Hits Of 58' col
   *MFP Hour Of Pleasure (EMI): HR 8175 (MC only)*
AROUND THE WORLD IN 80 DAYS (1956) Music: VICTOR YOUNG
   -S/T- *MCA (S.Scr) MCAD 31164 (CD) also COLL.292,307*
AROUND THE WORLD IN 80 DAYS (Michael Palin BBC1 14/7/91
   (11/10/89) Orig music: PADDY KINGSLAND *unavailable*
ARRIVAL (1991) Music score: RICHARD BAND -S/T- *INTRADA*
   *(Silva Screen): MAF 7032CD (CD)*
ARRIVAL The (1996) Mus: ARTHUR KEMPEL feat NORTHWEST
   SINFONIA *SILVA SCREEN (Koch): FILMCD 182 (CD)*
ART ATTACK (TVS 15/6/90) theme mus: PETER MILLER and
   IAN PORTER (Mr.Miller & Mr.Porter) *unavailable*
ART OF LANDSCAPE (C4 11/12/89-90) Various New Age and
   Classical Music Var.Arts. Coll: *NEW NOTE (Pinn):*
   *ALC(CD)11 (CD/MC :V1) ALC(CD)12 (CD/MC :V2)*
   'CLASSICAL LANDSCAPES' *LANDSCAPE (SM): ALCV 2 Vid*
ARTHUR (1980) Theme 'Best That You Can Do' (B.Bacharach
   C.B.Sager-C.Cross-P.Allen) by CHRISTOPHER CROSS
   *see COLLECTIONS 28,262,297,353,382*
ARTHUR C.CLARKE'S MYSTERIOUS UNIVERSE  (USA)/Discovery/
   Satellite) Music sco: ALAN HAWKSHAW -S/T- music on
   *HUNGRY HAWK (Grapevine/Polygram): HHCD 101 (CD)*
AS TIME GOES BY (BBC1 12/1/92) theme "As Time Goes By"
   (Herman Hupfeld) by JOE FAGIN on Coll 'Best Of on
   *Westmoor (BMG): CDWM 107(CD) CWM 107(MC)*
   *CDS 1(CDs) see also under* 'CASABLANCA'

AS YOU LIKE IT (1936) Music sc: WILLIAM WALTON select.
'Walton Film Music' LONDON PHILHARMONIC ORCHESTRA
conduct: CARL DAVIS *EMI: CDM 565585-2 (CD) also*
ACADEMY of ST.MARTIN-IN-THE-FIELDS (N.Marriner)
and 'HAMLET' *CHANDOS: CHAN 8842 (CD)*
ASK THE FAMILY (BBC2) *see COLLECTION 6*
ASPECTS OF LOVE -songs by Andrew Lloyd Webber-Charles
Hart and Don Black
  1.ORIG LONDON CAST 1989 *feat:* MICHAEL BALL-ANN CRUMB
    DIANA MORRISON-KEVIN COLSON *POLY: 841 126-2 / -4*
  2.SHOWS COLLECTION Studio 1993 *feat:* PAUL JONES with
    STEPHANIE LAWRENCE-DAVE WILLETTS-FIONA HENDLEY-CARL
    WAYNE-WEST END CONCERT ORCH. *plus music of* 'PHANTOM
    OF THE OPERA' *CARLTON: PWKS(PWKMC) 4164 (CD(MC)*
  3.ROYAL PHILH.ORCH *PLAY SUITES from* Aspects Of Love
    Cats/Joseph and The Amazing Technicolor Dreamcoat
    *Carlton: PWKS(PWKMC) 4115 (CD(MC)*
  4.Classic Musicals series *feat:* JOHN BARROWMAN-JANIS
    KELLY-SHONA LINDSAY-JOHN DIEDRICH + 'JESUS CHRIST
    SUPERSTAR' *KOCH INT: 34083-2 (CD)*
ASSAM GARDEN The (1985) Music sco: RICHARD HARVEY theme
    *see COLLECTION 181*
ASSASSIN The: Point Of No Return (1992) Music sco: HANS
    ZIMMER includes songs by NINA SIMONE -S/T- *MILAN
    (BMG): 14302-2 (CD) 14302-4 (MC)*
ASSASSINATION BUREAU The (1968) Music sco: RON GRAINER
    *see COLLECTION 7*
ASSASSINS (ORIG USA CAST 1991) Songs: STEPHEN SONDHEIM
    William Parry-Terence Mann *(BMG): RD 60737 (CD)*
ASSAULT ON PRECINCT 13 (1976) Music sc: JOHN CARPENTER
    *see COLLECTION 178*
ASSAULT The (1986) - *see under* 'CRY IN THE DARK'
ASSOCIATE The (1996) VARIOUS ARTISTS -S/T- on
    *MOTOWN (Poly): 530 747-2 (CD)*
ASTEROID (ITV1/3/97) music: SHIRLEY WALKER *unavailable*
ASTRO BOY (USA TV) *see COLLECTION 342*
ASTRONOMERS The (USA TV) Music score: J.A.C.REDFORD
    *INTRADA USA (Silva Screen): MAF 7018D (CD)*
AT THE DROP OF A HAT (Musical Revue 1958 Fortune)
    featuring MICHAEL FLANDERS and DONALD SWANN on
    *EMI: CDP 797465-2(CD) /* AT THE DROP OF ANOTHER HAT
    (Musical Revue 1960 Haymarket) MICHAEL FLANDERS-
    -DONALD SWANN *EMI: CDP 797466-2 (CD) ECC  (2MC)*
ATHLETICS (BBCTV 79-96) "World Series" KEITH MANSFIELD
    *deleted Also* used "Fanfare For The Common Man" (A.
    Copland) *see also* 'WORLD ATHLETICS CHAMPIONSHIPS'
ATHLETICS (ITV Sport) "Hot Foot" by ROD ARGENT & PETER
    VAN HOOKE *see COLLECTION 138*
ATLANTIC CITY (1981) Music score: MICHEL LEGRAND -S/T-
    *MUSIDISC Import (Discovery): 11907-2 (CD)*
ATLANTIC REALM (BBC1 8/1/89) Music comp.& performed by
    CLANNAD -S/T- *refs: RCA (BMG): 74321 31867-2 (CD)*
ATLANTIS (1991) Music score: ERIC SERRA -S/T- *VIRGIN
    Impt (Silva Screen): 869462 (CD) 50867 (MC)*

ATOM ANT SHOW (USA TV) see *COLLECTION 343*
ATTACK OF THE CRAB MONSTERS 1956 *Coll* NOT OF THIS EARTH
ATTACK OF THE 50FT WOMAN 1958 see 'NOT OF THIS EARTH'
ATTACK ON THE IRON COAST 1967 Music: GERARD SCHURMANN
  'Coastal Command' *S.SCREEN (Koch): FILM(C)(CD) 072*
AU REVOIR LES ENFANTS 1987 see *COLLECTION 75*
AUF WIEDERSEHEN, PET (C4 11/3/95 orig ITV 11/11/83)
  "That's Livin' Alright"/"Breakin'Away" (David Mac
  Kay-Ian La Frenais) sung by JOE FAGIN *reissued on*
  *WESTMOOR (BMG): WCD 10 (CDs) WECS 10 (MC)* also
  'Best Of J.Fagin' *WESTMOOR: CDWM 107(CD) CWM 107*
  *(MC) also* 'BEST OF AUF WIEDERSEHEN PET 1 & 2'
  *PRESTIGE-TRC (BMG): CDSGP 0201 (CD) see COLL.4,6*
AUGUST (1995) Music sco: ANTHONY HOPKINS arr/orch and
  conducted by GEORGE FENTON *featur: ANTHONY HOPKINS*
  *(piano) -S/T- DEBONAIR (Pinn): CDDEB 1003 (CD)*
AUNTIE: THE INSIDE STORY OF THE BBC (BBC1 28/10/97)
  Original music by DEBBIE WISEMAN *unavailable*
AUNTIE'S (NEW) BLOOMERS (BBC1 29/12/91 & BBC1 1/1/95)
  theme music by KEITH STRACHAN *unavailable*
AUNTIE'S SPORTING BLOOMERS (BBC1 11/7/95) music arr.
  by PHILIP POPE *unavailable*
AUSTIN POWERS:INTERNATIONAL MAN OF MYSTERY (1997) -S/T-
  Various Artists *POLYDOR (Poly): 162 112-2 (CD)*
AUTUMN SONATA 1978 see *COLLECTIONS 77,78*
AVALON (90) Music score: RANDY NEWMAN -S/T- on *WARNER*
  *BROS IMP (S.Screen): 926 437-2 (CD) 926 437-4(MC)*
AVENGERS The (ABCTV 65-69) music by LAURIE JOHNSON
  see *COLLECTIONS 2,3,100,109,138,246,294,318,340,*
  *356,357,364,368,372*
A.W.O.L.(LIONHEART) (1990) Music sco: JOHN SCOTT -S/T-
  *INTRADA USA (Silva Screen): MAF 7011D (CD)*
AWAKENINGS (1990) Music score: RANDY NEWMAN -S/T- on
  *REPRISE Import (S.Screen): 26466-2 (CD) deleted*

BABE (THE GALLANT PIG) (1995) Music Sco: NIGEL WESTLAKE
  "If I Had You" adapted from Symphony No.3 Op.78
  (Saint-Saens) sung by YVONNE KEELY-SCOTT FITZGERALD
  -S/T- *VARESE (Pinn): VSD 5661 (CD) deleted*
BABE (1992) Music score: ELMER BERNSTEIN -S/T- Import
  *MCA (S.Screen): MCAD 10576 (CD) MCAC 10576 (MC)*
BABES IN ARMS (1939) Songs: RICHARD RODGERS-LORENZ HART
  -S/T- *with* JUDY GARLANDO-MICKEY ROONEY *NEW WORLD*
  *(Harmonia Mundi): NW 386-2 (CD) NW 386-4 (MC)*
BABETTE'S FEAST (1988) Music score: PER NORGARD -S/T-
  *MILAN (Pinn): CDCH 333 (CD)*
BABY (ORIG BROADWAY CAST 1983) Mus: DAVID SHIRE Lyrics
  RICHARD MALTYBY JNR *feat:* Liz Callaway-Beth Fowler
  James Congdon-T.Graff *TER (Disc): CD(ZC)TER 1089*
BABY IT'S YOU (C4 25/5/94) theme music "Spiritu" by
  JOHN HARLE on 'Silencium' - see *COLLECTION 407*
BABY OF MACON The (1993) Classical music by MONTEVERDI
  CORELLI-TALLIS-BACH-CLAMER-FRESCOBALDI etc. -S/T-
  *KOCH International (Koch): 34014-2 (CD)*

BABYLON 5 (USA/C4 16/5/94) music: CHRISTOPHER FRANKE
  BERLIN SYPHONY ORCHESTRA cond: Christopher Franke
  VOLUME 1 - *SONIC IMAGES-CDS (Pinn): SI 8403-2 (CD)*
  VOLUME 2 - *SONIC IMAGES-CDS (Pinn): SI 8502-2 (CD)*
  see *COLLECTIONS 109,273,302*
BACK TO THE FLOOR (BBC2 28/10/97) m: MUSIC SCULPTORS.*NA*
BACK TO THE FUTURE (1985) Music score: ALAN SILVESTRI
  -S/T- *MCA MCLD 19151 (CD) see COLL.8,198,274,323*
BACK TO THE FUTURE 2 (1989) -S/T- *MCA: deleted*
BACK TO THE FUTURE 3 (1990) Mus: ALAN SILVESTRI -S/T-
  *VARESE (Pinn): VSD 5272 (CD) VSC 5272 (MC)*
BACKBEAT (1994) Beatles Early Years -S/T- songs:
  *VIRGIN (EMI): CD(TC)V 2729 (CD/MC/LP)* -S/T-
  score: (Don Was) *Virgin CDV(TCV)2740 (CD/MC)*
BACKDRAFT (1991) Mus: HANS ZIMMER Songs: Bruce Hornsby
  -S/T- *MILAN (BMG): CDCH 807 (CD) C 807 (MC)*
BACKUP (BBC1 7/9/95) music: JOHN LUNN *unavailable*
BAD BOYS (1995) Music score: MARK MANCINA -S/T- on
  *COLUMBIA (Sony): 480 453-2(CD) -4(MC) 476601(LP)*
BAD GIRLS (1993) Music score: JERRY GOLDSMITH -S/T-
  *MILAN (BMG): 22054-2 (CD)*
BAD INFLUENCE (1990) Music score: TREVOR JONES -S/T- +
  V.Arts *reissued SPECTRUM (Poly): 551 102-2 (CD)*
BAD MOON (1996) Music score: DANIEL LICHT -S/T- on
  *SILVA AMERICA (Koch): SSD 1068 (CD)*
BAD TASTE (1988) Music by various artists -S/T- on
  *NORMAL (Topic/Proj/Dir): QDKCD 002 (CD)*
BAGDAD CAFE (1988) Mus (B.Telson-P.Adlon-O.Ebner-L.Brue
  hr-Bach) Theme "Calling You" sung by JEVETTA STEELE
  -S/T- *ISLAND: IMCD 102 (CD) ICM 2005 (MC)*
BAKER'S WIFE The (ORIG LONDON CAST 1989) Songs (Stephen
  Schwartz) featuring Sharon Lee Hill *TER (Disc):
  CD2TER 1175 (2CD) ZCTED 1175 (2MC)*
BAKERSFIELD PD (USA 93/C4 6/10/94) title theme: CARL
  FINCH and performed by BRAVE COMBO *unavailable*
BALLAD OF LITTLE JO The (1993) Mus sco: DAVID MANSFIELD
  featuring songs by KATE & ANNA McGARRIGLE -S/T- on
  *INTRADA (Silva Screen): MAF 7053D (CD)*
BALLYKISSANGEL (BBC1 11/2/96) Music score: SHAUN DAVEY
  -S/T- *VIRGIN (EMI): VTCD 17 (CD) VTMC 17 (MC)*
BALTO (1995) Music score: JAMES HORNER -S/T- *MCA Impt
  (EMS): MCAD 11388 (CD)*
BAMBI - see WALT DISNEY INDEX p.343
BANACEK (USA) see *COLLECTION 246*
BANANA SPLITS (aka BANANA BUNCH) (USA68) theme "Tra La
  La Song" (Adams-Barkan) see *COLLECTIONS 343,370*
BAND OF GOLD (ITV 12/3/95) theme and music score by
  HAL LINDES *unavailable*
  song "LOVE HURTS" (Bryant) sung by BARBARA DICKSON
  from 'Dark End Of The Street' *TRANSATLANTIC
  (Castle-BMG): TRACD 117 (CD) TRAMC 117 (MC)*
BAND WAGON The 1953 Songs: Howard Dietz-Arthur Schwartz
  rtz) *feat:* FRED ASTAIRE-JACK BUCHANAN-CYD CHARISSE
  -S/T- (28 tracks) *EMI S/T: CDODEON 19 (CD) DELETED*

BANDIT QUEEN (1993) Music score: NUSRAT FATEH ALI KHAN
   -S/T- *MILAN (BMG): 74321 37811-2 (CD)*
BAPS (B.A.P.S.) (1997) Mus sc: STANLEY CLARKE -S/T- inc
   KOOL & THE GANG-KINSUI-VERONICA and CRAIG MACK-ALEC
   BROWN-GYRL etc. *MILAN (BMG): 74321 48684-2 (CD)*
BARABBAS (1962) Music score: MARIO NASCIMBENE / with
   'ALEXANDER THE GREAT' *DRG (Pinn): DRGCD 32964 (CD)*
   *see also COLLECTION 266*
BARAKA (1993) Music score: MICHAEL STERNS -S/T- on
   *MILAN (BMG): 15306-2 (CD) 15306-4 (MC)*
BARB WIRE (1996) Music score: MICHEL COLOMBIER -S/T-
   *LONDON (Poly): 828 746-2 (CD) 828 746-4 (MC)*
BARBARIANS The (Film) Music score: PINO DONAGGIO -S/T-
   *INTRADA (Koch): MAF 7008D (CD)*
BARCELONA (1994) Music score: MARK SUOZZO -S/T-
   *MILAN (BMG): 237 942 (CD) 237 944 (MC)*
BAREFOOT CONTESSA The (1954) Mus sco: MARIO NASCIMBENE
   -S/T- inc.scor: *'ROOM AT THE TOP'/'QUIET AMERICAN'*
   *DRG (Pinn): DRGCD 32961 (CD) see also COLLECT 266*
BARNABY JONES (USA) *see COLLECTIONS 12,341*
BARNARDO'S CHILDREN (BBC2 4/7/95) theme and incidental
   music "Dives and Lazarus" (Vaughan Williams) *vers:*
   ACADEMY OF ST.MARTIN-IN-THE FIELDS (N.Marriner) on
   *PHILIPS (Polyg): 442 427-2 (CD)*
BARNEY MILLER (USA 82 / C4 9/1/88) theme: JACK ELLIOT
   and ALLYN FERGUSON *see COLLECTION 341*
BARNUM - songs by Cy Coleman and Michael Stewart
   1.ORIG LONDON CAST 1981 *feat:* MICHAEL CRAWFORD & Comp
   *Chrysalis:CCD(ZCDL) 1348(CD/MC) CDL1348(LP) DELETED*
   2.ORIG BROADWAY CAST 1984 *feat:* JIM DALE and Company
   *Columbia (S.Screen): CK 36576 (CD) JST 36576 (MC)*
BARON The *see COLLECTION 357*
BARRETA (USA) *see COLLECTION 168,341,379*
BARRY LYNDON (1975) MD: LEONARD ROSENMAN *feat.Classics*
   -S/T- *reiss: WB (WEA): 7599 25984-2 (CD) SONY Fra.*
   *(Disc): SK(ST) 61684 (CD/MC) see COLLECTIONS 70,77*
BASHVILLE (OR.LONDON CAST 1984) Songs (Denis King-Benny
   Green) Peter Woodward-Christina Collier-Donal Pelme
   ar-Douglas Hodge *TER (Disc): (ZC)TER 1072 (MC/LP)*
BASIC INSTINCT (1992) Music sco: JERRY GOLDSMITH -S/T-
   *VARESE (Pinn): VSD(VSC) 5360 (CD(MC)* note: disco
   track "Rave The Rhythm" by CHANNEL X *not on -S/T-*
   *see also COLLECTION 404*
BASKETBALL DIARIES The (1994) Music sco: GRAEME REVELL
   -S/T- *ISLAND Poly (Polyg): 524 093-2 (CD) -4(MC)*
BASQUIAT (1996) Music score by JOHN CALE -S/T- on
   *ISLAND (Polyg): 524 260-2 (CD) 524 260-4 (MC)*
BAT MASTERSON (USA TV) *see COLLECTION 340*
BATHING BEAUTY (1944 MUSICAL) *feat* ESTHER WILLIAMS and
   RED SKELTON *incl.songs from* 'HERE COMES THE WAVES'
   + 'THIS GUN FOR HIRE' *TARGET (BMG): CD 60001 (CD)*
BATMAN (USATV 1966) Music: NEAL HEFTI - ORIG TV S-/T-
   *RAZOR & TIE (Koch): RE 2153 (CD)*
   *see COLLECTION 109,110,273,339,374,379*

BATMAN (FILM 1989) *Songs* comp & sung by PRINCE -S/T-
   *W.BROS (WEA): K.7599 25936-2 (CD) WX 281C (MC)*
   *Score:* DANNY ELFMAN *WEA 925977-2 CD deleted*
BATMAN AND ROBIN (1997) Music score: ELLIOT GOLDENTHAL
   V.ARTS -S/T- *W.BROS (WEA): 9362 46620-2 (CD) -4(MC)*
   *see also Coll* 'BATMAN TRILOGY' *(Varese: VSD 5766)*
BATMAN FOREVER (1994) Music: ELLIOT GOLDENTHAL -S/T-
   score: *ATLANTIC (WEA): 7567 82776-2 (CD) deleted*
   songs: *inc.*U2-P.J.HARVEY-BRANDY-SEAL-MASSIVE ATTACK
   EDDI REDER-MAZZY STAR-NICK CAVE-METHOD MAN-MICHAEL
   HUTCHENCE -S/T- *ATLANTIC (WEA) 7567 82759-2 / -4*
   *see also COLLECTIONS 30,34,82,134,274*
BATMAN: MASK OF PHANTASM (1993) Music: SHIRLFY WALKER
   -S/T- *WARNER Impt (S.Scr): WA 45484-2 (CD) -4(MC)*
BATTLE OF BRITAIN 1969 Mus: WILLIAM WALTON-RON GOODWIN
   selection of WALTON music *EMI: CDM 565585-2 (CD)*
   *see also COLLECTIONS 35,184,238,380*
BATTLE OF BRITAIN 1969 Mus: RON GOODWIN-WILLIAM WALTON
   Academy of St.Martin-in-the-Fields (N.Marriner) and
   'Escape me Never'/'Three Sisters'/'Spitfire Prelude
   & Fugue'/'Wartime Sketchbook' *CHANDOS:CHAN 8870*
BATTLESHIP POTEMKIN 1925 Mus.sco: EDMUND MEISAL + music
   from 'THE HOLY MOUNTAIN' Orch della Svizzera Italia
   na (Mark Abeas) *EDEL (S.Screen) 0029062EDL (2CD)*
BATTLESTAR GALACTICA (USA 78/ITV) Mus sco: STU PHILLIPS
   *see COLLECTIONS 12,55,110,273,301,333*
BAYWATCH (USA/ITV 13/1/90) Theme (95) "I'm Always Here"
   JIM JAMISON *unavailable* Theme 93 "Current Of Love"
   DAVID HASSELHOFF *ARISTA (BMG): 74321 17226-2 (CDs)*
   on 'Miracle Of Love' *Arista BMG 74321 17618-2 (CD)*
   orig theme "Save Me" (Cetera-Foster) PETER CETERA
   'One More Story' *FULL MOON-WEA: WX161(C)(CD)*
   *see also COLLECTION 12*
BAYWATCH NIGHTS (USA 95/ITV 4/5/96) "Baywatch Nights"
   sung by DAVID HASSELHOFF *unavailable*
BEACHES (1989) BETTE MIDLER (songs by Cole Porter-Randy
   Newman etc) "Wind Beneath My Wings" (Henley-Silbar)
   -S/T- *ATLANTIC (WEA): K.781933-2 (CD) -4 (MC)*
   *see also COLLECTIONS 116,134,218*
BEADLE'S HOT SHOTS (ITV 20/1/96) mus: STEPHEN GREEN..*NA*
BEAN (1997) Music sco: HOWARD GOODALL -S/T- with V.Arts
   *MERCURY-POLYGRAM TV: 553 774-2 (CD) -4 (MC)*
BEAST The (USA TV mini-series) Music score: DON DAVIS
   -S/T- *VARESE (Pinn): VSD 5731 (CD)*
BEAST WITH FIVE FINGERS The (1947) sco: MAX STEINER *new*
   *record feat* MOSCOW S.O.(Stromberg)+ 'VIRGINIA CITY'
   /'LOST PATROL' *MARCO POLO (Select): 8.223870 (CD)*
BEASTMASTER 2 (1991) Music score: ROBERT FOLK -S/T- on
   *INTRADA USA (Koch Int): MAFCD 7019 (CD)*
BEAT GIRL (1960) Music score: JOHN BARRY Featuring:
   Adam Faith-John Barry Seven + 4-Shirley Anne Field
   -S/T- *PLAY IT AGAIN (BMG-Con): PLAY 001 (CD) also*
   *contains* John Barry's 1961 "Stringbeat" album
BEAT THAT EINSTEIN (as above 3/11/94) music: MCASSO..*NA*

BEATLES - see 'ANTHOLOGY'
BEATRIX POTTER TV animated s -see also 'WORLD OF PETER
   RABBIT AND FRIENDS' and 'TALES OF BEATRIX POTTER'
BEAUTIFUL GIRL LIKE ME, A (1972-'Belle Fille.') Mus sc
   GEORGES DELERUE on COLL 'TRUFFAUT & DELERUE ON
   THE SCREEN' DRG (Pinn): 32902 (CD)
BEAUTIFUL THING (1997) Music score: JOHN ALTMAN with
   songs sung by MAMA CASS and The MAMAS & The PAPAS
   -S/T- MCA (BMG): MCD 60013 (CD) MCC 60013 (MC)
BEAUTY AND THE BEAST
   Songs: Alan Menken-Howard Ashman-Tim Rice
   1.FILM 1992 -S/T- WALT DISNEY (B.Vista): WD 71360-2
   (CD) -4(MC)
   2.ORIG BROADWAY CAST 1994
   WALT DISNEY: WD 60861-2 (CD)
BEAUTY AND THE BEAST (Belle Et La Bette, La) (1946) Mus
   score: GEORGES AURIC new recording: MOSCOW SYMPHONY
   ORCH. (Adriano) MARCO POLO (Select): 8.223765 (CD)
BEAUTY AND THE BEAST - see WALT DISNEY INDEX p.343
BEAUTY AND THE BEAST (USA TV) see COLLECTION 110
BEAVIS AND BUTTHEAD (USA/C4 13/1/95) 'Beavis & Butthead
   Experience' -S/T- GEFFEN-MCA (BMG): GED 24613 (CD)
BEAVIS AND BUTTHEAD DO AMERICA (1996) Sco:JOHN FRIZZELL
   -S/T- songs: GEFFEN (BMG): GED(GEC) 25002 (CD/MC)
   -S/T- score: MILAN (BMG): 74321 47536-2 (CD)
BECK (BBC1 2/10/96) Music score: DAEMION BARRY / end
   credits music by MORCHEEBA unavailable
BED AND SOFA - songs: POLLY PEN and LAURENCE KLAVAN
   ORIG USA CAST feat: TERRI KLAUSNER-MICHAEL X.MARTIN
   JASON WORKMAN and Co.VARESE (Pinn): VSD 5729 (CD)
BED OF ROSES (1995) Music sc: MICHAEL CONVERTINO songs
   "Independent Love Song" by SCARLET & "Ice Cream" by
   SARAH MacLACHLAN -S/T- MILAN (BMG): 74321 34863-2
BEDKNOBS AND BROOMSTICKS see WALT DISNEY INDEX p.343
BEDLAM (1946) Music score: ROY WEBB see Collect 'CURSE
   OF THE CAT PEOPLE'
BEETLEJUICE (1988) Music score: DANNY ELFMAN -S/T- and
   HARRY BELAFONTE GEFFEN-MCA (BMG):GFLD 19284 (CD)
   see also COLLECTIONS 110,129
BEFORE AND AFTER (1996) Music score: HOWARD SHORE -S/T-
   HOLLYWOOD (Poly): 162 039-2 (CD) deleted 96
BEGGAR BRIDE The (BBC1 24/8/97) music sco: COLIN TOWNS
   theme song "She's A Star" performed by JAMES on
   FONTANA (Poly): JIMCD 16 (CDs)
BEGGAR'S OPERA The (LIGHT OPERA by John Gay) dig.record
   ing feat: WARREN MITCHELL-MICHAEL HORDERN-JOAN SUTH
   ERLAND-KIRI TE KANAWA-ANGELA LANSBURY-STAFFORD DEAN
   ALFRED MARKS-JAMES MORRIS-REGINA RESNIK & National
   Phil.Orch (Richard Bonynge) DECCA:430 066-2 (2CDs)
BEIDERBECKE AFFAIR The (C4 4/93 orig 1985) music of BIX
   BEIDERBECKE performed by FRANK RICOTTI ALL-STARS &
   KENNY BAKER -S/T- DOORMOUSE (C.Wellard): DM20CD
   also 'Collection' on CASTLE (BMG): CCSCD 350 (CD)
BEIDERBECKE CONNECTION see COLLECTION 5

BEING HUMAN (1993) Music score: MICHAEL GIBBS -S/T- on
 *VARESE (Pinn): VSD 5479 (CD)*
BELLE ET LA BETTE, LA - see 'BEAUTY AND THE BEAST'
BELLE EPOQUE (1992) Music score: ANTOINE DUHAMEL -S/T-
 *MILAN (BMG): 74321 27931-2 (CD)*
BELIZAIRE THE CAJUN -S/T- *Arhoolie USA (Topic/Proj):*
 *ARHC 5038 (MC)*
BELLE OF NEW YORK The (1952) feat FRED ASTAIRE and VERA
 ELLEN *BLUE MOON (Discov): BMCD 7011 (CD)* including
 'BAND WAGON'
BELLY OF AN ARCHITECT (1987) Music score: WIM MERTENS
 -S/T- *CREPUSCULE (Discovery) TWI 8132 (CD)*
BEN CASEY (USA) (C4 4/1/97) theme music: DAVID RAKSIN
 *see COLLECTION 340*
BEN-HUR (silent 1925) New score: CARL DAVIS -S/T-
 *SILVA SCREEN (Koch): FILMC(CD) 043 (MC/CD)*
BEN HUR (1959) (1) Music score: MIKLOS ROSZA digitally
 re-mastered 75m.CD *EMI ODEON: CDODEON 18 (CD)*
 (2) MIKLOS ROSZA Orig sco + unissued material *MGM*
 *Imp (S.Screen): A2K 47020 (2CDs)* (3) *Nat.Phil* Orch
 *POLY:417849-2* 'MY KIND OF MUSIC' (4) Choral Pieces
 BEN HUR *Coll* 'MIKLOS ROZSA FILM MUSIC V.1' *PROMETH*
 *EUS (S.Scr): PCD 122 (CD)* (5) *see also COLLECTIONS*
 *62,63,81,140,159,203,296,385*
BENNY AND JOON (1993) music sco: RACHEL PORTMAN -S/T-
 *MILAN (BMG): 15168-2 (CD) 15168-4 (MC)*
BENNY HILL SHOW *see COLLECTION 344*
BENSON (USA TV) *see COLLECTION 344*
BERGERAC (BBC1 from 18/10/81) theme by GEORGE FENTON
 *see COLLECTIONS 4,100,388*
BEST FOOT FORWARD (ORIG OFF-BROADWAY CAST 1963) Songs
 (Hugh Martin-Ralph Blane) *feat* LIZA MINNELLI-RONALD
 CHRISTOPHER WALKEN etc.*DRG USA (Pinn) CD15003 (CD)*
BEST IN FOOTBALL (TV) m: TONY HATCH *see COLLECTION 182*
BEST LITTLE WHOREHOUSE GOES PUBLIC O.BROADWAY CAST 1978
 Songs (Carol Hall) *feat:* CARLIN GLYNN-HENDERSON FOR
 SYTHE-DELORES HALL-PAMELA BLAIR-JAY GARNER-CLINT AL
 LMON *VARESE Spotlight (Pinn): VSD 5542 (CD)*
BEST LITTLE WHOREHOUSE IN TEXAS (82)M: PATRICK WILLIAMS
 Songs: CAROL HALL *feat:* DOLLY PARTON-BURT REYNOLDS
 -S/T- *MCA USA (Silva Screen): MCAD 31007 (CD)*
BEST OF THE BEST 2 (1992) Mus sco: DAVID MICHAEL FRANK
 + songs -S/T-*IMPT (Silva Screen): CIN 22012 (CD)*
BEST SHOT 'Hoosiers' (1987) Mus: JERRY GOLDSMITH -S/T-
 *TER (Disc): CDTER 1141 (CD) ZCTER 1141 (MC)*
BETRAYED (1988) Music sco: BILL CONTI -S/T-
 *TER (Disc): CDTER 1163 (CD) ZCTER 1163 (MC)*
BETTY BLUE (1986) Music score: GABRIEL YARED -S/T- on
 *VIRGIN: (TC)V 2396 (MC/LP) CDV 2396 (CD)*
BETWEEN THE LINES (BBC1 from 4/9/92) theme music: HAL
 LINDES *see COLLECTIONS 303,352*
BEVERLY HILLBILLIES The (USA 62) Theme "The Ballad Of
 Jed Clampett" sung by LESTER FLATT & EARL SCRUGGS
 *see COLLECTION 339*

BEVERLY HILLS COP 1 1985 Music Sco: HAROLD FALTERMEYER
-S/T- *MCA (BMG): MCLD 19087 (CD) MCLC 19087 (MC)*
see also *COLLECTIONS 198,274*
BEVERLY HILLS COP 2 1987 V.Arts -S/T- *MCA deleted 93*
BEVERLY HILLS COP 3 1993 V.Arts -S/T- *MCA deleted 95*
BEVERLY HILLS 90210 (ITV 12/1/91)theme by JEFFREY Skunk
BAXTER & STACY WIDELITZ -S/T- inc.theme: JOHN DAVIS
'Vol.1'*GIANT (BMG):74321 14798-2(CD) -4(MC)* 'V.2'
*74321 20303-2(CD) -4(MC)*
see also *COLLECTIONS 12,345*
BEWITCHED (USA 60's) theme music by JACK KELLER and
HOWARD GREENFIELD see *COLLECTIONS 340,360,405*
BEYOND THE CLOUDS (C4 28/2/94) music: GEORGE FENTON
GEORGE FENTON TV -S/T- on *WESTMOOR (Target/BMG):*
*CDWM 109(CD) CWM 109(MC) CDS 3 (CDs) WCS 3 (MC)*
*note:* also used for C4 'SPIRITS GHOSTS AND DEMONS'
BEYOND THE FRINGE (The Complete) *REVUE 1961 Fortune The
atre London)* feat PETER COOK-DUDLEY MOORE-ALAN BENN
ETT-JONATHAN MILLER-PAXTON WHITEHEAD *and also ORIG
BROADWAY CAST 1962)* feat: PETER COOK-DUDLEY MOORE-
ALAN BENNETT-JONATHAN MILLER *EMI: CDBTF 61 (3CDs)*
BEYOND THE VALLEY OF THE DOLLS (1970) mus: STU PHILLIPS
-S/T- (V.Arts) *reissued with* 'GROUPIE GIRL' (1970)
*SCREEN GOLD (Greyhound): SGLDCD 0010 (CD)*
BHAJI ON THE BEACH (1993) Music sco: CRAIG PRUESS-JOHN
ALTMAN-KULJIT BHAMRA *feat V.Arts* -S/T- *KEDA/Grape
vine (Poly): KEDCD 23 (CD) KEDMC 23 (MC) deleted*
BIG BANG (YTV 15/4/96) mus: CHRIS NORTON *unavailable*
BIG BATTALIONS The (C4/Carnival 19/11/92) Music score
composed/conducted by CHRISTOPHER GUNNING -S/T-
*HIT LONDON (Poly): AHLCD 6 (CD) AHLMC 6 (MC)*
BIG BLUE The (1988) Music sco: ERIC SERRA -S/T- *VIRGIN
CDV 2541 (CD) (TC)V 2541 (MC/LP) MDV 2541 (MiniD)*
IMPORT EDITIONS *SILVA SCREEN:-* VOL.1 *30145*
*(CD) 50145 (MC)* VOL.2 *30667 (CD) 50667 (MC)* /
COMPLETE *30193 (2CDs) 40065 (2MC)*
BIG BREAK (BBC1 30/4/91) theme "The Snooker Song"
(Mike Batt) from Musical 'Hunting Of The Snark'
sung by CAPTAIN SENSIBLE *deleted*
BIG BREAKFAST The (C4/Planet 24 from 24/9/92) V/Arts
*ARCADE (Sony):ARC 3100082(CD) 3100094(MC) deleted*
"Cock A Doodle Do-It" (song) by EGGS ON LEGS
*AVEX (Sony): AVEXCD 18(CDs) AVEXMC 18(MC) deleted*
BIG CAT DIARY (BBC1 11/9/96) m: DAVID POORE*unavailable*
BIG CHILL The 1984 Music: MARVIN GAYE-TEMPTATIONS-FOUR
TOPS etc. -S/T- *MOTOWN (Poly): 530017-2(CD) -4(MC)*
BIG COUNTRY The (1958) Music score: JEROME MOROSS New
Digital Rec.- Philharmonia Orch *SILVA SCREEN (Koch)*
*FILMCD 030 (CD)* see also *COLLECTIONS 63,170,397,398*
BIG COUNTRY QUEST The (CST Prod/BBC1 25/7/94) theme mus
"Russian Dance" ('Nutcracker Suite')(TCHAIKOVSKY)
BIG DEAL (BBC1 14/10/84) title song composed/sung by
BOBBY G. see *COLLECTION 6*

BIG EASY The (1987) Music score: BRAD FIEDEL + V.Arts
-S/T- *re-issue SPECTRUM (Poly): 551 159-2 (CD)*
BIG GUNDOWN The (1966) Music sco ENNIO MORRICONE *Import
with* 'FACE TO FACE' *Mask (S.Screen): MK 701 (CD)*
BIG JAKE (1971) Music score: ELMER BERNSTEIN suite on
*VARESE (Pinn): VCD 47264 (CD)*
BIG MATCH The (ITV) Theme "Aztec Gold" ROD ARGENT-PETER
VAN HOOKE *see COLLECTIONS 6,167,317,358*
BIG MOUTH (Rapido/C4 19/3/96) title mus: SIMON BASS..*NA*
BIG NIGHT, A (1996) Music score: GARY De MICHELE -S/T-
V.Arts on *EDEL-CINERAMA (Pinn): 002278-2CIN (CD)*
BIG NIGHT OUT music: ROBERT FARNON *see COLLECTION 220*
BIG SWAP The (1996) Music: JASON FLINTER-CRAIG JOHNSON
-S/T- *OCEAN DEEP (Grapevine/Polyg): OCD 010 (CD)*
BIG VALLEY (USA) *see COLLECTIONS 170,343,398*
BIKER MICE FROM MARS (1993) Music Various Artists -S/T-
*GASOLENE ALLEY/MCA (BMG): MCD 10948 (CD)*
BILITIS (1977) Music sco: FRANCIS LAI theme *see Colls:*
'FRANCIS LAI-A MAN AND A WOMAN' *COLLECTION 236*
BILL AND TED'S BOGUS JOURNEY (1991) Music: DAVID NEWMAN
-S/T- *feat* STEVE VAI-MEGADETH-SLAUGHTER-KISS-WINGER
PRIMUS *reiss: INTERSCOPE-MCA (BMG): IND 91725 (CD)*
BILL The (Thames 16/10/84-96 also UKGold from 2/11/92)
theme "Overkill" ANDY PASK-CHARLIE MORGAN
*see COLLECTIONS 33,100,388*
BILLY (O.LONDON CAST 1974) Songs: JOHN BARRY-DON BLACK
*feat:* MICHAEL CRAWFORD-ELAINE PAIGE-AVIS BUNNAGE-
BILLY BOYLE and Company *SONY: 472818-2(CD)*
BILLY BUNTER OF GREYFRIARS SCHOOL (BBC 50's) theme "Sea
Songs" (V.WILLIAMS) *see COLLECTION 163*
BILLY CONNOLLY'S WORLD TOUR OF AUSTRALIA (BBC Sc/Sleepy
Dumpling/ BBC1 28/10/96) end theme song "Dreamtime"
(Ralph McTell) sung by BILLY CONNOLLY *unavailable*
other commiss.music by GRAHAM PRESKETT-RALPH McTELL
BILLY CONNOLLY'S WORLD TOUR OF SCOTLAND (BBC Sco/Sleepy
Dumpling/ BBC1 12/7/94) end theme mus "Irish Heartb
eat" sung by BILLY CONNOLLY on 'Musical Tour Of Sco
tland' *POLYGRAM TV: 529 816-2 (CD) -4(MC) also by*
VAN MORRISON on 'Inarticulate Speech Of The Heart'
on *POLYDOR (Poly): 839 604-2 (CD) -4 (MC)*
BIOGRAPH GIRL The (O.LONDON CAST 1980) Songs: David
Heneker-Warner Brown *fcat:* SHEILA WHITE-BRUCE BARRY
KATE REVILL-GUY SINER *TER (Disc): CDTER 1003 (CD)*
BIONIC WOMAN (USA TV) *see COLLECTION 343*
BIRD (1988) Music score: LENNIE NIEHAUS *feat music of*
Charlie Parker -S/T- *SONY: CBS 461002-2 (CD)*
CHARLIE PARKER (49) *POLYDOR 837176-2 (CD) -4 (MC)*
BIRD OF PREY (BBC1 22/4/82) theme mus: DAVE GREENSLADE
*see COLLECTION 6*
BIRD WITH THE CRYSTAL PLUMAGE (1969) Music sco: ENNIO
MORRICONE -S/T- inc 'FOUR FLIES ON GREY VELVET'
'CAT O'NINE TAILS' *DRG (Pinn): DRGCD 32911 (CD)*
BIRDCAGE The (1995) Music arr./adapt.by JONATHAN TUNICK
-S/T- *EDEL-Cinerama (Pinn): 002257-2 MCM (CD)*

BIRDING WITH BILL ODDIE (BBC2 21/2/97)m: XIAN VASSIE.*NA*
BIRDS OF A FEATHER (BBC1 16/10/89) Theme "What'll I Do"
(Irving Berlin) *TV version by* PAULINE QUIRKE-LINDA
ROBSON *unavailable*
BIRDY (1985) Music score: PETER GABRIEL -S/T- *CHARISMA*
*VIRGIN (EMI): CASCD 1167 (CD)*
BIT OF A DO, A (YTV 13/1/89) music: RAY RUSSELL theme
sung by GEORGE MELLY-John Chilton's Feetwarmers..*NA*
BIT OF FRY & LAURIE A (BBC2 9/3/90) End Theme "Finale"
from 'Carnival Of The Animals' (Saint-Saens) -S/T-
TV Cast on *BBC (Pinn): ZBBC 1538 (MC)*
BITEBACK (BBC1 17/11/91) m: RONALD DE JONG *unavailable*
BITTER SWEET (Musical Show 1988) Songs: NOEL COWARD New
Sadlers Wells Opera VALERIE MASTERSON *TER (Disc):*
*CDTER2 1160 (2CD)* / HIGHLIGHTS on *CD(ZC)TEO 1001*
BITTER SWEET (Musical Show 1929) *see COLLECTION 102*
BIZ The (BBC1 15/2/95) music: MICHAEL OMER *unavailable*
BJ AND THE BEAR (USA TV) *see COLLECTION 344*
BLACK AND WHITE MINSTREL SHOW The (BBC1 1950's-60's)
The George Mitchell Minstrels with DAI FRANCIS-TONY
MERCER-JOHN BOULTER-Margaret Savage-Eve Blanchard
'Down Memory Lane' *MFP (EMI):CC 223 (CD)* 'The Black
& White Minstrel Show' *EMI: CD(TC)IDL 105 (CD(MC)*
BLACK BAG (C4 19/2/91) m: AMANDA ALEXANDER *unavailable*
BLACK BEAUTY *(TV) see* 'ADVENTURES OF BLACK BEAUTY' and
*COLL* 'GREATEST TV THEMES'
BLACK BEAUTY (1993) Music score: DANNY ELFMAN -S/T- USA
*GIANT (WEA in UK): 45682 (CD)*
BLACK HEARTS IN BATTERSEA (BBC1 31/12/95) music compos
ed and performed by MARTIN KISZKO *unavailable*
BLACK HOLE (1979) JOHN BARRY *see COLLECTIONS 22,55*
see also WALT DISNEY INDEX p.343
BLACK RAIN (1989) Music score HANS ZIMMER songs by V/A
*VIRGIN: CDV 2607 (CD)*
BLACK ROBE (1991) Music score: GEORGES DELERUE -S/T-
*VARESE (Pinn): VSD 5349 (CD)*
BLACKADDER (BBC2 began 5/9/84) theme mus HOWARD GOODALL
on 'BLACKADDER THE THIRD' *BBC (Pinn):ZBBC 1270*
*(2MC)* BBC Videos: *BBCV 4782 (series 1) 4785 (2)*
*4786 (3) 4787 (4)* / *see also COLLECTION 229*
BLACKADDER'S CHRISTMAS CAROL Music: HOWARD GOODALL
*BBC (Pinn): ZBBC 1905CD (CD/MC) BBCV 4648 (VID)*
BLACKEYES (BBC2 29/11/89) Theme "Blackeyes" (Ferraris)
arr: Max Harris navailable / vers: PALM COURT THEA
ATRE ORCH 'Picnic Party' *Chandos: CHAN 8437(CD)*
BLADE RUNNER (1982) Music score: VANGELIS origin -S/T-
*EAST WEST (WEA): 4509 96574-2 (CD) -4 (MC)*
*see COLLECTIONS 37,202,273,357,404*
BLAKE'S 7 (UKGO 4/6/94 orig BBC1 2/1/78) Theme music
DUDLEY SIMPSON *see COLLECTIONS 5,109,273,301*
BLANKMAN (1993) Music score: MILES GOODMAN -S/T- *EPIC*
*Soundtrax (Sony Music): 476821-2 (CD) -4 (MC)*
BLEAK HOUSE (BBC2 1985) music scored and conducted by
GEOFFREY BURGON *see COLLECTION 40*

BLIND DATE (LWT 30/11/85-1995) theme: LAURIE HOLLOWAY
  see COLLECTION 33
BLIND MEN (LWT 21/11/97) theme m: "Winner Takes It All"
  (B.Ulvaeus-B.Andersson) TV version unavailable
  ABBA on 'GOLD' POLYDOR: 517 007-2 (CD) -4 (MC)
BLINK (93) Music sco: BRAD FIEDEL -S/T- MILAN (BMG):
  191902 (CD) 191904 (MC)
BLISS (1997) Music score: JAN A.P.KACZMAREK -S/T- on
  VARESE (Pinn): VSD 5836 (CD)
BLOCKBUSTERS (Central from 29/8/83) theme ED WELCH..on
  GRASMERE: GRASS 2 (7"s) with 'New Faces' deleted
BLONDEL - songs: Stephen Oliver and Tim Rice
  ORIG CAST 1983 feat: PAUL NICHOLAS-SHARON LEE HILL
  DAVID ALDER-CANTABILE-TRACY BOOTH-STEPHEN LANGHAM-
  ROGER LLEWELLYN reissue: MCA (BMG): MCD 11486(CD)
BLOOD AND GUNS (1969) Music sco: ENNIO MORRICONE -S/T-
  'Western Quintet' DRG (Pinn): DRGCD 32907 (2CD)
BLOOD AND SAND (1941) Music score: ALFRED NEWMAN
  Stanley Black DECCA (Poly): 417850-2 (CD) -4 (MC)
BLOOD AND SAND (70's) Music score ENNIO MORRICONE
  ENNIO MORRICONE ORCH on Coll 'An Ennio Morricone
  Quintet' DRG USA (Pinn): DRGCD 32907 (CD)
BLOOD BROTHERS - songs by Willy Russell
  1.ORIG LONDON CAST 1995 feat: STEPHANIE LAWRENCE & Co
  FIRST NIGHT (Pinn): CASTCD 49 (CD) CASTC 49 (MC)
  2.INTERNATIONAL CAST 1995 PETULA CLARK-DAVID & SHAUN
  CASSIDY & Co FIRST NIGHT: CAST(CD)(C) 50 (CD(MC)
  3.ORIG LONDON CAST 1988 feat: KIKI DEE and Comapny
  FIRST NIGHT (Pin):CASTC(CD)17 (MC/CD)
  4.ORIG LONDON CAST 1983 feat: BARBARA DICKSON & Comp.
  CASTLE CLASS.(BMG): CLACD 270 (CD) CLAMC 270 (MC)
BLOOD IS STRONG The (C4/Grampian 1/9/88) music composed
  & performed: CAPERCAILLE with KAREN MATHESON -S/T-
  SURVIVAL (Pinn): SURCD 014 (CD) SURMC 014 (MC)
BLOOMER GIRL (O.BROADWAY CAST 1944) Music: HAROLD ARLEN
  Lyrics: E.Y.HARBURG MCA USA Imp (Silva Screen)
  MCAD 10522 (CD) MCAC 10522 (MC)
BLOOMIN' MARVELLOUS (BBC1 8/9/97) title theme music by
  MICHAEL STOREY unavailable
BLOSSOM (USA TV) see COLLECTION 345
BLOTT ON THE LANDSCAPE (BBC2 6/2/85) see COLLECTION 5
BLOW-UP (1966) Music score: HERBIE HANCOCK / Songs by
  YARDBIRDS and TOMORROW -S/T- EMI: CDODEON 15 (CD)
BLUE (1993) Music score: SIMON FISHER TURNER + V.Arts.
  -S/T- MUTE (Pinn): CDSTUMM 49 (CD)
BLUE COLLAR (1978) Mus sco: JACK NITZSCHE -S/T- V.Arts
  CAPTAIN BEEFHEART-HOWLIN'WOLF-LYNYRD SKYNYRD-IKE &
  TINA TURNER on EDSEL-DEMON (Pinn): EDCD 435 (CD)
BLUE HAWAII (1961) feat: ELVIS PRESLEY remast. -S/T-
  (BMG): 07863 67459-2 (ltd CD) 07863 66959-2 (CD)
BLUE HEAVEN (C4 30/7/94) title music and songs: FRANK
  SKINNER / Steve Brown (mus director) unavailable
BLUE HEELERS (Australia 94/ITV 5/5/95) theme m: DANNY
  RUMOUR-JAMES ELLIOTT perf.by CRUEL SEA unavailab

BLUE IN THE FACE (1995) Music score: JOHN LURIE -S/T-
*WEA (WEA): 9362 45921-2 (CD)*
BLUE LAGOON The (1980) Music score: BASIL POLEDOURIS
-S/T- *SOUTHERN CROSS Silva Screen: SCCD 1018 (CD)*
BLUE MAX The (1966) Music score: JERRY GOLDSMITH -S/T-
*COLUMBIA (Sony Music): CK 57890 (CD)*
BLUE PETER (BBC1 27/10/58-1998) Theme "Barnacle Bill"
(Hornpipe) 95-96 heme by YES/NO PEOPLE *unavailable*
*Orig* SIDNEY ORCH ORCH *EMI* MIKE OLDFIELD *VIRGIN*
*EMI CDMOC 1 (2CD) see COLLECTION 381*
BLUE SKIES (1946) VARIOUS -S/T- SELECTIONS on
*GREAT MOVIE THEMES: (Targ-BMG): CD 60025 (CD)*
BLUE TRAIN The (ORIG LONDON CAST 1927) Songs (Robert St
oltz-Reginald Arkell) Addit.Songs (Ivy St.Helier)
*feat:* CICELY DEBENHAM-LILY ELSIE-BOBBY HOWES-ARTHUR
MARGETSON-JACK RAINE + *musicals 'DESERT SONG' (27)*
*'NEW MOON' (29) PEARL (Pavilion): GEMMCD 9100 (CD)*
BLUE VELVET (1987) Music sco: ANGELO BADALEMENTI -S/T-
*TER (Disc): CD(ZC)TER 1127 (CD/MC) VARESE (Pinn):*
*VCD 47277 (CD) see also COLLECTIONS 259,260,356*
BLUE WILDERNESS (C4 17/3/96) Music score: TANIA ROSE
theme music from 'Coral Sea Dreaming' courtesy of
NATURAL SYMPHONIES (Australia) *unavailable in UK*
BLUEBEARD (1972) Music score: ENNIO MORRICONE -S/T-
including music from 'LADY OF MONZA' (1969) on
*POINT IMP (Silva Screen): PRCD 121 (CD)*
BLUES ARE RUNNING The / KING MACKEREL (USA MUSICALS)
*SUGAR HILL USA (Koch): SHCD 8503 (CD) SH 8503(MC)*
BLUES BROTHERS (1980) *Featur:* RAY CHARLES-JAMES BROWN
ARETHA FRANKLIN-CAB CALLOWAY-BLUES BROTHERS -S/T-
*WEA: K4 50715 (MC) K2 50715 (CD) 756781471-5 (DCC)*
BLUES IN THE NIGHT (ORIG DONMAR WAREHOUSE THEATRE 1987)
DEBBY BISHOP-MARIA FRIEDMAN-CLARKE PETERS-CAROL WOO
DS & Co.*reiss FIRST NIGHT (Pinn): OCRCD 6029 (CD)*
BOAT The (DAS BOOT) (BBC2 17/9/89 orig 21/10/84) music
KLAUS DOLDINGER -S/T- *WB (WEA): K.58366 deleted*
*theme only on SILVA SCREEN (Koch): FILMCD 151 (CD)*
BOB HOPE SHOW (USA TV) *see COLLECTION 342*
BOB NEWHART SHOW (USA TV) *see COLLECTION 341*
BOCCACCIO '70 (1962) Music sco: NINO ROTA with ARMANDO
TROVAIOLI-PIERO UMILIANI "Soldi Soldi Soldi" sung
by Sophia Loren *ITALIAN IMP (S.Scr): OST 116(CD)*
BODGER & BADGER (BBC1 13/9/89) music PETER GOSLING.*NA*
BODIES REST AND MOTION (1993) Mus: MICHAEL CONVERTINO
-S/T- *WB IMPORT (S.Screen): 924 506-2 (CD) -4(MC)*
BODY BAGS (1993) Music score: JOHN CARPENTER-JIM LANG
-S/T- *VARESE (Pinn): VSD 5448 (CD)*
BODY HEAT (ITV 15/7/94) m: SIMON ETCHELL *unavailable*
BODY HEAT (1981) Music: JOHN BARRY *see COLLECTION 24*
BODY OF EVIDENCE (1992) Music sc: GRAEME REVELL -S/T-
SCORE on *MILAN (BMG): 12720-2 (CD) 12720-4 (MC)*
*also on IMPORT (Silva Screen): RC 66141-2 (CD)*
BODY PARTS (1991) Music score: LOEK DIKKER -S/T-
*VARESE (Pinn): VSD 5337 (CD)*

BODY The (1970) Mus: ROGER WATERS-RON GEESIN -S/T-
*EMI Premier (EMI): CZ 178 (CD)*
BODYGUARD (1992) *Songs:* WHITNEY HOUSTON-LISA STANSFIELD
JOE COCKER-SASS JORDAN-CURTIS STIGERS-KENNY G-AARON
NEVILLE -S/T- *ARISTA (BMG): 07822 18699-2CD  -4MC*
BODYWORK (LIGHT OPERA MUSICAL 1988) Mus/Lyrics: RICHARD
STILGOE featuring *The National Youth Music Theatre*
with LONNIE DONEGAN-CHAS & DAVE and JAKE THACKRAY
*FIRST NIGHT (Pinn): CASTCD 15 (CD) CASTC 15 (MC)*
BOLERO (1984) Music score: PETER BERNSTEIN -S/T- incl:
Elmer Bernstein prev.unreleased material *cond* Chris
topher Palmer *PROMETHEUS (S.Scr): PCD 124 (CD)*
BOLLYWOOD OR BUST (BBC2 1/1/94) mus HARJINDER BOPARI.*NA*
BOMBAY BLUE (C4 4/10/97) mus: MARTIN SWAN *unavailable*
BONANZA (USA 59) theme: DAVID ROSE (lyrics: Jay Living
ston-Ray Evans) *see COLLECTIONS 2,168,265,339,373*
BOOMERANG (1992) BABYFACE feat TONI BRAXTON etc. -S/T-
*ARISTA (BMG): 73008 26006-2 (CD) -4 (MC)*
BOON (Central 14/1/86-1992) theme "Hi Ho Silver" (Jim
Diamond-Chris Parren) sung by JIM DIAMOND on 'Jim
Diamond' *POLYDOR (Poly): 843 847-2 (CD) -4 (MC)*
BOOTY CALL (1996) -S/T- with Various Arts on
*JIVE-ZOMBA (Pinn): CHIP 182 (CD) HIP 182 (2LP)*
BORDELLO OF BLOOD (1996) Music score: CHRIS BOARDMAN
-S/T- *VARESE (Pinn): VSD 5728 (CD)*
BORGIAS The (BBC1 14/10/81) music sco: GEORGES DELERUE
*PROMETHEUS (S.Screen): PCD 109 (CD)*
BORN AND BRED (Thames 13/9/78) theme mus: RON GRAINER
*see COLLECTION 7*
BORN FREE (1965) Mus sco JOHN BARRY t.song (J.Barry-D.
Black) by MATT MONRO *see COLLECT 21,24,26,36,62,63*
BORN TO RUN (BBC1 25/5/97) "Hang It On Your Heart" sung
by MARIANNE FAITHFULL on *EMI UK: CDDISC 010 (CDs)*
incidental music by PHILIP APPLEBY *unavailable*
BORROWERS The (BBC1 8/11/92) music: HOWARD GOODALL..*NA*
BOSTON KICKOUT (1996) Music score: DAVID ARNOLD -S/T-
*SILVERTONE (Pinn): ORECD 543 (CD)*
BOTTOM (BBC2 17/9/91) theme music "BB's Blues" (B.B.
King) / "Last Night" (Branford) performed by The
BUM NOTES TV -S/T- *BBC (Pinn): ZBBC 1875CD (CD)*
*ZBBC 1875(MC) see COLLECTION 33*
BOUNCING BACK: Best Bits Of Johnny Ball (BBC1 4/7/96)
title mus: ANDY BLYTHE-MARTEN JOUSTRA *unavailable*
BOUNTY The (Mutiny On The Bounty) (1984) Mus: VANGELIS
theme *Coll* 'THEMES' *POLYDOR: 839518-2 (CD) -4 (MC)*
BOUQUET OF BARBED WIRE (LWT 9/1/76 & C4-83) theme mus
DENIS FARNON *see COLLECTION 175*
BOURNE IDENTITY The (TV USA 89) Theme & score: LAURENCE
ROSENTHAL cond Film Symphony Orchestra of Prague on
*INTRADA USA (Silva Screen): RVF 6005D (CD only)*
BOWLS - *see under* 'WORLD BOWLS'
BOX OF DELIGHTS The (BBC1 21/11/84) Theme "Carol Sympho
ny" (Hely-Hutchinson) PRO-ARTE ORCH (Barry Rose) on
*EMI: CDM 764131-2 (CD) -4 (MC)*

BOXING (Various) *see COLLECTION 155*
BOY FROM MERCURY The (1997) Music: Various Arts -S/T-
   *OCEAN DEEP (Grapev/Polyg): OCD 004 (CD)*
BOY MEETS GIRL (BBC 67) m. RON GRAINER *see COLLECTION 7*
BOY WHO GREW TOO FAST The (OPERA) Music &Libretto (Gian
   Carlo Menotti) Royal Opera House Orch/Chorus (David
   Syrus) - *TER (Disc): (CD)(ZC)TER 1125 (CD/MC)*
BOY WHO SANG 'O For The Wings Of A Dove' (C4 10/7/94)
   ERNEST LOUGH with TEMPLE CHURCH CHOIR and DR.GEORGE
   THALBEN-BALL organ *PEARL (Pavilion): GEMMCD 9102*
BOYFRIEND The - songs by Sandy Wilson
  1.30TH ANN.REVIV.LONDON CAST 1984 *feat:* ROSEMARY ASHE
   SIMON GREEN-JANE WELLMAN-ANNA QUAYLE-PETER BAYLISS
   PADDIE O'NEIL-DEREK WARING and Company
   <u>Highlights</u>: *SHOWTIME (MCI-THE): SHOW(CD)(MC) 027*
   <u>Complete</u>: *TER (Disc): CDTER 1095 (CD)*
  2.ORIG BROADWAY CAST 1954 *feat:* JULIE ANDREWS & Comp.
   *RCA (BMG): GD(GK) 60056 (CD/Ca)*
  3.CLASSIC MUSICALS SERIES *featur:* JANE WELLMAN-SIMON
   GREEN-ANNA QUAYLE-DEREK WARING-PETER BAYLIS *plus*
   *songs from* 'ME AND MY GIRL' *KOCH INT: 34080-2 (CD)*
BOYS (1995) Mus: STEWART COPELAND -S/T- *feat* "Wildwood"
   (Paul Weller) by PORTISHEAD, "Alright" by CAST and
   songs by SQUEEZE/DEL AMITRI/SUPERGRASS etc.
   *A.& M. (Poly): 540 489-2 (CD)*
BOYS FROM SYRACUSE -songs: Richard Rodgers-Lorenz Hart
  1.OFF-BROADWAY REV.CAST 63 *Angel EMI ZDM 764695-2 CD*
  2.USA STUDIO REC.53 *feat:* PORTIA NELSON-JACK CASSIDY
   BIBI OSTERWALD-HOLLY HARRIS-STANLEY PRAGER
   *Sony Broadway: SK 53329 (CD) DELETED 97*
BOYS ON THE SIDE (1994) M.sco: DAVID NEWMAN -S/T- V.Art
   *feat:* BONNIE RAITT-MELISSA ETHERIDGE-SHERYL CROW-ST
   EVIE NICKS-PRETENDERS-CRANBERRIES-ANNIE LENNOX etc.
   *ARISTA (BMG): 07822 18748-2 (CD) -4 (MC)*
BRADY BUNCH The (USA TV) *see COLLECTIONS 340,405*
BRADY BUNCH MOVIE The (1995) Music sco: GUY MOON -S/T-
   *MILAN (BMG): 27932-2 (CD)*
BRAIN DRAIN (BBC2/Hat T.19/9/92) mus: MATTHEW SCOTT..*NA*
BRAINDEAD (1992) Music sco: PETER DASENT Various Arts:
   -S/T- *NORMAL (Topic/Project/Dir): QDKCD 006 (CD)*
BRAINSPOTTING (C4 11/8/96) closing theme mus "Concerto
   For Cootie" by DUKE LELLINGTON ORCHESTRA / version
   'Great Paris Concert' *WB (WEA): 7567 81303-2 (CD)*
BRAMWELL (ITV 22/5/95) mus: STEPHEN WARBECK *unavailable*
BRANDED (USA) *see COLLECTION 339*
BRASS (Granada 21/2/83) music: KENYON EMRYS-ROBERTS..*NA*
BRASS EYE (C4 30/1/97) music: JONATHAN WHITEHEAD.....*NA*
BRASSED OFF (1996) Music score TREVOR JONES *feat* The
   GRIMETHORPE COLLIERY BAND conductor: JOHN ANDERSON
   -S/T- *RCA-CONIFER (BMG): 09026 68757-2 (CD)*
BRAVEHEART (1995) Music score: JAMES HORNER with London
   S.Orch -S/T- *ICON-LONDON (Poly): 448 295-2 (CD)*
BRAZIL (1985) Music score: MICHAEL KAMEN -S/T-
   *MILAN (BMG): 11125-2 (CD) 11125-4 (MC)*

BREAD (UKGO 3/11/92 and BBC 1/5/86-91) Theme mus "Home"
   DAVID MacKAY sung by The CAST *see COLLECTION 4*
BREAKFAST AT TIFFANY'S (1961) Music sco: HENRY MANCINI
   song "Moon River" (Lyr: Johnny Mercer) -S/T- *RCA*
   *ND 89905 (CD) see also COLLECTIONS 62,243,244,292*
BREAKFAST CLUB (1985) Music sco: KEITH FORSEY songs:
   Simple Minds-Wang Chung-Karlo De Vito-Jesse Johnson
   -S/T- *A.& M. (Poly): CDMID 179 (CD) AMC 5045 (MC)*
BREAKING AWAY (1979) *see COLLECTION 72*
BREAKING GLASS (1980) music composed & perf by HAZEL O'
   CONNOR -S/T- *reis: SPECTRUM (Poly): 551 356-2 (CD)*
BREAKING THE NEWS (BBC2 15/6/97) t.mus: JAMES ASHER.*NA*
BREAKING THE WAVES (1995) Music sco: JOACHIM HOLBEK
   -S/T- Var.Art *POLLYANNA (Pinn): POLLYPREM 001 (CD)*
BRIDE OF FRANKENSTEIN The (1935) Mus sco: FRANZ WAXMAN
   *see COLLECTIONS 61,63,206,390,393*
BRIDE OF THE RE-ANIMATOR (1990) Music sco: RICHARD BAND
   +'RE-ANIMATOR' -S/T- *S.SCREEN Koch: FILMCD 082(CD)*
BRIDES OF CHRIST (C4 23/1/92) Music score: MARIO MILLO
   -S/T- *ALHAMBRA (Pinn): A8936 (CD only)* / ALSO USED
   "Hosanna In Excelsis" from Mass in B.Min.(J.S.Bach)
   BERLIN RADIO SO (L.Maazel) *POLY: 426657-2PSL2(2CD)*
BRIDESHEAD REVISITED (Gra 12/10/81) mus GEOFFREY BURGON
   -S/T- *re-iss on MFP (EMI) CD(TC)MFP 6172 (CD/MC)*
   *see COLLECTIONS 40,213,267,382*
BRIDGE ON THE RIVER KWAI (1957) Music: MALCOLM ARNOLD
   LSO (R.Hickox) *CHANDOS: 9100 (CD)* "Colonel Bogey"
   (Kenneth Alford) *see COLLECTIONS 14,35,63,169,238*
BRIDGE The (1990) Music sco: RICHARD G.MITCHELL -S/T-
   *DEMON (Pinn): DSCD 5 (CD) DSCASS 5 (MC)*
BRIDGE TOO FAR A (1977) Music score: JOHN ADDISON
   *see COLLECTIONS 169,173,238*
BRIDGES OF MADISON COUNTY The (1995) Music sc: LENNIE
   NIEHAUS -S/T- *MALPASO-WB (WEA): 9362 45949-2 (CD)*
   *see also COLLECTIONS 32,59,66,126,139*
BRIEF ENCOUNTER (1945) Mus: RACHMANINOV new collect:
   'BRIEF ENCOUNTER: THE VERY BEST OF RACHMANINOV' on
   *ERATO (WEA): 0630 18061-2 (CD) -4 (MC)*
   *see also COLLECTIONS 62,65,69,97,171*
BRIEF SEASON, A (Ita.1968) Music sco: ENNIO MORRICONE
   -S/T- with 'SICILIAN CHECKMATE' (E.Morricone)
   *LEGEND Import (Silva Screen): LEGENDCD 26 (CD)*
BRIGADOON - songs - Alan Jay Lerner & Frederick Loewe
   1.ORIG 1954 FILM -S/T- w: GENE KELLY-CYD CHARISSE-VAN
     JOHNSON / 23 tracks *EMI PREMIER: CDODEON 16 (CD)*
   2.ORIG BROADWAY CAST 1947 w: DAVID BROOKS-MARION BELL
     PAMELA BRITTON-LEE SULLIVAN *(BMG): GD(GK) 81001*
   3.ORIG LONDON CAST 1988 *feat:* ROBERT MEADMORE-JACINTA
     MULCAHY-MAURICE CLARK-LESLEY MACKIE-ROBIN NEDWELL-
     IAN MACKENZIE STEWART *FIRST NIGHT (Pin) OCRCD 6022*
   4.STUDIO RECORDING 1991 Ambrosian Chorus & London Sin
     fonietta (John McGlynn)-Brent Barrett-Rebecca Luker
     Judy Kaye-John Mark Ainsley *EMI: CDC 754481-2 (CD)*
   5.STUDIO RECORDING 1997 *SHOWTIME (Disc): SHOWCD 056*

BRIGHT SPARKS (1/7/96) t.mus: DAVE ARNOLD *unavailable*
BRIMSTONE AND TREACLE (1982) Mus: STING-POLICE-SQUEEZE
    GO GO's -S/T- *A.& M.(Poly): CAM 64915 (MC)*
BRING ON THE NIGHT (1986) Music: STING on 'Bring On The
    Night' *A.& M. (Poly): BRIND 1 (2CD) BRINC 1 (2MC)*
BRIT AWARDS 1997 VARIOUS ARTISTS *Sony Music (Sony):*
    *SONYTV 23CD (CD) SONYTV 23MC (MC)*
BRITISH SONG CONTEST (BBC1 8/3/97) winning entry:
    "Love Shine A Light" (K.Rew) by KATRINA & THE WAVES
    *ETERNAL: WEA 106CD* see also EUROVISION SONG CONTEST
BRITT ALLCROFT'S MAGIC ADVENTURES OF MUMFIE (Quality
    Family Ent.USA/ITV 22/9/94) music: LARRY GROSSMAN
    songs (L.Grossman-John Kane) Theme music "Home"
    *MCI (THE): MUMFIE C1 (CDs) MUMFIE T1 (MC)*
BRITTAS EMPIRE The (BBC1 3/1/91) music: FRANK RENTON.*NA*
BROADWAY KIDS - *see COLLECTIONS*
BROADWAY MELODY OF 1936 (1935 MUSICAL) *feat:* JACK BENNY
    ELEANOR POWELL-ROBERT TAYLOR + 'BRO.MELODY OF 1940'
    *GREAT MOVIE THEMES (TARGET-BMG): CD 60007 (CD)*
BROADWAY MELODY OF 1940 (40 MUSICAL) *feat:* FRED ASTAIRE
    GEORGE MURPHY-ELEANOR POWELL + 'BRO.MELODY OF 1936'
    *GREAT MOVIE THEMES (TARGET-BMG): CD 60007 (CD)*
BROKEN ARROW (1996) Music score: HANS ZIMMER -S/T- on
    *MILAN (BMG): 74321 34865-2 (CD) -4 (MC)*
BROKER'S MAN The (BBC1 17/6/97) music: ALAN CLARK....*NA*
BRONCO (USA) *see COLLECTION 176,342*
BRONX TALE, A (1993) Various 60s Artists & songs -S/T-
    *EPIC (Sony): 474 806-2 (CD)*
BROOD The (1979) *see under* 'DEAD RINGERS'
BROOKSIDE (C4 2/11/82-1997) Theme music: DAVE ROYLANCE
    STEVE WRIGHT (USA TV) *see COLLECTION 367*
BROTHER FROM ANOTHER PLANET (1984) Music score: MASON
    DARING -S/T- *Daring (Direct): DRCD 1007 (CD)*
BROTHER SUN SISTER MOON (1972) Music sc: RIZ ORTOLANI
    -S/T- *reissue Imp (Silva Screen): MPCD 228 (CD)*
BROTHERS McMULLEN The (1995) Music score: SEAMUS EGAN
    -S/T- includ "I Will Remember You" sung by SARAH
    McLACHLAN  *ARISTA (BMG): 07822 18803-2 (CD) -4(MC)*
BROTHERS The (UKGold 6/11/92 orig BBC1 71) Theme music
    DUDLEY SIMPSON *see COLLECTION 2*
BROWNING VERSION The (1994) Music sc: MARK ISHAM -S/T-
    *MILAN (BMG): 213 012 (CD) 213 014 (MC)*
BRUSH STROKES (BBC1 12/10/87) theme "Because Of You" by
    DEXYS MIDNIGHT RUNNERS on 'Very Best Of Dexys..' on
    *MERCURY (Poly): 846 460-2 (CD) -4(MC) -1(LP)*
BRUTE FORCE (1947) Music score: MIKLOS ROZSA selection
    on 'LUST FOR LIFE' *VARESE (Pinn): VSD 5405 (CD)*
BUBBLING BROWN SUGAR (ORIG LONDON CAST 1977) Var comps
    feat: Billy Daniels-Helen Gelzer-Lon Satton-Elaine
    Delmar-Stephanie Lawrence-Clarke Peters-MiquelBrown
    Amii Stewart *DRG (Pin): CDSBL 13106 (CDx2)*
BUCCANEER The (1958) *see COLLECTION 372*
BUCCANEERS The (BBC1 4/1/95) orig music: COLIN TOWNS
    -S/T- *MERCURY (Poly): 526866-2 / -4  deleted96*

BUCK ROGERS IN THE 25TH CENTURY (USA 79 ITV) theme mus:
   STU PHILLIPS *see COLLECTIONS 12,273*
BUDDAH OF SUBURBIA The (BBC 3/11/93) title song and inc
   idental music (David Bowie) sung by DAVID BOWIE and
   ERDAL KIZILCAY feat LENNY KRAVITZ gtr -S/T- reissue
   *ARISTA (BMG): 74321 17004-2 (CD) -4 (MC)*
BUDDY (1997) Music score: ELMER BERNSTEIN -S/T- on
   *VARESE (Pinn): VSD 5829 (CD)*
BUDDY (ORIG LONDON CAST 95 'LIVE' RECORDING) on
   *FIRST NIGHT (Pinn): CASTCD 55 (CD) CASTC 55 (MC)*
BUDDY (ORIG LONDON CAST 89) PAUL HIPP-Gareth Marks-Enzo
   Squillino *FIRST NIGHT (Pinn):QUEUEC (CD)1 (MC/CD)*
BUDDY'S SONG (90) Featur: Chesney Hawkes-Roger Daltrey
   -S/T- *CHRYSALIS (EMI): CCD21 (CD) ZDD21 (MC)*
BUDGIE (LWT 9/4/71-72) theme "The Loner" NEIL HARRISON
   *see COLLECTIONS 4,175,320,360*
BUDGIE THE LITTLE HELICOPTER (Sleepy Kid/HTV/ 4/1/94)
   theme mus: PAUL K.JOYCE prod Dennis C.Brown Product
   -S/T- on *MFP (EMI): TCMFP 6117 (MC)*
BUGS (BBC1 1/4/95) o.music: GAVIN GREENAWAY *unavailable*
BUGS BUNNY SHOW (Cart.USA) *see COLLECTIONS 325,326,339*
BUGSY MALONE (Show 1997) Music and songs: PAUL WILLIAMS
   ORIG LONDON CAST *TER (DISC): CDTER 1246 (CD)*
BUGSY MALONE (Film 1976) Music and songs: PAUL WILLIAMS
   -S/T- *reissue RSO-POLYDOR (Poly): 831 540-2 (CD)*
BULLETPROOF (1996) Music score: ELMER BERNSTEIN
   -S/T- songs (VA) *MCA (BMG): MCAD 11498 (CD)DELET.97*
   -S/T- score Bernstein *VARESE (Pinn): VSD 5757 (CD)*
BULLETS OVER BROADWAY (1994) dir: WOODY ALLEN / -S/T-
   *SONY CLASSICAL: SK 66822 (CD)*
BULLITT (1968) Music sco: LALO SCHIFRIN -S/T- reissue
   *W.BROS (WEA): 9362 45008-2 (CD)*
BURKE'S LAW (USA) *see COLLECTIONS 110,342,374*
BURN (QUEIMADA) (1968) Music sc: ENNIO MORRICONE -S/T-
   *Italian Import (SILVA SCREEN): VCDS 7020 (CD)*
BUSTER (1988) Music score: ANNE DUDLEY w. PHIL COLLINS
   -S/T- *VIRGIN (EMI): CDV 2544 (CD) OVEDC 398 (MC)*
BUSY WORLD OF RICHARD SCARRY (Can/Fr.93/BBC2 9/10/94)
   theme: MILAN KYMLICKA score LAURENT PETITGERARD.*NA*
BUTCH CASSIDY AND THE SUNDANCE KID (1969) Music: BURT
   BACHARACH "Raindrops Keep Falling On My Head" (B.
   Bacharach-H.David) sung by B.J.THOMAS -S/T- reiss:
   *SPECTRUM (Poly): 551 433-2(CD) also COLLEC 173,358*
BUTTERFLY (1981) Music score ENNIO MORRICONE -S/T- on
   import on *PROMETHEUS (Silva Screen): PCD 108 (CD)*
BUTTERFLY BALL The (Film Musical 1974) Music sc: ROGER
   GLOVER / Roger Glover & Friends -S/T- *CONNOISSEUR
   (Pinn): VSOPCD 139 (CD) VSOLP(MC) 139 (Dbl LP/MC)*
BUTTERFLY KISS (BBC2 14/6/97) JOHN HARLE *see COLL.407*
BUTTERFLIES (BBC1 10/11/78-1983) theme "Love is Like A
   Butterfly" (Dolly Parton) *TV version sung by* CLARE
   TORRY *(EMI deleted)* / DOLLY PARTON version on Coll
   'Favourites' *CARLTON: PWKS 4116 (CD)* Park sequence
   Mus:'Adagio for Organ & Strings D.Minor' (ALBINONI)

BY JEEVES! (MUSICAL) Songs: ANDREW LLOYD WEBBER-ALAN AY
CKBOURN *feat:* STEVEN PACEY-MALCOLM SINCLAIR & Comp.
*POLYDOR (Polyg): 531 723-2 (CD unissued)*
BYE BYE BIRDIE (ORIG BROADWAY CAST 1960) Music (Charles
Strouse) Lyrics (Lee Adams) DICK VAN DYKE & Company
*CBS USA (S.Screen): CK 02025 (CD) JST 02025 (MC)*
BYE BYE BIRDIE (FILM MUSICAL 1963) feat: DICK VAN DYKE
*-S/T- Import (SILVA SCREEN): 1081-2 (CD)*
BYKER GROVE (BBC1 26/9/95) incid.music: SIMON ETCHELL
additional music by TOM ROBINSON *unavailable*
BYKER GROVE (BBC1 8/11/89-94) theme m: MARTIN BRAMMER-
DAVID BREWIS performed by THE KANE GANG *unavailable*
BYZANTIUM: THE LOST EMPIRE (C4 7/9/97) original music
HOWARD DAVIDSON *unavailable*

CABARET - songs by John Kander and Fred Ebb
  1.NEW LONDON CAST 1986 *feat:* WAYNE SLEEP-VIVIENNE
  MARTIN-CAROLINE CLARE-GRAZINA FRAME-KELLY HUNTER-OS
  CAR QUITAK etc.*FIRST NIGHT (Pinn): OCRCD 6010 (CD)*
  2.STUDIO RECORDING *featur:* JONATHAN PRYCE-JUDY DENCH
  MARIA FRIEDMAN-GREGG EDELMAN-JOHN MARK AINSLEY
  Complete: *TER (Disc): CDTER2 1210 (2CD)*
  Highlights: *SHOWTIME (MCI-THE): SHOW(CD)(MC) 021*
  3.ORIG LONDON CAST 1968 *feat:* JUDI DENCH-LILA KEDROVA
  KEVIN COLSON-BARRY DENNEN *SONY: SMK 53494 (CD)*
  4.FILM MUSICAL 1972 *featuring* LIZA MINNELLI -S/T-
  *MCA (BMG): MCLD 19088 (CD)*
  5.ORIG BROADWAY CAST 1966 *feat:* JILL HAWORTH-JACK
  GILFORD-BERT CONVY-LOTTE LENYA-JOEL GRAY-PEG MURRAY
  *CBS (S.Screen) CK 03040(CD) JST 03040 (MC)*
  6.SHOWS COLLECTION 1997 *feat:* TOYAH WILLCOX-NIGEL PLA
  NER & Comp.*CARLTON Shows: 3036 20039-2 (CD) -4 (MC)*
CABIN IN THE SKY (1943) *feat* LOUIS ARMSTRONG-LENA HORNE
  ETHEL WATERS-EDDIE ANDERSON *re-mastered -S/T- on
  EMI SOUNDTRACKS (EMI): CDODEON 31 (CD)*
CABIRIA (57-Italy) - *see under* 'LA STRADA'
CABOBLANCO (1980) Music score: JERRY GOLDSMITH -S/T-
  *PROMETHEUS Imp (Silva Screen): PCD 127 (CD)*
CADFAEL (Carlton/ITV 29/5/94) music: COLIN TOWNS -S/T-
  *EMI SOUNDTRACK: CDEMC 3735 (CD)*
CAGNEY AND LACEY (USA81 BBC1 9/7/82) Theme: BILL CONTI
  see *COLLECTIONS 12,51,100,101,242,344,373,388*
CAHILL US MARSHALL (1973) Music score: ELMER BERNSTEIN
  suite on *VARESE (Pinn): VCD 47264 (CD)*
CAINE MUTINY (1954) Music score: MAX STEINER
  see *COLLECTIONS 54,157*
CAL (1984) Music score: MARK KNOPFLER -S/T- *VERTIGO-
  Poly: VERHC 17 (MC) 822 769-2 (CD)*
CALAMITY JANE - songs: Sammy Fain-Paul Francis Webster
  1.STUDIO RECORDING 1996 *featuring:* GEMMA CRAVEN
  *CARLTON Shows Collection 30362 0030-2 (CD) -4 (MC)*
  2.STUDIO R.1995 *w:* DEBBIE SHAPIRO-TIM FLAVIN-SUSANNAH
  FELLOWS Highlights: *(MCI-THE): SHOW(CD)(MC) 036*
  Complete: *TER (Disc): CDTER2 1215 (2CD)*

3.FILM MUSICAL 1953  DORIS DAY -S/T- *SONY: 467610-2*
*(CD)* + -S/T- songs from 'THE PAJAMA GAME' also
*ENTERTAINERS: CD 343 (CD)*
CALIFORNIA DREAMS (USA C4 25/4/93) Rock Drama TV Ser
-S/T- re-issue: *GEFFEN MCA (BMG): GFLD 19301 (CD)*
CALL ME MADAM - songs by Irving Berlin
  1.ORIG LONDON CAST 1994 *feat:* TYNE DALY-DAVID KERNAN
   JOHN BARROWMAN *DRG Pinn: DRGCD(DRGMC) 94761*
  2.ORIG LONDON CAST 1952 *w:* BILLIE WORTH-ANTON BROOK-
   SHANI WALLIS-JEFF WARREN *TER (Disc) ZCTER 1062 MC*
  3.ORIG BROADWAY CAST 1950 *w:* ETHEL MERMAN-DICK HAYMES
   *MCA USA (S.Screen): MCAD 10521(CD) MCAC 10521(MC)*
CALL MY BLUFF (BBC1 13/5/96 revived series) theme music
  "Ciccolino" *see COLLECTION 1*
CALL RED (Thames 8/1/96) music: STEPHEN W.PARSONS and
  FRANCIS HAINES / song "Guardian Angel" sung by
  MARCELLA DETROIT *unavailable*
CALLAN (ITV 1967) *see COLLECTION 2*
CAMBERWICK GREEN (1966) *see COLLECTION 408*
CAMELOT - songs by Alan Jay Lerner & Frederick Loewe
  1.REVIVAL LONDON CAST 1982 *feat:* RICHARD HARRIS-FIONA
   FULLERTON-ROBERT MEADMORE-ROBIN BAILEY-MICHAEL HOWE
   <u>Highlights</u>: *SHOWTIME (MCI-THE): SHOW(CD)(MC) 013*
   <u>Complete</u>:   *TER (Disc): (CD)(ZC)TER 1030 (CD/MC)*
  2.ORIG LONDON CAST 1964 *w:* LAURENCE HARVEY-ELIZABETH
   LARNER-NICKY HENSON-JOSEPHINE GORDON-KIT WILLIAMS
   BARRY KENT *FIRST NIGHT: OCRC 4 (MC) deleted*
  3.ORIG BROADWAY CAST 1961 *feat:* JULIE ANDREWS-RICHARD
   BURTON-ROBERT GOULET-ROD.McDOWELL *CBS UK(40)70009*
   *(MC/LP)*+CBS USA (Silva S) *CK(JST) 32602 (CD/MC)*
  4.FILM MUSICAL 1967 w.RICHARD HARRIS-VANESSA REDGRAVE
   -S/T- *W.Bros (WEA): 7599 27325-2 (CD)*
  5.CLASSIC MUSICALS SERIES *featuring:* RICHARD HARRIS
   FIONA FULLERTON-ROBERT MEADMORE-MICHAEL HOWE etc.+
   songs from 'MY FAIR LADY' *Koch Int: 34079-2 (CD)*
CAMILLE CLAUDEL (1989) Music sco: GABRIEL YARED -S/T-
  *VIRGIN FRANCE (Discovery): 88098-2 (CD)*
CAMOMILE LAWN The (C4 5/3/92) music by STEPHEN EDWARDS
  based on 'String Quartet in F' (RAVEL). Recordings
  BRITTEN QUART.*EMI: CDC 754346-2 (CD) EL 754346-4*
  *(MC)* CHILINGIRIAN QUARTET *EMI: (CD)(TC)EMX 2156*
CAMPION (UKGO 9/1/93 orig BBC1 22/1/89) theme music by
  NIGEL HESS *see COLLECTIONS 6,192*
CAN-CAN (ORIG BROADWAY CAST 1953) Songs (Cole Porter)
  *feat:* GWEN VERDON-LILO-PETER COOKSON-HANS CONREID
  ERIK RHODES *ANGEL (EMI): ZDM 764664-2 (CD)*
CAN'T COOK WON'T COOK (BBC1 20/11/95) music composed
  by KEN BOLAM *unavailable*
CANDID CAMERA (USA TV) *see COLLECTION 342*
CANDIDE -songs by Leonard Bernstein-Stephen Sondheim
       Richard Wilbur and John Latouche
  1.ORIG BROADWAY CAST 1956 *w:* BARBARA COOK-MAX ADRIAN
   ROBERT ROUNSEVILLE-IRRA PETINA-WILLIAM OLVIS-LOUIS
   EDMONDS-C.BAIN *SONY Broadway: SK 48017 (CD)*

 2. MUSICAL OPERA 1988 Studio *feat:* SCOTTISH OPERA CAST
    *TER (Disc): CD(ZC)TER 1156* Highlights: *CD(ZC)1006*
 3. MUSICAL OPERA 1991 Studio Recording *w:* JERRY HADLEY
    JUNE ANDERSON-CHRISTA LUDWIG-ADOLPH GREEN-NICOLAI
    GEDDA-DELLA JONES-HURT OLLMANN & L.S.O. (Bernstein)
    *DG (Poly): 429734-2 (2CDs) -4 (2MC)*
 4. NEW BROADWAY CAST 1997
    *RCA VICTOR (BMG): 0902 668835-2 (CD)*
CANNON (USA) *see COLLECTION 246,343*
CAPEMAN The (MUSICAL 1997/8) All songs by PAUL SIMON
    *featuring* RUBEN BLADES-MARC ANTHONY-EDNITA NAZARIO
    *W.BROS (WEA): 9362 46814-2 (CD) -4 (MC)*
CAPITAL CITY (Thames 26/9/89) theme music: COLIN TOWNS
    -S/T- *FIRST NIGHT (Pinn): SCENE(CD)(C) 18 (CD/MC)*
CAPRICORN ONE (1978) Music sco: JERRY GOLDSMITH -S/T-
    so containing music from 'OUTLAND') on *GNP USA*
    *(Silva Screen): GNPD 8035 (CD) GNP-5 8035 (MC)*
    *see also COLLECTIONS 156,273,322*
CAPTAIN BLOOD (1935) *see COLLECTION 332*
CAPTAIN BLOOD (1952) Mus.sco: VICTOR YOUNG new record:
    BRANDENBURG S.ORCH.(Kaufman) with other items on
    *MARCO POLO (Select): 8.223607 (CD*
CAPTAIN BUTLER (C4 3/1/97) music: RICK FENN *unavailable*
CAPTAIN FUTURE (1995) Music score: CHRISTIAN BRUHN
    -S/T- *COLOSSEUM (Pinn): CST 8051 (CD) see COLL 302*
CAPTAIN KANGAROO (USA) *see COLLECTION 339*
CAPTAIN MIDNIGHT (USA TV) *see COLLECTION 342*
CAPTAIN PUGWASH (BBC 60s) "Trumpet Hornpipe" (Tradit)
    Captain Pugwash' Ships Crew QED with Firstmate H.
    *DINGLES SID 244 (7")*
CAPTAIN SCARLET AND THE MYSTERONS (BBC2 1/10/93 orig
    ITV 29/9/67) mus: BARRY GRAY *see COLLECTIONS 3,110*
    *135,162,273,357,364,368,372*
CAPTIVE (1986) Music sco: MICHAEL BERKLEY-The EDGE
    -S/T- *VIRGIN (EMI): CDV 2401 (CD)*
CAR 54 WHERE ARE YOU (USA TV) *see COLLECTION 340*
CAR WASH (1976) T.theme: NORMAN WHITFIELD sung by ROSE
    ROYCE -S/T- reissue: *MCA (BMG): MCD 11502 (CD)*
CARAVAGGIO 1610 (1986) Music: SIMON FISHER TURNER -S/T-
    *reissued on DEMON (Pinn): DSCD 10 (CD)*
CARD The - songs by Tony Hatch and Jackie Trent
    ORIG LONDON CAST 1973 *w:* JIM DALE-MILLICENT MARTIN
    JOAN HICKSON-MARTI WEBB-ELEANOR BRON-ALAN NORBURN
    JOHN SAVIDENT *FIRST NIGHT (Pinn): OCRCD 6045 (CD)*
CARDIAC ARREST (Island World/BBC1 21/4/94) music and
    sound design by DAVID MOTION & BOB LAST *unavailable*
CAREFREE (1938) FILM MUSICAL *feat* FRED ASTAIRE-GINGER
    ROGERS -S/T- *selection on* 'Let's Swing and Dance'
    +songs fr.'FOLLOW THE FLEET'/'TOP HAT'/'SWINGTIME'
    *GREAT MOVIE THEMES (Target-BMG): CD 60015 (CD)*
    *also available -S/T- + songs from 'SHALL WE DANCE'*
    *IRIS Mus-Chansons Cinema (Discov): CIN 007 (CD)*
CARLA'S SONG (1996) Music score: GEORGE FENTON -S/T- on
    *DEBONAIR Records (Pinn): CDDEB 1005 (CD)*

CARLITO'S WAY (1993) Mus sco: PATRICK DOYLE Songs V/A
   -S/T- (Songs) *EPIC (SM): 474 994-2 (CD)*
   -S/T- (Score) *VARESE (Pinn): VSD(VSC) 5463 CD/MC*
CARMEN - *mus:* Georges Bizet *libr:* H.Meilhac-L.Halevy
   1.FILM MUSICAL 1983 *w:* LAURA DEL SOL-PACO DE LUCIA
   ANTONIO GADES-CRISTINA HOYOS -S/T- *POLY (IMS):*
   *E.817 247-2 (CD)*
   2.FILM MUSICAL 1984 *w:* PLACIDO DOMINGO-JULIA MIGENES
   JOHNSON *ERATO: MCE 75113 (3MC) ECD 88037 (3CD)*
   3.STUDIO RECORDING *with* MARILYN HORNE as Carmen
   *DG (Poly): 427 440-2 (3CD's)*
CARMEN JONES songs by G.Bizet & Oscar Hammerstein II
   1.FILM MUSICAL 1954 *feat:* MARILYN HORNE-PEARL BAILEY
   LaVERN HUTCHINSON-MARVIN HAYES-OLGA JAMES-BERNICE
   PETERSON-BROCK PETERS -S/T- *(BMG): GD(GK) 81881*
   2.ORIG LONDON CAST 1991 *Direct.by:* SIMON CALLOW *with*
   WILHELMINA FERNANDEZ-SHARON BENSON-DAMON EVANS-
   MICHAEL AUSTIN-GREGG BAKER-KAREN PARKS-CLIVE ROWE
   DANNY JOHN JULES *EMI: CDJONES 1 (EL 754351-2)*
CARO DIARIO - see under DEAR DIARY
CAROUSEL - songs: Richard Rodgers-Oscar Hammerstein II
   1.FILM MUSICAL 1956 *feat:* GORDON McRAE-SHIRLEY JONES
   -S/T- Reissue *EMI ANGEL: ZDM 764 692-2 (CD)*
   2.ORIG LONDON CAST 1993 JOANNA RIDING-KATRINA MURPHY
   *FIRST NIGHT (Pinn): OCRCD 6042 (CD) CASTC 40 (MC)*
   3.SHOWS COLLECTION 1993 *feat:* DAVE WILLETTS-CLAIRE
   MOORE-SU POLLARD-IAN WALLACE-LINDA HIBBERD
   *CARLTON Shows: PWKS 4144 (CD) PWKMC 4144 (MC)*
   4.REVIVAL BROADWAY CAST 1965 *with* JOHN RAITT
   Import *(SILVA SCREEN): 6395-2 (CD)*
   5.ORIG BROADWAY CAST 1945 *with* JOHN RAITT-JAN CLAYTON
   JEAN DARLING-C.JOHNSON *MCA (BMG): MCLD 19152 (CD)*
   *also Imp (SILVA SCREEN): MCAD(MCAC) 10048 (CD/MC)*
CARRIE (1976) Music score: PINO DONAGGIO -S/T- *reiss +*
   *additional items RYKODISC (Vital): RCD 10701 (CD)*
   see also COLLECTIONS 210,355
CARRIED AWAY (1996) Music score: BRUCE BROUGHTON -S/T-
   *INTRADA (Koch): MAFCD 7068 (CD)*
CARRINGTON (1995) Music sco: MICHAEL NYMAN -S/T- incl:
   'Adagio' from String Quintet in C. (SCHUBERT) on
   *ARGO-DECCA (Poly): 444 873-2(CD) -4(MC) delet.96*
   see also Coll 'CINEMA CLASSICS COLLECTION' *(EMI)*
CARS THE STAR (BBC2 25/9/94) title music composed and
   performed by DAVID LOWE *unavailable*
CASABLANCA (1943) Mus: MAX STEINER *vocal:* DOOLEY WILSON
   -S/T- + *dialogue EMI SOUNDTR: 823 502-2 (CD)* also
   COLLECTIONS 29,54,62,63,81,140,157,216,286,292,380
CASINO (1995) Songs by Various Artists
   -S/T- (31 Tracks) on *MCA (BMG): MCAD 11389 (2CD)*
CASINO ROYALE (1967) Music score: BURT BACHARACH -S/T-
   *VARESE (Pinn): VSD 5265 (CD)* also COLLECTION 358
CASPER (1995) Music sco: JAMES HORNER / "Remember Me
   This Way" JORDAN HILL "Casper The Friendly Ghost"
   by LITTLE RICHARD -S/T- *MCA (BMG): MCD 11240 (CD)*

CASPER: A SPIRITED BEGINNING (1997) -S/T- feat Var.Arts
KC & SUNSHINE BAND-KOOL & THE GANG-BACKSTREET BOYS-
BOBBY McFERRIN-OINGO BOINGO-911-SHAMPOO-SUPERGRASS
EMI SOUNDTRACKS: 821 345-2 (CD) -4 (MC)
CASPER THE FIENDLY GHOST USA TV) see COLLECTION 339
CASTLE FREAK (1995) Music score: RICHARD BAND -S/T-
INTRADA (Silva Screen): MAF 7065 (CD)
CASTLES (BBC1 31/5/95) t.music: COLIN TOWNS unavailable
CASSANDRA CROSSING The (1977) Music sc: JERRY GOLDSMITH
feat song "I'm Still On My Way" sung by Ann Turkel
-S/T- CITADEL Imp (Silva Screen): OST 102 (CD)
CASUALTY (BBC1 6/9/86-98) theme music: KEN FREEMAN
see COLLECTION 33
CAT CRAZY (Meridian 24/7/97) music: LESTER BARNES....NA
CAT O'NINE TAILS (1980) Music: ENNIO MORRICONE -S/T-
inc 'FOUR FLIES ON GREY VELVET'/'BIRD WITH THE CRYS
TAL PLUMAGE' on DRG (Pinn): DRGCD 32911 (CD)
CAT PEOPLE (1982) Music: GIORGIO MORODER featur: DAVID
BOWIE -S/T- reissue MCA (BMG): MCLD 19302 (CD)
CATCHPHRASE (TVS 12/1/86) music: ED WELCH unavailable
CATHEDRAL (BBC1 7/9/97) theme "Anna Of The Five Towns"
by NIGEL HESS see COLLECTION 192
CATS - songs by Andrew Lloyd Webber and Trevor Nunn
1.ORIG LONDON CAST 1981 feat: ELAINE PAIGE & Comp
POLYDOR: 817 810-2 (CD) CATXC 001 (2MC)
'Highlights' 839415-2(CD) -1(LP) -4(MC) -5 (DCC)
2.ROYAL PHILH.ORCH PLAY SUITES from Aspects Of Love
Cats/Joseph and The Amazing Technicolor Dreamcoat
CARLTON Int: PWKS(PWKMC) 4115 (CD/MC)
3.CLASSIC MUSICALS SERIES feat: MARIA FRIEDMAN and
CLIVE CARTER w. MUNICH SYMPHONY ORCH (J.O.Edwards)
+songs 'PHANTOM OF THE OPERA' KOCH Int: 34078-2CD
CATWEAZLE (LWT 1/3/70-71) theme music: TED DICKS
see COLLECTIONS 3,320
CELEBRITY SQUARES (Central 8/1/93) theme: RICK TURK..NA
CELTS The (BBC2 14/5/87) Music score comp/performed by
ENYA -S/T-/- WEA: 4509 91167-2 (CD) WX 498C (MC)
WX 498 (LP) theme on WEA: YZ 705 (7"s)
CENTURY (1993) Music score: MICHAEL GIBBS -S/T- with
'CLOSE MY EYES' IONIC-MUTE (Pinn): IONIC 10 (2CD)
CESAR (1936) MARCEL PAGNOL'S TRILOGY (3) / music sco.by
VINCENT SCOTTO on Coll 'Films Of Marcel Pagnol' on
EMI FRA.(Discov): 855 883-2 (CD) / see also 'FANNY'
CHAIN REACTION (1996) Music score: JERRY GOLDSMITH
-S/T- VARESE (Pinn): VSD 5746 (CD)
CHAIRMAN The (1969) Music sc: JERRY GOLDSMITH -S/T- inc
'Ransom' (75) S.SCREEN (Koch): FILMCD 081 (CD)
CHALK (BBC1 20/2/97) music: HOWARD GOODALL unavailable
CHALLENGE The (O.L.CAST) TER (Disc): TERCD 1201 (2CD)
CHAMBER (1996) Music score: CARTER BURWELL -S/T- on
VARESE (Pinn): VSD 5758 (CD)
CHAMPION THE WONDER HORSE (USA 56)(BBC1 7/11/92) theme
song (Norman Luboff-Marilyn Keith) sung by FRANKIE
LAINE Coll 'HELLO CHILDREN VOLUME 2' deleted

CHAMPIONS (1984) Music sc: CARL DAVIS -S/T- *ISLAND*
   *deleted* "Sometimes" Elaine Paige *see COLLECT.280*
CHAMPIONS The (ITC 25/9/68 - 4/69) theme: EDWIN ASTLEY
   *see COLLECTIONS 3,182,357,358.364,372*
CHAMPIONS LEAGUE Football *see* 'EUROPEAN CHAMPIONS L...'
CHANCER (Central 6/3/90) theme (Jan Hammer) JAN HAMMER
   'Escape From Television' inc: 'Crockett's Theme'
   *MCA (BMG): MCAD 10410 (CD) MCAC 10410 (MC)*
CHANGE OF HABIT *see* ELVIS PRESLEY INDEX p.000
CHANGE THAT (BBC P.Mill 10/1/97) t.music: JIM PARKER.*NA*
CHANGING ROOMS (BBC2 4/9/96) title music: JIM PARKER.*NA*
CHAPLIN (1992) Music sco JOHN BARRY -S/T- reissue *EPIC*
   *(Sony M): 472 602-2 (CD) see COLLECTIONS 21,24,63*
CHARADE (1964) Music score: HENRY MANCINI
   *see COLLECTIONS 140,243,244,248*
CHARIOTS OF FIRE (1981) Music score: VANGELIS -S/T-
   *POLYDOR (Poly): POLDC (MC) 800 020-2 (CD) see also*
   *COLLECTIONS 55,63,75,90,155,203,285,324,333,353,382*
CHARLIE BROWN (A BOY NAMED) (USA 80's/BBC1) Mus score
   composed and performed by The VINCE GUARALDI TRIO
   *FANTASY (Complete): FCD 8430-2 (CD)*
CHARLIE GIRL - songs by David Heneker and John Taylor
   1.ORIG LONDON CAST 1965 *w:* JOE BROWN-HY HAZELL-ANNA
   NEAGLE-DEREK NIMMO-STUART DAMON-DAVID TOGURI-CHRIS
   TINE HOLMES *SONY WEST END (Sony): SMK 66174 (CD)*
   2.NEW LONDON CAST 1986 *w:* PAUL NICHOLAS-CYD CHARISSE
   MARK WYNTER-DORA BRYAN-NICHOL.PARSONS-KAREN DAVIES
   LISA HULL *FIRST NIGHT (Pinn): OCRCD 6009(CD)*
CHARLIE'S ANGELS (USA 76) theme: JACK ELLIOTT & ALLYN
   FERGUSON *see COLLECTIONS 100,168,341,360,379*
CHARRO! *see* ELVIS PRESLEY INDEX p.348
CHART SHOW The (Video Visuals/Twix/YTV 7/1/95) title
   mus: CHRIS ANDREWS & JONATHAN SORRELL *unavailable*
   'CHART SHOW ROCK ALBUM' *POLY:535489-2(CD) -4(MC)*
CHASERS (1996) music: DWIGHT YOAKAM-PETE ANDERSON -S/T-
   *MORGAN CREEK (Polyg): 002426-2 MCM (CD)*
CHASING THE DEER (1993) Theme music by JOHN WETTON on
   'Battle Lines" *CROMWELL (THE): CPCD 020 (CD)*
CHECKMATE (USA TV) *see COLLECTION 342*
CHEERS (USA C4 6/1/84-93) theme "Where Everybody Knows
   Your Name" GARY PORTNOY-Judy Hart Angelo
   *see COLLECTIONS 12,168,242,341,405*
CHEF! (BBC1 28/1/93) theme music "Serious Profession"
   by OMAR / incidental music: JAKKO M.JAKSZYK -S/T-
   *RESURGENCE-BLUEPRINT (Pinn): RES 118CD (CD)*
CHELSEA FLOWER SHOW 1996 (BBC2 22/5/96) theme mus from
   'Lakme'"The Flower Duet" (DELIBES) sung by MADY MES
   PLE and DANIELLE MILLET with Paris Opera Orchestra
   *EMI: 568 307-2 (CD)* 1994 (BBC2 25/5/94) theme music
   from 'The Celts' composed & performed by ENYA *WEA*
   *4509 91167-2(CD) WX 498C(MC)* 1993 (BBC2 26/5/93)
   closing mus. "The Mission" by ENNIO MORRICONE -S/T-
   *VIRGIN (EMI):CDV(TCV)(MDV)2402 (CD/MC/MD)* also used
*Continued next page...*

CHELSEA FLOWER SHOW 1996 *Continued...*

"Pomp And Circumstance No.2" (ELGAR) 1992 & 1991
(BBC2) mus.inc: PENGUIN CAFE ORCHEST "From The Colo
nies"(Broadcasting From Home) *EG-VIRGIN: EGCD 38CD*
"Air A Dancer"/"A Telephone And A Rubber Band"
from 'When In Rome'*EGCD 56 (CD)* "Sketch"/"Perpetuum
Mobile" from 'Signs Of Life' *EGCD 50 (CD)* *other mus*
*ic used* "Prelude" ('Holberg Suite Op.40) (E.GREIG)
CHELTENHAM FESTIVAL (BBC1 14/3/89) theme mus "Odissea"
(Gian Reverberi-L.Giordiano) RONDO VENEZIANO
*BMG (Discovery): 610.535 (CD)*
CHERRY HARRY & RAQUEL (1969 RUSS MEYER) -S/T- *QDK MEDIA*
*(Direct): QDKCD 014 (CD)* also music on Coll
'Russ Meyer Orig Soundtracks Vol.4' (various) on
*POP BIZ (Cargo-Greyhound): LP 014 (LP)*
CHESS *see under* 'WORLD CHESS CHAMPIONSHIPS 1993'
CHESS - songs: Benny Andersson-Bjorn Ulvaeus-Tim Rice
  1.1986 Chess Pieces: The Best Of Chess *feat:* ELAINE
  PAIGE-BARBARA DICKSON-MURRAY HEAD-TOMMY KORBERG-DEN
  IS QUILLEY-BJORN SKIFS-LONDON SYMPHONY ORCH-AMBROSI
  AN SINGERS *RCA (BMG): 74321 15120-2 (CD) -4 (MC)*
  2.ORIG BROADWAY CAST: *POLYDOR (Poly): 847 445-2 (CD)*
CHEYENNE  (USA TV) *see COLLECTION 342*
CHICAGO - songs: John Kander and Fred Ebb
  1.ORIG BROADWAY CAST (1996) *featuring:* ANN REINKING-
  BEBE NUEWIRTH-JAMES NAUGHTON-JOEL GRAY and Company
  *RCA (BMG): 09026 68727-2 (CD) -4 (MC)*
  2.ORIG LONDON CAST (1997) *feat:* RUTHIE HENSHALL-UTE
  LEMPER-HENRY GOODMAN-NIGEL PLANER *to be confirmed*
CHICAGO BLUES (Film 'Blues' Document) Muddy Waters &
  J.B.Hutto-Junior Wells-Mighty Joe Young-Koko Taylor
  Johnnie Young *CASTLE COMM (BMG): CLACD 425 (CD)*
CHICAGO HOPE (BBC1 1995) m: MARK ISHAM-S/T-*unconfirmed*
CHICKEN (1995) -S/T- *ICON (Pinn Imp):ICON 19962 (CD)*
CHICO AND THE MAN (USA 74) theme (Jose Feliciano) JOSE
  FELICIANO on *RCA: ND 90123 (CD) NK 89561 (MC)*
  *CARLTON Ess.Gold (CHE): 30359 00232 (CD) -4(MC)*
CHIGLEY (BBC1 1969) *see COLLECTION 408*
CHILDREN IN NEED (BBC1 21/11/97) song "PERFECT DAY"
  (L.Reed) V.ARTS *CHRYSALIS (Poly): CDNEED 001 (CDs)*
  *TCNEED 001 (MC) 7NEED 001 (7"s)* / song 1996 "When
  Children Rule The World"(A.Lloyd Webber-J.Steinman)
  by RED HILL CHILDREN *POLYD: 579726-2 (CDs) -4 (MC)*
  theme 1989-95 "If You Want To Help-Help Children In
  Need"(David Martin) FINCHLEY CHILDREN'S MUSIC GROUP
  *recording unconfirmed* (previous entries in TT 1991)
CHILDREN OF A LESSER GOD (1986) "Largo Ma Mon Tanto"
  2nd m/m 'Concerto D.Min For Violins' (BACH) / Music
  sco: MICHAEL CONVERTINO -S/T- *GNP (Silva Screen)*
  *GNPD(GNP5)(GNPS)8007 (CD/MC/LP) see COLLECTS.65,72*
CHILDREN'S HOSPITAL (BBC1 19/10/93) Theme mus.by DEBBIE
  WISEMAN on *BMG INT (BMG): 74321 47589-4 (MC*
  *see also COLLECTION 402*

CHILDREN'S THIEF The (Film Italy) Music score: FRANCO
    PIERSANTI -S/T- contains mus from 'ON MY OWN'(92)
    -S/T- *OST (Silva Screen): OST 117 (CD)*
CHILDREN'S WARD (Gran. 11/10/94) theme: DASHIELL RAE
    Incidental music: CHRIS COZENS *unavailable*
CHIMERA (Anglia 7/9/91) theme music "Rosheen Du" by
    NIGEL HESS sung by CHAMELEON
    *see COLLECTIONS 138,191,192*
CHINA 9 LIBERTY 37 (1978) Music sco: PINO DONAGGIO
    -S/T- *Import (SILVA SCREEN): PCD 117 (CD)*
CHINATOWN (1974) Music score: JERRY GOLDSMITH -S/T-
    *VARESE (Pinn): VSD 5677 (CD)*
CHIPS (USA 1980) theme: JOHN PARKER *see COLLECTIONS*
    *168,344*
CHITTY CHITTY BANG BANG (1968) Music and songs by
    RICHARD & ROBERT SHERMAN -S/T- *reissue + add.items*
    DICK VAN DYKE-SALLY ANN HOWES-LIONEL JEFFRIES etc.
    *RYKODISC (Vital): RCD 10702 (CD) RAC 10702 (MC)*
CHOIR The (BBC1 19/3/95) music sco: STANISLAS SYREWICZ
    featur: GLOUCESTER CATHEDRAL CHOIR and ANTHONY WAY
    *see COLLECTION 213*
CHORUS LINE, A   songs: Marvin Hamlisch-Edward Kleban
    1.FILM SOUNDTRACK 1985 *feat:* MICHAEL DOUGLAS-TERENCE
    MANN-ALYSON REED *reissue BGO (BMG): BGOCD 360 (CD)*
    2.ORIGINAL BROADWAY CAST 1975 *w:* KELLY BISHOP-PAMELA
    BLAIR-WAYNE CILENTO-KAY COLE-PATRICIA GARLAND-DONNA
    McKECHNIE *COLUMBIA (S.Scr): CK(JST) 33581 (CD/MC)*
CHRISTINE (1984) Music score: JOHN CARPENTER -S/T-
    John Carpenter's original music only on import
    *VARESE (Pinn): VSD 5240 (CD)*
CHRISTOPHER COLUMBUS (1949) Music sco: Sir ARTHUR BLISS
    Music from film and from 'Seven Waves Away' (56) on
    *MARCO POLO (Harmonia Mundi): 8223315 (CD)*
CHRISTOPHER COLUMBUS: THE DISCOVERY (1992) Music score
    CLIFF EIDELMAN -S/T- *VARESE (Pinn): VSD 5389 (CD)*
CHRONICLES OF NARNIA (UKGold 7/11/92 orig BBC 13/11/88)
    theme mus by GEOFFREY BURGON *see COLLECTION 40*
    *also avail BBC (Pinn) ZBBC 1109 and ZBBC 1110 (2MC)*
CHUCKLEVISION (BBC1 21/9/91) m: DAVE COOKE *unavailable*
CIMARRON STRIP (USA TV) *see COLLECTION 343*
CINDERELLA (Disney 1950) *see* WALT DISNEY INDEX p.343
CINDERFILA (MUSICAL SHOW 1957) with JULIE ANDREWS *Col.*
    *(Silva Screen): CK 02005 (CD) JST 02005 (MC)*
CINEMA PARADISO (1990) Music score ENNIO MORRICONE
    *DRG (Pinn): CDSBL 12598 (CD) SBLC 12598 (MC)*
CINERAMA SOUTH SEAS ADVENTURE (1958) Music score: ALEX
    NORTH *5th CONT.Australia (S.Screen): LXCD 2 (CD)*
CIRCUS The (1928) Music sco: CHARLES CHAPLIN *see Coll*
    'FILM MUS.OF CHARLES CHAPLIN' *RCA: 09026 68271-2*
CIRQUE DU SOLEIL - see 'SALTIMBANCO'
CITIZEN KANE (1941) Music: BERNARD HERRMANN (complete
    score) Australian Philh.Orch (Tony Bremner) with Ro
    samund Illing *5th CONT (S.Screen): PRCD 1788 (CD)*
    *see COLLECTIONS 63,185,187,188,190*

CITIZEN X (1995) Music score: RANDY EDELMAN -S/T- on
  *VARESE (Pinn): VSD 5601 (CD)*
CITIZEN'S ARREST (LWT/C4 17/9/96)mus: ANDREW MIDGLEY.*NA*
CITY HALL (1995) Music score: JERRY GOLDSMITH -S/T- on
  *VARESE (Pinn): VSD 5699 (CD)*
CITY LIGHTS (1931) Original Music composed by CHARLES
  CHAPLIN. New recording reconstructed from the orig
  manuscripts. City Lights Orch conductor: Carl Davis
  *S.SCREEN (Koch): FILMCD 078 also COLLEC 56,57,58,63*
CITY OF ANGELS (O.LONDON CAST 1993) Songs (Cy Coleman-
  Larry Gelbart) *feat:* MARTIN SMITH-ROGER ALLAM-HENRY
  GOODMAN-HADYN GWYNNE-SUSANNAH FELLOWS-JOANNE FARREL
  *FIRST NIGHT (Pinn): OCRCD 6034 (CD)*
CITY OF INDUSTRY (1996) Music score: STEPHEN ENDELMAN
  -S/T- with MASSIVE ATTACK-BOMB THE BASS-LUSH-TRICKY
  PHOTEX etc. *QUANGO-ISLAND (Poly): 524 308-2 (CD)*
CITY OF VIOLENCE (Citta Violenta) Music score: ENNIO
  MORRICONE -S/T- *IMPT (Silva Screen): OST 127 (CD)*
CITY SLICKERS (1991) Music score: MARC SHAIMAN -S/T-
  *VARESE (Pinn): VSD 5321 (CD)*
CITY SLICKERS 2 (1993) Music score: MARC SHAIMAN -S/T-
  *COLUMBIA (Sony M): 476 815-2 (CD) -4 (MC)*
CIVIL WAR The (BBC2 30/3/91) theme "Ashokan Farewell"
  by JAY UNGAR -S/T- incl: "Shenandoah"/"When Johnny
  Comes Marching Home" & others - KEN BURNS -S/T- on
  *ELEKTRA-NONESUCH (WEA): 7559-79256-2(CD) -4(MC)*
  ALSO AVAILABLE: "The Civil War-It's Music & Sounds"
  *MERCURY Living Presence (Poly): 432 591-2 MM2 (CD)*
  *see also COLLECTIONS 59,144*
CLAMBAKE *see* ELVIS PRESLEY INDEX p.348
CLARKSON'S STAR CARS (BBC1 12/7/93) theme "Peter Gunn"
  (Henry Mancini)CINCINNATI POPS ORCH (Erich Kunzel)
  'Mancini's G.Hits' *TELARC (BMG): CD 80183 (CD)*
CLARISSA EXPLAINS IT ALL (USA TV) *see COLLECTION 345*
CLASS (ITV/September Pr) 10/6/97) music: SIMON BRINT.*NA*
CLASSIC ADVENTURE (BBC1 11/5/92) mus: NIGEL HESS
  *see COLLECTIONS 138,191,192*
CLEAR AND PRESENT DANGER (1993) Music sc: JAMES HORNER
  -S/T- *MILAN (BMG): 22401-2 (CD) 22401-4 (MC)*
CLERKS (1994) Music sco: SCOTT ANGLEY -S/T- with V.Arts
  *COLUMBIA (Sony): 477 802-2 (CD)*
CLIENT The (USA) (C4 22/2/97) mus: STEPHEN GRAZIANO..*NA*
CLIVE ANDERSON ALL TALK (BBC1 6/10/96) title music "All
  Talk" comp/perf: ELVIS COSTELLO & ATTRACTIONS....*NA*
CLIVE ANDERSON ON TV (C4 17/3/89-96) theme m "Yaketty
  Yak" (Jerry Leiber-Mike Stoller) orig: COASTERS
CLIVE BARKER'S A-Z OF HORROR (BBC2 4/10/97) t.music by
  TOT TAYLOR on the 'WATERLAND' album
  *TWEED (3MV-Vital): TWEEDCD 001 (CD)*
CLIVE JAMES SHOW The (Carlton 21/5/95) theme music by
  MARK SAYER-WADE and TOLGA KASHIF *unavailable*
CLOCKWORK ORANGE A (1971) Electronic music score WALTER
  'Wendy' CARLOS V.Classics -S/T- *WB (WEA): CD 246127
  (CD) K.446127 (MC) see also COLLECT 69,70,71,110*

CLOCKERS (1995) Music sco (Stanley Clarke and Terence
    Blanchard) -S/T- feat: CHAKA KHAN-SEAL-MEGA BANTON
    MARC DORSEY-CROOKLYN DODGERS-REBELZ OF AUTHORITY..
    -S/T- *MCA (BMG): MCD 11304 (CD)*
CLOSE ENCOUNTERS OF THE THIRD KIND (1977) Music score
    JOHN WILLIAMS Nat.Phil.Orch *RCA: RCD 13650 (CD)*
    -S/T- *ALHAMBRA (S.Screen): A.8915 (CD) see also*
    *COLLECTIONS 173,200,273,301,322,323,329*
CLOSE MY EYES (1991) Music sco: MICHAEL GIBBS -S/T- +
    'CENTURY' on *IONIC-MUTE (Pinn): IONIC 10 (2CD)*
CLOSE SHAVE, A (Wallace & Gromit) (1995) Mus by JULIAN
    NOTT *Video: BBC (Pinn): BBCV 5766 (VHS) see also*
    'GRAND DAY OUT'/'WRONG TROUSERS'
CLOTHES SHOW The (BBC1 13/10/87-97)theme "In The Night"
    (Tennant-Lowe) PET SHOP BOYS on 'Disco' *EMI: CDP*
    *746450-2(CD) TC-PRG 1001(MC) TV version unavailable*
CLUELESS (1995) Music sco: DAVID KITAY  -S/T- w. V.Arts
    *CAPITOL (EMI): CDEST 2267 (CD)*
CLUELESS (USA) (ITV 4/1/97) mus: DAVID KITAY "Ordinary
    Girl" (C.Caffey-A.Waronker) sung by CHINA FORBES.*NA*
COASTAL COMMAND (1942) Music score: VAUGHAN WILLIAMS
    on 'Film Music' RTE CONCERT ORCH (Andrew Penny) on
    *MARCO POLO (Sel): 8.223665 (CD) see COLLECT 85,184*
COCKTAIL (1988) Music score: J.PETER ROBINSON -S/T- on
    *ELEKTRA (WEA): 960806-2 (CD) see also COLLECT.39*
COCOON (1985) Music score: JAMES HORNER Feat: Michael
    Sembello -S/T- *POLYDOR: 827 041-2 (CD)*
    *see also COLLECTIONS 268,322*
COCOON 2 'The Return' (1989) Music score: JAMES HORNER
    -S/T- *VARESE (Pinn): VSD 5211 (CD)*
COEUR EN HIVER, Un - see 'HEART IN WINTER, A'
COLBY'S The (USA TV) *see COLLECTION 344*
COLD HEAVEN (1992) Music score: STANLEY MYERS Suite on
    *INTRADA (S.Screen): MAF 7048D (CD) also includes*
    *Suite from film* 'TRUSTING BEATRICE' (S.MYERS)
COLD LAZARUS (BBC1 5/96) Music sco: CHRISTOPHER GUNNING
    -S/T- includes music from 'KARAOKE' and feat tracks
    by BING CROSBY-HANK WILLIAMS-CRAIG DOUGLAS etc.
    *SILVA SCREEN (Koch): FILM(CD)(C) 181 (CD/MC)*
COLD ROOM The (1994) Music score: MICHAEL NYMAN -S/T-
    *SILVA SCREEN (Koch): FILMCD 157 (CD)*
COLDITZ (BBC1 19/10/72) "Colditz March" ROBERT FARNON
    *see COLLECTIONS 2,35*
COLOR OF MONEY The (1986) Mus: ROBBIE ROBERTSON +songs
    -S/T- *MCA USA Imp (Silva Screen): MCAD 6189 (CD)*
    *see also COLLECTIONS 39,361*
COLOR PURPLE The (1986) Music sco: QUINCY JONES +Songs
    Tata Vega -S/T- *QWEST Imp (S.Scr): 925389-2 (2CDs)*
    *see COLLECTION 323*
COLT 45  (USA TV) *see COLLECTION 342*
COLTRANE IN A CADILLAC (Tiger Aspect/Meridian 4/5/93)
    theme mus "Benny Rides Again" BENNY GOODMAN ORCHES
    TRA *CHARLY (Koch): CPCD 82632 (CD)* also on 'BENNY
    GOODMAN PLAYS EDDIE SAUTER' *HEP (Pinn): HEPCD 1053*

COLTRANE'S PLANES AND AUTOMOBILES (C4 9/11/97) original
    music by JAMES FINNEGAN *unavailable*
COLUMBO (USA) - *see COLLECTION 2,101,246*
COME DANCING (BBC 1950-1996) *Coll* feat the ANDY ROSS
    ORCH *MFP (EMI): CD(TC)MFP 6183 / 92/93 ser.theme*
    (Stewart James-Bradley James) by ROSEMARIE FORD..*NA
    prev.theme* 25/6/90) "Dancing Feet" by ANDY ROSS
    *PRESID: PCOM(PTLC)(PTLS) 1107 (CD/MC/LP) Select.*
    ANDY ROSS ORCH *COLUMBIA (SM): 475642-2(CD) -4(MC)*
    *see COLLECTION 1*
COMEDY PLAYHOUSE (BBC1 1960s) theme "Happy Joe" by RON
    GRAINER *see COLLECTIONS 7,372*
COMMITMENTS The (1991) -S/T- (Various Atists covers)
    *MCAD 10286 (CD) MCAC 10286 (MC)* / ORIG ARTISTS on
    'SOUL CLASSICS' *Atl.(WEA) 7567 91813-2(CD) -4(MC)*
    COMMITMENTS 2 Second Album incl: "Hard To Handle"
    "Show Me"/"Too Many Fish In The Sea"/"Nowhere To
    Run" + 7 new tracks  *MCA (BMG): MCLD 19312 (CD)*
COMMON AS MUCK (BBC1 7/9/94) theme "Tasty Fish" by The
    Other Two (ex NEW ORDER) *spec.arr.not available*
COMMONWEALTH GAMES 1994 (BBC1 18/8/94) theme "Commanch
    ee Overture" (Steve Spiro) also used "Club Chant"
    by INTERNATIONAL FOOT LANGUAGE on 'The Brave' on
    *WEA: YZ 844CD (CDsin) YZ 844C (MC) YZ 844T (12")*
COMPANEROS (1970) Music score (E.Morricone) ENNIO MORR
    ICONE ORCHESTRA on Collection 'An Ennio Morricone
    Quintet' *DRG USA (Pinn): DRGCD 32907 (CD)*
COMPANY - songs: Stephen Sondheim
    1.ORIG LONDON CAST 1995/6 *w:*ADRIAN LESTER-SHEILA GISH
      SOPHIE THOMPSON-CLIVE ROWE-PAUL BENTLEY and Company
      *FIRST NIGHT (Pinn): CASTCD 57 (CD) CASTC 57 (MC)*
    2.ORIG BROADWAY CAST 1995
      *EMI PREM.West End (EMI): PRMFCD 2 (CD)*
    3.ORIG LONDON CAST 1972 *w:* ELAINE STRICH-BETH HOWLAND
      GEORGE COE-SUSAN BROWNING-LARRY KERT *SONY
      Broadway: SMK 53496 (CD) deleted*
    4.ORIG BROADWAY CAST 1970 *feat:* ELAINE STRITCH-DEAN
      JONES-BARBARA BARRIE-DONNA McKECHNIE and Company
      *Columb (S.SCREEN): CK 03550 (CD) JST 03550 (MC)*
COMPANY OF WOLVES The (1984) Mus: GEORGE FENTON -S/T-
    *TER (Disc): (CD)ZCTER 1094 (CD/MC)*
CON AIR (1997) Music score: MARK MANCINA & TREVOR RABIN
    song "How Do I Live" sung by TRISHA YEARWOOD on
    *MCA (BMG): MCSTD 48064 (CDs) MCSC 48064 (MC)*
    -S/T- (import only) *POLY: E.162 099-2 (CD)*
CONAN THE BARBARIAN (1981) Music sco: BASIL POLEDOURIS
    -S/T- *MILAN (BMG): 111 262 (CD) 111 264 (MC)* -
    *also available USA CD containing extra 20mins of
    prev.unreleased material VARESE: VSD 5390 (CD)*
CONAN THE DESTROYER (1983) Music sco: BASIL POLEDOURIS
    *VARESE (S.Screen): VSD 5392 (CD)*
    *see also COLLECTIONS 63,64,299,385*
CONE ZONE The (Tetra/Carlton 15/3/95) theme music by
    KIM GOODY-ALAN COATES-FRANCIS HAINES *unavailable*

**CONFESSIONAL The** (1995) Music: STEFAN GIRADET-SACHA
    PUTTMAN-ADRIAN UTTLEY -S/T- *feat* Various Artists
    *POLLYANNA-Grapevine (Poly): PPCD 001 (CD)*
**CONFESSIONS** (BBC1 1/4/95) mus: PHILIP POPE *unavailable*
**CONFESSIONS OF A POLICE CAPTAIN** (1971-Italy) *see under*
    'IN THE GRIP OF THE SPIDER'
**CONFIDENTIALLY YOURS** (1983 'Vivement Dimanche') Music
    GEORGES DELERUE *on Coll* 'TRUFFAUT & DELERUE ON
    THE SCREEN' *DRG (Pinn): 32902 (CD)*
**CONFORMIST The** (1970) Music sco: GEORGES DELERUE -S/T-
    with -S/T- score from 'TRAGEDY OF A RIDICULOUS MAN'
    *DRG (Pinn): DRGCD 32910 (CD)*
**CONNECTION The** (1961) Mus.by FREDDIE REDD-JACKIE McLEAN
    -S/T- *re-iss BOPLICITY (Complete): CDBOP 019 (CD)*
**CONQUEST OF THE AIR** (1938) Music sco: Sir ARTHUR BLISS
    *see COLLECTION 85*
**CONSENTING ADULTS** (1992) Music sco: MICHAEL SMALL -S/T-
    *MILAN (Pinn): 12479-2 (CD) 12479-4 (MC)*
**CONTACT** (1997) Music score: ALAN SILVESTRI -S/T- V.Arts
    *WB (WEA): 9362 46811-2 (CD) -4 (MC)*
**COOGAN'S RUN** (BBC2 17/11/95) theme & incidental music:
    DAVID MINDELL & DON GOULD (Mingles Mus) *unavailable*
**COOK THE THIEF HIS WIFE AND HER LOVER The** (1989) Music:
    MICHAEL NYMAN -S/T- *VIRGIN (EMI): (CD)(TC)VE 53*
**COOL HAND LUKE** (1967) Music score: LALO SCHIFRIN
    -S/T- *TSUMAMI Imp (Silva Screen): TSU 0130 (CD)*
**COOL McCOOL** (USA TV) *see COLLECTION 343*
**COOL RUNNINGS** (1993) Music score: HANS ZIMMER songs by:
    WAILING SOULS-JIMMY CLIFF-DIANA KING-TIGER etc.
    -S/T- reissue: *COLUMBIA (Sony): 474 840-2 (CD)*
**COOLEY HIGH** (1975) Music sc: FREDDIE PERREN -S/T- *feat*
    SMOKEY ROBINSON & MIRACLES-TEMPTATIONS-MARY WELLS-
    SUPREMES etc. *SPECTRUM (Poly): 551 547-2 (CD)*
**COP LAND** (1997) Music score: HOWARD SHORE -S/T-
    *RCA-MILAN (BMG): 74321 53128-2 (CD)*
**COPACABANA** (ORIG LONDON CAST 1994) Songs: BARRY MANILOW
    *feat* GARY WILMOT *FIRST NIGHT (Pinn): OCRCD 6047(CD)*
**COPS** (USA 90 SKY 91) theme "Bad Boys" (Inner Circle)
    'One Way' *RAS (Jetstar): RAS(CD)(MC)3030 deleted*
**COPYCAT** (1996) Music score: CHRISTOPHER YOUNG -S/T-
    *MILAN (BMG): 74321 33742-2 (CD)*
**CORNBREAD EARL AND ME** -S/T- *feat:* The BLACKBYRDS on
    *BGP/ACE (Pinn): CDBGPM 094 (CD) BGPD 1094 (LP)*
**CORONATION STREET** (Granada 9/12/60-1998) theme mus:
    ERIC SPEAR *see COLLECTIONS 2,33,367*
      'THE CORONATION STREET ALBUM' *feat* **The CAST** *with*
      *guests* CLIFF RICHARD-HOLLIES-MICHAEL BALL & DEUCE
      *EMI PREM: CD(TC)COROTV 1 (CD/MC)* also '25TH ANNI
      VERSARY ALB' *K-TEL: ECD 3115 (CD) EMC 2115 (MC)*
      'Best Of' V.Arts *EMI GOLD: CD(TC)MFP 6310 (CD/MC)*
**COSBY SHOW The** (USA C4 20/1/85) series theme mus by:
    STU GARDNER-BILL COSBY *see COLLECTIONS 12,242,345*
**COSI** (1996) Music score: STEPHEN ENDELMAN -S/T- Imp
    *ICON (Pinn.Imports): ICON 19961 (CD)*

COSMIC EYE - see 'JOURNEY TO NEXT'
COTTON CLUB The (1985) Music score: JOHN BARRY -S/T-
   reissue: GEFFEN USA (Sil.Screen): GEF 24062 (CD)
   see also COLLECTION 24
COUNT DRACULA (1970) Music sco: BRUNO NICOLAI -S/T-
   PAN Imprt (Silva Screen): PAN 2502 (CD)
COUNT DUCKULA (Thames 6/9/88) theme mus: MIKE HARDING
   vocal by Sarah Harding on Coll 'KID'S THEMES'
COUNT OF LUXEMBOURG The (OPERETTA) Music: FRANZ LEHAR
   English lyr:ERIC MASCHWITZ New Sadlers Wells Cast
   English Highlights TER (Disc): CDTER 1050 (CD)
COUNT OF MONTE CRISTO The (1976) Mus: ALLYN FERGUSON
   -S/T- includes 'MAN IN THE IRON MASK' mus (Allyn
   Ferguson) PROMETHEUS (Sil.Screen): PCD 130 (CD)
COUNTDOWN (C4 from 2/11/82-98) music: ALAN HAWKSHAW.NA
COUNTESS FROM HONG KONG A (1967) Music score: CHARLES
   CHAPLIN see COLLECTIONS 56,57
COUNTESS MARITZA (OPERETTA) Mus: EMERICH KALLMANN Engl
   ish lyr: NIGEL DOUGLAS  New Sadlers Wells Cast
   Highlights in English TER (Disc) (CD)(ZC)TER 1051
COUNTRY DIARY OF AN EDWARDIAN LADY see COLLECTION 353
COUNTRYMAN (1982) Reggae music -S/T- feat: BOB MARLEY &
   WAILERS-ASWAD-TOOTS & MAYTALS-LEE SCRATCH PERRY-
   -S/T- Reggae Refresh-ISLAND (Poly): RRCD 44(CD)
COURAGEOUS CAT AND MINUTE MOUSE (USA TV) see COLL.340
COURIER The (88) Music sco: DECLAN McMANUS (Elvis Cost
   ello) Songs: U2-Something Happens-Hothouse Flowers
   Cry Before Dawn -S/T- VIRGIN (EMI):CDV 2517 (CD)
COURT JESTER The (1955) Songs (Sylvia Fine-Sammy Cahn)
   with DANNY KAYE -S/T- also incl.songs from 'HANS
   CHRISTIAN ANDERSEN' VARESE (Pinn): VSD 5498 (CD)
COVER UP (USA 1985) theme "Holding Out For A Hero"
   see COLLECTION 168
COWBOYS The (1971) Music score: JOHN WILLIAMS -S/T-
   VARESE (Pinn): VSD 5540 (CD) see COLLECT 298,394
COWGIRLS (ORIG BROADWAY CAST RECORDING)
   VARESE (Pinn): VSD 5740 (CD)
CRACKER (Granada 22/10/95) theme & incidental music by
   RICK WENTWORTH (prev. JULIAN WASTALL) unavailable
CRADLE WILL ROCK The (ORIG CAST 1985) Songs: MARC BLITZ
   STEIN TER (Disc): CDTEM2 1105 (2CD)
CRAFT The (1995) Music sco: GRAEME REVELL 2 soundtracks
   music score -S/T- VARESR (Pinn): VSD 5732 (CD)
   songs V.Art -S/T- SONY: 484 152-2 (CD) -4(MC) feat:
   ELASTICA-HEATHER NOVA-OUR LADY PEACE-LOVE SPIT LOVE
CRAPSTON VILLAS (C4 27/10/95) orig mus: ROWLAND LEE..NA
CRASH (1996) Music score: HOWARD SHORE -S/T- on
   MILAN (BMG): 74321 40198-2 (CD)
CRASH AND BURN (1991) Music score: RICHARD BAND -S/T-
   INTRADA (Silva Screen): MAF 7033CD (CD)
CRAZY FOR YOU - songs by George and Ira Gershwin
   1.ORIG LONDON CAST 1993 w: RUTHIE HENSHALL-KIRBY WARD
   FIRST NIGHT (Pinn): CASTCD 37 (CD) CASTC 37 (MC)
   2.ORIG BROADWAY CAST 1992 EMI: CDC 754618-2 (CD)

CREATURE FROM THE BLACK LAGOON (54) Mus: Hans J.Salter
    + mus.from 'HITLER' (61) 'BLACK SHIELD OF FALWORTH'
    (54) 'INCREDIBLE SHRINKING MAN'(57) (Hans J.Salter)
    *VARESE (Pinn): VSD 5407 (CD)*
CREATURES THE WORLD FORGOT - see *COLLECTION 266*
CRICKET (BBC 1970's-98) Theme "Soul Limbo" by BOOKER T.
    & MG's see *COLLECTIONS 4,155,167*
CRIES AND WHISPERS (1972) see *COLLECTION 79*
CRIME BEAT (BBC1 11/3/96) theme music: CHRIS CAWTE...*NA*
CRIME STORY (USA ITV 89) Theme "Runaway" (Del Shannon
    Max Crook) by DEL SHANNON *TV version unavailable*
    DEL SHANNON original on various compilations
CRIME TRAVELLER (BBC1 1/3/97) music composed and
    performed by ANNE DUDLEY *unavailable*
CRIMEAN WAR The (C4 9/11/97) Music score: NEIL BRAND
    Russian music: PYOTR SAVCHENKO & THE RUSSIAN FOLK
    ENSEMBLE *unavailable*
CRIMES OF PASSION (1984) Music sco (Rick Wakeman) Songs
    "It's A Lovely Life" (theme) (R.Wakeman-N.Gimbel)
    "Dangerous Woman" (Bell-Crumley) by MAGGIE BELL
    -S/T- *PRESIDENT (BMG): RWCD 3(CD) RWK 3(MC)*
CRIMETIME (1996) Music: DAVID A.STEWART -S/T- inc V.Arts
    *POLLYANNA Prod (Pinn): POLLYPREM 002 (CD)*
CRIMEWATCH UK (BBC1 7/6/84-1998) Theme mus "Emergency"
    see *COLLECTION 6*
CRIMSON PIRATE (1952) see *COLLECTION 332*
CRIMSON TIDE (1995) Music score HANS ZIMMER -S/T- on
    *MILAN (Polyg): 162025-2 (CD)*
CRISSCROSS (1991) Music score: TREVOR JONES -S/T-
    *INTRADA USA (Silva Screen): MAFCD 7021 (CD)*
CROCODILE DUNDEE (1986) Music score: PETER BEST -S/T-
    *SILVA SCREEN (Koch): FILMCD 009 (CD)*
CROCODILE SHOES (BBC1 10/11/94) music: TONY McANANEY
    "Crocodile Shoes" sung by JIMMY NAIL -S/T- on
    *EAST WEST (WEA): 4509 98556-2 (CD) -4 (MC)* title
CROCODILE SHOES 2 (BBC1 14/11/96) *featur* JIMMY NAIL
    -S/T- *EAST WEST (WEA): 0630 16935-2 (CD) -4 (MC)*
CROSSFIRE (1947) Music score: ROY WEBB see *Coll*
    'CURSE OF THE CAT PEOPLE'
CROSSING DELANCEY (1988) Music sco: PAUL CHIHARA -S/T-
    *VARESE (Pinn) VSC 5201 (CD)*
CROSSROADS (Central 2/11/64 - 4/4/88 | 4510 episodes)
    Orig theme 'Crossroads' TONY HATCH 1964-1987 *also*
    by PAUL McCARTNEY & WINGS on 'VENUS and MARS'*(EMI)*
    see *COLLECTIONS 2,3,168,182,358,364,367,368,372*
CROW The (1993) Music score: GRAEME REVELL + Var.Arts
    -S/T- (score) *VARESE (Pinn): VSD 5499 (CD)*
    -S/T- (songs) *WB (WEA): 7567 82519-2(CD) 4(MC)*
CROW The (2): CITY OF ANGELS (1996) Music score: GRAEME
    REVELL -S/T- with V.Artists HOLE/FILTER/BUSHG/WHITE
    ZOMBIE/SVEN MARY THREE/ABOVE THE LAW with FROST etc
    *HOLLYWOOD-POLYDOR (Poly): 533 147-2 (CD) -4 (MC)*
CROW ROAD The (BBC2 4/11/96) theme and incidental music
    composed and performed by COLIN TOWNS *unavailable*

CROWN COURT (Granada 1972) closing theme music "Distant
    Hills" (Reno-Haseley) *see COLLECTION 357*
CROWS - *see Collections* 'SIMONETTI PROJECT'
CRUCIBLE The (1996) Music score: GEORGE FENTON -S/T- on
    *RCA Victor (BMG): 09026 68666-2 (CD)*
CRUEL SEA The (1953) *see COLLECTION 225*
CRUMB (BBC2 26/12/96) Music: DAVID BOEDDINGHAUS & CRAIG
    VENTRESCO -S/T- *RYKODISC (Vital): RCD 10322 (CD)*
CRY BABY (1989) Music score: PATRICK WILLIAMS -S/T- on
    *MCA: MCLD 19260 (CD)*
CRY FREEDOM (1987) Music: GEORGE FENTON-JONAS GWANGWA
    -S/T- *MCA (SIlva Screen): MCAD 6224 (CD)*
CRY IN THE DARK A (1988) Music sco: BRUCE SMEATON *also*
    Suites from 'The Assault' mus: Jurriaan Andriessen
    'The Rosegarden' (Egisto MACCHI) 'The Naked Cage'
    (Christopher L.STONE) *SIL.SCREEN: SIL 1527-2 (CD)*
CRY THE BELOVED COUNTRY (1995) Music score: JOHN BARRY
    -S/T- *EPIC (Sony): 483 551-2 (CD) -4 (MC)*
CRYING GAME The (1992) Music sc: ANNE DUDLEY Song "The
    Crying Game" (Geoff Stevens) -S/T- feat Var.Arts
    *reissue: POLYDOR: 517024-2 (CD)*
CRYSTAL MAZE The (C4 15/2/90) theme music by ZACK
    LAURENCE *unavailable*
CURDLED (1996) Music -S/T- feat Var.Arts: BLAZERS-SLASH
    JOSEPH JULIAN GONZALES-ROSANA-LATIN BROTHERS etc.
    *GEFFEN (BMG): GED 25103 (CD) DELETED 97*
CURE The (1995) Music score: DAVE GRUSIN -S/T- on
    *GRP / MCA (BMG): GRP 9828-2 (CD) DELETED 97*
CURSE OF THE CAT PEOPLE (1944) Music score: ROY WEBB
    *CLOUD NINE (Silva Screen): CNS 5008 (CD) see also
    Coll* 'CURSE OF THE CAT PEOPLE'
CUTTHROAT ISLAND (1995) Mus sco: JOHN DEBNEY w. LONDON
    SYMPHONY ORCH  *SILVA SCR (Koch): FILMCD 178 (CD)*
    *see also COLLECTION 332*
CYBERCITY OEDO 808 (Animated 94 MANGA/C4 19/8/95) Mus
    score (-) -S/T- issued  *DEMON (Pinn): DSCD 8 (CD)*
CYBILL (USA/C4 5/1/96) title song "Nice Work If You Can
    Get It" (G.& I.Gershwin) arr.by TOM SCOTT sung by
    CYBILL SHEPHERD / addit mus: TOM SCOTT *unavailable*
CYCLO (95) Music score: TON-THAT TIET with Var.Artists
    -S/T- *MILAN (BMG): 74321 30108-2 (CD) see also*
    *COLLECTIONS* 'MUSIC FROM THE ORIENT'
CYRANO DE BERGERAC (1950) Music score: DIMITRI TIOMKIN
    on Coll 'HIGH NOON' *RCA (BMG): 09026 62658-2 (CD)*
CYRANO DE BERGERAC (1990) Music sco: JEAN-CLAUDE PETIT
    -S/T- *COLOSSEUM (Pinn): CST 348046 (CD)*
    *see also* 'JEAN DE FLORETTE'
**D** AD (BBC1 25/9/97) theme "Tijuana Taxi" HERB ALPERT &
    HIS TIJUANA BRASS on 'The Very Best Of HERB ALPERT'
    *A.& M.(Poly): CDMID 170 (CD) CMID 170 (MC)*
DAD'S ARMY (BBC1 31/7/68-77) theme "Who Do Think You
    Are Kidding Mr.Hitler" (J.Perry-D.Taverner) sung by
    BUD FLANAGAN O.Cast Rec *BBC (Pinn): ZBBC 1140 (MC)*
    *see COLLECTIONS 2,3,31,168,372*

DAKTARI (USA TV) *see COLLECTION 340*

DALES DIARY The (YTV only) theme music "Overture" from
   'The Wasps' (VAUGHAN WILLIAMS) complete version on
   *EMI CLASSICS: CDM 565 130-2 (CD)*
DALLAS (UKGO 2/11/93 USA 80 / BBC1 1978-6/10/91) theme:
   JERROLD IMMEL *see COLLECT.159,168,341,373,382*
DALZIEL AND PASCOE (BBC1 16/3/96) original music by
   BARRINGTON PHELOUNG *unavailable*
DAMAGE (1993) Music score: ZBIGNIEW PREISNER -S/T- on
   *VARESE (Pinn): VSD 5406 (CD)*
DAMES (1934) *COLLECTION with* 'SAN FRANCISCO'/'SUZY' on
   *GREAT MOVIE THEMES (Targ-BMG): CD 60022 (CD)*
DAMES AT SEA - songs by Jim Wise with George Haimsohn
   and Robin Miller
   1.ORIG UK TOURING CAST 1989 *w:* BRIAN CANT-SANDRA DICK
   INSON-JOSEPHINE BLAKE *TER (Disc): CD(ZC)TER 1169*
DAMIEN: OMEN 2 (1978) Music score: JERRY GOLDSMITH
   -S/T- *SILVA SCREEN (Koch): FILMCD 002 (CD)*
DAMBUSTERS The (1955) Theme music: ERIC COATES
   *see COLLECTIONS 35,130,238,384*
DAMN YANKEES (FILM MUSICAL 1958) Songs: RICHARD ADLER-
   JERRY ROSS -S/T- *RCA Austr (S.Scr): 1047-2 (CD) -4*
DAMNED The (1969) Music sco: MAURICE JARRE on 'MAURICE
   JARRE TRILOGY' *DRG (Pinn): DRGCD 32906 (2CD)*
DANCE A LITTLE CLOSER (Musical) Music: CHARLES STROUSE
   Lyrics: ALAN JAY LERNER *Original Broadway Cast* on
   *TER (Disc): CDTER 1174 (CD)  ZCTER 1174 (MC)*
DANCE TO THE MUSIC OF TIME (C4 9/10/97) Music score by
   CARL DAVIS *unavailable* / theme song "20th Century
   Blue" (N.Coward) sung by NOEL COWARD (1931) 'The
   Compact Coward' *EMI: CZ 185 (CD)*
DANCES WITH WOLVES (1990) Music score: JOHN BARRY -S/T-
   *EPIC (SM): 467591-2(CD) -4(MC) ZK 66817 (CDspecial)*
   *see COLLECTIONS 21,24,26,55,63,201,319,397,398*
DANIEL BOONE (USA) *see COLLECTION 339*
DANCING IN THE STREET: A Rock'n'Roll History (BBC2 15/6
   /96) featuring VAR ARTISTS -S/T- *ELITE-CARLTON:
   (CHE): 30364 0016-2 (2CD) 30364 0016-4 (2MC)*
DANGER MAN (ITV 11/9/1960-68) Theme mus "High Wire" by
   EDWIN ASTLEY -S/T- *RAZOR & TIE (Koch): RF 21512(CD)*
   *see COLLECTIONS 3,4,109,356,357,364,368,372*
DANGERFIELD (BBC1 27/1/95) theme and incident.music by
   NIGEL HESS *see COLLECTIONS 5,33,192*
DANGEROUS GROUND (1997) Music sco: STANLEY CLARKE -S/T-
   *CHIPS-ZOMBA (Pinn): CHIP 181 (CD) HIP 181 (2LP)*
DANGEROUS LIAISONS (1988) Music Score: GEORGE FENTON
   -S/T- *VIRGIN (EMI): CDV 2583 (CD)*
   *see also COLLECTIONS 66,75,171*
DANGEROUS MINDS (1995) Music score composed & performed
   by WENDY and LISA -S/T- *feat:* Various Artists
   issued on *MCA (BMG): MCD 11228 (CD) MCC 11228 (MC)*
DANGEROUS MOONLIGHT (1941) Theme mus 'Warsaw Concerto'
   by RICHARD ADDINSELL *see COLLECTIONS 160,387*

DANTE'S PEAK (1997) Music score: JOHN FRIZZELL with the
    main theme composed by JAMES NEWTON HOWARD -S/T- on
    *VARESE (Pinn): VSD 5793 (CD)*
DANZON (1992) Music sco: DANZONERA DIMAS-FELIPE PEREZ
    -S/T- *DRG (Pinn): CDSBL 12605 (CD)*
DARK CITY (1950) *see COLLECTION 392*

DARK HALF The (1992) Music sco: CHRISTOPHER YOUNG -S/T-
    *VARESE (Pinn): VSD 5340 (CD)*
DARK SHADOWS (USA Soap 1966-70) "Quentin's Theme" by
    Charles Randolph Green / ROBERT COBERT ORCHESTRA
    -S/T-*VARESE: VSD 5702 (CD) see also COLLECTION 340*
DARK SKIES (USA96 / C4 13/1/97) theme: MICHAEL HOENIG
    *see COLLECTION 273*
DARK STAR (1974) Music score: JOHN CARPENTER -S/T-
    *VARESE (Pinn): VSD 5327 (CD)*
    *see COLLECTIONS 178,273,300*
DARKMAN (1990) Music score: DANNY ELFMAN -S/T- *Impt.*
    *MCA USA (Silva Screen): MCAD 10094 (CD)*
DARLING BUDS OF MAY The (Yorkshire 7/4/91) theme mus
    PIP BURLEY Incid.mus BARRIE GUARD conducting the
    ENGLISH LIGHT ORCH (Barrie Guard) *MFP S/T Music*
    *(EMI): CD(TC)MFP 6128 (CD/MC)* spokenword MC:
    *MCI (TBD): TALKMC 015 (2MC) 016 (2MC)*
DARTS (BBC1/2 All Competitions) Theme mus "Cranes" by
    DOUGLAS WOOD orig by DOUGLAS WOOD GROUP *deleted*
DAS BARBECU (00) ORIG CAST RECORDING -S/T-
    *VARESE (Pinn): VSD 5593 (CD)*
DAS BOOT (W.Germany) - *see under* 'BOAT The'
DASTARDLY AND MUTTLEY *see COLLECTIONS 341,370*
DAVE ALLEN (Carlton/Noel Gay 7/1/93) theme "Blarney's
    Stoned" ALAN HAWKSHAW *see COLLECTIONS 317,360*
DAVID DIMBLEBY'S INDIA (BBC2 12/7/97) m: RON DE JONG.*NA*
DAVID JASON IN HIS ELEMENT (YTV 28/10/97) orig music
    by BRIAN BENNETT *unavailable*
DAVY CROCKETT (1955) Theme s "Ballad Of Davy Crockett"
    (Tom BLackburn-George Bruns) sung by FESS PARKER
    on 'Americana' *COLUMBIA (SM): 468121-2(CD) -4(MC)*
DAWN OF THE DEAD (Film) - *see* under 'ZOMBIES'
DAY OF ANGER (1969) Music score: RIZ ORTOLANI + 'BEYOND
    THE LAW' (68) -S/T- *Impt (S.SCREEN): OST 110 (CD)*
DAY THE EARTH STOOD STILL The (1951) Music sco: BERNARD
    HERRMANN Suite on 'Great Film Music' *Coll DECCA*
    *Phase 4 (Poly): 443 899-2 (CD)* also incl JOURNEY TO
    THE CENTRE OF THE EARTH-SEVENTH VOYAGE OF SINBAD
    FAHRENHEIT 451-THREE WORLDS OF GULLIVER *also avail*
    *able:* Symphonic Suite (Nat.P.O.-Fred Steiner) with
    'The Kentuckian' *Imp PREAMBLE (S.Scr): PRCD 1777*
DAY THE FISH CAME OUT (1967) Music: MIKIS THEODORAKIS
    -S/T- *SAKKARIS (Pinn): SR 50088 (CD)*
DAY TODAY The (Talkback prod/BBC2 19/1/94) music by
    JONATHAN WHITEHEAD & CHRISTOPHER MORRIS *unavailable*
DAYLIGHT (1996) Music score: RANDY EDELMAN -S/T-
    *UNIVERSAL-MCA (BMG): UND 53024 (CD)*

DAYS AND NIGHTS OF MOLLY DODD (USA TV) *see COLLECT.345*
DAYS OF HOPE (Musical 91) Songs: HOWARD GOODALL Orig.
   London Cast *TER (Disc): (CD)ZCTER 1183 (CD/MC)*
DAYS OF MAJESTY (Granite Prod for YTV 2/6/93) orig mus
   BARRINGTON PHELOUNG  TV -S/T- on *LONDON (Polyg)*
   *828 427-2 (CD) 828 427-4 (MC)*
DAYS OF WINE AND ROSES The (62)  Music: HENRY MANCINI
   *see COLLECTIONS 27,177,218,243,244*
DAYTRIPPER (1996 Snowboarding Video) -S/T-
   *A.& M. (Poly): 540 677-2 (CD) -4 (MC)*
DAZED AND CONFUSED (1994) ALICE COOPER-DEEP PURPLE-KISS
   ZZ TOP -S/T- *GIANT (BMG): 4321 16675-2 (CD) -4(MC)*
DEACON BRODIE (BBC2 8/3/07) music: SIMON BOSWELL....*NA*
DEAD AGAIN (1991) Music score: PATRICK DOYLE -S/T-
   *VARESE (Pinn): VSD (VSC) 5339 (CD/MC)*
DEAD GOOD SHOW The (Gran 9/11/92) theme "Beat Girl" by
   JOHN BARRY *PLAY IT AGAIN (BMG-Con) PLAY 001 (CD)*
DEAD MAN (1995) Music score: NEIL YOUNG
   -S/T- *WB (WEA): 9362 46171-2 (CD)*
DEAD MAN WALKING (1995) T.song by BRUCE SPRINGSTEEN w
   JOHNNY CASH-SUZANNE VEGA-LY.LOVETT-MICHELLE SHOCKED
   -S/T- (songs) *COLUMB (Sony): 483 534-2(CD) -4(MC)*
   -S/T- (score) *COLUMB: 484107-2(CD) -4(MC)* delet 97
DEAD MEN DON'T WEAR PLAID (1981) Music sc: MIKLOS ROZSA
   -S/T- *PROMETHEUS (Silva Screen): PCD 126 (CD)*
DEAD POETS SOCIETY (1989) Music score: MAURICE JARRE
   *-S/T- MILAN (BMG): CDCH 558 (CD)* inc:'THE YEAR OF
   LIVING DANGEROUSLY' (M.Jarre)
   *see also COLLECTIONS 65,76,80,139,171,214*
DEAD PRESIDENTS (1995) Music score by DANNY ELFMAN
   -S/T- (score) *CAPITOL (EMI): 7248 35818-2 (CD)*
   -S/T- (songs 1) *EMI PREM: PRDCD 4 (CD)*
   -S/T- (songs 2) *EMI PREM: PRMDCD 5 (CD)*
DEAD RINGERS (1988) Music score: HOWARD SHORE + music
   from 'SCANNERS' (80) and 'The BROOD' (79) music by
   Howard Shore *SILVA SCREEN (Koch): FILMCD 115 (CD)*
DEAD SOLID PERFECT (1991) Music score: TANGERINE DREAM
   -S/T- *SILVA SCREEN (Koch): FILMCD 079 (CD)*
DEAD ZONE The (1983) Music score: MICHAEL KAMEN -S/T-
   *MILAN (BMG): 239 762 (CD) 239 764 (MC)*
DEADFALL (1968) Mus sco: JOHN BARRY / "My Love Has Two
   Faces" sung by SHIRLEY BASSEY / Guitar solo by
   RENATA TARREGO -S/T- *RETROGRADE: FSM 80124-2 (CD)*
DEADLY ADVICE (1993) Music score: RICHARD HARVEY theme
   on Coll on *SILVA SCREEN (Koch): FILMCD 172 (CD)*
DEADLY CARE (1992) Mus: EDGAR FROESE-CHRISTOPHER FRANKE
   TANGERINE DREAM-S/T- *S.SCREEN Koch: FILMCD 121(CD)*
DEAN MARTIN SHOW The (USA TV) *see COLLECTION 343*
DEATH AND THE MAIDEN (1994) Music sco: WOJCIECH KILAR
   -S/T- on *ERATO (BMG): 4509 99727-2 (CD)*
DEATH BECOMES HER (1992) Music sc: ALAN SILVESTRI
   -S/T- *VARESE (Silva Screen): VSD 5375 (CD)*
DEATH BEFORE DISHONOUR (1987) Music sc: BRIAN MAY
   -S/T- *PROMETHEUS (Silva Screen): PCD 118 (CD)*

DEATH IN BRUNSWICK (1991) Music sco: PHILIP JUDD -S/T-
  *ALHAMBRA Germany Imp. (Silva Screen): A.8933 (CD)*
DEATH IN VENICE (1971) Music: GUSTAV MAHLER (Symphony
  numbers 3 & 5) -S/T- *SONY Fra (Discov): SK 70097
  (CD) ST 70097 (MC) see also COLLECTIONS 68,97,258*
DEATH ON THE NILE - *see COLLECTION 62*
DEATH RIDES A HORSE (1969) Music score ENNIO MORRICONE
  -S/T- also inc.'A PISTOL FOR RINGO' + 'THE RETURN
  OF RINGO' *Import (SILVA SCREEN): OST 107 (CD)*
DEATH WARRANT (1990) - *see under* 'KICKBOXER'
DEATH WISH (1974) Music: HERBIE HANCOCK *selection also
  includes* 'DEATH WISH 4' (87-John Bisharat-Val McCal
  lum) 'TEN TO MIDNIGHT' (84-Robert O Ragland) 'MURPH
  Y'S LAW' (86-Marc Donahue-Val McCallum) 'TOUGH GUYS
  DON'T DANCE' (87-Angelo Badalamenti) 'X-RAY' (80-Ar
  lon Ober) *SILVA SCREEN: 1529-2 (CD)*
DEEP The (Doc.series)(C4 13/7/97) music: JAI YEN...*NA*
DEEP COVER (1992) Music sc: MICHEL COLOMBIER -S/T-
  Var.artists *EPIC (Sony M): 471669-2 (CD)*
DEEP RED (Profondo Rosso) *see COLLECTION 312*
DEERHUNTER The (1978) Music sco: STANLEY MYERS -S/T-
  *CAPITOL (S.Screen) 92058-2(CD) -4(MC)* 'Cavatina'
  perf: John WILLIAMS *see COLLS.35,79,169,267,285,362*
DEF-CON 4 (1985) Music sco: CHRISTOPHER YOUNG -S/T- and
  includes Music from "Avenging Angel" (85) "Torment"
  (85) "The Telephone" (88) Music (Christopher Young)
  on *INTRADA USA (Sil.Screen): MAF 7010D (CD) and*
DEFENCE OF THE REALM (BBC1 8/8/96) theme mus "School Of
  Mysteries" JOHN HARLE on 'SILENCIUM' *see COLL.407*
DEFENCE OF THE REALM (1985) Music score: RICHARD HARVEY
  theme on *SILVA SCREEN (Koch): FILMCD 172 (CD)*
DEKALOG (The Ten Commandments) (1988) Music: ZBIGNIEW
  PREISNER -S/T- *AMPLITUDE (Discov): AMP 709 (CD)*
DELERIA (1987) Music s: SIMON BOSWELL-STEFANO MAINETTI
  *LUCITOLA MEDIA (Backtrack/S.Scr): LMCD 002 (CD)*
DELIA SMITH'S SUMMER COLLECTION (BBC2 4/5/93) theme mus
  "Summertime" (George Gershwin) *BBC arr.unavailable*
DELIA SMITH'S WINTER COLLECTION (BBC2 11/10/95 theme
  "Winter Wonderland" arr. by SIMON WEBB *unavailable*
DELIVERANCE (1972) M: ERIC WEISSBERG "Duelling Banjos"
  feat STEVE MANDELL -S/T- *WB (WEA): K(2)(4)46214
  (CD/MC/LP) see also COLLECTION 361*
DELTA FORCE II: THE Columbian (1990) Music: FREDERICK
  TALGORN -S/T- *ALHAMBRA (Pinn): A.8921 (CD)*
DELUSION (1991) Music sco: BARRY ADAMSON *MUTE:
  IONIC 4 (LP) IONIC 4C (MC) IONIC 4CD (CD)*
DEMOLITION MAN (1993) Music s: ELLIOT GOLDENTHAL
  -S/T- *VARESE (Pinn): VSD 5447 (CD)*
DEMON HEADMASTER The (BBC1 2/1/96) Music sco: RICHARD
  ATTREE (BBC Radiophonic Workshop) *unavailable*
DEMON KNIGHT (1994) Various Artists -S/T-
  *ATLANTIC WEA 7567 82725-2 (CD) 7567 82725-4 (MC)*
DEMPSEY & MAKEPEACE (LWT 11/1/85) theme: ALAN PARKER
  *see COLLECTIONS 5,175,357*

DENNIS THE MENACE (USA) *see COLLECTION 339*
DEPARTMENT S (ITC 9/3/69) theme music: EDWIN ASTLEY
   *see COLLECTIONS 2,3,357,364,368,372*
DEPUTY The *see COLLECTION 2*
DES RES (LWT 17/4/97) music: DEBBIE WISEMAN *unavailable*
DESERT SONG - songs by Sigmund Romberg - Oscar Hammer
   stein II and Otto Harbach
   1. ORIG LONDON CAST 1927 *w:* EDITH DAY-PHEBE BRUNE-GENE
      GERRARD-CLARICE HARDWICKE-DENNIS HOEY-BARRY MACKAY
      *plus music from 'NEW MOON (1929) 'BLUE TRAIN' (27)*
      *PEARL (Pavilion): GEMMCD 9100(CD)*
   2. STUDIO RECORDING *w:* GORDON MacRAE & DOROTHY KIRSTEN
      *+ music from 'New Moon' and 'The Student Prince'*
      *HMV (EMI): CDM 769052-2 (CD)*
   3. STUDIO RECORDING *with:* MARIO LANZA *also music from*
      *The STUDENT PRINCE RCA (BMG) GD(GK)60048 (CD/MC)*
DESMOND'S (H.Barclay Prod/C4 5/1/89-1995) Theme "Don't
   Scratch My Soca" by TRIX WORRELL-JOHN COLLINS...*NA*
DESPERADO (1995) Music sco: LOS LOBOS -S/T- *feat* LATIN
   PLAYBOYS-TITO & TARANTULA-LINK WRAY-DIRE STRAITS
   *EPIC Soundtrax (Sony): 480 944-2 (CD)*
DESPERATE REMEDIES (1993) Music score: PETER SCHOLES
   feat music by Verdi-Berlioz-Strauss *feat soprano*
   CARMEL CARROLL -S/T- *MILAN (BMG): 887 938-2 (CD)*
DESEPERATELY SEEKING SUSAN (1985) Score: THOMAS NEWMAN
   +'Making Mr.Right' *VARESE (Pinn): VCD 47291 (CD)*
DESTRY RIDES AGAIN (O:LONDON CAST 1979) Songs: HAROLD
   ROME *featuring* JILL GASCOINE and Co. / Recording
   *TER (Disc): CDTER 1034 (CD) ZCTER 1034 (MC)*
DETECTIVE The (BBC 1968) Mus: RON GRAINER *see COLL.7*
DETECTIVES The (BBC1/Celador 27/1/93) theme music by
   KEITH and MATTHEW STRACHAN *unavailable*
DEUX ANGLAISES ET LE CONTINENT *see* 'TWO ENGLISH GIRLS'
DEVICES AND DESIRES (Anglia 4/1/91) theme mus "Elegy"
   RICHARD HARVEY *on Coll* 'SHROUD FOR A NIGHTINGALE'
   *SILVA SCREEN (Koch): FILMCD 172 (CD)*
DEVIL AND DANIEL WEBSTER The (aka 'All That Money Can
   Buy) (1941) music score: BERNARD HERRMANN / Suite
   on Coll 'CONCERTO MACABRE' *KOCH INT: 37609-2 (CD)*
DEVIL DOLL The (1936) *see COLLECTION 392*
DEVIL IN A BLUE DRESS (1995) Music sc: ELMER BERNSTEIN
   -S/T-JIMMY WITHERSPOON-I.BONE WALKER-DUKE ELLINGTON
   ROY MILTON-WYNONIE HARRIS-PEE WEE CRAYTON-THELONIO.
   MONK-BULLMOOSE JACKSON-AMOS MILBURN-MEMPHIS SLIM-
   LLOYD GLENN *COLUMBIA (SM): 481 379-2 (CD) -4 (MC)*
DEVIL RIDES OUT The (1968) Music sc: JAMES BERNARD *see*
   *Coll* 'DEVIL RIDES OUT' *S.SCREEN: FILMCD 174 (CD)*
DEVIL'S OWN The (1996) Music sco: JAMES HORNER -S/T-
   *TOMMY BOY (RTM-Disc): TBCD 1204 (CD)*
DEVIL'S TOOTHPICK The (1992) Doc.Brazilian/USA music:
   GILBERTO GIL-BILLY COBHAM-KENIA-LARRY CORYELL etc.
   *CTI-KUDU (New Note-Pinn): CTI 10122 (CD)*
DIABOLIQUE (1996) Music score: RANDY EDELMAN -S/T- on
   *EDEL-CINERAMA (Pinn): 002258-2CIN*

DIAMONDS ARE FOREVER (1971) Music sco: JOHN BARRY t.
   song (J.Barry-Don Black) sung by SHIRLEY BASSEY
   -S/T- *reiss EMI PREMIER: CZ 554 (CD)* see JAMES BOND
   FILM INDEX p.346 *and COLLECTIONS 20,25,26,29,305*
DIAL MIDNIGHT (LWT 95) theme music: SIMON MOORE - PHIL
   BINDING *see COLLECTION 33*

---

DIANA PRINCESS OF WALES FUNERAL SERVICE 6TH SEPTEM.1997
Official BBC Recording Of The Complete Funeral Service
Of DIANA PRINCESS OF WALES 1961-1997 All record company
profits to THE DIANA, PRINCESS OF WALES, MEMORIAL FUND
*BBC WORLDWIDE / POLYGRAM CLASS: 449 800-2 (CD) -4 (MC)*

---

DIARY OF ANNE FRANK The (1959) Music sco: ALFRED NEWMAN
   *TSUNAMI (Silva Screen): TSU 0122 (CD)*
DICK BARTON (ITV 78) theme mus "Devil's Galop" CHARLES
   WILLIAMS *see COLLECTIONS 44,96,137,163*
DICK EMERY SHOW (BBC1 70's) theme music: JACK POINT
   *see COLLECTION 229*
DICK POWELL THEATRE (USA61) *see COLLECTION 182*
DICK VAN DYKE SHOW (USA) *see COLLECTIONS 339,374*
DID YOU SEE (BBC2 80-93) orig ser.(1980-88 with Ludovic
   Kennedy) theme music 'Think Big' (Francis MONKMAN)
   *see COLLECTION 6* / (20/10/91-93 w.Jeremy Paxman)
   title theme (Anthony & Gaynor Sadler) *unavailable*
DIDIER (1997) Music score: PHILIPPE CHANY
   *XIII BIZ (Discovery): LBS 1097010-2 (CD)*
DIE HARD (1988) Music sco: MICHAEL KAMEN -S/T- *reissue
   Fox (BMG): (unconfirmed) see COLLECTIONS 69,97,258*
DIE HARD 2: DIE HARDER (1989) Mus: MICHAEL KAMEN -S/T-
   *VARESE (Pinn): VSD 5273CD* see also CINEMA CLASSICS2
DIE HARD 3: WITH A VENGEANCE (1995) Music sco: MICHAEL
   KAMEN w: V/A -S/T- *RCA (BMG): 09026 68306-2 (CD)*
DIFFERENT STROKES (USA TV) *see COLLECTION 344*
DIFFERENT WORLD, A (USA series C4 from 22/9/88) theme
   music (Stu Gardner-Bill Cosby-Dawnn Lewis) sung by
   ARETHA FRANKLIN  (USA TV) *see COLLECTION 345*
DINOSAURS The (USA TV Ser 93) music by PETER MELNICK
   TV -S/T- *NARADA Cinema (Pinn): ND 66004 (CD)*
DIRTY DANCING (1987) Music score: JOHN MORRIS + V.Arts
   -S/T- *RCA: BD 86408 (CD) BK 86408 (MC)*
   'MORE DIRTY DANCING' *74321 36915-2 (CD) -4 (MC)*
   'LIVE'  music *RCA (BMG): PK 90336 (MC)*
DIRTY DANCING (USA 90 ITV 18/10/91) theme "(I've Had)
   The Time Of My Life" sung by BILL MEDLEY-JENNIFER
   WARNES *entry above see also COLLECTIONS 17,292*
DISCLOSURE (1994) Music score ENNIO MORRICONE -S/T- on
   *VIRGIN Movie Music (EMI): CDVMM 16 (CD)*
DISORDERLIES (1987) Music: RAY PARKER JNR & others
   -S/T- *re-issued on SPECTRUM (Poly): 551 137-2 (CD)*
DISCWORLD (TERRY PRATCHETT'S) (C4) 'SOUL MUSIC' album
   *PLUTO (Direct): TH 030746 (CD)*
DISTINGUISHED GENTLEMAN (1992) Music sc: RANDY EDELMAN
   -S/T- *VARESE (Silva Screen): VSD 5402 (CD)*

DIVA (1982) Music score: VLADIMIR COSMA *feat* 'La Wally' sung by WILHEMLMENIA FERNANDEZ -S/T- *MILAN (Silva Screen): 950 622 (CD) see also COLLECTIONS 52,63 65,69,81,97,139,146,171,258,276*

DIVORCE ME DARLING - Music and lyrics by SANDY WILSON Chichester Festival Theatre 1997 *RECORDING featuring* DAVID ALDER-SIMON BUTTERISS-KEVIN COLSON-TIM FLAVIN-ROSEMARY FORD-ANDREW HALLIDAY-LINZI HATELY-RUTHIE HENSHALL-LILANE MONTEVECCHI-JOAN SAVAGE-JACK TRIPP-MARTIN WEBB *TER (MC-THE): CDTER 1245 (CD)*

DIXON OF DOCK GREEN (BBC1 50's-70's) theme "An Ordinary Copper" (Jeff Darnell) *see COLLECTIONS 1,2*

DJANGO (1966) Music score: LUIS BACALOV -S/T- *ALHAMBRA (Discovery): A.8930 (CD)*

DOBIE GILLIS (USA) *see COLLECTION 339*

DOC HOLLYWOOD (1991) Music score: CARTER BURWELL -S/T- *VARESE (Pinn): VSD 5332 (CD)*

DOCTOR AT LARGE (ITV 1971) theme "Bond Street Parade" by ALAN TEW *see COLLECTIONS 3,168*

DOCTOR AT THE TOP (BBC1 21/2/91) *see COLLECTIONS 3,168 see also 'DOCTOR IN THE HOUSE'*

DOCTOR DOLITTLE (1967) songs by LESLIE BRICUSSE -S/T- featur: REX HARRISON-SAMANTHA EGGAR-ANTHONY NEWLEY *reissued -S/T- on PHILIPS (Poly): 534 500-2 (CD)*

DOCTOR FAUSTUS (1967) Music sco: MARIO NASCIMBENE -S/T- w: 'FRANCIS OF ASSISI' *DRG (Pinn) DRGCD 32965 (CD)*

DOCTOR FINLAY (Scottish TV 5/3/93) mus: RICHARD HARVEY played by The Scottish Chamber Orch (R.Harvey) *see COLLECTION 181*

DOCTOR FINLAY'S CASEBOOK (BBC1 1962-71) theme music "March from 'A Little Suite' No 2 by TREVOR DUNCAN *see COLLECTIONS 1,2,5,43,44,45,130,163,181*

DOCTOR GIGGLES (1992) Music score (Brian May) -S/T- (SCORE) *INTRADA (Silva Screen): MAF 7043CD* -S/T- (SONGS) *Victor USA:* unconfirmed

DOCTOR IN THE HOUSE (LWT 70)*see COLLECTIONS 3,168,229*

DOCTOR JEKYLL AND MS.HYDE (1994) Music: MARK McKENZIE -S/T- *INTRADA (Silva Screen Imp): MAF 7063D (CD)*

DOCTOR JEKYLL & SISTER HYDE (1971) Mus: DAVID WHITAKER *on Coll 'Omen The: 50 Years Of...' deleted*

DOCTOR KILDARE (USA 61) Theme music: JERRY GOLDSMITH *see COLLECTIONS 2,342,373*

DOCTOR NO (1962) Music score: MONTY NORMAN-JOHN BARRY -S/T- *reiss EMI PREM (EMI):CZ 558 (CD) see also COLLECTION 62* + JAMES BOND FILM INDEX p.348

DOCTOR QUINN: MEDICINE WOMAN (USA/ITV 28/5/93) orig music by WILLIAM OLVIS *unavailable*

DOCTOR WHO (1996) (BBC1 27/5/96) Music sco: JOHN DEBNEY (orig theme by RON GRAINER) + additional music by JOHN SPONSLER and LOUIS SERBE *unavailable*

DOCTOR WHO (BBC1 23/11/63-93) orig theme by RON GRAINER *fur theme music see the following* COLLECTS.3,4,7,109,138,273,301,344,364,368,372,402

*Continued next page...*

DOCTOR WHO (BBC1 23/11/63-93) ...*Continued*
    'THIRTY YEARS AT THE RADIOPHONIC WORKSHOP' (BBC)
    Music Var.Arts *BBC (Pinn) BBCCD 871 (CD) see also*
    (1) 'DR.WHO - VARIATIONS ON A THEME' various comp.
    *SILVA SCREEN (Koch): FILMCD 706 (CD)*
    'DOWNTIME' (Doctor Who Video) music: IAN LEVENE
    *SILVA SCREEN (Koch): FILMCD 717 (CD)*
    'SHAKEDOWN' Music MARK AYRES
    *SILVA SCREEN (Koch): FILMCD 718 (CD)*
    DOCTOR WHO: EVOLUTION feat music by RON GRAINER-
    KEFF McCULLOCH and DOMINIC GREEN
    *PRESTIGE (THE): RDSGP 0320 (CD)*
    DOCTOR WHO: VENGEANCE ON VAROS
    *BBC (Pinn): ZBBC 1932 (2MC)*
    *see also listing in TELE-TUNES 1994 p.73*
DOCTOR ZHIVAGO (1965) Music score: MAURICE JARRE
    -S/T- *reissue: EMI Premier (EMI): CDODEON 1 (CD)*
    *see also COLLECTIONS 81,120,203,214,215*
DOCTORS The (BBC1 69) m: TONY HATCH *see COLLECTION 182*
DOIN' TIME ON PLANET EARTH - see 'ALLAN QUARTERMAIN'
DOLLY SISTERS The 1945 MUSICAL) BETTY GRABLE-JUNE HAVER
    includes songs from 'ROSE OF WASHINGTON SQUARE' and
    'GOLD DIGGERS OF 1933' *TARGET (BMG): CD 60009 (CD)*
DOLORES CLAIBORNE (1995) Music sco: DANNY ELFMAN -S/T-
    *VARESE (Pinn): VSD 5602 (CD)*
DON JUAN DE MARCO (1994) Music sco: MICHAEL KAMEN "Have
    You Ever Really Loved A Woman" (Adams_Lange-Kamen)
    by BRYAN ADAMS -S/T- *A.& M. (Poly): 540 357-2 (CD)*
DON QUIXOTE (Spanish TV mini-series) music score: LALO
    SCHIFRIN -S/T- *PROMETHEUS (S.Scr): PCD 132 (CD)*
DONNA REED SHOW (USA) *see COLLECTION 339*
DONNIE BRASCO (1997) Music score: PATRICK DOYLE
    -S/T- (songs) *HOLLYWOOD (Polyg): 162102-2 (CD)*
    -S/T- (score) *VARESE (Pinnacle): VSD 5834 (CD)*
DON'T BE A MENACE (1995) Music score:
    -S/T- *Island (Poly): 524 146-2 (CD) -4 (MC)*
DON'T FORGET YOUR TOOTHBRUSH (Ginger Prod C4 12/2/94)
    original music by DAVID ARNOLD *unavailable*
DON'T LOOK NOW (1973) Music sco: PINO DONAGGIO -S/T-
    *TER (Disc): CDTER 1007 (CD) ZCTER 1007 (MC)*
DON'T WAIT UP (UKGold 28/1/93 orig BBC1 25/10/83)
    theme music by NICK INGHAM *unavailable*
DOOGIE HOWSER MD (USA) *see COLLECTIONS 12,345*
DOOM GENERATION The (1996) Ambient music sco: DAB GATTO
    -S/T- *V/A RCA America (BMG): 74321 31872-2 (CD)*
DOOMSDAY GUN The (1994) Music sco: RICHARD HARVEY suite
    on Coll 'SHROUD FOR A NIGHTINGALE' *see Colls*
DOORS The (1991) Music sco: BUDD CARR Original songs by
    JIM MORRISON & DOORS -S/T- *ELEKTRA (WEA): 7599*
    *61047-2 (CD) EKT 85C (MC) EKT 85 (LP)*
DOSH (C4 31/10/95) title theme music by PHIL BINDING
    and SIMON MOORE *unavailable*
DOUBLE IMPACT (1991) Music score: ARTHUR KEMPEL -S/T-
    *S.SCREEN (Koch): FILMCD 110 (CD) see 'KICKBOXER'*

DOUBLE INDEMNITY (1944) Music sco: MIKLOS ROZSA / Suite
    on Coll 'FILM NOIR CLASSICS' with 'THE KILLERS' and
    'THE LOST WEEKEND' feat NEW ZEALAND SYMPH.ORCH.cond
    by JAMES SEDARES on KOCH INT (Koch): 37375-2 (CD)
DOUBLE LIFE OF VERONIKA The (1991) Music sco: ZBIGNIEW
    PREISNER Choral music by Van Den Budenmayer -S/T-
    Impt (SILVA SCREEN): SID 001 (CD) SID 201K (MC)
DOUBLE TROUBLE see ELVIS PRESLEY INDEX p.348
DOWN BY LAW (1987) Music sco: JOHN LURIE and TOM WAITS
    Lounge Lizards-Arto Lindsay-Nana Vasconcelos -S/T-
    also includes 'VARIETY' -S/T- music: JOHN LURIE
    MADE TO MEASURE (New Note-Pinn): MTM 14 (CD)
DOWNTIME - see DOCTOR WHO (Television Section)
DR. see under 'DOCTOR'
DRACULA - see COLLECTIONS 119,121,206,209,223,260,262,
    274,354,378,404 AND ITEMS LISTED BELOW
DRACULA (1992) Music sco: WOJCIECH KILAR -S/T- featur
    "Love Song For A Vampire" performed by ANNIE LENNOX
    COLUMBIA (Sony M): 472 746-2 (CD)
DRACULA (1973) Music score: ROBERT COBERT theme music
    see COLLCTION 378
DRACULA (HAMMER STORY featuring CHRISTOPHER LEE & The
    HAMMER CITY ORCHESTRA) BGO (Pinn): BGOCD 240 (CD)
DRACULA see COLLECTION 209
DRACULA PRINCE OF DARKNESS see COLLECTION 209
DRAGNET (USA 50s) theme: WALTER SCHUMANN
    see COLLECTION 100,101,108,339
DRAGON: THE BRUCE LEE STORY (1993) Mus: RANDY EDELMAN
    -S/T- MCA (BMG): MCAD(MCAC) 10827 (CD/MC)
DRAGONHEART (1996) Music score: RANDY EDELMAN -S/T-
    MCA (BMG): MCAD 11449 (CD)
DRAT THE CAT! (MUSICAL) songs: MILTON SCHAFER-IRA LEVIN
    ORIG 1997 USA STUDIO RECORDING featuring SUSAN EGAN
    JASON GRAAE-JONATHAN FREEMAN-JUDY KAYE on VARESE
    (Pinn):VSD 5721 (CD) see also COLL 'LOST IN BOSTON'
DRAUGHTSMAN'S CONTRACT The (1983) Music: MICHAEL NYMAN
    -S/T- CHARISMA (Virgin-EMI): CAS(MC)(CD) 1158
DRAW! (1984) Music sc: KEN WANNBERG -S/T- inc.mus.from
    'RED RIVER' PROMETHEUS (Silva Scr):PCD 129 (CD)
DREAM DEMON (1988) Music: BILL NELSON Theme on 'Duplex'
    COCTEAU (Pinn): CDJCD 22(CD) TCJCD 22(MC) JCD 22
DREAM IS ALIVE The - see 'BLUE PLANET'
DREAM LOVER (1994) Music score: CHRISTOPHER YOUNG -S/T-
    KOCH Screen Rec (Koch): 387002 (CD)
DREAM OF OLWEN The -see 'WHILE I LIVE' + COLLECTION 387
DRIFTWOOD (1996) Music score: CARL DAVIS -S/T- on
    OCEAN DEEP (Grapev/Polyg): OCD 003 (CD)
DRIVING MISS DAISY (1989) Music sco HANS ZIMMER songs
    Eartha Kitt-Louis Armstrong -S/T- VARESE (Pinn):
    VSD 5246 (CD) VSC 5246 (MC)
    see COLLECTIONS 65,79,146,276
DRIVING SCHOOL The (BBC1 10/6/97) mus: GLENN KEILES..NA
DROP THE DEAD DONKEY (Hat Trick/C4 9/8/90-96) title
    music: MATTHEW SCOTT incidental mus: PHILIP POPE.NA

**DROP ZONE** (1994) Music score HANS ZIMMER -S/T- on
*VARESE (Pinn): VSD 5581 (CD)*
**DROWNING BY NUMBERS** (1988) Music score: MICHAEL NYMAN
-S/T- *VENTURE (Virg-EMI): CD(TC)VE 23 (CD/MC)*
**DUBARRY WAS A LADY** (1943) *feat:*LUCILLE BALL-GENE KELLY
RED SKELTON-TOMMY DORSEY ORCH *inc.songs from* 'SKY'S
THE LIMIT'/'42ND STREET' *TARGET (BMG):CD 60010 (CD)*
**DUCHESS OF DUKE STREET** The (UKGold 2/11/92 orig BBC 76)
theme music: ALEXANDER FARIS *see COLLECTION 2*
**DUCK YOU SUCKER!** ('A FISTFUL OF DYNAMITE' 1972) Music
ENNIO MORRICONE-S/T- *ALHAMBRA (Pinn): A.8917 (CD)*
**DUCKMAN** (USA TV) *see COLLECTION 345*
**DUCKTAILS - THE MOVIE** *see* WALT DISNEY INDEX p.343
**DUDES** (1988) Music score: CHARLES BERNSTEIN -S/T- *MCA
(BMG): MCF(C) 3419 (LP/MC) MCAD 6212 (CD)*
**DUE SOUTH** (Canada 94/BBC1 9/5/95) mus: (Jack Lenz-John
-McCarthy-Jay Semko) theme performed by JAY SEMKO-
CRASH TEST DUMMIES *other mus.by* THE NORTHERN PIKES
SARAH MacLACHLAN-KLAATU-GUESS WHO-FIGGY DUFF-BLUE
RODEO-LOREENA McKENNITT and PAUL GROSS etc.
*'Due South' (Orig Soundtrack): Unforscene-Nettwerk
(Pinn): 6242840004-28 (CD) 6242840004-42 (MC)*
*see also COLLECTION 101*
**DUEL IN THE SUN** (1946) Music sc: DIMITRI TIOMKIN suite
*see COLLECTION 366*
**DUELLISTS** The (1977) *see COLLECTION 332* 'SWASHBUCKLERS'
**DUKES OF HAZZARD** (USA 79) Theme 'Good Ol'Boys' (WAYLON
JENNINGS) *see COLLECTIONS 168,344*
**DULCIMA** (Film 1971) Music score: JOHNNY DOUGLAS Theme
*DULCIMA (THE): DLCD 110 (CD) DLCT 110 (MC)*
**DUMB AND DUMBER** (1994) Music sc: TODD RUNGREN -S/T- inc
GIGOLO AUNTS-CRASH TEST DUMMIES-ECHOBELLY-PROCLAIM
ERS-PRIMITIVES and other artists *Revised Re-issue
RCA (BMG): 74321 48059-2 (CD) -4 (MC)*
**DUMBO** - *see* WALT DISNEY INDEX p.343
**DUNE** (1984) Music score: BRIAN ENO & TOTO -S/T- *re-iss
POLYDOR (IMS-Poly): E.823 770-2 (CD)*
*see also COLLECTIONS 273,301,333*
**DUNGEONS AND DRAGONS** (BBC2 83) theme: JOHNNY DOUGLAS
'On Screen' with JOHNNY DOUGLAS STRINGS *DULCIMA
(THE): DLCD 110 (CD) DLCT 110 (MC)*
**DYING YOUNG** (91) Music sco JAMES NEWTON HOWARD theme by
KENNY G. -S/T- also inc JEFFREY OSBORNE-KING CURTIS
*reissue: ARISTA (BMG): 261952 (CD) 411952 (MC)*
**DYNASTY** (UKGO 8/3/93 orig BBC1 82 (USA 80) theme music
BILL CONTI *see COLLECTIONS 159,168,341,373*

**E.** F.X. (USA STAGE SHOW 1995/96) *featur* MICHAEL CRAWFORD
*TELSTAR (WEA): TCD 2810 (CD) STAC 2810 (MC)*
**E.R.** (USA/C4 1/2/95) theme music: JAMES NEWTON HOWARD
-S/T- *WEA (WEA): 7567 82942-2 (CD) -4 (MC)*
**E.T.** (The Extra Terrestrial) (1982) Music comp & cond
by JOHN WILLIAMS -S/T- *MCA (BMG): MCLD 19021 (CD)*
*see also COLLECTIONS 48,62,63,200,301,319,323*

EARLY EDITION (ITV 15/3/97) theme: W.G.SNUFFY WALDEN.*NA*
EARTHQUAKE (1974) Music sco: JOHN WILLIAMS -S/T- *reiss*
    *VARESE (Pinn): VSD 5262 (CD)*
EAST OF EDEN (1954) Music score: LEONARD ROSENMAN *new*
    *Recording* LONDON SINFONIETTA (J.ADAMS) *with* 'REBEL
    WITHOUT A CAUSE' (1955 Leonard Rosenman) *NONESUCH*
    *(WEA): 7559 79402-2 (CD) also available:* LEONARD
    ROSENMAN complete score + 'GIANT'/'REBEL WITHOUT A
    A CAUSE' *CINERAMA (S.Scr): CIN 2206-2(2CD) -4(2MC)*
EASTENDERS (BBC1 19/2/85-1998) *theme*: SIMON MAY-LESLIE
    OSBORNE *Orig version* SIMON MAY ORCHESTRA
    *see COLLECTIONS 168,367,402*
    *2nd vers* SIMON MAY ORCH *on Coll* 'NEW VINTAGE' *del.*
    *ARC (BMG): CDART 102 (CD)* + "Every Loser Wins" sung
    by NICK BERRY Collections 'NEW VINTAGE' *deleted*
    *2nd vers.vocal theme "I'll Always Believe In You"*
    *sung by SHARON BENSON on POLYDOR: PZCD 268 (CDs)*
    *POCS 268 (MC) PO 268 (7"s) deleted*
EASTER PARADE (FILM MUSICAL (1948) Songs by IRVING
    BERLIN *featuring* FRED ASTAIRE-JUDY GARLAND -S/T-
    *reiss EMI Premier: CDODEON 4 (CD)*
EASY COME EASY GO *see* ELVIS PRESLEY INDEX p.348
EASY RIDER (1969) Music: STEPPENWOLF-ELECTRIC PRUNES-
    JIMI HENDRIX EXPERIENCE-BYRDS-ROGER McGUINN..-S/T-
    *MCA (BMG): MCLD 19153 (CD) MCLC 19153 (MC)*
EAT DRINK MAN WOMAN (1993) Music score: MADER -S/T-
    *VARESE (Pinn): VSD 5528 (CD)*
ECHO FOUR-TWO (Assoc.Rediff.24/8/61-25/10/61) theme mus
    LAURIE JOHNSON *see COLLECTION 372*
ED'S NEXT MOVE (1996) Jazz Music score by BENNY GOLSON
    -S/T- *MILAN (BMG): 74321 41336-2 (CD)*
EDDIE (1996) Music sco: STANLEY CLARKE -S/T- V.Artists
    *ISLAND (Poly): 524 243-2 (CD) -4 (MC)*
EDGE OF DARKNESS (BBC2 10/5/92 orig 4/11/85) Theme mus
    ERIC CLAPTON-MICHAEL KAMEN *BBC:12/ZCRESL178 delet*
    *version* 'IMAGES' *Quality (Pinn): QTVCD 002 (CD)*
EDUCATING RITA (1983) Music sco: DAVID HENTSCHEL -S/T-
    *reissue C5 (Pinn): C5CD 587 (CD) see also COLL 353*
EDWARD II (1991) Music score: SIMON FISHER TURNER -S/T-
    *MUTE (Pinn): IONIC 8CD (CD) IONIC 8LP (LP)*
EDWARD AND MRS.SIMPSON (ITV 8/11/78) Music: RON GRAINER
    *sec COLLECTION 7*
EDWARD SCISSORHANDS (1990) Music score: DANNY ELFMAN
    -S/T- *re-issued on MCA (BMG): MCLD 19303 (CD)*
    *see also COLLECTIONS 110,128*
EDWIN DROOD (MUSICAL 1986) *see* 'Mystery Of Edwin Drood'
EERIE INDIANA (USA) *see COLLECTION 12*
EGYPTIAN The (1954) Music sco: BERNARD HERRMANN-ALFRED
    NEWMAN -S/T- with Hollywood Symphony Orchestra on
    *VARESE (Pinn): VSD 5258 (CD)*
EIGER SANCTION The (1975) Music score: JOHN WILLIAMS
    -S/T- *reissue VARESE (Pinn): VSD 5277 (CD)*
EIGHT HEADS IN A DUFFELBAG (1997) Mus sco: ANDREW GROSS
    -S/T- *VARESE (Pinn): VSD 5835 (CD)*

EIGHTH DAY The (Le Huitieme Jour) (1996) Mus sc: PIERRE
    VAN DORMAEL -S/T- featuring Various Artists
    *MERCURY (Poly): 532 713-2 (CD)*
EL AMOR BRUJU (FILM BALLET 1986)-S/T- *EMI:CDC 747586-2*
EL CID (1961) Music score: MIKLOS ROZSA *New Recording*
    COMPLETE SCORE New Zealand Symphony Orchestra on
    *KOCH INTernat.Class (Koch): 37340-2 (CD) -4(MC)*
    *see also COLLECTIONS 201,296,385*
EL GRECO (1964) Music sco ENNIO MORRICONE with 'Giord
    ano Bruno' *Impt (SILVA SCREEN): OST 111 (CD)*
ELDORADO (BBC1 6/7/92- 9/7/93) theme music: SIMON MAY
    "When You Go Away" (S.May) sung by JOHNNY GRIGGS
    *Coll* 'NEW VINTAGE' *ARC (Tot-BMG): CDART 102 (CD)*
    instr.theme *Hit-Chrysal.(Poly): HLC3 (CDs) deleted*
ELECTRA (1975) Music score: MIKIS THEODORAKIS -S/T-
    *SAKKARIS (Pinn): SR 50090 (CD)*
ELECTRIC DREAMS (1984) m: GIORGIO MORODER-PHILIP OAKEY
    -S/T- *VIRGIN (EMI): CDVIP 127 (CD) TCVIP 127(MC)*
ELEGIES For Angels Punks and Raging Queens (ORIG LONDON
    CAST 1993) *First Night (Pinn): OCRCD 6035 (CD)*
ELEPHANT MAN The (1980) Music score: JOHN MORRIS plus
    'Adagio' (Samuel BARBER) sco *MILAN (BMG): 199862*
    *(CD) see also COLLECTIONS 68,171,258*
ELIZABETH AND ESSEX (1939) Mus: ERICH WOLFGANG KORNGOLD
    New: CARL DAVIS & Munich S.O. *MILAN: 873 122 (CD)*
ELLEN (USA93/C4 28/10/94) theme mus: W.G.SNUFFY WALDEN
    *unavailable*
ELLINGTON (YTV 26/10/94) orig music composed and perf
    ormed by JOHN ALTMAN *unavailable*
ELVIRA MADIGAN (1987) 'Piano Con.No.21'K.467' (MOZART)
    *see COLLECTIONS 70,97,171,258,310*
ELVIS PRESLEY TV SPECIAL *see* ELVIS PRESLEY INDEX p.348
EMERGENCY WARD 10 *see COLLECTIONS 2,5,163,381*
EMMA (1995) Music sco: RACHEL PORTMAN -S/T- *POLYGRAM*
    *Euro: 162 069-2 (CD)*
EMMA (JANE AUSTEN'S) (Meridian 24/11/96) Music composed
    and conducted by DOMINIC MULDOWNEY *unavailable*
EMMERDALE (FARM) (Yorkshire 16/10/72-1998) theme music
    by TONY HATCH *see COLLECTIONS 3,33,168,182.364,367*
    *372* + 'EMMERDANCE' album by The 'WOOLPACKERS' *feat:*
    "Hillbilly Rock Hillbilly Roll"/"Linedancing" etc.
    *RCA (BMG): 74321 44405-2(CD) 74321 42541-2(CDs)*
    'GREATEST LINE DANCE PARTY' *(BMG): 74321 51227-2 (CD)*
EMPIRE STRIKES BACK The (Star Wars 2) Music score by
    JOHN WILLIAMS / Special-Edition SOUNDTRACK (1997)
    *RCA (BMG): 09026 68747-2 (Deluxe 2CD)*
    *RCA (BMG): 09026 68773-2 (Slimline 2CD) -4 (2MC)*
    *see also under* 'STAR WARS 2'
    *see COLLECTIONS 48,212,273,300,322,323,330*
EMPTY NEST (USA TV) *see COLLECTION 345*
END OF THE VIOLENCE (1997) Music score: RY COODER
    -S/T- (score) *OUTPOST (BMG): OPD 30007 (CD)*
    -S/T- (songs) *OUTPOST (BMG): OPD 30008 (CD)*
ENEMY MINE *see COLLECTION 322*

ENGLAND MY ENGLAND (C4 25/12/95) Music of HENRY PURCELL
    feat: MONTEVERDI CHOIR & ORCHESTRA (John Eliot Gard
    ner) *ERATO (WEA): 0630 10700-2 (CD) -4 (MC)*
ENGLAND OF ELIZABETH The (1956 travel short)  Music by
    VAUGHAN WILLIAMS *MARCO POLO (Select) 8.223665(CD)*
ENGLISH PATIENT The (1996) Music sco: GABRIEL YARED
    -S/T- *FANTASY (Pinn): FCD 16001 (CD)*
    *see also COLLECTIONS 59,66,67*
ENTER THE DRAGON (1973) Music sco: LALO SCHIFRIN -S/T-
    *WB import WEA FRAnce (Discovery): 7599 26380-2 (CD)*
    *see COLLECTIONS 318,360*
ENTERTAINMENT USA (BBC2 15/4/83) theme "I'll Slap Your
    Face" JONATHAN KING *MCI (DISC): MCCD(MCTC) 108*
EQUALIZER The (USA 29/10/86) theme by STEWART COPELAND
    -TV S/T- *IRS: MIRFC 1029 (MC) DMIRF 1029 (CD)*
    *see COLLECTIONS 12,345*
EQUINOXE (1992) Music by Various Artists -S/T-
    *VARESE (Pinn): VSD 5424 (CD)*
ER - see E.R.beginning of E's
ESCAPE FROM L.A. (1996) Music sco: SHIRLEY WALKER-J.C.
    score -S/T- *MILAN (BMG): 74321 40951-2 (CD)*
    songs -S/T- *WEA: 7567 92714-2 (CD) -4 (MC)*
    Dance Re-mixes from the original score
    *MILAN (BMG): 74321 42639-1 (12"vinyl)*
ESCAPE FROM NEW YORK (1981) Music sco: JOHN CARPENTER-
    ALAN HOWARTH -S/T- *VARESE (Pinn): VCD 47224 (CD)*
ESCAPE ME NEVER (1947) Mus sco: ERICH WOLFGANG KORNGOLD
    "Ballet Fantasy": MOSCOW SYMPH.ORCH (Stromberg) and
    'ANOTHER DAWN' *MARCO POLO (Select): 8.223871 (CD)*
    suite also available on *CHANDOS: CHAN 8870 (CD)*
    *see also COLLECTIONS 164,224*
ESCORT The - see 'LA SCORTA'
ESTHER (BBC2 24/10/94) theme music: PETER OLDROYD and
    GARY SCARGILL *unavailable*
ET - see beginning of 'E's
EUROCOPS (C4 5/3/90) theme (Jan Hammer) JAN HAMMER on
    'Snapshots' *MCA (Poly): (D)MCG(C) 6039 (CD/MC)*
EUROPA (1992) Music sco: JOAKIM HOLBEK -S/T- *VIRGIN*
    *FRANCE (Discovery): 87781-2 (CD)*
EUROPA EUROPA (1991) Music score: ZBIGNIEW PREISNER
    -S/T- also inc.mus. 'OLIVIER OLIVIER' (Preisner)
    *DRG (Pinn): DRGCD 12606(CD) DRGMC 12606(MC)*
EUROPEAN CHAMPIONS LEAGUE Football (ITV Sport 25/11/92)
    "Champion League Anthem" (TONY BRITTEN) *unavailable*
EUROPEAN FIGURE SKATING CHAMPIONSHIPS (BBC 1/2) theme
    music "Mornings At Seven" (James Last) JAMES LAST
    ORCHESTRA on 'By Request' *POLYDOR (Polyg):*
    *831 786-2 (CD) -4 (MC) see also* 'ICE SKATING'
EUROPEAN FOOTBALL CHAMPIONSHIP 1996 (UK)
    BBC1 theme: "Ode To Joy" from Choral Symphony No.9
    (BEETHOVEN) *VIRGIN (EMI):VSCDT(VSC) 1591 (CDs/MC)*
    ITV  theme: "Jerusalem" (H.Parry-W.Blake) performed
    by CHARLIE SKARBEK feat MIRIAM STOCKLEY and PRAGUE
    PHILHARMONIC ORCH *WEEKEND (BMG): WEEKCD 107 (CDs)*

EUROPEAN FOOTBALL CHAMPIONSHIP 1992 (Sweden) 10/6/92
    ITV Coverage: *theme:* "You Are The Number One" by
    UNION featuring PAUL YOUNG (Mike & Mechanics) on
    *Coll* 'BEST OF BRITISH TELEVISION'
    BBC Coverage *theme:* "Ode To Joy" 4th m/ment 'Choral
    Symphony No.9' (BEETHOVEN) BERLIN PHILHARMONIC ORCH
    *DG-POLY: 415832-2 (CD) many versions available*
EUROVISION SONG CONTEST (VARIOUS) *see COLLECTION 359*

EUROVISION SONG CONTEST (1997) (Ireland) BBC1 3/5/1997)
    97 winning song: "Love Shine A Light" performed by
    KATRINA & THE WAVES UK scored 227pts (25 countries)
    on *ETERNAL (WEA): WEA 106(CD)(C)(T) (CDs/MC/12"s)*
    97 runner up: "Mysterious Woman" performed by MARC
    ROBERTS Ireland scored 157pts. recorded on *RITZ
    (Pinn): RITZCD 305 (CDs) RITZC 305 (MC)*
    Interval Music: composed by RONAN KEATING and perf.
    by BOYZONE
    *Other song entries unreleased in the UK*
EUROVISION SONG CONTEST (1996) (Norway) BBC1 18/5/96)
    96 winning song: "The Voice" perform: EIMEAR QUINN
    for IRELAND scored 162 pts (23 Countries) recorded
    *POLYDOR (Poly): 576 884-2 (CD) 576 884-4 (MC)*
    96 UK entry: "Ooh Aah Just A Little Bit" by GINA G.
    (77pts - 7th) *ETERNAL (WEA): WEA 041(CD)(C)(T)*
    Interval Music: composed by EGIL MONN-IVERSEN perf:
    NORWEGIAN RADIO ORCH conduct: FRODE THINGNAES....*NA*
    Morten Harket song "Heaven's Not For Saints (Let It
    Go) on *ARISTA (BMG): 74321 390112-2 (CDs) -4 (MC)*
EUROVISION SONG CONTEST (1995) (Ireland) BBC1 13/5/95)
    95 winning song: "Nocturne" perform: SECRET GARDEN
    for NORWAY scored 148 pts (25 Countries) recorded
    *POLYDOR: 856 978-2 (CD) 856 978-4 (MC)*
    95 UK entry: "Love City Groove" by LOVE CITY GROOVE
    (76pts - 10th) *PLANET 3: GXY 2003CD (CDs)*
    Interval Music: "Lumen" by MICHEAL O'SUILLEABHAIN
    *VENTURE VIRGIN (EMI): VENDX 5 (CDs) VENCX 5 (MC)*
EUROVISION SONG CONTEST (1994) (Ireland) (BBC1 30/4/94)
    94 winning song: "Rock'n'Roll Kids"(Brendan Graham)
    by PAUL HARRINGTON & CHARLIE McGETTIGAN for IRELAND
    scored 226pts (25 Countries) *Roc Kids M (Grapevine
    /Poly): RNRK(CD)(MC)(SP) 1 (CDs/MC/7"s) deleted*
    94 UK entry: "Lonely Symphony" (De Angelis-Dean) by
    FRANCES RUFFELLE (63pts-10th) *VIRGIN: VSCCD(VSC)
    (VS) 1499 (CDs/MC/7"s)* / Interval Music (1994)
    orch.dance sequence: "RIVERDANCE" by BILL WHELAN
    *SON-RTE (Tot-BMG): BUACD 1 (CDsing) BUASC 1 (MC)*
    *SEE ALSO UNDER* 'RIVERDANCE THE SHOW'
EUROVISION SONG CONTEST (1993) (Ireland) (BBC1 15/5/93)
    93 winning song: "In Your Eyes" (Jimmy Walsh) sung
    by NIAMH KAVANAGH for IRELAND scored 187 pts (25 Co
    untries) *ARISTA: 74321 15415-2(CDs) -4(MC) -7(7")*
    93 UK entry:"Better The Devil" (Dean Collinson-Red)
    SONIA (164 pts-2nd) *ARISTA (BMG): 74321 14687-2CDs*

EUROVISION SONG CONTEST (1992) (Sweden) (BBC1 9/5/92)
92 winning song: "Why Me"(Johnny Logan)LINDA MARTIN
scored 155 points (23 Countries) *Columbia (Sony)*
*658131-7 (7"s) 658131-4 (MC) deleted*
92 UK entry: "One Step Out Of Time" (Tony Ryan-Paul
Davies-Victor Stratton) MICHAEL BALL (139 pts- 2nd)
*Poly: PZCD 206 (CDs) PO 206 (7") POCS 206 deleted*
EUROVISION SONG CONTEST (1991) (Rome) (BBC1-4/5/91)
91 winning song: "Fangad Av En Stormvind' (Captured
By A Love Storm) CAROLA (Sweden) scored 146 points
(22 Countries) *RCA: PB 44649(7") PD 44650(CDs)*
also "Le Dernier Qui A Parle" (Last One Who Speaks)
AMINA (France) 146 Ppts *Philips: PH 45 (7")PHMC 45*
91 UK entry "A Message To Your Heart" (Paul Curtis)
SAMANTHA JANUS (47 Points-11th) *Hollywood (Pinn):*
*HWD(T)(CD)104 (7"/12"CDs) deleted*
EUROVISION SONG CONTEST (1990) (Yugoslav)(BBC1 5/5/90)
90 winning song "Insieme 1992" (All Together Now)by
TOTO COTUGNO (Italy) scored 149 pts (22 countries)
on *Odeon (EMI): (12)ODO 113 (12"s/7"s) deleted*
90 UK entry "Give A Little Love Back To The World"
(Paul Curtis) sung by EMMA (87 points placed 6th)
recorded on *Big Wave (BMG): BWR 33 (7"s) deleted*
EUROVISION SONG CONTEST (1989) (Switzerl) (BBC1-6/5/89)
89 winning song "Rock Me" sung by RIVA (Yugoslavia)
scored 137 points (1st)(22 countries) *unavailable*
89 UK entry "Why Do I Always Get It Wrong" (Second)
130pts (Brian Hodgson-John Beeby) perf: LIVE REPORT
*Brouhaha (Priority):CUE 7(7") 12CUE 7(12") deleted*
EUROVISION SONG CONTEST (1988) (Ireland) (BBC1-30/4/88)
1988 wining song:  "Ne Partez Pas Sans Moi" sung by
CELENE DION (Switzerland) - *unavailable in the UK*
scored 137 points (1st place) (21 countries in all)
1988 UK entry: "Go" sung by SCOTT FITZGERALD - 136
points (2nd) - on *PRT (PRT): PYS 10 (7"s) deleted*
EUROVISION SONG CONTEST (1987) (Belgium) (BBC1-9/5/87)
1987 winning song: "Hold Me Now" composed & sung by
JOHNNY LOGAN (Ireland) *Epic: Log 1 (7"s) 451073-1*
*(LP) 451073-4 (MC)* / 172 points / (1st place)
1987 UK entry: "Only The Light" (Richard Peebles)
RIKKI - *OK: OK 010 (7"s) OKL (12"s)* / 47 pts (13th)
EUROVISION SONG CONTEST (1986) (Norway) (BBC1-3/5/86)
1986 winning song: "Jaime La Vie" I Love Life - by
SANDRA KIM (Belgium)-*Carrere: CAR(T) 398 (7"/12s)*
*deleted* scor.176 points (1st)(20 countries in all)
1986 UK entry: "Runner In the Night" by RYDER *10*
*Virgin: TEN 1 (7") deleted* 72 points and placed 7th
EUROVISION SONG CONTEST (1985) (Sweden) (BBC1-4/5/85)
1985 winning song: "La Det Swinge"(Let It Swing)
BOBBY SOCKS *RCA: PB 40127 (7")*(123pts) 19countries
1985 UK entry: "Love Is" performed by VIKKI *PRT*
*7P/12P 326 deleted* scored 100 points / placed 4th

*1984-83-82-81 CONTESTS LISTED IN PREVIOUS EDITIONS*

EUROVISION THEME MUSIC "Te Deum In D.Major" (Marc-Antoi
ne Charpentier) Academy Of St.Martin-In-The Fields
(Neville Marriner) *EMI: CDC 754 284-2 (CD)* also
English Chamber Orch *EMI: CZS 767 425-2 (2CD)*
EVEN COWGIRLS GET THE BLUES (1993) Music & songs (k.d.
lang)-S/T- *Sire-WB (WEA): 9362 45433-2(CD) -4(MC)*
EVEN FURTHER ABROAD with Jonathan Meades (BBC2 19/2/97)
music: HOWARD J.DAVIDSON *unavailable*
EVENING SHADE (USA) *see COLLECTIONS 12,345*
EVENING STAR (1996) Music score: WILLIAM ROSS -S/T-
*Import (Silva Screen): ANG 54567 (CD)*
EVENT HORIZON (1997) Music sco: MICHAEL KAMEN + V.Arts.
-S/T- *INTERNAL (Poly): 828 939-2 (CD)*
EVER DECREASING CIRCLES (BBC1 29/1/84-1989) theme mus
"Prelude No.15 Op.34 Allegretto" (D.SHOSTAKOVICH)
EVERYBODY'S GOT ONE (BBC1 14/1/97) title music composed
by DUNCAN MILLAR *unavailable*
EVERYONE SAYS I LOVE YOU (1996) Mus: DICK HYMAN / Songs
on *RCA Victor (BMG): 09026 68756-2 (CD)*
EVIL DEAD (1985) Mus: JOSEPH LoDUCA *VSD 5362 deleted*
EVIL DEAD 2 (1987) Music score: JOSEPH LoDUCA -S/T-
*TER (Koch): CDTER 1142 (CD) ZCTER 1142 (MC)*
EVIL DEAD 3 (Army Of Darkness) (1992) m: JOSEPH LoDUCA
-S/T- *VARESE (Pinn): VSD 5411 (CD)*
EVITA - songs by Tim Rice and Andrew LLoyd Webber
   1.FILM 1996 *feat* MADONNA-JONATHAN PRYCE-ANTONIO BANDE
     RAS-JIMMY NAIL etc.-S/T- *SIRE (WEA): 9362 463462-2
     (CD) -4 (MC)* / "Don't Cry For Me Argentina" MADONNA
     *WEA: W.0384CD (CDs) W.0384C (MCs)*
   2.STUDIO RECORDING 1976 *with* JULIE COVINGTON and Comp
     *MCA (BMG): DMCXC 503 (CD)*
   3.ORIG BROADWAY CAST 1979 *feat:* PATTI LuPONE-MANDY
     PATINKIN-BOB GUNTON-MARK SYERS-JANE OHRINGER & Comp
     *MCA (BMG): MCDH 453 (2LP)*
   4.ORIG LONDON CAST 1978 *w:* ELAINE PAIGE-DAVID ESSEX
     *MCA (BMG): MCGC 3527 (MC) DMCG 3527 (CD)*
     *see COLLECT.32,59,105,174,216,232,267,281,282,382*
EXCALIBUR (1981) Music score incl.unused music cues
   TREVOR JONES *OLD WORLD MUSIC (Imp): OWM 9402 (CD)*
   *see COLLECTIONS 64,70,73,76,109,258,276*
EXECUTIVE DECISION (1995) Music score: JERRY GOLDSMITH
   *VARESE (Pinn): VSD 5714 (CD)*
EXIT (Film) Music score: TANGERINE DREAM -S/T-
   *VIRGIN (EMI): CDV 2212 (CD) OVEDC 166 (MC)*
EXIT TO EDEN (1994) Music score: PATRICK DOYLE -S/T-
   *VARESE (Pinn): VSD 5553 (CD)*
EXODUS (1960) Music score: ERNEST GOLD + score from
   'Judith' (KAPLAN) *TSUNAMI (Sil.Sc): TSU 0115 (CD)*
   *see also COLLECTIONS 203,216*
EXORCIST The (1973) Music sco: JACK NITZSCHE -S/T- inc.
   V.composers MIKE OLDFIELD-KRYSZTOF PENDERECKI-HANS
   WERNER HENZE-GEORGE CRUM-ANTON WEBERN-DAVID BORDEN
   *WB import WEA FRAnce (Discovery): 9362 46294-2 (CD)*
   *see also COLLECTIONS 210,274*

EXOTICA (1994) Music score: MYCHAEL DANNA -S/T- on
    *VARESE (Pinn): VSD 5543 (CD)*
EXPERIENCE (Rock 1968) JIMI HENDRIX EXPERIENCE feat:
    Jimi Hendrix-Noel Redding-Mitch Mitchell *reissue*
    -S/T- NECTAR (Pinn): NTRCD 036 (CD) NTRC 036 (MC)
EXPERIMENT IN TERROR (1962) Music score: HENRY MANCINI
    -S/T- *RCA Import (Discovery): 74321 48942-2 (CD)*
EXPLORERS The (1985) Music score : JERRY GOLDSMITH
    -S/T- *VARESE USA (Silva Screen): VSD 5261 (CD)*
EXPOSED (1983) *see COLLECTIONS 74,76*
EXTREME (USA/C4 22/8/95) music: PATRICK WILLIAMS and
    PHIL RAMONE additional music by Charles Pollard..*NA*
EXTREME MEASURES (1996) Music score: DANNY ELFMAN -S/T-
    *VARESE (Pinn): VSD 5767 (CD)*
EYE OF THE PANTHER Mus.sco: JOHN DEBNEY -S/T- incl 'NOT
    SINCE CASANOVA' *PROMETHEUS (S.Screen): PCD 140 (CD)*

**F** 1 (Formula One Grand Prix) (ITV 7/3/97) theme music
    "Cosmic Girl" (Kay-Stone) by JAMIROQUAI on *S2 (SONY
    Mus): 663829-2 (CDs) -4 (MC) TV version unavailable*
F.B.I.(USA) *see COLLECTION 339*
FABULOUS BAKER BOYS The (1989) Music score: DAVE GRUSIN
    -S/T- *GRP USA (Import): GRP 2002-2 (CD)*
FACE (1997) Music sco: ANDY ROBERTS-PAUL CONROY-ADRIAN
    CORKER -S/T- *feat V/A ISLAND (Poly): CID 8061 (CD)*
FACE / OFF (1997) Music score: JOHN POWELL  -S/T-
    *PHILIPS (Poly): 162 125-2 (CD)*
FACE TO FACE (BBC2 18/9/95) theme mus "Overture to Les
    Francs Juges" Op.3 (BERLIOZ) *version* Chicago S.Orch
    (Solti) *DECCA (Polygram): 417 705-2 (CD)*
FACE TO FACE (19067) Music score ENNIO MORRICONE *Import
    with* 'BIG GUNDOWN' *MASK (S.Screen): MK 701 (CD)*
FAHRENHEIT 451 (1966) Music sco: BERNARD HERRMANN Suite
    on 'Great Film Music' Coll *DECCA Phase 4 (Poly):
    443 899-2 (CD) with* JOURNEY TO THE CENTRE OF THE
    EARTH-SEVENTH VOYAGE OF SINBAD-DAY THE EARTH STOOD
    STILL-THREE WORLDS OF GULLIVER / *also available:*
    SEATTLE SYMPH ORCHESTRA *VARESE (Pinn): VSD 5551
    (CD) also* ORIG SOUNDTRACK on -S/T- *TSUNAMI Imp
    (Silva Screen): TSU 0136 (CD) COLLECTIONS 165,187*
FAIR GAME (YTV for C4 27/4/95) title mus: MIKE SCOTT.*NA*
FAITH IN THF FUTURE (LWT/ITV 1/12/95) theme "The World
    Is What You Make It" (P.Brady) sung by PAUL BRADY
    *MERCURY (Poly): 856 993-2 (CDs) or PB(CD)(MC) 5*
FALCON CREST (USA) *see COLLECTIONS 12,344,367*
FALL GUY The (USA TV) *see COLLECTION 344*
FALL OF BERLIN The (1949) - *see COLLECTION 261*
FALL OF THE ROMAN EMPIRE The (1964) Music sco: DIMITRI
    TIOMKIN -S/T- *CLOUD NINE (S.Screen): ACN 7016(CD)*
FALLEN ANGELS (USA/BBC2 4/8/95) title theme: ELMER and
    PETER BERNSTEIN series also contains various songs
    -S/T- *VERVE (IMS-Poly): E.519903-2 (CD)*
FALLEN IDOL (1948) Music score: WILLIAM ALWYN *suite by
    London S.O.(Richard Hickox) CHANDOS: CHAN 9243 (CD)*

FALLING IN LOVE (1985) Music score: DAVE GRUSIN Select
by Dave Grusin GRP USA (Pinn): GRPD 9018 (CD)
FAME (USA/BBC1 82-12/2/85) reissue of KIDS FROM FAME on
RCA (BMG): ND 90427 (CD) theme sung by Erica Gimpel
RCA: PK 89257 (MC) see COLLECTIONS 46,168,344,382
FAME (FILM MUSICAL 80) Mus: MICHAEL GORE-DEAN PITCHFORD
IRENE CARA -S/T- POLYDOR Imp E.800 034-2 (CD)
see COLLECTIONS 46,168,344,382
FAME (THE MUSICAL) (ORIG LONDON CAST 95) feat: LORRAINE
VELEZ-RICHARD DEMPSEY-SONIA SWABY and Company on
POLYDOR-RUG (Poly): 529 109-2 (CD) -4 (MC)
FAMILY AT WAR A (Gra+ 6/10/96 orig ITV 12/5/70) Theme:
Ist m/m Symphony No.6 in E.Minor (VAUGHAN WILLIAMS)
London Symp Or (A.Previn) RCA (BMG) RD 89883 (CD)
New Phil Or (A.Boult) HMV (EMI) CDC 747215-2(CD)
FAMILY MATTERS (USA TV) see COLLECTION 345
FAMILY MONEY (C4 16/3/97) mus.sco: CHRISTOPHER GUNNING
"Trouble In Mind" sung by NINA SIMONE from 'Pastel
Blue'/'Don't Let Me Be Misunderstood'albums deleted
FAMILY THING (95) -S/T- Edel (Pinn): 0022602 (CD)
FAMILY WAY The (66) Music score: PAUL McCARTNEY (arr.&
producer: George Martin) Suite on 'The Family Way'
(Variations Concertantes Opus 1) featur: CARL AUBUT
(gtr) Clare Marchand, Andre Moison & Claudel String
Quartet PHILIPS (Poly): 454 230-2 (CD)
FAMOUS FIVE The (ITV 1/7/96) music score: JOE CAMPBELL
and PAUL HART unavailable
FANNY (1932) MARCEL PAGNOL'S TRILOGY (2) / music sco.by
VINCENT SCOTTO on Coll 'Films Of Marcel Pagnol' on
EMI FRA.(Discov): 855 883-2 (CD) see also 'MARIUS'
FANNY CRADDOCK (BBC 1963) theme mus "Buttered Crumpet"
see COLLECTION 7
FANTASIA (1941) New Recording of the complete classical
film music from the Walt Disney/Leopold Stokowski
animated classic NAXOS (Select): 8551166 (CD)
see also WALT DISNEY INDEX p.343
see also COLLECTIONS 66,74,75,76,77,79
FANTASTICKS The- songs by Harvey Schmidt & Tom Jones
1.ORIG BROADWAY CAST 1960 with: JERRY ORBACH-RITA
GARDNER-KENNETH NELSON TER (Disc): CD(ZC)TER 1099
and also on POLY (IMS-Poly): AA 821 943-2 (CD) +
2.JAPAN TOUR CAST REC. DRG (Pinn) DRGCD 19005 (CD)
FANTASY FOOTBALL LEAGUE (Avalon/Gr.Slam/BBC2 14/1/94)
music by STEVE BROWN unavailable
FANTASY ISLAND (USA TV) see COLLECTION 344
FAR AND AWAY (1992) Music score: JOHN WILLIAMS also
The Chieftains and ENYA ("Book Of Days") -S/T- on
MCA: MCAD(MCAC) 10628 CD/MC deleted / end credits
music on SILVA SCREEN (Koch): FILMCD 152 (CD)
FAR FLUNG FLOYD (BBC2 13/7/93) theme " Waltz In Black"
The STRANGLERS on 'Meninblack" Fame (MFP-EMI):
CDFA 3208 (CD) TCFA 3208 (MC) see COLLECTION 337
FAR FROM HOME: ADVENTURES OF YELLOW DOG (1996) Music:
JOHN SCOTT -S/T- JOHN SCOTT (S.Scr): JSCD 118(CD)

FAREWELL TO ARMS, A (1957) Mus: MARIO NASCIMBENE -S/T-
+'SONS AND LOVERS' *DRG (Pinn): DRGCSD 32962 (CD)*
*also avail:* inc.mus. from 'The Barefoot Contessa'
on *LEGEND Import (Silva Screen): LEGENDCD 11 (CD)*
FAREWELL TO MY CONCUBINE (1993) Music sco: ZHAO JIPING
-S/T- *VARESE (Pinn): VSD 5454 (CD)*
FARINELLI: IL CASTRATO (1995) Classical music -S/T-
*AUVIDIS Travelling (Harmonia Mundi): K.1005 CD)*
FARMING (BBC 50's) theme music "A Quiet Stroll"
CHARLES WILLIAMS *see COLLECTION 163*
FAST SHOW The (BBC2 27/9/94) mus.dir.PHIL POPE / theme:
"Release Me" (Miller-Stevenson-Harris) arranged by
Phil Pope *unavailable* orig vers: (USA) Ray Price
FATAL ATTRACTION (1987) Music sco: MAURICE JARRE -S/T-
*GNP USA (Silva Screen) GNPD 8011 (CD) GNP-5 8011
(MC)* other m: "Un Bel Di"(Madam Butterfly)(Puccini)
*see COLLECTIONS 65,120,139,171,258*
FATAL FLAMES (Italian Horror Film) Music score AL FESTO
-S/T- *IMPRT (Silva Screen): VCDS 7022 (CD)*
FATHER CHRISTMAS (C4-25/12/91) music: MIKE HEWER perf:
Phoenix Chamber Orch (Julian Bigg) narrated by Mel
Smith -S/T- *COLUMBIA (SM): 469475-2 (CD)* -4(MC)
FATHER KNOWS BEST (USA TV) *see COLLECTION 342*
FATHER OF THE BRIDE (1991) Music score: ALAN SILVESTRI
-S/T- *VARESE (Pinn): VSD 5348 (CD)*
FATHER OF THE BRIDE 2 (1995) Music sco: ALAN SILVESTRI
-S/T- *HOLLYWOOD (Poly): 162 020-2 (CD) delet.96*
FATHER TED (C4 21/4/95) title music by the DIVINE
COMEDY *unavailable*
FAWLTY TOWERS (BBC2 75 rerun 95) theme: DENNIS WILSON
*see COLLECTIONS 229,402*
FEARLESS (1993) music sco: MAURICE JARRE -S/T- *ELEKTRA
NONESUCH (WEA): 7559 79334-2 (CD) -4 (MC)* also on
FEDS (1988) Music score and songs: RANDY EDELMAN -S/T-
*GNP (S.Screen) GNPD 8014 (CD)*
FEEL GOOD FACTOR (C4 26/8/97) t.mus: MUSIC SCULPTORS.*NA*
FELIX THE CAT (USA) *see COLLECTION 339*
FENN STREET GANG The (LWT 24/9/71) theme "The Dandy" by
DENIS KING *see COLLECTION 4*
FERRY CROSS THE MERSEY (Film Musical 1964) Feat GERRY &
PACEMAKERS-CILLA BLACK-FOURMOST -S/T- *(digitally re
mastered) EMI: DORIC 114 (CD)* -S/T- also on
*BEAT GOES ON (Pinn): BGOLP 10 (LP)*
FEVER PITCH (1996) Mus sc: NEIL MacCOLL & BOB HEWERDINE
-S/T- *BLANCO Y NEGRO (WEA): 0630 18453-2(CD) -4(MC)*
FIDDLER ON THE ROOF - songs Jerry Bock-Sheldon Harnick
  1.CARLTON SHOWS COLLECTION 1995 *feat:* ANTHONY NEWLEY
    TRACEY MILLER-MARION DAVIES-LINDA HIBBERT-NICK CURT
    IS-DAVID HITCHEN *CARLTON: 30362 0014-2(CD) -4(MC)*
  2.STUDIO RECORDING 1968 *featuring:*
    ROBERT MERRILL-MOLLY PICON-ROBERT BOWMAN-ANDY COLE
    MARGARET EAVES-SYLVIA KING-EDDIE LESTER & Company
    LONDON FESTIVAL ORCHESTRA (Stanley Black) *reissue:*
    *DECCA (Poly): 448 949-2 (CD)*

FIDDLER ON THE ROOF *Continued from previous page...*

3. ORIG LONDON CAST 1967 *feat:* TOPOL-MIRIAM KARLIN-SAN
   DOR ELES-HEATHER CLIFTON-LINDA GARDNER-CYNTHIA GREN
   VILLE.. *SONY West End (Sony):SMK(SMT)53499 (CD/MC)*
4. FILM MUSICAL 1971 *featuring:* TOPOL -S/T- *re-issue:*
   *UNITED ARTISTS (EMI): CDP 746091-2 (CD)*
5. ORIG BROADWAY CAST 1964 *with:* ZERO MOSTELL & MARIA
   KARNILOVA-BEATRICE ARTHUR-JULIA MIGENES *RCA (BMG):*
   *RD 87060 CD also Silva Screen Imp: RCD1 7060 (CD)*
FIDDLY FOODLE BIRD (BBC1 8/1/92) title song: BOB SAKER-
   JONATHAN HODGE + Stuart Leathwood-Julian Littman on
   *MFP (EMI): CDMFP 5958 (CD) TCMFP 5958 (MC)*
FIELD OF DREAMS (1989) Music score: JAMES HORNER -S/T-
   *RCA NOVUS (Silva Screen): 3060-2 (CD) 3060-4 (MC)*
FIELDS OF AMBROSIA songs: MARTIN SILVESTRI-JOEL HIGGINS
   ORIG LONDON CAST *feat:* CHRISTINE ANDREAS & Company
   *FIRST NIGHT (Pinn): CASTCD 58 (CD)*
FIERCE CREATURES-DON'T PET THEM (1996) Music sco: JERRY
   GOLDSMITH -S/T- *VARESE (Pinn): VSD 5792 (CD)*
FIFTEEN-TO-ONE (C4 11/1/88-98) mus.dir PAUL McGUIRE.. *NA*
FIFTH ELEMENT The (1997) Music sco: ERIC SERRA -S/T- on
   *VIRGIN (EMI): CDVIRX 63 (CD) MCVIRX 63 (MC)*
FIFTY-FIVE DAYS AT PEKING (1961) Music: DIMITRI TIOMKIN
   *Coll 'HIGH NOON' RCA (BMG): 09026 62658-2 (CD)*
FILM 98 (BBC1 72-98) *theme* "I Wish I Knew How It Would
   Feel To Be Free" (B.Taylor-D.Dallas) BILLY TAYLOR
   TRIO on Coll 'Blue Movies' *EMI: CDP 857748-2 (CD)*
   *see COLLECTIONS 31,285,402*
FINIAN'S RAINBOW - songs by Burton Lane & E.Y.Harburg
1. ORIGINAL BROADWAY CAST 1947 *feat:* ELLA LOGAN-ALBERT
   SHARPE-DONALD RICHARDS-DAVID WAYNE-ANITA ALVAREZ
   *COLUMBIA (S.Screen): CK 04062 (CD) JST 04062 (MC)*
2. REVIVAL BROADWAY CAST 1960 *with:* JEANNE CARSON & Co
   *RCA (Silva Screen): 1057-2 (CD) 1057-4 (MC)*
FINNEY (Zenith/Tyne-Tees 17/11/94) music composed by
   JOHN LUNN / music supervisor: Bob Last *unavailable*
FIORELLO (O.BROADWAY CAST 1959) Songs (Jerry Bock-Sheld
   on Harnick) *featuring:* TOM BOSLEY-PATRICIA WILSON-
   ELLEN HANLEY-HOWARD DA SILVA-MARK DAWSON & company
   *EMI ANGEL: ZDM 565 023-2 (CD)*
FIRE (1997 Deepa Mehta) Music score: A.R.RAHMAN -S/T-
   *COLOSSEUM (Pinn): CST 348068 (CD)*
FIRE DOWN BELOW (1997) Music score: NICK GLENNIE SMITH
   -S/T- *W.BROS (WEA): number to be confirmed (CD/MC)*
FIRE IN THE SKY (1992) Music score: MARK ISHAM -S/T-
   *VARESE (Pinn): VSD 5417 (CD)*
FIREBALL XL5 (ATV/ITV 25/3/63) theme song: BARRY GRAY
   sung by DON SPENCER *see COLLECTIONS 3,110,273,339*
   *357,364,368,372*
FIREFIGHTERS (BBC1 28/5/97) title m: HOWARD DAVIDSON. *NA*
FIREMAN SAM (BBC/SC4-88) theme: Ben Heneghan-Ian Lawson
   sung by MALDWYN POPE 'All In A Good Cause' Spoken
   Word *BBC(Pin): YBBC 1483 / see also COLLECTS 60,408*

FIREMAN SAM (MUSICAL VERSION OF ANIMATED TV SERIES)
  *EPIC (Sony): 480 689-4 (MC)*
FIRM The (1993) Music score: DAVE GRUSIN -S/T-*GRP USA*
  *NEW NOTE-MCA (BMG): GRLD 19358 (CD)*
FIRST BLOOD (82) Music sco: JERRY GOLDSMITH vocal by
  Dan Hill -S/T- *INTRADA (S.Screen): FMT 8001D (CD)*
  see also under 'RAMBO' and *COLLECTION 327*
FIRST GREAT TRAIN ROBBERY (1978) see 'WILD ROVERS'
FIRST KNIGHT (1994) Music score: JERRY GOLDSMITH -S/T-
  *EPIC Soundtrax (Sony): 480 937-2 (CD)*
FIRST MEN IN THE MOON The (1964) Music score: LAURIE
  JOHNSON *CLOUD NINE (S.Screen-Conif): ACN 7015 (CD)*
FIRST OF THE FEW (1942) Music incl: "Spitfire Prelude
  and Fugue" (WILLIAM WALTON) L.P.Orch (Sir A.Boult)
  *HMV: ED 2911129-4 (MC)* with 'Things To Come'
FIRST STRIKE (JACKIE CHAN'S) (1997) Music sco: J.PETER
  ROBINSON -S/T- V.Art *RCA (BMG): 74321 47734-2 (CD)*
FIRST WIVES CLUB The (1996) Music: MARC SHAIMAN -S/T-
  -S/T- (songs) *COLUMB (SM): 485 396-2 (CD) -4(MC)*
  -S/T- (score) *VARESE (Pinn): VSD 5781 (CD)*
FISHER KING The (1991) Music sco: GEORGE FENTON -S/T-
  arts include Harry Nilsson-Brenda Lee-Chill Rob.G
  *MCA (BMG): MCAD 10249 (CD) MCAC 10249 (MC)*
FIST GOES WEST, A (1980) Music score ENNIO MORRICONE
  ENNIO MORRICONE ORCH on Coll 'An Ennio Morricone
  Quintet' *DRG USA (Pinn): DRGCD 32907 (CD)*
FISTFUL OF DOLLARS A (1964) Music score ENNIO MORRICONE
  *see Collections 126,170,249,252,254,255,256,397*
FISTFUL OF DYNAMITE, A (Duck You Sucker!) (1971) Music
  ENNIO MORRICONE *DRG USA (Pinn) DRGCD 32907 (CD)*
  *see COLLECTIONS 251,398*
FIVE DAYS AND FIVE NIGHTS (FILM) Music: D.SHOSTAKOVICH
  music score + music from 'THE GADFLY' (1955) *NAXOS*
  *Select: 8.553299 (CD)* see also Coll 'MOVIE MADNESS'
FIVE EASY PIECES (1970) *see COLLECTION 73*
FIVE FINGER EXCERCISE (1962) *see COLLECTION 377*
FIVE GUYS NAMED MOE (O.LONDON CAST 1991) Song & Dance
  Review celebrating the music LOUIS JORDAN *feat:*
  CLARKE PETERS *FIRST NIGHT (Pinn): CAST(C)(CD) 23*
  'Five Guys Named Moe'(L.JORDAN) *MCA:MCLD 19048 CD*
  L.JORDAN & TYMPANY 5 *BANDSTAND (H.Mund):BDCD 1531*
FIVE HEARTBEATS The (1991) Various Arts -S/T- *VIRGIN*
  *Movie Music (EMI): CDVMM 4 (CD) TCVMM 4 (MC)*
FIX The (Musical 1997) ORIG LONDON CAST RECORDING
  *feat* JOHN BARROWMAN-PHILIP QUAST and Company
  *FIRST NIGHT (Pinn): CASTCD 62 (CD) CASTC 62 (MC)*
FLAMING STAR *see* ELVIS PRESLEY INDEX p.348
FLAMINGO KID The (1984) Music sco: CURT SOBELL + V/A
  -S/T- *re-issue SPECTRUM (Poly): 551 539-2 (CD)*
FLASH GORDON (1980) Music & Songs: QUEEN -S/T- reiss:
  *EMI: CD(TC)PCSD 137 (CD/MC) see COLLECTION  268*
FLASHDANCE (1983) Mus: GIORGIO MORODER t.song IRENE
  CARA -S/T- *CASABLANCA: 811 492-2(CD) PRIMC 111(MC)*
  *see COLLECTION 274*

FLASHPOINT (1985) Music score: TANGERINE DREAM -S/T-
   *ONE WAY (Greyhound): 18507 (CD)*
FLEMISH FARM The (1943) Music score: VAUGHAN WILLIAMS
   *MARCO POLO (Select): 8.223665 (CD)*
FLESH IS WEAK The *see COLLECTION 288*
FLETCH (1985) Music: HAROLD FALTERMEYER + STEPHANIE
   MILLS-KIM WILDE-DAN HARTMAN  *MCA: DMCF 3284(CD)*
FLIGHT OF THE CONDOR (BBC2 14/10/87) Theme 'Floreo De L
   lamas'(Marquez) INTI ILLIMANI & GUAMARY *BBC delet*
FLINTSTONES The (USA 61/85) "Meet The Flinstones" (Hoyt
   Curtin) TV-S/T- reiss: *MCI (MCI-THE): MCCD(MCTC)
   181 (CD/MC) see COLLECTIONS 339,370*
FLINTSTONES The (FILM 1993) Music: HOYT CURTIN & oth)
   *MCA (BMG): MCD 11045 (CD) and  MCA 11100 (CD)*
FLIPPER (USA 1964) *see COLLECTION 339*
FLIRTING WITH DISASTER (1996) Mus: STEPHEN ENDELMAN
   -S/T- *GEFFEN-MCA (BMG): GED 24970 (CD) DELETED 97*
FLORA THE RED MENACE - songs: John Kander & Fred Ebb
   OFF BROADWAY CAST 1987 *TER (Disc):CDTER 1159 (CD)*
FLORADORA (ORIG LONDON CAST 1899) Music (Leslie Stuart)
   Lyrics (Ernest Boyd-Jones &Paul Rubens) Louis Bradf
   field-Kate Cutler-Ada Reeve-Syney Barraclough on
   *PEARL (Harmonia Mundi): OPALCD 9835 (CD)*
FLOWER OF MY SECRET The (La Fleur De Mon Secret) (1995)
   Music score: ALBERT IGLESIAS -S/T- *feat* MILES DAVIS
   CAETANO VELOSO *SQUATT Sony:SQT 481444-2(CD) -4(MC)*
FLOWERING PASSIONS (C4 13/6/91) music by FRANCIS SHAW
   -S/T- *SILVA SCREEN (Koch): FILM(C)(CD) 116 (MC/CD)*
FLOWERS IN THE ATTIC (1988) Music: CHRISTOPHER YOUNG
   -S/T- *INTRADA USA (Silva Screen): MAF 7009D (CD)*
FLOYD ON....(BBC2 1986-94) theme music "Waltz In Black"
   also used "Peaches" by THE STRANGLERS 'Collection'
   *Fame (EMI): (CD)(TC)FA 3230 (CD/MC)*
   *see COLLECTION 337*
FLOYD COLLINS (Musical 1996 USA) Songs: ADAM GUETELL
   *w:* CHRISTOPHER INNVAR-JESSE LENAT-THERESA McCARTHY
   *NONESUCH (WEA): 7559 79434-2 (CD)*
FLUKE (C4 6/5/97) theme music: RICK TURK-TOM VINE....*NA*
FLY The (1986) Music score: HOWARD SHORE -S/T- on
   *VARESE (Pinn): VCD 47272 (CD)*
FLYING DOCTORS (BBC1 1/10/85) theme mus: GARRY McDONALD
   & LAURIE STONE *see COLLECTION 367*
FLYING DOWN TO RIO (1933 MUSICAL) *w:*FRED ASTAIRE-GINGER
   ROGERS-DOLORES DE RIO *includ.songs from* 'HOLLYWOOD
   HOTEL' *TARGET (BMG): CD 60008 (CD)*
FLYING VET (BBC2 4/9/96) orig music sco: ART PHILLIPS
   -S/T- *ABC Soundtracks (S.Screen): 479784-2 (CD)*
FOG The (1979) Music score: JOHN CARPENTER -S/T- Imp
   *VARESE (Pinn): VCD 47267 (CD)*
FOLLIES - songs by Stephen Sondheim
   1.ORIG LONDON CAST 1987 *feat:* JULIA McKENZIE-DIANA
     RIGG-DANIEL MASSEY-DAVIE HEALEY-DOLORES GRAY & Comp
     *FIRST NIGHT (Pinn): OCRCD 6019 (CD)*
   2.ORIG BROADWAY CAST 1971 *w:* ALEXIS SMITH-GENE NELSON

2.ORIG BROADWAY CAST 1971 *w:* ALEXIS SMITH-GENE NELSON
  DOROTHY COLLINS-JOHN McMARTIN-YVONNE DE CARLO & Com
  *EMI ANGEL: ZDM 764666-2 (CD)*
3.LIVE STUDIO RECORD. 1985 *also featuring:* 'STAVISKY'
  (Stephen Sondheim) *RCA (BMG): RD 87128 (2CD's)*
4.REVIVAL USA LINCOLN CENTER 1985 *w:* BARBARA COOK-
  GEORGE HEARN-MANDY PATINKIN-LEE REMICK-ELAINE STRIT
  CH-CAROL BURNETT & New York Philharmonic Orchestra
  *RCA (BMG) BK 87128 (MC) BD 87128 (CD)*
FOLLOW THAT DREAM *see* ELVIS PRESLEY INDEX p.348
FOLLOW THE BOYS (1944) VARIOUS -S/T- SELECTIONS on
  *GREAT MOVIE THEMES: (Targ-BMG): CD 60032 (CD)*
FOLLOW THE FLEET (1936) FILM MUSICAL *feat* FRED ASTAIRE
  GINGER ROGERS -S/T- *sel.on* 'Let's Swing and Dance'
  +songs from 'SWING TIME'/'TOP HAT'/'CAREFREE'
  *GREAT MOVIE THEMES (Target-BMG): CD 60015 (CD)*
  *also available -S/T- plus songs from* 'SWING TIME'
  *IRIS Mus-Chansons Cinema (Discovery):CIN 006 (CD)*
  *see COLLECTIONS 16,286*
FOLLYFOOT (ITV 1971) theme "Lightning Tree" (Steve Fra
  cis) sung by The SETTLERS *see COLLECTION 6*
  *and* "Meadow Mist" from Follyfoot *see COLLECTION 43*
FOOD & DRINK (BBC2) 93-98 series theme mus: SIMON MAY
  *COLL* 'NEW VINTAGE' *ARC Total: CDART 102 deleted*
FOOTBALL *see* EUROPEAN CHAMPIONS LEAGUE/MATCH OF T.DAY
FOOTBALL ITALIA (Chrysalis for C4 12/9/92) theme music
  "I'm Stronger Now" (Steve DuBerry-Ben Chapman) by
  DEFINITIVE 2 *DeCONSTRUCTION (BMG): 743211 2473-2*
  *(CDs) -1 (12"s) deleted*
FOOTLIGHT PARADE (1933 MUSICAL) *feat:* JAMES CAGNEY-JOAN
  BLONDELL-RUBY KELLER DICK POWELL *incl.songs from*
  'STAR SPANGLED RHYTHM' *TARGET (BMG): CD 60013 (CD)*
FOOTLOOSE (Rock Film 1984) Music: KENNY LOGGINS *feat:*
  BONNIE TYLER "Holding Out For A Hero" + other arts
  -S/T- *COLUMBIA: CBS 463000-2 (CD) 463000-4 (MC)*
FOR A FEW DOLLARS MORE (1965) Music: ENNIO MORRICONE
  *see COLLECTIONS 126,127,170,249,252,254,256*
FOR ME AND MY GAL (1942) *feat:* JUDY GARLAND-GENE KELLY
  reissued -S/T- *EMI ODEON: CDODEON 12 (CD)*
FOR RICHER OR POORER (1997) Music score: RANDY EDELMAN
  -S/T- *VARESE (Pinn): VSD 5891 (CD)*
FOR ROSEANNA - *see* 'ROSEANNA'S GRAVE'
FOR THE BOYS (1991) Music sco: DAVE GRUSIN with BETTE
  MIDLER -S/T- *ATLANTIC WEA: 756782329-2(CD) -4(MC)*
FOR THOSE I LOVED (BBC1 21/7/91) musis score: MAURICE
  JARRE *on Coll* 'Maurice Jarre Trilogy' with 'A Seas
  in Hell'/'The Damned'*DRG (Pinn): DRGCD 32906 (2CD)*
FOR YOUR EYES ONLY - *see* JAMES BOND FILM INDEX p.346
FORBIDDEN GAMES (1952) *see COLLECTION 78*
FORBIDDEN PLANET (1954) Music sco: LOUIS & BEBE BARRON
  -S/T- *GNP USA Imp (Silva Screen): PRD 001 (CD)*
FORBIDDEN WORLD (1982) - *see under* 'MUTANT'
FOREVER GREEN (LWT 26/2/89) theme: PATRICK GOWERS
  *see COLLECTIONS 138,175*

FOREVER KNIGHT (USA TV series) music sco: FRED MOLLIN
   -S/T- GNP (S.Screen): GNPD 8043 (CD) also COLL 378
FOREVER PLAID (O.LONDON CAST RECORDING 1993) American
   Hit Musical with songs from the 50's/60's featuring
   STAN CHANDLER-DAVID ENGEL-LARRY RABEN-GUY STROMAN
   and Company on FIRST NIGHT (Pinn):CAST(C)(CD) 33
FOREVER YOUNG (1992) Music score: JERRY GOLDSMITH -S/T-
   WB IMPT (Silva Screen): WA 24482-2 (CD) -4 (MC)
FORMULA 1 - see 'F1'
FORREST GUMP (1993) Music sco: ALAN SILVESTRI + V.Arts
   -S/T- (songs): EPIC (Sony): 476 941-2(2CD) 4(2MC)
   -S/T- (score): EPIC (Sony): 477 369-2 (CD)
   see also COLLECTIONS 17,59,82
FORSYTE SAGA The (BBC1 67) Theme mus "Elizabeth Tudor"
   from 'Three Elizabeths Suite' by ERIC COATES
   see COLLECTIONS 3,31,364,372
FORTEAN TV (C4 29/1/97) theme music "In The Hall Of The
   Mountain King" from 'Peer Gynt Suite Op.23' various
FORTY-SECOND STREET - see under 42ND STREET
FOUR FEATHER FALLS (Granada 59) theme song: BARRY GRAY
   MICHAEL HOLLIDAY 'EP Collect' SEE FOR MILES (Pinn)
   SEECD 311 (CD) see also COLLECTION 4
FOUR FLIES ON GREY VELVET (1971) Music sco: ENNIO MORR
   ICONE -S/T- inc 'BIRD WITH THE CRYSTAL PLUMAGE' +
   'CAT O'NINE TAILS' DRG (Pinn): DRGCD 32911 (CD)
FOUR IN THE MORNING (1965) Music sco: JOHN BARRY -S/T-
   PLAY IT AGAIN (Koch): PLAY 002 (CD)
FOUR WEDDINGS AND A FUNERAL (1993) Music score: RICHARD
   RODNEY BENNETT -S/T- VERTIGO (Poly):516 751-2 (CD)
   see also COLLECTIONS 66,78,171
FOURTH PROTOCOL (1987) Music score: LALO SCHIFRIN -S/T-
   FILMTRAX (Silva Screen): MOMCD 109 (CD)
FOX AND THE HOUND The - see WALT DISNEY INDEX p.343
FRANCES (1982) Music sco JOHN BARRY see COLLECTION 24
FRANCIS BISSELL'S WEST COUNTRY KITCHEN (C4 7/1/97) orig
   music: SIMON CHAMBERLAIN unavailable
FRANCIS OF ASSISI (1961) Mus sc: MARIO NASCIMBENE -S/T-
   with 'DOCTOR FAUSTUS' DRG (Pinn): DRGCD 32965 (CD)
FRANK AND JESSE (1994) Music score: MARK McKENZIE -S/T-
   INTRADA USA (Silva Screen): MAF 7959D (CD)
FRANK SKINNER SHOW (BBC2 3/9/95) mus "National Emblem"
   (E.E.Bagley) TV vers.arr.by Julian Stewart Lindsay
   ROYAL MARINES BAND on 'By Land and Sea' BANDLEADER
   (BMG-Con): BND 61030 (CD) BNA 5030 (MC)
FRANKENSTEIN    see COLLECT.61,63,110,119,206,354,390,393
   see also 'MARY SHELLEY'S FRANKENSTEIN'
FRANKENSTEIN CREATED WOMAN (1966) Music: JAMES BERNARD
   see COLLECTION 119
FRANKIE STARLIGHT (1995) Music score: ELMER BERNSTEIN
   -S/T- VARESE (Pinn): VSD 5679 (CD)
FRASIER (USA 93/C4 20/4/94) title music by BRUCE MILLER
   DARRYL PHINNESSEE perf: KELSEY GRAMMER unavailable
FRAUDS (1992) Mus: GUY CROSS -S/T- Mushroom (Tot-BMG)
   PTR 003 (CD)

FRED BBC2 1/10/84 and FRED DIBNAH STORY (BBC2 28/8/96)
  series theme mus "Carnival Of Venice" (Briccialdi)
  JAMES GALWAY,flute *RCA (BMG): PD(PK) 70260 (CD/MC)*
FREDDIE AS F.R.O.7 (1992) M: DAVID DUNDAS-RICK WENTWOR
  TH Lyr: Don Black-David Ashton-Jan Acevski "I'll
  Keep Your Dreams Alive" GEORGE BENSON-PATTI AUSTIN
  -S/T- *MCI (THE-DISC): FRO7 CD1(CD) FRO7 MC1(MC)*
FREDDY'S DEAD: THE FINAL NIGHTMARE (A NIGHTMARE ON ELM
  STREET 6)(1991) Mus: BRIAN MAY -S/T- *METAL BLADE
  (Pinn): CDZZORRO 33 (CD) ZORRO 33 (LP)* / IMPORT
  *VARESE (Pinn): VSD 5333 (CD)*
FREE WILLY (1993) Mus sco: BASIL POLEDOURIS -S/T- *MJJ
  (Sony Music): 474 264-2 (CD) deleted see COLL 32*
FREE WILLY 2: The Adventure Home (1995) Music: BASIL
  POLEDOURIS -S/T- *Sony:480 739-2(CD) -4(MC) deleted*
FREE WILLY 3: THE RESCUE (1997) Mus sco: CLIFF EIDELMAN
  -S/T- *VARESE (Pinn): VSD 5830 (CD)*
FREEJACK (1991) Music score: TREVOR JONES -S/T- *reiss
  MORGAN CREEK (Poly): 002247-2 (CD)*
FREEWHEELERS The (ITV 70's) theme music "Private Eye"
  LAURIE JOHNSON *see COLLECTION 4*
FRENCH KISS (1995) Music score: JAMES NEWTON HOWARD
  -S/T- *MERCURY (Poly): 528 321-2 (CD) -4 (MC)*
FRENCH LIEUTENANT'S WOMAN The (1981) Music: CARL DAVIS
  'Adagio' Sonata in D.K576 (MOZART) John Lill (pno)
  *-S/T-DRG (Pinn): DRGCD 6106 see also COLLECT 66,71*
FRENCH TWIST - see 'GAZON MAUDIT'
FRESH PRINCE OF BEL-AIRE (USA 1990/BBC2 14/1/91) music
  WILL SMITH *see COLLECTION 345*
FREUD (1962) Music score: JERRY GOLDSMITH
  -S/T- *TSUNAMI Imp (Silva Screen): TSU 0129 (CD)*
FRIDAY (1994) Music sco: HIDDEN FACES  -S/T- *PRIORITY
  VIRGIN (EMI): CDPTY 117 (CD) PTYMC 117 (MC)*
FRIDAY THE 13TH (Film 1980) Music sco: HARRY MANFREDINI
  *see COLLECTIONS 210,355*
FRIDAY THE 13TH (TV Series) (USA 89)(ITV-13/7/90) mus
  score by FRED MOLLIN  -S/T- on *GNP Crescendo USA
  (S.Screen): GNPD 8018 (CD) GNPS(5) 8018 (LP/MC)*
FRIED GREEN TOMATOES (1992) Music score: THOMAS NEWMAN
  -S/T- *MCA: MCAD 10461 (CD)*
FRIENDLY PERSUASION (1956) Music score: DIMITRI TIOMKIN
  t.song (D.Tiomkin-P.F.Webster) sung by PAT BOONE
  -S/T- *VARESE (Pinn): VSD 5828 (CD)*
FRIENDS (NZ/C4 28/4/95) theme music "I'll Be There For
  You" (Michael Skloff-Allee Willis) by REMBRANDTS
  *-S/T- (WEA): 9362 46008-2 (CD) 9362 46008-4 (MC)
  see also COLLECTION 405*
FRIGHT NIGHT (1985) Music score: BRAD FIEDEL selection
  *see COLLECTION 378*
FRIGHTENERS The (1996) Music score: DANNY ELFMAN -S/T-
  *MCA (BMG): MCAD 11469 (CD) DELETED 97*
FRITZ THE CAT (1971) Music sco: ED BOGAS-RAY SHANKLIN
  CHARLES EARLAND -S/T- inc 'Heavy Traffic' score
  *FANTASY (Pinn): FCD 24745 (CD)*

FROG PRINCE The (1984) Music score: ENYA -S/T- *re-iss*
  *SPECTRUM (Poly): 551 099-2 (CD)*
FROM DAWN TIL DUSK (1995) Music score: GRAEME REVELL
  -S/T- *feat* STEVIE RAY VAUGHN-ZZ TOP-THE BLASTERS..
  *EPIC Soundtrax (Sony): 483 617-2 (CD) -4 (MC)*
FROM RUSSIA WITH LOVE (1963) Music: JOHN BARRY title
  song (L.Bart) MATT MONRO -S/T- *re EMI: CZ 550 (CD)*
  *see also COLLECTIONS 25,26,38,108,132,,305,352 and*
FUGITIVE The (USA ABC/QM 1963-66) theme music: PETE
  RUGOLO *see COLLECTIONS 110,342,364,368,372,374*
FUGITIVE The (1993) Music score: JAMES NEWTON HOWARD
  -S/T- *ELEKTRA (WEA): 7599 61592-2 (CD)*
FULL CIRCLE (The Haunting Of Julia) (1976) Music score
  COLIN TOWNS -S/T- *KOCH Screen (Koch): 38703-2(CD)*
  *see COLLECTION 404*
FULL CIRCLE WITH MICHAEL PALIN (BBC1 31/8/97) title mus
  by PETER HOWELL + orig music by ELIZABETH PARKER.*NA*
  *BBC Radio Coll (Pinn): ZBBC 2016 (MC)*
FULL METAL JACKET (1987) Songs by various artists
  -S/T- *W.BROS (WEA): 925 613-2 (CD) -4 (MC)*
FULL MONTY The (1996) Music: ANNE DUDLEY -S/T- *featur:-*
  HOT CHOCOLATE-TOM JONES-M.PEOPLE-SERGE GAINSBOURG-
  STEVE HARLEY & COCKNEY REBEL-GARY GLITTER-WILSON
  PICKETT-IRENE CARA-DONNA SUMMER-SISTER SLEDGE etc.
  *RCA Victor (BMG): 09026 68904-2 (CD) -4 (MC)*
FULLY BOOKED (BBC1 Scot 22/4/95) t.music: JOHN COOK..*NA*
FUNKY BUNKER (ITV 10/1/97) title music: SIMON BASS...*NA*
FUN IN ACAPULCO *see* ELVIS PRESLEY INDEX p.348
FUNNY BONES (1995) Music score: JOHN ALTMAN -S/T- on
  *EDEL UK (Pinn): 002930-2EDL (CD)*
FUNNYBONES (BBC1 29/9/92) theme music: ERNIE WOOD
    *see COLLECTION 60*
FUNNY FACE (1957) Songs: GEORGE & IRA GERSHWIN *with:*
  AUDREY HEPBURN-FRED ASTAIRE-KAY THOMPSON-MICHEL
  AUCLAIR *VERVE (Poly): 531 231-2 (CD)*
FUNNY FACE see also Coll 'GERSHWIN MUSICAL OVERTURES'
FUNNY GIRL - songs by Jule Styne and Bob Merrill
    1.FILM SOUNDTRACK 1968 *feat:* BARBRA STREISAND -S/T-
    *COLUMBIA (Sony M): 462 545-2 (CD) -4 (MC)*
    2.ORIG BROADWAY CAST 1964 BARBRA STREISAND-JEAN STAP
    LETON-S.CHAPLIN-K.MEDFORD *EMI: ZDM 764661-2 (CD)*
FUNNY THING HAPPENED ON THE WAY TO THE THEATRE, A
    songs by Stephen Sondheim
    1.ORIG LONDON CAST 1963 *w:* FRANKIE HOWERD-ISLA BLAIR-
    KENNETH CONNOR-JOHN RYE-JON PERTWEE-MON.EDDIE GRAY
    LEON GREENE *EMI Angel: CDANGEL 3 (CD) DELETED 2.96*
    2.ORIG BROADWAY CAST 62 *w:* ZERO MOSTEL-JOHN CARRADINE
    JACK GILFORD-RAYMOND WALBURN-DAVID BURNS and Comp.
    *EMI ANGEL: ZDM 764770-2 (CD)*
FUNNY WOMEN (BBC2 4/10/97) theme song "Funny Face" (G.&
  I.Gershwin) sung by FRED ASTAIRE 'FUNNY FACE' -S/-T
  *VERVE (Poly): 531 231-2 (CD)*
FURY The (1978) Music sc: JOHN WILLIAMS / LONDON S.ORCH
  -S/T- import *VARESE (Pinn): VSD 5264 (CD)*

FUTURE FANTASTIC (BBC1 21/6/96) "Extremis" based on the
'Future Fantastic' theme by HAL mixed by QATTARA
spoken vocal by GILLIAN ANDERSON *VIRGIN (EMI): tbc*
FUTUREWATCH (BBC2 5/1/97) m: SWITCH & THE GINGER BP..*NA*

**G.**B.H. (C4 6/6/91) music: RICHARD HARVEY and ELVIS Cost
ello)-S/T- music by ELVIS COSTELLO & RICHARD HARVEY
*DEMON (Pinn): DSCD 4(CD) DSCASS 4(MC) DSLP4 (LP)*
*see COLLECTION 181*
G.I.BLUES (1960) featur ELVIS PRESLEY remastered -S/T-
*RCA (BMG): 07863 67460-2 (ltd ed CD) 07863 66960-2*
*(CD) -4 (MC) see also* ELVIS PRESLEY INDEX p.348
G.I.JANE (1997) Music score: TREVOR JONES -S/T- on
*POLYDOR: 162 109-2 (CD)*
GADFLY The (1955) Music Suite Op.97A (D.SHOSTAKOVICH)
score incl.music from 'FIVE DAYS AND FIVE NIGHTS'
*NAXOS (Select): 8.553299 (CD) recording also on*
*CFP (EMI) CDCFP 4463 (CD) -4 (MC)*
GAELIC GAMES (C4 8/7/95) theme mus "The Celts" (Enya)
ENYA *WEA (WEA): 4509 91167-2 (CD) WX 498C (MC)*
also 1993 series "Book Of Days" (Enya-Roma Ryan)
"Shepherd Moons" *WEA 9031 75572-2(CD)-4(MC)*
GALLIPOLI (1981) *see COLLECTION 65,69,258,263,384,*
GAMBLE The (1991) Mus sc: PINO DONAGGIO -S/T- *Italian*
*Import (Silva Screen): OST 106 (CD)*
GAMBLER The (1997) Mus: TCHAIKOVSKY adapt.by BRIAN LOCK
-S/T- *VIRGIN CLASSICS (EMI): VC 545 312-2 (CD)*
GAME The (1997) Music score: HOWARD SHORE  song "White
Rabbit" (G.Slick) performed by JEFFERSON AIRPLANE
-S/T- *LONDON (Poly): 458 556-2 (CD) -4 (MC)*
GAME OF DEATH (1979) Music score: JOHN BARRY c/w NIGHT
GAMES (Barry) *SILVA SCREEN (Koch):FILMCD 123 (CD)*
GAME ON (Hat-Trick for BBC2 27/2/95) theme music "When
I Find My Heaven" by The GIGOLO AUNTS on 'Flippin'
Out' *FIRE Records (Pinn): FIRECD 35 (CD) + on*
-S/T- 'DUMB & DUMBER' *RCA (BMG):07863 66523-2 (CD)*
GAME SET AND MATCH (Gran 3/10/88) *see COLLECTION 181*
GAMEKEEPER The (BBC1 28/7/95) Music by The IRON HORSE
-S/T- 'Voice Of The Land' - THE IRON HORSE on *KLUB*
*(Gord.Duncan/Ross/Topic): CD(ZC)LDL 1232 (CD/MC)*
GANGWAY (1937) md: Louis Levy / 4 songs on Coll 'LOUIS
LEVY - MUSIC FROM THE MOVIES' *KOCH: RAJCD 884*
GARDEN OF THE FINZI-CONTINIS The (1970) Music: MANUEL
DE SICA -S/T- *LEGEND (Silva Screen): OST 125 (CD)*
GARDEN The (1990) Music sco: SIMON FISHER TURNER -S/T-
*IONIC (Pinn): IONIC 5C (MC) IONIC 5CD (CD)*
GARDENER'S WORLD (BBC2/Catalyst) theme music 1993-98
series by NICK WEBB and GREG CARMICHAEL (ACCOUSTIC
ALCHEMY) from 'Morning Light' *label unconfirmed*
GARY RHODES (BBC2 6/11/97) m: DEBBIE WISEMAN *unavail.*
GAS FOOD AND LODGING (1992) Music sc: BARRY ADAMSON &
V.Arts) *IONIC (RTM/Pinn): IONIC 9(C)(CD) (MC/CD)*
GATE TO THE MIND'S EYE The (1994)(Animated) Music by
THOMAS DOLBY -S/T- *GIANT (BMG):74321 23386-2 (CD)*

GATTACA (1997) Music score: MICHAEL NYMAN -S/T-
   *VIRGIN VENTURE (EMI): CDVE 936 (CD)*
GAY 90'S MUSICAL The (ORIG 1997 USA CAST RECORDING)
   Songs: RON ABEL-TOM BROWN-DAN KAEL-HOLLY NEAR etc.
   *VARESE (Pinn): VSD 5867 (CD)*
GAZON MAUDIT (FRENCH TWIST) (1995) Music: MANUEL MALOU
   -S/T- *VIRGIN (EMI): CDVIR 49 (CD)*
GBH - see beginning of G's
GENDERQUAKE (C4 9/7/96) op.theme music "Ebben Ne Andro
   Lontano" from 'La Wally' (Catalini) sung by LESLEY
   GARRETT 'DIVA' *S.Screen (Koch): SONGCD 903 (CD)*
GENERAL HOSPITAL (ITV 70's series) theme *(1)* "Girl In
   The White Coat" DEREK SCOTT theme *(2)* "Red Alert"
   *see COLLECTION 368,372*
GENERAL HOSPITAL (USA TV) *see COLLECTION 343*
GENERATION GAME *see* 'JIM DAVIDSON'S GENERATION GAME'
GENEVIEVE (1953) Music score composed & performed by
   LARRY ADLER "Genevieve Waltz"/"Love Themes"/"Blues"
   'Best Of Larry Adler' *EMI GOLD: CD(TC)MFP 6259 also*
   "Genevieve Waltz" on *EMI: CD(TC)EMS 1543 (CD/MC)*
GENTLE BEN (USA TV) *see COLLECTION 343*
GENTLE TOUCH The (LWT 1/9/84) theme (Roger Webb) ROGER
   WEBB ORCH *see COLLECTION 175*
GENTLEMEN PREFER BLONDES - songs: Jule Styne-Leo Robin
 1.REVIVAL BROADWAY RECORDING 1995 *with:* K.T.SULLIVAN
   *DRG (Pinn): DRGCD (DRGMC) 94762 (CD/MC)*
GEOFF HAMILTON'S PARADISE GARDENS (BBC2 76/1/97) front
   title music: SYMBIOSIS *unavailable*
GEORGE OF THE JUNGLE (USA TV) *see COLLECTION 340*
GERMINAL (1993) Music: JEAN LOUIS ROCQUES with ORCHES
   TRE NAT.DE LILLE -S/T- *VIRGIN (EMI) CDVIR 28 (CD)*
GET ON THE BUS (1996) Music sc: TERENCE BLANCHARD -S/T-
   V.Arts: STEVIE WONDER-D'ANGELO-A TRIBE CALLED QUEST
   CURTIS MAYFIELD *INTERSCOPE/MCA (BMG): IND 90089(CD)*
GET SHORTY (1996) Music score: JOHN LURIE -S/T- V.Arts
   US3-BOOKER T.& MG's-MORPHINE-GREYBOY etc.
   *ANTILLES-ISLAND (Poly): 529 310-2 (CD) -4 (MC)*
GET SMART (USA TV 60s) *see COLLECTIONS 339,379*
GET WELL SOON (BBC1 2/11/97) title theme song "In Over
   My Head" by CHRISTIE HENNESSEY sung by ALED JONES
   *COALITION (WEA): COLA 032CD (CDs) COLA 032C (MC)*
GHOST (1990) Music sco: MAURICE JARRE feat "Unchained
   Melody" (Alex North-Hy Zaret) - RIGHTEOUS BROTHERS
   -S/T- *re-issue MILAN (BMG): 4321 34278-2 (CD)*
   *see COLLECTIONS 63,80,120,214,218,262,274*
GHOST AND MRS.MUIR (1947) Music score: BERNARD HERRMANN
   score recording on *VARESE (Pinn): VSD 5850 (CD)*
GHOST AND MRS.MUIR (USA TV) *see COLLECTION 343*
GHOSTBUSTERS (1984) Music sco: ELMER BERNSTEIN Title
   song: Ray Parker Jnr. songs by Various Arts -S/T-
   *ARISTA (BMG) 258720 (CD) see COLLECTIONS 17,46,268*
GHOSTBUSTERS 2 (1989) Music score: RANDY EDELMAN -S/T-
   also includes "Love Is A Cannibal" by Elton John
   *MCA (BMG): MCD 06056 (CD)*

GHOSTS OF THE CIVIL DEAD (1991) Music: NICK CAVE-BLIXA
    BARGOED-MICK HARVEY -S/T- *Mute (RTM/Pinn):(-)(CD)*
G.I.BLUES *see ELVIS PRESLEY INDEX p.348*
GIANT (1956) Music: DIMITRI TIOMKIN suite on 'Western
    Film World Of D.Tiomkin' with LONDON STUDIO S.ORCH.
    (L.Johnson) *U.KANCHANA (H.Mundi) UKCD 2011 (CD)*
    *also avail:* complete score + 'EAST OF EDEN'/'REBEL
    WITHOUT A CAUSE' *TSUNAMI (S.Screen):TSU 0201 (CD)*
GIDGET (USA TV) *see COLLECTION 340*
GIGI - songs by Alan Jay Lerner and Frederick Loewe
    1.FILM MUSICAL 1958 *w:* LESLIE CARON-MAURICE CHEVALIER
      -S/T- *42 tracks MGM (EMI Premier): CDODEON 10 (CD)*
    2.ORIG LONDON CAST 1985 *w:* SIAN PHILLIPS-BERYL REID-
      AMANDA WARING-JEAN PIERRE AUMONT-GEOFFREY BURRIDGE-
      JOHN AARON *FIRST NIGHT (Pinn): OCRCD 6007 (CD)*
      *see also COLLECTIONS 180,319*
GILBERT & SULLIVAN OVERTURES LIGHT OPERA PRO-ARTE ORCH.
    (Sir M.Sargent) *CFP (EMI): CD(TC)CFP 4529 (CD/MC)*
GILLIGAN'S ISLAND (USA) *see COLLECTION 339*
GIRL 6 (96)   PRINCE -S/T- *WEA:9362 46239-2(CD) -4(MC)*
GIRL CRAZY (1943) Songs by GEORGE & IRA GERSHWIN *feat:*
    JUDY GARLAND-MICKEY ROONEY-TOMMY DORSEY ORCHESTRA
    *EMI SOUNDTRACKS: CDODEON 30 (CD)* new recording on
    *VIRGIN (EMI): VM 561247-2 (CD) see also Collect*
    'GERSHWIN MUSICAL OVERTURES'
GIRL FRIEND The (COLCHESTER MERCURY THEATRE REVIVAL 86)
    Songs: R.Rodgers-L.Hart *feat:* BARBARA KING-MARK HUT
    CHINSON-AMANDA DAINTY *TER (Disc): CD(ZC)TER 1148*
GIRL FRIDAY (BBC1 26/11/94) music by SIMON BRINT
    *see COLLECTION 33*
GIRL FROM U.N.C.L.E. (USA TV) *see COLLECTION 343*
GIRL HAPPY *see ELVIS PRESLEY INDEX p.348*
GIRL ON A MOTORCYLE (1968) Music score comp/arranged
    by LES REED -S/T- *re-issue (limited edition) on*
    *RPM (Pinn): RPM 171 (CD)*
GIRL WHO CAME TO SUPPER The - songs by Noel Coward
    1.NOEL COWARD SINGS HIS SCORE (1963)
    *DRG (Pinn): DRGCD 5178 (CD)*
GIRLS GIRLS GIRLS *see ELVIS PRESLEY INDEX p.348*
GIRLY SHOW The (C4 26/1/96) title music: SIMON BASS..*NA*
GIVE MY REGARDS TO BROAD STREET (1984) PAUL McCARTNEY
    J.LENNON -S/I- *EMI:CDP 746043-2(CD) TCPCTC 2(MC)*
GLADIATORS (ITV 9/96) theme "The Boys Are Back In Town"
    (P.Lynnot) GLADIATORS *RCA (BMG):74321 41699-2(CDs)*
    (LWT 10/92 series) theme mus (Muff Murfin)
    'GLADIATORS ALBUM' (Var.Art) *POLYG: 515 877-2 (CD)*
    *-4(MC)*   VOLUME 2 'RETURN' *516 517-2(CD) -4(MC)*
    *see COLLECTION 33*
GLASS MOUNTAIN The (1949) Music sco: NINO ROTA 'Legend
    Of The Glass Mountain' (NINO ROTA) MANTOVANI ORC
    *HORATIO NELSON (THE): CDSIV 6128(CD) SIV 1128(MC)*
    *see also COLLECTIONS 62,160*
GLENN MILLER STORY The (1954) Universal Studio Orch
    -S/T- *MCA (BMG): MCLD 19025 (CD)*

GLOBAL SUNRISE (BBC 1/1/97) Music score: BRIAN BENNETT
　-S/T- *OCEAN DEEP (Grapev/Poly): OCD 002 (CD)*
GLORY (1989) Music score: JAMES HORNER w. Boys Choir
　Of Harlem -S/T- *VIRGIN: CDV(TCV)V 2614 (CD/MC)*
GLORY OF MY FATHER (LA GLOIRE DE MON PERE)(90) Music:
　VLADIMIR COSMA + 'MY MOTHER'S CASTLE' (CHATEAU DE
　MA MERE)(90) -S/T-*Imp (S.Scr) 50050(CD) 40050(MC)*
GMTV (ITV) theme music by DAVID ARCH *see COLLECTION 33*
GO INTO YOUR DANCE (1935) Film Musical songs: AL DUBIN
　HARRY WARREN *feat* AL JOLSON and RUBY KEELER & Comp
　-S/T- including songs from 'MELODY FOR TWO'/'YOU
　CAN'T HAVE EVERYTHING'/'YOU'LL NEVER GET RICH' on
　*GREAT MOVIE THEMES (Target-BMG): CD 60014 (CD)*
GOBLIN MARKET (ORIG OFF BROADWAY CAST 87) Songs: POLLY
　PENN *TER (Disc):(CD)(ZC)TER 1144*
GODFATHER The (1972) Mus sc: NINO ROTA -S/T- *MCA (BMG)*
　*MCLD 19022 (CD)* SUITE: *S.Screen (Koch): FILMCD 077*
GODFATHER II (1974) Music sco: NINO ROTA -S/T- *MCA USA*
　*(Silva Screen): MCAD 10232 (CD)*
GODFATHER III (1991) M: CARMINE COPPOLA. Theme: NINO
　ROTA. v: HARRY CONNICK JR -S/T- *SONY: 467 813-2 CD*
　*see COLLECTIONS 63,70,97,154,171,244,276,277*
GODSPELL - songs by Stephen Schwartz
　1.FILM -S/T- 1973 *feat:* VICTOR GARBER-DAVID HASKELL-
　　JERRY STOKA-LYNNE THIGPEN-ROBIN LAMONT *-S/T-*
　　*ARIOLA (S.Screen): ARCD 8337 (CD) ACB6 8337 (MC)*
　2.ORIG BROADWAY CAST 1971 *feat:* DAVID HASKELL-LAMAR
　　ALFORD-JOHANNE JONAS-ROBIN LAMONT-SONIA MANZANO
　　JEFFREY MYLETT-STEPHEN NATHAN and Comp *Orig Cast*
　　*ARIOLA (S.Screen): ARCD 8304 (CD) ACB6 8304 (MC)*
　3.CARLTON SHOWS: GODSPELL / JESUS CHRIST SUPERSTAR
　　STUDIO HIGHLIGHTS 1994 Various Arts *CARLTON Shows*
　　*Coll: PWKS 4220 (CD) PWKMC 4220 (MC)*
　4.STUDIO RECORDING 1993 *w:* JOHN BARROWMAN-CLAIRE BURT
　　JACQUELINE DANKWORTH-RUTHIE HENSHALL-GLYN KERSLAKE
　　PAUL MANUEL-CLIVE ROWE-SAMANTHA SHAW-DARREN DAY
　　Highlights: *SHOWTIME (MCI-THE): SHOW(CD)(MC) 012*
　　Complete: *TER (Disc): CD(ZC)TER 1204 (CD/MC)*
GOING ALL THE WAY (1996) Music by TOMandANDY -S/T-
　*VERVE (Poly): 537 908-2 (CD)*
GOING FOR A SONG (BBC1 71) Theme "Prelude" -'The Birds'
　(RESPIGHI) *several classical recordings available*
GOING STRAIGHT (BBC1 1978) - *see COLLECTION 402*
GOLD (ITV 27/10/97) theme and incid.music: HAL LINDES
　*unavailable. see also* 'BAND OF GOLD'
GOLD DIGGERS (1995) Music score: JOEL McNEELY -S/T-
　*VARESE (Pinn): VSD 5633 (CD)*
GOLD DIGGERS OF 1933 (33 MUSICAL) DICK POWELL-RUBY KEEL
　ER-JOAN BLONDELL-GINGER ROGERS *includes songs from*
　'ROSE OF WASHINGTON SQUARE' and 'THE DOLLY SISTERS'
　*TARGET (BMG): CD 60009 (CD)*
GOLD RUSH The (1925) Music: CHARLES CHAPLIN *see Coll*
　'FILM MUS.OF CHARLES CHAPLIN' *RCA: 09026 68271-2*
　MAX TAK ORCH *BASTER (Direct): BASTER 309050 (CD)*

GOLDEN BOY (O.BROADWAY CAST 1959) Songs (Charles Stro
    use-Lee Adams) *feat:* SAMMY DAVIS JNR.-BILLY DANIELS
    PAUL WAYNE-KENNETH TOBEY-TED BENIADES-LOUIS GOSSETT
    *EMI ANGEL (EMI): ZDM 565 024-2 (CD)*
GOLDEN GIRLS The (USA)(C4 1/8/86) Theme "Thank You For
    Being a Friend" (Andrew GOLD) *see COLLECTION 344*
GOLDEN MOUNTAINS (1931) - *see COLLECTION 261*
GOLDEN VOYAGE OF SINBAD (1973) *see COLLECTION 332*
GOLDENEYE - *see JAMES BOND FILM INDEX p.346*
GOLDFINGER (1964) Mus: JOHN BARRY title song (J.Barry
    L.Bricusse-A.Newley) sung by SHIRLEY BASSEY -S/T-
    -S/T- *reissue EMI PREMIER (EMI): CZ 557 (CD)*
    *see COLLECTIONS 20,25,26,27,28,29,203*
    *see also JAMES BOND FILM INDEX p.*
GOLDRING AUDIT (C4/Juniper 8/3/97) t.mus: DAVID ARCH.*NA*
GOLF (BBC1/2) theme mus "Chase Side Shoot Out" (Brian
    Bennett) by BRIAN BENNETT *see COLLECTION 155*
GOMER PYLE (USA TV) *see COLLECTION 340*
GONDOLIERS The - songs by Gilbert and Sullivan
    1.D'OYLY CARTE OPERA COMPANY - New Symph Orchestra
      (Isadore Godfrey) *LONDON (Poly): 425 177-2 (CDx2)*
    2.NEW SADLERS WELLS OPERA - *TER (Disc): ZCTED 1187
      (2MC) CDTER2 1187 (2CD)*
    3.PRO-ARTE ORCHESTRA (Malcolm Sargent) & GLYNDEBOURNE
      FESTIVAL CHOIR Soloists: Geraint Evans-Alexander Yo
      ung-Owen Brannigan-R.Lewis *EMI:CMS 764394-2 (2CDs)*
GONE WITH THE WIND (1939) Music sco: MAX STEINER -S/T-
    with addition.unissued items *digitally re-mastered*
    *EMI ODEON (EMI): CDODEON 27 (2CD)* also available:
    National Philharmonic Orchestra (Charles Gerhardt)
    *RCA RED SEAL (BMG): GD 80452 (CD) GK 80452 (MC)*
    *see COLLECTIONS 62,63,81,136,140,157,160,171,173,*
    *203,230,292,319*
GOOD GUYS The (Thames 3/1/92) mus: DEBBIE WISEMAN *see
    Colls* 'FAVOURITE TV THEMES'/'GREATEST TV THEMES'
GOOD LIFE The (BBC1 4/4/75) theme music: BURT RHODES
    *see COLLECTION 229*
GOOD MORNING AND GOOBYE (1967 RUSS MEYER) music on Coll
    'Russ Meyer Orig Soundtracks Vol.4' (various) on
    *POP BIZ (Cargo-Greyhound): LP 014 (LP)*
GOOD MORNING VIETNAM (1988) Music score: ALAN MASON +
    Var.Arts -S/T- *A.& M: CDMID 163 (CD) CMID 163 (MC)*
GOOD NEWS! MUSIC THEATRE OF WICHITA Songs B.G.DeSylva
    Lew Brown-Ray Henderson *feat* KIM HUBER-ANN MORRISON
    LINDA MICHELE-MICHAEL GRUBER *TER (Disc):CDTER 1230*
GOOD ROCKIN'TONITE (O.LONDON CAST 1992) *JACK GOOD'S* no
    stalgic look back at the 50's *with* PHILIP BIRD-TIM
    WHITNALL-GAVIN STANLEY-JOE BROWN and Company on
    *FIRST NIGHT (Pinn): OCRCD 6026 (MC/CD)*
GOOD THE BAD & THE UGLY (1966) Music: Ennio Morricone
    -S/T- *LIBERTY (S.Screen): 46408-2 (CD) see COLLECT*
    *62,126,127,170,173,251,252,254,256,352,353,358*
GOOD GUYS The (ITV 3/1/92) theme music: DEBBIE WISEMAN
    *see COLLECTION 138,175*

GOODBYE AGAIN (1961) Music score: GEORGES AURIC
  *see COLLECTION 73*
GOODBYE GIRL ORIG LONDON CAST 1996 (Marvin Hamlisch-Don
  Black) *featuring* GARY WILMOT-ANN CRUMB and Company
  *FIRST NIGHT (Pinn): SCORECD 44*
GOOBYE MR.CHIPS (O.CHICHESTER CAST 1979) *w:* JOHN MILLS
  *TER (DISC):CD(ZC)TER1025 see Coll* RICHARD ADDINSELL
GOODFELLAS The (1990) Music score: CHRISTOPHER BROOKS
  Song "Roses Are Red" (Al Byron-Paul Evans) sung by
  Bobby Vinton-S/T- *ATLANTIC (WEA): 7567 82152-2(CD)*
GOODNIGHT SWEETHEART (BBC1 18/11/93) theme (Ray Noble)
  mus (Anthony & Gaynor Sadler) sung by NICK CURTIS
  *unavailable* orig: AL BOWLLY *EMI: CDP 794341-2 (CD)*
GOOFY MOVIE The (1995) Music: DON DAVIS + V.Artsists
  -S/T- *W.DISNEY (B.Vista): WD 76400-2 (CD) -4 (MC)*
GORKY PARK (1983) Music sco: JAMES HORNER -S/T- reiss:
  *VARESE (Pinn): VCD 47260 (CD)*
GOSPEL ACCORDING TO ST.MATTHEW (1964) Mus: LUIS BACALOV
  and BACH/MOZART/PROKOFIEV plus excerpts from 'MISSA
  LUBA' and song "Sometimes I Feel Like A Motherless
  Child" by ODETTA *IMPORT Silva Screen: OST 132 (CD)*
GOTHIC (1987) Music: THOMAS DOLBY feat Screaming Lord
  Byron (Tim Spall) -S/T- *VIRGIN (EMI): CDV 2417*
GOTHIC DRAMAS (1977 Italian TV) mus: ENNIO MORRICONE
  TV -S/T- *DRG/New Note (Pinn): DRGCD 32916 (CD)*
GOWER'S CRICKET MONTHLY (BBC2 15/5/95) m.STEVE SPIRO.*NA*
GRACE OF MY HEART (1996) M.sco: LARRY GRAY songs: ELVIS
  COSTELLO-BURT BACHARACH-SHAUN COLVIN-WILLIAMS BROS.
  -S/T- feat Var.Artists on *MCA (BMG): MCD 11554 (CD)*
GRADUATE The (1967) Songs: PAUL SIMON & ART GARFUNKEL
  -S/T- *COLUMBIA (Sony): 40-32359 (MC) CD 32359 (CD)*
GRAFFITI BRIDGE (1990) Mus: PRINCE -S/T- *Paisley Park
  WB (WEA): 759927493-2 (CD) WX(C) 361 (LP/MC)*
GRAND The (Gran 4/4/97) music: JULIAN NOTT *unavailable*
GRAND CANYON (1992) Music score: JAMES NEWTON HOWARD
  -S/T- *MILAN (BMG): 262493 (CD) 412493 (MC)*
GRAND DAY OUT, A (Wallace & Gromit) music: JULIAN NOTT
  v/o PETER SALLIS -S/T- with 'The Wrong Trousers'
  *BBC (Pinn): ZBBC 1947 (MC)   BBC Video: BBCV 5155*
  (Grand Fay Out) *BBCV 5155* (Wrong Trousers) *(VHS)*
GRAND HOTEL (BROADWAY CAST RECORDING) with John Wylie-
  Henry Grossman-Willm Ryall-David Elledge and Comp.
  *RCA Vic (BMG): 09026 61327-2(CD) -4 (MC) -5 (DCC)*
GRAND NATIONAL (BBC Grandstand) opening music theme
  from film "Champions"1983 (CARL DAVIS) *unavailable*
GRAND NIGHT FOR SINGING, A (O.BROADWAY CAST 1994) on
  *VARESE (Pinn): VSD 5516 (CD)*
GRAND PRIX (BBC 78-96) theme "The Chain" originally
  FLEETWOOD MAC from 'Rumours' *WEA: K2 456344
  (CD) K2 56344 (CD) see COLLECTIONS 155,167,382*
  from 1997 see F1 (FORMULA 1) (ITV)
GRANDSTAND (BBC1 began 8/10/58 - 1998) *THEME MUSIC
  1976-98* KEITH MANSFIELD *see COLLECTIONS 4,155,167
  1958 theme* "News Scoop" LEN STEVENS *see COLLECT.6,*

GRANGE HILL (BBC1 1978-96) *theme mus (78-89)* "Chicken
Man" (ALAN HAWKSHAW) *see COLLECTIONS 360,406*
*1990-98 theme* PETER MOSS *unavailable*
GRANPA (Film Car C4/31/12/89) Music: HOWARD BLAKE with
SARAH BRIGHTMAN and PETER USTINOV -S/T- *COLUMBIA*
*(Sony Music) CDHB 1 (CD) HBC 1 (MC) HB 1 (LP)*
GREASE - songs by Jim Jacobs-Warren Casey-Gibb Bros-
John Farrar-Louis St.Louis-S.Simon and others
  1.FILM MUS. 1978 *w:* JOHN TRAVOLTA-OLIVIA NEWTON JOHN
  FRANKIE VALLI-STOCKARD CHANNING-FRANKIE AVALON etc.
  *POLYDOR: 817 998-2 (CD) 817 998-4 (MC) -5 (DCC)*
  2.ORIG LONDON CAST 1993 CRAIG McLACHLAN-DEBBIE GIBSON
  VOYD EVANS & Co *Epic (SM): 474 632-2 (CD) -4 (MC)*
  3.STUDIO RECORDING 1994 JOHN BARROWMAN-SHONA LINDSAY
  ETHAN FREEMAN-MARK WYNTER & Company
  Highlights: *SHOWTIME (MCI-THE): SHOW(CD)(MC) 007*
  Complete: *TER (Disc): CD(ZC)TER 1220 (CD/MC)*
  *see also Tele-Tunes 1995 p.188 for other records*
  4.CARLTON SHOWS COLL (Studio 93) CARL WAYNE-MICHAELA
  STRACHAN *CARLTON: PWKS(PWKMC) 4176 (CD/MC)*
  5.NEW BROADWAY CAST 1994 *RCA (BMG): 09026 62703-2 CD*
  6.STUDIO RECORDING VARIOUS ARTISTS *HALLMARK (CHE):*
  *30395-2 (CD) -4 (MC)*
GREAT CARUSO The (1950) Sung by MARIO LANZA  *RCA GOLD*
*SEAL (BMG): GD(GK)(GL) 60049 (CD/MC/LP)*
GREAT DAY IN HARLEM, A (1995) Various Arts / spin-off
CD (not -S/T-) inc.tracks by ART BLAKEY-GENE KRUPA
DUKE ELLINGTON-DIZZY GILLESPIE-COUNT BASIE-CHARLES
MINGUS etc. on *SONY JAZZ (SM): 460500-2 (CD)*
GREAT DICTATOR (1940) *see Coll* 'CHARLIE'
GREAT ESCAPE The (1962) Mus sco: ELMER BERNSTEIN -S/T-
*INTRADA USA (Koch Int): MAFCD 7025 (CD)*
*see COLLECTIONS 35,62,63,140,199,201,238*
GREAT EXPECTATIONS (ORIG CAST THEATR CLWYD, MOLD 1993)
Songs: MIKE READ  Adap:Christopher G.Sandford *feat*
DARREN DAY-CHRIS CORCORAN-ELIZABETH RENEHAN-TAMARA
USTINOV *TER (Disc): CDTER 1209(CD) TERZC 1209(MC)*
GREAT JOURNEYS (BBC2 16/11/94) t.music: ROGER BOLTON.*NA*
GREAT MUPPET CAPER The (1981) Music & Songs: JOE RAPOSO
*feat* JIM HENSON-FRANK OZ-DAVE GOELZ -S/T- *ARISTA*
*KIDZ (BMG): 74321 18246-2 (CD) 74321 18246-4 (MC)*
GREAT ORMAND STREET HOSPITAL (BBC1 2/2/94) music by
JULIAN STEWART LINDSAY *unavailable*
GREAT RAILWAY JOURNEYS (BBC2 3/9/96) series title music
IAN LYNN. incidental episode music by COLIN WINSTON
FLETCHER-CHRIS WHITTEN-DAVID POORE plus various lib
rary production music *unavailable*
GREAT ROCK AND ROLL SWINDLE (1980) Music: SEX PISTOLS
-S/T- *full VIRGIN (EMI): TCVD 2510(2MC) CDVD 2510
(2CDs) highlights: OVED 234 (LP) OVEDC 234 (MC)*
GREAT TRAIN ROBBERY (FIRST) - *see under* 'WILD ROVERS'
GREAT WHITE HYPE The (1996) Music: MARCUS MILLER -S/T-
*V/A EPIC (Sony): 484 294-2(CD) -4(MC) deleted 1997*
GREAT WHITE The - *see* 'ACT OF PIRACY'

GREATEST AMERICAN HERO (USA TV) *see COLLECTION 341*
GREEN ACRES (USA) *see COLLECTIONS 339,405*
GREEN CARD (1991) Music score HANS ZIMMER -S/T-
    *VARESE (Pinn): VSD 5309 (CD) VSC 5309 (MC)*
GREEN HORNET The (USA TV) *see COLLECTIONS 340,379*
GREENWILLOW (ORIG N.Y.CAST 1960) Songs: FRANK LOESSER
    *feat:* ANTHONY PERKINS-CECIL KELLAWAY-PERT KELTON-
    ELLEN McKOWN-WILLIAM CHAPMAN-GROVER DALE *on*
    *DRG USA (Pinn): DRGCD 19006 (CD)*
GREY FOX The (1982) Music score: MICHAEL CONWAY -S/T-
    *DRG (Pinn): CDSL 9515 (CD) see COLLECTION 79*
GREYSTOKE: THE LEGEND OF TARZAN LORD OF THE APES (1984)
    *see COLLECTION 77*
GRIDLOCK'D (1997) Mus score: STEWART COPELAND -S/T- on
    *MERCURY (Poly): 534 684-2 (CD) -4 (MC)*
GRIFF (USA) *see COLLECTION 246*
GRIND (O.BROADWAY CAST 1985) Songs (LARRY GROSSMAN and
    ELLEN FITZHUGH) *with* Ben Vereen-Leilani Jones & Co
    *TER (Disc): (CD)(ZC)TER 1103 (CD/MC)*
GRIZZLY ADAMS - *see* 'LIFE AND TIMES OF GRIZZLY ADAMS'
GROSSE POINT BLANK (1997) Music sco: JOE STRUMMER -S/T-
    (Various Artisrs) *LONDON (Poly): 828 867-2 (CD)*
GROUND FORCE (BBC2 19/9/97) mus: JIM PARKER *unavailable*
GROUNDHOG DAY (1092) Music score: GEORGE FENTON -S/T-
    *Imp (S.Scr): CB 53760 (CD) deleted / see COLLECT.97*
GROUPIE GIRL (1970) Various Artists -S/T- *reissue with*
    'BEYOND THE VALLEY OF THE DOLLS' (1970) Var.Artists
    *SCREEN GOLD (Greyhound): SGLDCD 0010 (CD)*
GROVE FAMILY The (BBC 50s) *see COLLECTION 381*
GROWING PAINS (BBC1 16/5/92) theme music: NIGEL HESS
    *see COLLECTION 191*
GROWN UPS (BBC2 7/1/97) music by ROBERT HARTSHORNE and
    lyrics by JON SAYERS *unavailable*
GRUMPIER OLD MEN (1995) Music sco: ALAN SILVESTRI -S/T-
    *LONDON (Poly): 535 482-2 (CD) -4 (MC)*
GULLIVERS TRAVELS (C4 7/4/96) mus score: TREVOR JONES
    -S/T- *RCA (Silva Screen): RCA 68475-2 (CD)*
GUMBY SHOW The (USA TV) *see COLLECTION 342*
GUN LAW (also known as GUN SMOKE)(USA 55-75) theme mus
    (Koury-Spencer) *see COLLECTIONS 170,342*
GUNSMOKE - see GUN LAW
GUNS OF NAVARONE The (1961) Music sco: DIMITRI TIOMKIN
    -S/T- suite on *UNICORN KANCHANA: DKPCD 9047 (CD)*
GUYS AND DOLLS - songs by Frank Loesser
  1.REVIVAL LONDON NATIONAL THEATRE CAST 1982: IAN CHAR
    LESON-JULIE COVINGTON-DAVID HEALY-BOB HOSKINS-JULIA
    McKENZIE  *reiss MFP (EMI): CD(TC)MFP 5978 (CD/MC)*
  2.FILM MUSICAL 1955  FRANK SINATRA-MARLON BRANDO-JEAN
    SIMMONS-VIVIAN BLAINE *MCA (BMG): MCLD 19155 (CD)*
  3.ORIG BROADWAY CAST 1950  ROBERT ALDA-VIVIENE BLAINE
    STUBBY KAYE *MCA (S.Scre): MCAD(MCAC) 10301 (CD/MC)*
  4.REVIVAL LONDON NATIONAL THEATRE CAST 1982 IAN CHAR
    LESON-JULIE COVINGTON-DAVID HEALY-BOB HOSKINS-JULIA
    McKENZIE  *reiss MFP (EMI): CD(TC)MFP 5978 (CD/MC)*

5.NEW BROADWAY CAST 1991 Walter Bobbie-John Carpenter
  Steve Ryan-Ernie Sabella-Herschel Sparber-Ruth Will
  iamson *RCA (BMG): 09026 61317-2(CD) -4(MC) -5(DCC)*
6.CARLTON SHOWS COLLECTION 1995  DENNIS LOTIS-BARBARA
  WINDSOR-KEITH MICHELL-BERNARD CRIBBINS and Company
  *CARLTON SHOWS Collect: 30362 0013-2 (CD) -4 (MC)*
7.STUDIO RECORDING 1995  EMILY LOESSER-GREGG EDELMAN
  TIM FLAVIN-DAVID GREEN-KIM CRISWELL-DON STEPHENSON
  <u>Complete:</u> *TER (Disc): CDTER 1228 (CD)*
  <u>Highlights:</u> *SHOWTIME (MCI-THE): SHOW(CD)(MC) 034*
GYPSY - songs by Jules Styne and Stephen Sondheim
  1.ORIG BROADWAY CAST 1959 w.ETHEL MERMAN and Company
    *COLUMBIA (S.Screen): CK 32607 (CD) JST 32607 (MC)*
  2.ORIG LONDON CAST 1973 ANGELA LANSBURY-DEBBIE BOWEN
    JUDY CANNON-ZAN CHARISSE-BARRIE INGHAM on *RCA IMP*
    *(Silva Screen): 60571-2 (CD) 60571-4 (MC)*
  3.REVIVAL BROADWAY CAST 1990 *with* TYNE DALY *ELEKTRA*
    *NONESUCH (S.Screen): 79239-2 (CD) -4 (MC) deleted*

HACKERS (1996) Music score: SIMON BOSWELL -S/T- *featur:*
  STEREO MCs-ORBITAL-LEFTFIELD-UNDERWORLD-PRODIGY...
  *EDEL-CINERAMA (Pinn): 002256-2 CIN (CD)*
HADLEIGH (Yorkshire 29/10/69-76) theme mus: TONY HATCH
  *see COLLECTIONS 3,182,372*
HAIR - songs by Galt McDermott-Jerome Ragni-James Rado
  1.FILM MUS.1979 -S/T- *RCA (S.Scr): 3274-2(CD) -4(MC)*
  2.ORIG BROADWAY CAST 1968 *w:* STEVE CURRY-RONALD DYSON
    MELBA MOORE *RCA Victor (BMG): BD 89667 (CD)*
  3.ORIG LONDON CAST 1968 *with* PAUL NICHOLAS-VINCE EDWA
    RDS-OLIVER TOBIAS  *POLYDOR 519 973-2 (CD) -4 (MC)*
  4.REV. LONDON CAST 1993 *w:* PAUL HIPP-JOHN BARROWMAN
    SINITTA-PEPSI LAWRIE DEMACQUE-ANDREE BERNARD-FELICE
    ARENA-PAUL J.MEDFORD *EMI: CDEMC 3663(CD) delet.96*
  5.CARLTON SHOWS COLLECTION 1995 *w.* CARL WAYNE-NICOLA
    DAWN-BOBBY CRUSH-JOHN HOWARD *prod by* Gordon Lorenz
    *CARLTON Shows Collect: 30362 0015-2 (CD) -4 (MC)*
  6.STUDIO RECORDING - SHOWS COLLECTION
    *SHOWTIME (Disc): SHOWCD 055 (CD)*
HAIR BEAR BUNCH (USA71) "Help It's The Hair Bear Bunch'
  theme (Hoyt Curtain-Jo.Roland-Denby Williams)
  *see COLLECTION 370*
HALF A SIXPENCE (O.LONDON CAST 1963) Songs: DAVID HENE
  KER *feat* TOMMY STEELE *DERAM (Poly): 820 589-2 (CD)*
HALF COCKED (1995) *feat* VARIOUS ARTISTS -S/T- *MATADOR*
  *(Vital): OLE 152-2 (CD) -1 (LP)*
HALLOWEEN (THE BEST OF HALLOWEEN 1-6) S/track Master
  *VARESE (Pinn): VSD 5773 (CD)*
  *see also COLLECTIONS 37,109,178,206,210,355*
HALLOWEEN 1 (1978) Music sco: JOHN CARPENTER -S/T- Imp
  *VARESE USA (Pinn): VCD 47230 (CD)*
HALLOWEEN 2 (1981) Music sco: JOHN CARPENTER -S/T  Imp
  *VARESE USA (Pinn): VCD 47152 (CD)*
HALLOWEEN 3 (1983) Mus: ALAN HOWARTH-J.CARPENTER -S/T-
  *VARESE (Pinn): VSD 5243 (CD)*

HALLOWEEN 4 (1988) Music sco: ALAN HOWARTH -S/T- Imprt
   *VARESE (Pinn: VSD 5205 (CD)*
HALLOWEEN 5 (1989) Music sco: ALAN HOWARTH -S/T- Imprt
   *VARESE (Pinn): VSD 5239 (CD)*
HALLOWEEN 6 (1995) Music score: ALAN HOWARTH -S/T- on
   *VARESE (Pinn): VSD 5678 (CD)*
HAMISH MACBETH (BBC1 Scot 26/3/95) music: JOHN LUNN..*NA*
HAMLET (1948) Music score: WILLIAM WALTON inc.mus.from
   'As You Like It' *CHANDOS (Chandos): CHAN 8842 (CD)*
   *see also COLLECTION 306*
HAMLET (1964 USSR) Music: SHOSTAKOVICH score performed
   by BELGIAN RADIO SYMPHONY ORCHESTRA (Shostakovich)
   *RCA Navigator Classics (BMG): 74321 24212-2 (CD)*
   *see also COLLECTION 261*
HAMLET (1990) Music score ENNIO MORRICONE -S/T-
   *VIRGIN (EMI): CDVMM 3 (CD)*
HANCOCK (BBC1 60's) theme mus: DEREK SCOTT
   *see COLLECTIONS 3,368,372*
HANCOCK'S HALF HOUR (BBC1 60s) theme ANGELA MORLEY
   *see COLLECTION 229*
HAND THAT ROCKS THE CRADLE (1991) Music: GRAEME REVELL
   -S/T- *reiss HOLLYWOOD (S.Screen): HWD 161304 (CD)*
HANDFUL OF DUST A (1988) Music score: GEORGE FENTON
   -S/T- *OCEAN DISQUE (Pinn): CDLTD 071 (CD)*
HANDMAID'S TALE The (1990) Music sco: RYUICHI SAKAMOTO
   -S/T- *GNP (S.Screen):GNPD 8020(CD) GNP-5 8020(MC)*
HANGOVER SQUARE (1945) Music score: BERNARD HERRMANN
   Suite on 'CONCERTO MACABRE' *KOCH INT: 37609-2 (CD)*
   -S/T- with 'HATFUL OF RAIN'/'ON DANGEROUS GROUND'
   *TSUNAMI Imp (Silva Screen): TCI 0610 (CD)*
HANNAH 1939 (ORIG USA CAST) Songs: BOB MERRILL
   *TER (Disc): CDTER 1192 (CD) ZCTER 1192 (MC)*
HANNAH AND HER SISTERS (1986) Music: COUNT BASIE Orch +
   HARRY JAMES ORCH -S/T- *MCA (BMG): IMCAC 6190(MC)*
   *see COLLECTIONS 66,68,72*
HANS ANDERSEN - songs by Frank Loesser
   1.FILM MUSICAL 1952 *feat:* DANNY KAYE on 'Very Best Of
   *MCA (BMG): MCLD 19049 (CD) MCLC 19049(MC)* also on
   *VARESE (Pin): VSD 5498 (CD) with* 'THE COURT JESTER'
   2.ORIG LONDON CAST 1974/77 *wi:* TOMMY STEELE-SALLY ANN
   HOWES-ANTHONY VALENTINE-SIMON ANDREWS-LILA KAYE-MIL
   O O'SHEA-COLETTE GLEASON-BOB TODD *reiss on 1 CD on*
   *DRG-New Note (Pinn): DRGCD 13116 (CD)*
HAPPY DAYS (USA 74 / re-run C4 27/2/89) *orig opening*
   *theme* "Rock Around The Clock" (Jimmy De Knight-Max
   Freedman) BILL HALEY & THE COMETS *MCA Rec (BMG)*
   *Title theme* "Happy Days"(Norman Gimbel-Charles Fox)
   PRATT & McLAIN *see COLLECTIONS 168,341*
HAPPY TRAILS (USA) *see COLLECTION 339*
HARD BOILED (1993) music score: MICHAEL GIBBS -S/T- on
   *IONIC-MUTE (RTM-Pinn): IONIC 11CD (CD)*
HARD DAY'S NIGHT A (1964) Songs: JOHN LENNON-PAUL McCAR
   TNEY / Beatles & George Martin -S/T-*PARLOPHONE EMI:*
   *PCS 3058 (LP) TCPCS 3058 (MC) CDP 746437-2 (CD)*

HARD TARGET (1993) Music score: GRAEME REVELL -S/T- on
*VARESE (Pinn): VSD 5445(CD) see also COLLECTION 78*
HARDCASTLE AND McCORMICK (USA TV) *see COLLECT.12,344*
HARDER THEY COME The (1971) Music & songs: JIMMY CLIFF
-S/T- *MANGO ISLAND: RRCD 11 (CD) RRCT 11 (MC)*
HARDY BOYS & NANCY DREW MYSTERIES (USA) *see COLLEC.344*
HARPIST The (1997) Music score: BRIAN BENNETT -S/T- on
*OCEAN DEEP (Grapevine/Polyg): OCD 011 (CD)*
HARRY AND THE HENDERSONS (USA 90 BBC1 27/9/91) theme
"Your Feet's Too Big" (Ada Benson-Fred Fisher & Ink
Spots) TV vers.sung by LEON REDBONE *unavailable*
INK SPOTS on *FLAPPER (Pinn): PASTCD 9757 (CD)*
HARRY ENFIELD'S TELEVISION PROGRAMME (BBC2 2/4/92)theme
mus: KATE SI.JOHN additional music by SIMON BRINT
*BBC (Pinn): ZBBC 15877CD (2CD)*
HARRY O (USA) *see COLLECTION 246*
HARRY'S GAME (Yorkshire 25/10/82) music: PAUL BRENNAN
CLANNAD 'Ultimate Coll.'*(BMG) 74321 48674-2 (CD)*
*see COLLECTIONS 168,267,352,382*
HARRY'S MAD (Central 4/1/93) mus: NIGEL-BEAHAM POWELL &
BELLA RUSSELL *SPOKEN WORD MC BBC (Pinn):YBBC 1395*
HART TO HART (USA TV) *see COLLECTION 341*
HARVEST (Regain) (1937) Music: ARTHUR HONEGGER suite
on *MARCO POLO (Select): 8.223467 (CD)*
HARVEY GIRLS The (1946) Songs: HARRY WARREN-JOHNNY
MERCER *feat:* JUDY GARLAND-RAY BOLGER-JOHN HODIAK
-S/T- *reissue:* EMI PREMIER: *CDODEON 11 (CD)*
HATARI! (62) Music: HENRY MANCINI *see COLLECT 177,243*
HAUNTED (1995) Music score: DEBBIE WISEMAN -S/T-
*SILVA SCREEN (Koch): TRXCD 2002 (CD)*
HAUNTED SUMMER (1989) Music: CHRISTOPHER YOUNG -S/T-
*SILVA SCREEN (Koch): FILMCD 037 (CD)*
HAVE GUN-WILL TRAVEL (USA 57) theme "Ballad Of Paladin"
(Richard Boone-J.Western-Sam Rolfe)- JOHNNY WESTERN
*on* 'Americana' *COLUMBIA Sony: 468121-2(CD) -4(MC)*
*see COLLECTIONS 265,340*
HAVE I GOT NEWS FOR YOU (BBC2 28/9/90-1998 theme tune
performed by BIG GEORGE *see COLLECTION 402*
HAVE YOUR CAKE AND EAT IT (BBC1 15/3/97) music score by
JEREMY SAMS *unavailable*
HAWAII 5-0 (USA 1968-80) theme music: MORTON STEVENS
*see COLLECTIONS 2,100,101,109,168,246,339,356,379*
HAWAIIAN EYE (USA TV) *see COLLECTION 340*
HEAD (1968) Music performed by The MONKEES featuring:
MICKEY DOLENZ-DAVY JONES-MIKE NESMITH-PETER TORK
-S/T- *RHINO/ATLANTIC (WEA): 4509 97659-2 (CD)*
HEAD OF THE CLASS (USA TV) *see COLLECTION 373*
HEAR MY SONG (1991) Music: JOHN ALTMAN Josef Locke's
voice VERNON MIDGLEY -S/T- *WEA: 7599 24456-2 (CD)*
*-4 (MC)* JOSEF LOCKE recordings are on 'Hear My
Song' *EMI (EMI):CDGO 2034 (CD) TCGO 2034 (MC)*
HEART CONDITION (1990) Music score: PATRICK LEONARD
song "Have A Heart" sung by Bonnie Raitt from 'Nick
Of Time' *CAPITOL: (CD)(TC)EST 2095 (CD/MC/LP)*

HEART IN WINTER, A (Un Coeur En Hiver) (1991) Music sco
   (Philippe Sarde)'Sonata for Piano,Violin & Cello'
   (RAVEL) Complete mus *ERATO (WEA): 4509 92408-2(CD)*
   *see also Coll* 'CINEMA CLASSICS 9'
HEART OF MIDNIGHT (1988) Music score: YANNI -S/T-
   *SILVA SCREEN (Koch): FILMCD 119 (CD)*
HEART OF THE MATTER (BBC1 (1979-98) *1995-98 theme by*
   JUSTIN NICHOLLS *see COLLECTION 33*
   series 89-94 *title mus:* JONATHAN GIBBS *unavailable*
HEARTBEAT (YTV 10/4/92) theme "Heartbeat" (N.Petty-Bob
   Montgomery) NICK BERRY 'HEARTBEAT' *Columbia Sony:*
   *471900-2 (CD) -4 (MC)* + VOL.2 *475529-2 (CD) -4 (MC)*
   BUDDY HOLLY on *Pickwick: PCD 888(CD) HSC 3199 (MC)*
   BILL MAYNARD on *Seven (Pinn): MMM 01(CD)(MC)(S)*
   'BEST OF HEARTBEAT' *Sony: MOOD(CD)(C) 37 (CD/MC)*
   'HEARTBEAT-FOREVER YOURS' *Sony TV:SONYTV 8(CD)(MC)*
   'BEST OF BRITISH TELEVISION' *MCI(THE):MCCD 225(CD)*
   'NUMBER ONE LOVE SONGS' Var.Arts *Global TV (BMG):*
   *RADCD 46 (2CD) RADMC 46 (2MC)*
   'LOVE ME TENDER' *Global TV (BMG): RADCD(MC) 72*
   *see also COLLECTIONS 33,100*
HEARTBREAK HIGH (Aust.94/BBC2 27/9/94) Various Music
   -S/T- *WEA (WEA): 4509 99938-2 (CD)*
HEARTBREAKERS (1984) Music sco: TANGERINE DREAM -S/T-
   *SILVA SCREEN (Koch): FILMCD 163 (CD)*
HEARTBURN (1986) *see COLLECTION 77*
HEARTS AND SOULS (1993) Music score: MARC SHAIMAN *feat:*
   FRANKIE VALLI-STEPHEN BISHOP-RAY CHARLES-B.B.KING
   -S/T- *MCA (S.Screen): MCAD(MCAC) 10919 (CD/MC)*
HEAT (1995) mus: ELLIOT GOLDENTHAL *WEA: 9362 46144-2*
HEAT AND DUST (1982) *see COLLECTION 68*
HEATHCLIFF - songs by John Farrar and Tim Rice
   1.LIVE 1996 RECORDING *feat* CLIFF RICHARD *with* HELEN
     HOBSON-SARA HAGGERTY and GORDON GILTRAP *(guitar)*
     *EMI UK: CD(TC)EMD 1099 (2CD/MC)*
   2.STUDIO ALBUM 1995 *featuring* CLIFF RICHARD *with*
     OLIVIA NEWTON JOHN-KRISTINA NICHOLS and others
     *EMI: CD(TC)EMD 1091 (CD/MC)*
HEAVENLY CREATURES (1994) Music: PETER DASENT + V/Arts
   -S/T- *MILAN (BMG): 253 502-2 (CD)*
HEAVEN'S PRISONERS (1995) Music score: GEORGE FENTON
   -S/T- (songs) *CODE BLUE-WEA: 7567 82848-2 / -4*
   -S/T- (score) *DEBONAIR (Pinn): CDDEB 1004 (CD)*
HEAVY (1994) Music score: THURSTON MOORE -S/T- on
   *CINERAMA-EDEL (Pinn): 0022642CIN (CD)*
HEAVY METAL (1981) Mus.sco: ELMER BERNSTEIN + Var.Arts:
   SAMMY HAGAR-RIGGS-DEVO-CHEAP TRICK-DONALD FAGEN-CHE
   AP TRICK-BLACK SABBATH-NAZARETH-JOURNEY-DON FELDER-
   STEVIE NICKS *-S/T- reiss.COL.(SONY): 486 749-2 (CD)*
HEAVY TRAFFIC (1973) Music sco: ED BOGAS-RAY SHANKLIN-
   CHARLES EARLAND -S/T- inc 'Fritz The Cat' score on
   *FANTASY (Pinn): FCD 24745 (CD)*
HEIDI (1968) Music score: JOHN WILLIAMS -S/T- *Imp.on*
   *COLUMBIA USA (Silva Screen): LXE 707 (CD)*

HELLO DOLLY - songs by Jerry Herman
1. ORIG BROADWAY CAST 1964 *with:* CAROL CHANNING-DAVID
   BURNS-EILEEN BRENNAN-SONDRA LEE-CHARLES NELSON REI
   LLY-JERRY DODGE-GORDON CONNELL-IGORS GAVON-ALICE
   PLAYTEN-DAVID HARTMAN *VARESE (Pinn): VSD 5557 (CD)*
2. BROADWAY MUSICAL 1967 *w:* Pearl Bailey-Cab Calloway
   *RCA Victor (BMG): GD 81147 (CD)*
3. FILM MUSICAL 1969 -S/T- *featuring* BARBRA STREISAND
   *CASABLANCA (S.Screen): 810368-2 (CD) -4 (MC)*
   *see also COLLECTIONS 136,172,248,269*
HELLO GIRLS The (BBC1 5/9/96) opening theme "Busy Line"
   (Murray Semos-Frank Stanton) sung by BBC CAST....*NA*
   various closing themes (original 50's/60's songs)
HELLRAISER (1987) Music score: CHRISTOPHER YOUNG -S/T-
   *S.SCREEN (Koch): FILMCD 021(CD) see COLLEC 210,355*
HELLRAISER 2 'Hellbound' (1988) Mus: CHRISTOPHER YOUNG
   -S/T- *GNP (BMG-Con): GNP(C)(D) 8015 (LP/MC/CD)*
HELLRAISER III 'Hell On Earth'(92) Music: RANDY MILLER
   -S/T- (SCORE) *GNP (S.Screen): GNPD 8233 (CD) GNP5
   8233 (MC)* (SONGS) S.Screen: 480007-2(CD) -4(MC)
HELLRAISER IV: BLOODLINE (95) Music score: DANIEL LICHT
   *feat* Northwest Sinfonia and Chorus (Pete Anthony)
   -S/T- *SILVA SCREEN (Koch): FILMCD 179 (CD)*
HELP (1965) Songs: JOHN LENNON-PAUL McCARTNEY -S/T-
   *EMI: CDP 746 439-2 (CD) TC-PCS 3071 (MC) PCS (LP)*
HEMINGWAY'S ADVENTURES OF A YOUNG MAN (1962) Music by
   FRANZ WAXMAN 'Sayanora' *BMG: 09026 662657-2 (CD)*
HENRY PORTRAIT OF A SERIAL KILLER (1990) Music by JOHN
   McNAUGHTON-KEN HALE -S/T- *QDK (SRD):EFA 11910 (CD)*
HENRY V (1944) Music sco: WILLIAM WALTON sel.on 'WALTON
   FILM MUSIC' LONDON PHILHARM.ORCH cond by CARL DAVIS
   *EMI: CDM 565585-2 (CD)* also BOURNEMOUTH SYMPHONY OR
   CHESTRA (Litton) *LONDON DECCA (Poly):448 134-2(CD)*
HENRY V (1989) Music sco: PATRICK DOYLE C.B.S.O.(Simon
   Rattle) -S/T- *EMI: CDC(EL) 749919-2 (CD) -4(MC)*
   *see also COLLECTIONS 64,66,78,293,306,385*
HENRY V AT THE GLOBE (C4 15/6/97) M.Dir: PHILIP PICKETT
   selection of music on Coll 'SHAKESPEARE'S MUSICK'
   *PHILIPS (Poly): 446 687-2 (CD) -4 (MC)*
HENRY'S CAT (BBC 1984) *see COLLECTION 408*
HERCULES (1997, WALT DISNEY) Music: ALAN MENKEN song
   "Go The Distance" sung by MICHAEL BOLTON -S/T- on
   *DISNEY (Carlton/Poly): WD 60864-2 (CD) -4 (MC)*
   *see also* WALT DISNEY INDEX p.343
HERCULES The Legendary Journeys (TV 95) mus sco: JOSEPH
   LoDUCA -S/T- *VARESE (Pinn): VSD 5660 (CD) (Vol.1)
   VSD 5884 (CD) (Vol.2) see also COLLECTIONS 110,302*
HERE AND NOW (BBC1 15/9/97) title mus: GEORGE FENTON.*NA*
HERE COME THE WAVES (1945 MUSICAL) *feat* BING CROSBY and
   BETTY HUTTON *incl.songs from* 'BATHING BEAUTY' and
   'THIS GUN FOR HIRE' *TARGET (BMG): CD 60001 (CD)*
HERE WE GO ROUND THE MULBERRY BUSH (1967) Music: STEVIE
   WINWOOD and The SPENCER DAVIS GROUP -S/T- re-issue:
   *RPM (Pinn): RPM 179 (CD)*

HERE'S HARRY (BBC1 1960's) theme "Comedy Hour" IVOR SL
   ANEY *see COLLECTION 4*
HETTY WAINTHROP INVESTIGATES (BBC1 3/1/96) theme music:
   NIGEL HESS *see COLLECTIONS 5,33,192*
HIDEAWAY (1994) Music score: TREVOR JONES -S/T- on
   *INOIC-MUTE/RTM (Disc): IONIC 12CD (CD)*
HIDER IN THE HOUSE (1989) Music sco: CHRISTOPHER YOUNG
   -S/T- *INTRADA USA (Silva Screen): MAF 7007D (CD)*
HIGH AND THE MIGHTY The music score: DIMITRI TIOMKIN
   on 'HIGH NOON' *RCA (BMG): 09026 62658-2 (CD)*
   *see COLLECTIONS 63,204,394*
HIGH CHAPARRAL The (USA BBC1 67) music: DAVIS ROSE
   *see COLLECTIONS 168,176,343,373*
HIGH NOON (1952) Music score: DIMITRI TIOMKIN suite on
   'Western Film World Of D.Tiomkin' LONDON STUDIO SO.
   (L.Johnson) *UN.KANCHANA (H.Mundi) UKCD 2011 (CD)*
   *Song* "Do Not Forsake Me" (Ned Washington-Dimitri Ti
   omkin) by TEX RITTER *BEAR FAMILY: BCD 15625 (CD)*
   *see also COLLECTIONS 62,81,170,265,365,366*
HIGH SCHOOL HIGH (1996) Music: IRA NEWBORN *-S/T- feat*
   The BRAXTONS-BRAIDS-FAITH EVANS-JODECI and others
   *BIG BEAT/EAST WEST (WEA): 7567 92709-2(CD) -4(MC)*
HIGH SOCIETY - songs by Cole Porter
  1.FILM MUSICAL 1956 SOUNDTRACK *with* BING CROSBY-GRACE
   KELLY-FRANK SINATRA-CELESTE HOLM and Company -S/T-
   *CAPITOL EMI: CDP 793787-2 (CD)*
  2.CARLTON SHOWS COLLECTION 1994 Studio Recording
   *feat:* KENNY BALL & HIS JAZZMEN-DENNIS LOTIS-CARL
   WAYNE-TRACY COLLIER-West End Concert Orch (Matthew
   Freeman) *CARLTON Shows Coll: PWKS(PWKMC) 4193*
HIGH SPIRITS (1988) Music score: GEORGE FENTON -S/T-
   *GNP (S.Screen) GNPD 8016 (CD) GNP5 8016 (MC)*
HIGH SPIRITS (O.LONDON CAST 1964) Songs (Tim Gray-Hugh
   Martin) *feat* Cicely Courtneidge-Dennis Quilley-Jack
   Waters-Marti Stevens *DRG (Pinn): CDSBL 13107 (CD)*
HIGH VELOCITY (1977) Music score: JERRY GOLDSMITH -S/T-
   *PROMETHEUS (Silva Screen): PCD 134 (CD)*
HIGHER AND HIGHER (1943 MUSICAL) *feat* FRANK SINATRA-MEL
   TORME-VICTOR BORGE *includ.songs from* 'STEP LIVELY'
   *TARGET (BMG): CD 60004 (CD)*
HIGHLANDER (1986) Music score: MICHAEL KAMEN Songs by
   by Queen (6 from 'A Kind Of Magic' inc. title trk
   *PARLOPHONE: (TC)EU 3509 (MC/LP) CDP 746267-2 (CD)*
HIGHLANDER: Final Dimension (1994) Mus: PETER ROBINSON
   -S/T- *Edel (Pinn): EDL 28892 (CD)*
HIGHLANDER (TV series 1992) theme song "Princes Of The
   Universe" by QUEEN from album 'A Kind Of Magic'
   *EMI: CDP 746 267-2 (CD)*
HIGHWAY (TTees 9/84) 'Highway Companion' Harry Secombe
   Bernard Cribbins-Wendy Craig-Guards Chapel Choir &
   ROD THOMSON (theme) *Word: WRDC 3033 (MC)*
HIGHWAY PATROL (USA) *see COLLECTIONS 101,342*
HIGHWAY TO HEAVEN (USA)(ITV 7/6/87) theme: DAVID ROSE
   *see COLLECTIONS 12,344*

HILL STREET BLUES (USA 80-ITV/C4 80s) theme: MIKE POST
    see COLLECTIONS 12,51,100,101,159,168,242,341,353
    357,360,382,388,405
HISTORY OF BRITISH ART (BBC2 21/4/96) title mus: DAVID
    BOWIE arranged by DOMINIC MULDOWNEY unavailable
HISTORY OF MR.POLLY (1949) Music score: WILLIAM ALWYN
    Suite from film played by London Symphony Orch
    (Richard Hickox) on CHANDOS: CHAN 9243 (CD)
HITCHER The (1986) Music score: MARK ISHAM -S/T-
    SILVA SCREEN (Koch): FILMCD 118 (CD)
HITCHHIKERS GUIDE TO THE GALAXY (UKGO 23/3/93 orig BBC2
    BBC2 81) theme: TIM SOUSTER other mus: PADDY KINGS
    LAND BBC:ZBBC 1035 (MC set) BBCCD 6001(CD set)
    see COLLECTIONS 110,273
HMS BRILLIANT (BBC1 26/7/95) music: JOHN HARLE / title
    theme "Light" sung by SARAH LEONARD see COLL.407
HMS PINAFORE - (operetta) songs by Gilbert & Sullivan
  1.New Sadlers Wells 1987 NIKOLAS GRACE-LINDA ORMISTON
    Highlights: SHOWTIME (MCI-THE): SHOW(CD)(MC) 022
    Complete: TER (Disc): CDTER(ZCTED) 1150 (2CD/2MC)
  2.D'OYLY CARTE OPERA COMPANY - New Symphony Orchest
    (I.Godfrey) LONDON (Poly): 414 283-2 (CDx2)
  3.PRO-ARTE ORCH Malcolm Sargent GLYNDEBOURNE FESTIV.
    CHOIR  GEORGE BAKER-JOHN CAMERON-RICHARD LEWIS-OWEN
    BRANNIGAN+'TRIAL BY JURY' EMI: CMS 764397-2 (2CD)
HOBSON'S CHOICE (1953) Music sco: MALCOLM ARNOLD suite
    +other MALCOLM ARNOLD works KOCH Int: 37266-2 (CD)
    Suite 'Film Music' London Symphony Orchest (Richard
    Hickox) CHANDOS: CHAN 9100 (CD)
HOFFA (1992) Music sco: DAVID NEWMAN -S/T- on FOX IMPT
    (Silva Screen): FOX 11001-2 (CD) FOX 11001-4 (MC)
HOGAN'S HEROES (USA TV) see COLLECTION 340
HOLD THE BACK PAGE (BBC1 12/11/85) see COLLECTION 153
HOLDING ON (BBC2 8/9/97) music: NICK BICAT unavailable
HOLDING THE BABY (Granada 24/1/97) mus: STEVE NIEVE..NA
HOLIDAY 92/93/94/95/96/97/98 (BBC1) theme music by
    PAUL HARDCASTLE unavailable  89/90/91 series theme
    "Holiday Romance" GORDON GILTRAP see COLLECTION 153
    86/87/88 "Holiday Suite" by The SIMON MAY ORCHESTRA
    'NEW VINTAGE' ARC (Total): CDART 102 (CD) deleted
    80-85 "Heartsong" GORDON GILTRAP see COLLECTS 6,153
HOLIDAY REPS (BBC1 13/11/97) theme mus "There She Goes"
    The LA'S GO DISCS (Poly): 828 202-2 (CD) -4 (MC)
HOLLOW REED The (1996) Music score: ANNE DUDLEY -S/T-
    RCA (BMG): 09026 68630-2 (CD)
HOLLYOAKS (Mersey Productions/C4 23/10/95) theme music
    STEVE WRIGHT-GORDON HIGGINS unavailable
HOLLYWOOD CANTEEN (1944) VARIOUS -S/T- SELECTION on
    GREAT MOVIE THEMES (Targ-BMG): CD 60024 (CD)
HOLLYWOOD HOTEL (1937 MUSICAL) w: DICK POWELL-ROSEMARY
    & LOLA LANE includ.songs from 'FLYING DOWN TO RIO'
    TARGET (BMG): CD 60008 (CD)
HOLLYWOOD LOVERS (ITV 8/1/97) title mus: INFINITE PROD
    additional music: MICHAEL CONN unavailable

HOLLYWOOD PETS (ITV 18/4/96) music: SIMON BRINT with
    additional music by MICHAEL CONN *unavailable*
HOLLYWOOD WIVES (USA 4/9/89) title song (Jan Buckingham
    Jeff Silbar) LAURA BRANIGAN / music: LALO SCHIFRIN
    *see COLLECTION 242*
HOLLYWOOD WOMEN (Carlton 2/12/93) title theme: GRAHAM
    De WILDE-NIGEL MARTINEZ sung by JOSIE JAMES......*NA*
HOMBRE (USA) *see COLLECTION 170*
HOME ALONE (1990) Music score: JOHN WILLIAMS -S/T- on
    *COLUMBIA (Sony): MK 46595 (CD) deleted*
HOME ALONE 2 (1992) -S/T- w.BETTE MIDLER-DARLENE LOVE-
    LITTLE STEPHEN & E.ST.BAND-WAS NOT WAS-ALAN JACKSON
    ATLANTIC STARR  *ARISTA (BMG): 07822 11000-2(CD) -4*
HOME AND AWAY (Australia)(ITV from 13/2/89) -S/T- inclu
    ding theme (Mike Perjanik) sung by KAREN BODDINGTON
    & MARK WILLIAMS *MUSHROOM (Pinn.Imps): D.93463 (CD)*
    *see COLLECTION 367*
HOME FOR THE HOLIDAYS (1995) Music score: MARK ISHAM
    -S/T- feat V.Arts *MERCURY (Poly): 528 871-2 (CD)*
HOME FRONT (BBC2 12/4/94) mus: JAMES TAYLOR Quartet..*NA*
HOMEBOY (1988) Music score: ERIC CLAPTON-MICHAEL KAMEN
    -S/T- *VIRGIN (EMI): CDV 2574 (CD)*
HOMEWARD BOUND (1993) Music sco: BRUCE BROUGHTON -S/T-
    *INTRADA (Silva Screen): MAF 7041D (CD)*
HOMICIDE: LIFE ON THE STREET (USA/C4 15/11/93) theme
    LYNN F.KOWAL + incid.score by JEFF RONA *unavailable*
HOMME ET UNE FEMME Un - *see under* 'MAN & A WOMAN, A'
HONEY I BLEW UP THE KID (1992) Music: BRUCE BROUGHTON
    -S/T- *INTRADA (Koch/S.Screen): MAFCD 7030 (CD)*
HONEYMOONERS The (USA TV) *see COLLECTION 340*
HONG KONG PHOOEY (USA TV) *see COLLECTIONS 343,370*
HOODLUM (1996) Music score: ELMER BERNSTEIN -S/T-
    *INTERSCOPE (BMG): INTD 90131 (CD)*
HOOK (1991) *see COLLECTION 332*
HOOSIERS (1987) - *see under* 'Best Shot' (UK Title)
HOPALONG CASSIDY (USA TV) *see COLLECTION 342*
HORIZON (BBC2) title music: WILFRED JOSEPHS other mus
    ELIZABETH PARKER (BBC Radiop.Workshop) *unavailable*
HORROR OF DRACULA *see COLLECTION 209*
HORRORS OF THE BLACK MUSEUM *see COLLECTIONS 206,207*
HORSE OF THE YEAR SHOW (BBC1) theme m: "A Musical Joke"
    in F (K.522) 'Musikalischer Spass' 4th m/m (MOZART)
    *see COLLECTION 167*
HORSEMAN ON THE ROOF The (1995) Music sco: JEAN CLAUDE
    PETIT -S/T- *AUVIDIS-TRAVELLING (Koch): 1139-2 (CD)*
HORSEMAN RIDING BY. A (UKGO 18/4/93 orig BBC 24/9/78)
    Theme "A Country Canter" (MICHAEL HANKINSON) *see*
    *Coll* 'FAMOUS THEMES REMEMBER THESE'
HOSPITAL WATCH (BBC1 fr.17/8/86) theme "La Serenissima"
    (Gian P.Reverberi-L.Giordano) by RONDO VENEZIANO on
    'Venezia 2000' *BMG Italy (Discovery): 610 299 (CD)*
    also on 'Scaramucce' *BMG (Discovery): 610 193 (CD)*
HOSTAGES (Granada 23/9/92) m: RICHARD HARVEY *see Coll:*
    'SHROUD FOR A NIGHTINGALE' *(Koch): FILMCD 172 (CD)*

HOT GADGETS (BBC1 25/6/97) theme music: RAVAGGIO.....*NA*
HOT MIKADO (ORIG LONDON CAST 1995) *feat:* SHARON BENSON-
    LAWRENCE HAMILTON-ROSS LEHMAN-PAULETTE IVORY & Comp
    *FIRST NIGHT (Pinn): OCRCD 6048 (CD)*
HOT SHOE SHUFFLE (ORIG AUSTRALIAN CAST 1993)*feat:* DAVID
    ATKINS-RHONDA BURCHMORE-JACK WEBSTER & TAP BROTHERS
    *FIRST NIGHT (Pinn): OCRCD 6046 (CD)*
HOT SHOTS (1991) Music score: SYLVESTER LEVAY -S/T- on
    *VARESE (Pinn): VSD 5338 (CD)*
HOT SPOT The (1991) Music sco: JACK NITZSCHE + V.Arts
    -S/T- *ANTILLES (Poly): ANCD 8755(CD) ANC 8755(MC)*
HOT TO TROT (1988) *see COLLECTION 70*
HOTEL (BBC1 3/11/97) t.music: MARK T.WHITE *unavailable*
HOUR OF THE GUN (1967) Music score: JERRY GOLDSMITH
    -S/T- *INTRADA (Koch/Silva Screen): MAFCD 7020 (CD)*
HOUSE OF AMERICA (1997) Music sco: JOHN CALE -S/T- *feat*
    VELVET UNDERGROUND & NICO-BLUR-TOM JONES-TEENAGE
    FANCLUB-DRUGSTORE-LINOLEUM-PRODIGY-SUPERGRASS-MANIC
    STREET PREACHERS-CATATONIA-DUBSTAR and JOHN CALE
    *EMI SOUNDTRACKS (EMI); PRMDCD 29 (CD)*
HOUSE OF CARADUS The (Granada 78) theme: JOHNNY PEARSON
    *see COLLECTION 285*
HOUSE OF ELLIOT The (BBC1 31/8/91-1994) music theme
    and score: JIM PARKER -S/T- on *EMI Soundtrack Ser
    (EMI): CDSTM 5 (CD) TCSTM 5 (MC) DELETED 96*
HOUSE OF FRANKENSTEIN (1944) Music sco: HANS SALTER &
    PAUL DESAU *new recording* MOSCOW SYMPHONY ORCHESTRA
    (Stromberg) *MARCO POLO (Select): 8.223748 (CD)*
HOUSE OF THE SPIRITS The (1994) Music sco HANS ZIMMER
    -S/T- *VIRGIN (USA): number unconfirmed*
HOUSE ON SONORITY ROW (1985) Music: RICHARD BAND -S/T-
    *INTRADA (S.Screen): MAF 7046D (CD) also cont
    ains -S/T-* to 'THE ALCHEMIST' by RICHARD BAND
HOUSE PARTY 2 (1993) Music by Various Artists -S/T- on
    *MCA (BMG): MCLD 19246 (CD)*
HOUSE STYLE (Gran 7/1/97) music score: ANDY WHITMORE.*NA*
HOW BUILDINGS LEARN (BBC2 10/7/97) o.mus: BRIAN ENO..*NA*
HOW GREEN WAS MY VALLEY (1941) Music sco: ALFRED NEWMAN
    -S/T- *FOX-ARISTA (BMG): 07822 11008-2 (CD)*
HOW THE WEST WAS WON (1962) Music score: ALFRED NEWMAN
    -S/T- *deleted / see COLLECTIONS  170,211,394,397*
HOWARDS FND (1992) Music score: RICHARD ROBBINS -S/T-
    *NIMBUS (Nimbus): NI 5339 (CD) NC 5339 (MC)*
HOWARDS' WAY (BBC1 1/9/85-25/11/90) theme: SIMON MAY-
    LESLIE OSBORNE / SIMON MAY ORCH "Barracuda" theme
    and *vocal vers.* "Always There" sung by MARTI WEBB
    *see COLLECTIONS 168,402*
HOWDY DOODY! (USA) *see COLLECTION 339*
HR PUFF'N STUFF (USA TV) *see COLLECTION 343*
HUCKLEBERRY HOUND (USA TV) *see COLLECTIONS 340,370*
HUDSON HAWK (1991) Music: MICHAEL KAMEN-ROBERT KRAFT
    -S/T- *VARESE (Pinn): VSD 5323 (CD)*
HUMAN JUNGLE The (ITC 63/C4 87) theme: BERNARD EBBING
    HOUSE by JOHN BARRY ORCH *see COLLECTIONS 5,374*

HUMANOID The (1979) Music score ENNIO MORRICONE -S/T-
incl.music from 'NIGHTMARE CASTLE' (65-E.Morricone)
*ITALIAN IMPT. (Silva Screen): OST 118 (CD)*
HUNCHBACK OF NOTRE DAME (1996, Disney) Mus ALAN MENKEN
Lyr STEPHEN SCHWARTZ song "Someday" sung by ETERNAL
*EMI FIRST AVENUE: CDEMS 439 (CDs) TCEM 439 (MC)*
*-S/T- W.DISNEY (Technic): WD 77190-2 (CD) -4(MC)*
HUNDRED ACRES A (Antelope West/C4 23/2/90) theme by
NIGEL HESS *see COLLECTION 138,191*
HUNGER The (1982) Music: MICHAEL RUBINI-DENNY JAEGER
+music "Lakme" (DELIBES) "Solo Cello Suites" (BACH)
*VARESE (Pinn): VSD 47261(CD) -S/T- also available*
*MILAN (BMG): CDCH 004 (CD) inc.* 'THE YEAR OF LIVING
DANGEROUSLY' *see also COLLECTIONS 146,206,378*
HUNT FOR RED OCTOBER The (1989) Music: BASIL POLEDOURIS
*-S/T- MCA (BMG): MCLD 19306 (CD) see also COLL.199*
HUNTER (USA77)(ITV 5/85) mus: MIKE POST-PETE CARPENTER
*see COLLECTIONS 12,168,344*
HUNTERS: THE WORLD OF PREDATORS AND PREY (Discovery 95)
Mus: The RESIDENTS -S/T- *MILAN (BMG): 31169-2 (CD)*
HUNTING OF THE SNARK The (O.LONDON CAST 1991) Songs by
MIKE BATT.  Kenny EVERETT-David McCALLUM-Veronica
HART-John PARTRIDGE *FIRST NIGHT (Pinn): CASTCD 24*
HURRICANE (1979) Music sc: NINO ROTA score select.with
'THIS ANGRY AGE' *LEGEND (S.Screen): LEGENDCD 22*
HYPERSPACE (Film) Music score: DON DAVIS on *PROMETHEUS*
*(S.Screen): PCD 120 (CD) also contains SUITE FROM*
*TV SERIES* 'BEAUTY AND THE BEAST'
**I** AND ALBERT (O.LONDON CAST 1972) Songs: **Charles Strou**
**se-Lee Adams** *feat:* POLLY JAMES-SVEN BERTIL TAUBE-
LEWIS FIANDER-RAEWYN BLADE *TER (Disc): CDTER 1004*
I CAN GET IT FOR YOU WHOLESALE (O.BROADWAY CAST 1962)
Songs (Harold Rome) featur: BARBRA STREISAND & Co
*COLUMBIA (Sony M): 474 903-2 (CD)*
I DO I DO - songs: Harvey Schmidt and Tom Jones
1.ORIG BROADWAY CAST 1966 *feat* ROBERT PRESTON & Comp
*RCA (Silva Screen): 1128-2 (CD) 1128-4 (MC)*
2.ORIG USA CAST *feat:* KAREN ZIEMBA & DAVID GARRISON
*VARESE (Pinn): VSD 5730 (CD)*
I DREAM OF JEANNIE (USA 60s) *see COLLECTIONS 339,360*
I KNOW WHAT YOU DID LAST SUMMER (1997) Mus: JOHN DEBNEY
-S/T- *incl:* KULA SHAKER-TOAD THE WET SPROCKET-TYPE
O NEGATIVE-SOUL ASYLUM-FLICK-ADAM COHEN-OFFSPRING-
*COLUMBIA (Sony): 488 663-2 (CD) 488 663-2 (MC)*
I LOVE LUCY (USA 1950s) *see COLLECTIONS 339,405*
I LOVE MY WIFE (O.BROADWAY CAST) Songs by CY COLEMAN-
MICHAEL STEWART *DRG (Pinn): CDRG 6109 (CD)*
I LOVE YOU PERFECT (TVM 1989) Music score: YANNI -S/T-
*SILVA SCREEN (Koch): FILMCD 122 (CD)*
I LOVE YOU YOU'RE PERFECT NOW CHANGE (USA REVUE 1996)
O.CAST RECORDING *VARESE (Pinn): VSD 5771 (CD)*
I MARRIED JOAN (USA TV) *see COLLECTION 340*
I REMEMBER MAMA (MUSICAL 1985) Songs: Richard Rodgers
Martin Charnin  *World premiere record w:* Sally Anne

HOWES-George HEARN-Ann MORRISON-Sian PHILLIPS-Gay
SOPER-Patricia ROUTLEDGE *TER (Disc):CD(ZC)TER 1102*
I SHOT ANDY WARHOL (1996) Music score: JOHN CALE -S/T-
*EAST WEST/TAG (WEA): 7567 792690-2(CD) -4(MC)*
I SPY (USA) *see COLLECTIONS 108,246,340*
I WENT DOWN (1997) Music score: DARIO MARIANELLI -S/T-
*OCEAN DEEP (Grapevine-Polyg): OCD 008 (CD)*
IAN HISLOP'S SCHOOL RULES (C4 7/9/97) t.music "Jupiter"
- 'The Planets' (G.Holst) *many recordings available*
IBIZA UNCOVERED (SKY1 6/7/97) theme music "Magic Carpet
Ride" by The MIGHTY DUB KATZ on *LONDON-FRR (Poly):
FCD 306(CDs) FX 306(12"s)* / 'IBIZA UNCOVERED' with
VARIOUS ARTISTS on *VTDCD 168 (CD) VTDMC 168 (MC)*
ICE CASTLES (1978) Music score: MARVIN HAMLISCH -S/T-
*ARISTA (S.Screen): ARCD 8317 (CD) ACB6 8317 (MC)*
ICE SKATING (BBC 78-97) theme "Mornings At Seven" JAMES
LAST ORCH 'By Request' *POLY: 831 786-2(CD) -4(MC)*
ICE SKATING (OLYMPIC GAMES 1994) see 'TORVILL & DEAN'
IF (1968) Music sco: MARC WILKINSON *score unavailable
also used* "African Sanctus" from 'MISSA LUBA'
(Congolese African Mass) available version on
*PHILIPS (Poly): 426 836-2 (CD) -4 (MC)*
IGNATIO (Film) Music VANGELIS -S/T- *813 042-2 (CD)*
IL POSTINO - *see* 'POSTMAN The'
I'LL DO ANYTHING (1993) Music score HANS ZIMMER -S/T-
*VARESE (Pinn): VSD 5474 (CD)*
I'LL FLY AWAY (USA TV) *see COLLECTION 345*
I'M GETTING MY ACT TOGETHER AND TAKING IT ON THE ROAD
Songs: Nancy Ford-Gretchen Cryer O.LONDON CAST 1981
DIANE LANGTON-BEN CROSS *TER (Disc):CD(ZC)TER 1006*
I'M NO ANGEL (1933) *see COLLECTION 396*
IMAGINE - THE MOVIE (1988) Mus: JOHN LENNON -S/T- *PARL
OPHONE (EMI):(TC)PCSP 722 (2LP/MC) CDPCSP 722(CD)*
IMMORTAL BELOVED (1994) Music extr.(Beethoven-Rossini)
LONDON S.O.(Sir George Solti) + other arts -S/T-
*Sony: SK 66301 (CD) deleted 97 see COLLECT. 59,65*
IN CUSTODY (1993) Indian M -S/T- *EMI: CDQ 5550972(CD)*
IN HARM'S WAY - *see COLLECTION 394*
IN LIKE FLINT - *see under* 'OUR MAN FLINT'
IN LOVE AND WAR (1958) Music sco: HUGO FRIEDHOFER Symp
honic Suite - National Philh.Orch (Fred Steiner) on
'The Kentuckian' *PREAMBLE (S.Scr) PRCD 1777 (CD)*
IN LOVE AND WAR (1996) Music score: GEORGE FENTON -S/T-
*RCA Victor (BMG): 09026 68725-2 (CD)*
IN SEARCH OF ANGELS (USA TV special 94) title music by
TIM STORY *also feat:* WIM MERTENS-MARK ISHAM-JANE SI
BERRY-kd lang *WINDHAM HILL (BMG): 01934-11153 (CD)*
IN SEARCH OF HAPPINESS (BBC1 15/10/95) theme music arra
ngement of SIDNEY BECHET'S "Si Tu Vois Ma Mere" by
BIG GEORGE *unavail / orig: VOGUE Imp: 600026 CD*
IN SUSPICIOUS CIRCUMSTANCES (Granada 30/3/92) series
theme music: MATTHEW SCOTT *unavailable*
IN THE ARMY NOW (1993) Music score: ROBERT FOLK -S/T-
*INTRADA (Silva Screen): MAF 7058CD (CD)*

IN THE BLOOD (BBC2 13/5/96) t.music: GILES SWAYNE -S/T-
   *RYKODISC (Vital): RCD 20172(CD) RACS 20174(MC)*
IN THE GRIP OF THE SPIDER (*aka* WEB OF THE SPIDER)(72)
   Music (Riz Ortolani) inc 'CONFESSIONS OF A POLICE
   CAPTAIN' (71-Italy) *OST (S.Screen): OST 114 (CD)*
IN THE HEAT OF THE NIGHT (USA TV) *see COLLECTION 345*
IN THE LINE OF DUTY (TV) music sc: MARK SNOW  TV -S/T-
   *INTRADA (Koch Int): MAFCD 7034 (CD)*
IN THE MOUTH OF MADNESS (1994) Music sc: JOHN CARPENTER
   -S/T- *DRG USA (Pinn): DRGCD 12611 (CD)*
IN THE NAME OF THE FATHER (1993) Music: TREVOR JONES
   -S/T- *ISLAND (Poly): IMCD 208 (CD) ICT 8026 (MC)*
IN TOWN TONIGHT (BBC 1950s) *see COLLS: 45,130,163,402*
INCHON (1981 Music sco: JERRY GOLDSMITH -S/T-
   *FANTASY (Silva Screen): FMT 8002D (CD)*
INCOGNITO (1996) -S/T- *RCA (BMG): 09026  68971-2 (CD)*
INCREDIBLE HULK The (USA 1978) theme music: JOE HARNELL
   *see COLLECTIONS 12,168,344*
INCREDIBLE JOURNEYS (BBC1 2/1/97) mus: MIKE MARSHALL.*NA*
INCREDIBLE SHRINKING MAN The (1957) *see under* 'CREATURE
   FROM THE BLACK LAGOON'
INCREDIBLE TRUE ADVENTURES OF TWO GIRLS IN LOVE (1996)
   M: TERRY DAME -S/T-*Milan (BMG): 74321 33743-2 (CD)*
INDEPENDENCE DAY (1996) Music score: DAVID ARNOLD -S/T-
   *RCA-20th Century Fox (BMG): 09026 68564-2 (CD)*
INDIAN IN THE CUPBOARD (1995) Music sco: RANDY EDELMAN
   -S/T- *SONY Classical (Sony M): SK 68475 (CD)*
INDIANA JONES & THE LAST CRUSADE (1989) Music score:
   JOHN WILLIAMS -S/T- *WB (WEA): K925883-2(CD) -4(MC)*
INDIANA JONES & THE TEMPLE OF DOOM (1984) Music: JOHN
   WILLIAMS *see COLLECTIONS 48,200,212,298,323*
INDIFFERENT The (1988) Music score: ENNIO MORRICONE
   ENNIO MORRICONE *sel: RCA (BMG): 74321 31552-2 (CD)*
INFERNO (1980) Music sco: KEITH EMERSON -S/T- *CINEVOX
   ITA (S.Screen): CDCIA 5022 (CD) CIAK 75022 (MC)*
INFINITY (1996) Music score: BRUCE BROUGHTON -S/T- on
   *INTRADA Import (Silva Screen): MAF 7072 (CD)*
INFORMER The (1935) *see* 'STREETCAR NAMED DESIRE'
INKWELL The (1994) -S/T- featuring Various Artists on
   *RCA (BMG): 74321 21568-2 (CD) 74321 21568-4 (MC)*
INN OF THE SIXTH HAPPINESS The (1958) Mus sco: MALCOLM
   ARNOLD Suite on 'Film Music' London Symphony Orch
   (R.Hicox) *CHANDOS: CHAN 9100 (CD)*
INNOCENT The (L' Innocente) (1976) Music score: FRANCO
   MANNINO -S/T- score includes 'THE STRANGER'
   *DRG (Pinn): DRGCD 3292-2 (CD)*
INNOCENT SLEEP THE (1995) Music sco: MARK AYRES conduct
   ed by Nic Raine / vocalist LESLEY GARRETT -S/T-
   *SILVA SCREEN (Koch): FILMCD 167 (CD)*
INS AND THE OUTS The (Uns Et Les Autres Les) (Fra 1981)
   Music score (Francis Lai/Michel Legrand/Ravel)-S/T-
   *EDITIONS 23 (S.Screen): 80043-2 (CD) 80042-4 (MC)*
INSIDE OUT (USA MUSICAL) Songs: ADRYAN RUSS / ORIG CAST
   RECORDING on *DRG (Pinn): DRGCD 19007 (CD)*

INSIDERS (BBC1 19/2/97) m: STEWART COPELAND *unavailable*
INSPECTOR MORSE (ITV 1987-93) theme:BARRINGTON PHELOUNG
    *Collection reissue:* 'INSPECTOR MORSE III' theme and
    incidental classical music selection on
    *VIRGIN (EMI): CDVIP 178 (CD) TCVIP 178 (MC)*
    'PASSION OF MORSE' BARRINGTON PHLOUNG compilat.plus
    'Politician's Wife'/'Truly Madly Deeply'/'Saint-Ex'
    *TRING Int (Tring): TRING 003 (CD) MCTRING 003 (MC)*
    'ESSENTIAL INSPECTOR MORSE COLLECTION' *VIRGIN
    (EMI): VTCD 62 (CD) VTMC 62 (MC)*
    *see COLLECTIONS 100,138,213,267,352,388*
    spoken word 4 MC: *MCI (TBD): TALKMC 013/014*
INSPECTOR GADGET (USA TV) *see COLLECTION 341*
INSPECTOR WEXFORD - *see* 'RUTH RENDELL MYSTERIES The'
INTERNATIONAL ATHLETICS - *see under* 'ATHLETICS'
INTERNATIONAL DETECTIVE *see COLLECTION 5*
INTERNATIONAL SHOWJUMPING *see under* 'HORSE OF THE YEAR'
INTERNATIONAL TENNIS (BBC Maj.Competitions) "Brave New
    World" from 'War Of The Worlds' (JEFF WAYNE)
    *SONY CDX (40)96000 (MC/CD) see also* WIMBLEDON
INTERVIEW WITH THE VAMPIRE (1994) M: ELLIOT GOLDENTHAL
    -S/T- *GEFFEN (BMG): GED 24719 (CD) GEC 24719 MC*
INTOLERANCE (Film Silent 1916 D.W.Griffiths) New Score
    by CARL DAVIS played by Luxembourg Symphony Orchest
    (Carl Davis): *PROMETHEUS (S.Screen): PCD 105 (CD)*
INVADERS The (USA 66) theme music: DOMINIC FRONTIERE
    (USA TV) *see COLLECTION 343*
INVENTING THE ABBOTT (1997) Music score: MICHAEL KAMEN
    -S/T- *COLOSSEUM (Pinn): CST 348062 (CD)*
INVESTIGATION OF A CITIZEN ABOVE SUSPICION (1970) Music
    score ENNIO MORRICONE -S/T- with IL GIOCATTOLO
    *CINEVOX ITALY (Silva Screen): CDCIA 5086 (CD)*
INVISIBLE MAN RETURNS The (1940) Music sco: HANS SALTER
    FRANK SKINNER *new recording* MOSCOW SYMPHONY ORCHEST
    (Stromberg) on *MARCO POLO (Select): 8.223748 (CD)*
    *also includes* THE WOLF MAN and SON OF FRANKENSTEIN
IOLANTHE (operetta) songs by Gilbert and Sullivan
    1.D'OYLY CARTE OPERA COMPANY New Symph Orch Of London
      (I.Godrey) *LONDON (Poly): 414 145-2 (2CD) -4 (MC)*
    2.PRO-ARTE ORCHESTRA (Malcolm Sargent) & GLYNDEBOURNE
      FESTIVAL CHOIR Soloists: George Baker-Ian Wallace-
      Alex.Young-Owen Brannigan *EM1: CMS 764400-2 (2CDs)*
    3.D'OYLE CARTE OPERA (JOHN PRYCE JONES, musical dir)
      *feat:* JILL PERT-RICHARD STUART-ELIZABETH WOOLLETT-
      PHILIP BLAKE-JONES *TER (Disc): CDTER2 1188 (2CD)*
IRENE (BROADWAY REVIVAL CAST 1973) Songs (Var) *featur:*
    DEBBIE REYNOLDS-PATSY KELLY-GEORGE S.IRVING & Comp
    *SONY BROADWAY (Sony Mus): CD 32266 (CD)*
IRON AND SILK (1991) Music score: MICHAEL GIBBS -S/T-
    *IONIC (RTM/Pinn): IONIC 7C (MC) IONIC 7CD (CD)*
IRON EAGLE III (ACES) (1991) Music: HARRY MANFREDINI
    -S/T- *INTRADA USA (Silva Screen): MAFCD 7022 (CD)*
IRON WILL (1993) -S/T- Music score: JOEL McNEELY -S/T-
    *VARESE (Pinn): VSD 5467 (CD)*

IRONCLADS (1991) Music score: ALLYN FERGUSON / suite on
    Coll 'FILM MUSIC OF ALLYN FERGUSON III' also incl:
    'APRIL MORNING' *PROMETHEUS (S.Screen): PCD 141 (CD)*
IRONSIDE *see COLLECTIONS 2,339*
IS PARIS BURNING (1965) Music sco: MAURICE JARRE -S/T-
    *IMPRT (Silva Screen): 476842-2 (CD) deleted*
ISLAND OF DR.MOREAU (1996) Music sco: GARY CHANG-ZBIGNI
    EW PREISNER -S/T- *MILAN (BMG): 74321 40955-2 (CD)*
ISLAND OF GHOSTS: *see under* 'MADAGASCAR'
ISLAND RACE (BBC1 5/9/95) music: PADDY KINGSLAND.....*NA*
IT COULD HAPPEN TO YOU (1994) Music sco: CARTER BURWELL
    *feat:* FRANK SINATRA-TONY BENNETT etc. -S/T- on
    *COLUMBIA (Sony M): 476 817-2 (CD) 476 817-4 (MC)*
IT HAPPENED AT THE WORLD'S FAIR *see* ELVIS PRESLEY FILM
    INDEX p.348
IT TAKES A THIEF (USA) *see COLLECTIONS 246,343*
IT'LL BE ALLRIGHT ON THE NIGHT (Thames 1981-95) theme
    music: ROD ARGEN and PETER VAN HOOKE *unavailable*
IT'S A MAD MAD MAD MAD MAD WORLD (1963) Music: ERNEST GOLD
    -S/T- *reiss+addit. RYKODISC (Vital): RCD 10704 (CD)*
IT'S ABOUT TIME (USA TV) *see COLLECTION 340*
IT'S ALIVE 2 'It Lives Again' (1978) Music sco: BERNARD
    HERRMANN -S/T- *SILVA SCREEN (Koch): FILMCD 074 (CD)*
IT'S GARRY SHANDLING SHOW (USA TV) *see COLLECTION 345*
IT'S MY PARTY (1995) Music sco: BASIL POLEDOURIS -S/T-
    *VARESE (Pinn): VSD 5701 (CD)*
ITN NEWS (Orig 60's-70 theme) 'Non Stop' JOHN MALCOLM
    *see COLLECTIONS 163,381 - see also NEWS AT TEN*
ITV ATHLETICS - *on Coll* 'FAVOURITE TV THEMES' *deleted*
ITV SPORTS CLASSICS (London Sports Prod for LWT 7/1/95)
    theme "World Of Sport March" (Don Harper) *see Coll*
    'A-Z OF BRITISH TV THEMES VOLUME 3'
IVAN THE TERRIBLE (1943) Music by PROKOFIEV *new vers:*
    FRANKFURT RADIO SYMPHONY ORCH (Dmitri Kitoenko)
    *RCA VICTOR Red Seal (BMG): 09026 61954-2 (CD)*
    other recordings: Philharmonia Orch (Neeme Jarvi)
    Linda Finnie (mezzo-sop) Nikita Storojev (bass-bar)
    *CHANDOS (Chandos): CHAN 8977 (CD)*
    Philharmonic Orch (Riccardo Muti) Ambrosian Chorus
    (J.McCarthy) Irina Arkhipova-Boris Morgunov-Anatoly
    Mokrenko *EMI: CDM 769584-2 (CD) EG 769584-4 (MC)*
IVANHOE (BBC1 12/1/97) orig music score: COLIN TOWNS.*NA*
IVANHOE (1951) Music sco: MIKLOS ROZSA *new digital rec*
    *ording featur:* Sinfonia of London (Bruce Broughton)
    *INTRADA (Silva Screen): MAF 7055CD (CD)*
IVOR THE ENGINE (BBC1 77) theme: VERN ELLIOTT  Stories
    and music from the series on *BBC: ZCM 517 (MC)*

**J**ACK (1996) Music sc: MICHAEL KAMEN song "Star" sung by
    BRYAN ADAMS -S/T-*HOLLYWOOD (Poly Euro): 162063-2 CD*
JACK AND SARAH (1995) Music score: SIMON BOSWELL -S/T-
    *POLYDOR (Polyg): 527 925-2 (CD)*
JACOB'S LADDER (1990) Music sco: MAURICE JARRE -S/T-
    *VARESE (Pinn): VSD(VSC) 5291 (CD/MC)*

JACKIE GLEASON SHOW (USA TV) *see COLLECTION 340*
JACQUES COUSTEAU (BBC) *see COLLECTION 1*
JAILHOUSE ROCK (1957) feat ELVIS PRESLEY remaster.-S/T-
    *RCA (BMG): 07863 67453-2 (CD) 07863 67453-4 (MC)*
    *see also* ELVIS PRESLEY INDEX p.348
JAKE'S PROGRESS (C4 12/10/95) music by RICHARD HARVEY
    & ELVIS COSTELLO -S/T- *DEMON (Pinn): DSCD 14 (CD)*
    *see COLLECTION 181*
JAMAICA INN (ITV 9/5/83) Music score: FRANCIS SHAW
    *see COLLECTION 6*
JAMES AND THE GIANT PEACH (1995) M/Songs: RANDY NEWMAN
    -S/T- *W.DISNEY (B.Vista): WD 68120-2 (CD) -4 (MC)*
JAMES BOND FILMS - *see* JAMES BOND FILM INDEX p.346
JANE EYRE (ITV/LWT 9/3/97) music sco: RICHARD HARVEY.*NA*
JANE EYRE (1943) Music score: BERNARD HERRMANN new 1994
    recording by The SLOVAK RADIO SYMPHONY ORCHESTRA on
    *MARCO POLO (Select): 8.223535 (CD) also available*
    *w.*'LAURA' (D.RAKSIN) *Fox-Arista (BMG):07822 11006-2*
JASON AND THE ARGONAUTS (1963) Mus: BERNARD HERRMANN
    *see COLLECTIONS 186,188,190,395*
JASON KING (ITC 15/7/71-72) theme LAURIE JOHNSON
    *see COLLECTIONS 109,294,318,357*
JAWS (1975) Music score: JOHN WILLIAMS -S/T- *re-iss:*
    *MCA MASTERS (BMG): MCLD 19281 (CD)*
    *see COLLECTIONS 63,173,200,203,298,323*
JAWS 2 (1978) Music score: JOHN WILLIAMS -S/T-
    *VARESE (Pinn): VSD 5328 (CD) VSC 5328 (MC)*
JAZZ AGE (BBC 1969) mus: RON GRAINER *see COLLECTION 7*
JAZZ SINGER The (1980) *feat:* NEIL DIAMOND -S/T- *reiss:*
    *COLUMBIA (Sony M): 483 927-2 (CD) -4 (MC)*
JEAN DE FLORETTE (1987) Music score: JEAN-CLAUDE PETIT
    main theme adap.from "La Forza Del Destino" (Verdi)
    Orchestra De Paris w.Toots Thieleman *plus* 'CYRANO
    DE BERGERAC' (90) *PLAYTIME (Discovery): 302330 (CD)*
    *see also* COLLECTIONS 66,74,80,139,277
JEEVES AND WOOSTER (Granada 22/4/90) mus: ANNE DUDLEY
    -S/T- *EMI:CD(TC)3623 (CD/MC) deleted*
    *vers.by* GRAHAM DALBY & THE GRAHAMOPHONES on Coll
    'Transatlantique' *PRESIDENT: PCOM 1128 (CD)*
    *see also* 'BY JEEVES' (Musical)
JEFFERSON IN PARIS (1994) Music score: RICHARD ROBBINS
    -S/T *EMI (EMI): CDQ 555311-2 (CD) DELETED 97*
    *see also COLLECTIONS 65,139*
JEFFERSONS The (USA TV) *see COLLECTION 341*
JEFFREY (1995) Music score: STEPHEN ENDELMAN -S/T- on
    *VARESE (Pinn): VSD 5649 (CD)*
JELLY'S LAST JAM (ORIG BROADWAY CAST 1993) GREGORY
    HINES as Jelly Roll Morton / Import on
    *POLYDOR (IMS-Polyg): AA 314 510 846-2 (CD)*
JENNIFER EIGHT (1992) Music sco: CHRISTOPHER YOUNG
    -S/T- *USA Imp (S.Screen): 66120-2 (CD) 66120-4 (MC)*
JEOPARDY (USA TV) *see COLLECTIONS 340,405*
JEREMY CLARKSON'S MOTORWORLD (BBC2 5/1/95) title music
    DAVID LOWE *unavailable*

JERRY McGUIRE (1996) Mus sco: DANNY BRAMSON -S/T- feat:
    THE WHO-NEIL YOUNG-PAUL McCARTNEY-ELVIS PRESLEY-
    BOB DYLAN-BRUCE SPRINGSTEEN-NANCY WILSON on *EPIC*
    *(Sony Music): 486 981-2 (CD) -4 (MC)*
JERRY'S GIRLS (O.BROADWAY C.1984) Songs: Jerry Herman
    CAROL CHANNING-LESLIE UGGAMS *TER: CDTER2 1093 2CD*
JESUS CHRIST SUPERSTAR - songs by Tim Rice and Andrew
    LLoyd Webber
  1.ORIG LONDON CAST 1996 *feat:* STEVE BALSALMO-ZUBIN
    VARTA-JOANNA AMPILL and Company
    *REALLY USEFUL-Polydor: 533 735-2 (CD) -4 (MC)*
    Highlights *REALLY USEFUL: 537 686-2 (CD) -4 (MC)*
  2.FILM MUSICAL 1973 *w:* YVONNE ELLIMAN-TED NEELY-CARL
    ANDERSON-BARRY DENNEN  *MCA (BMG): MCXC 502 (2MC)*
  3.ORIG LONDON CAST 1972 *w:* PAUL NICHOLAS-DANA GILLESP
    IE-PAUL JABARA & Comp *MCA (BMG): MCFC 2503 (MC)*
  4.STUDIO RECORD 1972 *w:* MURRAY HEAD-IAN GILLAN-YVONNE
    ELLIMAN *MCA (BMG): MCXC 501 (2MC) DMCX 501 (CD)*
  5.HIGHLIGHTS FROM 20TH ANNIVERSARY (1992)
    *with:* PAUL NICHOLAS-CLAIRE MOORE-KEITH BURNS & Comp
    *FIRST NIGHT (Pinn): OCRCD 6031 (CD)*
  6.CARLTON SHOWS COLL 1994 *with* GODSPELL Various Arts.
    *CARLTON Shows Collect: PWKS(PWKMC) 4220 (CD/MC)*
  7.STUDIO RECORD 1995 *w:* DAVE WILLETTS-CLIVE ROWE-ISSY
    VAN RANDWYCK-BILLY HARTMAN-ETHAN FREEMAN-ANDREW NEW
    EY-CHRISTOPER BIGGINS-ANDREW HALLIDAY-JAY MARCUS...
    *SHOWTIME (THE-Disc): SHOW(CD)(MC) 026 (CD/MC)*
  8.CLASSIC MUSICALS SERIES *feat:* DAVE WILLETS-CLIVE RO
    WE-ISSY VAN RANDWYCK-CHRISTOPER BIGGINS and Company
    + *songs* 'ASPECTS OF LOVE' *KOCH Int: 34083-2 (CD)*
  9.ORIG MASTERWORKS EDIT.*feat* DAVE WILLETTS-CLIVE ROWE
    ISSY VAN RANDWYCK-ETHAN FREEMAN-CHRISTOPER BIGGINS
    *TER (Disc): CDTER 9026 (2CD)*
JETSONS The (USA62) - *see COLLECTIONS 339,370.405*
JEWEL IN THE CROWN (C4 1/6/97 orig: ITV/Gran 9/1/84)
    music score by GEORGE FENTON -S/T- *reissued on*
    *EMI PREMIER: PRMCD 33 (CD) see COLLECTION 353*
JIM DAVIDSON'S GENERATION GAME (BBC1 21/10/95) title
    music: STEPHEN GREEN *unavailable*
JIM'LL FIX IT (BBC1 1975) - *see COLLECTION 408*
JIMMY'S (YTV for C4 22/5/95) series theme music by
    ERNIE WOOD *unavailable*
JOAN AND LESLIE (BBC 1950s) theme "Miss Melanie" RONALD
    BINGE *see COLLECTION 42*
JOE 90 (ATV/ITC 29/9/68-69) theme mus: BARRY GRAY *see*
    *COLLECTIONS 110,135,162,273,356,357,364,368,372*
JOHN & JEN: MUSICAL -S/T- *VARESE (Pinn): VSD 5688 (CD)*
JOHNNY GUITAR (1953) Music score: VICTOR YOUNG -S/T-
    *VARESE (Pinn): VSD 5377 (CD)*
JOHNNY AND THE DEAD (LWT 11/4/95) mus: STEFAN GIRADET
    -S/T- *Weekend (FLy Direct) CD(MC)WEEK 106 (CD/MC)*
    *see COLLECTION 33*
JOHNNY STACCATO (USA 1959) theme mus: ELMER BERNSTEIN
    *see COLLECTIONS 2,108,246*

JOHNS (1996) music score by CHARLES BROWN -S/T- on
  *VARESE (Pinn): VSD 5778*
JOLSON STORY The (1946) V.ORIG -S/T- songs *Collection*
  *GREAT MOVIE THEMES: (Targ-BMG): CD 60021 (CD)*
JOLSON: THE MUSICAL (1995) Victoria Palace London *with*
  BRIAN CONLEY and Company - ORIG CAST RECORDING on
  *FIRST NIGHT (Pinn): CASTCD 56 (CD) CASTC 56 (MC)*
JONATHAN CREEK (BBC1 10/5/97) title music "Variations
  On A Theme" 'Danse Macabre' (Saint-Saens) arranged
  by JULIAN STEWART LINDSAY *TV version unavailable*
JONATHAN LIVINGSTON SEAGULL (1973) Music: NEIL DIAMOND
  -S/T- re-issue *SONY: 467607-2 (CD)* available with
  'BEAUTIFUL NOISE'/'JAZZ SINGER'*SONY: 488676-2 (3CD)*
JONNY BRIGGS (BBC1 3/4/96) - *see COLLECTION 408*
JONNY QUEST (USA TV) *see COLLECTION 340*
JOSEPH and THE AMAZING TECHNICOLOR DREAMCOAT - songs
  by Tim Rice and Andrew Lloyd Webber
  1.ORIG LONDON REVIVAL CAST 1991 *with:* JASON DONOVAN
    *POLYDOR-REALLY USEFUL (Poly):511 130-2(CD) -4(MC)*
    (Jason Donovan & Company) *also available* "Any Dream
    Will Do"/"Close Every Door To Me"/"Pharaoh's Story"
    (Phillip Schofield) *POLY: RUR(CD)(CS)11(7"/CDs/MC)*
  2.ORIG LONDON CAST 1973 *w:* GARY BOND-PAUL BROOKE-IAN
    CHARLESON-JOAN HEAL-JEREMY JAMES TAYLOR-GAVIN REED
    *MCA (BMG): MCLD 19023(CD) MCLC 19023(MC deleted)*
  3.CARLTON SHOWS COLL with ROBIN COUSINS-JACQUI SCOTT
    NICK CURTIS-STEVE BUTKER-BOBBY CRUSH and Company
    *CARLTON: PWKS 4163 (CD) PWKMC 4163 (MC)*
  4.STUDIO RECORD. *w:* PAUL JONES-TIM RICE-GORDON WALLER
    MIKE SAMMES SINGERS and GEOFF LOVE & HIS ORCHESTRA
    *CFP (EMI): CC 242 (CD) HR 8200 (MC)*
  5.ROYAL PHILH.ORCH *PLAY SUITES from* Aspects Of Love/
    Cats/Joseph and The Amazing Technicolor Dreamcoat
    *CARLTON INT (Carlton): PWKS(PWKMC) 4115 (CD/MC)*
JOSIE AND THE PUSSYCATS *see COLLECTIONS 341,370*
JOUR DE FETE (Jacques Tati 1948) Music sco: JEAN YATOVE
  -S/T- selection on 'Orig Music From His Films' on
  *POLY (Discov): 836 983-2 (CD) see also* MON ONCLE
JOURNEY TO THE CENTRE OF THE EARTH (59) Music score:
  BERNARD HERRMANN + 4 songs sung by PAT BOONE
  *VARESE (Pinn): VSD 5849 (CD) also COLLECTION 165*
JOY LUCK CLUB The (1993) Music sc: RACHEL PORTMAN -S/T-
  Songs -S/T- *ARISTA (BMG): 74321 18456-2(CD) -4(MC)*
  Score -S/T- *HOLLYWOOD (S.Screen): HR 61561-2 (CD)*
JUBILEE (1978) *V.A.* BRIAN ENO-ADAM & ANTS-WAYNE COUNTY
  & THE ELECTRIC CHAIRS-CHELSEA-SUZI PINNS-MANEATERS
  AMILCAR -S/T- *reissued EG-POLYG: EGCD 34 (CD)*
  *also CAROLINE (Vital/Cargo/Greyhound): 1112 (CD)*
JUDE (1996) Music score: ADRIAN JOHNSTON -S/T-
  *IMAGINARY ROAD/Philips (Poly): 534 116-2 (CD)*
JUDICIAL CONSENT (1995) Music sco: CHRISTOPHER YOUNG
  -S/T *INTRADA (Silva Screen): MAF 7062D (CD)*
JUDITH (1965) Music score: SOL KAPLAN with score from
  'Exodus' (E.GOLD) *TSUNAMI (Silva S): TSU 0115 (CD)*

JUICE (1992) Music sco HANK SHOCKLEE & The Bomb Squad
-S/T- Naughty By Nature-Erik B.& Rakim-Big Daddy
Kane-Salt'n'Pepa *reiss: MCA (BMG): MCLD 19308 (CD)*

JUKE BOX JURY 1989 (BBC2 24/9/89) theme "Hit And Miss"
(J.Barry) COURTNEY PINE *Antilles (Poly) deleted*

JUKE BOX JURY 1959 (BBC1) theme "Hit and Miss" by JOHN
BARRY 7 + 4 *see COLLECTIONS 4,26,27,402*

JULES ET JIM (1961) Music score: GEORGES DELERUE -S/T-
*PROMETHEUS (S.Screen): PCD 103 (CD) COLLECTION 115*

JULIET BRAVO (UKGold 5/11/92 orig 30/8/80) theme: DEREK
GOOM arr.of melody by Bach *see COLLECTIONS 100,388*

JULIUS CAESAR (1953) Music sco: MIKLOS ROZSA *new digit
recording* SINFONIA OF LONDON cond: Bruce Broughton
*INTRADA (Silva Screen): MAF 7056D (CD)*
*see also COLLECTION 306* 'SHAKESPEARE FILM MUSIC'

JUMANJI (1995) Music score: JAMES HORNER -S/T- *SONY
481 561-2(CD) -4(MC) deleted 97 see COLLECTION 34*

JUMPIN'JACK FLASH (1986) Music score: THOMAS NEWMAN
-S/T- *reissued on SPECTRUM (Poly): 551 138-2 (CD)*

JUNGLE BOOK The (1940) Music score: MIKLOS ROZSA
-S/T- with 'THIEF OF BAGHDAD' *COLOSSEUM (Pinn):
CST 348044 (CD)* also -S/T- music from 'SPELLBOUND'
(Miklos Rozsa) *FLAPPER (Pinn): PASTCD 7093 (CD)*

JUNGLE BOOK (1967) Songs: RICHARD & ROBERT SHERMAN sung
by LOUIS PRIMA-PHIL HARRIS-STERLING HOLLOWAY etc.
-S/T- *W.DISNEY (B.Vista): WD 70400-2 (CD) -4 (MC)*
*see also* WALT DISNEY INDEX p.343

JUNGLE BOOK (1994) Music score: BASIL POLEDOURIS -S/T-
*MILAN (BMG): 74321 24861-2 (CD)*

JUNGLE FEVER (1991) Mus & songs: STEVIE WONDER "If She
Breaks Your Heart" sung by Kimberly Brewer -S/T-
*POLYDOR: 530000-2 (CD) 530000-4 (MC) 530000-1(LP)*

JUNIOR (1994) Music: JAMES NEWTON HOWARD -S/T- on
*VARESE (S.Screen): VSD 5558 (CD)*

JURASSIC PARK (1993) Music score: JOHN WILLIAMS -S/T-
*MCA (BMG): MCD 10859(CD) MCC 10859 MC deleted 95*
*see COLLECTIONS 63,82,200,273,298,319,323*

JUST CAUSE (1994) Music sc: JAMES NEWTON HOWARD -S/T-
*VARESE (Pinn): VSD 5596 (CD)*

JUST GOOD FRIENDS (BBC1 22/9/83) theme (John Sullivan)
PAUL NICHOLAS *FIRST NIGHT (Pinn): CAST(C)(CD) 43*

JUST WILLIAM (Talisman/BBC1 13/11/94 music composed &
directed by NIGEL HESS *see COLLECTIONS 5,33,192*

JUSTICE GAME The (BBC1 7/4/89) "Waterfront" (Jim Kerr)
SIMPLE MINDS 'Sparkle In The Rain' *VIRGIN (Poly)
CDV 2300 (CD) V 2300 (LP) TCV 2300 (MC)*

JUSTINE (1969) Music score: JERRY GOLDSMITH -S/T- *Imp
TSUNAMI (Silva Screen): TSU 0119 (CD)*

**K**2 (1991) Music score: HANS ZIMMER -S/T-
*VARESE (Pinn): VSD 5354 (CD)*

KAMA SUTRA (1997) Mus sco: MYCHAEL DANNA / the Sarangi
played by ARUNA NARYAN KALLE -S/T- issued on
*COLOSSEUM (Pinn): CST 348063 (CD)*

KANSAS CITY (1997) VAR.JAZZ ARTS Collection (inspired
   by the film) *GIANTS OF JAZZ/DELTA (BMG): CD 53300*
KARAOKE (BBC1 28/4/96) Music score: CHRISTOPHER GUNNING
   -S/T- includes music from 'COLD LAZARUS' and tracks
   by BING CROSBY-HANK WILLIAMS-CRAIG DOUGLAS etc.
   *SILVA SCREEN (Koch): FILM(CD)(C) 181 (CD/MC)*
KAVANAGH QC (ITV 3/1/95) music by ANNE DUDLEY and JOHN
   KEANE -S/T- *VIRGIN (EMI): VTCD(VTMC) 134 (CD/MC)*
KAZAAM (1996) Music sco: CHRISTOPHER TYNG -S/T- V.Arts
   *A.& M.(Poly): 549 027-2 (CD)*
KEEPER OF THE CITY (1991) Music sco: LEONARD ROSENMAN
   Utah Symph Orc -S/T- *INTRADA (S.Scr) MAFCD 7024*
KEEPING MUM (BBC1 17/4/97) theme mus: STEFAN GIRADET.*NA*
KEEPING UP APPEARANCES (BBC1 from 29/10/90-95) title
   theme music by NICK INGMAN *unavailable*
KENTUCKIAN The (1955) Music score: BERNARD HERRMANN
   *PREAMBLE (SILVA SCREEN): PRCD 1777 (CD)*
KERN GOES TO HOLLYWOOD (ORIG LONDON CAST 85) Songs by
   Jerome Kern-Dorothy Fields etc. *feat* ELAINE DELMAR
   DAVID KERNAN-ELISABETH WELCH-LIZ ROBERTSON & Comp.
   *FIRST NIGHT (Pinn): OCRCD 6014 (CD)*
KEY LARGO (1948) M: MAX STEINER *see COLLECTION 54*
KEY TO REBECCA The (USATV mini-ser 85) mus sco: J.A.C.
   REDFORD -S/T- *PROMETHEUS (Silva S): PCD 123 (CD)*
KEYS OF THE KINGDOM (1944) Music score: ALFRED NEWMAN
   re-recorded *TSUNAMI IMPT (S.Scr): TSU 0134 (CD)*
KICKBOXER (1989) Music score: PAUL HERTZOG + songs/mus
   from 'BLOODSPORT'(87) 'CYBORG' (89-Kevin Bassinson)
   'DEATH WARRANT' (90) 'DOUBLE IMPACT' (91-A.Kempel)
   *SILVA SCREEN (Koch): FILMCD 103 (CD)*
KID GALAHAD *see* ELVIS PRESLEY INDEX p.348
KID The (1921) Music score: CHARLES CHAPLIN *see Coll:*
   'FILM MUSIC OF CHARLES CHAPLIN' *RCA: 09026 68271-2*
KIDNAPPED (LWT 1978) m: VLADIMIR COSMA "David's Theme"
   *see Coll see COLLECTION 168* ('David Balfour' track)
KIDS (1996) Music & songs by: LOUIS BARLOW-JOHN DAVIS
   V.Arts -S/T- *LONDON (Poly): 828 640-2 (CD) -4(MC)*
KIDS ARE ALRIGHT The (Documentary Film Of THE WHO) Mus:
   (Pete Townshend & others) *BMG Vid: 74321 20087-30*
KIDS IN THE HALL BRAIN CANDY (1996) Mus: CRAIG NORTHEY-
   DOUG ELLIOTT-PAT STEWARD -S/T- *MATADOR (Vital):*
   *OLE 1832(CD) OLE 1831(LP) see also COLLECTION 345*
KIKA (1993) music of various artists -S/T- *Import on*
   *IMPORT MUSIC SERVICES (IMS-Pol): E.517 572-2 (CD)*
KILLER TONGUE The (1996) Music and songs by FANGORIA
   -S/T- on *EDEL-CINERAMA (Pinn): 002269-2CIN (CD)*
KILLERS The (1946) Music sco: MIKLOS ROZSA selection
   'LUST FOR LIFE' *VARESE (Pinn): VSD 5405 (CD)*
   *Coll* 'FILM NOIR CLASSICS' *see* 'DOUBLE INDEMNITY'
KILLING FIELDS The (1984) Music sco: MICHAEL OLDFIELD
   -S/T- *VIRGIN (EMI): OVEDC 183 (MC) CDV 2328 (CD)*
   *sec also COLLECTION 66*
KILLING ZOE (1994) Music score (TOMandANDY) -S/T- on
   *MILAN (BMG): 232 102 (CD)*

KILROY (BBC1 12/10/87-1998) theme music composed and
     arranged by ROBERT HOWES *unavailable*
KIND HEARTS AND CORONETS (1949) *see COLLECTIONS 77,225*
KINDERGARTEN COP (1990) Music sco: RANDY EDELMAN -S/T-
     *VARESE (Pinn): VSD(VSC) 5305 (CD/MC)*
KING AND I The - songs by R.Rodgers & O.Hammerstein II
   1.FILM MUSICAL 1956 *w:* YUL BRYNNER-DEBORAH KERR *(sung
     by MARNI NIXON)* RITA MORENO-TERRY SAUNDERS -S/T-
     reissue *EMI Broadway Classics: EG 764 693-2 (CD)*
   2.ORIG BROADWAY CAST 1951 *feat:* YUL BRYNNER-GERTRUDE
     LAWRENCE-DORETTA MORROW-LARRY DOUGLAS & Company
     *MCA (BMG): MCLD 19156 (CD)*
   3.STUDIO RECORDING 1992 *w:* JULIE ANDREWS-BEN KINGSLEY
     LEA SALONGA-PEABO BRYSON-MARILYN HORNE-ROGER MOORE-
     MARTIN SHEEN-HOLLYWOOD BOWL SO.cond.by JOHN MAUCERI
     *PHILIPS: 438 007-2 (CD) -4( MC) -5 (DCC) -1 (LP)*
   4.STUDIO RECORD.1994 *w:* VALERIE MASTERSON-CHRISTOPHER
     LEE-JASON HOWARD-HARRY WILLIAMS-TINUKE OLAFIMIHAN-
     SALLY BURGESS-BEA JULAKASIUN and Company
     *SHOWTIME (MCI-THE): SHOW(CD)(MC) 024*
   5.CLASSIC MUSICALS SERIES *feat:* VALERIE MASTERSON
     THOMAS ALLEN-MURIEL DICKINSON & MUNICH SYMPH.ORCH.
     *+ songs from* 'OKLAHOMA!' *KOCH Int: 34077-2 (CD)*
   6.NEW BROADWAY CAST 1995 *featur* LOU DIAMOND PHILLIPS
     DONNA MURPHY / NEW BROADWAY CAST RECORDING
     *VARESE (Pinn): VSD 5763 (CD)*
   7.SHOWS COLLECTION VARIOUS ARTISTS
     *CARLTON SHOWS Collect: 39362 0041-2 (CD) -4 (MC)*
KING CREOLE (1958) feat ELVIS PRESLEY remastered -S/T-
     *RCA (BMG): 07863 67454-2 (CD) 07863 67454-4 (MC)*
     *see also* ELVIS PRESLEY INDEX p.348
KING IN NEW YORK A (1957) Music score (Charles Chaplin)
     *see COLLECTION 56*
KING KONG (1933) Music score: MAX STEINER New recording
     National Philharm Orch (Fred Steiner) *S.SCREEN Imp
     LXCD 10 / see also COLLECTIONS 372,319*
KING KONG (1976) Music score: JOHN BARRY -S/T-
     *IMP (S.Screen): MK 702 (CD) / see COLLECTION 25*
KING MACKEREL / THE BLUES ARE RUNNING (USA MUSICALS)
     *w:*COASTAL COHORTS: DON DIXON-BLAND SIMPSON-JIM WANN
     *SUGARHILL USA (Koch): SHCD 8503 (CD) SH 8503 (MC)*
KING OF KINGS (1961) Music sco: MIKLOS ROZSA
     *see COLLECTION 296*
KING RAT (1965) Music score: JOHN BARRY -S/T- *re-issue:*
     *COLUMBIA (Sony Music): CK 57894 (CD)*
KING SOLOMON'S MINES (1985) Music sco: JERRY GOLDSMITH
     -S/T- *INTRADA USA (S.Screen): FMT 8005D (CD)*
KINGS GO FORTH (1958) Music score: ELMER BERNSTEIN also
     inc -S/T- to SOME CAME RUNNING (58-Elmer Bernstein)
     *CLOUD NINE/SILVA PROD: CNS 5004 (CD)*
KING'S ROW (1942) Music score: ERICH WOLFGANG KORNGOLD
     -S/T- score *VARESE (Pinn): VCD 47203 (CD)*
KING'S THIEF (1955) Music sc: MIKLOS ROZSA new record:
     BRANDENBURG S.O. *MARCO POLO (Sel): 8.223607 (CD)*

KINSEY (BBC1 2/4/91) theme music: DAVE GREENSLADE
   see COLLECTION 6
KISMET - songs by Robert Wright and George Forrest
   adapted from the music of Alexander Borodin
   1.ORIG -S/T- 1955 reissue EMI ODEON: CDODEON 23 (CD)
   2.STUDIO 1964 reissue LONDON (Poly): 452 488-2 (CD)
   3.ORIG BROADWAY CAST 1953 with: ALFRED DRAKE and Comp
   COLUMBIA (S.Screen): CK 32605 (CD) JST 32605 (MC)
   4.STUDIO REC.1990 w: VALERIE MASTERSON-DONALD MAXWELL
   DAVID RENDALL-ROSEMARY ASHE-BONAVENTURA BOTTONE-RIC
   HARD VAN ALLAN  Philharmonia Orch:John Owen Edwards
   Highlights: SHOWTIME (MCI-THE): SHOW(CD)(MC) 014
   Complete:  TER: CDTER2-1170 (2CD)
   5.STUDIO REC.1992 with: SAMUEL RAMEY-JULIA MIGENES-
   JERRY HADLEY-MANDY PATINKIN-DOM DE LUISE-RUTH ANN
   SWENSON SONY BROADWAY: SK 46438 (CD)
KISS ME KATE - songs by Cole Porter
   1.ORIG FILM -S/T- 1953 w: KATHRYN GRAYSON-HOWARD KEEL
   ANN MILER etc. EMI ODEON (EMI): CDODEON 25 (CD)
   2.ORIG BROADWAY CAST 1948 with: LISA KIRK-PATRICIA
   MORISON-ALFRED DRAKE-HARRY CLARK-HAROLD LANG & Comp
   EMI Angel (EMI):ZDM 764760-2 (CD)
   3.ORIG LONDON CAST 1987 w: FIONA HENDLEY-PAUL JONES-
   EARLENE BENTLEY-JOHN BARDEN-TIM FLAVIN-PETE LEDBURY
   NICHOLA McAULIFFE-CYRIL NRI-EMIL WOLK and Company
   reissued on FIRST NIGHT (Pinn): OCRCD 6020 (CD)
   4.STUDIO RECORD.1991 with: JOSEPHINE BARSTOW-THOMAS
   HAMPSON-KIM CRISWELL-GEORGE DVORSKY & Company.
   EMI: CDS 754 033-2 (2CDs) EX 754 033-4 (2 MC)
   5.STUDIO RECORD.1995 with THOMAS ALLEN-DIANA MONTAGUE
   GRAHAM BICKLEY SHOWTIME (MCI): SHOW(CD)(MC) 032
   Complete:   TER (Disc): CDTER2 1212 (2CD)
   6.STUDIO RECORDING 1996 with EDMUND HOCKRIDGE
   JANINE ROEBUCK-JACKIE JEFFERSON prod: GORDON LORENZ
   CARLTON SHOWS Coll (CHE): 30362 00332 (CD) -4(MC)
KISS OF DEATH (1995) Music score: TREVOR JONES -S/T- on
   MILAN (BMG): 28020-2 (CD)
KISS OF THE SPIDER WOMAN (ORIG LONDON CAST 1992) feat:
   CHITA RIVERA-BRENT CARVER-ANTHONY CRIVELLO & Comp:
   reissued on FIRST NIGHT (Pinn): OCRCD 6030 (CD)
KISS OF THE VAMPIRE (1964) Music sco: JAMES BERNARD see
   Coll 'DEVIL RIDES OUT' SILVA SCR: FILMCD 174 CD
KISS THE GIRLS (1997) Music score: MARK ISHAM -S/T-
   MILAN: catalogue number to be confirmed
KISSIN' COUSINS see ELVIS PRESLEY INDEX p.348
KNIFE IN THE WATER (1962) Mus sc: KRZYSZTOF KOMEDA also
   'CRAZY GIRL' POWER BROS (Harm.Mundi): PB 00145 (CD)
KNIGHT RIDER (USA 82 ITV) theme (G.A.LARSON-S.PHILLIPS
   see COLLECTIONS 12,168,344
KNIGHT SCHOOL (ITVC 2/9/97) music : PAUL K.JOYCE.....NA
KNOTS LANDING (USA BBC1 79) theme music: JERROLD IMMEL
   see COLLECTIONS 341,373
KOJAK (USA 73) theme music: BILLY GOLDENBERG see COLL
   2,101,109,110,159,168,246,341,360,388

KOLCHAK THE NIGHT STALKER (USA TV) *see COLLECTION 343*
KOLYA (1997) Music score: ODREJ SOUKUP inc.Classical m.
    -S/T- *PHILIPS (Poly): 456 432-2 (CD)*
KONGA - *see under COLLECTION 207*
KOYAANISQATSI (1982) Music score: PHILIP GLASS -S/T-
    *ANTILLES (Island-Poly): IMCD 98 or ANCD 8707 (CD)*
KRAMER V KRAMER (1979) Mus:.'Concerto in G.Maj' for two
    mandolins, strings & organ (VIVALDI) + 'Concerto in
    C.Maj' for mandolins, strings,harpsichord (VIVALDI)
    'Sonata D.Maj' trumpet,strings & continuo (PURCELL)
    -S/T- *SONY FR.(Discov): SK 73945(CD) ST 73945 (MC)*
KREMMEN THE MOVIE featuring KENNY EVERETT *reissued on*
    *EMI GOLD-LFP (EMI): LFPS 1554 (MC)*
KRYPTON FACTOR The (Granada 28/8/95) title music: ANNE
    DUDLEY incid.music by MIKE WOOLMANS *unavailable*
KULL THE CONQUEROR (1997) Music score: JOEL GOLDSMITH
    -S/T- *VARESE (Pinn): VSD 5862 (CD)*
KUNDUN (1997) Music score: PHILIP GLASS -S/T- on
    *Nonesuch (WEA): 7559 79460-2 (CD) -4 (MC)*
KUNG FU (USA 1971) mus: JIMMY HELMS *see COLLECTION 168*


**L**'AMANT *see 'LOVER The'*
L.A.CONFIDENTIAL (1997) Music score: JERRY GOLDSMITH
    -S/T- score *VARESE (Pinn): VSD 5885 (CD)*
    -S/T- songs *RESTLESS (BMG): 74321 52596-2 (CD)*
L.A.LAW (USA)(ITV 7/9/88) theme music: MIKE POST
    *see COLLECTIONS 12,168,341,388*
LA BAMBA (1987)  Music: MILES GOODMAN-CARLOS SANTANA
    feat Los Lobos -S/T- *SLASH-LONDON: 828 058-2 (CD)*
    *Orig Ritchie Valens songs on ACE: CDCHD 953 (CD)*
LA DERNIER METRO *see 'LAST METRO The'*
LA DOLCE VITA (1960) *see COLLECTIONS 63,295*
LA FEMME D'A COTE *see 'WOMAN NEXT DOOR The'*
LA FETE SAUVAGE (TV Sountrack) Music by VANGELIS -S/T-
    *Polydor Impt (Discovery): 841 198-2 (CD)*
LA FLEUR DE MON SECRET - see FLOWER OF MY SECRET
LA FOLIE, A (1994) Music: MICHAEL NYMAN feat MICHAEL
    NYMAN BAND -S/T- *Imprt (DISCOVERY): 839949-2 (CD)*
LA GLOIRE DE MON PERE - *see under* 'GLORY OF MY FATHER'
LA HAINE (Hate)(1995) m: ISAAC HAYES-BOB MARLEY-GAP
    BAND + -S/T- 'Metisse' *MILAN (BMG): 31966-2 (CD)*
LA MACHINE (1996) Music score: MICHEL PORTAL -S/T-
    *Import POLYGRAM: 444 789-2 (CD)*
LA PASSIONE (1996) Music by CHRIS REA -S/T- on
    *EAST WEST (WEA): 0630 16695-2 (CD) -4 (MC)*
LA REINE MARGOT - see 'QUEEN MARGOT'
LA REVOLUTION FRANCAISE 1789-1794 (SHOW 1990) Songs:
    Alain Boublil and Claude Michel Schonberg / Orig
    PARIS Cast on *FIRST NIGHT (Pinn): OCRCD 6006 (CD)*
LA SCORTA (The Escort) (1993) Mus: ENNIO MORRICONE
    -S/T- *EPIC Italian Impt (Discovery): 474187-2 (CD)*
LA STRADA (1954-Italy) Music sc: NINO ROTA *also incl:*
    'NIGHTS OF CABIRIA The' (1957-Italy) (Nino ROTA)
    *LEGEND (Silva Screen): LEGEND CD 7 (CD)*

LABYRINTH (1986) Music score: TREVOR JONES-DAVID BOWIE
    -S/T- *re-issue FAME-MFP (EMI): CDFA 3322 (CD)*
LADY AND THE TRAMP - *see* WALT DISNEY INDEX p.343
LADY BE GOOD (ORIG BROADWAY CAST) Songs (George and Ira
    Gershwin) *ELEKTRA NONESUCH (WEA):7559 79308-2 / -4*
LADY CHATTERLEY (BBC1 6/6/93) music from "Appalachia"
    (DELIUS) / "Hammersmith Prelude" (HOLST) / "Venus"
    from 'The Planets' (HOLST) London Philharmonic Orch
    cond: Barry Wordsworth *vers:* "Appalachia" by ROYAL
    PHILH.ORCH *DECCA (Poly): 425 156-2 (CD) -4(MC)*
    "Hammersmith Prelude" *MERCURY (Poly):432 009-2 CD*
LADY KILLERS The (Granada 26/7/95) theme "The Rose" by
    MICHAEL BALL 'First Love' *Sony: 483 499-2(CD)-4(MC)*
LADY SINGS THE BLUES The (1972) Music: MICHEL LEGRAND
    *Songs of Billie Holiday* sung by DIANA ROSS -S/T- on
    *re-issued MOTOWN-POLYDOR (Poly): 530 135-2 (2CD)*
LADYHAWKE (1985) Mus sc: ANDREW POWELL -S/T-
    *GNP-Silva Screen: GNPD 8042 (CD)*
LADYKILLERS The (1955) Music: TRISTRAM CARY other mus
    'Minuet No.5 In E.String Quintet Op.11'(BOCCHERINI)
    *see COLLECTIONS 74,225*
LAKES The (BBC1 14/9/97) Music score: SIMON BOSWELL
    -S/T- inc "Walk Away" by CAST and other V.ARTISTS
    *TELSTAR TV (WEA): TTVCD 2923 (CD) TTVMC 2923 (MC)*
LAND AND FREEDOM (1994) Music score: GEORGE FENTON
    -S/T- *DEBONAIR (Pinn): CDDEB 1001 (CD)*
LAND BEFORE TIME The (1988) Music score: JAMES HORNER
    and Diana Ross -S/T- *MCA (S.Screen) MCAD 6266 (CD)*
LAND BEFORE TIME 2 (1997) Songs from the film on
    *UNIVERSAL-MCA (BMG): UMD 80388 (CD) UMC 80388 (MC)*
LAND OF SMILES The (OPERETTA) Songs (Franz LEHAR-Ludwig
    Herzer-Fritz Lohner Beda) French Highlights +'MERRY
    WIDOW' etc. *EMI BELLE EPOQUE: CZS 767 872-2 (2CD)*
LAND OF THE GIANTS (USA 68 / C4 10/1/93) theme music by
    JOHN WILLIAMS *see COLLECTIONS 110,343*
LAND OF THE LOST (USA TV) *see COLLECTION 343*
LAND OF THE PHAROAHS (1955) Music sco: DIMITRI TIOMKIN
    -S/T- *TSUNAMI (Silva Screen): TCI 0608 (CD)*
LAND OF THE TIGER (BBC2 17/11/97) orig music specially
    composed & performed by NICHOLAS HOOPER *unavailable*
LAND RAIDERS (69) Music score: BRUNO NICOLAI -S/T- on
    *PROMETHEUS (Silva Screen): PCD 128 (CD)*
LAND WITHOUT MUSIC (FILM OPERETTA 1936) Music: Oscar
    STRAUSS and featuring songs sung by Richard Tauber
    -S/T- excerpts on *PEARL (H.Mundi): GEMM 263 (LP)*
LARAMIE (USA 59) theme CYRIL MOCKRIDGE *see COLLECT.170*
LARGER THAN LIFE (1996) Music sco: MILES GOODMAN -S/T-
    *MILAN (BMG): 74321 44282-2 (CD)*
LARKRISE TO CANDLEFORD (NAT.THEATRE STAGE PROD.1978)
    Mus: ALBION BAND *CHARISMA/VIRGIN: CDSCD 4020 (CD)*
LASSIE (USA TV) *see COLLECTION 342*
LAST CHANCE LOTTERY (C4 25/1/97) theme based on "Creep"
    *TV vers.by* PATRICK KIELTY *unavailable / original:*
    RADIOHEAD from 'Pablo Honey' *EMI: CD(TC)PCS 7360*

LAST DANCE (1996) Music score: MARK ISHAM -S/T- on
*HOLLYWOOD (Silva Screen): HW 62055-2 (CD)*

LAST DAYS OF CHEZ NOUS (1992) Music sc: PAUL GRABOWSKY
-S/T- *DRG USA (Pinn): DRGCD 12607 (CD)*

LAST EMPEROR The (1988) Mus: DAVID BYRNE-RYUICHI SAKAMO
TO-CONG SU -S/T- *VIRGIN: CDV 2485 (CD) OVEDC 366*

LAST EXIT TO BROOKLYN (1989) Music score: MARK KNOPFLER
-S/T- *VERTIGO (Poly): 838 725-2(CD) -4(MC)*

LAST GOVERNOR The (BBC1 3/7/97) music: RICHARD HARVEY
and STEPHEN BAKER *unavailable*

LAST MAN STANDING (1996) Music score & songs: RY COODER
-S/T- *VERVE-POLYDOR (Poly): 533 415-2 (CD)*
also avail: 'LAST MAN STANDING' (music inspired by
film) ELMER BERSTEIN *VARESE (Pinn):VSD 5755 (CD)*

LAST METRO The (1980)+ 'THE WOMAN NEXT DOOR' (1981) Mus
GEORGES DELERUE *on COLL* 'TRUFFAUT & DELERUE ON
THE SCREEN' *DRG (Pinn): 32902 (CD)*

LAST NIGHT OF THE PROMS 1994 (BBC1 10/9/94)100th Season
BBC Symphony Orchestra (Andrew Davis) BRYN TERFEL-
EVELYN GLENNIE-MICHAEL DAVIS-BBC Singers and Chorus
*TELDEC (WEA): 4509 97868-2 (CD) -4 (MC)*

LAST OF ENGLAND The (1987) Music: SIMON FISHER TURNER
Song "Skye Boat Song" sung by Marianne Faithfull
-S/T- *MUTE: IONIC 1 (LP) CDIONIC 1 (CD)*

LAST OF THE HIGH KINGS The (1996) Mus: MICHAEL CONVERT
INO -S/T- (V.Arts) *EMI PREMIER: PRMD(CD)(TC) 26*

LAST OF THE MOHICANS (1992) Music: TREVOR JONES-RANDY
EDELMAN -S/T- *reis: MORGAN CREEK (Pinn): 002241-2
MCM (CD)* FILMSUITE *SILVA SCREEN: FILMCD 155 (CD)*

LAST OF THE SUMMER WINE The (BBC1 12/11/73-1996) theme
RONNIE HAZLEHURST *RH RECORDS (Pinn): RH1CD (CD)
RH1MC (MC)* also 'TV Cast Recording *BBC (Pinn):
ZBBC 1727 (2MC)* see also COLLECTION 1

LAST STAND AT SABRE RIVER (1998) Music: DAVID SHIRE
-S/T- *INTRADA (Koch): number to be confirmed*

LAST STARFIGHTER The (1984) Music sc: CRAIG SAFAN -S/T-
reissue *INTRADA (Silva Screen): MAF 7066 (CD)*

LAST TEMPTATION OF CHRIST (1988) Music: PETER GABRIEL
-S/T-'Passion' *R.WORLD-VIRG: RW(CD)(MC)(LP)(MD) 1*

LATE SHOW The (1976) Music score: KEN WANNBERG -S/T-
selection with 'THE AMATEUR'/'OF UNKNOWN ORIGIN'
*PROMETHEUS (Silva Screen): PCD 137 (CD)*

LATE SHOW REVIEW The (BBC2 6/94) theme "Cantaloop" US 3
*Coll* "Jazz Classics" *TELSTAR (WEA): TCD(STAC) 2722*

LATE SHOW WITH DAVID LETTERMAN (USA TV) *see COLLECT.345*

LATER (WITH JOOLS HOLLAND) (BBC2) Compilation featuring
BLUE/OASIS/PAUL WELLER/SUPERGRASS/ELASTICA etc. on
*ISLAND (Poly): CID 8053 (CD)*

LAURA (1944) Music score: DAVID RAKSIN -S/T- re-issue
with 'JANE EYRE' (1943) *FOX-ARISTA (BMG): 07822
11006-2(CD)* see also COLLECTIONS 136,216,311

LAVERNE AND SHIRLEY (USA TV) *see COLLECTION 341*

LAW AND ORDER (USA TV) *see COLLECTIONS 345,388*

LAWMAN (USA TV) *see COLLECTION 342*

LAWRENCE OF ARABIA (1962) Music score: MAURICE JARRE
  -S/T- *VARESE (Pinn): VSD 5263 (CD) VSC 5263 (MC)*
  *SILVA SCREEN (Koch): FILMC(CD)036 (MC/CD) see also*
  *COLLECT.35,62,63,120,140,169,173,203,214,215,292*
LAWNMOWER MAN 2: BEYOND CYBERSPACE (95) Music score:
  ROBERT FOLK -S/T- *VARESE (Pinn): VSD 5698 (CD)*
LE CHATEAU DE MA MERE - *see under* 'GLORY OF MY FATHER'
LE HUITIEME JOUR - see EIGHTH DAY
LE JOUR ET LA NUIT (1997) Music score: MAURICE JARRE
  -S/T- *imp WEA FRANCE (Discovery): 0630 18006-2 (CD)*
LE MANOIR (C4 YTV 24/7/92) theme music "Images For Orch
  estra" (Debussy) played by The CBSO (Simon Rattle)
  *EMI: CDC 749947-2 (CD) -4 (MC) other incidental*
  *music:* "Prelude A L'Apres-Midi D'Faun" (Debussy)
  LSO (Andre Previn) *EMI: CDC 747001-2 (CD) -4 (MC)*
LE NOTTE BLANCHE *on COLL 'FILM MUS.OF NINO ROTA' delet*
LEADING MAN The (1996) Music score: EDWARD SHEARMUR
  -S/T- Various Arts: GARY BARLOW-DUBSTAR-GERRY & THE
  PACEMAKERS-TALKING HEADS-PETER SKELLERN-MILLA-PETER
  SARSTEDT-LONDON MET.ORCH *EMI PREMIER: PRMDCD 23(CD)*
LEAP OF FAITH (1992) Music score: CLIFF EIDELMAN -S/T-
  *MCA (BMG): MCD 10671 (CD) MCC 10671 (MC)*
LEAVE IT TO BEAVER (1997) Music sc: RANDY EDELMAN -S/T-
  *VARESE (Pinn): VSD 5838 (CD)*
LEAVE IT TO BEAVER (USA TV) *see COLLECTION 339*
LEAVING HOME (C4 29/9/96) 20th Century Orchestral music
  CITY OF BIRMINGHAM SYMPHONY ORCH cond: SIMON RATTLE
  -S/T- music from the 7 part series on *EMI CLASSICS*
  *CDM 566 136-2 (2CD's) and CDM 566 137-2 (2CDs)*
LEAVING LAS VEGAS (1994) Music sco: MIKE FIGGIS + V.Arts
  -S/T- *IRS-A.& M.(Poly): 540 476-2 (CD)*
LEAVING OF LIVERPOOL The (Austr/BBC Co Pr BBC1 15/7/93)
  music score: PETER BEST -S/T- *ONE M ONE Australia*
  *(Silva Screen): IMICD 1019 (CD)*
LEGACY OF REGINALD PERRIN The (BBC1 22/9/96) theme mus:
  RONNIE HAZLEHURST *POLYDOR: 2384 107 (LP deleted)*
LEGEND (1986) *note: this film can be heard with 2 -S/T-*
  Mus *(1)* JERRY GOLDSMITH  Lyrics (John Bettis) -S/T-
  *SILVA SCREEN (Koch): FILMCD 045 (CD)* / Mus *(2)*
  TANGERINE DREAM *and also feat* "Is Your Love Strong
  Enough" by BRYAN FERRY / "Loved By The Sun" by JON
  ANDERSON -S/T- *re-iss: VARESE (Pinn): VSD 5645 (CD)*
LEGEND OF THE GLASS MOUNTAIN *see* 'GLASS MOUNTAIN The'
LEGEND OF JESSE JAMES (USA TV) *see COLLECTION 342*
LEGEND OF WYATT EARP *see* LIFE AND LEGEND OF WYATT EARP
LEGENDS OF THE FALL (1994) Music sc: JAMES HORNER -S/T-
  *EPIC (Sony Music): 478 511-2 (CD)*
LEON (The Professional) (1994) Music score: ERIC SERRA
  -S/T- *COLUMBIA (Sony): 478 323-2 (CD) -4 (MC)*
LES MISERABLES - songs by Alain Boublil-Claude Michel
  Schonberg with English lyrics by Herbert Kretzmer
  *Recordings:*
  1.ORIG LONDON CAST 1985 *with:* PATTI LuPONE and Comp
  *ENCORE CD1 (CD) ENCORE C1 (2MC)*

LES MISERABLES *Continued...*

2. ORIG FRENCH CAST *FIRST NIGHT (Pinn):* DOCRCD 1 (2CD)
   COMPLETE SYMPHONIC RECORDINGS LONDON P.O.and UK/USA
   Casts *FIRST NIGHT (Pinn):* MIZCD1 (3CDs) MIZC1 (3MC)
3. FIVE OUTSTANDING PERFORMANCES From Les Miserables:
   *FIRST NIGHT (Pinn):* SCORCD 17 (CD)   Highlights from
   Int.Cast *FIRST NIGHT (Pinn):CAST(C)(CD)20 (MC/CD)*
4. MANCHESTER 1992 CAST RECORDING   *FIRST NIGHT (Pinn):*
   SCORECD 34 (CDep)
5. CARLTON SHOWS COLLECTION 1993 STUDIO RECORD *with:*
   DAVE WILLETTS-CLAIRE MOORE & West End Concert Orch
   *CARLTON SHOWS:* PWKS 4175 (CD) PWKMC 4175 (MC)
6. ROYAL PHILHARMONIC ORCHESTRA *PLAY SUITES from*
   Miss Saigon and Les Miserables
   *CARLTON Shows:* PWKS(PWKMC) 4079 (CD/MC)
7. 10TH ANNIVERARY LONDON STAGE SHOW 1995
   *FIRST NIGHT (Pinn):ENCORECD 8 (2CD) ENCOREC 8(2MC)*

LES SILENCES DU PALAIS - see 'SILENCES OF THE PALACE'
LES UNS ET LES AUTRES - see under 'INS AND THE OUTS'
LES VALSEUSES (1974 Fra) Music sco: STEPHANE GRAPPELLI
   -S/T- *MUSIDISC (Discovery): 10870-2 (CD)*
LET 'EM EAT CAKE *see COLLECTION 151*
LET IT BE (1970) Songs: JOHN LENNON-PAUL McCARTNEY
   *PARLOPHONE: (TC)PCS 7096 (MC/LP) CDP 746447-2(CD)*
LET'S DO IT! (Chichester Festival Prod 1994) Songs by
   (Noel Coward and Cole Porter) *feat:* DAVID KERNAN-
   LIZ ROBERTSON-LOUISE GOLD-ROBIN RAY-PETER GREENWELL
   PAT KIRKWOOD *SILVA SCREEN (Koch): SONG(C)(CD) 910*
LEVIATHAN (1989) Music score: JERRY GOLDSMITH -S/T-
   *VARESE (Pinn):* VCD 5226 (CD)
LEXX: THE DARK ZONE STORIES (SKY1 8/97) Music score by
   MARTY SIMON -S/T- *COLOSSEUM (Pinn):* CST 348064 (CD)
   *see COLLECTION 302*
LIAR LIAR (1997) Mus score: JOHN DEBNEY -S/T- (V.Arts)
   *MCA (BMG):* MCD 11618 (CD) *DELETED 97*
LICENCE TO KILL - see *COLLECTIONS 202,262,274*
   *see also* JAMES BOND FILM INDEX p.346
LIDO LADY (ORIG LONDON CAST 1926) Songs (Richard Rodge
   rs-Lorenz Hart) *feat:* CICELY COURTNEIDGE-BOBBY COM
   BER-PHYLLIS DARE-JACK HULBERT-HAROLD FRENCH +
   *musicals* 'SHOWBOAT' (1928) and 'SUNNY' (1926) on
   *PEARL (Pavilion):* GEMMCD 9105 (CD)
LIEBESTRAUM (1991) Music score: MIKE FIGGIS and tracks
   by Earl Bostic & His Orch and Bennie Moiseiwitsch
   -S/T- *VIRGIN (EMI):* CDV 2682 (CD) TCV 2682 (MC)
LIFE AFTER BIRTH (C4 17/5/96) music: PHILIP POPE / song
   "Sparky's Dream" performed by TEENAGE FANCLUB on
   *CREATION (Pinn):* CRESCD 201 (CDs) CRESC 201 (MC)
LIFE AND LEGEND OF WYATT EARP (USA TV) *see COLLECTION*
   176,342
LIFE AND TIMES OF DAVID LLOYD GEORGE (BBC2 4/3/81)
   theme music 'Chi Mai' ENNIO MORRICONE
   *see COLLECTIONS 213,251,267,284,285,333*

LIFE AND TIMES OF GRIZZLY ADAMS (USA 78) theme "Maybe"
   THOM PACE) instrumental version ('The Man From The
   Mountains') *see COLLECTIONS 168,343*
LIFE LESS ORDINARY, A (1997) Music score: DAVID ARNOLD
   -S/T- *inc* BECK-UNDERWORLD-REM-ELVIS PRESLEY-PRODIGY
   DUSTED-BOBBY DARIN-CARDIGANS-ASH-FAITHLESS & others
   *A.& M. (Poly): 540 837-2 and LIFECD 1 (CD) -4 (MC)*
LIFE WITH FRED (BBC2 10/3/94) theme music "Carnival Of
   Venice" (Briccialdi) version by JAMES GALWAY on
   *RCA (BMG): PD 70260 (CD) PK 70260 (MC)*
LIFEBOAT (1) (BBC1 27/4/94) orig mus: MICHAEL STOREY
   title song sung by TERRY NEASON *WEA: YZ830(CD)C)*
   *other music used* "Safe and Sound" CHORALE (orig
   issued 11/83 on *RCA 371 (7"s) now deleted*
LIFEBOAT (2) (Central 27/4/93) music: ANTHONY PHILLIPS
   "Lifeboat Suite" / 'Missing Links V2 The Sky Road'
   on *BRAINWORKS/Voiceprint (Vital): BWKD 212 (CD)*
LIFEFORCE *see COLLECTION 322*
LIFESTYLES OF THE RICH & FAMOUS (USA TV) *see COLL.344*
LIGHT OF EXPERIENCE The (BBC2 76-87) theme "Doina De
   Jale" GHEORGE ZAMFIR *Coll* 'REFLECTIONS' *deleted*
LIKE WATER FOR CHOCOLATE (93) Music score: LEO BROWER
   -S/T- *Milan (BMG): 887 797 (CD)*
LILAC TIME (ORIG LONDON CAST 1922) Mus (Franz SCHUBERT)
   Lyr (Adrian ROSS) *feat:* CLARA BUTTERWORTH-DOROTHY
   CLAYTON-EDMUND GWENN + *RIO RITA (1930) SOUTHERN
   MAID (1920) PEARL (Pavilion): GEMMCD 9115 (CD)*
LILIES OF THE FIELD (1963) Music sco: JERRY GOLDSMITH
   -S/T- *TSUNAMI Imp (Silva Screen): TSU 0101 (CD)*
LILLIE (GRA+5/10/96 orig ITV 24/9/1978) theme music:
   JOSEPH HOROVITZ *see COLLECTION 175*
LILIES (1997) Music score: MYCHAEL DANNA -S/T- on
   *VARESE (Pinn): VSD 5868 (CD)*
LILLIPUT IN ANTARCTICA (Cousteau Society/BBC1 2/8/93)
   theme music "Antarctica" (Vangelis) VANGELIS on
   'Themes' *POLYDOR (Poly): 839 518-2 (CD) -4 (MC)*
LILY WAS HERE *see COLLECTION 267*
LIMELIGHT (1937) 4 songs on Coll 'LOUIS LEVY-MUSIC
   FROM T.MOVIES' *EMPRESS (Koch): RAJCD 884*
LIMELIGHT (1952) Music score: CHARLES CHAPLIN
   *see COLLECTIONS 56,57,160,230*
LINGUINI INCIDENT The (1992) Music sco: THOMAS NEWMAN
   -S/T- *VARESE (Pinn): VSD 5372 (CD) VSC 5372 (MC)*
LION KING The  (1994) *see* WALT DISNEY INDEX p.343
LION OF THE DESERT (1981) Music score: MAURICE JARRE
   L.Symph Orch *SILVA SCREEN (Koch): FILMCD 060 (CD)*
   *also inc music from* 'THE MESSAGE' (1977) (JARRE)
LIONHEART (1987) Music score: JERRY GOLDSMITH -S/T-
   *VARESE (Pinn): VCD 47282 (CD-V1) VCD 47288 (CD-V2)*
   also 'BEST OF' *VARESE (Pinn): VSD 5484 (CD)*
LIONHEART (1990) - *see* 'A.W.O.L.'
LIONS TOUR 93 (ITV Sport/Scottish Prov 26/6/93) theme:
   CHARLIE SKARBEK arr.of Holst's "Jupiter" vocal by
   KIRI TE KANAWA "World In Union" *see* WORLD CUP RUGBY

LIPSTICK ON YOUR COLLAR (C4 21/2/93) opening title song
    (Edna Lewis-George Goehring) sung by CONNIE FRANCIS
    closing music "The Man With The Golden Arm" played
    by BILLY MAY ORCH. *SOUNDTRACK select.of 28 oldies
    POLYGRAM TV (Poly): 516 086-2 (CD) -4(MC) deleted
    see also* 'PENNIES FROM HEAVEN'/'SINGING DETECTIVE'
LIQUID TELEVISION (USA TV) *see COLLECTION 345*
LITTLE BUDDAH (1992) Mus score: RYUICHI SAKAMOTO -S/T-
    *reissue MILAN (BMG): 74321 18031-2 (CD)*
    *see COLL 264* 'MUSIC FROM THE ORIENT' -S/T- also on
    *MILAN (BMG): 180 312 (CD) 180 314 (MC) also avail*
    'secret score' on *MILAN (BMG): 22745-2 (CD)*
LITTLE HOUSE ON THE PRAIRIE (USA 74 rpt C4-13/10/91)
    theme: DAVID ROSE *see COLLECTIONS 12,168,341*
LITTLE MAN TATE (1991) Music score: MARK ISHAM -S/T-
    *VARESE Impt (S.Screen): VSD 5343 (CD)*
LITTLE MARY SUNSHINE (O.LONDON CAST 1962) Songs: RICK
    BESOYAN *feat:* ED BISHOP-JOYCE BLAIR-ERIK CHITTY-TE
    RENCE COOPER-BERNARD CRIBBINS-ANNA DAWSON-PATRICIA
    ROUTLEDGE-GITA DENISE.*DRG (Pinn): CDSBL 13108 CD*
LITTLE ME - songs by Cy Coleman and Carolyn Leigh
    1.ORIG BROADWAY CAST 1962 *w* Sid Caesar-Virginia Mart
      in-Nancy Andrews-Mort Marshall-Peter Turgeon-Micky
      Deems-Joey Faye *RCA Vict (BMG): 09026 61482-2 (CD)*
    2.ORIG LONDON CAST 1964 *w:* BRUCE FORSYTH-AVRIL ANGERS
      JACK FRANCOIS-EILEEN GOURLAY-DAVID HENDERSON TATE-
      BERNARD SPEAR-SVEN SVENSON *DRG (Pin): CDSBL 13111*
LITTLE MERMAID The (89) *see* WALT DISNEY INDEX p.343
LITTLE NIGHT MUSIC, A - songs by Stephen Sondheim
    1.NATIONAL THEATRE PROD 1996 *feat* JUDI DENCH-PATRICIA
      HODGE-SIAN PHILLIPS-SEAN MATHIAS & Com ORIG.CAST on
      *TRING Int (THE): TRING 001 (CD) MCTRING 001 (MC)*
    2.ORIG BROADWAY CAST 1973 *with* GLYNIS JOHNS & Company
      *CBS USA (S.Scr): CK 32265(CD) JST 32265(MC)*
    3.ORIG LONDON CAST 1975 *with:* JEAN SIMMONS-HERMOINE
      GINGOLD-JOSS ACKLAND and Company
      *RCA (Silva Screen) 5090-2 (CD) 5090-4 (MC)*
    4.STUDIO RECORDING *w:* SIAN PHILLIPS-SUSAN HAMPSHIRE
      ELISABETH WELCH arrang.& cond.by JOHN OWEN EDWARDS
      *TER (Disc): CDTER(ZCTER) 1179 (CD/MC)*
    5.STUDIO RECORDING *feat* TERRY TROTTER (solo piano)
      *VARESE (Pinn): VSD 5819 (CD)*
LITTLE ODESSA (1994) Classical Music from & inspired by
    the film -S/T- *PHILIPS (Polyg): 446 391-2 (CD)*
LITTLE PRINCESS, A (19) Music score: PATRICK DOYLE
    -S/T- *VARESE (Pinn): VSD 5628 (CD)*
LITTLE RASCALS (USA TV) *see COLLECTION 339*
LITTLE SHOP OF HORRORS (FILM MUSICAL 1987) Songs (Alan
    Menkin-Howard Ashman) Orig Film sco: MILES GOODMAN
    -S/T- *GEFFEN-MCA (BMG): GFLD 19289 (CD)*
LITTLE WOMEN (94) Music score: THOMAS NEWMAN LONDON SO
    -S/T- *Sony Classical: SK 66922-2 (CD) DELETED 1997*
LITTLEJOHN (LWT 95) theme "House Of Fun" BOOM!
    *see COLLECTION 33*

LIVE A LITTLE LOVE A LITTLE *see* ELVIS PRESLEY FILM IND.
LIVE AND KICKING (BBC1 2/10/93) theme music by DAVID
   ARNOLD and PAUL HART *unavailable*
LIVE AND LET DIE (1993) Music sco: GEORGE MARTIN title
   song (Paul & Linda McCartney) by PAUL McCARTNEY
   -S/T- *reissue EMI PREMIER (EMI): CZ 553 (CD)*
   *see* JAMES BOND FILM INDEX p.346 *see also* COLL.305
LIVE FOR LIFE 'Vivre Pour Vivre' (1967) Music score:
   FRANCIS LAI incl: 'A Man And A Woman' (1966) -S/T-
   *DRG (New Note-Pinn): DRGCD 12612 (CD)*
LIVER BIRDS The (BBC1 6/5/96) theme mus re-recorded by
   MIKE McCARTNEY &Fuzzy "On A Mountain Stands A Lady"
   (trad.) performed by SCAFFOLD / orig BBC1 series
   (BBC1 14/4/69-5/1/79) *see COLLECTIONS 2,4,402*
LIVES OF JESUS (BBC1 01/12/96) original music by: GLENN
   KEILES -S/T- *MCA (BMG): MCD(MCC) 60030 (CD/MC)*
LIVING DAYLIGHTS The - *see* JAMES BOND FILM INDEX p.346
   *see COLLECTIONS 79,274*
LIZA WITH A 'Z' (USA TV Concert 1972) -S/T- featur LIZA
   MINNELLI reissue *SONY Coll: 982994-2 (CD) -4 (MC)*
LOADED (1994) Music score: SIMON FISHER TURNER -S/T- on
   *OCEAN DEEP (Grapev/Polyg): OCD 001 (CD)*
LOCAL HERO (1982) Music: MARK KNOPFLER -S/T- *Vertigo*
   *(Poly): 811038-2 (CD) see also* COLLECTIONS 262,303
LOCKSMITH The (BBC1 25/9/97) Music composed and conduct
   ed by COLIN TOWNS *unavailable*
LODGER The (1944) Music score: HUGO FRIEDHOFER / Suite
   on Coll *with* 'RAINS OF RANCHIPUR'/'SEVEN CITIES OF
   GOLD'/'ADV.OF MARCO POLO' The MOSCOW SYMPHONY ORCH
   (W.T.Stromberg) *MARCO POLO (Select): 8.223857 (CD)*
LODOSS WAR 1/2/3 (Japan 95) Animated MANGA Film -S/T-
   *Animanga-New Note (Pinn): AM 3 / 4 / 8 (CDs)*
LOIS AND CLARK see 'NEW ADVENTURES OF SUPERMAN'
LOLITA (1961) Music sco: BOB HARRIS *feat:* NELSON RIDDLE
   *complete -S/T- EMI SOUNDTRACKS: 821 978-2 (CD)*
LONDON BRIDGE (Carlton 11/4/96) mus: CRAIG ARMSTRONG.*NA*
LONDON MARATHON The (BBC1 13/5/84-98) theme "The Trap"
   by RON GOODWIN *see COLLECTIONS 158,159*
LONDON'S BURNING (LWT 20/2/88-96) theme m "Blue Watch"
   SIMON BRINT-RODDY MATTHEWS on 'LONDON'S BURNING'
   *EMI: CDEMC 3729 (CD)* see also *COLLECTIONS 138,175*
LONE RANGFR The (USA 1949 re-run C4 88) theme "William
   Tell Overture" (ROSSINI) *see COLLECTIONS 309,339*
LONE STAR (1996) Music score: MASON DARING -S/T-
   *Daring (Direct): DARINGCD 3023 (CD)*
LONE WOLF McQUADE (1983) Music sco: FRANCESCO DI MASI
   -S/T- *VARESE (Pinn): VSD 5573 (CD)*
LONELY PLANET (C4 from 28/9/94) theme mus: IAN RITCHIE
   MICHAEL CONN sel.of World Music on 'Music For The
   Lonely Planet' *KAZ (BMG): KAZ(CD)(MC) 223 (CD/MCs)*
   *new:*'MORE MUSIC FROM THE LONELY PLANET' *KAZ-Castle*
   *Comm (BMG): KAZCD 224 (2CD) KAZMC 224 (2MC)*
   *also available* 'LISTEN TO THE PLANET' Var.Artists
   *MILAN (BMG): 74321 37243-2 (CD)*

LONESOME DOVE (USA TV/BBC1 30/8/93) music score: BASIL
    POLEDOURIS -S/T- *IMP (Sil.Screen): CFM 972.2 (CD)*
LONG GOOD FRIDAY The (1980) Music sco: FRANCIS MONKMAN
    feat KEVIN PEEK-TRISTRAM FRY-HERBIE FLOWERS (SKY)
    -S/T- *SILVA SCREEN (Koch): FILMCD 020 (CD)*
    *see also COLLECTION 356*
LONG KISS GOODNIGHT The (1996) Music: ALAN SILVESTRI
    -S/T- *MCA (BMG): MCD 11526 (CD)*
LONGEST DAY The (1962) Music score: PAUL ANKA
    *see COLLECTIONS 35,140,169,173,238,380,383,384*
LOONEY TUNES (USA TV) *see COLLECTION 340*
LORD OF ILLUSIONS (1995) Music sco: SIMON BOSWELL -S/T-
    *IONIC/MUTE/RTM (Disc): IONIC 13CD (CD)*
LORD OF THE DANCE 1996 SHOW Music: RONAN HARDIMAN feat
    MICHAEL FLATLEY and Comp / Music cond and orch by
    ANNE DUDLEY *POLYGRAM TV: 533 757-2 (CD) -4 (MC)*
LORD OF THE FLIES (1990) Music score: PHILIPPE SARDE
    London Symphony Orch & The Trinity Boys Choir
    -S/T- *SILVA SCREEN (Koch): FILMCD 067 (CD)*
LORD OF THE RINGS The (1978) Music: LEONARD ROSENMAN
    -S/T- *FANTASY/INTRADA (S.Screen): FMTCD 8003 (CD)*
LORENZO'S OIL (1992) Classical music -S/T- *MCA (BMG):
    MCD 10782 (CD) deleted 1994 - see COLLECTION 74*
LOST BOYS The (1987) Music score: THOMAS NEWMAN -S/T-
    *ATLANTIC (WEA): 781767-2 (CD) -4(MC)*
LOST CHILD The (BBC2 29/6/97) Violin Sonatas (FREDERICK
    DELIUS) performed by TASMIN LITTLE with BOURNEMOUTH
    SO (R.Hickox) *CONIF.CLASS (BMG): 75605 51315-2 (CD)*
LOST CIVILIZATIONS (1995) Music score: JOE DELIA -S/T-
    *VARESE (Pinn): VSD 5650 (CD)*
LOST CONTINENT The *see* 'HORRORS OF THE BLACK MUSEUM'
LOST EMPIRES (Granada 24/10/86) music: DEREK HILTON
    *TER (Disc): (CD)(ZC)TER 1119 (CD/MC)*
LOST GARDENS OF HELIGAN The (C4 14/3/97) music score
    by ELIZABETH PARKER *unavailable*
LOST HIGHWAY (1996) Music score: ANGELO BADALAMENTI
    Var.Arts -S/T- *INTERSCOPE-MCA (BMG): IND 90090 (CD)*
LOST HORIZON (1937) Mus sco: DIMITRI TIOMKIN conduct.by
    MAX STEINER -S/T- *TSUNAMI (S.Screen): TSU 0135 (CD)*
LOST IN SPACE (USA) *see COLLECTIONS 110,273,339,343*
LOST IN THE STARS (O.BROADWAY CAST 1949) Music (Kurt
    Weill) Ly:(Maxwell Anderson) *feat:* Todd Duncan-Les
    lie Banks-Warren Coleman-Inez Matthews-Frank Roane
    *MCA USA (S.Scr): MCAD 10302 (CD) MCAC 10302 (MC)*
LOST PATROL The (1934) Music: MAX STEINER *new recording*
    *feat* MOSCOW SO (Stromberg) + 'BEAST WITH 5 FINGERS'
    /'VIRGINIA CITY' *MARCO POLO (Select): 8.223870 (CD)*
LOST WEEKEND The (1945) Music sco: MIKLOS ROZSA / Suite
    on Coll *'FILM NOIR CLASSICS' see* 'DOUBLE INDEMNITY'
LOST WORLD The: Jurassic Park 2 (1997) M: JOHN WILLIAMS
    -S/T- *MCA (BMG): MCAD 11628 (CD) MCC 11628 (MC)*
LOTUS EATERS The (UKGO 12/9/93 orig BBC 71) theme "Ta
    "Ta Trena Pou Fyghan" STAVROS XARAHAKOS
    *see COLLECTION 31*

LOU GRANT (USA 77/C4 84) theme mus: PATRICK WILLIAMS
    *see COLLECTION 12,51,242*
LOUISIANA PURCHASE (USA CAST RECORDING 1996) on
    *DRG-NEW NOTE (Pinn): DRGCD 94766 (CD)*
LOVE AFFAIR (1994) Music score ENNIO MORRICONE -S/T-
    *WB IMP (Silva Screen): WA 45810-2 (CD) -4 (MC)*
LOVE AND DEATH (1975) *see COLLECTION 77*
LOVE BITES (LWT/Granada 15/3/97) theme mus: DUBSTAR..*NA*
LOVE BOAT (USA TV) *see COLLECTION 341*
LOVE FOR LYDIA (LWT 30/9/77) theme: HARRY RABINOWITZ
    *see COLLECTION 175*
LOVE JONES (1996) -S/T- featuring Various Artists on
    *COLUMBIA (Sony Music): 487 230-2 (CD) -4 (MC)*
LOVE ME TENDER (56) - see ELVIS PRESLEY INDEX p.348
LOVE STORY (1944) Music score: HUBERT BATH
    *see COLLECTION 387*
LOVE STORY (1970) Music score: FRANCIS LAI -S/T-
    *MCA (BMG) MCLD 19157 (CD) see COLLECTIONS:*
    *29,38,62,140,160,173,203,226,243,244,284,285*
LOVE STORY (TV 1970's) theme music: TONY HATCH
    *see COLLECTION 182,321*
LOVE VALOUR COMPASSION (1997) Music sco: HAROLD WHEELER
    -S/T- *DECCA (Poly): 455 644-2 (CD)*
LOVE YOU 'TIL TUESDAY (1969) C4 14/2/88  Music by
    DAVID BOWIE -S/T- *CARLTON: PWKS 4131P(CD)*
LOVED BY YOU (ITV 11/3/97) title mus: DEBBIE WISEMAN.*NA*
LOVED UP (BBC2 23/9/95) Rave mus BANCO DE GAIA-ORBITAL
    PRODIGY-LEFTFIELD -S/T- on *PRIMAVERA (Vital):*
    *PRIMACD 002 (CD) PRIMAMC 002(MC) PRIMALP 002 (LP)*
LOVERS The (L'Amant) (1991) Music score: GABRIEL YARED
    -S/T- *CIRCA / VIRGIN (EMI): CDVMM 9 (CD)*
LOVEJOY (BBC1 10/1/86-1994) theme music: DENIS KING
    *see COLLECTION 5*
LOVING YOU (1957)  feat ELVIS PRESLEY remastered -S/T-
    *RCA (BMG): 07863 67452-2 (CD) 07863 67452-4 (MC)*
    see also ELVIS PRESLEY INDEX p.348
LOW DOWN DIRTY SHAME (1994) Music: V.Arts -S/T- *JIVE*
    *(BMG): CHIPCD 156 (CD) HIPC 156 (MC) HIP 156 (LP)*
LULLABY OF BROADWAY (1950) *MGM (EMI): CDODEON 8 (2CD)*
    *see also COLL*
LUNATIC The (1991) Music sco: WALLY BADAROU + V.Arts
    -S/T- *MANGO ISLAND (Poly): CIDM(MCT) 1086 (CD/MC)*
LUST FOR LIFE (1956) Music score: MIKLOS ROZSA -S/T-
    *VARESE (Pinn): VSD 5405 (CD)*
LUV (BBC1 9/3/93) theme mus 'Intermezzo from Cavalleria
    Rusticana' (Mascagni) *see COLLECTIONS 65,70,83,*
    *86,93,276,277,310*

**M** BUTTERFLY (1993) Music score: HOWARD SHORE -S/T- on
    *VARESE (Pinn): VSD 5435 (CD)*
M.SQUAD (USA TV 1957-60) theme mus: COUNT BASIE (series
    2/3) STANLEY WILSON (1) 'Music From M.SQUAD' Collect
    *RCA Victor (BMG): 74321 43397-2 (CD)*
    *see COLLECTIONS 246,342*

MacARTHUR (1977) Music sco: JERRY GOLDSMITH -S/T- IMPT
    *VARESE (S.Screen): VSD 5260 (CD)*
McCALLUM (ITV 28/12/95) music score: DAEMION BARRY...*NA*
    "Cry Me A River" (A.Hamilton) sung by MARI WILSON
    from 'On The Beat' *CASTLE (BMG): PIPCD 032 (CD)*
McCLOUD - *see COLLECTIONS 2,246*
MacGREGOR ACROSS SCOTLAND (BBC1/Wildview Prod 18/7/92)
    theme music: JIMMIE MacGREGOR incidental music by
    DOUGIE MacLEAN examples on 'Craigie Dhu' album on
    *DUNKELD Celtic Music/Topic): DUN 001 (CD/MC)*
MacGYVER (USA-88)(BBC1 8/4/89) theme mus: RANDY EDELMAN
    *see COLLECTIONS 12,344,373*
McHALE'S NAVY (USA TV) *see COLLECTION 339*
McMILLAN AND WIFE (USA) *see COLLECTION 246*
McVICAR (1980) Music score: JEFF WAYNE featuring ROGER
    DALTREY-JEFF WAYNE-PETE TOWNSHEND -S/T- *re-issue:*
    *POLYDOR (Polyg): 527 341-2 (CD)*
MACBETH (FILM OPERA 1986) Mus: VERDI Dir:Claude D'Anna
    feat:Leon Nucci-Shirley Verrett-Samuel Ramsey -S/T-
    *DECCA (Poly): 417 525-4 (MC) 417 525-2 (CD)*
MACK AND MABEL - songs by Jerry Herman
    1.ORIG REVIVAL LONDON CAST 1995 *with:* HOWARD McGILLIN
      CAROLINE O'CONNOR-KATHRYN EVANS and Company
      *EMI PREMIER (EMI): CDEMC 3734 (CD)*
    2.ORIG BROADWAY CAST 1974 *w* ROBERT PRESTON-BERNADETTE
      PETERS *MCA (BMG): MCLD 19089 (CD)*
    3.LIVE IN CONCERT RECORDING UK 1988 Various Artists
      *First Night (Pinn): OCRCD 6015 (CD)*
MACKENNA'S GOLD (69) Music score: QUINCY JONES title
    song sung by JOSE FELICIANO -S/T- *TSUNAMI Import*
    *(Silva Screen): TSU 0123 (CD)*
MACROSS PLUS 2 (Japanese Animated MANGA video) -S/T-
    *DEMON (Pinn): DSCD 13 (CD)*
MAD CITY (1997) Music score: THOMAS NEWMAN -S/T-
    *VARESE (Pinn): VSD 5887 (CD)*
MAD DOG AND GLORY (1992) Music score: ELMER BERNSTEIN
    -S/T- *VARESE (Pinn): VSD 5415 (CD)*
MAD LOVE (1995) Music sco: ANDY ROBERTS -S/T- inc V/A:
    7 YEAR BITCH-THRONEBERRY-GRANT LEE BUFFALO-FLUORESC
    EIN-ROCKET FROM THE CRYPT-HEAD CANDY-MADDER ROSE &
    KIRSTY MacCOLL *DEDICATED (RTM/DISC):DEDCD 022 (CD)*
MAD MAX (1979) Music score: BRIAN MAY -S/T- Import on
    *VARESE (Pinn): VCD 47144 (CD)*
MAD MAX 2 (1981) Music score: BRIAN MAY -S/T- *VARESE*
    *(Pinn) VCD 47262 (CD) see also COLLECTION 268*
MAD MAX 3 'Beyond Thunderdome' (1985) Mus MAURICE JARRE
    -S/T- *GNP (Silva Screen): GNPD 8037 (CD)*
    *see COLLECTIONS 28,109,201,274*
MADAGASCAR: ISLAND OF GHOSTS (SURVIVAL) Anglia 13/11/91
    Original music by ROSSY on 'Island Of Ghosts' on
    REAL WORLD (Virgin): CDRW 19 (CD) RWMC 19 (MC)
MADAME SOUSATZKA (1988) Music score: GERALD GOURIET
    -S/T- *VARESE (Pinn): VSD 5204 (CD)*
    *see COLLECTIONS 74,76*

MADNESS OF KING GEORGE The (94) Mus sco: GEORGE FENTON
  adapting the music of G.F.HANDEL) with BAROQUE ORCH
  -S/T- *EPIC (Sony): 478477-2 (CD) deleted 96*
  *see COLLECTIONS 65,249,171*
MAGDALENE (1988) Music score: CLIFF EIDELMAN -S/T- on
  *INTRADA (Koch/S.Screen): MFCD 7029 (CD)*
MAGIC ADVENTURES OF MUMFIE - see 'BRITT ALLCROFT'S..'
MAGIC IN THE WATER (1995) Music score: DAVID SCHWARTZ
  -S/T- *VARESE (Pinn): VSD 5659 (CD)*
MAGIC ROUNDABOUT The (BBC1 64) theme: ALAIN LEGRAND
  VIDEOS: *BBC: BBCV 4278, 4494 see also COLLECT.357*
MAGICAL MYSTERY TOUR (1967) Feat music by The BEATLES
  -S/T- *PARLOPHONE (EMI): PCTC 255 (LP) TC-PCS 3077*
  *(MC) CD-PCTC 255 (CD)  SMMT 1 (2 x 7" singles)*
MAGICIAN The (USA TV) *see COLLECTION 343*
MAGILLA GORILLA (USA TV) *see COLLECTION 339*
MAGNIFICENT AMBERSONS The (1942) Mus: BERNARD HERRMANN
  -S/T- *5TH CONTINENT (Silva Screen): PRCD 1783 (CD)*
MAGNIFICENT SEVEN The (1960) Music sc: ELMER BERNSTEIN
  -S/T- also containing music from sequel 'RETURN OF
  THE M...' *TSUNAMI Germ (S.Screen): TSU 0102 (CD)*
  *see COLLECTIONS 23,62,63,81,140,173,211,397,398*
MAGNUM; P.I. (USA 1980) theme: MIKE POST-PETE CARPENTER
  *see COLLECTIONS 12,51,100,168,242,341,360,388*
MAHABARAHTA (C4 9/12/90 Music composed and performed by
  TOSHI TCHUCHITORI -S/T- *REAL WORLD-VIRGIN (EMI):*
  *CDRW 9 (CD) RWLP 9 (LP) RWMC 9 (MC)*
MAHABARAT (BBC2 14/4/90) 91 pt Hindi serial / Playback
  singer: MAHENDRA KAPOOR on "Dillan Dee Gal" on
  *STAR (Backs): SSRLP 5106 (LP) SC 5106 (MC)*
MAHOGANY (1975) Music sc: MICHAEL MASSER theme "Do You
  Know Where You're Going To" (M.Masser-G.Goffin) by
  DIANA ROSS -S/T- *MOTOWN (Poly): E.530 277-2(CD)*
  *see also COLLECTIONS 28,280*
MAIGRET (BBC1 1961) theme music: RON GRAINER
  *see COLLECTIONS 1,3,100,364,372*
MAIGRET (Granada 9/2/1991) theme mus: NIGEL HESS *EAGLE*
  *(BMG): EAGLE 14 (7")* vocal by OLIVE SIMPSON
  *see COLLECTIONS 6,191,192*
MAINLY FOR WOMEN (BBC 50s) m: "Jockey On The Carousel"
  ROBERT FARNON *see COLLECTION 220*
MAJOR BARBARA (1941) Music sco: Sir WILLIAM WALTON  New
  Recording by Academy Of St.Martin-In-The Fields
  (Sir Neville Marriner) *CHANDOS: CHAN 8841 (CD)*
  + Music from 'Richard III' & 'Macbeth'
MAJOR DAD (USA TV) *see COLLECTION 345*
MAJOR DUNDEE (1965) Music score: DANIELE AMFITHEATROF
  -S/T- *TSUNAMI Germany (S.Screen): TSU 0111 (CD)*
MAJOR LEAGUE (1989) Music score: JAMES NEWTON HOWARD
  -S/T- *MOTOWN (BMG): ZD(ZK) 74277 (CD/MC)*
MAKING THE GRADES - see 'ALLAN QUARTERMAIN'
MALCOLM (1986) Mus: SIMON JEFFES PENGUIN CAFE ORCHESTRA
  'Penguin Cafe Orch' *EG-VIRG: EGED 11(CD)* Music From
  The PCO' *EGED 27* 'Broadcasting From Home' *EGED 38*

**MALICE** (1993) Music score: JERRY GOLDSMITH -S/T-
  *VARESE (Pinn): VSD 5442 (CD)*
**MALICE AFORETHOUGHT** (BBC2 15/3/79) music: RON GRAINER
  *see COLLECTION 7*
**MAMA I WANT TO SING** (Musical 95) *w* CHAKA KHAN as DORIS
  TROY / OCR *EMI CD(TC)EMC 3709 (CD/MC) DELETED DORIS
  TROY 'Just One Look' Ichiban (Koch): SCLCD 2504(CD)*
**MAMBO KINGS** The (1992) Music by various artists -S/T-
  *ELEKTRA (WEA): 755961 240-2 (CD) 755961 240-4 (MC)*
**MAME** - songs by Jerry Herman
  1.ORIG BROADWAY CAST 1966) *with* ANGELA LANSBURY & Co.
  *CBS USA (Sil.Screen) CK 03000 (CD) JST 03000 (MC)*
**MAN** ABOUT THE HOUSE (UKGO 7/2/94 orig Thames 73) theme
  "Up To Date" (JOHNNY HAWKESWORTH)
  *see COLLECTIONS 4,229,318,360*
**MAN** ALIVE (BBC2) theme m: TONY HATCH *see COLL.3,182,372*
**MAN** AND A WOMAN A 'Un Homme Et Une Femme' (1966) Music
  by FRANCIS LAI incl: 'Live For Life' (67) -S/T-
  *DRG (N.Note-Pinn): DRGCD 12612 (CD) + COLLS 226,358*
**MAN** CALLED IRONSIDE, A (USA) *see COLLECTION 101,109,246*
**MAN** FROM U.N.C.L.E. The (USA/NBC/MGM 1964-1967) reshown
  (BBC2 fr 11/9/92) theme music: JERRY GOLDSMITH
  *ORIG TV -S/T- RAZOR & TIE (Koch): RE 2133 (CD)*
  HUGO MONTENEGRO OR -S/T-*RCA (BMG):74321 24179-2(CD)*
  *see also COLLECTIONS 12,100,168,339,356,357,374,379*
**MAN** IN A SUITCASE (ITC 27/9/67-68) theme: RON GRAINER
  *see COLLECTIONS 3,7,357,358,364,372*
**MAN** IN THE IRON MASK The (1976) Music: ALLYN FERGUSON
  -S/T- includes 'COUNT OF MONTE CRISTO' music (Allyn
  Ferguson) *PROMETHEUS (Silva Screen): PCD 130 (CD)*
**MAN** IN THE NEWS (LWT 69) mus: RON GRAINER *see COLLECT.7*
**MAN** OF LA MANCHA - songs by Mitch Leigh and Joe Darion
  1. COMPLETE STUDIO RECORDING 1996 *feat* PLACIDO DOMINGO
  MANDY PATINKIN-SAMUEL RAMEY-JERRY HADLEY-CAROLANN
  PAGE-ROBERT WHITE-ROSALIND ELIAS and Orchestra
  *SONY Classical (Sony): SK 46436 (CD) ST 46436 (MC)*
  2.ORIG BROADWAY CAST 1965 *with*: RICHARD KILEY-JOAN DI
  ENER-IRVING JACOBSON-RAY MIDDLETON-ROBERT ROUNSEVI
  LLE-JON CYPHER *MCA USA (S.Screen): MCAD 31065 (CD)*
  3. ORIG FRENCH CAST "L'Homme De La Mancha" *w*: JACQUES
  BREL-JOAN DIENER & Comp *(S.Screen): 839 586-2 (CD)*
**MAN** TROUBLE (1992) *see COLLECTIONS 75,77*
**MAN** WHO KNEW TOO LITTLE The (1997) Music: CHRISTOPHER
  YOUNG -S/T- *VARESE (Pinn): VSD 5886 (CD)*
**MAN** WHO MADE HUSBANDS JEALOUS (ITV 6/6/97) incidental
  music by HUGHES & MURPHY *not available* "Mad About
  The Boy" (N.Coward) sung by CONNIE LUSH *unavailable*
  other songs performed by KIM CRISWELL *unavailable*
**MAN** WHO MISTOOK HIS WIFE FOR A HAT (1987) Mus: MICHAEL
  NYMAN -S/T- *COLUMBIA (Sony): CD44669 (CD) 40-(MC)*
**MAN** WITH THE GOLDEN GUN The (1974) Music: JOHN BARRY
  title song (John Barry-Don Black) sung by LULU
  -S/T- *reissue EMI PREMIER: CZ 552 (CD)*
  *see JAMES BOND FILM INDEX p.346*

MAN WITHOUT A FACE The (1993) Music sco: JAMES HORNER
  -S/T- *IMPT (Silva Screen): 518 244-2 (CD) -4 (MC)*
MAN'S TRAGEDY, A (1981) Music score ENNIO MORRICONE on
  'BERNARDO BERTOLUCCI DOUBLE FEATURE' Collection on
  *DRG (Pinn): DRGCD 32910 (CD)*
MANDELA (1996) -S/T- featuring VARIOUS ARTISTS on
  *MANGO-ISLAND (Poly): CIDM(MCT) 1116*
MANGALA THE INDIAN GIRL Film Soundtrack -S/T-
  *Club Du Disques Arabe (HARMONIA MUNDI): AAA121(CD)*
MANHATTAN (1979) Music score: GEORGE GERSHWIN -S/T-
  *SONY: MK 36020(CD) see COLLECTIONS 15,66,70,97,276*
MANNAJA / TEDEUM (Italian Spaghetti Westerns) Music:
  G.& M.DeANGELIS *IMPORT (S.Screen): OST 1212 (CD)*
MANNIX (USA/1967-74) theme music: LALO SCHIFRIN
  *see COLLECTIONS 246,339,374*
MANON DES SOURCES (1987) Music score: JEAN CLAUDE PETIT
  -S/T- *MILAN (BMG): CDCH 241 (CD) deleted*
  CD also inc music from 'JEAN DE FLORETTE' (Film 87)
MARCUS WELBY, MD (USA TV) *see COLLECTION 341*
MARIUS (1931) MARCEL PAGNOL'S TRILOGY (1)/ music sco.by
  FRANCIS GROMON on Coll 'Films Of Marcel Pagnol' on
  *EMI FRA.(Discov): 855 883-2 (CD) see also 'FANNY'*
MARK OF ZORRO (1940) *see COLLECTION 332*
MARK TULLY'S FACES OF INDIA (C4 30/8/97) original music
  by MARK POORE *unavailable*
MARLENE: A TRIBUTE TO DIETRICH (ORIG CAST RECORD 1997)
  *PLAYBACK (Pinn): PBMARCD 1 (CD) PBMART 01 (MC)*
MARNIE (1964) Mus: BERNARD HERRMANN *see COLLECTION 196*
MARRYING MAN The - see 'TOO HOT TO HANDLE'
MARS ATTACKS! (1996) Mus sco: DANNY ELFMAN / song "It's
  Not Unusual" (G.Mills) sung by TOM JONES -S/T- on
  *W.BROS (WEA): 7567 82992-2 (CD)*
MARTIN GUERRE songs: Alain Boublil-CLaude Michel Schon
  berg-Edward Hardy O.LONDON CAST 1996: IAIN GLENN-
  JULIETTE CATON-MATTHEW RAWLE-JEROME PRADON-ANN
  EMERY & Co *FIRST NIGHT (Pinn): CAST(CD)(C) 59*
MARY HARTMAN, MARY HARTMAN (USA TV) *see COLLECTION 343*
MARY POPPINS (1964) *see WALT DISNEY INDEX p.343*
MARY QUEEN OF SCOTS (1971) Music score: JOHN BARRY
  *see COLLECTION 24*
MARY REILLY (1996) Music sco: GEORGE FENTON cond: I.S.O.
  -S/T- *ElFKTRA-Sony CLs: SK 62259 (CD) DELETED 1997*
MARY SHELLEY'S FRANKENSTEIN (1994) Mus s: PATRICK DOYLE
  -S/T- *EPIC (Sony): 477 987-2(CD) -4 (MC) deleted 96*
MARY TYLER MOORE SHOW (USA TV) *see COLLECTIONS 340,405*
M*A*S*H (FILM 1970) Mus sco: JOHNNY MANDEL-MIKE ALTMAN
  -S/T- *reissue: Columbia (Sony): CK 66804 (CD)*
M*A*S*H (TV-USA 71-84 BBC2: 20/5/73) theme mus "Suicide
  Is Painless" (J.Mandel-M.Altman) TV -S/T- *reissue
  SONY: 983380-2(CD) see COLLECTIONS 110,168,341,361
  373,382,405*
MASK The (1994) Music by Var.Arts incl. HARRY CONNICK
  JNR-VANESSA WILLIAMS-JIM CARREY -S/T- on *COLUMBIA
  Chaos (Sony M): 477316-2 (CD) deleted 1997*

**MASSACRE IN ROME** (Italy-73) Music sc: ENNIO MORRICONE
-S/T- includes 'The BATTLE OF ALGIERS' (Italy-65)
*ITALIAN import (Silva Screen): OST 105 (CD)*

**MASTERCHEF** (BBC1 2/7/90) and 'JUNIOR MASTERCHEF' music
by RICHARD G.MITCHELL *unavailable*

**MASTERMIND** (BBC 1972-97 theme mus "Approaching Menace"
NEIL RICHARDSON *see COLLECTION 6*

**MATCH OF THE DAY** (BBC1 fr.1970) theme "Offside" BARRY
STOLLER *see COLLECTIONS 31,137,167,168*

**MATCH The Coca-Cola Cup** theme "You Are The Number One"
(Charlie Skarbek) UNION feat Paul Young *JIVE (BMG)
JIVECD 309 (CDs) see also COLLECTION 138*

**MATEWAN** (1987) Music score: MASON DARING -S/T- Import
*DARING (Topic/Proj/DIR/CMD): DARINGCD 1011 (CD)*

**MATT HOUSTON** (USA TV) *see COLLECTION 344*

**MAVERICK** (TV USA 57) title theme: PAUL FRANCIS WEBSTER
and DAVID BUTTOLPH *see COLLECTIONS 170,340*

**MAX HEADROOM** (TV) *see COLLECTION 345*

**MAXIMUM RISK** (1996) Music score: ROBERT FOLK -S/T- on
*VARESE (Pinn): VSD 5756 (CD)*

**MAY TO DECEMBER** (BBC1 3/4/89) theme m "September Song"
(K.Weill-Maxwell Anderson) *TV version unavailable*

**MAYERLING** (1935) Music score: ARTHUR HONEGGER Suite on
*MARCO POLO (Select): 8.223467 (CD)*

**ME AND MY GIRL** - songs by Noel Gay and Douglas Furber
  1.ORIG LONDON CAST 1985   ROBERT LINDSAY-EMMA THOMPSON
    FRANK THORNTON and Company *EMI: CDP 746393-2 (CD)*
  2.ORIG BROADWAY CAST 1987 *with* ROBERT LINDSAY-MARYANN
    PLUNKETT & Co *TER (Disc): CDTER 1145 (CD)*
  3.CARLTON SHOWS COLL STUDIO *with:* DAVID KERNAN-JACQUI
    SCOTT-TRACEY COLLIER-JOHN HOWARD-MASTER SINGERS
    *CARLTON: PWKS(PWKMC) 4143 (CD/MC)*
  4.CLASSIC MUSICALS SERIES *feat:* ROBERT LINDSAY
    MARYANN PLUNKETT-JANE SUMMERHAYS-GEORGE S.IRVING
    *+songs from* 'THE BOYFRIEND' *KOCH Int: 34080-2 (CD)*

**MEDIC** (USA 1955) theme "Blue Star" by VICTOR YOUNG
*see COLLECTIONS 160,342*

**MEDICAL CENTER** (USA TV) *see COLLECTIONS 340,379*

**MEET ME IN ST.LOUIS** (FILM 1944) *featuring JUDY GARLAND
-S/T- reissue EMI PREMIER: CDODEON 2 (CD)*

**MEET ME IN ST.LOUIS** (O.BROADWAY CAST 1990) Songs (Hugh
Martin-Ralph Blane) at Gershwin Theatre)
*DRG USA (Pinn): CDSBL 19002 (CD) SBLC 19002 (MC)*

**MEET THE FEEBLES** (1991) Music sco: PETER DASENT + V/A
-S/T- *NORMAL (Topic-Project-Dir): QDKCD 003 (CD)*

**MEETING VENUS** (1991) Mus (WAGNER) incid.score: RACHEL
PORTMAN -S/T- *feat* KIRI TE KANAWA-RENE KOLLO with
'Tannhauser' *TELDEC (WEA): 229246336-2 (CD) -4 MC
see also COLLECTIONS 75,78*

**MELISSA** (BBC TV 1973) *see COLLECTION 1*

**MELODY FOR TWO** (1937) Film Musical - VARIOUS ARTISTS
-S/T- includ.songs from 'GO INTO YOUR DANCE'/'YOU
CAN'T HAVE EVERYTHING'/'YOU'LL NEVER GET RICH' on
*GREAT MOVIE THEMES (Target-BMG): CD 60014 (CD)*

MELROSE PLACE (USA TV/SKY1 94) TV Soundtrack feat Var.
   Artists on *GIANT (BMG): 74321 22608-2(CD) -4(MC)*
   *see COLLECTIONS 12,345*
MEMORIES   (Japan 95) Animated MANGA Film -S/T-
   *ANIMANGA-New Note (Pinn): AM 7 (CD)*
MEMPHIS BELLE (1990) Music score: GEORGE FENTON -S/T-
   *VARESE (Pinn): VSD(VSC) 5293 (CD/MC)*
   "Danny Boy" by Mark Williamson on: *VS 52937 (7"s)*
MEN BEHAVING BADLY (BBC1 1/7/94) theme music by ALAN
   LISK on COLL 'MEN BEHAVING BADLY' *REMEDIA (Pinn):*
   *REP 001CD (CD)   see also COLLECTION 229*
MEN FROM SHILOH (USA TV) *see COLLECTION 343*
MEN IN BLACK The (1996) M.sco: DANNY ELFMAN -S/T- V.Art
   "Men In Black" composed and sung by WILL SMITH
   -S/T- *COLUMBIA (SM): 488 122-2 (CD) -04(MC) -1(LP)*
MEPHISTO WALTZ The (1971) Music score: JERRY GOLDSMITH
   score w: 'The OTHER' *VARESE (Pinn): VSD 5851 (CD)*
MERRIE MELODIES (USA TV) *see COLLECTION 340*
MERRILY WE ROLL ALONG (CAST RECORDING) Songs by STEPHEN
   SONDHEIM  Highlights:  *TER (Disc): CD(ZC)TER 1225*
   Complete: *TER (Disc): CDTEM2 1203 (2CD) also on*
   *VARESE (Pinn): VSD 5548 (CD)*
MERRY CHRISTMAS MR.LAWRENCE (1983) M: RYUICHI SAKAMOTO
   *reiss: MILAN (BMG): 74321 22048-2 (CD) also on*
   *VIRGIN: CDV 2276 (CD) OVEDC 237 see COLLECTIO 267*
MERRY WIDOW The (operetta) - songs by Franz Lehar
  1.Studio Recording 1994 COMPLETE Operetta in German
   without dialogue *with:* BARBARA BONNEY-BRYN TERFEL-
   BOJE SKOVHUS-CHERYL STUDER-RAINER TROST-KARL MAGNUS
   FREDRIKSSON with Vienna Philh.Orch (Gardiner)
   *DG (Polygram): 439 911-2 (CD) -4 (MC)*
  2.Studio Recording 1995 HIGHLIGHTS in English by
   SCOTTISH OPERA CHORUS & SCOTTISH NATIONAL ORCHESTRA
   (A.Gibson) *CFP (EMI): CDCFPSD 4742 (2CD)*
  3.NEW SADLERS WELLS 1986 CAST (2 versions)
   Highlights 1: *SHOWTIME (THE-Disc): SHOW(CD)(MC)037*
   Highlights 2: *TER (Disc):CD(ZC)TEO 1003 (CD/MC)*
   Complete: *TER (Disc): (CD)(ZC)TER 1111 (CD/MC)*
  4.Studio Recording HIGHLIGHTS + songs from 'Land Of
   Smiles' on *EMI BELLE EPOQUE: CZS 767 872-2 (2CD)*
MESSAGE The (MOHAMMED MESSENGER OF GOD)(1977) Music
   score: MAURICE JARRE Royal P.Orch on *SILVA SCREEN*
   *(Koch): FILMCD 060 (CD)* + mus 'Lion Of The Desert'
MESSAGE TO LOVE: THE ISLE OF WIGHT FESTIVAL 1970 (BBC2
   26/8/95) *feat:* JIMI HENDRIX-FREE-BOB DYLAN-EMERSON
   LAKE & PALMER-JETHRO TULL-MILES DAVIS-THE DOORS-
   THE WHO-TINY TIM *ESSENTIAL (BMG): EDFCD 327 (CD)*
METEOR MAN (1993) Music score: CLIFF EIDELMAN -S/T-
   *IMS-POLYGRAM: AA 374 636 364-2 (CD)*
METROPOLIS (1925 rest.1984 ver.with contemporary score
   Giorgio Moroder) songs by PATA BENATAR-FREDDIE MER
   CURY-ADAM ANT-BONNIE TYLER-JON ANDERSON-LOVERBOY-
   CYCLE V-BILLY SQUIER and GIORGIO MORODER -S/T- *(84)*
   *reiss: COLUMBIA (Sony): 460204-2 (CD) deleted 1996*

**METROPOLIS** (O.LONDON CAST 1988) Music (Joe Brooks) Lyr
ics (Joe Brooks-Dusty Hughes) *with* Brian Blessed-Ju
dy Kuhn-Graham Bickley-Jonathan Adams and Company
*TER (Disc) CDTER2 1168 (CDx2)*

**MIAMI VICE** (USA orig BBC1 4/2/85) theme: JAN HAMMER
'Best Of Miami Vice' *MCA: 241 746-2/-4/-1(CD/MC)*
'MIAMI VICE 1'inc theme + items by Glenn Frey-Chaka
Khan-Tina Turner-Phil Collins-Mel Melle
*MCA (BMG): MCLD 19024 (CD) see also COLLECTIONS:
55,100,101,110,168,179,267,333,341,352*

**MICHAEL** (1997) Mus sco: RANDY NEWMAN -S/T- with DON HEN
LEY-MAVERICKS-ARETHA FRANKLIN-VAN MORRISON-AL GREEN
BONNIE RAITT-WILLIE NELSON-NORMAN GREENBAUM etc.
*REVOLUTION (BMG): 74321 41880-2 (CD)*

**MICHAEL BALL** (Carlton 8/7/93) music dir (Michael Reed)
album "Always" *POLYDOR: 519 666-2 (CD) -4 (MC)*
'BEST OF MICHAEL BALL' *Polygram TV: 523 891-2 (CD)*
'THE MUSICALS' *Polygam TV: 533 892-2 (CD) see COLL*

**MICHAEL BARRYMORE'S MY KIND OF PEOPLE** (ITV 26/10/95)
music director: TREVIR BROWN *unavailable*

**MICHAEL COLLINS** (96) Music score: ELLIOT GOLDENTHAL
-S/T- *Atlantic (WEA): 7567 82960-2 (CD) -4 (MC)*

**MICHAEL WINNER'S TRUE CRIMES** - *see* 'TRUE CRIMES'

**MICHURIN** (FILM Score) Suite Op.78 (Shostakovich) USSR
RADIO & TV ORCH *Melodiya (BMG): 74321 32041-2 CD*

**MICKEY'S CHRISTMAS CAROL** *see* WALT DISNEY INDEX p.343

**MIDDLEMARCH** (BBC2 12/1/94) orig mus: STANLEY MYERS and
CHRISTOPHER GUNNING *unavailable* / piano piece
"Song Without Words" (MENDELSSOHN) *var.recordings*

**MIDNIGHT CALLER** (USA)(BBC 28/1/89) theme: BRAD FIEDEL
*see COLLECTIONS 12,345,373*

**MIDNIGHT COWBOY** (1969) Music score: JOHN BARRY t.song
"Everybody's Talkin'" (Fred Neil) by NILSSON -S/T-
reiss: *EMI PREMIER: PRMCD 6 (CDP 748409-2)(CD)*
*see also COLLECTIONS 17,20,21,24,25,38,62,63,198
243,244,356,358*

**MIDNIGHT EXPRESS** (1978) Music: GIORGIO MORODER -S/T-
*CASABLANCA (Poly): 824206-2 (CD)*
*see COLLECTIONS 55,110,213,303,333*

**MIDSOMER MURDERS** (ITV 23/3/97) music by JIM PARKER...*NA*

**MIDSUMMER NIGHT'S SEX COMEDY** (1982) music MENDELSSOHN
*see COLLECTIONS 73,75*

**MIDWEEK** *see COLLECTION 5*

**MIGHTY APHRODITE** (1996) Music arr/cond: DICK HYMAN
-S/T- on *SONY Classics (SM): SK 62253 (CD)*

**MIGHTY MORPHIN POWER RANGERS: THE MOVIE** (1995)
-S/T- songs *ATANTICc WEA: 7567 82777-2 (CD) -4(MC)*
-S/T- score *VARESE (Pin): VSD 5672 (CD)*

**MIGHTY MOUSE** (USA TV) *see COLLECTION 340*

**MIKADO The** (operetta) - songs by Gilbert and Sullivan
1.D'OYLY CARTE OPERA COMPANY 1989 (Jonathan Miller)
*featuring* LESLIE GARRETT-ERIC IDLE-FELICITY PALMER
Highlights: *SHOWTIME (MCI-THE): SHOW(CD)(MC) 005*
Complete: *TER: CDTER2 1178 (2CD) ZCTED 1178 (2MC)*

2.SADLER'S WELLS OPERA ORCH & CHORUS (A.FARIS) JOHN
  HOLMES-JOHN WAKEFIELD-CLIVE REVILL-DENIS DOWLING
  JOHN HEDDLE NASH-MARION STUDHOLME-PATRICIA KERN-
  *CFP (EMI): CDCFPD(TCCPFD)4730 (2CDs/2MC)*
3.PRO-ARTE ORCHEST (Malcolm Sargent) GLYNDEBOURNE
  FESTIVAL CHOIR Soloists OWEN BRANNIGAN-RICHARD LEW
  IS-GERAINT EVANS-IAN WALLACE *EMI:CMS 764403-2  2CD*
4.HIGHLIGHTS feat National Opera Company
  *TER (Disc): CDTER 1121 (CD)*
5.D'OYLY CARTE OPERA COMPANY - Royal Philharm Orch
  (R.Nash) - *LONDON (Poly): 425 190-2 (CDx2)*
MIKE & ANGELO (Thames 17/10/91) mus: KIM GOODY and
  ALAN COATES (prev.DAVID STAFFORD) *unavailable*
MIKE HAMMER (USA 83 revival) theme "Harlem Nocturne"
  (Earle Hagen) KEN MACKINTOSH ORCH on 'Mac's Back'
  *President: PLCD 532 (CD) see COLLECTION 51,108,242*
MILLENNIUM (BBC2 UK/Canada Co-Prod 3/1/93) music score
  HANS ZIMMER arranged & performed by MARK MANCINA
  -S/T- *NARADA Cinema (Pinn): ND 66001 (CD)*
MILLENNIUM (ITV 29/6/97) theme m: MARK SNOW *unavailable*
MILLER'S CROSSING (1990) Music s: CARTER BURWELL -S/T-
  *VARESE (Pinn): VSD(VSC) 5288 (CD/MC) deleted 95*
MILOU IN MAY (1989) Music sco: STEPHANE GRAPPELLI -S/T-
  *SONY Europe (Discovery): 466 285-2 (CD)*
MIMIC (1997) Music score: MARCO BELTRAMI -S/T- on
  *VARESE (Pinn): VSD 5863 (CD)*
MIND TO KILL, A (C5 30/8/97) music: MARK THOMAS......*NA*
MINDER (Thames 11/9/80) "I Could Be So Good For You"
  (Gerard Kenny-Pat Waterman) sung by DENNIS WATERMAN
  *see COLLECTIONS 168,360*
MIRACLE ON 34TH STREET (1994) Music sc: BRUCE BROUGHTON
  -S/T- inc NATALIE COLE-DIONNE WARWICK-ELVIS PRESLEY
  *ARISTA (BMG): 07822 11022-2 (CD) -4 (MC)*
MIRROR HAS TWO FACES The (96) Mus sco: MARVIN HAMLISCH
  -S/T- *feat:* BARBRA STREISAND-RICHARD MARX-LUCIANO
  PAVAROTTI *COLUMBIA (Sony M): 485 395-2 (CD) -4 (MC)*
MISFITS The (1961) Music sco: ALEX NORTH -S/T- *Import*
  *TSUNAMI (Silva Screen): TCI 0609 (CD)*
MISHIMA 'A Life In Four Chapters' (1985) Music: PHILIP
  GLASS -S/T- *ELEKTRA Nonesuch (WEA): 7559 79113-2*
MISS MARPLE (BBC1 from 26/12/84) theme: ALAN BLAIKLEY-
  KEN HOWARD *see Colls* 'COPS'
MISS SAIGON - songs by Alain Boublil - Claude Michel
  Schonberg and Richard Maltby Jnr.
  1.ORIG LONDON CAST 1989 *w:* LEA SALONGA-JONATHAN PRYCE
    SIMON BOWMAN-PETER POLYCARPOU & Company
  2.HIGHLIGHTS: *FIRST NIGHT (Pinn): CAST(C)(CD) 38*
  3.SYMPHONIC SUITES: *KIMCD1 (2CD) KIMC1 (MC) also on*
    *CASTCD 39 (CD) CASTC 39 (MC)*
  4.ROYAL PHILHARMONIC ORCHESTRA *PLAY SUITES from*
    Miss Saigon and Les Miserables
    *CARLTON INT: PWKS(PWKMC) 4079 (CD/MC)*
  5.INTERNATIONAL CAST RECORDING (HIGHLIGHTS)
    *FIRST NIGHT (Pinn): CASTCD 60 (CD) CASTMC 60 (MC)*

MISS WORLD (BBC/ITV) *see COLLECTION 318*
MISSA LUBA (AFRICAN MASS) - KENYAN FOLK MELODIES By The
    MUUNGANO NATIONAL CHOIR directed by Boniface MGANGA
    *PHILIPS (Poly): 426 836-2 (CD) -4 (MC)*
MISSING (1982) Music score: VANGELIS  available vers:
    VANGELIS on 'Themes' *POLYDOR: 839518-2 (CD) -4(MC)*
    SHADOWS on 'Diamonds' *CARLTON: PWKS 4018P (CD)*
    ELAINE PAIGE (vocal) 'Cinema' *CARLTON: PWKS 545 CD*
MISSING POSTMAN The (BBC1 29/3/97) m: DEBBIE WISEMAN.*NA*
MISSION IMPOSSIBLE (ORIG TV ser.) theme: LALO SCHIFRIN
    TV -S/T- *reissue: MCA (BMG): MCLD 19320 (CD)*
    *see also COLLECTIONS 2,100,108.109,246,302,339,*
    *356,357,363,373*
MISSION IMPOSSIBLE (1996) Music sco: DANNY ELFMAN orig
    theme (Lalo Schifrin) version by Larry Mullen and
    Adam Clayton (U2) -S/T- *feat* PULP-GARBAGE-BJORK-
    MASSIVE ATTACK-CAST-GAVIN FRIDAY-MULLEN & CLAYTON
    *MOTHER-ISLAND (Poly): 531 682-2 (CD) -4 (MC)*
MISSION IMPOSSIBLE (USA 60s re-r BBC2 87) theme: LALO
    SCHIFRIN plus NEW 91 series music: JOHN E.DAVIS
    -S/T- *GNP (S.Screen): GNPD(GNP-5) 8029 (CD-MC)*
MISSION The (1986) Music sco ENNIO MORRICONE -S/T-
    *Virgin (EMI): TCV 2402 (MC) CDV 2402 (CD) MDV*
    *2402 (MiniD) see also COLLECTIONS 32,62,63,64,*
    *171,244,251,252,267,324,400*
MISSISSIPPI BURNING (1988) Music sco: TREVOR JONES
    -S/T- *re-iss.on Spectrum (Poly): 551 100-2 (CD)*
MISTER - see under 'MR.'
MO' BETTER BLUES (1990) Music score: BILL LEE featur:
    B.Marsalis - *SONY: 467160-2 (CD) -4 (MC)*
MO' MONEY (1992) Various artists  -S/T- *PERSPECTIVE*
    *A.& M.(Polyg): 361004-2 (CD) 361004-4 (MC)*
MOBY DICK (O.LONDON CAST 1992) Songs (Robert Longdon-
    Hereward Kaye) *with* TONY MONOPOLY-HOPE AUGUSTUS-THE
    RESA KARTEL & Co *FIRST NIGHT (Pinn): DICKCD 1 (CD)*
MOD SQUAD (USA TV) *see COLLECTIONS 339,374*
MODERN TIMES (1936) *see COLLECTIONS 56,57,58*
MODERNS The (1988) Music score: MARK ISHAM Songs by
    Charles Couture -S/T- *VIRGIN (EMI): CDV 2530 (CD)*
MOLL FLANDERS (ITV 1/12/96) Original music composed
    and directed by JIM PARKER *unavailable*
MOLL FLANDERS (FILM 1996) Music score: MARK MANCINA
    -S/T- *Import LONDON (Poly): 452 485-2 (CD)*
MOLL FLANDERS (O.LONDON CAST 1993) Songs (George Stiles
    -Paul Leigh) *feat* JOSIE LAWRENCE-ANGELA RICHARDS
    *FIRST NIGHT (Pinn): OCRCD 6036 (CD)*
MON ONCLE (Jacques Tati 1956) Music sco: ALAIN ROMAINS
    -S/T- selection on 'Original Music from His Films'
    incl. 'JOUR DE FETE' and 'MONSIEUR HULOT'S HOLIDAY'
    *POLYGRAM (Discovery): 836 983-2 (CD)*
MONA LISA (1986) *see COLLECTIONS 68,243*
MONDO TOPLESS (1966 RUSS MEYER) music on Collection
    'Russ Meyer Orig Soundtracks Vol.4' (various) on
    *POP BIZ (Cargo-Greyhound): LP 014 (LP)*

MONEY PROGRAMME The (BBC2 4/66-88 & 95-97) 'theme from
    Carpetbaggers': ELMER BERNSTEIN on 'The Cat' JIMMY
    SMITH *VERVE (Poly): 810 046-2 (CD)* 89-94 theme...*NA*
MONEY TALKS (1997) V/A *inc:* BARRY WHITE & FAITH EVANS-
    LISA STANSFIELD-MARY J.BLIGE-SWV-ANGIE STONE-DEVOX
    -S/T- *RCA (BMG): 07822 18975-2 (CD) -4 (MC) -1 (LP)*
MONEY TRAIN (1995) Music score: MARK MANCINA -S/T-
    *COLUMBIA (Sony M): 481 562-2 (CD) -4 (MC)*
MONKEES The (USA 1966) theme (Boyce-Hart) MONKEES 'Then
    & Now Best Of' *ARISTA: 257874 (CD) 407874 (MC)*
    *see COLLECTION 340*
MONSIEUR HULOT'S HOLIDAY (Jacques Tati 1953) Mus score
    (A.ROMAINS-Franck BARCELLINI) 'Original Music from
    His Films' *POLYGRAM (Discovery): 836 983-2 (CD)*
MONSIEUR VERDOUX (1947) M: C.CHAPLIN *see COLLECTION 56*
MONTH IN THE COUNTRY, A (1987) *see COLLECTION 77'*
MONTY PYTHON AND THE HOLY GRAIL (1975) Mus: NEIL INNES
    -S/T- *VIRGIN (EMI): VCCCD 004 (CD) VCCMC 004 (MC)*
MONTY PYTHON'S FLYING CIRCUS (BBC2 5/10/69-1974) theme
    music "Liberty Bell March" (John Phillip SOUSA)
    "INSTANT MONTY PYTHON CD COLLECTION" (6CD Box set)
    *VIRGIN: CDBOX 3 (CDx6)* "Ultimate MONTY PYTHON Rip
    Off" *VIRGIN (EMI): CDV(TCV) 2748 (CD/MC)*
    *see COLLECTIONS 110,229,340*
MONTY PYTHON'S LIFE OF BRIAN (1979) Music sc: GEOFFREY
    BURGON Songs: ERIC IDLE feat: Monty Python Team
    *VIRGIN (EMI): VCCCD 009 (CD) VCCMC 009 (MC)*
MONTY PYTHON'S MEANING OF LIFE (1983) M: JOHN DU PREZ
    ERIC IDLE *VIRGIN EMI: VCCD 010(CD) VCCMC 010(MC)*
    *see also COLLECTION 332*
MOONLIGHTING (USA BBC2 29/5/86) t.theme (Al Jarreau-
    Lee Holdridge) AL JARREAU 'Moonlighting'
    *see COLLECTIONS 168,344*
MOONRAKER (1979) Music score: JOHN BARRY title song
    (John Barry-Hal David) sung by SHIRLEY BASSEY
    -S/T- *EMI PREMIER: CZ 551 (CD) see* also p.346
MOONSTRUCK (1987) *see COLLECTIONS 71,72,276*
MOONWALKER (1988) Music score: BRUCE BROUGHTON Songs by
    Michael Jackson  "Bad" *EPIC: 450290-2(CD) -4(MC)*
    'Moonwalker Suite' (Bruce BROUGHTON) "Fantastic
    Journey" *TELARC (BMG-Con): CD 80231 (CD)*
MORE (1969) Music score comp/performed by PINK FLOYD
    -S/T- *reiss: EMI: CDEMD 1084 (CD) TCEMD 1084 (MC)*
MORE THAN A MIRACLE (1967) Music score: PIERO PICCIONE
    -S/T- *Import (SILVA SCREEN): CDST 304 (CD)*
MORECAMBE & WISE SHOW The (BBC1 66-84) Various themes:
    "Bring Me Sunshine"/"Positive Thinkin'"/"We Get Alo
    ng So Easily Don't You Agree" sung by MORECAMBE and
    WISE on 'Get Out Of That' *EMI: ECC 29 (MC only)*
    'Bring Me Sunshine' - *see COLLECTION 402*
MORK AND MINDY (USA 78 / C4 16/3/93) theme music by
    PERRY BOTKIN JNR *see COLLECTIONS 12,344*
MORTAL KOMBAT (1995) Music sco: GEORGE S.CLINTON -S/T-
    + V.Arts *LONDON (Polyg): 828 715-2 (CD) -4 (MC)*

MORTAL KOMBAT (1995) Music sco: GEORGE S.CLINTON -S/T-
   'MORE KOMBAT' on *EDEL (Pinn): 0022672CIN (CD)*
MOST HAPPY FELLA The - songs by Frank Loesser
  1.NEW BROADWAY CAST 1991 *w:* SPIRO MALAS-SOPHIE HAYDEN
   CLAUDIA CATTANIA *RCA (BMG):09026 61294-2 CD* del.95
MOTHER NIGHT (1996) Music score: MICHAEL CONVERTINO
   -S/T- *VARESE (Pinn): VSD 5780 (CD)*
MOTOR MONTH (BBC2 24/3/97) t.music based on "The Chain"
   (Fleetwood Mac) by STEVE SPIRO and WIX *unavailable*
MOTOR RACING *see* GRAND PRIX (BBC) 'F1'(FORMULA 1 (ITV)
MOUNTAIN ROAD The (1960) Music score: JEROME MOROSS
   *see COLLECTION 377*
MOUSE HUNT (1997) Music score: ALAN SILVESTRI -S/T- on
   *VARESE (Pinn): VSD 5892 (CD)*
MOVING STORY (ABTV Prod for Carlton 26/5/94) music sc:
   ROGER JACKSON t.song by KIRSTY MacCOLL *unavailable*
MR.& MRS. (Border 18/1/84) theme music "Be Nice To Each
   Other" (T.Hatch-Jackie Trent) TONY HATCH & JACKIE
   TRENT *see COLLECTIONS 182,372 also* "Music To Drive
   By" ALAN MOOREHOUSE *see also COLLECTION 317*
MR.BLOBBY - *see under* NOEL'S HOUSE PARTY / on *COLL*
   '100% KIDS PARTY' *TELSTAR: TCD(STAC) 2874 deleted*
MR.CINDERS (REVIV.LONDON CAST 1983) Songs (Vivian Ellis
   Richard Myers-Clifford Grey-Leo Robin) *with* Graham
   Hoadly-Andrea Kealy-Dennis Lawson-Diana Martin-Chri
   stina Matthews-Steven Pacey / Michael Reed (md) on
   *TER (Disc): CDTER 1069 (CD): ZCTER 1069 (MC)*
MR.ED (USA 60s) *see COLLECTIONS 339,405*
MR.HOLLAND'S OPUS (1995) Mus sco: MICHAEL KAMEN + V/A:
   -S/T-(songs) *POLYDOR (Poly): 529 508-2 (CD)*
   -S/T-(score) *POLYDOR (Poly): 452 062-2 (CD) -4(MC)*
MR.LUCKY (USA) theme: HENRY MANCINI *see COLLECTION 374*
MR.MAGOO (USA TV) *see COLLECTION 341*
MR.MEN & LITTLE MISSES (BBC1 76) Arthur LOWE-Pauline CO
   LLINS-J.ALDERTON *MSD: KIDM 9002/3 (MC) also avail:*
   'BEST MR.MEN ALBUM IN THE WORLD..EVER' inc: THEME
   *VIRGIN (EMI): VTCD 166 (CD) VTMC 166 (MC)*
MR.RELIABLE (1996) Music score: PHILIP JUDD -S/T-
   *POLYDOR (Polyg): 516 820-2 (CD) -4 (MC)*
MR.ROSE (Granada 17/2/67-5/12/68) theme music "Mr.Rose
   Investigates" (Snow) *see COLLECTION 372*
MR.SATURDAY NIGHT (1992) Music sco: MARC SHAIMAN -S/T-
   *MILAN (BMG): 12468-2 (CD) 12468-4 (MC)*
MR.WONDERFUL (O.BROADWAY CAST 1956) Songs (Jerry Bock-
   George Weiss-Larry Holfencor) *with* Sammy Davis Jnr
   *MCA USA (S.Screen): MCAD 10303(CD) MCAC 10303(MC)*
MRS.BROWN (1997) Music score: STEPHEN WARBECK -S/T- on
   *MILAN (BMG): 74321 51072-2 (CD)*
MRS.COHEN'S MONEY (C4 7/4/97) t.mus DEBBIE WISEMAN..*NA*
MRS.DOUBTFIRE (1993) Music score: HOWARD SHORE -S/T-
   *ARISTA (BMG): 07822 11015-2 (CD) -4 (MC)*
   *see COLLECTIONS 66,97*
MRS.PARKER AND THE VICIOUS CIRCLE (1994) Music: MARK
   ISHAM -S/T- *VARESE (Pinn): VSD 5471 (CD)*

MRS.WINTERBOURNE (1996) Music sco: PATRICK DOYLE -S/T-
   *VARESE (Pinn): VSD 5720 (CD)*
MUCH ADO ABOUT NOTHING (1993) Music sco: PATRICK DOYLE
   -S/T- *EPIC (Sony M): MOOCD 30 (CD) MOODC 30 (MC)*
MULHOLLAND FALLS (1996) Music score: DAVE GRUSIN -S/T-
   *EDEL-Cinerama (Pinn): 002259-2CIN (CD)*
MUMFIE see BRITT ALLCROFTS MAGIC ADVENTURES OF MUMFIE
MUNSTERS The (USA 63) title theme: JACK MARSHALL
   see *COLLECTIONS 12,339,374*
MUPPET SHOW The (ITV 76/BBC1 86) theme: SAM POTTLE
   see *COLLECTIONS 168,341*
MUPPET MOVIE The (1979) Music and songs: PAUL WILLIAMS
   KENNY ASCHER *feat:* JIM HENSON-FRANK OZ-DAVE GOELZ
   *reiss: ARISTA (BMG): 74321 18247-2 (CD) -4 (MC)*
MURDER ON THE ORIENT EXPRESS - see *COLLECTION 62*
MURDER ONE (USA 95/BBC2 5/3/96) music theme composed
   and performed by MIKE POST *unavailable*
MURDER SHE WROTE (USA) theme: JOHN ADDISON see *COLL 12*
MURDER WAS THE CASE (1994) Mus by SNOOP DOGGY DOGG + VA
   -S/T- *INTERSCOPE-MCA (BMG): IND 92484 (CD) also on*
MURIEL'S WEDDING (1994) Music sco: PETER BEST *featur:*
   ABBA-DUSTY SPRINGFIELD-THE CARPENTERS -S/T- on
   *POLYDOR (Poly): 527 493-2 (CD) 527 493-4 (MC)*
MURPHY BROWN (USA TV) see *COLLECTION 345*
MURPHY'S LAW (86) - *see under* 'DEATH WISH'
MUSIC AND THE MIND (C4 5/5/96) feat The MEDICI STRING
   QUARTET / PAUL ROBERTSON (speaker) music to accomp
   any the series *KOCH SCHWANN (Koch): 36437-2 (CD)*
MUSIC IN MINIATURE (BBC) theme "Elizabethan Serenade"
   RONALD BINGE see *COLLECTIONS 42,130,137*
MUSIC LOVERS The (1970) see *Coll* CINEMA CLASSICS 6 & 9
MUSIC MAN The Songs by Meredith Willson
   1.FILM MUSICAL 1962 ROBERT PRESTON-SHIRLEY JONES
      -S/T- *WB USA (S.Screen): 1459-2 (CD) M5 1459 (MC)*
   2.ORIG LONDON CAST 1961 *with* VAN JOHNSON-PATRICIA
      LAMBERT-RUTH KETTLEWELL-MICHAEL MALNICK and Comp
      *LASERLIGHT POP-TARGET (BMG): 12447 (CD)*
MUSIC TEACHER The (1990) -S/T- Operatic Classical Mus
   *PRESIDENT (BMG): PCOM(PTLC) 1109 (CD/MC)*
MUTANT (1982) Music sco: RICHARD BAND perf.by National
   Philharm.Orch *INTRADA (S.Screen):MAF 7052D (CD)*
MUTINY ON THE BOUNTY (1984) - *see under* 'BOUNTY'
MY BEST FRIEND'S WEDDING (1997) Music sco:JAMES NEWTON
   HOWARD -S/T- (V.Arts) *SONY: 488 115-2 (CD) -4 (MC)*
MY COUSIN RACHEL (1952) see *COLLECTION 392*
MY COUSIN VINNY (1991) Music score: RANDY EDELMAN -S/T-
   *VARESE (Pinn): VSD 5364 (CD)*
MY DINNER WITH ANDRE (1981) see *COLLECTION 75*
MY FAIR LADY - songs Alan Jay Lerner & Frederick Loewe
   1.FILM MUSICAL 1964 *with:* REX HARRISON-AUDREY HEPBURN
      *sung by* MARNI NIXON -S/T- *SONY: CD 70000 (CD) and
      also SK(S1) 66711 (CD/MC)*
   2.O.LONDON CAST 1958 REX HARRISON-JULIE ANDREWS-STANL
      EY HOLLOWAY *COL (S.Screen): CK 02105(CD) 02105 (MC)*

MY FAIR LADY *Continued...*
  3. ORIG BROADWAY CAST 56 *w:* REX HARRISON-JULIE ANDREWS
     *COLUMBIA (S.Screen): CK(JST) 05090 (CD/MC)*
  4. STUDIO RECORD 1987 *w:* KIRI TE KANAWA-JEREMY IRONS-
     WARREN MITCHELL-JOHN GIELGUD *DECCA: 421 200-2 CD*
  5. CARLTON SHOWS COLLECT.STUDIO 1994 *w:* DENNIS QUILLEY
     LIZ ROBERTSON-IAN WALLACE-NICK CURTIS and Company
     *CARLTON SHOWS: PWKS(PWKMC) 4174 (CD/MC)*
  6. CLASSIC MUSICALS SERIES *w:* ALEC McCOWEN and TINUKE
     OLAFIMIHAN-RON MOODY-HENRY WICKMAN & others
     + *songs from* 'CAMELOT' *KOCH INT: 34079-2 (CD)*
  7. ORIG MASTERWORKS EDIT. *w:* ALEC McCOWEN-BOB HOSKINS
     TINUKE OLAFIMIHAN-DUCLIE GRAY-HENRY WICKHAM-MICHAEL
     DENISON *TER (Disc): CDTER2 1211 (2CD)*
MY FAVORITE MARTIAN (USA TV) *see COLLECTION 340*
MY GEISHA (1962) *see Colls* 'CINEMA CLASSICS 5'/'LEGENDS
  OF HOLLYWOOD'
MY GIRL (1991) Music score: JAMES NEWTON HOWARD V.Arts
  -S/T- *EPIC (SM): 469213-2 (CD) -4 (MC) deleted 96*
MY GIRL 2 (1994) Music score: CLIFF EIDELMAN with V/A
  -S/T- *COLUMBIA (SM): 475 734-2(CD) -4(MC) deleted*
MY LEFT FOOT (1989) *see COLLECTIONS 72,79,258,276*
MY MOTHER THE CAR (USA TV) *see COLLECTION 340*
MY MOTHER'S CASTLE (1990)(Chateau De Ma Mere) *see also*
  'GLORY OF MY FATHER'(La Gloire De Mon Pere)
MY NAME IS NOBODY (1973) Music score ENNIO MORRICONE
  ENNIO MORRICONE ORCH on Coll 'An Ennio Morricone
  Quintet' *DRG USA (Pinn): DRGCD 32907 (CD)*
MY SO CALLED LIFE (C4 26/7/95) theme mus: W.G.SNUFFY
  WALDEN -S/T- *WEA: 7567 82721-2 (CD) -4 (MC)*
  *see COLLECTION 345*
MY THREE SONS (USA TV) *see COLLECTIONS 339,374*
MY TWO DADS (USA C4 from 10/5/90) theme "You Can Count
  On Me" (GREG EVIGAN-Lenny Macallso-Michael Jacobs)
  *see COLLECTION 345*
MY WILDERNESS REPRIEVED (BBC2 8/4/93) theme music "Minu
  et" from 'A Downland Suite' (John Ireland) ENGLISH
  CHAMBER ORCH (David Garforth) *CHANDOS: CHAN 8390 CD*
MYSTERIES OF EDGAR WALLACE The (ITV 60's) Theme "Man Of
  Mystery" (Michael Carr) by THE SHADOWS 'In The 60s'
  *MFP (EMI): CDMFP 6076 (CD) (TC)MFP 5873 (MC/LP)*
MYSTERIES WITH CAROL VORDERMAN (BBC1 7/10/97) title
  music: TERRY DAY *unavailable*
MYSTERIOUS ISLAND (1961) Mus sc: BERNARD HERRMANN -S/T-
  *CLOUD NINE (S.Screen): ACN 7017 (CD)*
MYSTERIOUS UNIVERSE - see under 'ARTHUR C.CLARKE'S...'
MYSTERY MOVIE (USA TV) *see COLLECTION 340*
MYSTERY OF EDWIN DROOD ORIG BROADWAY CAST recording
  *VARESE (Pinn): VSD 5597 (CD)*
MYSTERY TRAIN (1989) Music score: JOHN LURIE and V.Arts
  -S/T- *MILAN (BMG): CDCH 509 (CD)*
NAKED CAGE The (1985) - *see under* 'CRY IN THE DARK, A'
NAKED CITY The (1948) Music sco: MIKLOS ROZSA select.
  on 'LUST FOR LIFE' *VARESE (Pinn): VSD 5405 (CD)*

NAKED CITY The (USA 1958-63) theme music by BILLY MAY
    *versions by* KEN MACKINTOSH 'Mac's Back' *PRESIDENT:*
    *PLCD 532 (CD) see COLLECTIONS 182,342,374*
NAME OF THE GAME (USA TV) *see COLLECTION 246,341*
NAME OF THE ROSE (1986) Music sco: JAMES HORNER -S/T-
    *VIRGIN France (Discovery): 88085-2 (CD)*
NAPOLEON (1927) 1982 Score composed and conducted by
    CARL DAVIS *SILVA SCREEN (Koch): FILMCD 149 (CD)*
    *also with* S.C.Orchestra *CFP (EMI): CDCFP 4542 (CD)*
NASH BRIDGES (USA) (ITV 6/1/97) music: ELIA CMIRAL...*NA*
NATIONAL LAMPOON'S ANIMAL HOUSE (1978) Music: ELMER
    BERNSTEIN -S/T- re-iss *MCA (BMG): MCLD 19086 (CD)*
NATIONAL LOTTERY (BBC1 19/11/94) theme composed and
    arranged by ED WELCH *unavailable*
NATIONWIDE (BBC 70's) theme music "The Good Word" by
    JOHN SCOTT *see COLLECTIONS 2,5,318*
NATURAL BORN KILLERS (1994) feat music by LEONARD COHEN
    PATTI SMITH-COWBOY JUNKIES-PATSY CLINE-L7-BOB DYLAN
    NINE INCH NAILS-PETER GABRIEL etc. -S/T- reiss.on
    *INTERSCOPE (MCA/BMG): IND 92460-2 (CD)*
NATURAL HEALTH SHOW (ITV 2/9/97) music: DAVID KESTER.*NA*
NATURAL The (1984) Music score: RANDY NEWMAN -S/T- Imp
    *W.BROS USA (Silva Screen) 925116-2  -4 (CD/MC)*
NAZIS: A WARNING FROM HISTORY (BBC2 10/9/97) opening m:
    'German Requiem' Op.45 (BRAHMS) *version by* VIENNA
    PHIL.ORCH (Haitink) *Philips (Poly): 446 681-2 (CD)*
    also used: "Kline Dreigschenmusik" (arrangement of
    'Moritat'("Mack The Knife"- 'The Threepenny Opera')
    (Weill-Brecht-Blitzstein) *BBC ARCHIVE not available*
NEAR DARK (1988) Music score: TANGERINE DREAM -S/T-
    *SILVA SCREEN (Koch): FILMCD 026 (CD)*
NEEDFUL THINGS (1993) Music score: PATRICK DOYLE -S/T-
    *VARESE (Pinn): VSD 5438 (CD)*
NEIGHBOURS (Austr.85/BBC1 27/10/86-98) *theme* by JACKIE
    TRENT-TONY HATCH) *orig vers.*sung by BARRY CROCKER
    *See COLLECTION 367*
NELL (1994) Music: MARK ISHAM. solo flute (Jim Walker)
    -S/T- *LONDON (Poly): 444 818-2(CD) -4(MC) delet.96*
NET The (1995) Music score: MARK ISHAM -S/T- on
    *VARESE (Pinn): VSD 5662 (CD)*
NETWORK FIRST (THE VISIT) (Man Alive Prod for Carlton)
    (7/12/94) theme music "Caribbean Blue" by ENYA
    'Shepherd Moons' *WEA: 9031 75572-2 (CD) -4 (MC)*
NEVADA SMITH (1966) Music score: ALFRED NEWMAN
    -S/T- *TSUNAMI Germ (Silva Screen): TSU 0113 (CD)*
NEVER CRY WOLF (1983) Mus: MARK ISHAM *see* 'MRS.SOFFEL'
NEVER MIND THE BUZZCOCKS (BBC2 12/11/96) title music:
    SWITCH AND THE GINGER GP *unavailable*
NEVER SAY NEVER AGAIN - *see* JAMES BOND INDEX p.346
NEVERWHERE (BBC2 12/9/96) Music score: BRIAN ENO -S/T-
    *BBC REC (Pinn): ZBBC 1944CD (CD) 7BBC 1944 (MC)*
NEW ADVENTURES OF BLACK BEAUTY (Pro Films Australia/
    BBC1 11/4/94) theme "Galloping Home" by DENIS KING
    *see COLLECTIONS 138,175,358*

NEW ADVENTURES OF SUPERMAN (WBTV USA/BBC1 8/1/94) orig
　　music: JAY GRUSKA *see COLLECTION 345*
NEW AVENGERS The (ITV 22/10/76-78) theme mus: LAURIE
　　JOHNSON *see COLLECTION 4,33,294,357,358*
NEW JACK CITY (91) Music score: MICHEL COLOMBIER -S/T-
　　*reiss feat* V.ARTS: *GIANT (BMG): 74321 15104-2 (CD)*
NEW JERSEY DRIVE (1994) *feat:* Var.RAP & R.& B. -S/T-
　　*TOMMY BOY (Pinn): TB(CD)(C)(V) 1114 (CD/MC/2LP)*
　　*TOMMY BOY (Pinn): (Volume 2) - 1130 (CD/MC/2LP)*
NEW MOON - songs by Sigmund Romberg-Oscar Hammerstein
　1.ORIG LONDON CAST 1929 *with* EVELYN LAYE-GENE GERRARD
　　DOLORES FARRIS-JACK LIVESEY-VERA PEARCE-HOWETT WORS
　　TER-BEN WILLIAMS *+ musicals 'DESERT SONG (1927) and*
　　*'BLUE TRAIN' (1927) PEARL (Pavil): GEMMCD 9100(CD)*
　2.STUDIO RECORDING *with* GORDON MacRAE-DOROTHY KIRSTEN
　　*see under* 'DESERT SONG'
NEW ORLEANS (1947) *featur* LOUIS ARMSTRONG & ALL STARS
　　BILLIE HOLIDAY-WOODY HERMAN ORCHESTRA and others
　　-S/T- *JASMINE (BMG-Con): GOJCD 1025 (CD)*
NEW SCOOBY DOO MOVIES *see COLLECTION 370*
NEW TWILIGHT ZONE (USA TV) *see COLLECTION 344*
NEW YORK NEW YORK - songs by John Kander and Fred Ebb
　1.FILM MUSICAL 1977 *with:* LIZA MINNELLI-Georgie Auld
　　Diahanne Abbott-Larry Kent-Robert de Niro-Mary Kay
　　Place-Ralph Burns Or -S/T- *LIBERTY EMI Eur (Disc):*
　　*746 090-2 (CD) + LIBERTY (S.Screen): 46090-4 (MC)*
NEW YORK ROCK (ORIG NEW YORK CAST RECORDING) *featuring*
　　YOKO ONO *CAPITOL (EMI): CDP 829 843-2 (CD)*
NEW YORK UNDERCOVER (1995) Various Artists -S/T-
　　*MCA (BMG): MCD 11342 (CD) MCC 11342 (MC)*
NEWCOMERS The *see COLLECTION 5*
NEWS AT TEN (ITN 3/7/67-93) theme "The Awakening" '20th
　　Century Portrait' by JOHNNY PEARSON orig vers.on
　　*Coll* 'SOUNDS VISUAL' *deleted see also* 'ITN NEWS'
NEWSNIGHT (BBC2 28/1/80-98) theme music composed by
　　GEORGE FENTON *unavailable*
NICHOLAS NICKLEBY Life & Advent. ORIG LONDON CAST 1982
　　Songs: STEPHEN OLIVER *with* Royal Shakespeare Comp
　　*TER (Disc): CDTER 1029 (CD)*
NICK & NORA (O.BROADWAY CAST 1991) Music: CHARLES STRO
　　USE Lyrics: RICHARD MALTBY JNR *TER (Disc): CDTER*
　　*1191 (CD) ZCTER 1191 (MC)*
NIGHT AT THE OPERA, A (1935) *see Coll* CINEMA CLASSICS 9
　　*and Coll* 'OPERA AT THE MOVIES'
NIGHT COURT (USA/ITV 91) theme music: JACK ELLIOTT
　　*see COLLECTIONS 12,168,344*
NIGHT DIGGER (1971) Mus.sco: BERNARD HERRMANN with
　　TOMMY REILLY harm. *5th Cont (S.Scre):LXCD 12 (CD)*
NIGHT FEVER (C5 6/9/97) music by RICK TURK *unavailable*
NIGHT GALLERY (USA TV) *see COLLECTION 343*
NIGHT MAIL (1936 Post Office) Mus s: BENJAMIN BRITTEN
　　score select.*HYPERION (Select): CDA 66845 (CD)*
NIGHT OF THE GENERALS (1966) Music sco: MAURICE JARRE
　　-S/T- *FANTASY/INTRADA (Silva Sc): FM 8004D (2CD)*

NIGHT PASSAGE (1957) Music sco: DIMITRI TIOMKIN theme
    on Coll 'Western Film World Of Dimitri Tiomkin'
    with LONDON STUDIO S.O. (Laurie Johnson)
    *UNICORN KANCHANA (H.Mundi): UKCD 2011 (CD)*
NIGHTCROSSING (1987) Music sco: JERRY GOLDSMITH -S/T-
    *INTRADA USA (Silva Screen) RVF 6004D (CD)*
NIGHTINGALE (O.LONDON CAST 1982) Songs Charles Strouse
    *w:* SARAH BRIGHTMAN-GORDON SANDISON-SUSANNAH FELLOWS
    *TER (Disc): CDTER2 1031 (2CD) ZCTED 1031 (MC)*
NIGHTMARE CASTLE (1965) - *see under* 'HUMANOID,The'
NIGHTMARE ON ELM STREET 1 (1984) Mus: CHARLES BERNSTEIN
NIGHTMARE ON ELM STREET 2: Freddy's Revenge (1985) Mus
    CHRISTOPHER YOUNG *both Soundtracks VARESE (Pinn)*
    *VSD 47255 (CD)*
NIGHTMARE ON ELM STREET 3: Dream Warriors (1987) Mus:
    ANGELO BADALAMENTI -S/T- *VARESE: VCD 47293 (CD)*
NIGHTMARE ON ELM STREET 4: Dream Master (1988) Music
    CRAIG SAFAN -S/T- *VARESE (Pinn): VSD 5203 (CD)*
NIGHTMARE ON ELM STREET 5: Dream Child (1989) Music:
    JAY FERGUSON -S/T- *VARESE (Pinn): VSD 5238 (CD)*
NIGHTMARE ON ELM STREET 6: Freddie's Dead (1991) Mus:
    BRIAN MAY -S/T- *VARESE (Pinn): VSD 5333 (CD)*
    *see also* 'FREDDIE'S DEAD - THE FINAL NIGHTMARE'
NIKITA (1989) Music score: ERIC SERRA -S/T-
    *VIRGIN (EMI): CDVMM 2 (CD) TCVMM 2 (MC)*
NINE - songs by Maury Yeston
    ORIG LONDON CONCERT CAST 1992 *with:* JONATHAN PRYCE
    ELAINE PAIGE   *TER (Disc): CDTER2 1193 (2CD)*
NINE MONTHS (1995) Music sco HANS ZIMMER *feat* "Time Of
    Your Life" sung by LITTLE STEVEN + tracks by MARVIN
    GAYE-TYRONE DAVIS -S/T- *MILAN (BMG): 30110-2 (CD)*
NO BANANAS (BBC1 5/3/96) mus: JOHN ALTMAN -S/T- V.Arts
    *new numb: VIRGIN (EMI): CDVIP 176(CD) TCVIP 176(MC)*
NO HIDING PLACE (ITV 16/9/59-67) theme: LAURIE JOHNSON
    *see COLLECTIONS 3,100,372*
NO HONESTLY (ITV 4/10/84) theme by LYNSEY DE PAUL
    *see COLLECTIONS 2,168*
NO NO NANETTE - songs by Vincent Youmans - Otto Harbach
    and Irving Caesar
    1. REVIVAL CAST 1971 *with* RUBY KEELER *COLUMBIA Imp*
    *(Silva Screen): CK 30563 (CD) JST 30563 (MC)*
    2. ORIG LONDON REVIVAL CAST 1973 *w:* ANNA NEAGLE-TONY
    BRITTON-ANNE ROGERS-PETER GALE-BARBARA BROWN-ELAINE
    HOLLAND...*SONY West End (SM): SMK 66173 (CD)*
NO RETREAT NO SURRENDER (1985) Music sco: PAUL GILREATH
    -S/T- *SILVA SCREEN (Koch): FILMCD 150 (CD)*
NO SWEAT (BBC1 3/4/97) music by NORTH AND SOUTH "I'm A
    Man Not A Boy" on *RCA (BMG):*
NO WAY HOME (1997) Mus sc: RICK GIOVINAZZO -S/T- *OCEAN
    DEEP (Grapev/Polyg): OCD 005(CD) TBCD 7785(CDs) TBC
    7785 (MC)* -S/T- *TOMMY BOY (RTM-Disc): TBCD 1169(CD)*
NO WAY TO TREAT A LADY (ORIG USA CAST) songs: (DOUGLAS
    J.COHEN) *f:* ALIX KOREY-ADAM GRUPPER-MARGUERITE MAC
    INTYRE-PAUL SCHOEFFLER *VARESE (Pinn): VSD 5815 (CD)*

NO WAY OUT (1988) Mus: MAURICE JARRE -S/T- inc 'Year Of
   Living Dangerously' *ER (Koch) CD(ZC)TER 1149*
NOAH'S ARK (ITV 8/9/97) Music: COLIN TOWNS *unavailable*
NODDY BBC1 17/9/92) music: PAUL K.JOYCE *see COLLECT.60*
NOEL AND GERTIE (O.LONDON CAST 1986) Songs NOEL COWARD
   *with* Lewis FIANDER-Patricia HODGE and Company
   *TER (Disc): CDTER 1117 (CD)*
NOEL'S HOUSE PARTY (BBC1 fr.23/11/91) md Ernie Dunstall
   theme *not available* / "Mr.Blobby The Album" *Destiny*
   *(BMG): DMUSCD(DMUSMC) 106 (CD/MC) see* 'MR.BLOBBY'
NOMADS OF THE WIND (BBC2 9/1/94) mus: BRIAN BENNETT
   TV -S/T- *Karussell (Poly): 450 147-2 (CD) -4 MC)*
   *see COLLECTION 303*
NORMA JEAN AND MARILYN (TVM 1996) Music: CHRISTOPHER
   YOUNG -S/T- *INTRADA (S.Screen): MAF 7070 (CD)*
NORTH AND SOUTH (USA) *see COLLECTION 12*
NORTH BY NORTHWEST (1959) Music sco: BERNARD HERRMANN
   -S/T- *re-issue EMI PREMIER (EMI): CDODEON 6 (CD)*
   *see COLLECT.18,63,81,187,189,194,196,197,360,363*
NORTH STAR (1996) Music score: JOHN SCOTT -S/T- on
   *JOHN SCOTT Records (Silva Screen): JSCD 120 (CD)*
NORTHERN EXPOSURE (USA/C4 16/3/92)theme:DAVID SCHWARTZ
   -S/T- *with Var.Arts MCA (BMG): MCD 10685 (CD)*
   -S/T- 'More Music' *MCA (BMG): MCLD 19350 (CD)*
   *see COLLECTIONS 12,361*
NOSFERATU 1. (1922) Music sco: HANS ERDMANN orchestral
   version on *RCA (BMG): 09026 68143-2 (CD)*
NOSFERATU 2. (MUSICAL) Songs: BERNARD TAYLOR Orig Cast
   PETER KARRIE-CLAIRE MOORE-BARRY JAMES-MARIO FRANG
   OULIS *DRESS CIRCLE (Silver Sounds): NVDC 2 (CD)*
NOSTROMO (BBC2 1/2/97) Music score: ENNIO MORRICONE on
   *POLYDOR (Polyg): 533 658-2 (CD)*
NOT OF THIS EARTH (1957) *see COLLECTION 271*
NOT ONLY...BUT ALSO... (BBC2 4/11/90 orig 1965) theme
   "Goodbyee" (P.Cook-Dudley Moore) PETE & DUD 'The
   Clean Tapes' on *RIO (AMT): RDC 1206 (MC)*
NOT SINCE CASANOVA Mus.sco: JOHN DEBNEY -S/T- incl 'EYE
   OF THE PANTHER' *PROMETHEUS (S.Screen): PCD 140 (CD)*
NOT THE NINE O'CLOCK NEWS (BBC2 16/10/79) theme mus:
   NIC ROWLEY *TV Cast Rec BBC (Pinn): ZBBC 1009 2MC*
NOT WITHOUT MY DAUGHTER (1991) Music: JERRY GOLDSMITH
   -S/T- *SILVA SCREEN (Koch): FILM(C)(CD) 091*
NOTHING TO LOSE (1996) Music score: ROBERT FOLK / song
   "C U When U Get There" perform.by COOLIO *TOMMY BOY*
NOUVELLE VAGUE (1990) Music: DINO SALUZZI-DAVID DARLING
   PAUL HINDEMITH-ARNOLD SCHOENBERG-PAUL GIGER-PATTI
   SMITH-MEREDITH MONK-HEINZ HOLLIGER -S/T- on
   *ECM (New Note-Pinn): 449 891-2 (2CD)*
NOW AND THEN (95) Music sco: CLIFF EIDELMAN -S/T- (2)
   score: *VARESE (Pinn): VSD 5675 (CD)*
   songs: *COLUMBIA (Sony): 481 606-2 (CD) -4 (MC) inc:*
   BADFINGER/MONKEES/STEVIE WONDER/FREDA PAYNE/ARCHIES
   JACKSON 5/DIANA ROSS & SUPREMES & TEMPTATIONS/FREE/
   TONY ORLANDO & DAWN/VANITY FAYRE and SUSANNA HOFFS

NOW VOYAGER! (1942) *see* 'STREETCAR NAMED DESIRE A'
NOWHERE (1997) Various Arts -S/T- including RADIOHEAD-
    ELASTICA-CHEMICAL BROTHERS-MASSICE ATTACK etc.
    *MERCURY (Poly): 534 522-2 (CD)*
NUNSENSE - songs by Dan Goggin
    1.ORIG LONDON CAST 1987 *w* HONOR BLACKMAN-ANNA SHARKEY
      LOUISE GOLD   *TER (Disc): CDTER 1132 (CD)*
    2.ORIG OFF-BROADWAY CAST 1986 *w:* CHRISTINE ANDERSON
      SEMINA de LAURENTIS-MARILYN FARINA-EDWINA LEWIS-
      SUZI WINSTTON & Comp *DRG (Pinn): SBLC 12589 (MC)*
    3.ORIG CAST RECORDING *details unconfirmed*
      *DRG USA (Pinn): DRGCD 12608 (CD) DRGMC 12608 (MC)*
NUTTY PROFESSOR The (1995) Music score: DAVID NEWMAN
    Rap Songs *(INSPIRED BY THE FILM) feat:* CASE-MONTELL
    JORDAN-TRIGGER THE GAMBLER-AZ YET-LL COOL J-MONICA
    DEF SQUAD *MERCURY-Def Jam (Poly): 531 911-2 /-4*
NYPD BLUE (USA 93/C4 15/1/94) theme music: MIKE POST
    *see COLLECTIONS 101,345,388*
O LUCKY MAN (1973) Music sco: ALAN PRICE -S/T- *reiss:*
    *WARNER BROS (WEA): 9362 46137-2 (CD)*
O PIONEERS! (1991) Music score: BRUCE BROUGHTON -S/T-
    *INTRADA USA (Silva Screen): MAFCD 7023 (CD)*
O ZONE The (BBC2 18/9/95) music The SHAMEN *unavailable*
OAKIE DOKE (BBC1 11/9/95) theme music by ERNIE WOOD
    *see COLLECTION 60*
OBJECTIVE BURMA! (1944) Music score: FRANZ WAXMAN *see*
    *COLLECTION 389*
OBSESSION (1976) Music sco: BERNARD HERRMANN conducting
    NAT.PHILHARMONIC ORCH *see COLLECTION 190*
OCEANO - *see under* 'The ROVER'
OCTOPUSSY (1983) Music score: JOHN BARRY / theme song:
    "All Time High" sung by RITA COOLIDGE -S/T- *reissue*
    *+ additional items RYKODISC (Vital): RCD 10705 (CD)*
    *see also* 'JAMES BOND FILM INDEX' *also COLLECT 305*
ODD COUPLE The (USA 70 BBC rerun 89) theme: NEAL HEFTI
    *see COLLECTIONS 168,340,373,374*
ODD MAN OUT (1946) Music score: WILLIAM ALWYN Suite LSO
    (Richard Hickox) *CHANDOS: CHAN 9243 (CD)*
OF LOVE AND SHADOWS (1994) Music score: JOSE NIETO
    JOSE NIETO with Middle Slovak Philharmonic Orchest
    -S/T- *CUBE-FLY (FLY Direct): FLYCD 107 (CD)*
OF MEN AND DEMONS - *see* 'JOURNEY TO NEXT'
OF UNKNOWN ORIGIN (1983)  Music sco: KEN WANNBERG -S/T-
    selection with 'LATE SHOW'/'THE AMATEUR' on Imprt
    *PROMETHEUS (Silva Screen): PCD 137 (CD)*
OH DOCTOR BEECHING (BBC1 1/7/96) theme song sung by SU
    POLLARD & CAST *(unavailable)* based on song 'Oh Mr.
    Porter' (George & Thomas Le Brun) *version (1931) by*
    NORAH BLANEY on 'Glory Of The Music Hall Vol.3' on
    *PEARL (Pavillion): GEMMCD 9477 (CD)*
OKLAHOMA! - songs: Richard Rodgers-Oscar Hammerstein II
    1.FILM MUSICAL 1955 *with:* GORDON MacRAE-SHIRLEY JONES
      GLORIA GRAHAM-ROD STEIGER-GENE NELSON- and Company
      -S/T- *EMI:  ZDM 764 691-2 (CD)*

OKLAHOMA! *Continued...*

2. ORIG LONDON CAST 1980 *with:* JOHN DIEDRICH-ROSAMUND
SHELLEY-MADGE RYAN-MARK WHITE-ALFRED MOLINA-JILLIAN
MACK-LINAL HAFT and Co.
<u>Highlights:</u> *SHOWTIME (MCI-THE): SHOW(CD)(MC) 001*
<u>Complete:</u> *TER (Disc): (CD)(ZC)TEM 1208 (CD/MC)*

3. ORIG BROADWAY CAST 1943 *Theatre Guild Prd with:*
ALFRED DRAKE-JOAN ROBERTS-CELESTE HOLME-LEE DIXON
*MCA (BMG): MCLD 19026 (CD)*

4. STUDIO RECORD USA 1952 *w:* NELSON EDDY-VIRGINIA HASK
INS-KAYE BALLARD-PORTIA NELSON-LEE CASS-DAVID ATKIN
SON-DAVID MORRIS *SONY Broadway (SM): SK 53326 (CD)*

5. BROADWAY CAST RECORDING 1979 *with:* LAURENCE GUTTARD
CHRISTINE ANDREAS-MARY WICKES *RCA(BMG):RD 83572(CD)*

6. CLASSIC MUSICALS SERIES *feat:* JOHN DIEDRICH
MADGE RYAN-ROSAMUND SHELLEY-MARK WHITE-ALFRED MOLINA
+ *songs from* 'THE KING & I' *KOCH INT: 34077-2 (CD)*

OLD BEAR STORIES (Carlton 22/9/93) music:PAUL CASTLE.*NA*

OLD GREY WHISTLE TEST (BBC2 Rock Series 70s-80s) theme
"Stone Fox Chase" (Buttrey-Haley-McCoy) orig by
AREA CODE 615 *Polyd deleted see also* WHISTLE TEST

OLD GRINGO (89) Music score: LEE HOLDRIDGE Suite on
'LONESOME DOVE' *SILVA SCREEN (Koch): FILMCD 176 CD*

OLD MAN AND THE SEA The (Yorkshire / 90) music: BRUCE
BROUGHTON -S/T- *INTRADA (S.Screen): RVF 6008D (CD)*

OLIVER! - songs by Lionel Bart

1. FILM MUSICAL 1968 *w:* HARRY SECOMBE-RON MOODY-SHANI
WALLIS-JACK WILD -S/T- *RCA: ND(NK) 90311 (CD/MC)*

2. NEW LONDON CAST 1994 *w:* JONATHAN PRYCE-SALLY DEXTER
*FIRST NIGHT (Pinn): CASTCD 47 (CD) CASTC 47 (MC)*

3. CARLTON SHOWS COLLECTION Studio 1994 *w* IAN WALLACE
BONNIE LANGFORD-GARETH STRINGER-VICTOR SPINETTI &
West End Concert Orch & Chorus (Matthew Freeman)
*CARLTON SHOWS: PWKS(PWKMC) 4194 (CD/MC)*

4. STUDIO RECORD 1991 *w:* JOSEPHINE BARSTOW-JULIAN FORS
YTHE-SHEILA HANCOCK-STUART KALE-RICHARD VAN ALLAN
National Symphony Orchestra (JOHN OWEN EDWARDS)
<u>Highlights:</u> *SHOWTIME (MCI-THE): SHOW(CD)(MC) 004*
<u>Complete:</u> *TER (Disc): (CD)(ZC)TER 1184 (CD/MC)*

5. LONDON STUDIO RECORD 1962 *w:* STANLEY HOLLOWAY-ALMA
COGAN-DENNIS WATERMAN-LESLIE FYSON-VIOLET CARSON-
CHARLES GRANVILLE-TONY TANNER *with* RITA WILLIAMS
SINGERS and TONY OSBORNE ORCH *EMI Broaway Classics*
*ZDM 764890-2 (CD) EG 764890-4 (MC) deleted 97*

6. LONDON STUDIO RECORD 1966 *w:* JON PERTWEE-JIM DALE
NICOLETTE ROEG-BLANCHE MOORE-TOMMY MANN-FRED LUCAS
CHARLES GRANVILLE and GEOFF LOVE & HIS ORCHESTRA
*MFP (EMI):CC 8253 (CD) HR 8253 (MC)*

7. ORIG BROADWAY CAST 1963 CLIVE REVILL-GEORGIA BROWN
*RCA (BMG): GD 84113 (CD) GK 84113 (MC)*

8. ORIG LONDON CAST 1960 *w:* RON MOODY-GEORGIA BROWN-
PAUL WHITSUN JONES-HOPE JACKMAN-DANNY SEWELL & Co
*DERAM (Poly): 820 590-2 (CD) -4 (MC) deleted*

OLIVER AND CO (1989) *see* WALT DISNEY INDEX p.343
OLIVER TWIST (BBC 1962) music: RON GRAINER peformed by
   The EAGLES *see COLLECTION 7*
OLIVIER OLIVIER (1991) Music: ZBIGNIEW PREISNER incl
   'EUROPA EUROPA' -S/T- *DRG (Pinn): DRG(CD)(MC) 12606*
OLYMPIC GAMES 1996 (JULY) (themes and trailer music)
   (BBC1) "Tara's Theme" from 'Gone With The Wind' (M.
   STEINER) *TV ver:* SPIRO & WIX *EMI Premier: PRESCD 4
   (CDs) PRESTC 4 (MC) PRES 4 (7"s)* also on 'MOTION'
   *EMI Premier: PRMDCD 8 (CD) PRMDTC 8 (MC)*
   (SKYTV) Trailer theme "Yeha Noha" (Wishes Of Happin
   ess) from SACRED SPIRIT *VIRGIN (EMI):CDV(TCV) 2753*
   (USA: SUMMON THE HEROES: Official Olympic Theme) by
   JOHN WILLIAMS on 'Summon The Heroes' *Sony Class
   SK(ST) 62622 (CD/MC)* see also under COLLECTIONS
OLYMPIC GRANDSTAND Lillehammer Norway 1994 BBC2 12/2/94
   theme "Pop Looks Bach" SAM FONTEYN *see* 'SKI SUNDAY'
OLYMPIC WINTER GAMES *see* 'WINTER OLYMPIC GAMES'

OLYMPUS ON MY MIND (O.USA CAST 1996) Songs: Grant Stur
   iale-Barry Harman) *TER (Disc): CD(ZC)TER 1131*
OMEN The (1976) M: JERRY GOLDSMITH -S/T- *VARESE (Pinn)
   VSD 5281* 'O Fortuna' "Carmina Burana" (CARL ORFF)
   *see also COLLECTIONS 55,64,109*
OMEN II 'Damien' (1978) Music score: JERRY GOLDSMITH
   -S/T- *SILVA SCREEN: FILMCD 002 (CD)*
OMEN III 'Final Conflict' (1981) Mus: JERRY GOLDSMITH
   -S/T- *VARESE (Pinn): VCD 47242 (CD) VSC 5282 (MC)*
OMEN IV The Awakening' (1991) Music: JONATHAN SHEFFER
   -S/T- *VARESE (Pinn): VSD(VSC) 5318 (CD/MC)*
ON A CLEAR DAY YOU CAN SEE FOREVER (1970) Mus (Burton
   LANE) Lyrics (Alan Jay LERNER) - BARBRA STREISAND
   -S/T- *COLUMBIA (Sony: 474 907-2 (CD)*
ON BORROWED TIME (39) *see COLLECTION 392*
ON DANGEROUS GROUND (1951) Music: BERNARD HERRMANN
   -S/T- with 'HANGOVER SQUARE'/'A HATFUL OF RAIN'
   *TSUNAMI Imp (Silva Screen): TCI 0610 (CD)*
ON DEADLY GROUND (1993) Music score: BASIL POLEDOURIS
   -S/T- *VARESE (Pinn): VSD 5468 (CD)*
ON HER MAJESTY'S SECRET SERVICE (1969) Music sco: JOHN
   BARRY title song (J.Barry-Hal David) sung by LOUIS
   ARMSTRONG -S/T- *rcissue EMI PREMIER: CZ 549 (CD)*
   *see also* JAMES BOND INDEX p.346
ON MY OWN (1992) Music: FRANCO PIERSANTI -S/T- *Imp
   (Sil.Screen): OST 117(CD)* with 'CHILDREN'S THIEF'
ON SIDE (BBC1 27/10/97) t.mus: JIM MEACOCK *unavailable*

ON THE BUSES (ITV 28/2/69) theme music: TONY RUSSELL
   *see COLLECTIONS 6,229,360*
ON THE LINE *see COLLECTION 138*
ON THE MOVE (BBC) *see COLLECTION 2*
ON THE RECORD (BBC1 1988-96) theme "Allegro" (Divertis
   mento No.5 in C, K187)(MOZART) *vers:* Philharmonia
   Orchestra (Wright) *NIMBUS: NI 5121 (CD)*

ON THE TOWN (1949) -S/T- score *Imp* + 'ANCHORS AWEIGH'
   *BLUE MOON (Discovery): BMCD 7007 (CD)*
ON THE TOWN - songs by Leonard Bernstein-Betty Comden
   and Adolph Green
   1. STUDIO RECORD ST.LOUIS SYMPHONY ORCH Felix Slatkin
      *with:* CANDIDE/FANCY FREE.*EMI Eminence:CDEMX 2242 CD*
   2. ORIG BROADWAY CAST 1944 VARIOUS ARTISTS
      *CBS USA (S.Screen): CK(JST) 02038 (CD/MC)*
   3. ORIG LONDON CAST 1963 *w:* CAROL ARTHUR-ELLIOTT GOULD
      ROSAMUND GREENWOOD..*SONY BROADWAY:SMK 53497 (CD)*
   4. ORIG MASTERWORKS EDIT (First Complete R) *feat* GREGG
      EDELMAN-TIM FLAVIN-ETHAN FREEMAN-KIM CRISWELL-JUDY
      KAYE-VALERIE MASTERSON *TER (Disc):CDTER2 1217 (2CD)*
ON THE UP (BBC1 from 4/9/90) Opening music "Concerto Gr
   ossi in A.op.6 no.11" 1st m/m (Handel) by GUILDHALL
   STRING ENSEMBLE - *RCA (BMG): RD(RK) 87921 (CD/MC)*
   Closing theme comp.& sung by DENNIS WATERMAN.....*NA*
ON THE WATERFRONT (ORIG BROADWAY CAST) Music (David Amr
   am) *VARESE (Pinn): VSD 5638 (CD)*
ON YOUR TOES (REVIVAL BROADWAY CAST 1983) Mus R.RODGERS
   L.HART *TER (Disc): ZCTED 1063(2MC) CDTER 1063(CD)*
ON YOUR TOES (CLASSIC MUSICALS SERIES) *feat:* EUGENE J.
   ANTHONY-BETTY ANN GROVE-MARY C.ROBARE-LARA TEETER
   + *songs from* 'PAL JOEY' *KOCH INT: 34082-2 (CD)*
ONCE ON THIS ISLAND songs: Lynn Ahrens-Stephen Flaherty
   1. ORIG LONDON CAST 1994 VARIOUS ARTISTS
      *TER (Disc): CDTER 1224 (CD)*
   2. ORIG BROADWAY CAST 1990 VARIOUS ARTS *RCA IMPORT*
      *(Silva Screen) 60595-2 (CD) 60595-4 (MC)*
ONCE UPON A MATTRESS (Musical Comedy by MARY RODGERS &
   MARSHALL BAREN) NEW BROADWAY CAST featuring SARAH
   JESSICA PARKER *RCA Victor (BMG): 09026 68728-2 (CD)*
ONCE UPON A TIME IN AMERICA (1984) Mus: ENNIO MORRICONE
   -S/T- *MERCURY (Poly):  822 334-2 (CD)*
   *see COLLECTIONS 63,244,251,252,255,303,360,400*
ONCE UPON A TIME IN THE WEST (1969) M: ENNIO MORRICONE
   -S/T- *RCA (Silva Screen): 4736-2 (CD) 4736-4 (MC)*
   *see COLLECTIONS 63,170,202,249,251,252,255,*
ONCE WERE WARRIORS (1994) Music sco: MURRAY GRINDLEY &
   MURRAY McNABB -S/T- feat Various Artists on
   *MILAN (BMG): 74321 24902-2 (CD)*
ONE AGAINST THE WIND (1992) Music sco: LEE HOLDRIDGE
   -S/T- *INTRADA (S.Screen): MAF 7039D (CD)*
ONE BORN EVERY MINUTE - see 'FLIM FLAM MAN'

ONE EYED JACKS (1961) Music score: HUGO FRIEDHOFER
   -S/T- *TSUNAMI Germ (Silva Screen): TSU 0114 (CD)*
ONE FINE DAY (1996) Mus sco: JAMES NEWTON HOWARD -S/T-
   *COLUMBIA (Sony Music): 486 910-2 (CD) -4 (MC)*
ONE FLEW OVER THE CUCKOO'S NEST (1975) Music sco: JACK
   NITZSCHE -S/T- *FANTASY Imp FCD 4531 (CD) deleted*
ONE FOOT IN THE GRAVE (BBC1 4/1/90-95) theme mus (Eric
   Idle) ERIC IDLE and VICTOR MELDREW (Richard Wilson)
   *VICTA-Total (BMG):CD(CAV)(12)VICTA 1  deleted*

ONE FOOT IN THE PAST (BBC2 4/6/93) series theme music:
ROGER BOLTON *unavailable*
ONE FROM THE HEART (1982) Mus/Songs: TOM WAITS-CRYSTAL
GAYLE -S/T- re-iss *SONY MUSIC (SM):467 609-2 (CD)*
ONE GAME The (Central 4/6/88) theme music "Saylon Dola"
NIGEL HESS sung CHAMELEON *see COLLECTIONS 5,138,192*
ONE MAN AND HIS DOG (BBC2 1976-1997) title theme music
composed by ALAN BENSON *unavailable*
ONE MILLION YEARS BC (1966) Music sc: MARIO NASCIMBENE
+ 'WHEN DINOSAURS RULED THE EARTH'/'CREATURES THE
WORLD FORGOT' *LEGEND (S.Screen): LEGEND CD13 (CD)*
ONE NIGHT STAND (1997) Music score: MIKE FIGGIS -S/T-
*VERVE (Poly): 539 025-2 (CD)*
ONE TRICK PONY (1980) Music score: PAUL SIMON -S/T-
*WB (WEA): K4-56846 (MC) K2-56846 (CD)*
ONEDIN LINE The (UKGold 5/11/92 orig BBC1 15/10/71) mus
theme 'Adagio' from Spartacus Ballet (KHACHATURIAN)
*see COLLECTION 2,31*
ONLY FOOLS AND HORSES (BBC1 8/9/81-96) theme composed
and performed by JOHN SULLIVAN *unavailable*
ONLY THE LONELY The Roy Orbison Story (O.LONDON CAST
1995) *featuring:* LARRY BRANSON and Company on
*FIRST NIGHT (Pinn): CASTCD 51 (CD) CASTC 51 (MC)*
ONLY WHEN I LARF (1968) *see COLLECTION 7*
ONLY YOU (94) Music score: RACHEL PORTMAN -S/T- on
*Sony Music (SM): 476818-2 (CD) -4 (MC) DELETED 96*
OPERA (1987,Italy) - *see COLLECTION 312*
OPERA (Terror At The Opera) (87) Music by ROGER & BRIAN
ENO-BILL WYMAN & extracts from various Operas -S/T-
*CINEVOX Italy Import (Silva Screen): CIA 5074 (CD)*
OPERA SAUVAGE FRENCH TV Music score: VANGELIS -S/T- on
import: *POLYDOR (IMS-Poly): E.829 663.2 (CD)*
ORANGES ARE NOT THE ONLY FRUIT (BBC2 10/1/90) music by
RACHEL PORTMAN - *2 Story MC BBC (Pinn): ZBBC 1151*
*see COLLECTION 6*
OPERATION DUMBO DROP (95) Music score: DAVID NEWMAN
-S/T- *Hollywood (Polyg): 162 032-2 (CD)*
OPRAH WINFREY SHOW The (USA/BBC2 96/97) end theme song
"Ten Years" composed/sung by PAUL SIMON on Collect:
'CARNIVAL!' *RCA Vict (BMG):74321 44769-2(CD) -4(MC)*
ORCA - KILLER WHALE (1977) Music score ENNIO MORRICONE
-S/T- *LEGEND IMPT (Silva Screen): CD 10 (CD)*
ORCHESTRA! (C4 6/1/91) Sir GEORG SOLTI and DUDLEY MOORE
Orchestral Music -S/T- *DECCA:430 838-2(CD) -4(MC)*
ORCHESTRA WIVES (1942 MUSICAL) *with* GLENN MILLER BAND &
RAY EBERLE *includ.*songs from 'SUN VALLEY SERENADE'
*TARGET (BMG): CD 60002 (CD)*
ORDINARY PEOPLE (1980) Theme 'Canon In D' (PACHELBEL)
on *COLLECTIONS 69,83,86,94,310*
ORIENT EXPRESS (1979) Music score: ENNIO MORRICONE
ENNIO MORRICONE -S/T- selection on 'TV FILM MUSIC'
*RCA (BMG): /4321 31552-2 (CD)*
ORIGINAL GANGSTAS (1996) RAP FILM -S/T- *feat:* LUNIZ-ICE
T-SMOOTH-JUNIOR MAFIA *VIRGIN (EMI): CDVUS 104 (CD)*

ORPHEUS IN THE UNDERWORLD (MUSICAL OPERETTA) Music by
    Jacques OFFENBACH / English text by S.Wilson- D.
    Pountney - *English National Opera* (Mark Elder) on
    *TER (Disc):CDTER 1134* HIGHLIGHTS: *CD(ZC)TEO 1008*
OSCAR'S ORCHESTRA (ITV 12/9/95) various classical music
    Mozart-Glinka-Chopin-Tchaikovsky-Rimsky Korsakov-JS
    Bach-Beethoven-Holst-Grieg etc. -S/T- *available on*
    *ERATO (WEA Classics): 0630 11865-2 (CD) -4 (MC)*
OTHELLO (1995-O.Parker) Music: CHARLIE MOLE -S/T-
    *VARESE (Pinn): VSD 5689 (CD)*
OTHELLO (1951-O.Welles) Music score: FRANCESCO LAVAGNINO
    ALBERTO BARBERIS -S/T- *VARESE (Pinn): VSD 5420 CD*
OTHER The (1972) Music score: JERRY GOLDSMITH score w:
    'MEPHISTO WALTZ' *VARESE (Pinn): VSD 5851 (CD)*
OUR FRIENDS IN THE NORTH (BBC2 15/1/96 and 19/7/97)
    theme music and incidental score by COLIN TOWNS..*NA*
    -S/T- *(V.ARTS)* BOB DYLAN-ANIMALS-KINKS-TROGGS-BARRY
    McGUIRE-SMALL FACES-WHO-ELTON JOHN-CHIC-REAL THING-
    BLONDIE-RUTS-CLASH-UNDERTONES-CULTURE CLUB-SMITHS-
    EURYTHMICS-PULP *TELSTAR TV (WEA): TTV(CD)(MC) 2922*
OUR HOUSE (ITV 1960 series) theme music (Maxim-Hudis)
    *see COLLECTIONS 368,372*
OUR TUNE (SIMON BATES, RADIO 1) "Love Theme from Romeo
    and Juliet" (NINO ROTA) *on COLLECT* 'HOLLYWOOD'S
    GREATEST HITS' *TELARC (Conif-BMG): CD 80168 (CD)*
OUT OF AFRICA (1986) Music JOHN BARRY + Melissa Manche
    ster-Al Jarreau -S/T- *MCA (BMG): MCLD(MCLC) 19092*
    new recording by ROYAL SCOTTISH NATIONAL ORCHESTRA
    (Joel McNeely,cond) on *VARESE (Pinn): VSD 5816 (CD)*
    *see COLLECT.21,24,62,65,68,81,97,139,171,291,203*
OUT OF IRELAND (1995) *feat* SEAMUS EGAN-MICK MOLONEY-
    EILEEN IVOR *SHANACHIE (Koch): SH(CD)(MC) 79092*
OUT OF THE BLUE (BBC1 23/5/95) theme and incidental
    music: JOHN HARLE *unavailable*
OUT OF THIS WORLD (1) songs: Cole Porter
  1.ORIG NEW YORK CAST 1995 *featur:* ANDREA MARTIN-MARY
    ANN LAMB-ERNIE SABELLA-GREGG EDELMAN-MARIN MAZZIE-
    PETER SCOLARI-LA CHANZE-KEN PAGE-ROB FISHER COFFEE
    CLUB ORCHEST *DRG (New Note-Pinn): DRGCD 94764 (CD)*
  2.ORIG BROADWAY CAST 1950 *feat:* CHARLOTTE GREENWOOD-
    WILLIAM REDFIELD-WILLIAM EYTHE-PRISCILLA GILLETTE-
    BARBARA ASHLEY-DAVID BURNS *SONY: SK 48223 (CD)*
OUT OF THIS WORLD (2) (ITV 24/6/62) *see COLLECTION 182*
OUTBREAK (1995) Music score: JAMES NEWTON HOWARD -S/T-
    *VARESE (Pinn): VSD 5599 (CD)*
OUTER LIMITS The (USA 95/BBC2 1/5/95) theme mus: MARK
    MANCINA-JOHN VAN TONGREN incidental score & other
    music by FRED MOLLIN-J.PETER ROBINSON and others.*NA*
    *ORIG USA 63/64 theme:* DOMINIC FRONTIERE TV -S/T-
    *GNP USA (S.Screen-Conif): GNPD(GNP5) 8032 (CD/MC)*
    *see COLLECTIONS 110,340*
OUTLAND (1981) Music sc: JERRY GOLDSMITH -S/T- (also
    containing music from 'CAPRICORN ONE') on *GNP USA*
    *(Silva Screen): GNPD 8035 (CD) GNP-5 8035 (MC)*

OUTSIDE CHANCE: - see BRIAN CONLEY
OUTSIDE EDGE (Central from 24/3/94) mus: FIACHRA TRENCH
   -S/T- *ECHO (Pinn): LBWCD 1 (CD) LBWMC 1 (MC)*
OVERLANDERS The (1946) Music sco: DIMITRI TIOMKIN West
   Australian S.O.(David MEASHAM) *UNICORN KANCHANA
   (Harmonia Mundi): UKCD 2062 (CD)*
OWEN MD (BBC1 70) theme mus: "Sleepy Shores" by JOHNNY
   PEARSON *see COLLECTIONS 2,4,31,168,284*
OZ Film -S/T- *Animanga-New Note (Pinn): AM 2 (CD)*

**P.**D.JAMES Thrillers (Anglia TV) *see* 'UNNATURAL CAUSES'
   *see COLLECTION 181*
PACIFIC OVERTURES - songs by Stephen Sondheim
   1.ORIG BROADWAY CAST 1976 *w:* MAKO-SOON TECK OH-YUKI
   SHIMODA-SAB SHIMONO-ISAO SATO and Company
   *RCA (S.Screen) RCD14407(CD) CBK14407(MC)*
   2.ENGLISH NATIONAL OPERA CAST PROD *TER (Disc): CDTER
   1151 (CD Highlights) CDTER2 1152 (2CD Complete)*
PADDINGTON (BBC1 74) theme "Size Ten Shuffle" HERBERT
   CHAPPELL *Coll* 'TV TUNES FOR KIDS 2'/ Spoken word MC
   with Michael Hordern on *BBC (Pinn): YBBC 1481 (MC)*
PAGEMASTER The (1994) Music: JAMES HORNER. Song "Dream
   Away" perf.by BABYFACE and LISA STANSFIELD -S/T- on
   *ARISTA (BMG): 07822 11019-2(CD) 07822 11019-4(MC)*
PAGNOL, Marcel TRILOGY - *see* 'MARIUS'/'FANNY'/'CESAR'
PAINT YOUR WAGON (FILM MUSICAL 1969) (ALAN JAY LERNER-
   FREDERICK LOEWE) Feat: LEE MARVIN-CLINT EASTWOOD
   -S/T- *reissued on MCA (BMG): MCLD 19310 (CD)*
PAJAMA GAME The - Songs by RICHARD ADLER and JERRY ROSS
   1.First Complete Recording *feat:* JUDY KAYE-RON RAINES
   KIM CRISWELL-AVERY SALTZMAN-BROOKE ALMY-DAVID GREEN
   NATIONAL SYMPHONY ORCHESTRA cond: JOHN OWEN EDWARDS
   *TER (MCI-THE): CDTER2 1232 (2CD)*
   2.FILM MUSICAL 1957 *with:* DORIS DAY -S/T- songs
   *SONY 467610-2 (CD)* + 'CALAMITY JANE' (1953) also
   on *ENTERTAINERS (BMG): CD 343 (CD)*
   3.ORIG BROADWAY CAST 1954 *w:* John Raitt-JANIS PAIGE-
   EDDIE FOY JNR-CAROL HANEY-RETA SHAW-RALPH DUNN
   *COLUMBIA (S.Screen): CK 32606 (CD) JST 32606 (MC)*
PAL JOEY - songs by Richard Rodgers and Lorenz Hart
   1.REVIVAL LONDON CAST 1980 *with:* SIAN PHILLIPS-DENIS
   LAWSON and Company
   Highlights: *SHOWTIME (MCI-THE): SHOW(CD)(MC) 008*
   Complete: *TER (Disc): (CD)(ZC)TER 1005 (CD/MC)*
   2.ORIG BROADWAY CAST 1940  GENE KELLY-VIVIENNE SEGAL
   *CBS USA (Sil.Screen) CK 04364 (CD) JST 04364 (MC)*
   3.BROADWAY CAST OF 1952 *w:* HAROLD LANG-VIVIENNE SEGAL
   HELEN GALLAGHER-LIONEL STANDER-PATRICIA NORTHROP-
   ELAINE STRITCH *EMI ANGEL:: ZDM 764696-2 (CD)*
   4.STUDIO RECORDING 1995 *w:* NEW YORK'S CITY CENTRE MU
   SICALS IN CONCERT PROD *DRG (Pinn): DRGCD 94763(CD)*
   5.CLASSIC MUSICALS SERIES *feat:* DENIS LAWSON-
   SIAN PHILLIPS-DANIELLE CARSON-DARLENE JOHNSON etc
   *+ songs from* 'ON YOUR TOES' *KOCH INT: 34082-2 (CD)*

PALLISERS The (BBC1 19/1/74) music: HERBERT CHAPPELL
    *see COLLECTION 2*
PANORAMA (BBC1 11/11/53-1997) Various Themes including:
    80-97 Theme "Today It's You"Aujourd Hui C'est Toi"
    from 'A MAN AND A WOMAN' (66-FRANCIS LAI) available
    *-S/T- MUSIDISC (Pinn): 10129-2 (CD) -4 (MC)*
    Orig 50s Theme "Openings & Endings" ROBERT FARNON
    *see COLLECTION 220*
PAPER CHASE (USA TV) *see COLLECTION 344*
PAPILLON (1973) Music score: JERRY GOLDSMITH -S/T-
    *SILVA SCREEN (Koch): FILMCD 029 (CD)*
PARADINE CASE The (1947) Music score: FRANZ WAXMAN sel:
    'Hollywood Piano Concertos' *Koch Int: 37225-2 (CD)*
PARADISE ROAD (1996) Music: DVORAK and other classics
    *-S/T- SONY CLASSICS: SK 63026 (CD)*
PARIS S'EVEILLE (1991) Music score: JOHN CALE -S/T-
    *YELLOW MOON (Grapevine/POLY): YMCD 007 (CD)*
PARIS TEXAS (1984) Original Songs by RY COODER -S/T-
    *W.BROS (WEA): 925 270-2 (CD) 925 270-4 (MC)*
PARK IS MINE The (1991) Music score: TANGERINE DREAM
    *-S/T- SILVA SCREEN (Koch): FILMCD 080 (CD)*
PARKINSON (BBC1 1970-81 & 1997/98) *see COLLECTION 402*
PARTNERS IN CRIME (LWT 16/10/83) mus: JOSEPH HOROVITZ
    performed by RICHARD RODNEY BENNETT and MARIAN
    MONTGOMERY *see COLLECTION 175*
PARTRIDGE FAMILY The (USA TV 70s) *see COLLECTION 340*
PARTY OF 5 (1997) Music sco: STEVEN CAHILL -S/T- V.Arts
    *WEA: 9362 46431-2(CD) / -S/T- EMI UK: PRMDCD 32(CD)*
PARTY PARTY (1983) Music by Various Arts -S/T- *reiss:*
    *SPECTRUM (Poly): 551 440-2 (CD)*
PASSAGE TO INDIA A (1985) Music score: MAURICE JARRE
    *see COLLECTIONS 63,120,214,215*
PASSION Songs by STEPHEN SONDHEIM
    (1) O.LONDON CAST 1996- MICHAEL BALL-MARIA FRIEDMAN
    *FIRST NIGHT (Pinn): CASTCD 61 (CD) CASTC 61 (MC)*
    (2) O.BROADWAY CAST 1994 *w:* DONNA MURPHY & Company
    *EMI CLASSICS: CDQ 555 251-2 (CD)*
PASSION FISH (1993) Music score: MASON DARING -S/T- inc
    BALFA BROTHERS-DUKE LEVINE GROUP-JOHN DELAFOSE& THE
    EUNICE PLAYBOYS-JAMES MACDONELL-ZYDECO EXPRESS-LE
    TRIO CADIEN *DARING (Project-CMD-ADA):DRCD 3008 CD*
PASSPORT TO PIMLICO (1949) *see COLLECTION 225*
PAT GARRETT & BILLY THE KID (1973) Songs: BOB DYLAN
    -S/T- reiss *SONY M: CD 32098 (CD) 40-32098 (MC)*
PATCH OF BLUE, A (1965) Music score: JERRY GOLDSMITH
    *Imp* + 'PATTON' *TSUNAMI (S.Screen): TCI 0606 (CD)*
PATIENCE (operetta) - songs by Gilbert and Sullivan
    1.D'OYLE CARTE OPERA CHORUS AND ORCHESTRA 1994
      *TER (Disc): CD(ZC)TER2 1213 (2CD/2MC)*
    2.PRO-ARTE ORCHEST (Malcolm Sargent) and GLYNDEBOURNE
      FESTIVAL CHOIR Soloists: JOHN SHAW-TREVOR ANTHONY-
      ALEX YOUNG-GEORGE BAKER *EMI: CMS 764406-2 (2CDs)*
    3.D'OYLY CARTE OPERA COMPANY New Symphony Orch Of Lond
      on (Is.Godfrey) *LONDON (Poly): 425 193-2 (CDx2)*

PATLABOR 2 (95 MANGA VIDEO) Music:(-)
   -S/T- *DEMON (Pinn): DSCD 15 (CD)*
PATTON (70) Music score: JERRY GOLDSMITH + *music from*
   'TORA TORA TORA' by ROYAL SCOTTISH NATIONAL ORCH.
   *VARESE (Pinn): VSD 5796 (CD) also*
   'A PATCH OF BLUE' *Tsunami (S.Scre): TCI 0606 (CD)*
   *see also COLLECTIONS 199,238,383*
PATTY DUKE SHOW (USA TV) *see COLLECTION 339*
PAUL MERTON'S IN GALTON AND SIMPSONS...(ITV 2/9/97)
   original music by STEFAN GIRADET *unavailable*
PAUL TEMPLE (BBC1 23/11/69) theme music: RON GRAINER
   *see COLLECTIONS 7,44,163,168*
PEACEMAKER The (1997) Music score: HANS ZIMMER
   -S/T- *DREAMWORKS (BMG): DRDS 0027 (CD)*
PEAK PRACTICE (Central 10/5/93) orig mus: JOHN ALTMAN
   -S/T- *EMI SOUNDTRACK: PRMFCD 1 (CD)*
PEANUTS (USA TV) *see COLLECTION 340*
PEANUTS BANK FOOTS THE BILL (1995) -S/T- Import on
   *COLOSSEUM (Pinn): CST 348053 (CD)*
PEARL & DEAN theme - *see COLLECTION 358*
PEBBLE MILL AT ONE (70's-80's) theme "As You Please"
   *see COLLECTION 31*
PEG (O.LONDON CAST 1984) Songs: DAVID HENEKER *featur:*
   SIAN PHILLIPS *TER (Disc): CD(ZC)TER 1024 (CD/MC)*
PELICAN BRIEF The (1993) Music sco: JAMES HORNER -S/T-
   *WARNER IMPT (Sil.Screen): WA 24544-2 (CD) -4 (MC)*
PENNIES FROM HEAVEN (BBC2 7/2/90 prev.shown 1/12/1978)
   1930's music re-recorded from orig 78's / 65 songs
   *CONNOISS (Pinn): POTTCD 300 (2CD) POTTMC 300 (2MC)*
   *see also entry* 'SINGING DETECTIVE'
PEOPLE: A MUSICAL CELEBRATION OF DIVERSITY (1995) incl:
   PEABO BRYSON & LEA SALONGA "How Wonderful We Are" +
   HEAVY D-AL JARREAU-CHAKA KHAN-VANESSA WILLIAMS etc.
   *LIGHTYEAR ENT (Pinn Imps): 54150-2 (CD)*
PEOPLE IN LONDON (ITV 1964) theme mus "Spanish Armada"
   LES REED *see COLLECTION 6*
PEOPLE PEOPLE PEOPLE - *see* 'JOURNEY TO NEXT'
PEOPLE Vs LARRY FLYNT (1996) Music score: THOMAS NEWMAN
   -S/T- *EMI PREMIER (EMI): PRMDCD 32 (CD)*
PEOPLE'S CENTURY (BBC2 13/9/95) title music by ZBIGNIEW
   PRIESNER other mus by ORLANDO GOUGH-FIACHRA TRENCH
   DEBBIE WISEMAN -S/T- *VIRGIN (EMI): CD(TC)VIP 177*
   *(CD/MC) see also COLLECTION 213*
PEOPLE'S COURT (USA TV) *see COLLECTION 344*
PERCY (1971) Music: RAY DAVIES Songs sung by The KINKS
   -S/T- *CASTLE Classics (Castle-BMG): CLACD 164 (CD)*
PERFECT SCOUNDRELS (TVS from 22/4/90) mus (2nd ser) by
   NIGEL HESS *see COLLECTIONS 191,192*
PERFECT STATE, A (BBC1 27/2/97) mus: MICHAEL STOREY..*NA*
PERFECT STRANGERS (USA TV) *see COLLECTIONS 344,373*
PERFORMANCE (1970) Music score: JACK NITZSCHE Songs by
   RANDY NEWMAN-RY COODER-MERRY CLAYTON-BUFFY SAINTE
   MARIE-LAST POETS -S/T- *WB (WEA): 7599 26400-2 (CD)*
PERFECT STRANGERS (USA TV) *see COLLECTIONS 344,373*

PERILS OF PENELOPE PITSTOP *see COLLECTION 370*
PERRY MASON *see COLLECTION 100,101,109,246,339,360*
PERSUADERS The (ITV 17/9/71-72) theme mus: JOHN BARRY
  *see COLLECTIONS 2,4,21,26,109,168,357*
PET POWER (Meridian 14/1/97) music: ANDREW DAVIES....*NA*
PET SEMATARY (1989) Music sco: ELLOIT GOLDENTHAL -S/T-
  *VARESE (Pinn): VSD 5227 (CD)*
PETE KELLY'S BLUES (USA TV) *see COLLECTION 342*
PETER AND THE WOLF (1996) SERGEI PROKOFIEV *feat.voices*
  KIRSTIE ALLEY-ROSS MALINDER-LLOYD BRIDGES *with the*
  RCA SYMPHONY ORCHESTRA (cond;Daughterty)
  *RCA VICTOR Gold Seal (BMG): 74321 31869-2 (CD)*
PETER GUNN (USA 58) theme music: HENRY MANCINI
  TV -S/T- *FRESH SOUNDS (Disc): FSCD 2009 (CD) also*
  'MORE MUSIC FROM PETER GUNN' Henry Mancini on
  *RCA Victor (BMG): 74321 29857-2 (CD)*
  *see COLLECTIONS 108,168,243,340,352*
PETER PAN *see WALT DISNEY INDEX p.343*
PETER PAN (ORIG LONDON CAST 1994) *featuring:*
  RON MOODY-NICOLA STAPLETON & Company
  *FIRST NIGHT (Pinn): CASTCD 46 (CD) CASTC 46 (MC)*
PETER PAN (The British Musical) ORIG CAST RECORDING
  *EMI (EMI): CDEMC 3696 (CD)*
PETER PAN (ORIG USA TV PROD 54) Music (Moose Charlap)
  Lyr (Carolyn Leigh) add.mus/songs (Leonard Bernst
  tein Jule Styne-Bette Comden-Adolph Green) *feat:*
  MARY MARTIN *RCA (S.Screen): 3762-2(CD) 3762-4(MC)*
PETER PRINCIPAL The (BBC1 2/6/97) music score by
  MARK RUSSELL *unavailable*
PETER'S FRIENDS (1992) The Album (Various Artists)
  *EPIC (Sony): MOODCD 27 (CD) MOODC 27 (MC)*
  *see COLLECTIONS 78,171,262,276*
PETE'S DRAGON - *see WALT DISNEY INDEX p.343*
PETTICOAT JUNCTION )USA TV) *see COLLECTION 339*
PEYTON PLACE (USA) *see COLLECTIONS 168,343,367,389*
PHAEDRA (1961) Music score: MIKIS THEODORAKIS -S/T- on
  *Sakkaris Imprt (Pinn): SR 50060 (CD)*
PHANTOM The (1996) Music score: DAVID NEWMAN -S/T- on
  *MILAN (BMG): 74321 39325-2 (CD)*
PHANTOM: The American Musical Sensation (O.CAST 1993)
  Songs (Maury YESTON) *feat:* Glory Crampton-Richard
  White-Paul Schoeffler-Jack Dabdoub and Company
  *RCA Victor (BMG): 09026 61660-2 (CD)*
PHANTOM OF THE OPERA (1) songs by Andrew Lloyd Webber
  Charles Hart and Richard Stilgoe
  1.ORIG LONDON CAST 1986 *with:* MICHAEL CRAWFORD-SARAH
    BRIGHTMAN & Company *POLYDOR: 831 273-2 (2CD) also*
  2.HIGHLIGHTS *831563-2(CD) -5(DCC) POLH(C) 33(MC/LP)*
  3.STUDIO RECORD 1993 *w:*GRAHAM BICKLEY-JOHN BARROWMAN
    CLAIRE BURT Munich Symph Orch (John Owen Edwards)
    <u>Highlights</u>: *SHOWTIME (MCI-THE): SHOW(CD)(MC) 002*
    <u>Complete</u>: *TER (Disc): CDTEM 1207 (CD)*

*Continued next page...*

    4. CARLTON SHOWS COLL.1993 Studio Record w:PAUL JONES
       STEPHANIE LAWRENCE-CARL WAYNE-FIONA HENDLEY & Comp
       *CARLTON: PWKS 4164 (CD) PWKMC 4164 (MC)*
       *also contains songs from 'ASPECTS OF LOVE'*
    5. CLASSIC MUSICALS SERIES *feat:*GRAHAM BICKLEY-CLAIRE
       MOORE-JOHN BARROWMAN-MUNICH SYMPH.ORCH+ *songs from*
       'CATS' *KOCH Int: 34078-2 (CD)*
PHANTOM OF THE OPERA (2) ORIG STAGE MUSICAL 1992 Lyrics
    by KEN HILL with add.Music.by ALASDAIR MacNEILL and
    set to Music by VERDI-DONIZETTI-GOUNOD-MOZART-OFFEN
    BACH and BIZET / *Directed by* KEN HILL *and featuring*
    Christina Collier-Richard Tate-Michael McLean-Peter
    Straker (Phantom)-Steven Pacey-Haluk Bilginer-Toni
    Palmer-Reginald Marsh-Tracy Gillman-Jacquel.Barron
    *D.SHARP (Pinn): DSHCD 7005 (CD) DSHMC 7005 (MC)*
PHANTOM OF THE OPERA (3) (1925 FILM *featur.*LON CHANEY)
    1. (1996 restoration) Music by Carl Davis conducting
       The CITY of PRAGUE PHILHARMONIC, organ: JOHN BIRCH
       *SILVA SCREEN (Koch): FILMCD 193 (CD)*
    2. (Studio Recording 1995) music by Rick Wakeman on
       'Phantom Power' *AMBIENT (AMT): A10M2(CD) A10MC2(MC)*
    3. (1977 version) Music: Gaylord Carter organ 'Mighty
       Wurlitzer' *NEW WORLD (Conifer): NW 227 (LP) deleted*
PHANTOM OF THE OPERA (1989 FILM feat: Robert Englund)
    Symphonic music score by Mischa Segal -S/T- on
    *SILVA SCREEN (Koch): FILMCD 069 (CD)*
PHANTOM OF THE OPERA ON ICE (1996) Mus: ROBERTO DANOVA
    -S/T- *Roberto Danova-PLAZA (Pinn): PZA 008(CD(MC)*
PHAT BEACH (1996) -S/T- *EDEL (Pinn): 0022622CIN (CD)*

PHENOMENA aka CREEPERS (1984) Music by IRON MAIDEN
    SIMON BOSWELL TURNER-BILL WYMAN-GOBLIN-MOTORHEAD
    *CINEVOX ITALY (Silva Screen): CDCIA 5062 (CD)*
    *also DCMDF 303 (CD) see COLLECTION 312*
PHENOMENON (1996) Music score: THOMAS NEWMAN -S/T-
    *REPRISE (WEA): 9362 46360-2 (CD)*
PHIL KAY FEELS..(C4 19/4/97) m: GREG WHITE *unavailable*
PHILADELPHIA (1994) Music score: HOWARD SHORE opening
    song by BRUCE SPRINGSTEEN 2 Soundtracks available
    -S/T- Songs *EPIC (SM): 474998-2(CD) -4(MC) -8(MD)*
    -S/T- Score *EPIC (SM): 475800-2(CD) 4(MC) delet*
    *see COLLECTIONS 65,139,171,276*
PHILADELPHIA EXPERIMENT The (1984) Mus: KEN WANNBERG
    -S/T- *also contains score from 'MOTHER LODE' on*
    *PROMETHEUS (S.Screen): PCD 121(CD) see COLLECT.268*
PHILADELPHIA STORY The (1940) Music score: FRANZ WAXMAN
    *see COLLECTION 393*
PHOENIX AND THE CARPET The (BBC1 16/11/97) Music score
    by PAUL HART *unavailable*
PIAF (ORIG LONDON CAST 1994) *featuring* ELAINE PAIGE
    *WB (WEA): 4509 94641-2 (CD) -4 (MC)*
PIANO The (1993) Music score: MICHAEL NYMAN -S/T- on
    *VENTURE-VIRGIN (EMI): CD(TC)VE 919 (CD/MC)*
    *see also COLLECTIONS 62,65,139,171,324*

PICKWICK THE MUSICAL CHICHESTER FESTIVAL THEATRE 1993
    Songs (Cyril ORNADEL-Leslie BRICUSSE) *featuring:*
    HARRY SECOMBE-ALEXANDRA BASTEDO-ROY CASTLE-RUTH
    MADOC-GLYN HOUSTON-DAVID CARDY-MICHAEL HOWE & Comp
    <u>Highlights</u>: *SHOWTIME (MCI-THE): SHOW(CD(MC) 023*
    <u>Complete</u>: *TER (Disc): CDTER 1205 (CD)*
    <u>Classic Musicals series</u> *feat:* HARRY SECOMBE
    RUTH MADOC-ROY CASTLE-DAVID CARDY-ROBERT MEADMORE
    *+ songs from* 'SCROOGE' *KOCH INT: 34081-2 (CD)*
PICNIC (1956) Music sco: GEORGE DUNING -S/T- *MCA USA*
    *Import (Silva Screen): MCAD 31357 (CD)*
    *see also COLLECTIONS 204,218*
PICNIC AT HANGING ROCK *see COLLECTIONS 76,263*
PICTURE BRIDE (1995) Music score: CLIFF EIDELMAN
    -S/T- *VARESE (Pinn): VSD 5651 (CD)*
PICTURE PARADE (BBC 1950s) *see COLLECTION 381*
PIE IN THE SKY (BBC1 13/3/94) music theme and score by
    COLIN TOWNS *unavailable*
PILGRIM'S REST (BBC1 31/7/97) theme music composed by
    COLIN WINSTON-FLETCHER *unavailable*
PILLOW BOOK The (1996) Music score: BRIAN ENO -S/T- on
    *XIII BIS (Discovery): LBS 197101 (CD)*
PILLOW TALK (1959) Mus sco: FRANK DE VOL -S/T- *feat*
    DORIS DAY *Bear Family (Topic/Proj): BCD 15913 2CD*
PINGU (BBC1 27/9/91) theme music *see COLLECTION 60*
PINK PANTHER The (TV BBC1-2 USA 64) theme music: HENRY
    MANCINI 'In The Pink' *RCA (BMG): 74321 24283-2 CD*
    *see COLLECTION 109,243,340,352,358*
PINK PANTHER The (FILM 1963) Mus: HENRY MANCINI *-S/T-*
    *(SPECIAL AUDIO LP EDITION) Import (VIVANTI dist)*
    *AUDIOLP LSP 2795 (LP Audio Quality) -S/T- also on*
    *RCA: ND(NK) 80832 (CD/MC)*
PINKY AND PERKY (BBC 60's) Song compilation on *EMI:*
    *CD(TC)EMS 1470 (CD/MC)*
PINOCCHIO (1939) M: LEIGH HARLINE-P.SMITH-N.WASHINGTON
    -S/T- *DISNEY (B.Vista): WD 75430-2 (CD) -4 (MC)*
    *see also* WALT DISNEY INDEX p.343
PINOCCHIO (1996) Music sco: RACHEL PORTMAN -S/T- *feat:*
    STEVIE WONDER-JERRY HADLEY & SISSEL and BRIAN MAY
    *DECCA (Polyg): 452 740-2 (CD) -4 (MC)*
PIRATES OF PENZANCE (operetta) songs by W.S.Gilbert
    and A.Sullivan
   1.D'OYLY CARTE OPERA COMPANY 1989 STUDIO RECORDING
    *with:* MARILYN HILL SMITH and Company
    <u>Highlights</u>: *SHOWTIME (MCI-THE): SHOW(CD)(MC) 010*
    <u>Complete</u>:*TER (Disc): CDTER2 (ZCTED)1177 (2CD/MC)*
   2.PRO-ARTE ORCHEST (Malcolm Sargent) and GLYNDEBOURNE
    FESTIVAL CHOIR Soloists:George Baker-James Milligan
    John Cameron-Richard Lewis *EMI: CMS 764409-2 (2CDs)*
   3.D'OYLY CARTE OPERA COMP with R.P.O. cond: I.Godfrey
    *LONDON (Poly): 425 196-2 (CDx2) 425 196-4 (MC)*
PISTOL FOR RINGO A - *see under* 'DEATH RIDES A HORSE'
PIXIE AND DIXIE - *see COLLECTION 370*
PLANET ISLAM (BBC2 3/8/97) title mus: DAVID STEVENS..*NA*

PLANET OF THE APES (1968) Music score: JERRY GOLDSMITH
    score on *VARESE (Pinn): VSD 5848 (CD)*
PLANET SHOWBIZ (C4 30/4/97) title music: DAVID BALL and
    INGO VAUK / incid. music by SIMON BRINT *unavailable*
PLATOON 1.(1986) Mus: GEORGES DELERUE (rejected orig
    score) *PROMETHEUS (Silva Screen): PCD 136 (CD)*
    *also contains complete score 'SALVADOR'*
PLATOON 2. (1986) Music: GEORGES DELERUE Main theme
    'Adagio For Strings' (Samuel BARBER) Vancouver S.O.
    -S/T- *ATLANTIC (WEA): 781 742-2(CD) WX 95(MC) see*
    *COLLECTIONS 65,68,97,116,139,169,171,258,361,384*
PLATOON LEADER (1988) Music score: GEORGE S.CLINTON
    -S/T- *CRESCENDO (S.Screen): GNPD 8013 (CD)*
PLAY AWAY / PLAY SCHOOL (BBC1-2 / 1964-88) *Songs from*
    *both series featuring* Jonathan Cohen-Brian Cant-Don
    Spencer-Johnny Ball-Rick Jones-Lucie Skeaping-Carol
    Chell-Floella Benjamin-Lionel Morton-Toni Arthur-Jo
    hnny Silvo-Chloe Ashcroft / *MFP: TC-DL 1114 (2MC)*
PLAY ON! (ORIG BROADWAY CAST RECORDING) featuring the
    songs of DUKE ELLINGTON in 'TWELFTH NIGHT' setting
    ORIG BROADWAY CAST *VARESE (Pinn): VSD 5837 (CD)*
PLAY YOUR CARDS RIGHT (Talbot TV/LWT/The Sun 18/3/94)
    theme: ALYN AINSWORTH  *see COLLECTION 33*
PLAYDAYS: Lizzie Singalong (BBC) *BBC (Pinn): YBBC 1490*
    *theme on Coll 'TV TUNES FOR KIDS' see Coll / also*
    *avail:* 'PLAYDAYS LIVE ON STAGE' *BMG Kidz: 74321*
    *24486-4 (MC)* PLAYDAYS (BBC2) CHRISTMAS SONGS AND
    STORIES *LFP (EMI): LFPK 2019 (MC) see COLLECT 60*
PLAYER The (1991) Music score: THOMAS NEWMAN -S/T-
    *VARESE USA (Pinn): VSD 5366 (CD)*
PLAYING GOD (1998) Music score: RICHARD HARTLEY -S/T-
    *MILAN (catalogue number to be confirmed)*
PLEASE SAVE MY EARTH  (Japan 1995) Animated MANGA Film
    -S/T- *ANIMAMGA-New Note (Pinn): AM 6 (CD)*
PLEASE SIR (LWT 68) theme music: SAM FONTEYN
    *see COLLECTIONS 3,360*
PLOTLANDS (BBC1 18/5/97) Music: JOHN KEANE *unavailable*
PLYMOUTH ADVENTURE (1952) Music score: MIKLOS ROZSA
    -S/T- *TSUNAMI Imp (Silva Screen): TSU 0132 (CD)*
POCAHONTAS (1995) Music score: ALAN MENKEN Songs (Alan
    MENKEN-Stephen SCHWARTZ) including "Colours Of The
    Wind" sung: VANESSA WILLIAMS -S/T- *DISNEY Records*
    -S/T- *W.DISNEY (B.Vista): WDR 75462-2 (CD) -4 (MC)*
    *Sing-A-Long: Walt Disney: DISCD(MC) 481 (CD/MC)* /
    Story and Song: *Disney: PDC 316 (CD) see also*
    WALT DISNEY INDEX p.343
POINT BREAK (1991) Music: MARK ISHAM + JIMI HENDRIX
    PIL-RATT-LA GUNS-WESTWORLD-LIQUID JESUS-WIRETRAIN
    *re-iss: MCA GEFFEN (BMG): MCLD 19327 (CD)*
POINT OF NO RETURN - see under 'ASSASSIN, The'
POINT The (1970) Music and songs by NILSSON / reissue
    *EDSEL (Pinn): EDCD 340 (CD) ED 40 (LP) deleted*
POINTS OF VIEW (BBC 2/10/61-98) 1991-98 theme by the
    BBC Radiophonic Workshop *unavailable*

POIROT *see under* 'AGATHA CHRISTIE'S POIROT'
   *see also COLLECTIONS 5,138,175,388*
POLDARK (BBC1 5/10/75) theme mus: KENYON EMRYS-ROBERTS
   *see COLLECTION 2*
POLDARK (HTV 2/10/96) Music theme and incidental
   music by IAN HUGHES *unavailable*
POLICE ACTION LIVE! (ITN-Carlton ITV 18/11/95) music
   by DAVID HEWSON *unavailable*
POLICE CAMERA ACTION (Carlton 4/10/95) / POLICE STOP!
   (Carlton 2/1/95) music by DAVID LOWE *unavailable*
POLICE SQUAD (USA) *see COLLECTIONS 110,344*
POLICE STORY (USA) *see COLLECTIONS 12,343,379*
POLICE WOMAN (USA) *see COLLECTIONS 100,101,246,343,379*
POLITICIAN'S WIFE The (C4 16/5/95|) music: BARRINGTON
   PHELOUNG on compilation 'PASSION OF MORSE' also inc
   'Inspector Morse'/'Truly Madly Deeply'/'Saint-Ex'
   *TRING INT (Tring): TRING 003 (CD) MCTRING 003 (MC)*
POLTERGEIST (1982) Music score: JERRY GOLDSMITH -S/T-
   *reissue: EMI SOUNDTRACKS (EMI): 821 957-2 (CD)*
   *see COLLECTIONS 61,210,355*
POPEYE (USA Cart 40s) theme song "I'm Popeye The Sailor
   Man" (Sammy Lerner) *see COLLECTION 339*
POPPIE NON GENA (MUSICAL 83) JOE BOYD / ORIG S.AFRICAN
   CAST *reissued May 96 HANNIBAL-RYKODISK (Vital):
   HNCD 1351 (CD) HNBC 1351 (MC)*
PORGY AND BESS - songs by George and Ira Gershwin
                              with DuBose Heyward
   1.FILM MUSICAL 1959  DOROTHY DANDRIDGE-SIDNEY POITIER
     -S/T- *SONY Europe (Discovery): CD 70007 (CD)*
   2.Studio HIGHLIGHTS *w* LEONTYNE PRICE-WILLIAM WARFIELD
     JOHN W.BUBBLES-McHENRY BOATWRIGHT.+Symphonic Dances
     to WEST SIDE STORY  *RCA (BMG): 74321 24218-2 (CD)*
   3.ORIG BROADWAY CAST 1942 *w:* Todd Duncan-Anne Brown-
     Edward Matthews-Helen Dowdy *MCA (BMG):MCLD 19158 CD*
   4.GLYNDEBOURNE FESTIVAL OPERA 1988 WILLARD WHITE-CYNT
     HIA HAYMON-DAMON EVANS-BRUCE HUBBARD-L.P.O.(Simon
     Rattle) *EMI ANGEL: CDS 556 220-2 (3CDs-Complete) or
     LDB 491 131-2 (2CDs) or CDC 754 325-2 (Highlights)*
   5.Houston Grand Opera: DONNIE RAY ALBERT-CLAMMA DALE
     ANDREW SMITH-WILMA SHAKESNIDER-BETTY LANE and Comp
     Complete Rec: *RCA Red Seal (BMG): RD 82109 (3 CDs)*
     Highlights Only: *RCA Red Seal (BMG): RD 84680 (CD)*
   6.STUDIO HIGHLIGHTS (1975) *with* WILLARD WHITE-BARBARA
     HENDRICKS and Comp with CLEVELAND ORCH & CHOIR cond
     LORIN MAAZEL *DECCA (Poly): 436 306-2DH (CD)*
PORKPIE (C4 13/11/95) theme music: TRIX WORRELL & JOHN
   COLLIN / incid.music by JOHN COLLINS *unavailable*
PORRIDGE (BBC1 5/9/74) theme music: MAX HARRIS
   *see COLLECTION 229*
PORTERHOUSE BLUE (C4 3/6/87) Title theme by Rick Lloyd
   sung by FLYING PICKETTS *see COLLECTION 6*
PORTRAIT OF A LADY (1996) Music score: WOJCIECH KILAR
   plus additional music by FRANZ SCHUBERT -S/T- on
   *DECCA (Poly): 455 011-2 (CD) -4 (MC)*

POSTMAN PAT (BBC1 from 5/7/82-1996) music: BRYAN DALY
    narrated and sung by KEN BARRIE *POST MUSIC (Pinn):*
    *PPCD 101 (CD) PMC 101 (MC)* also available with
    KEN BARRIE-CAROL BOYD *BBC (Pinn): YBBC 1491 (MC)*
    VOL.2 *POST MUS (Pinn):PPCD 102 (CD) PPMC 102 (MC)*
    *see COLLECTION 60*
POSTMAN PAT (MUSICAL VERSION OF ANIMATED TV SERIES)
    *EPIC (Sony Music): 480 686-4 (MC)*
POSTMAN The (Il Postino) (95) Mus score: LUIS E.BACALOV
    -S/T- *POLYDOR (Poly): 162209-2 (CD)* also available
    -S/T- *HOLLYWOOD (Silva Screen): HW 62029-2 (CD)*
POT BLACK / JUNIOR POT BACK (BBC2 72-86) "Black & White
    Rag" (George Botsford) WINIFRED ATWELL *PRESIDENT:*
    *PLCD 531 (CD) (TC)PLE 531 see also COLLECTION 167*
POTTER'S WHEEL (BBC 1950's) *see COLLECTIONS 137,163*
POWAQQATSI (1988) Music score: PHILIP GLASS -S/T- on
    *ELEKTRA NONESUCH (WEA): 7559 79192-2 (CD) -4(MC)*
POWDER (1995) Music score: JERRY GOLDSMITH
    -S/T- *Import (Silva Screen): HW 20384-2 (CD)*
    *also available via European Music Services (EMS)*
POWER GAME The (ITV 65) theme music: CYRIL STAPLETON
    *see COLLECTIONS 3,364,372*
POWER The (1967) Music score: MIKLOS ROZSA Suite + mus
    ic from 'BEN HUR'/'KING OF KINGS' 12 choral pieces
    *PROMETHEUS (Silva Screen): PCD 122 (CD)*
PRAYER FOR THE DYING A (1988) Orig score: JOHN SCOTT
    *(replaced by BILL CONTI score)* - John Scott version
    available on *JOS (Silva Screen): JSCD 102*
    *(CD)* inc John Scott's score 'WINTER PEOPLE' (1989)
PREACHER'S WIFE The (1996) Music sco: HANS ZIMMER songs
    comp/produced by Annie LENNOX/David FOSTER/Trevor
    HORN/BABYFACE and performed by WHITNEY HOUSTON
    -S/T- *ARISTA (BMG): 07822 18951-2 (CD) -4 (MC)*
PREACHING TO THE PEVERTED (1997) Various Arts -S/T- on
    *NAKED (Pinn): PERVCDLP 001 (CD) PERVMCLP 001 (MC)*
PREDATOR - on COLL 'UNIVERSAL SOLDIER' *deleted*
PREDATOR 2 (1990) Music score: ALAN SILVESTRI -S/T- on
    *VARESE (Pinn): VSD 5302 (CD)*
PRELUDE TO A KISS (1992) Music sco: HOWARD SHORE -S/T-
    *MILAN (BMG): 11125-2 (CD) 11125-4 (MC)*
PRESIDENCY (BBC2 23/2/97) music: GUY SIGSWORTH.......*NA*
PRESTON FRONT (BBC1 16/7/95) theme song "Here I Stand"
    sung by The MILLTOWN BROTHERS on album 'Slinky'
    *A.& M. (Poly): 395 346-2 (CD) 395 346-4 (MC)*
PRESUMED INNOCENT (1990) Music score: JOHN WILLIAMS
    -S/T- *VARESE (Pinn): VSD 5280 (CD)*
PRET-A-PORTER (1994) Music: INA KAMOZE-TERENCE TRENT D'
    ARBY-CRANBERRIES-M.PEOPLE-JANET JACKSON etc.-S/T-on
    *COLUMBIA (Sony): 478 226-2 (CD) see COLLECT.17,356*
PRETTY IN PINK (1986) Music score: MICHAEL GORE songs by
    V/A  -S/T- *A.& M.(Poly): (C)(CD)MID 157 (MC/CD)*
PRETTY WOMAN (1989) Music sco JAMES NEWTON HOWARD -S/T-
    *EMI USA (EMI): CDP 793492-2 (CD) TCMTL 1052 (MC)*
    *see also COLLECTIONS 28,74,97,139,171,274*

PRETTYBELLE (ORIG USA STAGE CAST) Songs by JULE STYNE
    *feat* ANGELA LANSBURY *VARESE (Pinn): VSD 5439 (CD)*
PRIDE AND PREJUDICE (BBC1 24/9/95) orig mus.composed
    and conducted by CARL DAVIS -S/T- *featuring*
    MELVYN TAN (fortepiano) on *EMI: CDEMC 3726 (CD)*
    *TCEMC 3276 (MC)* or *EMI: 72438 36090-2 / -4*
PRIDE AND THE PASSION The (1957) Music: GEORGE ANTHEIL
    *with* 'AGONY & THE ECSTASY' (ALEX NORTH) 75m
    *CLOUD NINE (BMG-Con): CNS 5001 (CD)*
PRIMAL FEAR (1996) Music sco: JAMES NEWTON HOWARD -S/T-
    *MILAN (BMG): 74321 35545-2 (CD)*
PRIME SUSPECT (Gran 7/4/91) (2) 15/12/92 (3) 19/12/93)
    theme music: STEPHEN WARBECK *deleted*
PRINCE AMONG ISLANDS, A (ITV 10/5/92) mus CAPERCAILLIE
    "Coisich A Ruin" featuring KAREN MATHIESON
    *see COLLECTION 303* also -S/T- selection on
    *SURVIVAL (BMG): ZT 45394 (MC)*
PRINCE AMONG MEN, A (BBC1 15/9/97) m: JAMIE MARSHALL.*NA*
PRINCE AND THE PAUPER The (1937) Music sco: ERICH WOLFG
    ANG KORNGOLD performed by BRANDENBURG PHILHARMONIC
    ORCH (William T.Stromberg) *also feat* 'ADVENTURES OF
    MARK TWAIN' (STEINER) *RCA (BMG): 09026 62660-2 (CD)*
PRINCE AND THE SHOWGIRL 1957 *see COLL* RICHARD ADDINSELL
PRINCE OF DARKNESS (1988) Music: JOHN CARPENTER & ALAN
    HOWARTH -S/T- *VARESE (Pinn): VCD 47310 (CD)*
PRINCE VALIANT (1954) Music sco: FRANZ WAXMAN *see Coll*
    'SUNSET BOULEVARD' *RCA (BMG): RD 87017 (CD)*
PRINCESS BRIDE The (1987) Music score: MARK KNOPFLER
    -S/T- *VERTIGO: VERH 53C (MC) 832864-2 (CD)*
PRINCESS CARABOO (1994) Music: RICHARD HARTLEY -S/T-
    *VARESE (Pinn): VSD 5544 (CD)*
PRISCILLA: QUEEN OF THE DESERT (1994) Mus: GUY CROSS
    -S/T- *MOTHER (Poly): 516937-2 (CD) 516937-4 (MC)*
PRISONER The (C4 23/9/92 prev:19/9/83 orig:ITV 29/9/67)
    Music by RON GRAINER & Albert Elms etc. *S.Screen
    (Koch): FILMCD 042* (Vol.1) *FILMCD 084* (Vol.2 feat
    music of Philip Green-Robert Farnon-J.S.Petit +
    "The Age Of Elegance") *FILMCD 126* (Vol.3). addit.
    item 'PRISONER THEME"+'DANGER MAN' (Edwin Astley)
    & "DRY BONES" (Four Lads) *BAM CARUSO (Rev-APT):
    NRIC 112 (CDs) see also COLLECTIONS 7,109,357*
PRISONER CELL BLOCK H (Australia 79-87)(UK 84-93) theme
    "On The Inside" (Alan Caswell) sung LYNNE HAMILTON
    *see COLLECTION 367*
PRISONERS OF CONSCIENCE (BBC2 27/11/89) theme "Fragile"
    (G.Sumner) STING from 'Nothing Like The Sun'
    *A.& M. CDA 6402 (CD) AMA 6402 (LP) AMC 6402 (MC)*
PRIVATE LIVES OF ELIZABETH AND ESSEX *see COLLECT.332*
PRIVATE PARTS (1996) Score: VAN DYKE PARKS -S/T- V.Arts
    *W.BROS (WEA): 9362 46477-2 (CD)*
PRIZZI'S HONOR (1987) Music score: ALEX NORTH
    *see COLLECTIONS 72,277*
PRODUCERS The (1968,Mel Brooks) music sco: JOHN MORRIS
    -S/T- + dialogue *RAZOR & TIE (Koch): RE 2147 (CD)*

PROFESSIONAL The - see 'LEON'
PROFESSIONALS The (LWT 30/12/77-1983/Granada+ 15/2/97)
    theme: LAURIE JOHNSON. LAURIE JOHNSON'S LONDON BIG
    BAND *VIRGIN (EMI): VSCDT 1643 (CDs) VST 1643 (12")*
    *see also COLLECTIONS 5,138,175,294,357,360*
PROFESSIONALS The (1966) Music sco: MAURICE JARRE -S/T-
    *SILVA TREASURY (Koch): SSD 5002 (CD)*
PROFIT (BBC2 9/11/97) theme mus: MIKE POST *unavailable*
PROFUNDO ROSSO (Horror Film) Music score: GOBLIN -S/T-
    *CINEVOX (S.Screen) CIAK 75005 (MC) CIA 5005 (LP)*
PROMISED LAND The (BBC2 22/9/96)Mus: TERENCE BLANCHARD
    -S/T- *Columbia (Sony): 478 585-2 (2CD) -4 (2MC)*
PROOF (1991) Music comp/perf. by NOT DROWNING WAVING
    -S/T- *ALHAMBRA Imp (S.Screen): A.8927 (CD) deleted*
PROPRIETOR The (1995) Music score: RICHARD ROBBINS
    -S/T- (V.Art) *EPIC Sony: 486 673-2 (CD) delet.97*
PROSPERO'S BOOKS (1991) Music: MICHAEL NYMAN -S/T-
    *PHILIPS (Polyg): 425224-2 (CD) 425224-4 (MC)*
PROTECTORS The (ITC orig 29/9/72) theme music "Avenues
    & Alleyways" (Mitch Murray-Pete Callander) sung by
    TONY CHRISTIE *MCA (BMG): MCLD(MCLC) 19204 (CD/MC)*
    *see COLLECTIONS 2,357,358*
PROVOS: IRA AND SINN FEIN (BBC2 23/9/97) theme music:
    DAVID FERGUSON *unavilable*
PSYCHO (1960) Music sco: BERNARD HERRMANN NATIONAL PHI
    LHARMONIC ORCH (B.Herrmann) Studio Recording on
    *UNICORN KANCHANA (H.Mundi): UKCD 2021 (CD)*
    new recording by ROYAL SCOTTISH NATIONAL ORCH cond,
    Joel McNEELY *VARESE (Pinn): VSD 5765 (CD)*
    *see COLLECT.61,63,187,189,190,194,195,196,355,404*
PSYCHODERELICT (Rock Opera 93) Songs: PETER TOWNSHEND
    *ATLANTIC/EAST WEST (WEA): 7567 82494-2(CD) -4(MC)*
PUBLIC EYE (1992) Music score: MARK ISHAM -S/T-
    *VARESE (Pinn): VSD 5374 (CD) VSC 5374 (MC)*
PULP FICTION (1993) Music by Various Artists -S/T- on
    *MCA (BMG): MCD 11103 (CD) MCC 11103 (MC)*
    *see COLLECTIONS 28,134,259,260,356,361*
PUMP UP THE VOLUME (1990) -S/T- feat: CONCRETE BLONDE
    "Everybody Knows" (L.Cohen) - COWBOY JUNKIES-SONIC
    YOUTH-PIXIES-LIQUID JESUS-SOUND GARDEN -S/T- reiss
    *MCA (BMG): MCD 06121 (CD)*
PURE COUNTRY (1992) Music comp/perf. by GEORGE STRAIT
    -S/T- *MCA (BMG): MCD 10651 (CD) MCC 10651 (MC)*
PURPLE RAIN (1984) Music: PRINCE & REVOLUTION -S/T-
    *WB (WEA): 759 925 110-2 (CD) -4 (MC) -5 (DCC)*
PURSUIT (USA) *see COLLECTION 12*
PUSHER (1997) Music score: PETER PETER-POVI KRISTIAN
    -S/T- VARIOUS ARTISTS *MCA (BMG): MCD 85013 (CD)*
PUTTING IT TOGETHER (O.USA CAST 1993) Songs (Stephen
    SONDHEIM) *featuring* JULIE ANDREWS-STEPHEN COLLINS
    CHRISTOPHER DURANG-MICHAEL RUPERT-RACHEL YORK & Co
    *RCA (BMG): 09026 61729-2 (CD) -4 (MC) see COLLECT*
PYROMANIAC'S LOVE STORY, A (1994) Music score: RACHEL
    PORTMAN -S/T- *VARESE (Pinn): VSD 5620 (CD)*

**Q** MILLIGAN (BBC2 5/9/93) "Q Theme": SPIKE MILLIGAN on
    'BRITISH COMEDY CLASSICS' *EMI: ECC 7 (2MC)*
Q THE WINGED SERPENT (1982) Music sco: ROBERT O.RAGLAND
    -S/T- *reiss: CAM (SSD): CSE 800128 (CD)*
QB VII (74 Mini-series) Music by JERRY GOLDSMITH -S/T-
    *INTRADA (S.Screen): MAF 7061D (CD)*
QUADROPHENIA (1979) Songs: PETE TOWNSHEND Feat The WHO
    *POLYDOR (Polyg):  813 074-2 (2CD's) also available*
    -S/T- *POLYDOR (Poly): 519 999-2 (CD)*
QUANTUM LEAP (USA 89)(BBC2 13/2/90) theme: MIKE POST
    -S/T- *GNP (S.Screen) GNPD 8036(CD) GNP-5 8036(MC)*
    *see COLLECTIONS 12,345*
QUATERMASS AND THE PIT *see COLLECTION 288*
QUATERMASS EXPERIMENT The (1955) Music: JAMES BERNARD
    *see COLLECTIONS 119 /* BBC TV ser.Main theme "Mars"
    'Planets Suite' HOLST - *see COLLECTION 402*
QUATERMASS II (1957) Music sco: JAMES BERNARD *see COLL*
    'DEVIL RIDES OUT' *SILVA SCREEN: FILMCD 174 (CD)*
    *see also COLLECTION 6,119*
QUEEN MARGOT (La Reine Margot) (1994) Music sco: GORAN
    BREGOVICH "Elohi" performed by OFRA HAZA -S/T- Imp
    *(SILVA SCREEN): 522 655-2 (CD)*
QUEEN'S NOSE The (BBC1 15/11/95) music composed and
    and conducted by CARL DAVIS *unavailable*
QUEIMADA - see BURN
QUEST (1996) Music score: RANDY EDELMAN -S/T- on
    *VARESE (Pinn): VSD 5716 (CD)*
QUESTION OF SPORT, A (BBC1 1970-98) current theme by
    RICHIE CLOSE *see COLLECTIONS 155,167*
    Competition Music "There Are More Questions Than
    Answers" JOHNNY NASH 'Gr.Hits' *EPIC 465306-2 (CD)*
QUESTION TIME (BBC1 25/9/79-98) theme music composed
    by STANLEY MYERS *unavailable*
QUICK AND THE DEAD The (1994) Music sco: ALAN SILVESTRI
    -S/T- *VARESE (Pinn): VSD 5595 (CD)*
QUICK DRAW McGRAW  (USA TV) *see COLLECTIONS 342,370*
QUICKSILVER (1986) Music sco: TONY BANKS + music 'Lorca
    & The Outlaws' *Charisma (VIRGIN): CASCD 1173 (CD)*
QUIET AMERICAN The (1958) Music score: MARIO NASCIMBENE
    -S/T- +scores *'ROOM AT THE TOP'/'BAREFOOT CONTESSA'*
    *DRG (Pinn): DRGCD 32961 (CD)  also COLLECTION 266*
QUIEN SABE - see under 'BULLET FOR THE GENERAL'
QUIET MAN The (1952) Music sco: VICTOR YOUNG *complete*
    *orig score* DUBLIN SCREEN ORCH (K.Alwyn) *SCANNAN*
    *(Koch): SFC 1501 (CD) also inc* 'SAMSON & DELILAH'
    *VARESE: VSD 5497 (CD) see COLLECTIONS 63,307,394*
QUIGLEY DOWN UNDER (1990) Music score: BASIL POLEDOURIS
    -S/T- *INTRADA (S.Screen): MAF 7006(D)(C) (CD/MC)*
QUINCY (USA 76) theme mus: GLEN A.LARSON-STU PHILLIPS
    *see COLLECTIONS 168,341*
QUITE CONTRARY (BBC) *see COLLECTION 1*
QUO VADIS (1951) Music sco: MIKLOS ROZSA *DECCA (Poly)*
    *421265-4 (MC) / theme* TER: (Con) (CD)(ZC)TER 1135
    *see also COLLECTIONS 63,296*

RAB C.NESBITT (BBC2 27/9/90) series theme music by
    DAVID McNIVEN *unavailable*
RACE FOR THE YANKEE ZEPHYR (1981) / SURVIVOR (1980)  M:
    BRIAN MAY *ONEMONE (S.Screen):1MI 1008 (CD)*
RACHEL RACHEL (1968) Music score: JEROME MOROSS
    *see COLECTION 377*
RACING FROM AINTREE (BBC1 5/4/90) theme "The Mission"
    ENNIO MORRICONE *see* FILMS & SHOWS 'THE MISSION'
RADIO GALS (ORIG USA CAST RECORD)
    *VARESE (Pinn): VSD 5604 (CD)*
RAG NYMPH The (ITV 3/10/97) Music score: COLIN TOWNS.*NA*
RAGE OF THE HEART (ORIG CONCEPT ALBUM) Songs (Enrico
    Garzilli) *feat* MICHAEL BALL and JANET MOONEY
    *FIRST NIGHT (Pinn): OCRCD 6025 (CD)*
RAGING BULL (1980) "Intermezzo" 'Cavalleria Rusticana'
    (MASCAGNI) *see COLLECTIONS 65,70,276*
RAGING PLANET (C4 8/11/97) mus: MARK THOMAS *unavaiable*
RAIDERS OF THE LOST ARK (1981) Music: JOHN WILLIAMS
    *SILVA SCREEN (Koch): RAIDERS 001 (CD)*  -S/T- *Imp*
    *(S.Screen): 821 583-4 (MC) see also COLLECTIONS:*
    *8,48,63,81,173,199,200,201,212,323*
RAILWAY CHILDREN The (1970) Music score: JOHNNY DOUGLAS
    *also feat* LIONEL JEFFRIES -S/T- reissue: MFP (EMI):
    *CDMFP 6373 (CD and 7243 857005-2) TCMFP 6383 (MC)*
    *also* 'On Screen' *DULCIMA: DLCD 110* 'Dancing Feet'
    Andy ROSS ORCH *PRESIDENT: PCOM(PTLC)1107 (CD/MC)*
RAIN MAN (1989) Music sco: HANS ZIMMER plus:Belle Stars
    Delta R.Boys-Etta James-Ian Gillan-Roger Glover etc
    -S/T-*CAPITOL EMI: CZ456 (CD) TCATAK 180 (MC)*
    *see also COLLECTIONS 39,55*
RAINBOW (Thames 1974-88) theme mus "Rainbow" FRASER-
    PORTNOW-THOMAS *on Coll* 'TV TUNES FOR KIDS'
RAINBOW DAYS (ITV 8/1/96) mus: KIM GOODY-ALAN COATES.*NA*
RAINBOW The (1989) Music score: CARL DAVIS Philharmonia
    & Graunke Orchestra of Munich (Carl DAVIS) -S/T-
    *SILVA SCREEN (Koch): FILMCD 040 (CD)*
RAINS OF RANCHIPUR (1955) Music score: HUGO FRIEDHOFER
    Suite on Coll *with* 'ADV.OF MARCO POLO'/'THE LODGER'
    'SEVEN CITIES OF GOLD' by MOSCOW SYMPHONY ORCHESTRA
    (W.T.Stromberg) *MARCO POLO (Select): 8.223857 (CD)*
RAISE THE RED LANTERN (1991) Music score: ZHAO JIPING
    *see COLLECTION 264* 'MUSIC FROM THE ORIENT'
RAISE THE TITANIC (1980) Music sco JOHN BARRY suite
    *see COLLECTION 21*
RAISIN (O.BROADWAY CAST 1973) Songs:Judd Woldin-Robert
    Brittan) *feat:* VIRGINia Capers-Joe Morton-Ernestine
    Jackson-Ralph Carter *SONY Broadway:CD 32754 (CD)*
RAKE'S PROGRESS (48) Music: WILLIAM ALWYN 'Calypso'
    from film played by LONDON Symphony Orch (Richard
    Hickox) on *CHANDOS: CHAN 9243 (CD)*
RALLY REPORT (BBC2 19/11/89) theme "Duel" (PROPAGANDA)
    *ZTT (Isl Poly) ZCIQ 3 (MC) CID 126 (CD) deleted*
RAMBLING ROSE (1991) Music score: ELMER BERNSTEIN -S/T-
    *VIRGIN Movie Music (EMI): CDVMM 5(CD) TCVMM 5(MC)*

RAMBO 'FIRST BLOOD PART 1' (1982) Mus: JERRY GOLDSMITH
  *IMPORT (Silva Screen): FMT 8001D (CD)*
RAMBO 'FIRST BLOOD PART 2' (1985) Mus: JERRY GOLDSMITH
  -S/T- *COLOSS.(Pinn):CST 348005(CD) CST 8005SMC(MC)*
RAMBO III (1988) Music sco: GIORGIO MORODER -S/T- *POLY*
  *834 929-2 (CD) POLD 5227 (LP) deleted / Full Orch*
  *tral Score:* Imp *INTRADA (Silva Sc): RVF 6006D (CD)*
  *see also COLLECTIONS 8,327*
RANDALL AND HOPKIRK (DECEASED) (ITV 26/9/69) theme mus
  EDWIN ASTLEY *see COLLECTIONS 6,109,357*
RANSOM (1996) Music score: JAMES HORNER -S/T- *HOLLYWOOD*
  *(Polyg): 162 086-2 (CD)*
RANSOM (aka The Terrorists) (1975) Music: JERRY GOLDS
  MITH -S/T- includes 'The Chairman' (69) reissued
  *SILVA SCREEN (Koch): FILMCD 081 (CD)*
RAPA NUI: The Centre Of The World (1993) Mus: STEWART
  COPELAND -S/T- *MILAN (BMG): 214 402 (CD)*
RAPID FIRE (1992) Music score: CHRISTOPHER YOUNG -S/T-
  *VARESE (Pinn): VSD 5388 (CD)*
RAT CATCHERS The (ITV 2/2/66) theme mus: JOHNNY PEARSON
  *see COLLECTION 318*
RAT PATROL (USA TV) *see COLLECTION 340*
RATTLE AND HUM (1988) Music by U2 -S/T- *ISLAND (Polyg):*
  *U 27 (Dbl LP) UC 27 (MC) CID U27 (CD)*
RAUMPATROUILLE (Euro TV Sci-Fi series 1960s) Music by
  PETER THOMAS SOUND ORCHESTRA -S/T- *BUNGALOW-CITY*
  *SLANG/RTM (Disc): RTD 3460009-2 (CD) -1 (LP)*
RAW DEAL (1986) Music sco and songs: TOM BAHLER + V/A
  -S/T- *VARESE (Pinn): VSD 47286 (CD)* note: 2nd m/m
  'Piano Conc.No.3 in C.min' (BEETHOVEN) *not on -S/T-*
RAWHIDE (USA 57) title song (D.Tiomkin-Ned Washington)
  FRANKIE LAINE *vers.on* 'Round-Up' *TELARC (BMG-Con):*
  *CD 80141 (CD) see also Coll* 'MY RIFLE MY PONY & ME'
  *see COLLECTIONS 2,170,265,340,365,398*
RE-ANIMATOR / BRIDE OF THE RE-ANIMATOR (1985/86) Music
  RICHARD BAND -S/T- *S.SCREEN (BMG) FILMCD 082 (CD)*
REACH FOR THE SKY (1956) Music: JOHN ADDISON *see Coll*
  'BIG WAR THEMES' *(MFP)* 'WORLD WAR 2 THEMES' *(MFP)*
READY STEADY COOK (BBC2 24/10/94) music: KEN BOLAM...*NA*
REAL McCOY (1993) Music score: BRAD FIEDEL -S/T-
  *VARESE (Pinn): VSD 5450 (CD)*
REAL McCOYS (USA TV) *see COLLECTION 342*
REALITY BITES (1993) -S/T- incl LENNY KRAVITZ-JULIANA
  HATFIELD 3-INDIANS-WORLD PARTY-DINOSAUR JNR-POSIES-
  SQUEEZE-KNACK-LISA LOEB-ETHAN HAWKE-BIG MOUNTAIN
  -S/T- *RCA (BMG): 07863 66364-2 (CD) -4 (MC)*
REBECCA (1940) Music score: FRANZ WAXMAN *see Collect*
  'Sunset Boulevard' *RCA: RD 87017 (CD)*
REBECCA (BBC2 17/1/79) m:DEBUSSY adapted by RON GRAINER
  *see COLLECTION 7*
REBECCA (ITV 5/1/97) music score CHRISTOPHER GUNNING.*NA*
REBEL (USA TV) *see COLLECTION 340*
REBEL WITHOUT A CAUSE (1955) Music sc: LEONARD ROSENMAN
  *new Recording* LONDON SINFONIETTA (J.ADAMS) *with*

'EAST OF EDEN' (1954 Leonard Rosenman) *NONESUCH (WEA): 7559 79402-2 (CD)* + 'GIANT' & 'EAST OF EDEN' *CINERAMA-EDEL (Pinn): CIN 2206-2 (CD) -4 (MC)*

RECKLESS (ITV 6/1/97) music: HAL LINDES *unavailable*

RED DAWN (1984) Music sco: BASIL POLEDOURIS -S/T- IMPT *INTRADA USA (Silva Screen): RVF 6001D (CD)*

RED DWARF (BBC2 15/2/88-1997) music and theme song by HOWARD GOODALL *see COLLECTIONS 109,273*

RED HEAT (1988) Music score: JAMES HORNER -S/T- *VIRGIN (EMI): CDV 2558 (CD)*

RED KNIGHT WHITE KNIGHT (1989) Mus: JOHN SCOTT -S/T- *INTRADA (Koch/Silva Screen): MAF 7016D (CD)*

RED RIVER (1948) Music score: DIMITRI TIOMKIN *see COLLECTIONS 237,366*

RED RIVER (1988) Music score: KEN WANNBERG -S/T- also includes music from 'DRAW!' (Ken Wannberg) *IMPT PROMETHEUS (Silva Screen): PCD 129 (CD) deleted*

RED SCORPION (1989) Music score: JAY CHATTAWAY -S/T- *VARESE (Silva Screen): VSD 5230 (CD) deleted see also COLL* 'UNIVERSAL SOLDIER'

RED SHOE DIARIES (Films) Music (George Clinton) GEORGE CLINTON on 'Music Of The RED SHOE DIARIES' on *WIENERWORLD/GRAPEVINE (Discov): WNRCD 6001 (CD)*

RED SHOES The (1948) Music score: BRIAN EASDALE *see Coll* 'CLASSIC BRITISH FILM MUSIC' *(SILVA SCREEN)*

RED TENT The (1970) Music score ENNIO MORRICONE -S/T- *LEGEND IMPT (Silva Screen): LEGEND CD 5 (CD)*

REGAIN - see 'HARVEST'

REILLY-ACE OF SPIES (Thames 9/83) theme from 'Romance' (Shostakovich) arr Harry Rabinowitz *see COLLECTION 168*

REMAINS OF THE DAY (1993) Music sco: RICHARD ROBBINS -S/T- *EMI: CDQ 555029-2 (CD) 4DQ 555029-4 (MC) see COLLECTIONS 62,65*

REMINGTON STEELE (USA)(BBC1 3/9/83) mus: HENRY MANCINI *see COLLECTION 12*

REN AND STIMPY SHOW The (USA/BBC1 10/1/94) theme song "Dog Pound Hop" *see COLLECTION 345*

RENAISSANCE MAN (1993) Music score HANS ZIMMER -S/T- *VARESE (Pinn): VSD 5502 (CD)*

RENT - songs: Jonathan Larson / Orig 1996 Broadway Cast *DREAMWORKS-MCA (BMG): DRD 50003 (CD)*

REPO MAN (1984) Mus by IGGY POP-CIRCLE JERKS-PLUGZ -S/T- *re-issued on MCA (BMG): MCLD 19311 (CD)*

REQUIEM (ROCK REQUIEM 1985) Music: ANDREW LLOYD WEBBER Placido DOMINGO-Sarah BRIGHTMAN-Paul Miles KINGSTON ENGLISH CHAMBER ORCH *EMI: EL 270 242-2/-4/ (CD/MC)*

RESCUERS The / RESCUERS DOWN UNDER - *see* DISNEY p.343

RESERVOIR DOGS (1992) -S/T- featuring VARIOUS ARTISTS *MCA (BMG): MCD 10793 (CD) MCC 10793 (MC) see COLLECTIONS 259,274,356*

RESORT TO MURDER (BBC1 27/7/95) music sco: BILL CONNOR -S/T- *Debonair (Pinn): CDDEB 1002 (CD) see also COLLECTION 6*

RESTORATION (1995) Music score: JAMES NEWTON HOWARD and
    selections from the works of HENRY PURCELL
    -S/T- *MILAN (BMG): 4321 35522-2 (CD)*
RETURN OF DRACULA (1958) Music score: GERALD FRIED
    *see COLLECTION 378*
RETURN OF RINGO The - *see under* 'DEATH RIDES A HORSE'
RETURN OF SHERLOCK HOLMES The (Granada 9/7/86) *see
    under* 'SHERLOCK HOLMES'
RETURN OF THE JEDI (Star Wars 3) Mus sco: JOHN WILLIAMS
    Special-Edition ORIG SOUNDTRACK Recording (1997)
    *RCA (BMG): 09026 68748-2 (Deluxe 2CD)*
    *RCA (BMG): 09026 68774-2 (Slimline 2CD) -4 (2MC)*
    *see also COLLECTIONS 199,212,268,273,300,330*
RETURN OF THE SAINT The (ITV 78) theme: IRVING MARTIN-
    BRIAN DEE *see COLLECTIONS 3,357,360,364,368,372*
RETURN OF THE SEVEN The (1966) *sequel to* 'MAGNIFICENT
    SEVEN' *see* 'MAGNIFICENT SEVEN'
RETURN TO THE FORBIDDEN PLANET (ORIG LONDON CAST 1989)
    Bob CARLTON'S Sci-Fi Musical *VIRGIN: CDV(TCV) 2631*
REVENGE (1990) Music score: JACK NITZSCHE -S/T- on
    *SILVA SCREEN (Koch): FILMC(CD) 065 (MC/CD)*
RHAPSODY IN BLUE (1945) VARIOUS -S/T- SELECTIONS on
    *GREAT MOVIE THEMES: (Targ-BMG): CD 60028 (CD)*
RHODES (BBC1 9/96) Music sco: ALAN PARKER / prd: GRAHAM
    WALKER -S/T- *MCA (BMG): MCD(MCC) 60040 DELETED 97*
    *see also COLLECTION 402*
RHODES AROUND BRITAIN (BBC2 31/5/94) title theme mus
    by JAMES SIMPSON *unavailable*
RHYTHM ON THE RIVER (1940) VARIOUS -S/T- SELECTIONS on
    *GREAT MOVIE THEMES: (Targ-BMG): CD 60025 (CD)*
RICH MAN POOR MAN (USA-ITV 75) music score: ALEX NORTH
    *see COLLECTION 168*
RICHARD III (1955) Music: WILLIAM WALTON / Academy Of
    St.Martin-In-The-Fields (Neville MARRINER) with Sir
    John GIELGUD *CHANDOS: CHAN 8841 (CD)*
RICHARD III (1995) Music score: TREVOR JONES
    -S/T- *LONDON (Poly): 828 719-2 (CD) -4 (MC)*
    *see also Coll* 'SHAKESPEARE FILM MUSIC'
RICHIE RICH (1994) Music score: ALAN SILVESTRI -S/T-
    *VARESE (Pinn): VSD 5582 (CD)*
RICK STEIN'S TASTE OF THE SEA (BBC2 12/9/95) music by
    CROCODILE MUSIC *see COLLECTION 337*
RICKI LAKE (USA 93-C4 5/10/94) series theme music by
    JELLEYBEAN BENITEZ *unavailable*
RIDICULE (1996) Music sco: ANTOINE DUHAMEL -S/T- *DECCA
    (Poly): 452 990-2 (CD) also Poly: 452 697-2 (CD)*
RIFLEMAN The (USA TV 60s) *see COLLECTION 339*
RIGHT STUFF The (1983) Music sco: BILL CONTI+ mus from
    'NORTH & SOUTH' -S/T- *VARESE (Pinn): VSD 47250 (CD)*
    *see also Coll* 'SPACE AND BEYOND'
RIN TIN TIN (USA TV) *see COLLECTION 339*
RING The (Danielle Steel's) (96 TV mini-s) Music score
    MICHEL LEGRAND cond: CITY OF PRAGUE PHILHARM.ORCH.
    -S/T- *SILVA AMERICA (Koch): SSD 1072 (CD)*

RINK The - songs by John Kander and Fred Ebb
  1.ORIG LONDON CAST 1987/88) *w* DIANE LANGTON-JOSEPHINE
    BLAKE & COMP *TER (Disc): CDTERS 1155 (CD)*
  2.ORIG BROADWAY CAST 1983 *with* LIZA MINNELLI and COMP
    *TER (Disc): CDTER 1091 (CD) ZCTER 1091 (MC)*
RIO BRAVO (1959) Music score: DIMITRI TIOMKIN
    Title theme (D.Tiomkin-P.F.Webster) by DEAN MARTIN
    *MFP EMI: CDMFP 6032 (CD) also COLLECTIONS 265,366*
RIO CONCHOS (1964) Music score: JERRY GOLDSMITH -S/T-
    *INTRADA (Sil.Screen): RVF 6007D(CD)* also includes
    prelude from 65 film 'The Agony & The Ecstasy'
RIO GRANDE (1950) Music score: VICTOR YOUNG -S/T-
    *VARESE (Pinn): VSD 5378 (CD)*
RIO RITA (ORIG LONDON CAST 1930) Songs (Harry Tierney-
    Joseph McCarthy) *feat:* EDITH DAY-MARIA DE PIETRO-
    GEORGE GEE-GEOFFREY GWYTHER-RITA PAGE-LESLIE SARONY
    *+ musicals LILAC TIME (1922) 'SOUTHERN MAID'(1920)*
    *PEARL (Pavilion): GEMMCD 9115 (CD)*
RISING DAMP (YTV orig 1974) ORIG TV CAST RECORDING on
    *MAGMASTERS (Koch): MSE 011 (MC)*
    *see COLLECTION 229*
RISING SUN (1993) Music sco: TORU TAKEMITSU + Various
    Artists -S/T- *ARISTA (BMG): 07822 11003-2 (CD)*
RISKY BUSINESS (1983) Mus: TANGERINE DREAM-BOB SEGER
    -S/T- *VIRGIN (EMI): CDV 2302 (CD) OVEDC 240 (MC)*
RIVER OF SOUND, A (BBC2 27/12/95) featur: MICHEAL O'
    SUILLEABHAIN + various artists -S/T-
    *VIRGIN (EMI): CDV 2776 (CD) TCV 2776 (MC)*
RIVER RUNS THROUGH IT, A (1992) Music sco: MARK ISHAM
    -S/T- *MILAN (BMG): 12469-2 (CD) 12469-4 (MC)*
RIVER WILD The (1994) Music sco: JERRY GOLDSMITH -S/T-
    *RCA IMPT (S.Screen): 07863 66459-2 (CD)*
RIVERDANCE SHOW The (1995) music by BILL WHELAN *reissue*
    *CELTIC HEARTBEAT (BMG): UND(UMC) 53076 / 53106*
    New Version (Oct 95) on *WEA 7567 82816-2(CD) -4(MC)*
    *see also COLLECTIONS 144,213,267*
RIVERDANCE (TRIBUTE TO) 'THIS LAND' Various Artists
    *MFP (EMI): CDMFP 6237 (CD) TCMFP 6237 (MC)*
ROAD HOUSE (1989) Music: MICHAEL KAMEN + JEFF HEALEY
    BAND-BOB SEGER-OTIS REDDING-LITTLE FEAT-PATRICK SW
    AYZEE-KRIS McKAY -S/T- *ARISTA (BMG): 259.948 (CD)*
ROAD RUNNER (USA TV) *see COLLECTION 340*
ROAD TO WELLVILLE The (1994) Music sco: RACHEL PORTMAN
    -S/T- *VARESE (Pinn): VSD 5512 (CD)*
ROB ROY (1995) Music: CARTER BURWELL Songs performed
    by CAPERCAILLIE featuring KAREN MATHIESON
    -S/T- *VIRGIN (EMI): CDVMM 18 (CD) TCVMM 18 (MC)*
ROBE The (1953) Mus: ALFRED NEWMAN -S/T- *FOX-ARISTA*
    *(BMG): 07822 11011-2 (CD) and Import version on*
    *VARESE (Silva Screen): VARESE: VSD 5295 (CD)*
ROBERT AND ELIZABETH  songs: Ron Grainer-Ronald Miller
  1.ORIG CHICHESTER THEATRE CAST 1987 *with:* MARK WYNTER
    GAYNOR MILES-JOHN SAVIDENT and Company
    *FIRST NIGHT (Pinn): OCRCD 6032 (CD)*

ROBERT AND ELIZABETH *Continued from previous page...*

2.ORIG LONDON CAST 1965 *w* KEITH MICHELL-JUNE BRONHILL
ANGELA RICHARDS-JEREMY LLOYD & Orchestra (A.Faris)
*EMI Angel (EMI):CDANGEL 2(CD) DELETED 2.96*
ROBIN AND MARIAN (1976) *see COLLECTION 332*
ROBIN HOOD (1973 Cartoon) *see* WALT DISNEY INDEX p.343
ROBIN HOOD (1991) (*w*: Patrick Bergin) Music: GEOFFREY
BURGON -S/T- *SILVA SCREEN (Koch)= FILMCD 083 CD*
ROBIN HOOD 'The Adventures Of' *see* ADVENTURES OF ROBIN
ROBIN HOOD: MEN IN TIGHTS (1993) Music sc: HUMMIE MANN
-S/T- *MILAN (BMG): 17639-2 (CD) 17639-4 (MC)*
ROBIN HOOD: PRINCE OF THIEVES (1991) Music sco: MICHAEL
KAMEN song "(Everything I Do) I Do It For You" (B.
Adams-R.Lange-M.Kamen) BRYAN ADAMS *(A.& M):AMCD 789
-S/T- reiss: MORGAN CREEK (Poly): 002249-2 MCM (CD)*
*see COLLECTIONS 243,297,332,400*
ROBIN OF SHERWOOD (HTV 28/4/84) theme music "Robin The
Hooded Man)" CLANNAD *RCA (BMG): 74321 48674-2 (CD)
-4 (MC) see also COLLECTION 303*
ROBINSON CRUSOE (Adventures of) (BBC1 12/10/65) Music
score: ROBERT MELLIN-GIAN PIERO REVERBERI Original
TV S/TRACK *reissued w.ADDITIONAL unreleased music
SILVA SCREEN (Koch): FILMCD 705 (CD)*
ROBINSON CRUSOE & MAN FRIDAY (Filmed TV Mini ser.88)
music score: MAURICE JARRE -S/T- *PROMETHEUS Imp
(Silva Screen): PST 501 (LP)*
ROBOCOP (1987) Music score: BASIL POLEDOURIS -S/T-
*VARESE: (Pinn) VSD 47298 (CD) reissue / also on
ESSENTIAL (BMG):ESSCD 285(CD) ESSMC 285(MC)*
also -S/T- *TER (Disc): (CD)ZCTER 1146 (CD/MC)*
*see also COLLECTION 8*
ROBOCOP: THE TV SERIES (ITV 7/9/96) Ser.Soundtrack feat
JOE WALSH-LITA FORD-THE BAND-DAVE EDMUNDS-TODD RUND
GREN etc. *ESSENTIAL-CASTLE (BMG): ESMCD 491 (CD)*
ROBOCOP 2 (1990) Music score: LEONARD ROSENMAN -S/T-
*VARESE USA (Pinn): VSD 5271 (CD)*
ROBOCOP 3 (1993) Music score: BASIL POLEDOURIS -S/T-
*VARESE USA (Pinn): VSD 5416 (CD)*
ROBOTJOX (1989) Mus: FREDERIC TALGORN with PARIS PHIL
ORCH (Talgorn) *PROMETHEUS (S.Scr): PCD 125 (CD)*
ROCCO & HIS BROTHERS *on COLL* 'FILM MUSIC OF NINO ROTA'
*Italian Import (Silva Screen): VCDS 7001 (CD)*
ROCK The (1996) Music: NICK GLENNIE SMITH-HANS ZIMMER
HARRY GREGSON WILLIAMS -S/T- *HOLLYWOOD Records
(USA IMPT): HR 62062-2 (CD)*
ROCKERS (1978) Music score (Reggae) featur PETER TOSH
GREGORY ISAACS-THE MIGHTY DIAMONDS and others -S/T-
*REGGAE REFRESHERS-ISLAND (Poly): RRCD 45 (CD)*
ROCKETEER The (1991) Music score: JAMES HORNER -S/T-
*HOLLYWOOD Imp (S.Screen): HWD 161117 (CD)*
*see also COLLS:* 'CULT FILES'
ROCKFORD FILES (USA 75) theme: MIKE POST-PETE CARPENTER
*see COLLECTIONS 12,100,168,242,246,341,373*

ROCKY 1 (1976) Music: BILL CONTI Song "Gonna Fly Now"
(B.Conti-C.Connors-A.Robbins) Frank Stallone -S/T-
re-issue *EMI EUROPE (Discovery): 746081-2 (CD) &
LIBERTY (Silva Screen) 46081-2 (CD) 46081-4 (MC)*
see also COLLECTIONS 8,63,198,202,203,274,327
ROCKY 2 (1979) Music sco: BILL CONTI -S/T- *LIBERTY USA
(Silva Screen): 46082-2 (CD) 46082-4 (MC)* see also
*Colls: 'CINEMA CENTURY'*
ROCKY 3 (1982) Music sco: BILL CONTI song "Eye Of The
Tiger" by SURVIVOR -S/T- *EMI EUROPE (Discovery):
746561-2 (CD)* also *(S.Screen): 46561-2(CD) -4(MC)*
see also Colls 'ACTION THEMES'/'NUMBER 1 MOVIES...'
ROCKY 4 (1985) Music score: VINCE DI COLA Songs V.Arts
-S/T- *Imp (SILVA SCREEN):75240-2(CD) -4(MC)*
ROCKY 5 (1991) Music sco: BILL CONTI Songs V.Arts -S/T-
*CAPITOL: CDEST 2137 (CD) deleted 94*
ROCKY AND BULLWINKLE (USA TV) *see COLLECTION 340*
ROCKY HORROR SHOW The - songs by Richard O'Brien
  1.FILM MUSICAL 1975 (Rocky Horror Picture Show) *with:*
    TIM CURRY-LITTLE NELL-MEATLOAF-SUSAN SARANDON -S/T-
    *Castle Comm (BMG): ROCKY 1 (4CDs inc.O.LONDON Cast)*
  2.ORIG LONDON CAST 1973 *w:* TIM CURRY-RICHARD O'BRIEN-
    LITTLE NELL- *First Night (Pinn): OCRCD 6040 (CD)*
  3.CARLTON SHOWS COLLECTION 1995 *w:* CHERYL BAKER-ROBIN
    COUSINS-TRACEY MILLER-NICK CURTIS *prd* Gordon Lorenz
    *CARLTON SHOWS Collect: 30362 0016-2 (CD) -4 (MC)*
  4.STUDIO REC.1995 *w:* ANITA DOBSON-TIM FLAVIN-KIM CRIS
    WELL-HOWARD SAMUELS-AIDAN BELL-ISSY VAN RANDWYCK-CH
    RISTOPHER LEE <u>Complete:</u> *TER (Disc): CDTER 1221 (CD)*
    <u>Highlights:</u> *SHOWTIME (MCI-THE):SHOW(CD)(MC) 025*
  5.REVIVAL LONDON CAST 1990 *with:* TIM McINNERNY-ADRIAN
    EDMONDSON-GINA BELLMAN and Company / *reissued on*
    *MFP (EMI): CD(TC)MFP 5977 (CD/MC)*
ROGER AND THE ROTTENTROLLS (BBC1 13/9/96) music: ROBERT
  HOWES and ROD ARGENT *spoken word cassette on*
  *LISTEN FOR PLEASURE (EMI Gold): LFPK 2017 (MC)*
ROLLERBALL (1975) *see COLLECTION 72,79*
ROMANCE ROMANCE (O.BROADWAY CAST 1988) Songs: KEITH HE
  RRMANN-BARRY HARMON *TER (Disc): CDTER 1161 (CD)*
ROMEO AND JULIET (1996) Music score: CLIFF EIDELMAN
  -S/T- songs (volume 1) *CAPITOL (EMI): PRMDCD 28*
  -S/T- songs (volume 2) *CAPITOL (EMI): PRMDCD 34*
  -S/T- (score) *VARESE (Pinn): VSD 5752 (CD)*
ROMEO AND JULIET (1968) Music score: NINO ROTA -S/T-
  *CLOUD NINE (S.Scr): CNS 5000 (CD) deleted* / note
  'Love Theme' also used for 'SIMON BATES-OUR TUNE'
  see COLLECTIONS 160,203,243,244
ROMPER STOMPER (1992) Music score: JOHN CLIFFORD WHITE
  "Pearl Fishers Duet" (Bizet) ERNEST BLANC-NICOLAI
  GEDDA -S/T- *PICTURE THIS (Greyhound): PTR 002 (CD)*
ROMY AND MICHELE'S HIGH SCHOOL REUNION (1997) -S/T-
  *HOLLYWOOD (Poly): 162 098-2 (CD)*
ROOBARB (BBC1 70's) music: JOHNNY HAWKSWORTH
  *orig theme see COLLECTION 360*

ROOM AT THE TOP (1958) Music score: MARIO NASCIMBENE
-S/T- inc. 'BAREFOOT CONTESSA'/'THE QUIET AMERICAN'
*DRG (Pinn): DRGCD 32961 (CD)*

ROOM WITH A VIEW A (1986) Music score: RICHARD ROBBINS
-S/T- *DRG (Pinn): CDSBL 12588 (CD) see COLLECTIONS
63,65,68,71,73,102,103,139,146,171,274,276,277*

ROOTS (USA TV) *see COLLECTION 344*

ROSE The (1979) *featuring* BETTE MIDLER -S/T- on
*ATLANTIC (WEA): K2 50681 (CD) K4 50681 (MC)*

ROSE GARDEN The (1989) - *see under* 'CRY IN THE DARK, A'

ROSE OF WASHINGTON SQUARE (1939 MUSICAL) *w:* ALICE FAYE
AL JOLSON-TYRONE POWER *inc.songs fr* 'DOLLY SISTERS'
'GOLD DIGGERS OF 1933' *TARGET (BMG): CD 60009*

ROSEANNA'S GRAVE (1996) Music score: TREVOR JONES with
London Symphony Orch (Nick ingman) 'For Roseanna'on
*RCA VICTOR (BMG): 09026 68836-2 (CD)*

ROSEANNE (USA C4 from 27/1/89) theme mus: DAN FOLIART
HOWARD PEARL *see COLLECTIONS 12,345*

ROSEMARY'S BABY (1968) Music score: CHRISTOPHER KOMEDA
*re-issue* on *TSUNAMI (Silva Screen): TSU 0116 (CD)
see COLLECTION 79*

ROSIE AND JIM (Cent 3/9/90) mus: ANDREW McCRORIE-SHAND
'Rosie & Jim's Song Party' *MFP EMI:CDMFP 5964 (CD)
TCMFP 5964 (MC)* 'Rosie & Jim's Christmas' *MFP:
TCMFP 6100 (MC) theme on Coll* 'TV TUNES FOR KIDS'

ROTHSCHILD'S VIOLIN (Film Score) Music: FLEISCHMANN com
leted & orchestrated by SHOSTALOVICH. The ROTTERDAM
PHILHARMONIC ORCH *RCA V (BMG): 09026 68434-2 (CD)*

ROULA: HIDDEN SECRETS (1996) Music sco: DIETER SCHLEIP
-S/T- *COLOSSEUM (Pinn): CST 34 8056 (CD)*

ROUND MIDNIGHT (1986) Mus sco: HERBIE HANCOCK w: DEXTER
GORDON -S/T- reiss *(SM): 486799-2 (CD)* also 'OTHER
SIDE OF ROUND MIDNIGHT' *BLUENOTE: CDP 746386-2 CD*

ROUSTABOUT *see* ELVIS PRESLEY INDEX p.348

ROUTE 66 (USA) *see COLLECTIONS 246,340*

ROWAN AND MARTIN'S LAUGH-IN (USA TV) *see COLLECT.343*

ROYAL ASCOT (BBC1 20/6/95) theme "Odissea" (Reverberi-
Farina) by RONDO VENEZIANO on 'Odissea' *BMG Italy
(Select): 610 529 (CD)* also used 'Regata Dei Dogi'
RONDO VENEZIANO *BMG ITALY (Select): 610 535 (CD)*

ROYALS AND REPTILES (C4 19/10/97) original music by
HOWARD DAVIDSON *unavailable*

RUDDIGORE (operetta) songs by W.S.Gilbert & A.Sullivan
1.NEW SADLERS WELLS OPERA COMPANY *KOCH Int (Koch):
340342 (CD) 240344 (MC)* also on *TER: CDTER2 1128
(2CD) ZCTED 1128 (2MC)*
2.PRO-ARTE ORCHEST (Malcolm Sargent) and GLYNDEBOURNE
FESTIVAL CHOIR Soloists: GEORGE BAKER-RICHARD LEWIS
OWEN BRANNIGAN-HAROLD BLACKBURN *EMI:764412-2 (2CDs)*

RUGBY SPECIAL (BBC2 78-90) "Holy Mackerel" by BRIAN
BENNETT *see COLLECTIONS 4,167*

RUGBY UNION 5 NATIONS CUP (BBC1 20/1/96) trailer music
"Adiemus" (KARL JENKINS) from 'Songs Of Sanctuary'
*VIRGIN (EMI): CD(TC)VE 925 (CD/MC)*

RUGBY WORLD CUP 1995 (ITV 25/5/95) Anthems: "World In Union"/"Sakura" with LADYSMITH BLACK MAMBAZO & PJ POWERS *POLYGRAM TV: 527 807-2 (CD) -4 (MC) RUGBY 2 (CDs) RUGBY 4 (MC) RUGBY 7 (7")* also:- "Swing Low Sweet Chariot" by CHINA BLACK *POLYGRAM: SWLOW 2 (CDs) SWLOW 4 (MC) SWLOW 7 (7"s)*

RUMBLE FISH (1983) Music score: STEWART COPELAND -S/T- *A.& M. (IMS-Polyg): AA 750 214983-2 (CD) reissue*

RUNNING MAN The (1988) Music score: HAROLD FALTERMEYER -S/T- reissue *COLOSSEUM (Pinn): CST 348032 (CD)*

RUPERT (ITV 70's) theme "Rupert The Bear" (Ron Roker & Len Beadle) sung by JACKIE LEE *see Coll* '100% KIDS PARTY'*TELSTAR(WEA): TCD(STAC) 2874 (CD/MC) deleted*

RUSSIA HOUSE The (1990) Music score: JERRY GOLDSMITH -S/T- *MCA USA (S.Screen): MCAD(MCAC) 10136 (CD/MC)*

RUTH RENDELL MYSTERIES The (TVS 19/6/88) music by BRIAN BENNETT -'The Ruth Rendell Mysteries' (Var.Arts) *EMI Soundtrack: CD(TC)STM 2 (CD/MC) deleted 96* ALSO Brian Bennett (1) *Pickwick: PWKS 546 (CD) HSSC 3286* see COLLECTIONS 5,138,388

RUTHLESS! THE MUSICAL (LOS ANGELES CAST RECORDING 1994) *VARESE (Pinn): VSD 5476 (CD)*

RUTLES The (1978 'All You Need Is Cash' sequel) 'ARCHAE OLOGY' *VIRGIN (EMI): CDVUS 119 (CD) VUSMC 119 (MC)*

**S.**W.A.T. (USA) *see COLLECTION 246*

SABRINA (1995) Music score: JOHN WILLIAMS -S/T- *A.& M. Records (Poly): 540 456-2 (CD) deleted 96*

SABRINA THE TEENAGE WITCH (USA96/ITV 23/11/96) music by GARY STOCKDALE *unavailable*

SAFE (1994) Music score: ED TOMNEY -S/T- issued on *MUTE-Fine Line (RTM-Pinn): IONIC 14CD (CD)*

SAGA OF LIFE The (C4 30/11/96) o.mus: DEBBIE WISEMAN.*NA*

SAIL THE WORLD WHITBREAD ROUND THE WORLD YACHT RACE 94 (ITV 19/3/94) music score: ANTHONY PHILLIPS -S/T- *RESURGENCE-BLUEPRINT (Pinn): RES 102CD (CD)*

SAINT ELMO'S FIRE (1985) Music sco: DAVID FOSTER *feat* JOHN PARR -S/T- *ATLANTIC (WEA): 7567 81261-2 (CD)* see also COLLECTION 134

SAINT ELSEWHERE (USA) theme music by DAVE GRUSIN see COLLECTION 12,51,242,341

SAINT EX (BBC2 25/12/96) music: BARRINGTON PHELOUNG on compilation 'PASSION OF MORSE' also includes 'The Politician's Wife'/'Truly Madly Deeply'/'Saint-Ex' *TRING INT (Tring): TRING 003 (CD) MCTRING 003 (MC)*

SAINT The (1997 Val Kilmer) Music score: GRAEME REVELL -S/T- V.Arts: ORBITAL-CHEMICAL BROTHERS-UNDERWORLD-DAVID BOWIE-DAFT PUNK *VIRGIN (EMI): CDVUS 126 (CD) VUSMC 126 (MC)* + ORBITAL *Fffr (Poly): FCD 296 (CDs)*

SAINT The (ITC 4/10/62-69) theme music: EDWIN ASTLEY see COLLECTIONS 2,3,109,340,356,357,368,372 *TV -S/T- RAZOR & TIE (Koch): RE 21562 (CD)*

SALAAM BOMBAY! (1988) Music score: L.SUBRAMANIAM -S/T- *DRG (Pinn): CDSBL 12595 (CD)*

SALAD DAYS songs by Julian Slade and Dorothy Reynolds
1. REVIVAL LONDON CAST *with:* ELIZABETH SEAL-SHEILA
   STEAFEL-CHRISTIINA MATTHEWS-ADAM BAREHAM & Company
   <u>Highlights:</u> *SHOWTIME (MCI-THE): SHOW(CD)(MC) 009*
   <u>Complete:</u> *TER (Disc): (CD)(ZC)TER 1018 (CD/MC)*
2. ORIG LONDON CAST 1954 *w:* ELEANOR DREW-JOHN WARNER-
   JAMES CAIRNCROSS-PAT HEYWOOD-MICHAEL ALDRIDGE-DOROT
   THY REYNOLDS.. *SONY West End (Sony): SMK 66176 (CD)*
3. 40th Anniv.STUDIO Record 1994 *inc* SIMON GREEN-JANIE
   DEE-TIMOTHY WEST-JOSEPHINE TEWSON-PRUNELLA SCALES-
   VALERIE MASTERSON-JOHN WARNER-TONY SLATTERY *and Co*
   *EMI: CDC 555200-2 (CD) EL 555200-4 (MC)*
4. 5TH ANNIVERSARY PROD *FIRST NIGHT: SCORECD 43 (CD)*
SALTIMBANCO (1996) Music by RENE DUPERE  performed by
   CIRQUE DU SOLEIL (Circus Of The Sun) ORIG CAST REC
   *RCA VICTOR (BMG): 74321 25707-2 (CD) -4 (MC)*
SALVADOR (1986) Music score: GEORGES DELERUE -S/T- and
   'WALL STREET' *TER (Disc): CD(ZC)TER 1154 (CD/MC)*
SAMMY GOING SOUTH *see COLLECTION 288*
SAMSON AND DELILAH (1949) Music: VICTOR YOUUNG -S/T-
   incl. 'THE QUIET MAN' *VARESE (Pinn): VSD 5497 (CD)*
SAND PEBBLES The (1966) Music score: JERRY GOLDSMITH
   new recording includ.previously unreleased material
   *VARESE (Pinn): VSD 5795 (CD)*
SANDPIPER The (1965) Music sc: JOHNNY MANDEL song "The
   Shadow Of Your Smile"(J.Mandel-P.F.Webster) -*S/T*-
   *VERVE (Poly): 531 229-2 (CD) see COLL 38,136,218*
SANFORD AND SON (USA TV) *see COLLECTION 341*
SAN FRANCISCO (1936) *COLLECTION with* 'DAMES'/'SUZY' on
   *GREAT MOVIE THEMES (Targ-BMG): CD 60022 (CD)*
SANTA CLAUSE The (1995) Music sco: MICHAEL CONVERTINO
   "Jingle Bells" YELLO -*S/T-Milan (BMG):32364-2 (CD)*
SANTA SANGRE (1990) Mus: SIMON BOSWELL + Circus Orgo
   Silver Hombre-Concha Y Fenix *PRESID: PCOM 1104 CD*
SAPPHIRE AND STEEL (ITV 10/7/79) theme music: CYRIL
   ORNADEL *see COLLECTION 357*
SARAFINA: THE SOUND OF FREEDOM (1992) Mus: STANLEY
   MYERS -S/T- V.Ars *WB (WEA) 9362 45060-2 (CD)*
SARTANA (1968) Music sco: PIERO PICCIONE -S/T- *Imprt*
   *POINT (Silva Screen): PRCD 124 (CD)*
SATURDAY NIGHT FEVER (1978) Music by BEE GEES -S/T-
   *RSO (Poly): 825 389-2 (CD) see COLECTIONS 198,244*
SATURDAY NIGHT LIVE (USA TV) *see COLLECTION 341*
SAVAGE EARTH (ITV 18/11/97) mus: HOWARD DAVIDSON... *NA*
SAVED BY THE BELL (NBC USA/C4 1/1/95) theme music by
   SCOTT GALE and RICH EAMES *see COLLECTION 345*
SAYONARA (1957) Music sco: FRANZ WAXMAN orch.suite
   *RCA Red Seal (BMG): 09026 62657-2 (CD)*
SCANNERS (1980) - *see under* 'DEAD RINGERS'
SCARAMOUCHE (1952) Music: VICTOR YOUNG **new recording**
   BRANDENBURG S.ORCH.(KAUFMAN) with other items on
   *MARCO POLO (Select): 8.223607 (CD)*
SCARLET LETTER The (1995) Music sco: JOHN BARRY -S/T-
   *EPIC (Sony Music): 483 577-2 (CD) -4 (MC)*

SCARLETT (Sky One 13/12/94) music score: JOHN MORRIS
    theme "Love Hurts" (B.Bryant) performed by NAZARETH
    with Munich P.O. + City Of Prague Philh.Orch. (John
    Morris) -S/T- *POLYDOR (IMS-Poly): E.523 867-2 (CD)*
SCARS OF DRACULA (1970) Music score: JAMES BERNARD *see*
    *Coll* 'DEVIL RIDES OUT' *SILVA SCREEN: FILMCD 174 CD*
SCENT OF A WOMAN (92) Music score: THOMAS NEWMAN -S/T-
    *MCA (BMG): MCD(MCC) 10759 (CD/MC) deleted 95*
SCHINDLER'S LIST (1993) Music: JOHN WILLIAMS / Violin
    sol: Itzhak PERLMAN -S/T- *MCA (BMG): MCD(MCC) 10969*
    *COLLEC:32,63,65,139,169,171,200,267,298,323,384,400*
SCHOFIELD'S QUEST (LWT 26/6/94) theme mus (Toby Jarvis)
    MCASSO PRODUCT *see COLLECTION 33*
SCOOBY DOO (USA TV) *see COLLECTION 341*
SCOOBY DOO WHERE ARE YOU *see COLLECTION 370*
SCREAM (1997) Music sco: MARCO BELTRAMI -S/T-  V.Arts
    *EDEL (Pinn): 0022822CIN (CD)*
SCRIMPERS (Third Eye Prod/C4 3/10/94) orig mus: HOWARD
    DAVIDSON solo cornet: Steve Sidwell. theme song
    "Waste Not" comp/performed by FRED WARD *unavailable*
SCROOGE (ORIG LONDON CAST) Songs: LESLIE BRICUSSE *feat:*
    ALBERT FINNEY *TER (Disc): CD(ZC)TER 1194 (CD/MC)*
SCROOGE (Classic Musicals series) *feat:* ANTHONY NEWLEY
    TOM WATT-GEORGE ASPREY-TANYA COOKE-JON PERTWEE etc
    + *songs from* 'PICKWICK' *KOCH INT: 34081-2 (CD)*
SEA HAWK The (1940) Music sco: ERICH WOLFGANG KORNGOLD
    *TER (Disc): ZCTER 1164 (MC) CDTER 1164 (CD) also*
    *VARESE (Pinn): VSD 47304 (CD)*
    *see also COLLECTION 332*
SEA HUNT (USA TV) *see COLLECTION 340*
SEA OF LOVE (1989) Music score: TREVOR JONES -S/T-
    *SPECTRUM (Polygram): 550130-2 (CD) -4 (MC)*
SEAFORTH (BBC1 9/10/94) Music sco: JEAN-CLAUDE PETIT
    -S/T- *D.SHARP-JADEAN (Pinn): DSCHCD(DSHMC) 7016*
SEAQUEST DSV (USA/ITV 16/10/93) Mus: JOHN DEBNEY -S/T-
    *VARESE (Pinn): VSD 5565 (CD) see COLLECT 109,302*
SEARCHERS The - *see COLLECTION 394* 'TRUE GRIT'
SEASON IN HELL A (1971) Music sco: MAURICE JARRE suite
    'MAURICE JARRE TRILOGY' *DRG Pinn: DRGCD 32906 (2CD)*
SECRET AGENT - see 'DANGER MAN'
SECRET GARDEN The (1992) Music sco: ZBIGNIEW PREISNER
    "Winter Light" (Z.Preisner-L.Ronstadt-E.Kaz) sung
    by LINDA RONSTADT -S/T- *VARESE (Pinn):VSD 5443 (CD)*
SECRET GARDEN The (BBC1 75 & 85) theme "The Watermill"
    *see COLLECTION 42,44*
SECRET GARDEN The (Musical of Frances Hodson Burnett's
    novel) *featur:* BARBARA COOK-JOHN CULLUM-MAX SHOWALT
    ER-JUDY KAYE *VARESE Spotlight (Pinn): VSD 5451 (CD)*
SECRET LIFE OF MACHINES The (Artifax/C4 from 15/11/88)
    theme mus "The Russians Are Coming" based on 'Take
    5' (Paul Desmond) by VAL BENNETT on Coll 'Rebel Mus
    ic' *Trojan (Pinn): CDTRD 403 (2CD) TRLD 403 (2LP)*
SECRET OF MY SUCCESS The (1987) Music sc: DAVID FOSTER
    -S/T- *MCA IMPORT (Silva Screen): MCAD 6205 (CD)*

SECRET OF NIMH The (1982) Mus: JERRY GOLDSMITH Songs:
    PAUL WILLIAMS -S/T- *VARESE (Pinn): VSD 5541 (CD)*
    *also on TER (Disc): CDTER 1026 (CD)*
SECRET OF THE ICE CAVE (1989) *see* 'FIELD OF HONOR'
SECRET OF THE SAHARA (RAI/ZDF/TFI Co.Prod ITV 12/9/93)
    music score: ENNIO MORRICONE vocal by AMII STEWART
    -S/T- on *RCA (BMG): 74321 34226-2 (CD) also on COLL*
    *TV FILM MUSIC (COLL) RCA (BMG): 74321 31552-2 (CD)*
SECRET SQUIRREL (USA TV) *see* COLLECTIONS 343,370
SECRETS OF THE MOORS (C4 HTV/Forum 23/7/92) theme and
    incid.music from 'The Wasps' (VAUGHAN WiLLIAMS)
    LONDON PHILHARMONIC ORCH (Sir Adrian Boult)
    *EMI: CDM 764020-2 (CD) EG 764020-4 (MC)*
SEE YOU FRIDAY (YTV 9/5/97) orig music: JIM PARKER...*NA*
SEESAW (Musical 1973) Songs: CY COLEMAN-DOROTHY FIELDS
    Orig BROADWAY Cast *DRG USA (Pinn): CDRG 6108 (CD)*
SEINFELD (USA 90)(BBC2 6/10/93) mus: JONATHAN WOLFF
    *see COLLECTION 345*
SELFISH GIANT The (O.CAST RECORD 1993) Songs: MICHAEL
    JENKINS-NIGEL WILLIAMS *featur:* GRAHAM TREW-ALISON
    CAIN-RICHARD TILEY & Co *TER (Disc): CDTER 1206 (CD)*
SENSE AND SENSIBILITY (1996) Music sco: PATRICK DOYLE
    -S/T- *SONY CLASSICS: SK 62258 (CD) ST 62258 (MC)*
SENZA PELLE - see 'NO SKIN'
SEPTEMBER SONG (ITV 1/3/93) series music composed by
    RICHARD HARVEY *unavailable*
SERIAL MOM (1993) Music score: BASIL POLEDOURIS -S/T-
    *MCA Imp (SIlva Screen): MCAD(MCAC) 11052 (CD/MC)*
SERIOUSLY FUNNY (C4 4/2/97) orig music: MARK SAYER WADE
    and TOLGA KASHIF *unavailable*
SERPICO (1973) Mus score: MIKIS THEODARAKIS *see Coll*
    'CINEMA CLASSICS 11'
SESAME STREET (USA 70's) theme: JOE RAPOSO-Stone-Hart)
    *see COLLECTIONS 168,341*
SET IT OFF (1996) Music sco: CHRISTOPHER YOUNG  2-S/T-
    songs: *E.WEST (WEA) 7559 61995-2(CD) -4(MC) -1LP*
    score: *VARESE (Pinn): VSD 5779 (CD)*
SEVEN (1994) Music score: HOWARD SHORE -S/T- including:
    STATLER BROS-MARVIN GAYE-GRAVITY KILLS-GLORIA LYNNE
    HAIRCUT100-BILLIE HOLIDAY-CHARLIE PARKER-THELONIOUS
    MONK etc.*CINERAMA/TVT/EDEL UK (Pinn): 002243-2(CD)*
SEVEN BRIDES FOR SEVEN BROTHERS - songs: Johnny Mercer
    Gene De Paul + additional music by Adolph Deutsch
    1.ORIG FILM -S/T- 1954 *with* HOWARD KEEL-JANE POWELL-
      JEFF RICHARDS-RUSS TAMBLYN-TOMMY RALL -S/T- *27 trks*
      *EMI PREMIER (EMI): CDODEON 17 (CD)*
    2.ORIG LONDON CAST 1986 *with new songs by* Al Kasha-
      Joel Hirschhorn *w:* RONI PAGE-STEVE DEVEREAUX-GEOFF
      STEER-PETER BISHOP-JACKIE CRAWFORD and Company
      *FIRST NIGHT (Pinn): OCRCD 6008 (CD)*
    3.CARLTON SHOWS COLLECTION (STUDIO RECORDING 1994)
      *with* EDMUND HOCKRIDGE-BONNIE LANGFORD-MASTERSINGERS
      *CARLTON SHOWS Coll (Carlton): PWKS(PWKMC) 4209*
    4.SHOWTIME SERIES *SHOWTIME (Disc): SHOWCD 051 (CD)*

SEVEN CITIES OF GOLD (1955) Mus score: HUGO FRIEDHOFER
   Suite on Coll *with* 'THE RAINS OF RANCHIPUR' + 'THE
   LODGER' by The MOSCOW SYPHONY ORCH (W.T.Stromberg)
   *MARCO POLO (Select): 8.223857 (CD)*
SEVEN FACES OF WOMAN *see COLLECTIONS 2,138*
SEVEN WAVES AWAY (1956) Music score: Sir ARTHUR BLISS
   *see under* 'CHRISTOPHER COLUMBUS'
SEVEN YEAR ITCH The (1955) *see COLLECTION 69*
SEVEN YEARS IN TIBET (1997) Music score: JOHN WILLIAMS
   -S/T- *SONY CLASSICS: number to be confirmed*
SEVENTH VOYAGE OF SINBAD (1958) Music: BERNARD HERRMANN
   *see COLLECTIONS 165,186,190,332*
SEVENTY GIRLS 70 - songs by John Kander and Fred Ebb
   1.ORIG LONDON CAST 1991 *with* DORA BRYAN and Company
   *TER (Disc): CDTER 1186 (CD) ZCTER 1186 (MC)*
   2.ORIG BROADWAY CAST 1971 *with:* MILDRED NATWICK-HANS
   CONREID-LILLIAN ROTH-GIL LAMB-LILLIAN HAYMAN-LUCIE
   LANCASTER-GOLDYE SHAW *SONY BROADWAY: SK 30589 (CD)*
SEX LIES & VIDEOTAPE (1989) Music sco: CLIFF MARTINEZ
   -S/T- *VIRGIN (EMI): CDV 2604 (CD)*
SEXTON BLAKE (BBC 67) theme music: FRANK CHACKSFIELD
   *see COLLECTION 5*
SHADOW The (1993) Music score: JERRY GOLDSMITH -S/T-
   *ARISTA (BMG): 0782218763-2 (CD) 0782218763-4 (MC)*
SHADOW CONSPIRACY (1996) Mus sco: BRUCE BROUGHTON -S/T-
   *INTRADA Import (Silva Screen): MAF 7073 (CD)*
SHADOW OF THE NOOSE (BBC2 1/3/89) *see COLLECTION 6*
SHADOWLANDS (1993) Music score: GEORGE FENTON -S/T-
   *EMI: CDQ 555093-2 (CD) -4 (MC) see also COLLECT.65*
SHADY TALES (ITV-M.Mansfield 92) theme music played by
   GORDON GILTRAP *see COLLECTION 153*
SHAFT (1971) Music: ISAAC HAYES Theme: *see COLL*
   'THIS IS CULT FICTION' *VIRGIN (EMI) VTCD 59 (CD)*
SHAKA ZULU *featuring* LADYSMITH BLACK MAMBEZO -S/T- on
   *WB (WEA): 7599 25582-2 (CD) WX 94C (MC)*
SHAKA ZULU (ITV 22/6/91) music composed & performed by
   DAVE POLLECUTT TV-S/T- *Imp: CDC 1002 (CD) deleted*
SHAKEDOWN (1994) Doctor Who *Video* Spin-off / Music
   Sco: MARK AYRES *SILVA SCREEN Koch: FILMCD 718(CD)*
SHAKEN AND STIRRED - *see COLLECTION 305*
SHAKESPEARE: ANIMATED TALES (BBC 9/11/92) mus: MICHAIL
   MEEROVICH-IGOR KRASILNIKOV with SYMPHONY ORCHESTRA
   OF MOSFILM CORPORATION *unavailable*
SHAKESPEARE REVUE (CHRISTOPHER LUSCOMBE-MALCOLM McKEE)
   *feat:* SUSIE BLAKE-MARTIN CONNOR-JANIE DEE-C.LUS
   COMBE-MALCOLM McKEE *TER (Disc): CDTEM2 1237 (CD)*
SHALL WE DANCE (1937) FILM MUSICAL *feat* FRED ASTAIRE &
   GINGER ROGERS -S/T- *also incl.songs from* 'CAREFREE'
   *IRIS Mus-Chansons Cinema (Discov): CIN 007 (CD)*
SHALL WE DANCE (STUDIO RECORDING 1995) *featuring:-*
   VALERIE MASTERSON-CHRISTOPHER LFF-LIZ ROBERTSON-ANN
   MORRISON-TINUKE OLAFIMHAN-JULIA SHORE-CHRISTINE AND
   REAS-ROBERT LINDSAY-ADAM BAREHAM-PAUL COLLIS & Comp
   *SHOWTIME (THE-Disc): SHOW(CD)(MC) 029 (CD/MC)*

SHANE (Film 1953/TV 1966) "Call Of The Faraway Hills"
(Victor YOUNG-Mac DAVID) *see Coll* 'SHANE-A TRIBUTE
TO VICTOR YOUNG' *KOCH INT: 3-7365-2H1 (CD)*
*see also COLLECTIONS 170,307*
SHANGHAI TRIAD (1995) Music score: ZHANG GUANGTIAN
-S/T- *VIRGIN (EMI): CDVIR 44 (CD)*
SHAPE OF THE WORLD (ITV 1991) music: RICHARD HARVEY
*see COLLECTION 181*
SHARKFIGHTERS The (1956) Music score: JEROME MOROSS
*see COLLECTION 377*
SHARPE (ITV 05/5/93-96) Music: JOHN TAMS and DOMINIC
MULDOWNEY *Collection* 'Music from Sharpe' (Various)
*VIRGIN (EMI): VTCD 81 (CD) VTMC 81 (MC)*
SHAWSHANK REDEMPTION The (1994) Music: THOMAS NEWMAN
-S/T- inc: INK SPOTS-HANK WILLIAMS & DEUTSCH OPERA
*EPIC Soundtrax (Sony): 478332-2 (CD)*
SHE (1965) Music score: JAMES BERNARD *see Coll*
'DEVIL RIDES OUT' *SILVA SCREEN: FILMCD 174 (CD)*
SHE LOVES ME - songs by Jerry Bock-Sheldon Harnick
  1.ORIG LONDON CAST 1994 *with:* JOHN GORDON SINCLAIR-
    RUTHIE HENSHALL and DAVID DE KEYSER-TRACIE BENNETT
    BARRY JAMES    *FIRST NIGHT (Pinn): CAST(CD)(C) 44*
  2.ORIG BROADWAY CAST 1963 Songs *with:* BARBARA COOK &
    DANIEL MASSEY *VARESE (Pinn): VSD 5464 (CD)*
  3.ORIG LONDON CAST 1964 *with:* GARY MILLER-RITA MORENO
    GARY RAYMOND-ANNE ROGERS-JOAN RYAN-PETER SALLIS-GRE
    GORY PHILIPS *EMI ANGEL: CDANGEL 6 (CD) deleted 96*
SHE WORE A YELLOW RIBBON (1949) Music score: RICHARD
HAGEMAN ad others *see COLLECTION 394* 'TRUE GRIT'
SHE'S THE ONE (1995) Music by TOM PETTY -S/T- on
*WEA (WEA): 9362 46285-2 (CD) -4 (MC)*
SHELLEY (UKGO 12/7/93 prev Thames 28/7/92 orig 1979)
theme music by RON GRAINER *unavailable*
SHELTERING SKY The (1990) Music sco: RYIUCHI SAKAMOTO
-S/T- *VIRGIN (EMI): CDV 2652 (CD)*
SHERLOCK HOLMES (Granada) 'Adventures'/'Return'/'Sign'
music: PATRICK GOWERS St.Paul's Cathedral Choir &
Gabrieli String Qu.& Wren Or.*TER: (CD)(ZC)TER 1136*
*see COLLECTION 308*
SHERLOCK HOLMES The Musical (ORIG LONDON CAST 92) Songs
(Leslie Bricusse) *feat:* ROBERT POWELL-ROY BARRACLOU
GH-LOUISE ENGLISH *TER (Disc):CD(ZC)TER 1198 (CD/MC)*
SHETLAND SESSIONS The (BBC2 2/9/92) VARIOUS ARTISTS on
'Shetland Sessions V.1-2' *LISMOR (Gordon Duncan)*
*LCOM 7021/7022 (CD) LICS 7021/7022 (MC)* Themes:
"The Constitution" / "Scalloway Lasses" (ALY BAIN)
SHILOH (1997) Music score: JOEL GOLDSMITH
song "Are There Angels" sung by SHEENA EASTON -S/T-
*VARESE (Pinn): VSD 5893 (CD)*
SHINE (1996) Mus score: DAVID HIRSCHFELDER *piano music*
*perf:* DAVID HIRSCHFELDER-DAVID HELFGOTT-RICKY EDWAR
DS-WILHELM KEMPF -S/T- *PHILIPS (Poly): 454 710-2 CD*
*454 710-4 (MC) / also avail:* 'BRILLIANTISSIMO' feat
DAVID HELFGOTT *RCA (BMG): 74321 46725-2 (CD) -4(MC)*

SHIRLEY VALENTINE (1989) Music: WILLY RUSSELL-GEORGE
    HATZINASSIOS "The Girl Who Used To Be Me" (Marvin
    HAMLISCH) sung by PATTI AUSTIN -S/T- on
    *Silva Screen (Koch): FILMCD 062 (CD)*
SHIRLEY'S WORLD (ATV 1971) "Shirley's Theme"/"Rickshaw
    Ride" by LAURIE JOHNSON *see COLLECTION 294*
SHOES OF THE FISHERMAN (1968) Music score: ALEX NORTH
    -S/T- *Imp. TSUNAMI (Silva Screen): GAD 94009 (CD)*
SHOESTRING (UKGold 2/11/92 / BBC1 30/9/79) theme music
    GEORGE FENTON *see COLLECTIONS 5,382*
SHOOT LOUD LOUDER..I DON'T UNDERSTAND (1966) Music:
    NINO ROTA score on *DRG (Pinn): DRGCD 32914 (CD)*
SHOOTING FISH (1997) Mus sco: STANISLAS SYREWICZ -S/T-
    SPACE-STRANGELOVE-DAVID McALMONT-JACKIE DE SHANNON-
    WANNADIES-BLUETONES-SUPERNATURALS-DUBSTAR-DIONNE
    WARWICK-DIVINE COMEDY-SILVER SUN-PASSION STAR etc.
    *EMI PREM.SOUNDTRACKS: PRMDCD 35 (CD) PRMDTC 35 (MC)*
SHOOTING PARTY The (1985) Music sco: JOHN SCOTT Royal
    Phil Orch (J.Scott) *JS (limited ed) JSCD 113 (CD)*
SHOOTING STARS (BBC2 22/9/95) title music by
    PETE BAIKIE *unavailable*
SHOOTIST The (1976) Music sco: ELMER BERNSTEIN suite
    *VARESE (Pinn): VCD 47264 (CD)*
SHOP TILL YOU DROP (C4 27/2/97) theme m: JULIEN-PIERRE
    McKENZIE and MATHEW POULTON *unavailable*
SHORT EYES (1977) Music: CURTIS MAYFIELD song "Break
    It Down" performed by FREDDY FENDER -S/T- reissue
    *CHARLY (Koch): CPCD 8183 (CD)*
SHORTLAND STREET (ITV 6/12/93) title theme music by
    Graeme Bollard sung by TINA CROSS *unavailable*
SHOT IN THE DARK, A - *see COLLECTION 62*
SHOW BOAT - songs by Jerome Kern-Oscar Hammerstein II
    1.FILM SOUNDTRACK 1951 *feat:* HOWARD KEEL-AVA GARDNER
      KATHRYN GRAYSON -S/T- *29tks EMI PREM.CDODEON 5*
    2.STUDIO RECORDING 1993 National Symphony Orchestra
      (John Owen Edwards) *w:* BRIAN GREENE-FRAN LANDESMAN
      JASON HOWARD-JANIS KELLY-WILLARD WHITE-SALLY BURGE
      SS-SHEZWAE POWELL-CAROLINE O'CONONOR-SIMON GREEN-
      JAMES BULLER-GARETH SNOOK and Company
      Highlights: *SHOWTIME (MCI-THE): SHOW(CD)(MC) 011*
      Complete: *TER (Disc): CDTER2 1199 (2CD) ZCTED (MC)*
    3.CARLTON SHOWS COLL Studio Record 1993 *with* GEMMMA
      CRAVEN-DENIS QUILLEY-DAVID KERNAN-TRACEY MILLER
      *CARLTON Shows Coll: PWKS 4161(CD) PWKMC 4161(MC)*
    4.REVIVAL USA CAST 1991 LINCOLN CENTER THEATRE
      *RCA (BMG): 09026 61182-23 (CD)*
    5.STUDIO RECORDING 1988 *1st complete with:* FREDERICA
      VON STADE-JERRY HADLEY-TERESA STRATAS-BRUCE HUBBARD
      KARLA BURNS-DAVID GARRISON-PAIGE O'HARA-ROBERT NICH
      OLS-NANCY KULP-LILLIAN GISH with the AMBROSIAN CHOR
      US and the LONDON SINFONIETTA (John McGlinn)
      *EMI HMV: TCRIVER 1 (3MC) CDRIVER 1 (3CD)*
      HIGHLIGHTS: *EMI CDC 749847-2(CD) EL 749847-4(MC)*
                              *Continued next page>...*

SHOW BOAT...*Continued from previous page*

6. STUDIO USA CAST 1962 *with:* JOHN RAITT-BARBARA COOK
   *COL (Silva Screen): CK 02220 (CD) JST 02220 (MC)*
7. ORIG BROADWAY REVIVAL CAST 1946 *with:* JAN CLAYTON-
   Carol Bruce-Charles Fredericks-Kenneth Spencer-Col
   ette Lyons *SONY BROADWAY: SK 53330 (CD)*
8. ORIG LONDON CAST 1928 *with:* MARIE BURKE-COLIN CLIVE
   VIOLA COMPTON-EDITH DAY-CEDRIC HARDWICKE-PAUL ROBES
   ON-LESLIE SARONY-HOWETT WORSTER + *mus 'LIDO LADY'* &
   *'SUNNY' (1926) PEARL (Pavilion): GEMMCD 9105 (CD)*
9. ORIG LONDON CAST 1971 *with* CLEO LAINE-ANDRE
   JOBIN-LORFNA DALLAS-THOMAS CAREY-ENA CABAYO & Comp.
   *LASERLIGHT POP-TARGET (BMG): 12446 (CD)*
SHOW JUMPING - *see under* 'HORSE OF THE YEAR SHOW'
SHOW The (1995 Hip Hop Dance Movie) Music: LL COOL J
   WARREN G.-MARY J.BLIGE and others -S/T- *DEF JAM /
   ISLAND (Poly): 529 021-2 (CD) -4 (MC) -1 (LP)*
SHOWSTOPPERS (BBC1 29/10/95) theme "Wilkommen" (Kander
   Ebb) from 'Cabaret' and selection of songs featur:
   GARY WILMOT with The LONDON SYMHONY ORCHESTRA 'The
   Album' *CARLTON (Pinn): 30360 0009-2 (CD) -4 (MC)*
SICILIAN CHECKMATE (Ita.1968) Music: ENNIO MORRICONE
   -S/T- with 'A BRIEF SEASON' (Ennio Morricone)
   *Legend (Silva Screen): LEGENDCD 26 (CD)*
SIESTA (1988) Music sco: MARCUS MILLER-MILES DAVIS
   -S/T- *WB (WEA) K925655-4 (MC) -2 (CD)*
SILENCE OF THE LAMBS The (1991) Music: HOWARD SHORE
   -S/T- *MCA (Silva Screen): MCAD 10194 (CD) deleted*
SILENCES OF THE PALACE (Les Silence Du Palais) (1994)
   Music sc: ANOUR BRAHEM -S/T- *VIRGIN: CDVIR 35 (CD)*
SILENT FALL (1995) Music score: STEWART COPELAND -S/T-
   *MORGAN CREEK (Poly): 002250-2 MCM (CD)*
SILENT WITNESS (BBC1 21/2/96) theme mus (series 2 & 3)
   by JOHN HARLE on 'SILENCIUM' *see COLLECTION 407*
   orig.series theme by GEOFFREY BURGON *unavailable*
SILENTS The (C4 series 1988) music score: CARL DAVIS
   *VIRGIN Classics (Poly): VC 790785-2 (CD) -4 (MC)*
SILK ROAD The (ITV 23/6/87) 'Silk Road Suite' KITARO *w:*
   L.S.O. 'Silk Road 1' *Domo (Pinn): DOMO 71050-2 (CD)*
   *-4 (MC)* 'Silk Road 2' *Domo: 71051-2 (CD) -4 (MC)*
SILK STOCKINGS (O.BROADWAY CAST 1955) *with* DON AMECHE
   *IMPORT (Silva Screen): 1102-2 (CD) 1102-4 (MC)*
SILKWOOD (1983) Music sco: GEORGES DELERUE -S/T- *reiss*
   *DRG (Pinn): DRGCD 6107 (CD)*
SIMON AND SIMON (USA 82) theme music: MICHAEL TOWERS-
   BARRY DE VORZON *see COLLECTIONS 51,168,242,241*
SIMON BATES OUR TUNE - see under 'OUR TUNE'
SIMPLE MAN, A (BBC2 1987) Music by CARL DAVIS (Ballet)
   about L.S.LOWRY *FIRST NIGHT (Pinn): OCRCD 6039 (CD)*
SIMPLE TWIST OF FATE, A (1994) Music: CLIFF EIDELMAN
   -S/T- *VARESE (Pinn): VSD 5538 (CD)*
SIMPSONS The (Sky 90/BBC1 23/11/96) theme: DANNY ELFMAN
   score: RICHARD GIBBS /'Simpsons Sing The Blues' +

"Do The Bartman" *GEFFEN (BMG): GEFD 24308 (CD)*
"Songs In The Key Of Springfield" VAR.ARTS *RHINO (WEA): 8122 72723-2 (CD) see COLLECTION 345*
SINCE YOU WENT AWAY (1944) Music sco: MAX STEINER -S/T- *reissue TSUNAMI IMPT (Silva Screen): TSU 0133 (CD) see also 'STREETCAR NAMED DESIRE A'*
SINGIN' IN THE RAIN (FILM 1952) Songs: ARTHUR FREED -NACIO HERB BROWN *-S/T- reiss EMI ODEON: CDODEON 14 (CD) also: Impt.sco.+ -S/T- 'AN AMERICAN IN PARIS' BLUE MOON (Discovery): BMCD 7008 (CD)*
SINGIN' IN THE RAIN (O.LONDON CAST 1983) TOMMY STEELE-ROY CASTLE-SARAH PAYNE-DANIELLE CARSON & Company MD:Michael Reed *FIRST NIGHT (Pinn): OCRCD 6013 (CD) see also COLLECTIONS 62,145,172,351*
SINGING DETECTIVE The (BBC1 16/11/86 + 6/88 + 11/7/94) *theme music* "Peg O' My Heart" (F.Fisher-A.Bryan) by Max Harris & His Novelty Trio -S/T- reissued on *CONNOISSEUR (Pinn): POTT(CD)(MC) 200 (2CD/MC)*
SINGLES (1992) -S/T- feat Various Artists *EPIC (Sony): 471 438-2 (CD)*
SIR FRANCIS DRAKE (ABC/ATV 12/11/61-29/4/62) theme mus: (Ventura) *see COLLECTION 372*
SIR HENRY AT RAWLINSON END (1980) Mus: VIVIAN STANSHALL *featur:* TREVOR HOWARD-PATRICK MAGEE-DENISE COFFEY-J.G.DEVLIN and VIVIAN STANSHALL -S/T- *re-issued on VIRGIN (EMI): VCCCD 18 (CD) VCCMC 18 (MC)*
SIRENS (1994) Music score: RACHEL PORTMAN -S/T- on *MILAN (BMG): 213 022 (CD)*
SISTER ACT / SISTER ACT 2 (1992/93) Various Artists *HOLLYWOOD Records (Silva Screen): HWD 162080 (2CD)*
SISTER ACT (1992) Music sco: MARC SHAIMAN -S/T- *reiss: POLYDOR (Poly): 161334-2 (CD)*
SIX DEGREES OF SEPARATION (1993) Music: JERRY GOLDSMITH -S/T- *Imp (SILVA SCREEN) EA 61623-2 (CD) -4(MC)*
SIX MILLION DOLLAR MAN *see COLLECTIONS 246,343,360*
SIX WEEKS (1982) Music score by DUDLEY MOORE on *GRP (BMG): GRP 96612 (CD) GRP 96614 (MC)*
SKELETON COAST (BBC2 7/1/97) title mus: JON ATTARD and additional music by WENTWORTH NORMAN *unavailable*
SKI SUNDAY (BBC2 72-93) theme mus "Pop Goes Bach" SAM FONTEYN *see COLLECTIONS 5,155,167,360*
SKIN The (LA PELLE/LA PEAU)(81) Mus sco: LALO SCHIFRIN -S/T- *CINEVOX Ita (Silva Screen): CDCIA 5095 (CD)*
SKIPPY THE BUSH KANGAROO (Austral.TV 1966-68) theme by ERIC JUPP *see COLLECTION 343*
SKY AT NIGHT The (BBC1 24/4/57-97) theme "At The Castle Gate" from 'Pelleas et Melisande' Op.46 (SIBELIUS) *see COLLECTION 31*
SKY'S THE LIMIT (1943 MUSICAL) *feat:* FRED ASTAIRE and JOAN LESLIE *inc.songs from* 'DUBARRY WAS A LADY' and '42ND STREET' *TARGET (BMG):CD 60010 (CD)*
SLAB BOYS The (1997) Music arrang.by JACK BRUCE *featur:* EDWYN COLLINS-PAT KANE-PROCLAIMERS-LULU-EDDI READER -S/T- *OCEAN DEEP (Grapevine-Poly): OCD 006 (CD)*

SLAUGHTERHOUSE 5 (1972) *see COLLECTION 73*
SLEDGEHAMMER (USA 88 ITV 12/1/89) theme: DANNY ELFMAN
   *see COLLECTIONS 12,345*
SLEEPERS (1996) Music: JOHN WILLIAMS orchestral -S/T-
   *PHILIPS (Poly): 454 988-2 (CD)*
SLEEPING BEAUTY (1959) MD: GEORGE BRUNS -S/T- songs on
   *DISNEY (Buena Vista): WDR 75622 (CD) WDR 75624 (MC)*
   *see also under* WALT DISNEY INDEX p.343
SLEEPING WITH THE ENEMY *see COLLECTIONS 71,258*
SLEEPLESS IN SEATTLE (1993) Music: MARC SHAIMAN -S/T-
   *feat:*J.DURANTE-L.ARMSTRONG-N.KING COLE-DR.JOHN-GENE
   AUTRY *EPIC (Sony): 473 594-2 (CD) -4 (MC) -8 (MD)*
   *see COLLECTION 28*
SLEEPWALKERS (1992) Music score: NICHOLAS PIKE -S/T-
   *Milan (import BMG): 10132-4 (MC) 10132-2 (CD)*
SLICE OF SATURDAY NIGHT, A (O.LONDON CAST 1989) Arts
   Theatre Club / M.D.(Keith Hayman) *with* BINKY BAKER
   DAVID EASTER-CLAIRE PARKER-MITCH JOHNSON-ROY SMILES
   *reissue: FIRST NIGHT (Pinn): OCRCD 6041 (CD)*
SLIVER (1993) Music score: HOWARD SHORE var.arts inc:
   UB40 "Can't Help Falling In Love With You" & NENEH
   CHERRY-MASSIVE ATTACK-SHAGGY-ENIGMA etc. -S/T- on
   *VIRGIN Movie Mus (EMI): CD(TC)VMMX 11 (CD/MC)*
SMALL DANCE, A (ITV 3/6/92) music: RICHARD HARVEY
   *see COLLECTION 181*
SMASHIE & NICEY: END OF AN ERA (BBC1 14/6/95) theme
   "You Ain't Seen Nothin'Yet" (Randy Bachman) BACHMAN
   TURNER OVERDRIVE on 'Roll On Down The Highway' on
   *SPECTRUM (Poly): 550 421-2 (CD) 550 421-4 (MC)*
SMILE LIKE YOURS, A (1997) VARIOUS ARTISTS -S/T- on
   *W.BROS (WEA): 7559 62093-2 (CD)*
SMILLA'S FEELING FOR SNOW (1997) Music by HANS ZIMMER-
   HARRY GREGSON WILLIAMS + "Stabat Mater" (PERGOLESI)
   -S/T- *TELDEC (WEA): 063017872-2 (CD)*
SMOKE (1995) Music score: RACHEL PORTMAN -S/T- on
   *POLYDOR (Poly): 162 024-2 (CD)*
SMOKEY JOE'S CAFE songs: Jerry Leiber-Mike Stoller
   ORIG BROADWAY CAST RECORDING *Various Artists*
   -S/T- *ATLANTIC (WEA): 7567 82765-2 (CD) -4 (MC)*
SMURFS The (Cart 74) *see COLLECTIONS 168,341*
SNAGGLEPUSS - *see COLLECTION 370*
SNAP (C4 16/7/97) music: SIMON PAYNE *unavailable*
SNAPPER The (BBC2 4/4/93) theme "Can't Help Falling In
   Love With You" (George Weiss-Hugo & Luigi) perf.by
   LICK THE TINS *MOONCREST (BMG): CRESTCD 012 (CD)*
SNOOKER (BBC Sport) theme music "Drag Racer" by the
   DOUGLAS WOOD GROUP *see COLLECTION 167*
   *see also under* 'WORLD SNOOKER'
SNOOKER:THE CRUCIBLE (BBC2 3/4/97) mus: JIM MEACOCK.*NA*
SNOOPY THE MUSICAL (O.LONDON CAST 1982) Songs: LARRY
   GROSSMAN-HAL HACKADY *feat:* Teddy KEMPNER-Zoe BRIGHT
   *TER (Disc): CD(ZC)TER 1073 see* 'CHARLY BROWN' (TV)
SNOOPY THE MUSICAL (ORIG USA CAST RECORDING 1981) on
   *DRG USA (Pinn): CDRG 6103 (CD)*

SNOW WHITE & THE SEVEN DWARFS (1937) Sgs: FRANK CHURCHI
LL-LEIGH HARLINE-PAUL SMITH feat: ADRIANA CASELOTTI
-S/T- *DISNEY (B.Vista): WD 74540-2 (CD) -4 (MC)*
*see also* W.DISNEY INDEX p.343
SNOWMAN The (C4 Cartoon 24/12/85) music: HOWARD BLAKE
Narr: Bernard Cribbins with The Sinfonia Of LONDON
Song *"Walking In The Air"* sung by PETER AUTY -S/T-
*COLUMBIA (Sony) 71116-2 (CD) 40-71116 (MC)*
*see COLLECTION 303*
SNOWS OF KILIMANJARO The (1952) Mus: BERNARD HERRMANN
score select *SILVA SCREEN (Koch): FILMCD 162 (CD)*
*also on* 'Citizen Kane' *DECCA 417852-2 (CD)-4 (MC)*
SNOWY RIVER: The McGregor Saga (Austr.93/BBC1 2/10/94)
original music by FRANK STRANGIO *unavailable*
SNUG AND COZI (ITV 1/11/96) music: PAUL RUTTER - "Pink
Heads CD" *Vulcan (BMG): MSM 9702 (CDs) MSM9703 (MC)*
SOAP (USA) *see COLLECTIONS 168,344,367*
SOFTLY SOFTLY (BBC1) - *see COLLECTION 2,31,246*

SOLDIER SOLDIER (Central fr.10/6/91) music: JIM PARKER
*EMI SOUNDTRACK (EMI): CDSTM 8 (CD)*
*other mus* "Unchained Melody" (Alex North-Hy Zaret)
by ROBSON & JEROME *RCA (BMG): 74321 28436-2 (CDs)*
*-4 (MC) -7 (7"s)* "Cry Me A River" (Hamilton) /
"You Don't Have To Say You Love Me" (Pino Donaggio
-Napier Bell-Wickham) sung by DENISE WELCH on
*VIRGIN (EMI): VSCDT(VSC)1569 (CDs/MC) see COLL.213*
SOLO (UKGO 2/4/93 orig BBC2 11/1/81) theme "Air Russe"
'Op.107 Variation for Flute & Piano' (BEETHOVEN)
SOLOMON AND SHEBA (1959) Music score: MARIO NASCIMBENE
new recording of score with 'The Vikings' music on
*DRG-New Note (Pinn): DRGCD 32963 (CD)*
SOME KIND OF WONDERFUL (1987) Music by Var.Arts -S/T-
*Beat Goes On (Pinn): BGO(CD)(MC) 178 (CD/MC) also*
*MCA USA (S.Screen): MCAD 6200 (CD) MCAC 6200 (MC)*
SOME LIKE IT HOT (O.LONDON CAST 1992) Songs Jule STYNE
BoB MERRILL w.TOMMY STEELE-BILLY BOYCE-ROYCE MILLS
MANDY PERRYMENT *First Night (Pinn): OCRCD 6028 CD*
SOME MOTHER'S DO 'AVE 'EM (BBC 70's) theme music by
RONNIE HAZLEHURST *see COLLECTION 229*
SOME MOTHER'S SON (1996) Music sco: BILI WHELAN -S/T-
*WB (WEA): 7567 82956-2 (CD) -4 (MC)*
SOME PEOPLE music: RON GRAINER *see COLLECTION 7*

SOMEONE TO WATCH OVER ME (1987) *see COLLECTIONS 78,96,*
*276,313,334*
SOMETHING TO TALK ABOUT (1995) Music: HANS ZIMMER and
GRAHAM PRESKETT -S/T- *VARESE (Pinn): VSD 5664 (CD)*
SOMETHING WILD (1987) Music score: DAVID BYRNE *Featur*
FINE YOUNG CANNIBALLS/UB 40 others -S/T- on
*MCA (Silva Screen): MCAD 6194 (CD) MCAC 6194 (MC)*
SOMEWHERE IN TIME (1980) Music: JOHN BARRY -S/T- on
*BEAT GOES ON (Pinn): BGO(CD)(MC) 222 & MCA (Sil.Sc)*
*MCAD 31164 (CD) see COLLECTIONS 21,24,66,*

SOMMERSBY (1993) Music score: DANNY ELFMAN -S/T-
*ELEKTRA (WEA): 7559 61491-2 (CD) -4 (MC)*
SON OF DARKNESS TO DIE FOR II (1991) Mus: MARK McKENZIE
-S/T- *PROMETHEUS (S.Screen): PCD 110 (CD)*
SON OF FRANKENSTEIN (1939) Music score: FRANK SKINNER
*new recording* MOSCOW SYMPHONY ORCHESTRA (Stromberg)
on *MARCO POLO (Select): 8.223748 (CD) also includ:*
INVISIBLE MAN RETURNS-THE WOLF MAN
SONDHEIM: A MUSICAL TRIBUTE ORIG BROADWAY CAST *with*
DOROTHY COLLINS-CHITA RIVERA-ANGELA LANSBURY etc.
*RCA Vict: RD 60515 (2CDs)*
SONG AND DANCE - songs: Andrew Lloyd Webber-Don Black
  1. ORIG LONDON CAST 1982 *with:* MARTI WEBB & Company
*POLYDOR: 843 619-2 (CD) PODVC 4 (2Cas)*
  2. SONG AND DANCE / TELL ME ON A SUNDAY (STUDIO 1984)
*with* SARAH BRIGHTMAN and WAYNE SLEEP and Company
*RCA (BMG) BD 70480 (CD) BK 70480 (MC)*
*see also* EUROVISION SONG CONTEST
SONG OF NORWAY (STUDIO RECORDED MUSICAL) Songs (Robert
Wright-George Forrest adapted from music by Edvard
Grieg) *feat:* VALERIE MASTERSON-DONALD MAXWELL-DIANA
MONTAGUE-AMBROSIAN CHORUS-PHILH.ORCH (John Owen Edw
ards) *TER (Disc) CDTER2 1173 (2CD) ZCTED 1173 (MC)*
SONG OF SINGAPORE (ORIGINAL USA CAST) *DRG USA (Pinn):*
*CDSBL 19003 (CD)*
SONG OF THE SOUTH - *see* WALT DISNEY INDEX p.343
SONGBOOK (ORIG LONDON CAST 1979) Songs by Monty Norman
& Julian More *feat:* GEMMA CRAVEN-DAVID HEALY-DIANE
LANGTON-ANTON RODGERS-ANDREW C.WADSWORTH *reissue:*
*DRG (New Note-Pinn): DRGCD 13117 (CD)*
SONGS FOR A NEW WORLD (1996)Songs by JASON ROBERT BROWN
ORIG BROADWAY CAST on *RCA (BMG): 09026 68631-2 (CD)*
SONGS OF PRAISE (BBC1 12/9/93) Organ theme by ROBERT
PRIZEMAN recorded by STEPHEN CLEOBURY on Coll
'Splendour Of Kings' *COLLINS (Koch): 14012 (CD)*
Collection of hymns recorded at Old Trafford (BBC)
*EMI ALLIANCE (EMI): ALD 026 (CD) ALC 026 (MC)*
SONS AND DAUGHTERS (Australia ITV 19/10/83) title song
(Peter Pinne-Don Battye) sung by KERRI & MICK
*see COLLECTION 367*
SONS AND LOVERS (1960) Music: MARIO NASCIMBENE -S/T- +
'A FAREWELL TO ARMS' *DRG (Pinn): DRGCSD 32962 (CD)*
SONS OF KATIE ELDER The (1965) Music: ELMER BERNSTEIN
-S/T- *TSUNAMI Imp (Silva Screen): TSU 0104 (CD)*
SOOTY SHOW The (ITV 5/1/83-93) theme: MATTHEW CORBETT
'SOOTY & CO.' *MFP (EMI): TCMFP 6103 (MC)*
SOPHIE'S CHOICE (1983) Orig mus: MARVIN HAMLISCH -S/T-
*SOUTHERN CROSS (S.Screen) SCCD 902 (CD)*
SOPHISTICATED LADIES (ORIG BROADWAY CAST) *feat* Duke Ell
ington songs *IMPT (S.Screen): 56208-2(CD) -4(MC)*
SORCERER The - *see under* 'Wages Of Fear' (1978)
SOUL FOOD (1997) -S/T- featuring VARIOUS ARTISTS on
*LaFACE-RCA (BMG): 73008 26041-2 (CD) -4 (MC) -1(LP)*
SOUL MAN (1986) Music sco: TOM SCOTT + V.Artists -S/T-

*re-issued on SPECTRUM (Poly): 551 431-2 (CD)*
SOUL MUSIC (TERRY PRATCHETT'S) - see under 'DISCWORLD'
SOUND BARRIER The (1952) Mus: MALCOLM ARNOLD "Rhapsody"
'Film Music' LSO (R.Hickox) *CHANDOS: CHAN 9100 CD*
SOUND OF MUSIC The - songs by Richard Rodgers and
Oscar Hammerstein II
1. FILM MUSICAL 1965 *with:* JULIE ANDREWS-CHRISTOPER
PLUMMER -S/T- *collector's 30th anniversary edition*
*on RCA (BMG): 077863 66587-2 (CD) -4 (MC)*
2. CARLTON SHOWS COLLECT STUDIO 1993 *w:* DENIS QUILLEY
LIZ ROBERTSON-LINDA HIBBERD-MASTER SINGERS & Comp
*CARLTON SHOWS: PWKS 4145(CD) PWKMC 4145 (MC)*
3. ORIG BROADWAY CAST 1959  MARY MARTIN-THEODORE BIKEL
PATRICIA NEWAY-KURT KASZNAR-MARION MARLOWE-LAURIE
PETERS-BRIAN DAVIES *SONY BROADWAY: SK 53537 (CD)*
4. ORIG LONDON CAST 1961 *with* JEAN BAYLESS-CONSTANCE
SHACKLOCK-OLIVE GILBERT-SYLVIA BEAMISH-LYNN KENNIN
GTON *LASERLIGHT (BMG): 12448 (CD) also on*
*FIRST NIGHT (Pinn): OCRC 2 (MC)*
SOUTH BANK SHOW The (LWT 1978-97) theme "Caprice In A.
Minor No.24" 'Themes and Variations 1-4' (PAGANINI)
ANDREW & JULIAN LLOYD WEBBER *MCA: MCLD 19126 (CD)*
SOUTH PACIFIC - songs by Richard Rodgers and Oscar
Hammerstein II
1. FILM MUSICAL 1958 *with:* MITZI GAYNOR-ROSSANO BRAZZI
*(sung by* Giorgio Tozzi*)* JOHN KERR-JUANITA HALL *sung*
*by* Muriel Smith*)* -S/T- *RCA (BMG): (ND)(NK)NL 83681*
2. REVIVAL LONDON CAST 1988 *w:* GEMMA CRAVEN-BEATRICE
READING *FIRST NIGHT (Pinn): OCRCD 6023 (CD)*
3. STUDIO RECORDING 1986 *with:* KIRI TE KANAWA-JOSE CAR
reras-Sarah Vaughan-Mandy Patinkin-Ambrosia Singers
L.S.O.(Jonathan Tunick) *SONY: CBSCD 42205 (CD)*
4. CARLTON SHOWS COLLECTION *with:* GEMMA CRAVEN-DAVID
KERNAN-LINDA HIBBERD-MASTER SINGERS-NIC CURTIS etc.
*CARLTON SHOWS Coll: PWKS 4162(CD) PWKMC 4162(MC)*
5. ORIG BROADWAY CAST 1949 *with* MARY MARTIN-EZIO PINZA
JUANITA HALL-BARBARA LUNA-MICHAEL DeLEON-MYRON McCO
RMICK-WILLIAM TABBERT-BETTA St.JOHN and Company
*SONY BROADWAY (Sony Music): SK 53327 (CD)*
6. STUDIO RECORDING 1996) *feat* PAIGE O'HARA
JUSTINO DIAZ-SHEZWAE POWELL-SEAN McDERMOTT with The
NATIONAL SYPHONY ORCH conductor: JOHN OWEN EDWARDS
TER (MCI-Disc): CDTER 1242 (2CD)
SOUTH RIDING (ITV 16/9/74) m: RON GRAINER *see COLLECT.7*
SOUTHERN MAID (O.LONDON CAST 1920) Songs: H.FRASER
SIMPSON-DION CLAYTON CALTHROP-HARRY GRAHAM with
*additional songs by* IVOR NOVELLO and DOUGLAS FURBER
*feat* GWENDOLINE BROGDEN-ERNEST BERTRAM-JOSE COLLINS
CLAUDE FLEMMING-MARK LESTER-BERTRAM WALLIS+*musicals*
*'LILAC TIME' (1922) and 'RIO RITA' (1930) on*
*Pearl (Pavilion): GEMMCD 9115 (CD)*
SPACE 1999 (ITC 4/9/75-77) music: BARRY GRAY
*see COLLECTIONS 110,135,301,357*
SPACE...ABOVE AND BEYOND (USA) *see COLLECTION 110*

SPACE JAM (1996) Music score: JAMES NEWTON HOWARD
   -S/T- songs: *ATLANTIC (WEA): 7567 82961-2(CD)-4(MC)*
   -S/T- score: *ATLANTIC (WEA): 7567 82979-2(CD)*
SPACE PRECINCT (Gerry Anderson's) (BBC2 18/9/95) orig
   music by CRISPIN MERRELL *unavailable*
SPARTACUS (USA-60/renovated 91) Music score: ALEX NORTH
   -S/T- reiss *MCA (BMG): MCLD 19347 (CD) also through*
   *(S.Screen): MCAD 10256 (CD)* additional music on *Imp*
   *TSUNAMI (S.Screen): TSI 0603 (CD)*
SPARTACUS (Jeff Wayne's Musical Version 1992)
   *Columbia (Sony): 472030-4 (2 MC) 472030-2 (2CD)*
SPAWN (1997) Music score: GRAEME REVELL -S/T- (Various
   Artists) *SONY SOUNDTRAX: 488 188-2 (CD) -4 (MC)*
   *488 118-0 (3LP's)*
SPECIALIST The (1994) Music sc JOHN BARRY 2 Soundtracks
   Songs reissue  *EPIC (SM): 477 666-2 (CD)* Songs Spec
   ial.Re-mixes *EPIC: 477 809-2(CD) -4(MC)*
   Score *EPIC : 477 810-2 (CD) -4 (MC) all deleted 96*
SPECIES (1994) Music sco: CHRISTOPHER YOUNG / symphonic
   suite *see COLLECTION 322* 'SPACE AND BEYOND'
SPEED (94) Music score: MARK MANCINA V.Arts -S/T- feat
   BILLY IDOL-PLIMSOULS-GIN BLOSSOMS-PAT BENATAR-RIC
   OCASEK-GARY NUMAN-KISS-SAINT ETIENNE etc *reissued*
   Songs: *ARISTA (BMG): 07822 11018-2 (CD) -4 (MC)*
   Score: *MILAN (BMG): 234 652 (CD)*
SPEED 2: CRUISE CONTROL (1997) Music sco: MARK MANCINA
   V.Arts -S/T- with UB40-SHAGGY-TAMIA-MARK MORRISON-
   TK-CARHINOS BROWN-MAXI PRIEST-LEAH ANDREONE-COMMON
   SENSE-JIMMY CLIFF *VIRGIN (EMI): CDVUS 129 (CD)*
SPEEDWAY *see ELVIS PRESLEY INDEX p.348*
SPELLBOUND (1945) Music score: MIKLOS ROSZA -S/T- with
   music from 'JUNGLE BOOK' (Miklos ROSZA) on *FLAPPER*
   *(Pinn): PASTCD 7093 (CD) see also COLL* 'CINEMA 100'
SPENDER (BBC1 8/1/91) theme music composed & performed
   by TONY McANANEY *unavailable*
SPENSER FOR HIRE (USA 85)(BBC1 12/9/89) theme: STEVE
   DORFF-LARRY HERBSTRITT *see COLLECTION 12*
SPIDER! (BBC1 26/9/91) music by JEFF STEVENSON -S/T-
   *BMG Kidz (BMG): 74321 24642-4 (MC) deleted*
SPIDER BABY (1964) - *see COLLECTION 271*
SPIDERMAN (USA TV) *see COLLECTION 340*
SPINAL TAP - *see under* 'THIS IS SPINAL TAP'
SPINOUT *see ELVIS PRESLEY INDEX p.348*
SPIRITS GHOSTS AND DEMONS (C4 27/9/94) orig music by
   GEORGE FENTON - *see* 'BEYOND THE CLOUDS' entry
SPITFIRE GRILL The (1996) Music sco: JAMES HORNER -S/T-
   *SONY CLASSICS USA: SK 62776 (CD)*
SPITTING IMAGE (Central 6/86) 'Spit In Your Ear' V.Arts
   *VIRGIN (EMI) CDVIP 110 (CD) TCVIP 110 (MC)*
SPORTSNIGHT (BBC1 70-97) title theme: TONY HATCH
   *see COLLECTIONS 3,155,167,182,364,372*
SPORTSVIEW (BBC 1954-68) theme music "Saturday Sports"
   by WILFRED BURNS *see COLLECTION 6*
SPOT (BBC Children's TV) *see COLLECTION 60*

SPRUNG (1997) Various Artists -S/T- on
   *WEA (WEA): 9362 46557-2 (CD) -4 (MC)*
SPY WHO LOVED ME The (1977) Music sco: MARVIN HAMLISCH
   title song (M.Hamlisch-Carole Bayer Sager) sung by
   CARLY SIMON -S/T- *reissue EMI PREMIER: CZ 555 (CD)*
   *see also COLLECT.78,305* and JAMES BOND FILM INDEX
SPYSHIP (BBC1 9/11/83) theme "A Cold Wind" by RICHARD
   HARVEY vocal by JUNE TABOR *K-TEL: ONCD 3435 (CD)*
ST. - *see under 'SAINT...'*
STAND The (1993) Music score: W.G.SNUFFY WALDEN -S/T-
   *VARESE (Pinn): VSD 5496 (CD)*
STAND BY ME (1987) Music sco: JACK NITZSCHE+ Var.Arts
   *ATLANTIC (WEA): CD 7567 781 677-2 (CD) WX 92C(MC)*
STAR! (1968) feat JULIE ANDREWS as Gertrude Lawrence
   -S/T- *FOX-ARISTA (BMG): 07822 11009-2 (CD)*
STAR DUST (1940) VARIOUS -S/T- SELECTIONS on
   *GREAT MOVIE THEMES: (Targ-BMG): CD 60032 (CD)*
STAR IS BORN A (54) *with* JUDY GARLAND-JAMES MASON -S/T-
   *CBS USA (S.Screen): CK 44389 (CD) JST 44389 (MC)*
STAR IS BORN A (76) *with:* BARBRA STREISAND-KRIS KRISTOF
   FERSON -S/T- *COLUMBIA Sony: 474905-2 (CD) -4 (MC)*
STAR SPANGLED RHYTHM (1942 MUSICAL) *feat:* BETTY HUTTON
   BING CROSBY-DICK POWELL *incl.songs from* 'FOOTLIGHT
   PARADE' *TARGET (BMG): CD 60013 (CD)*
STAR TREK (TV)
STAR TREK (USA 66) theme music: ALEXANDER COURAGE *note*
   30TH BIRTHDAY EDITION (Coll) Music taken from best
   STAR TREK 1966-1968 ROYAL PHILHARMONIC ORCHESTRA
   orchest.by FRED STEINER *VARESE: VSD 25762 (2CD)*
   25TH ANNIVERSARY (The Astral Symphony) Featur music
   inc theme *Milan (BMG): 262 832 (CD) 412 832 (MC)*
   CLASSIC SERIES V.1 *GNPD 8006 (CD) GNP-5 8006 (MC)*
   CLASSIC SERIES V.2 *GNPD 8025 (CD) GNP-5 8025 (MC)*
   CLASSIC SERIES V.3 *GNPD 8030 (CD) GNP-5 8030 (MC)*
   SOUND EFFECTS (60) *GNPD 8010 (CD) GNP-5 8010 (MC)*
   STAR TREK *GNP (Vivanti): GNP 8006 (LP Audio Qual)*
   TV SCORES V.1 with R.P.Orch *CBS USA: LXE 703 (CD)*
   TV SCORES V.2 with R.P.Orch *CBS USA: LXE 704 (CD)*
   *see also COLLECTIONS 2,109,159,168,268,273,301,*
   *302,322,339,379,405*
STAR TREK: FIRST CONTACT (1996) Mus sc: JERRY GOLDSMITH
   -S/T- *GNP-Silva Screen (Koch): GNPD 8052 (CD)*
   *GNPD 8052-4 (MC)*
STAR TREK: THE NEXT GENERATION (USA 88)(BBC2-26/9/90)
   New theme: JERRY GOLDSMITH-ALEXANDER COURAGE plus
   music by DENNIS McCARTHY *all dist.by Silva Screen*
   Volume 1 - *GNPD 8012 (CD) GNP-5 8012 (MC)*
   Volume 2 - *GNPD 8026 (CD) GNP-5 8026 (MC)*
   Volume 3 - *GNPD 8031 (CD) GNP-5 8031 (MC)*
   *see COLLECTIONS 12,268,273,322,345*
STAR TREK: DEEP SPACE NINE (USA/BBC2 ?8/9/95) music:
   DENNIS McCARTHY-JAY CHATTAWAY -S/T- *GNP (Silva*
   *Screen): GNPD 8034 (CD) GNP-5 8034 (MC)*
   *see COLLECTION 268*

STAR TREK: VOYAGER (USA 94/BBC 6/95) theme m: JERRY
    GOLDSMITH score: JAY CHATTAWAY -S/T- *GNPD 8041*
    *(CD) GNP-5 8041 (MC) see COLLECTION 273,322*
STAR TREK (1) Motion Picture 1979 Mus: JERRY GOLDSMITH
    -S/T- *Sony: CK 66134 (CD) deleted*
STAR TREK (2) The Wrath Of Khan (1982) Mus sco: JAMES
    HORNER) -S/T- *GNP USA IMPT (S.Screen): GNPD 8022*
    *(CD) GNP-5 8022 (MC)* with orig Alex.Courage theme
STAR TREK (3) Search For Spock (1984) M: JAMES HORNER
    -S/T- *GNP-58023 (MC)*
STAR TREK (4) The Voyage Home (1987) Mus sco: LEONARD
    ROSENMAN -S/T- *reiss: MCA (BMG): MCLD 19349 (CD)*
STAR TREK (5) The Final Frontier (1989) Mus sc: JERRY
    GOLDSMITH -S/T- *EPIC: 465925-2(CD) -4(MC) deleted*
STAR TREK (6) The Undiscovered Country (1991) Mus sco
    CLIFF EIDELMAN -S/T- *MCA (BMG): MCLD 19348 (CD)*
STAR TREK (7) Generations (1994) Mus sc: DENNIS McCAR
    THY -S/T- *GNP (Sil.Scr): GNPD(GNP5) 8040 (CD/MC)*
STAR WARS (1) (1977) Music score: JOHN WILLIAMS -S/T-
    *RSO 2679 092 (LP) 800 096-2 (CD) also available*
    *on RCA RCD 13650 (CD) c/w 'Close Encounters..'*
STAR WARS (2) The Empire Strikes Back (1981) Mus sco
    JOHN WILLIAMS -S/T-*Imp (S.Screen): 827580-4 (MC)*
STAR WARS (3) Return Of The Jedi (1983) Music score:
    JOHN WILLIAMS - National Philharmonic Orchestra
    (Charles Gerhardt) -*RCA Vict (BMG): GD 60767 (CD)*
    -S/T- *RCA: RK 14748 (MC) RCD 14748 (CD)*
STAR WARS (A NEW HOPE) Music score: JOHN WILLIAMS
    Special Edition ORIG SOUNDTRACK RECORDING (1997)
    *RCA (BMG): 09026 68746-2 (Deluxe 2CD)*
    *RCA (BMG): 09026 68772-2 (Slimline 2CD) -4 (2MC)*
    *also available -S/T- VARESE (Pinn): VSD 5794 (CD)*
STAR WARS TRILOGY - The ORIGINAL SOUNDTRACK ANTHOLOGY
    Music score by JOHN WILLIAMS / also containing the
    20th Cent.Fox Fanfare with Cinemascope Extention
    (Alfred Newman) *this collect. contains previously*
    *UNRELEASED mus FOX-Arista (BMG): 07822 11012 4CDs*
STAR WARS TRILOGY Sel.mus.from 3 films + 'Close Encou
    nters' UTAH SYMPH OR *VARESE (Pinn): VCD 47201(CD)*
STARCRASH - *see* 'UNTIL SEPTEMBER'
STARGATE (1994) Mus: DAVID ARNOLD -S/T- *MILAN (BMG):*
    *74321 24901-2(CD) -4(MC) see also* 'CINEMA 100'
STARLIGHT EXPRESS - songs by Andrew Lloyd Webber and
    Richard Stilgoe
    1.ORIG LONDON CAST 1993 *Apollo Victoria Cast*
    *POLYDOR 519 041-2 (CD) 4 (MC) -1 (LP) -5 (Mini-D)*
    2.ORIG LONDON CAST 1984 STEPHANIE LAWRENCE-RAY SHELL
    LON SATTON *POLYDOR: LNCER 1 (2MC) 821597-2 (2CD)*
STARMAN (1985) Mus: JACK NITZSCHE -S/T- *TER (Disc):*
    *CD(ZC)TER 1097 also VARESE (Pinn): VCD 47220 (CD)*
STARS FELL ON HENRIETTA (1995) Music sco: DAVID BENOIT
    -S/T- *VARESE (Pinn): VSD 5667 (CD)*
STARSHIP TROOPERS (1997) Music score: BASIL POLEDOURIS
    -S/T- *VARESE (Pinn): VSD 5877 (CD)*

STARSKY & HUTCH (USA 75) theme "Gotcha" TOM SCOTT
  see *COLLECTIONS 101,168,341,360,379,388*
STARTING HERE STARTING NOW songs: David Shire-Richard
  Maltby Jr O.LONDON CAST *TER (Disc): CDTER 1200*
STATE FAIR songs: Richard Rodgers-Oscar Hammerstein II
  USA BROADWAY CAST 1996 *feat:* JOHN DAVIDSON-DONNA
  McKECHNIE-KATHRYN CROSBY-SCOTT WISE-ANDREA McARDLE
  BEN WRIGHT *DRG (Pinn): DRG(CD)(MC) 94765 (CD/MC)*
STATE OF GRACE (1990) Music sco: ENNIO MORRICONE -S/T-
  *MCA USA (S.Screen): MCAD 10119 (CD)*
STAY AWAY JOE *see* ELVIS PRESLEY INDEX p.348
STAY TUNED (1992) Music sco: BRUCE BROUGHTON + Various
  Arts -S/T- *MORGAN CREEK (Poly): 002251-2 MCM (CD)*
STAYING ALIVE (1983) Music score: JOHNNY MANDEL feat:
  BEE GEES *reissued* -S/T- *RSO (Poly): 813269-2 (CD)*
STAYING ALIVE (ITV 1/11/96) theme "Coming Around Again"
  (C.Simon) sung by JESSICA STEVENSON *unavailable*
STEAL BIG STEAL LITTLE (1996) Music sco: WILLIAM OLVIS
  -S/T- *MILAN (BMG): 74321 32722-2 (CD)*
STEALING BEAUTY (1995) Music sco: RICHARD HARTLEY -S/T-
  *feat Var.Arts:* PORTISHEAD/HOOVER/STEVIE WONDER-JOHN
  LEE HOOKER/LIZ PHAIR/AXIOM FUNK with BOOTSY COLLINS
  NINA SIMONE/BILLIE HOLIDAY/MAZZY STAR/COCTEAU TWINS
  LORI CARSON/SAM PHILLIPS
  *EMI PREMIER:PRMD(CD)(TC) 3*
STEALING HEAVEN (1989) Music score: NICK BICAT -S/T- on
  *TER (Disc): CDTER 1166 (CD) ZCTER 1166 (MC)*
STEEL PIER (ORIG BROADWAY CAST RECORDING)
  *RCA Victor (BMG): 09026 68878-2 (CD)*
STEP LIVELY (1944 MUSICAL) *feat* FRANK SINATRA-ADOLPHE
  MENJOU-GLORIA DE HAVEN *incl.songs from* 'HIGHER AND
  HIGHER' *TARGET (BMG): CD 60004 (CD)*
STEPHEN HAWKING'S UNIVERSE (BBC2 31/8/97) music by
  CYNTHIA MILLAR *unavailable*
STEPTOE & SON (BBC 5/1/62) theme "Old Ned" RON GRAINER
  see *COLLECTIONS 3,7,229,372*
  Original Cast Recording on *BBC: ZBBC 1145 (MC)*
STING The (1973) Music: MARVIN HAMLISCH-SCOTT JOPLIN
  -S/T-*MCA (BMG): MCLD 19027(CD) see COLLECTION 62*
STINGRAY (ATV/ITC 6/10/64 reshown BBC2 11/9/92) music
  BARRY GRAY (vocal: *GARRY MILLER*)
  *see COLLECTIONS 3,110,135,162,273,343,357,364,372*
STOLEN HEARTS (1996) Mus: NICK GLENNIE SMITH-PADDY MOL
  ONEY (CHIEFTAINS) "Haunted" perf: SHANE MacGOWAN-
  SINEAD O'CONNOR -S/T- *M.CREEK (Pinn) 002253-2 MCM*
STONE KILLER The (1973) Music score: ROY BUDD -S/T-
  *(Silva Screen Import): LEGEND CD6 (CD)*
STONES OF THE RAJ (C4 16/8/97) music composed by The
  FRATELLI BROTHERS *unavailable*
STOP IN THE NAME OF LOVE (ORIG LONDON CAST 1990) *with*
  Fabulous Singlettes Live From The Piccadilly on
  *FIRST NIGHT (Pinn): OCRCD 6017 (CD)*
STOP MAKING SENSE (1984) Music by TALKING HEADS -S/T-
  *EMI: EJ 240243-1/-4 (LP/MC) CDP 746064-2 (CD)*

STOP THE WORLD I WANT TO GET OFF (ORIG LONDON CAST 61)
  1. Songs: Anthony Newley-Leslie Bricusse w: ANTHONY NEW
     LEY-ANNA QUAYLE-MARTI WEBB *DECCA (Poly):820958-2CD*
  2. *with* MIKE HOLOWAY-LOUISE GOLD and The NSO ENSEMBLE
     (Martin Yates, MD) *TER (MCI-Disc): CDTER 1226 (CD)*
STORMY MONDAY (1988) Music sco: MIKE FIGGIS also music
     by B.B.KING -S/T- *VIRGIN (EMI): CDV 2537 (CD)*
STORMY WEATHER (1943) M: BENNY CARTER *feat:* LENA HORNE
     BILL ROBINSON-FATS WALLER-CAB CALLOWAY-ADA BROWN
     -S/T- *FOX-ARISTA (BMG): 07822 11007-2 (CD)*
STORY OF RUTH The (1960) Music sco: FRANZ WAXMAN -S/T-
     -S/T- *TSUNAMI Imp (Silva Screen): TCI 0614 (CD)*
     *see also COLL* 'LEGENDS OF HOLLYWOOD'
STORY OF THREE LOVES The (1953) 'Rhapsody On A Theme Of
     Paganini' (RACHMANINOV) on 'CLASSIC EXPERIENCE'
     *EMI PREMIER (EMI): CDCLEXP 1 (2CD) TCLEXP 1 (2MC)*
STRADIVARI (1989) -S/T- Classical M: TELEMANN-H.PURCELL
     VIVALDI-PACHELBEL-HANDEL -S/T- *PHIL: 422849-2 (CD)*
STRAIGHT TO HELL (1987) Mus: POGUES-JOE STRUMMER-ELVIS
     COSTELLO-PRAY FOR RAIN-ZANDER SCHLOSS -S/T- on
     *RERERTOIRE (Pinn): REP 4224WY (CD)*
STRANGE DAYS (1995) Music sco: GRAEME REVELL -S/T- inc
     "While The Earth Sleeps" PETER GABRIEL-DEEP FOREST
     *EPIC (Sony M): 480 984-2 (CD) -4 (MC)*
STRANGE REPORT (ITV 21/9/68) theme music by ROGER WEBB
     *see COLLECTIONS 357,358*
STRANGER THAN PARADISE (1986) plus 'The Resurrection of
     Albert Ayler' Music sco: JOHN LURIE -S/T- score
     *MADE TO MEASURE (New Note-Pinn): MTM 7 (CD)*
STRANGER The (Lo Straniero) (1967) Music score: PIERO
     PICCIONE -S/T- score includes 'THE INNOCENT'
     *DRG (Pinn): DRGCD 3292-2 (CD)*
STREET SCENE (ORIG LONDON CAST 1991) Music: KURT WEILL
     Lyrics (Langston Hughes) w.English National Opera
     Orch (Carl Davis) *TER: (DISC): CD(ZC)TER2 1185*
STREETCAR NAMED DESIRE A (1951) Music score: ALEX NORTH
     Orchestral score: NATIONAL PHILHARMONIC ORCH cond.
     by JERRY GOLDSMITH *VARESE (Pinn): VSD 5500 (CD)*
     *also avail.on CLOUD NINE (S.Screen): CNS 5003 (CD)*
     *with* symphonic suites from 'The INFORMER' (35-Max
     Steiner) 'NOW VOYAGER' (42-Max STEINER) & 'SINCE
     YOU WENT AWAY' (44-Max STEINER) *Archive Series*
STREETFIGHTER (1994) Music sco: GRAEME REVELL 2 -S/T-
     Songs: *VIRGIN: CDPTY(PTYMC)(PTYLP) 114 (CD/MC/LP)*
     Score: *VARESE (Pinn): VSD 5560 (CD)*
STREETHAWK (USA 84 ITV)theme by TANGERINE DREAM *see*
     *see COLLECTIONS 12,336*
STREETS OF FIRE (1984) Songs: JIM STEINMAN -S/T- *reiss:*
     *Beat Goes On (Pinn): BGO(CD)(MC) 220 (CD/MC) also*
     *Import: MCA USA (Silva Screen) MCAD 5492 (CD)*
STREETS OF SAN FRANCISCO (USA) *see COLLECTIONS 100,101*
     *110,246,341,356,379*
STRICTLY BALLROOM (1992) Music sco: DAVID HIRSCHFELDER
     -S/T- reissue *COLUMBIA (Sony): 472300-2*

STRIKE UP THE BAND (40) Songs: GEORGE & IRA GERSHWIN
   new recording on *VIRGIN (EMI): VM 561247-2 (CD)*
   ORIG USA CAST Brent Barrett-Rebecca Luker-Don Chas
   tain-J.Mauceri *ELEKTRA-Nones: 7559 79273-2(CD) -4*
STRIPPER The (1963) Music score: JERRY GOLDSMITH -S/T-
   -S/T- *TSUNAMI Imp (Silva Screen): TCI 0613 (CD)* +
   -S/T- to 'The TRAVELLING EXCECUTIONER' (GOLDSMITH)
STRIPTEASE (96) Music sco: HOWARD SHORE -S/T- *feat V/A*
   BLONDIE/CHYNNA PHILLIPS/PRINCE/B.IDOL/EURYTHMICS..
   *EMI PREMIER (EMI): CDEMC 3751 (CD)*
STUDENT PRINCE The - songs by Sigmund Romberg
   1.FILM MUSICAL 1954 *with:* MARIO LANZA *RCA Red Seal*
     *(BMG): GD(GK) 60048 (CD/MC) with:* The DESERT SONG
   2.STUDIO REC.1990 *with:* NORMAN BAILEY-MARILYN HILL
     SMITH-DIANA MONTAGUE-DAVID RENDALL-ROSEMARY ASHE
     Highlights 1: *SHOWTIME (MCI-THE): SHOW(CD)(MC)033*
     Highlights 2: *TER (Disc): CD(ZC)TEO 1005 (CD/MC)*
     Complete: *TER (Disc): CDTER2(ZCTED)1172 (2CDs/MC)*
   3.STUDIO RECORDING *with:* GORDON MacRAE and Company
     *see under* 'DESERT SONG The'
STUFF THE WHITE RABBIT (Granada 3/6/96)theme "I Put A
   Spell On You" (Jay Hawkins) NINA SIMONE on Coll
   'The 60's Vol.1' *MERCURY (Poly): 838 543-2 (CD)*
STUPIDS The (1996) Music sco: CHRISTOPHER STONE -S/T-
   *INTRADA USA (Silva Screen) MAF 7071 (CD)*
SUBURBIA (1996) Music by ELASTICA-SONIC YOUTH-BUTTHOLE
   SURFERS-SKINNY PUPPY-GENE PITNEY etc.-S/T- V.Arts:
   *GEFFEN-MCA (BMG): GED 25121 (CD) DELETED 97*
SUBWAY (1985)(European version) Music score: ERIC SERRA
   -S/T- *VIRGIN: OVED 223 (LP)* / IMPT (Silva Screen)
   *GMD 9702 (CD) GMK 9702 (MC)* song "A Lucky Guy" Ri
   ckie Lee Jones on 'Pirates' *WB: K2(4)56816 (CD/MC)*
   (USA version) M: BILL CONTI *currently unavailable*
SUDDEN DEATH (1995) Music score: JOHN DEBNEY -S/T- on
   *VARESE (Pinn): VSD 5663 (CD)*
SUGAR BABIES (O.BROADWAY C.1989) Songs: DOROTHY FIELDS-
   JIMMY McHUGH etc.*feat:* MICKEY ROONEY-ANN MILLER-SID
   SID STONE-JACK FLETCHER-ANN JILLIAN-BOB WILLIAMS on
   *VARESE (Pinn): VSD 5453 (CD)*
SUGARFOOT (aka TENDERFOOT) (USA) *see COLLECTION 176*

SULLIVANS The (Australia 79) theme music: GEOFF HARVEY
   *see COLLECTION 367*
SUMMER HOLIDAY (FILM MUSIC.1963) CLIFF RICHARD-Shadows
   -S/T- *MFP (EMI): TCMFP 5824 (MC) CDMFP 6021 (CD)*
   *see also Coll* 'CLIFF RICHARD: AT THE MOVIES'
SUMMER HOLIDAY (MUSICAL 96 Opera House Blackpool 1996)
   w:DARREN DAY-CLARE BUCKFIELD-ROSS KING-FAITH BROWN
   *RCA (BMG): 74321 45616-2 (CD) -4 (MC)*
   DARREM DAY *MEDLEY: RCA (BMG): 74321 38447-2 (CDs)*
   *74321 38447-4 (MC) 74321 38447-7 (7"s)*
SUMMER MAGIC - *see* WALT DISNEY INDEX p.343
SUMMER'S LEASE (BBC2 1/11/89) theme m: "Carmina Valles"
   NIGEL HESS sung CHAMELEON *see COLLECTIONS 138,192*

SUN VALLEY SERENADE (1941 MUSICAL) *w* GLENN MILLER BAND
    and TEX BENEKE *includ.songs from* 'ORCHESTRA WIVES'
    *TARGET (BMG): CD 60002 (CD)*
SUNDAY BLOODY SUNDAY (71) *see COLLECTIONS 69,276*
SUNDAY IN THE PARK WITH GEORGE (O.BROADWAY CAST 1984)
    Songs: STEPHEN SONDHEIM *w:*Mandy Patinkin-Bernadette
    Peters *RCA (Silva Scr): RCD1 5042 (CD) HBE1 5042
    (MC) also RCA (BMG):RD 85042 (CD) RK 85042 (MC)*
SUNDOWN (1989) Music score: RICHARD STONE selection
    *see COLLECTION 378* 'VAMPIRE CIRCUS'
SUNDOWN: THE VAMPIRE IN RETREAT (1990) Music: RICHARD
    STONE -S/T- *SILVA SCREEN (Koch): FILMCD 044 (CD)*
SUNNY (ORIG LONDON CAST 1926) Songs (Jerome Kern-Oscar
    Hammerstein II) *feat:* JACK BUCHANAN-BINNIE HALE-
    *PEARL (Pavilion): GEMMCD 9105 (CD)*
SUNNYSIDE FARM (BBC2 18/4/97) theme music: DAMON ALBARN
    PHIL DANIELS (lyr) performed by BLUR *unavailable*
SUNSET (O.OFF-BROADWAY CAST 1984) Music: GARY WILLIAM
    FRIEDMAN Words: WILL HOLT *feat* Tammy Grimes-Ronee
    Blakley-Kim Milford-Walt Hunter and Company
    *TER (Disc): CDTER 1180 (CD) ZCTER 1180 (MC)*
SUNSET BOULEVARD - songs by Andrew Lloyd Webber
  1a ORIG LONDON CAST 1993 *w:* PATI LuPONE-KEVIN ANDERSON
    *REALLY USEFUL (Poly): 519 767-2 (2CD) -4 (2MC)*
  1b Highlights *POLYDOR (Poly): 527 241-2 (CD) -4 (MC)*
  2. USA STAGE CAST 1994 *with:* GLENN CLOSE and Company
    *REALLY USEFUL (Poly): 523507-2 (2CD) -4 (2MC)*
SUNSET BOULEVARD (1950) Music sco: FRANZ WAXMAN on Col
    'Sunset Boulevard' *RCA (BMG): RD 87017 (CD only)*
SUNSET PARK (1995) Music by Various Artists
    *EAST WEST (WEA): 7559 61904-2 (CD) -4 (MC)*
SUPER MARIO BROS. (1993) Music of Various Arts -S/T-
    *CAPITOL: CDESTU 2201 (CD)*
SUPERCAR (ITV 9/61) mus: BARRY GRAY  Charles Blackwell
    Orch *see COLLECTIONS 4,357*
SUPERCOP (1996) -S/T- feat "Kung Fu Fighting" by TOM
    JONES plus tracks by WARREN G-BLACK GRAPE-DEVO etc.
    *INTERSCOPE-MCA (BMG): IND 90088 (CD) INC 90088 (MC)*
SUPERGIRL (1984) Music score: JERRY GOLDSMITH -S/T-
    *SILVA SCREEN (Koch): FILMCD 132 (CD)*
SUPERMAN (1978) Music score: JOHN WILLIAMS -S/T- Impt
    *WB USA (S.Screen): 3257-2 (CD) and K2.66084 (CD)*
    *see COLLECTIONS 109,110,168,339*
SUPERSTARS (BBC 80s) *see COLLECTION 358*
SUPERTED! - *see COLLECTION 408*
SURGERY The (C4 7/4/97) mus: COLIN WINSTON FLETCHER..*NA*
SURVIVAL: THE MUSIC OF NATURE (Anglia TV) Various Arts.
    *VIRGIN (EMI): VTCD 148 (CD) see also* 'MADAGASCAR'
    and 'DESERT SONG' *music by various composers*
SURVIVING PICASSO (1996) Mus: RICHARD ROBBINS -S/T-
    V.Arts *EPIC Soundtrax (SM): 486 820-2 (CD)*
SUSPIRIA (1976) Music score: DARIO ARGENTO by GOBLIN
    -S/T- *CINEVOX Ita (Silva Screen): CDCIA 5005 (CD)
    CIAK 75005 (MC) see also COLL* 'SIMONETTI PROJECT'

SUTHERLAND'S LAW (UKGO 18/2/95 orig BBC1 6/6/73) theme
    music (Hamish MacCunn) SCOTTISH NATIONAL ORCHESTRA
    conduct: Alexander Gibson *CHANDOS: CHAN 8379 (CD)*
SUZY (1936) *COLLECTION with* 'SAN FRANCISCO'/'DAMES' on
    *GREAT MOVIE THEMES (Targ-BMG): CD 60022 (CD)*
SWAN DOWN GLOVES The (O.LONDON CAST 1982) Songs: NIGEL
    HESS-BILLIE BROWN and The Royal Shakespeare Comp.
    *TER (Disc): CDTER 1017 (CD) ZCTER 1017 (MC)*
SWAN PRINCESS The (1994) Songs: LEX DE AVEZEDO & DAVID
    ZIPPEL *feat* LIZ CALLOWAY *SONY WOND: 483772-2 (CD)*
SWAP SHOP - *see COLLECTION 408*
S.W.A.T. (USA TV) *see COLLECTIONS 341,379*
SWEENEY The (Thames 2/1/75) theme music: HARRY SOUTH
    *see COLLECTIONS 2,5,100,246,356,357,388*
SWEENEY TODD (O.BROADWAY CAST 1979) Songs: STEPHEN
    SONDHEIM *feat:* ANGELA LANSBURY-LEN CARIOU *RCA Imp
    (Silva Screen): 3379-2 (2CD) CBK2 3379 (2MC)*
    HIGHLIGHTS on *RCD1 5033 (CD)*
SWEET CHARITY - songs by Cy Coleman and Dorothy Fields
    1.FILM MUSICAL 1969 *w* SHIRLEY MacLAINE-SAMMY DAVIS JR
      CHITA RIVERA -S/T- *EMI AMERICA: CDP 746562-2 (CD)*
    2.STUDIO RECORD 1995 *w:* JACQUELINE DANKWORTH-GREGG
      EDELMAN-JOSEPHINE BLAKE-SHEZWAE POWELL-DAVID HEALEY
      *SHOWTIME (MCI-THE): SHOW(CD)(MC) 035*
    3.ORIG BROADWAY CAST 1966 *with:* GWEN VERDON & Company
      *CBS USA (S.Screen): CK 02900 (CD) JST 02900 (MC)*
    4.ORIG LONDON CAST 1967 *w* JULIET PROWSE-ROD MacLENNAN
      JOSEPHINE BLAKE-ROGER FINCH-PAULA KELLY-JOHN KESTON
      etc.*SONY WEST END (SM): SMK 66172 (CD)*
SWEET HEREAFTER The (1997) Music score: MYCHAEL DANNA
    -S/T- (VAR.ARTS) *VIRGIN (EMI): CDVIR 68 (CD)*
SWELL PARTY (O.LONDON CAST 1991) Music & Songs Of COLE
    PORTER *S.Screen (Koch): SONG(C)(CD) 905 (MC/CD)*
SWING KIDS (1993) Music score: JAMES HORNER -S/T-
    *MILAN (BMG): 14210-2 (CD) 14210-4 (MC) see also
    Coll* 'CINEMA CLASSICS 7'
SWING TIME (1936) FILM MUSICAL *feat* FRED ASTAIRE-GINGER
    ROGERS -S/T- *selection on* 'Let's Swing and Dance'
    +songs from 'FOLLOW THE FLEET'/'TOP HAT'/'CAREFREE'
    *GREAT MOVIE THEMES (Target-BMG): CD 60015 (CD)*
    *also available recording with* 'FOLLOW THE FLEET' on
    *IRIS Mus-Chansons Cinema (Discov): CIN 006 (CD)*
    *see also COLL* 'FRED ASTAIRE SONGS FROM THE MOVIES'
SWINGERS (1996) Music score: JUSTIN REINHARDT -S/T- with
    Various Artists *POLYDOR (Poly): 162 091-2 (CD)*
SWITCH (USA TV) *see COLLECTION 343*
SWORD IN THE STONE - *see* WALT DISNEY INDEX p.343
SWORDSMAN OF SIENNA (1962) *see COLLECTION 332*


TAFFETAS The (O.OFF-BROADWAY CAST 1988) by RICK LEWIS
    *with* Jody ABRAHAMS-Karen CURLEE-Melanie MITCHELL-
    Tia SPEROS *TER (Disc): (CD)(ZC)TER 1167 (CD/MC)*
TAGGART (Scottish TV began 2/7/85) music: MIKE MORAN

TAGGART (Scottish TV began 2/7/85) music: MIKE MORAN
    "No Mean City" sung by MAGGIE BELL *see COLLECT 388*
TAKE ME HIGH (1973) songs TONY COLE *feat* CLIFF RICHARD
    *EMI: CDEMC 3641 (CD)* with 'HELP IT ALONG' album
    *see also Coll* 'CLIFF RICHARD: AT THE MOVIES'
TAKE ME HOME (BBC1 2/5/89) theme "The Very Thing" from
    'Raintown' DEACON BLUE *SONY: 450549-2 (CD) -4 (MC)*
TAKE THREE GIRLS (BBC2 1971) theme "Light Flight" by
    PENTANGLE from 'Basket Of Light'
    *Transatlantic-Essential (BMG): ESMCD 406 (CD)*
TALENT TO AMUSE, A (SHOW 1995) Songs: NOEL COWARD *feat:*
    PETER GREENWELL *rec.at Swan Theatre STRATFORD-UPON-
    AVON SIL.SCREEN (Koch): SILVAD(SILKC) 3009 (CD/MC)*
TALE OF TWO CITIES, A (1958) *see COLL* RICHARD ADDINSELL
TALES FROM THE CRYPT (USA TV) *see COLLECTION 345*
TALES FROM THE DARKSIDE-THE MOVIE (90) Music (Donald B
    Rubinstein-Pat Regan-Jim Manzie-Chaz Jankel) -S/T-
    *GNP (S.Screen): GNPD 8021(CD) GNP-5 8021 (MC)*
TALES OF BEATRIX POTTER (1971) Music: JOHN LANCHBERRY
    ROYAL OPERA HOUSE ORCHESTRA (John Lanchbery) -S/T-
    re-issued on *EMI ANGEL: CDC 754537-2 (CD)*
    *see also* TV SECT 'WORLD OF PETER RABBIT & FRIENDS'
TALES OF PARA HANDY (BBC1 Scotland 31/7/94) original
    music by PHIL CUNNINGHAM *unavailable*
TALES OF THE UNEXPECTED (Ang.79-87) theme: RON GRAINER
    *see COLLECTIONS 4,7,138,357,360,404*
TALKING TELEPHONE NUMBERS (Celador-Carlton 28/2/94)
    music by KEITH STRACHAN *unavailable*
TAP DANCE KID The (O.BROADWAY CAST 1984) Songs: HENRY
    KRIEGER-ROBERT LORICK *feat* GAIL MELSON-JIMMY TAPE
    *TER (Disc): CDTER 1096 (CD) ZCTER 1096 (MC)*
TARZAN (USA) *see COLLECTION 340*
TASTE THE BLOOD OF DRACULA *see COLLECTIONS 121,206,209*
TATIE DANIELLE (France 1990) - *see* 'AUNTIE DANIELLE'
TAXI (USA 1979/BBC1 17/4/80) Mus: BOB JAMES 'The Genie:
    Themes & Variations from TV Series TAXI'+ "Angela"
    (theme mus) *ESSENTIAL-CASTLE (BMG): ESMCD 465 (CD)*
    *see also COLLECT.12,51,168,242,341,360,373,382,405*
TAXI DRIVER (1976) Music sco: BERNARD HERRMANN -S/T-
    *ARISTA BMG: 258774(CD) COLLS: 63,81,109,187,190,356*
TEENAGE OPERA, A (1967 unrel.musical) songs: MARK WIRTZ
    *feat* KEITH WEST & others. *RPM (Pinn): RPM 165 (CD)*
TELETUBBIES (BBC1 31/3/97) mus dir:ANDREW McCRORY-SHAND
    'Fun With The TELETUBBIES' *BBC (Pinn):YBBC 2063(MC)*
    "Eh-Oh!" *BBC Worldwide BMG: WMXS 00092(CDs) -94(MC)*
TELEVISION NEWSREEL (BBC 1950's) theme "Girls in Grey"
    CHARLES WILLIAMS *see COLLECTIONS 45,137,163,381*
TELL ME ON A SUNDAY (STUDIO RECORDING 1979) Songs: DON
    BLACK-ANDREW LLOYD WEBBER *with* MARTI WEBB & Company
    *POLYDOR: 833 447-2 (CD) see also COLLECTIONS
    36,105,106,232,233,235,395*
TELLY ADDICTS (BBC1 3/9/85) theme mus: GEORGE FENTON.*NA*
TELLYSTACK (Zenith North/UKGO 22/7/96) music by PAUL
    RIORDAN and SIMON STIRLING *unavailable*

TEN (1979) *see COLLECTION 71*
TEN COMMANDMENTS The (1956) Music sco: ELMER BERNSTEIN
     -S/T- *TSUNAMI Imp (Sil.Screen): TSU 0123 (CD) and*
     -S/T- *MCA USA (Silva Screen): MCAD 42320 (CD)*
TEN TO MIDNIGHT (1983) - *see under* 'DEATH WISH'
TENANT OF WILDFELL HALL The (BBC1 17/11/96)
     Music score: RICHARD G.MITCHELL -S/T- on
     *Trident-New Mill. (Pinn): KCCD 4 (CD) KCMC 4 (MC)*
TENDERFOOT (aka SUGARFOOT) (USA) *see COLLECTION 176*
TENDERLOIN (ORIG BROADWAY CAST 1960) Songs: JERRY BOCK-
     SHELDON HARNICK *feat:* MAURICE EVANS and Company
     *EMI Angel: ZDM 565 022-2 (CD)*
TENEBRAE (1982) Music score composed and performed by
     GOBLIN -S/T- *CINEVOX (S.Screen): CDCIA 5035 (CD)*
     *inc* 'Zombie' *see also COLLECTION 312*
TENKO (BBC1 22/10/81) theme: JAMES HARPHAM *unavailable*
TERMINATOR The (1984) Music score: BRAD FIEDEL -S/T-
     *SILVA SCREEN (Koch): FILM(C)(CD) 101 (LP/MC/CD)*
     DEFINIT.EDIT.*Imp (Silva Sc): 0022082CIN (CD)deleted*
     *see COLLECTIONS 8,63,202,268,299*
TERMINATOR 2 (1991) Music sco: BRAD FIEDEL -S/T- score
     *VARESE (Pinn): VSD(VSC) 5335 (CD/MC)*
     special edition *VARESE (Pinn): VSD 5861 (CD)*
     *see collections 55,274,299,300*
TERMS OF ENDEARMENT (1983) Music sc: MICHAEL GORE -S/T-
     *CAPITOL (S.Screen): 46076-2 (CD) see COLL 203,353*
TERROR AND THE TRUTH (BBC2 13/7/97)m: DEBBIE WISEMAN.*NA*
TERROR The (1963) - *see COLLECTION 271*
TERRORISTS The - *see under* 'RANSOM'
TERRY AND JUNE (BBC1 24/10/79) theme music "Bell Hop"
     JOHN SHAKESPEARE *see COLLECTIONS 5,229*
TERRY PRATCHETT'S DISCWORLD see DISCWORLD / SOUL MUSIC
TESTAMENT (C4 6/11/88) theme mus: NIGEL HESS
     *see COLLECTION 192*
TESTAMENT: THE BIBLE IN ANIMATION (BBC2 16/10/96) theme
     music "Adiemus" by KARL JENKINS from 'ADIEMUS-SONGS
     OF SANCTUARY' *VIRGIN (EMI): CD(TC)VE 925 (CD/MC)*
TESTAMENT OF YOUTH (BBC2 4/11/79 re-shown BBC2 3/10/92)
     theme music: GEOFFREY BURGON *see COLLECTION 40*
TESTIMONI (1996-Italy) Music score: PAOLO VIVALDI -S/T-
     *Import (SILVA SCREEN): HP 7001 (CD)*
TFI FRIDAY (Ginger Pr/C4 9/2/96) opening mus "Man In A
     Suitcase" by RON GRAINER *see* 'MAN IN A SUITCASE'
THANK YOUR LUCKY STARS (ATV 60's) theme music: PETER
     KNIGHT *see COLLECTIONS 3,372*
THAT THING YOU DO (1996) Mus score: HOWARD SHORE -S/T-
     *EPIC (Sony Music): 486 551-2 (CD) -4 (MC)*
THAT'S ENTERTAINMENT (1974) VARIOUS ART.COMPILATION
     -S/T- *16 tracks EMI SOUNDTRACK: CDODEON 21 (CD)*
THAT'S ENTERTAINMENT 3 (1994) Music: MARC SHAIMAN -S/T-
     *EMI: CDQ 555215-2 (CD) -4 (MC)*
THAT'S SHOWBUSINESS (BBC1 1/4/96) tm: HELEN MUDDIMAN.*NA*
     previous themes by DEBBIE WISEMAN and ED WELCH...*NA*
THAT'S THE WAY IT IS *see* ELVIS PRESLEY INDEX p.348

THELMA & LOUISE (1991) Music score: HANS ZIMMER -S/T-
    *reissue MCA (BMG): MCLD 19313 (CD)*
THEY THINK IT'S OVER (BBC1 14/9/95) theme music by
    STEVE BROWN *unavailable*
THEY'RE PLAYING OUR SONG - songs by Marvin Hamlisch
    and Carole Bayer Sager
    1.ORIG LONDON CAST 1980 *with:* GEMMA CRAVEN-TOM CONTI
      Highlights: *SHOWTIME (MCI-Disc): SHOW(CD)(MC) 027*
      Complete: *TER (Disc): (CD)(ZC)TER 1035 (CD/MC)*
    2.ORIG BROADWAY CAST 1979 *with:* LUCIE ARNAZ-ROBERT
      KLEIN *CASABLANCA (IMS-Poly):AA826 240-2 (CD)*
THIEF (aka Violent Streets)(1981) Mus: TANGERINE DREAM
    -S/T- TANGERINE DREAM  *VIRGIN (EMI): TAND 12 (CD)*
THIEF OF BAGHDAD The (1940) Music: MIKLOS ROZSA -S/T-
    with 'JUNGLE BOOK' *COLOSS (Pinn):CST 348044 (CD)*
THIEF TAKERS The (Carlton 25/1/96) theme music by
    HAL LINDES *unavailable*
THIN LINE BETWEEN LOVE AND HATE, A (1995) V.Arts inc:
    LBC CREW-TEVIN CAMPBELL-R.KELLY-ADINA HOWARD etc.
    -S/T- *WB (WEA): 9362 46134-2 (CD) -4 (MC)*
THIN BLUE LINE The (1989) Music score: PHILIP GLASS
    -S/T- *ELEKTRA NONESUCH (WEA): 7559 79209-2 (CD)*
THIN BLUE LINE The (BBC1 13/11/95) theme music by
    HOWARD GOODALL *unavailable*
THING CALLED LOVE (1993) -S/T- Var.COUNTRY Artists
    *GIANT (BMG): 74321 15793-2 (CD)*
THING The (1982) Music score ENNIO MORRICONE -S/T-
    *VARESE (Pinn): VSD 5278 (CD) VSC 5278 (MC)*
THINGS TO COME *see COLLECTIONS 62,164,329*
THINGS TO DO IN DENVER WHEN YOU'RE DEAD (1995) Mus:
    MICHAEL CONVERTINO -S/T- featur.Various Artists
    *A.& M. (Poly): 540 424-2 CD*
THINNER (1996) Music score: DANIEL LICHT -S/T-
    *VARESE (Pinn): VSD 5761 (CD)*
THIRD MAN The *see COLLECTION 62*
THIRD ROCK FROM THE SUN (USA 95/BBC2 24/10/96) music by
    BEN VAUGHN. music supervisor LANA HALE *unavailable*
THIRST (1979) Mus: BRIAN MAY *see COLLECTION 378*
THIRTYSOMETHING (USA)(C4 18/1/89) theme: W.G.SNUFFY
    WALDEN-STEWART LEVIN *see COLLECTIONS 168,345*
THIS ANGRY AGE (1957) Mus: NINO ROTA score select.with
    'HURRICANE' *LEGEND (Sil.Screen):LEGENDCD 22 (CD)*
THIS EARTH IS MINE (1959) Music score: HUGO FRIEDHOFER
    *with* 'THE YOUNG LIONS' *VARESE (Pinn): VSD 5403 CD*
THIS GUN FOR HIRE (1942) MUSICAL *feat* VERONICA LAKE and
    ALAN LADD *incl.songs from* 'BATHING BEAUTY' & 'HERE
    COMES THE WAVES' *TARGET (BMG): CD 60001 (CD)*
THIS IS MY LIFE (1992) Music score & songs: CARLY SIMON
    -S/T- *QWEST (WEA): 7599 26901-2 (CD) -4 (MC)*
THIS IS SPINAL TAP (1984) Music composed/sung by SPINAL
    TAP -S/T- *RAZOR (Castle-BMG): LUSLP(MC)2 (LP/MC)*
THIS IS YOUR LIFE (BBC1 94-98/Thames 68-93) theme music
    "Gala Performance" LAURIE JOHNSON
    *see COLLECTIONS 5,33,168,294,358,381*

THIS LIFE (BBC2 18/3/96) title music: MARK ANDERSON &
    CLIFF FREEBORN performed by The WAY OUT *unavailable*
THIS MORNING (Gran 3/10/88-98) theme music by DAVID
    PRINGLE and RAY MONK *unavailable*
THIS WEEK (Thames) theme "Alla Marcia 3 -Karelia Suite"
    (Sibelius) - Academy of Saint Martin-in-the-Fields
    (Neville Marriner) PHILIPS (Poly): 412727-2 (CD)
THIS WORLD THEN THE FIREWORKS (1997) Orig.Jazz score by
    PETE RUGOLO / *songs* "The Thrill Is Gone" and "You
    Don't Know" performed by CHET BAKER -S/T- on
    *VARESE (Pinn): VSD 5860 (CD)*
THOMAS AND SARAH (LWT 14/1/79) theme: HARRY RABINOWITZ
    *see COLLECTION 175*
THOMAS AND THE KING Songs: John Williams-James Harbert
    ORIG LONDON CAST *feat:* JAMES SMILOE-DILYS HAMLETT-
    LEWIS FIANDER *TER (Disc): CDTER 1009 (CD)*
THOMAS CROWN AFFAIR *see COLL* CINEMA 100 / SUMMER PLACE
THOMAS THE TANK ENGINE & FRIENDS (ITV 25/2/92) theme m
    JUNIOR CAMPBELL-MIKE O'DONNELL *MFP (EMI): TCMFP*
    *6104 (MC)* theme also on *Coll* 'TV TUNES FOR KIDS'
THORN BIRDS The (USA BBC1 8/1/84) music: HENRY MANCINI
    *see COLLECTION 168,243,244,352,353*
    'Cathedral' music "Panis Angelicus" (Cesar FRANCK)
THORN BIRDS 2: Missing Years (1995) M: GARRY MacDONALD
    LAURIE STONE -S/T- *VARESE (Pinn): VSD 5712 (CD)*
THOSE WERE THE DAYS (USA) *see COLLECTION 168*
THOUSAND ACRES, A (1997) Music score: RICHARD HARTLEY
    -S/T- *VARESE (Pinn): VSD 5870 (CD)*
THREE COINS IN THE FOUNTAIN (1954) t.song (Sammy CAHN-
    Jule STYNE) sung by FRANK SINATRA 'Screen Sinatra'
    *MFP (EMI): CD(TC)MFP 6052 (CD/MC) see COLLECT.313*
THREE COLEURS: BLEU-BLANC-ROUGE (1993-94) Mus: ZBIGNIEW
    PREISNER *VIRGIN Fra (EMI): CDVMM 15 (3 CDbox set)*
THREE COLOURS: BLUE (1993) Music sc: ZBIGNIEW PREISNER
    *VIRGIN France (EMI): CDVMM 12 (CD)*
THREE COLOURS: RED  (1994) Music sc: ZBIGNIEW PREISNER
    *VIRGIN Fra (EMI): CDVMM 14 (CD) or 839 784-2 (CD)*
THREE COLOURS: WHITE (1993) Music s: ZBIGNIEW PREISNER
    *VIRGIN France (EMI): 839 472-2 (CD)*
THREE DAYS OF THE CONDOR (1975) Music sco: DAVE GRUSIN
    -S/T- *LEGEND Impt.(Silva Screen): LEGENDCD 27 (CD)*
THREE MUSKETEERS The (1935) Music sco: MAX STEINER **new**
    record BRANDENBURG S.ORCH. (Kaufman) + other items
    *MARCO POLO (Select): 8.223607 (CD)*
THREE MUSKETEERS The (1993) Music score: MICHAEL KAMEN
    Song "All For Love" (M.Kamen-B.Adams-R.Lange) sung
    by BRYAN ADAMS ROD STEWART and STING. -S/T- on
    *A.& M. (Poly): 540 190-2 (CD) 540 190-4 (MC)*
THREE O'CLOCK HIGH (1987) Music score: TANGERINE DREAM
    -S/T- *VARESE (Pinn): VCD 47307 (CD)*
THREE SISTERS (1970) Music sco: Sir WILLIAM WALTON New
    Recording by Academy of St.Martin-in-the-Fields
    (Neville Marriner) *CHANDOS: CHAN 8870 (CD)*
THREE STOOGES The (USA) *see COLLECTION 340*

THREE TENORS CONCERT 1994 (BBC1 17/7/94) JOSE CARRERAS
  PLACIDO DOMINGO-LUCIANO PAVAROTTI and ZUBIN MEHTA
  (cond) *TELDEC (WEA): 4509 96200-2 (CD) -4 (MC)
  -5 (MD) 4509 962013 (VHS Video)*
THREE TENORS CONCERT 1990 (C4 7/9/90) JOSE CARRERAS
  PLACIDO DOMINGO-LUCIANO PAVAROTTI and ZUBIN MEHTA
  (cond) *DECCA (Poly): 430 433-2 (CD) -4 (MC)*
THREE WORLDS OF GULLIVER (1959) Music score by
  BERNARD HERRMANN *see COLLECTIONS 165,186,190*
THREE'S COMPANY (USA TV) *see COLLECTION 341*
THREEPENNY OPERA 1.(ORIG DONMAR WAREHOUSE CAST 1994/5)
  Songs: KURT WEILL-MARC BLITZSTEIN *w:* TARA HUGO-TOM
  MANNION-SHARON SMALL-TOM HOLLANDER-SIMON DORMANDY
  *TER (Disc): CDTER 1227 (CD)*
THREEPENNY OPERA 2.(ORIG BROADWAY CAST 1954) Songs by:
  KURT WEILL-MARC BLITZSTEIN *feat* LOTTE LENYA & Comp
  *TER (Disc): CDTER 1101 (CD)*
THREESOME (1994) Music score: THOMAS NEWMAN -S/T-
  also contains score 'AMERICAN BUFFALO' (T.NEWMAN)
  *VARESE (Pinn): VSD 5751 (CD)*
  SONGS -S/T- *EPIC SONY 476 578-2(CD) -4(MC) deleted*
THUNDERBALL (1965) Music sco: JOHN BARRY title song by
  John Barry-Don Black) sung by TOM JONES -S/T- reiss
  *EMI: CZ 556 (CD) see COLLECTIONS 20,25,26,305 see
  also* JAMES BOND FILM INDEX p.346
THUNDERBIRDS! (ATV/ITC 30/9/65-66 reshown BBC2 20/9/91)
  theme: BARRY GRAY *see COLLECTIONS 2,3,110,135,162,
  273,343,357,364,368,372*
THUNDERHEART (1991) Music score: JAMES HORNER -S/T- Imp
  *INTRADA USA (Silva Screen): MAFCD 7027 (CD)*
TICKLE ME *see* ELVIS PRESLEY INDEX p.348
TIGER BAY (BBC1 21/7/97) theme: DANNY CHANG *unavailable*
TIGHTROPE (USA TV) *see COLLECTION 342*
TIME MACHINE The (1960) Music (Russell Garcia) -S/T-
  *GNP (S.Screen) GNPD(GNP5) 8008 (CD/MC)*
TIME OF THE GYPSIES (1989) Music score: GORAN BREGOVICH
  -S/T- *Imprt (SILVA SCREEN): 515862-2 (CD) -4 (MC)*
TIME TO KILL, A (1996) Music score: ELLIOT GOLDENTHAL
  -S/T- *ATLANTIC (WEA): 7567 82959-2 (CD) -4 (MC)*
TIME TUNNEL (USA 66) theme music: JOHN WILLIAMS
  *see COLLECTIONS 110,273.340*
TIMECOP (1993) Music score: MARK ISHAM -S/T- on
  *VARESE (Pinn): VSD 5532 (CD)*
TIMEWATCH (BBC2 6/11/94) opening title mus "In Trutina"
  from 'Carmina Burana' CARL ORFF *version by* LUCIA
  POPP on *EMI Studio Plus: CDM 764328-2 (CD)*
TIN CUP (1996) Music score: WILLIAM ROSS -S/T- V.Arts
  *EPIC Soundtrax (SONY): 484 293-2 (CD)*
TINKER TAILOR SOLDIER SPY (BBC1 10/9/79) theme "Nunc Di
  mittis" GEOFFREY BURGON Seaford Coll. Chapel Choir
  *see COLLECTIONS 6,40*
TISWAS (ATV 70s) *see COLLECTION 357*
TITANIC (FILM 1997) Music: JAMES HORNER -S/T- V.Artists
  *ARTFUL (TRC-Pinn:): ARTFULCD 11 (CD)*

TITANIC (MUSICAL 1997) Songs by MAURY YESTON./ ORIGINAL
    BROADWAY CAST *RCA Victor (BMG): 09026 68834-2 (CD)*
TITFIELD THUNDERBOLT The (1952) *see COLLECTION 225*
TITMUS REGAINED (ITV 3/9/91) see COLLECTION 191
TJ HOOKER (USA) *see COLLECTIONS 101,344*
TO DIE FOR (1995) Music score: DANNY ELFMAN -S/T-
    *VARESE (Pinn): VSD 5646 (CD)*
TO DIE FOR (1989) Music score: CLIFF EIDELMAN / also
TO DIE FOR 2: SON OF DARKNESS)(1991) Mus: MARK McKENZIE
    *see COLLECTION 378*
TO HAVE AND HAVE NOT (1945) Music score: FRANZ WAXMAN
    see 'CASABLANCA' *COLLECTION 286*
    also VARIOUS -S/T- SELECTIONS *GREAT MOVIE THEMES:*
    *(Targ-BMG): CD 60032 (CD)*
TO HAVE AND TO HOLD (1995) Mus: NICK CAVE-BLIXA BARGOED
    MICK HARVEY -S/T- *MUTE-RTM (Disc): IONIC 15CD (CD)*
TO HAVE AND TO HOLD (LWT 29/8/86) theme by JOHN WORTH
    sung CATHERINE STOCK *see COLLECTION 175*
TO KILL A MOCKINGBIRD (1962) Music sco: ELMER BERNSTEIN
    rec.by ROYAL SCOTTISH NATIONAL ORCH (E.Bernstein)
    *VARESE (Pinn): VSD 5754 (CD)*
TO LIVE AND DIE IN L.A. (1986) Music: WANG CHUNG -S/T-
    *GEFFEN-MCA Goldline (BMG): GED 24081 (CD)*
TO THE ENDS OF THE EARTH (Film Document.84) Music sco:
    JOHN SCOTT -S/T- *PROMETHEUS (S.Scr) PCD 102(CD)*
TO WONG FOO (1995) var.artists inc SALT.N.PEPA-CRYSTAL
    WATERS-TOM JONES-CYNDI LAUPER-LABELLE -S/T- on
    *MCA (BMG): MCD 11231 (CD)*
TODAY *see COLLECTION 2*
TOM AND VIV (1993) Music score: DEBBIE WISEMAN -S/T-
    *SONY Masters: SK 64381 (CD) DELETED 1997*
TOM BROWN'S SCHOOLDAYS 1950 *see COLLECTION 41*
TOM JONES (BBC1 9/11/97) Music score: JIM PARKER -S/T-
    *OCEAN DEEP (Poly): OCD 012 (CD)*
TOMBSTONE (1993) Music score: BRUCE BROUGHTON -S/T- on
    *INTRADA USA (Silva Screen): MAF 7038D (CD)*
TOMMY (FILM ROCK OPERA 1975) Music: PETE TOWNSHEND *Feat*
    The WHO-ELTON JOHN etc.-S/T- *POLYD 841 121-2 (CD)*
    *RE-MASTERED VERSION 1996 on POLYD 531 043-2 (CD)*
TOMMY (ROCK OPERA) LONDON SYMPH ORCH / PETE TOWNSHEND
    Roger DALTREY-Maggie BELL-Rod STEWART-Sandy DENNY-
    Ringo STARR-John ENTWISTLE-Steve WINWOOD-R.HAVENS
    *ESSENTIAL-CASTLE (BMG): ESMCD 404 CD)*
TOMMY (ORIG BROADWAY CAST 1993) Songs: PETE TOWNSHEND
    *RCA VICTOR (BMG): 09026 6187402 (CD)*
TOMORROW NEVER DIES (1997) Music score: DAVID ARNOLD
    title song by SHERYL CROW with end song by k.d.lang
    -S/T- *A.& M (Polyg): 540 830-2 (CD) 540 830-4 (MC)*
TOMORROW PEOPLE The (Thames 30/4/73-79) music: DUDLEY
    SIMPSON and BRIAN HODSON *see COLLECTION 301*
TOMORROW'S WORLD (BBC1) 1997/1988 series theme by
    DIVINE COMEDY. 1995/96 theme MARIUS DE VRIES. 1991-
    94 theme CHRIS BLACKWELL. *all unavailable* 1986-91
    theme "Halley's Comet" PAUL HART *see COLLECTION 31*

TONIGHT (BBC1 50's/60's) theme music "Today's Tonight"
*see COLLECTION 1*
TONITE LET'S ALL MAKE LOVE IN LONDON (FILM MUSICAL1967)
*SEE FOR MILES (Pinn): SEECD(SEEK) 258 (CD/MC)*
TOOL STORIES (C4 15/7/97) mus: JASON OSBORN *unavailable*
TOP CAT (USA 62/BBC UKtitle 'Boss Cat') md HOYT CURTIN
"Top Cat" theme (W.Hanna-J.Barbera-Evelyn Timmens)
*see COLLECTIONS 339,370*
TOP GEAR (BBC2 70's-98) *Opening theme* "Jessica" ALLMAN
BROTHERS BAND on 'Brothers and Sisters' album
*CAPRICORN (Polyg): 825 092-2 (CD) Closing theme*
"Blue Moves" (Elton John-Bernie Taupin) ELTON JOHN
*ROCKET (Poly): 822 818-2 (CD) 822 818-4 (MC)*
*also available Coll of Mus from series 'Top Gear'*
*EPIC (Sony): MOODCD 33 (CD) MOODC 33 (MC)*
TOP GEAR RALLY REPORT (BBC2 22/11/96) theme "Duel" by
PROPAGANDA *ZTT (Isl-Poly) ZCIQ 3 (MC) CID 126 (CD)*
TOP GUN (1986) Mus: HAROLD FALTERMEYER "Take My Breath
Away" (Berlin) -S/T- *COLUMBIA (SONY): CD 70296(CD)*
*40-70296 (MC) MD 70296 (MD)* see COLL.8,39,262,384
TOP HAT (1935) FILM MUSICAL *feat* FRED ASTAIRE-GINGER
ROGERS -S/T- *sel.on* 'Let's Swing and Dance'+ songs
from 'FOLLOW THE FLEET'/'SWING TIME'/'CAREFREE'
*GREAT MOVIE THEMES (Target-BMG): CD 60015 (CD)*
*also available recoring with* 'THE GAY DIVORCEE'
*IRIS-Mus-Chansons Cinema (Discovery): CIN 005 (CD)*
TOP HAT with Yehudi Menuhin (violin) Stephane Grappelli
(violin/piano) + N.Riddle *CFP (EMI):CDCFP 4509 (CD)*
TOP OF THE FORM (BBC2 60's) theme "Marching Strings"
(Ross) *see COLLECTIONS 1,31,163,402*
TOP OF THE POPS (BBC1 1/1/64-1998) various theme mus:
(from 2/2/95) theme: VINCE CLARKE *unavailable*
(from 3/10/91) "Get Out Of That" by TONY GIBBER..*NA*
(from 1986-91) "The Wizard" PAUL HARDCASTLE *deleted*
(from 1981-85) "Yellow Pearl" (M.URE-PHIL LYNOTT)
*VERTIGO (Poly): PRICE(PRIMC) 88 (LP/MC)*
(from 1974-80) "Whole Lotta Love" CCS *see COLL 361*
(orig by *LED ZEPPELIN ATLANTIC (WEA): K(2)(4)40037*
(from 1969-74) theme arrangement by JOHNNY PEARSON
(from 1965-69 o.theme: JOHNNIE STEWART-HARRY RABIN
OWITZ version by BOBBY MIDGLEY (2 versions)..... *NA*
TOP OF THE POPS 2 (BBC2 17/9/94) theme: BILL PADLEY..*NA*
TOP SECRET (ITV 11/8/61-62) "Sucu Sucu" LAURIE JOHNSON
*see COLLECTIONS 3,372*
TORA! TORA! TORA! (1970) music score: JERRY GOLDSMITH
score with 'PATTON' new recording by ROYAL SCOTTISH
NATIONAL ORCHESTRA (Jerry Goldsmith, conducting)
*VARESE (Pinn): VSD 5796 (CD)*
TORN CURTAIN (1966) rejected score: BERNARD HERRMANN
*SILVA SCREEN (Koch): FILMCD 162 (CD)* -S/T- reissue
*VARESE (Silva Screen): VSD 5296 (CD)*
*see also COLLECTIONS 187,189,190,197*
TORVILL & DEAN (Olympic Games 94 Lillehammer)(Ice Dance
Mus) Free Dance: 'LET'S FACE THE MUSIC' (I.Berlin)

Set Piece (Rhumba) 'HISTORY OF LOVE' (C.Almaran) +
mus: from MACK AND MABEL/SUMMERTIME/BARNUM/BOLERO/
CAPRICCIO ESPAGNOL/VENUS/LOVE DUET FROM FIRE & ICE
SNOW MAIDEN/DOLENCIAS(Missing)/OSCAR TANGO ICEWORKS
(Tilt)/SKATERS WALTZ/MEDLEY 94 GALA on Collection
'FACE THE MUSIC' POLYDOR: 845065-2 (CD) -4 (MC)
TOTAL ECLIPSE (1995) Music: JAN A.P.KACZMAREK -S/T-
Var.Arts SONY Classics (SM): SK 62037 (CD)
TOTAL RECALL (1989) Music score: JERRY GOLDSMITH -S/T-
VARESE (Pinn): VSD 5267 (CD) VSC 5267 (MC)
see COLLECTIONS 156,268,299,300,301
TOTO THE HERO (1991) Music sco: PIERRE VAN DORMAEL song
"Boum" (Char.Trenet-Roma Campbell Hunter) sung by
CHARLES TRENET EMI: CDP 794 464-2 (CD)
TOTS TV (Ragdoll Prod/Central 4/1/93) theme "I'm A Tot"
ANDREW McCRORIE SHAND TV -S/T- MFP (EMI): TCMFP
6148 (MC) theme also on 'TV TUNES FOR KIDS 2' BMG
-S/T- 'Tilly's Disco' MFP (EMI): (CD)(TC) 6154
TOUCH OF CLASS, A (1973) Music score by JOHN CAMERON
song "All That Love Went To Waste" (Sammy Cahn-Geo
rge Barrie) sung by MADELINE BELL -S/T- reissue on
DRG-NEW NOTE (Pinn): DRGCD 13115 (CD)
TOUCH OF EVIL, A (1958) Music sco: HENRY MANCINI -S/T-
VARESE (Pinn): VSD 5414 (CD) + DISCOVERY: MSCD 401
TOUCH OF FROST A (YTV 6/12/92) music composed/performed
by BARBARA THOMPSON and JON HISEMAN unavailable
TOUCH OF SCANDAL, A see COLLECTION 242
TOUCHE TURTLE - see COLLECTION 370
TOUGH GUYS DON'T DANCE (1987) - see under 'DEATH WISH'
TOUR DE FRANCE (TSL/C4 1991-98) theme music composed
and peformed by PETER SHELLEY (p.Virgin) unavailable
note: earlier theme see COLLECTION 155
TOUS LE MATINS DU MONDE (France 1992) Music sco: JORDI
SAVALL -S/T- AUVIDIS Valoir (Koch): AUV 4640 (CD)
AUV 54640 (MC) see also COLLECTION 73
TOY STORY (1996) Mus.songs: RANDY NEWMAN "You've Got A
Friend In Me" (R.Newman) sung by RANDY NEWMAN -S/T-
DISNEY (Technicolor): WD 77130-2(CD) WD 771304(MC)
TOYS (1992) Music score: HANS ZIMMER-TREVOR HORN -S/T-
WB-ZTT (WEA): 4509 91603-2 (CD) 91603-4 (MC)
TRACEY ULLMAN SHOW The (USA TV) see COLLECTION 345
TRACKS (BBC2 P.Mill 18/5/94) orig music composed and
performed by DAVID LOWE unavailable
TRADING PLACES (1983) see COLLECTIONS 76,276
TRAFFIK (C4 22/6/89) theme arr.by FIACHRA TRENCH part
of Chamber Symph.For Strings Op.110A (SHOSTAKOVICH)
CHANDOS: CHAN 8357 (CD)
TRAGICALLY HIP (1995) -S/T- MCA (BMG): MCLD 19314 (CD)
TRAINSPOTTING (1995) -S/T- V/A: BLUR-ELASTICA-BRIAN ENO
LEFTFIELD-IGGY POP-SLEEPER-PULP-LOU REED-UNDERWORLD
DAMON ALBARN-NEW ORDER-BEDROCK KYO EMI Premier :
CDEMC 3739 (CD) TCEMC 3739 (MC) EMC 3739 (2LPs)
'TRAINSPOTTING VOL.2' Various Arts
EMI SOUNDTRACKS: PRMDCD 36 (CD) PRMDTC 36 (MC)

TRANSYLVANIA TWIST (1991) Music score: CHUCK CIRINO
    see *COLLECTION 378*
TRANSYLVANIA 65000 (1985) Music score: LEE HOLDRIDGE
    see *COLLECTION 378*
TRAP The (1966) Music sco: RON GOODWIN *theme also used*
    *for* BBCTV 'LONDON MARATHON' coverage / Film -S/T-
    *IMP (S.Screen): LXE 708 (CD) see COLLECTS.158,159*
TRAPPER JOHN, MD (USA TV) *see COLLECTION 344*
TRAVEL SHOW The (BBC2 9/5/96) orig music: SIMON LAW and
    VIVIENNE McKONE music research: ANDREW MORGAN....*NA*
    previous ser.theme "Two Nations" HOWARD DAVIDSON.*NA*
TRAVELLER (1997) -S/T- V.A. *WB (WEA): 7559 62030-2 (CD)*
TRAVELLING MAN (Granada 3/9/85) theme: DUNCAN BROWNE &
    SEBASTION GRAHAM JONES *see COLLECTION 6*
TRAVELS WITH PEVSNER (BBC1 15/3/97) m: ORLANDO GOUGH.*NA*
TREAD SOFTLY STRANGER *see COLLECTION 288*
TREATY The (Thames/RTE/ABC 15/1/92) music sco: MICHEAL
    O'SUILLEABHAIN from the album 'Oilean' on
    *VIRGIN Venture: CDVE 40(CD) TCVE 40(MC) VE 40(LP)*
TREASURE OF THE SIERRA MADRE The (1948) Music score:
    MAX STEINER *see COLLECTION 54* 'CASABLANCA'
TREES LOUNGE (1996) Music sco: EVAN LURIE / Var.Arts
    -S/T- on *MCA (BMG): MCD 11539 (CD)*
TRESPASS (1993) Music score: RY COODER (2 -S/T-)
    score -S/T- *SIRE (WEA): 759 926978-2 (CD) -4 (MC)*
    songs -S/T- *WB (WEA):   936 245220-2 (CD) -4 (MC)*
TRIAL BY JURY - *D'Oyly Carte Opera Company* (GILBERT &
    SULLIVAN) +'Yeomen Of The Guard' *Lond: 417 358-2CD*
TRIALS OF LIFE (BBC1 3/10/90) mus score: GEORGE FENTON
    *PRESTIGE (BMG): CDSGP 030 (CD) CASSGP 030 (MC)*
    see *COLLECTION 5*
TRIANGLE (BBC1 81) theme music by JOHNNY PEARSON
    see *COLLECTION 285*
TRIBUTE TO THE BLUES BROTHERS A (O.LONDON CAST 1991)
    *feat* Con O'Neill-Warwick Evans & Company
    *FIRST NIGHT (Pinn): CASTCD 25 (CD) CASTC 25 (MC)*
TRIPODS The (BBC1 15/9/84) theme and incidental music:
    KEN FREEMAN -S/T- *G.R.FORRESTER (Pin):GERCD 1(CD)*
TROMEO AND JULIET (1996) Music score: WILLIE WISELY
    -S/T- *TROMA (Greyhound): 42907 (CD)*
TROUBLE WITH GIRLS The *see* ELVIS PRESLEY INDEX p.348
TROUBLE WITH HARRY *see COLLECTION 196*
TROUBLESHOOTER 2 (BBC2 10/11/92) and TROUBLESHOOTER
    RETURNS (BBC2 31/5/95) theme m: MICHAEL NYMAN..*NA*
TROUBLESOME CREEK: A MID-WESTERN (1995) Music score by
    SHELDON MIROWITZ and DUKE LEVENE -S/T-
    *Daring Rec.(Pinn/Topic): DARINGCD 3024 (CD)*
TRUE BLUE (1996) Music: STANISLAS SYREWICZ -S/T- V/A
    *DECCA (Polygram): 455 012-2 (CD) -4 (MC)*
TRUE GRIT (1969) Music sco: ELMER BERNSTEIN title song
    (Bernstein-Black) by GLEN CAMPBELL on 'Country Boy'
    *MFP EMI:CD(TC)MFP 6034 (CD/MC) see COLL* TRUE GRIT
TRUE LIES (1994) Music score: BRAD FIEDEL -S/T- reissue
    *EPIC SOUNDTRAX (SM): 476939-2 (CD)*

TRUE ROMANCE (1993) Music: HANS ZIMMER & MARK MANCINA
   -S/T- *reiss: MORGAN CREEK (Poly): 002242-2MCM (CD)*
TRUE STORIES (1986) Music: DAVID BYRNE / TALKING HEADS
   -S/T- *EMI: TC-EMC 3520 (MC) CDP 746345-2 (CD)*
TRUE WOMEN (TVM) Music score: BRUCE BROUGHTON -S/T- on
   *INTRADA (Koch): MAFD 7077 (CD)*
TRULY MADLY DEEPLY (BBC2 1/3/92) m: BARRINGTON PHELOUNG
   on compilation 'PASSION OF MORSE' also includ: 'The
   Politician's Wife'/'Inspector Morse' and 'Saint-Ex'
   *TRING INT (Tring): TRING 003 (CD) MCTRING 003 (MC)*
TRUMPTON (BBC1 1967) Mus: FREDDIE PHILLIPS *see COLL.408*
TRUSTING BEATRICE (Film) Music score: STANLEY MYERS
   with Suite from 'COLD HEAVEN' (Stanley MYERS) on
   *INTRADA Imprt (Silva Screen): MAF 7048D (CD)*
TRUTH ABOUT CATS AND DOGS The (1996) Music sco: HOWARD
   SHORE -S/T- *A.& M.(Poly): 314 540507-2 (CD)*
TUBE The (C4 Tyne Tees 82-84) theme "Star Cycle" (JEFF
   BECK) 'Best Of Beckology' *EPIC: 471348-2 (CD) -4MC*
TUNE IN TOMORROW (1991) Music score by WYNTON MARSALIS
   -S/T- *COLUMBIA (Sony): 467785-2(CD) -4(MC) -1(LP)*
TURNING POINT (1977) *see COLLECTION 79*
TURTLE BEACH (1991) Music sco: CHRIS NEAL theme *on COLL*
   'BLADE RUNNER' *SILVA SCREEN (Koch): SILVAD 3008(CD)*
TV NEWSREEL (BBC 50's) Theme "Girls In Grey" CHARLES
   WILLIAMS *see COLLECTIONS 45,163,381*
TWELFTH NIGHT (1996) Music sco: SHAUN DAVEY recorded by
   IRISH NATIONAL FILM ORCHESTRA cond: FIACHRA TRENCH
   *SILVA SCREEN (Koch): FILMCD 186 (CD)*
TWELVE MONKEYS (1995) Music sco: PAUL BUCKMASTER -S/T-
   with VARIOUS ARTISTS *MCA (BMG): MCD 11392 (CD)*
TWILIGHT ZONE The (TV USA 60's) theme: BERNARD HERRMANN
   BEST OF TWILIGHT ZONE *VARESE (Pinn): VCD 47233 (CD)*
   VOL.2' *VCD 47247 (CD)* NOTE: 1986 ser theme by
   GRATEFUL DEAD & MERL SAUNDERS *unavailable*
   *see COLLECTIONS 61,110,273,339,374,404*
TWILIGHT'S LAST GLEAMING (1977) Music: JERRY GOLDSMITH
   -S/T- *SILVA SCREEN (Koch): FILMCD 111 (CD)*
TWIN PEAKS (USA 90)(BBC2-23/10/90) music score: ANGELO
   BADALMENTI) songs (David Lynch-Angelo Badalamenti)
   "Falling" sung by JULEE CRUISE 'Music From Twin
   Peaks' *WEA: 7599 26316-2 (CD) -4 (MC) / for theme*
   *see COLLECTIONS 12,55,267,333,345,356,357,404*
TWIN PEAKS: FIRE WALK WITH ME (1992) Music: ANGELO
   BADALAMENTI) + Various Artists -S/T- *WB (WEA):
   9362 45019-2 (CD) -4 (MC) / SEE ALSO TV SECTION*
TWIN TOWN (1997) Music sco MARK THOMAS / Var.Artists
   -S/T- on *A.& M. (Poly): 540 718-2 (CD)*
TWIST OF SAND, A *see COLLECTION 288*
TWISTER (1996) Music score: MARK MANCINA -S/T-
   *WEA: 9362 46265-2 (CD) -4 (MC)*
TWO DAYS IN THE VALLEY (1996) Music: ANTHONY MARINELLI
   -S/T *V.Arts:* WILSON PICKETT-JUNIOR WELLS-OTIS REDD
   ING-MORPHINE-ERIN O'HARA-TAJ MAHAL-LYLE LOVETT etc.
   *EDEL (Pinn): 0029772EDL (CD)*

TWO FAT LADIES (BBC2 9/10/96) theme music: PETE BAIKIE
    JENNIFER PATERSON & CLARISSA DICKSON-WRIGHT voc..*NA*
TWO HEADED SPY The (1958) Music score: GERARD SCHURMANN
    *on COLLECTION* 'COASTAL COMMAND' *deleted*
TWO MOON JUNCTION (1988) Music: JONATHAN ELIAS -S/T-
    *VARESE (Pinn): VSD 5518 (CD)*
TWO POINT FOUR CHILDREN (BBC1 3/9/91-1997) theme music
    composed by HOWARD GOODALL *see COLLECTION 229*
TWO RONNIES The (BBC1 70s-80s) (The DETECTIVES 'Charley
    Farley and Piggy Malone') *see COLLECTIONS 317,360*


U.F.O. (ATV/ITC 16/9/70-73) music: BARRY GRAY
    *see COLLECTIONS 110,135,357*
UK-DK (1983) Punk Video Film with Various Punk Groups
    -S/T- *re-issue: CHERRY RED (Pinn): CDPUNK 47 (CD)*
ULYSSES (1954) Music score: ALESSANDRO CICOGNINI -S/T-
    *LEGEND Imp (Silva Screen): LEGEND CD 8 (CD)*
ULYSSES GAZE (1995) Music sco: ELENI KARAINDROU -S/T-
    *ECM NEW NOTE (Pinn): 449 153-2 (CD) -4 (MC)*
UMBRELLAS OF CHERBOURG (1964) Music sco: MICHEL LEGRAND
    Song "I Will Wait For You" (Lyrics Norman GIMBEL)
    -S/T- *ACCORD (Discovery): 10326-2 (CD) also through
    SILVA SCREEN: 834 139-2 (CD) see COLLECTION 400*
UN COEUR EN HIVER - see 'HEART IN WINTER, A'
UN HOMME ET UNE FEMME - see 'MAN AND A WOMAN, A'
UNDER MILK WOOD (South Bank Show) *ORIGINAL CAST RECORD*
    ANTHONY HOPKINS-JONATHAN PRYCE-FREDDIE JONES-NERYS
    HUGHES-WINDSOR DAVIES-GERAINT EVANS-SIAN PHILLIPS
    RUTH MADOC-GEMMA JONES-HARRY SECOMBE + *music by*
    MARY HOPKIN-BONNIE TYLER and TOM JONES *reissued on*
    *EMI GOLD-LFP: LFPC 7997 (2MC)*
UNDER SIEGE (1992) Music score: GARY CHANG -S/T-
    *VARESE (Pinn): VSD 5409 (CD) VSC 5409 (MC)*
UNDER SIEGE 2: Dark Territory (1995) Music score: BASIL
    POLEDOURIS -S/T- *VARESE (Pinn): VSD 5648 (CD)*
UNDER THE CHERRY MOON (1986) Music: PRINCE -S/T- on
    *WB (WEA): 925 395-2 (CD)*
UNDER THE CRESCENT (C4 4/10/97) title music by TALAT
    AZAZ and CARL GARDINER *unavailable*
UNDERGROUND (IL ETAIT UNE FOIS UN PAYS) (1995) Music:
    GORAN BREGOVICH -S/T- *POLYD (IMS): E.528 910-2 (CD)
    POLYGRAM France (Discovery): 528 910-2 (CD)*
UNDERNEATH (1995) Music score: CLIFF MARTINEZ -S/T-
    *VARESE (Pinn): VSD 5587 (CD)*
UNDERNEATH THE ARCHES (O.LONDON CAST 1982) The Songs of
    FLANAGAN & ALLEN *feat:* ROY HUDD-CHRISTOPHER TIMOTHY
    *TER (Disc): CDTER 1015 (CD) ZCTER 1015 (MC)*
UNDERWORLD (C4 4/11/97) mus: MATTHEW SCOTT *unavailable*
UNE FEMME FRANCAISE (1995) Music score: PATRICK DOYLE
    -S/T- *WEA France: 4509 99630-2 (CD)*
UNFORGIVEN (1992) Music score: LENNIE NIEHAUS -S/T-
    *VARESE (Pinn): VSD 5380 (CD)*
UNINVITED The (ITV 25/9/97) Music score: MARTIN KISZKO
    -S/T- *OCEAN DEEP (Poly): OCD 007 (CD)*

UNITED KINGDOM (BBC2 24/6/97) series title music by
   NIGEL HESS *unavailable*
UNIVERSAL SOLDIER (1992) Music sco: CHRISTOPHER FRANKE
   -S/T- *VARESE (Pinn): VSD 5373 (CD*
   *see also Coll* 'UNIVERSAL SOLDIER'
UNIVERSITY CHALLENGE (BBC2 21/9/94) theme "College Boy"
   DEREK NEW (new arrangement) *unavailable*
UNLAWFUL ENTRY (1992) Music score: JAMES HORNER -S/T-
   *INTRADA (S.Screen): MAFCD 7031 (CD)*
UNNATURAL CAUSES (Anglia 2/1/93) theme music "Elegy"
   by RICHARD HARVEY *Coll* 'SHROUD FOR A NIGHTINGALE'
   *SILVA SCREEN (Koch): FILMCD 172 (CD)*
UNS ET LES AUTRES Les  *see under* 'INS AND THE OUTS The'
UNSTRUNG HEROES (1995) Music score: THOMAS NEWMAN -S/T-
   *HOLLYWOOD (IMS-Poly): E.162 035-2 (CD)*
UNTAMED (1955) - *see COLLECTION 392*
UNTAMED HEART (1992) Music score: CLIFF EIDELMAN -S/T-
   *VARESE (Pinn): VSD 5404 (CD) VSC 5404 (MC)*
UNTIL SEPTEMBER (1984) and STARCRASH (1979-Ita) Music:
   JOHN BARRY  *Silva Scr: FILMCD 085 (CD) DELETED*
   *see also* John Barry *Collections* 'MOVIOLA' etc.
UNTOUCHABLES The (1987) Music score ENNIO MORRICONE and
   "Vesti La Giubba" from 'I Pagliacci' (LEONCAVALLO)
   -S/T- *A.& M.(IMS-Poly): E.393909-2 (CD) see Colls*
   'CINEMA CLASSICS 5'/'OPERA AT THE MOVIES'
   *see COLLECTIONS 108,246,342*
UP CLOSE AND PERSONAL (1995) Music sco: THOMAS NEWMAN
   -S/T- inc V.Artists *POLYDOR (Poly): 162 053-2 (CD)*
UP ON THE ROOF (1997) Music score: ALAN PARKER -S/T-
   *OCEAN DEEP (Poly): OCD 009 (CD)*
UPSTAIRS DOWNSTAIRS (LWT 70 rep C4-13/11/82) theme mus
   "The Edwardians" by ALEXANDER FARIS
   *see COLLECTIONS 2,4,138,168,175*
URBANISSIMO - *on COLL* 'JOURNEY TO NEXT'
URGA (1990) Music score: EDWARD ARTEYMEV -S/T- *Import*
   *PHILIPS (Discovery): 510 608-2 (CD)*
URSUS/URSUS IN THE VALLEY OF LIONS/URSUS IN THE LAND OF
   FIRE/THE THREE INVICIBLES (Italian films 60s) Music
   scores: ROMAN VLAD-RIZ ORTOLANI-CARLO SAVINA-ANGELO
   FRANCESCO LAVAGNINO *CINEVOX (S.Sc):CDCIA 5090 (CD)*
US GIRLS (BBC1 27/2/92) theme music: NIGEL HESS
   *see COLLECTION 191*
USED PEOPLE (1992) Music score: RACHEL PORTMAN -S/T-
   *BIG SCREEN (S.Screen)): WA 924481-2 (CD) -4 (MC)*
USUAL SUSPECTS The (1995) Music score: JOHN OTTMAN
   -S/T- *MILAN (BMG): 30107-2 (CD)*
UTILIZER The (USA TV Sci-fi) Music sco: DENNIS McCARTHY
   -S/T- *INTRADA (Silva Screen): MAF 7067 (CD)*

**V:** THE SERIES (USA 84 ITV 2/1/89) theme music: DENNIS
   McCARTHY Orchestral score by JOF HARNELL on Import
   *FJCD 001/2 (2CD) (limited) see COLLECTIONS 12,344*
VAGRANT (1991) Music score: CHRISTOPHER YOUNG -S/T-
   *INTRADA (Silva Screen): MAFCD 7028 (CD)*

VALIANT YEARS The (USA TV) see COLLECTION 380
VALLEY OF GWANGI The (1968) Music score: JEROME MOROSS
   COLLECTION 377-SILVA SCREEN (Koch): FILMCD 161 (CD)
VALLEY OF THE DOLLS (1967) t.song (Andre & Dory PREVIN)
   sung by DIONNE WARWICKE on 'Love Songs Collection'
   PICKWICK CARLTON: PWKS 525 (CD) HSC 3258 (MC)
VALMOUTH (O.LONDON CAST 1958) Songs: SANDY WILSON feat:
   MARCIA ASHTON-CLEO LAINE-FENELLA FIELDING-PETER GIL
   MORE-IAN BURFORD & Co DRG (Pinn): CDSBL 13109 (CD)
VALMOUTH (ORIG CHICHESTER CAST P) feat: BERTICE READING
   FENELLA FIELDING-D.HARE TER (Disc): CD(ZC)TER 1019
VALOUR AND THE HORROR The (Galafilms Canada-C4 31/8/94)
   "Requiem Op.48" (Gabriel FAURE) performed by ROYAL
   PHILHARMONIC ORCH (R.Hickox) with ALED JONES (sopr)
   RPO-PICKWICK (Pickw-Koch): CD(ZC)RPO 8004 (CD/MC)
VAMP (1987) Music score: JONATHAN ELIAS selection
   see COLLECTION 378 'VAMPIRE CIRCUS'
VAMPIRE CIRCUS (1971) Music score: DAVID WHITTAKER
   see COLLECTION 378 'VAMPIRE CIRCUS'
VAN DER VALK (ITV 73) theme "Eye Level" (JACK TROMBEY)
   SIMON PARK ORCHESTRA see COLLECTIONS 2,4,168,357
VANITY FAIR (BBC1 6/9/87) music by NIGEL HESS
   see COLLECTION 192
VARIETY - see 'DOWN BY LAW'
VEGAS (USA) see COLLECTION 168
VERTIGO (1958) Mus sco: BERNARD HERRMANN -S/T- original
   restored 1958 score conducted by Muir Mathieson on
   VARESE (Pinn): VSD 5759 (CD) / ALSO AVAILABLE:
   new 1995 recording by Royal Scottish National Orch
   (Joel NcNeely) on VARESE (Pinn): VSD 5600 (CD)
   COLLECT.187,189,190,194,195,196,197,210,319,355,404
VERY BRITISH COUP A (C4 19/6/88) theme from 'Great Mass
   in C.Minor" K.427 (MOZART) New Phil Orc (R.LEPPARD)
   Ileana Cotrubas-Kiri Te Kanawa-John Alldis Choir on
   EMI: CDC 747385-2 (CD) EG 290277-1/-4 (LP/MC)
VERY GOOD EDDIE (REV.BROADWAY CAST 1975) Songs: JEROME
   KERN-SCHUYLER GREENE DRG (Pinn): CDRG 6100 (CD)
VETS IN PRACTICE (BBC1 26/8/97) and VET'S SCHOOL (BBC1
   14/10/96) orig music by DEBBIE WISEMAN unavailable
VICAR OF DIBLEY (BBC1 10/11/94) music: HOWARD GOODALL
   GEORGE & THE CHOIR LONDON: DIB(CD)(MC)1 deleted
   ORIG TV CAST -S/T- BBC (Pinn): ZBBC 2113 (2MC)
VICTOR VICTORIA O.BROADWAY CAST RECORDING with JULIE
   ANDREWS-TONY ROBERTS-MICHAEL NOURI-RACHEL YORK
   PHILIPS (Poly): 446 919-2 (CD) 446 919-4(MC)
VICTOR VICTORIA (1982) Music: HENRY MANCINI Lyrics by
   LESLIE BRICUSSE feat JULIE ANDREWS-ROBERT PRESTON
   -S/T- GNP CRESCENDO (Silva Screen): GNPD 8038 (CD)
VICTORIA WOOD AS SEEN ON TV (BBC2 1986) mus: VICTORIA
   WOOD on 'BBC RADIO COLLECTION' sketches & songs on
   BBC (Pinn): ZBBC 1263 (2MC)
VICTORY AT SEA (USA 50's) music score: RICHARD RODGERS
   arr/cond: Robert Russell BENNETT version on
   TELARC USA (BMG): CD 80175 see COLLECTION 35

VIDEO GIRL -S/T- *Animanga-New Note (Pinn): AM 2 (CD)*
VIDEO GIRL A1 2ND *Animanga-New Note (Pinn): AM 9 (CD)*
VIEW TO A KILL A - *see* JAMES BOND FILM INDEX p.346
VIETNAM A TV HISTORY (USA TV) *see COLLECTION 344*
VIKINGS The (1958) Music score: MARIO NASCIMBENE new
    recording of score with 'Solomon and Sheba' music
    *DRG-NEW NOTE (Pinn): DRGCD 32963 (CD) see COLLECT
    64,266,385*
VILLAGE OF THE DAMNED (1994) Music sco: JOHN CARPENTER
    *VARESE (Pinn): VSD 5629 (CD)*
VIOLENT STREETS ('THIEF') (1981) Mus: TANGERINE DREAM
    *VIRGIN (EMI): CDV 2198 (CD)*
VIRGINIA CITY (1940) Mus sco: MAX STEINER *new recording*
    MOSCOW S.O.(Stromberg) *inc:* 'BEAST WITH 5 FINGERS'
    'LOST PATROL' *MARCO POLO (Select) 8.223870 (CD)*
VIRGINIAN The (USA 68) theme music: PERCY FAITH
    *see COLLECTIONS 2,168,170,340*
VISION ON (BBC1 1964-76) orig theme "Left Bank Two" by
    WAYNE HILL *see COLLECTIONS 4,318,360*
VIVA LAS VEGAS *see* ELVIS PRESLEY INDEX p.348

VIVRE POUR VIVRE - *see* 'LIVE FOR LIFE' + 'UN HOMME ET
    UNE FEMME' (MAN AND A WOMAN, A)
VOLCANO (1997) Music score: ALAN SILVESTRI -S/T- score
    *VARESE (Pinn): VSD 5833 (CD)*
VON RYAN'S EXPRESS (1965) Music score: JERRY GOLDSMITH
    score including music from 'OUR MAN FLINT'/'IN LIKE
    FLINT' *TSUNAMI IMPT (S.Screen): TCI 0602 (CD)*
VOYAGE OF TERROR (The Achille Lauro Affair) (1990) Mus
    ENNIO MORRICONE -S/T- selection on 'TV FILM MUSIC'
    *RCA (BMG): 74321 31552-2 (CD)* -S/T- import also on
    *RCA (S.Screen): OST 101 CD*
VOYAGE TO NEXT - *see* 'JOURNEY TO NEXT'

VOYAGE TO THE BOTTOM OF THE SEA (USA)
    *see COLLECTIONS 110,340*

WACKY RACES (USA68/BBC 70's) theme music (Hoyt Curtin-
    W.Hanna-J.Barbera) (USA TV) *see COLLECTIONS 343,370*
WAGES OF FEAR (1978)'The Sorcerer' Mus: TANGERINE DREAM
    -S/T- *MCA (BMG): MCLD 19159 (CD) also available on
    MCA Imp (Silva Screen): MCAD 10842 (CD)*
WAGON TRAIN (USA 57-C4 2/89) Theme (1)"Roll Along Wagon
    Train" (Fain-Brooks) *vocal version by* ROBERT HORTON
    'TV CLASSICS 4' *CASTLE (BMG): MBSCD 412 (4CDset)*
    Theme (2) "Wagons Ho!" JEROME MOROSS *see COLL 377*
    *also* GEOFF LOVE *MFP: HR 418109-4 (MC)* Theme (3)
    "Wagon Train" (Rene-Russell) JOHNNY GREGORY *deleted*
    *see COLLECTIONS 2,170,340,368,372,377*
WAITING FOR GOD (BBC1 28/6/90) theme 'Piano Quintet in
    A'("Trout") D.667 (Schubert) Alan Berg Quartet with
    Elisabeth Leonskaja-Georg Hortnagel *HMV: CDC 747
    448-2 (CD) -4(MC)  TV version not available*
    *see also Coll* 'CLASSIC THEMES FROM TV AND RADIO'

WAITING TO EXHALE (1995) *featuring* WHITNEY HOUSTON
    -S/T- *ARISTA (BMG): 07822 18796-2(CD) -4(MC)*
WALK IN THE CLOUDS, A (1995) Music score: MAURICE JARRE
    -S/T- *MILAN (BMG): 28666-2 (CD)*
WALKABOUT (1970) Music JOHN BARRY *see COLLECTION 24*
WALKING THUNDER (1996) Music sco: JOHN SCOTT -S/T- on
    *JS (Silva Screen): JSCD 117 (CD)*
WALL The (1981) Music: PINK FLOYD -S/T-
    *Harvest (EMI): CDS 746036-8(2CD) TC2SHDW 411(2MC)*
WALL STREET (1988) Music sc: STEWART COPELAND -S/T-
    *TER (Disc):CDTER 1154  see COLLECTION 70*
WALLACE AND GROMIT - see under 'GRAND DAY OUT'/'WRONG
    TROUSERS'/'CLOSE SHAVE'
WALLY GATOR   (USA TV) *see COLLECTIONS 342,370*
WALTONS The (USA 1972-81) theme mus: JERRY GOLDSMITH
    *see COLLECTIONS 12,341,367*
WANDERERS The (1979) Songs by V.Artists -S/T- reissue
    *SEQUEL (BMG): NEMCD 765 (CD)*
WAR AND PEACE (1956) *COLL* 'FILM MUSIC OF NINO ROTA'
    *Ital.IMPT (Silva Screen): VCDS 7001 (CD)*
WAR AND REMEMBRANCE (ITV (USA) 3/9/89) music sco: BOB
    COBERT spin-off 'Winds Of War' (ITV 9/83) TV -S/T-
    *TER: (ZC)TER 1070 (MC/LP) deleted. see COLLECT.380*
WAR LORD The (1965) Music: JEROME MOROSS -S/T- *reissue*
    *VARESE (Pinn): VSD 5536 (CD) - also available with*
    'THE CARDINAL' *TSUNAMI (S.Screen): TSU 0117 (CD)*
WAR OF THE BUTTONS (1994) Music score: RACHEL PORTMAN
    -S/T- *VARESE (Pinn): VSD 5554 (CD)*
WAR OF THE WORLDS (1952) Music sc: LEITH STEVENS -S/T-
    *reissue with* 'WHEN WORLDS COLLIDE'
    *TSUNAMI Import (Silva Screen): TCI 0612 (CD)*
WAR OF THE WORLDS (JEFF WAYNE'S Musical Concept Album)
    *COLUMBIA (Sony): CDX 96000 (2CD) 4096000 (2MC)*
    *Highlights on SONY: CDX 32356 (CD)*
WAR REQUIEM (1988) Music: BENJAMIN BRITTEN based on
    'War Requiem Op.66' C.B.S.O.(Simon RATTLE) *EMI:*
    *CDS 747 034-8 (2CDs)* LONDON SYMPH.ORCH (B.BRITTEN)
    *DECCA (Poly): 414 383-2DH2 (2CD) K27K22 (MC)*
WARLOCK: THE ARMAGEDDON (1993) Music sco: MARK McKENZIE
    -S/T- *INTRADA (Silva Screen): MAF 7049D (CD)*
WARRIORS The (1979) Music sco: BARRY DE VORZON + V/Arts
    -S/T- *re-issued on SPECTRUM (Poly): 551 169-2 (CD)*
WATCHDOG: FACE VALUE (BBC1 6/1/97) original theme music
    TOBY LANGTON-GILKS *unavailable*
WATERLOO BRIDGE (1940) VARIOUS -S/T- SELECTIONS on
    *GREAT MOVIE THEMES: (Targ-BMG): CD 60032 (CD)*
WARRIORS OF VIRTUE (1997) Music score: DON DAVIS -S/T-
    *KID RHINO (WEA): 8122 72640-2 (CD)*
WASHINGTON SQUARE (1997) Music score: JAN A.P.KACZMAREK
    -S/T- *VARESE (Pinn): VSD 5869 (CD)*
WATERLOO (1970) Music score: NINO ROTA -S/T- Import
    *LEGEND Italy (Silva Screen): LEGENDCD 20 (CD)*
WATERWAYS (RTE / C4 12/1/93) original music by
    RONAN HARDIMAN *unavailable*

WAVELENGTH (ITV 4/6/97) music: PETER DAVIS *unavailable*
WAVELENGTH (1982) Music score by TANGERINE DREAM -S/T-
    *VARESE (Pinn): VCD 47223 (CD)*
WAY OF THE LAKES (BBC1 6/8/93) incidental music "The
    Watermill" RONALD BINGE *see Colls* '40 YEARS OF BBC
    TV THEMES'/'BRITISH LIGHT MUSIC: RONALD BINGE'
    'BRITISH LIGHT MUSIC CLASSICS'
WAY WE WERE The (1973) Mus: MARVIN HAMLISCH  Lyr: ALAN
    /MARILYN BERGMAN -S/T- feat BARBRA STREISAND on
    *Sony: 474911-2 (CD) 474911-4 (MC) see COLLECT 280*
WAYNE'S WORLD 2 (1993) V.Artists including ROBERT PLANT
    4 NON BLONDES-DINOSAUR JUNIOR-AEROSMITH -S/T- on
    *WARNER BROS (WEA): 9362 45485-2 (CD) -4 (MC)*
WE'LL MEET AGAIN (LWT 19/2/82) theme: DENIS KING *on*
    COLL 'LOVEJOY' *deleted*
WEB OF THE SPIDER *see under* 'IN THE GRIP OF THE SPIDER'
WEDDING BANQUET The (1993) Music sco: MADER + 3rd m/m
    Piano Sonata in A.Major 'Turkish March' (MOZART)
    -S/T- *Import LDM (Discovery): LDM 1093 (CD)*
WEDDING BELL BLUES (1996) Music by Var.Artists -S/T-
    *VARESE (Pinn): VSD 5853 (CD)*
WEDLOCK - *see under* 'DEADLOCK'
WEEKEND WORLD (LWT 87) theme "Nantucket Sleighride" (Fe
    lix Pappalardi-Leslie West) MOUNTAIN 'Best Of Mount
    ain' *BEAT GOES ON (Pinn): BGO(CD)(LP) 33 (CD/LP)*
WELCOME BACK KOTTER (USA TV) *see COLLECTION 341*
WELCOME TO SARAJEVO (1997) Music score: ADRIAN JOHNSTON
    -S/T- *feat:* VAN MORRISON-STONE ROSES-BOBBY McFERRIN
    TEENAGE FAN CLUB-HOUSE OF LOVE-HAPPY MONDAYS-BLUR
    *EMI SOUNDTRACKS: 493 014-2 (CD)*
WEST SIDE STORY - songs by Leonard Bernstein and
    Stephen Sondheim
  1.FILM MUSICAL 1961 *with:* NATALIE WOOD *sung by Marnie
    Nixon* RICHARD BEYMER *sung by Jim Bryant* RITA MORENO
    *by Betty Wand* CHITA RIVERA-GEORGE CHAKIRIS-RUSS TAM
    BLYN *COLUMBIA (Sony): 467606-2 (CD) -4(MC) and
    Import: SONY BROADWAY: SK 48211 (CD) ST 48211(MC)
    -S/T- (SPECIAL AUDIO LP EDITION) IMPT (VIVANTI)
    AUDIOLP LSP 2362 LP Audio Quality*
  2.STUDIO RECORD 1984 TV-BBC1 10/5/1985 *with:* KIRI TE
    KANAWA-JOSE CARRERAS-TATIANA TROYANOS-KURT OLLMAN-
    MARILYN HORN and LEONARD BERNSTEIN *DG-POLYGRAM:
    415253-2(2CD) -4(MC) Highl: 431027-2 (CD) -4(MC)*
  3.STUDIO RECORD 1993 *with* MICHAEL BALL-BARBARA BONNEY
    LA VERNE WILLIAMS-CHRISTOPHER HOWERD-MARY CAREWE-JE
    NNY O'GRADY-LEE GIBSON-R.P.Orch: BARRY WORDSWORTH
    *CARLTON-IMG (Carlton): IMGCD(IMGMC)1801 (CD/MC)*
  4.LEICESTER HAYMARKET THEATRE PROD 1993 *with* National
    Symph.Orch (John Owen Edwards) PAUL MANUEL-TINUKE
    OLAFIMIHAN-CAROLINE O'CONNOR-NICK FERANTI and Comp.
    Highlights: *SHOWTIME (MCI-THE): SHOW(CD)(MC) 006*
    Complete: *TER: CDTER2 1197 (2CD) ZCTER2 1197(2MC)*
  5.STUDIO RECORD 1989 *with:* KATIA & MARIBELLEe LaBEQUE
*Continued next page...*

WEST SIDE STORY ...*Continued from previous page*

5. STUDIO RECORD 1989 *with:* KATIA & MARIBELLEe LaBEQUE
   'Symphonic Dances and Songs From West Side Story'
   arr for 2 pianos by Irwin Kostal *CBSCD 45531 (CD)*
6. ORIG BROADWAY CAST 1957 *w* CAROL LAWRENCE-LARRY KERT
   CHITA RIVERA *COL (S.Screen): CK(JST)32603 (CD/MC)*
7. ORIG NEW YORK CAST 1957 *with:* CAROL LAWRENCE-LARRY
   KERT-CHITA RIVERA-ART SMITH-MICKEY CALIN-KEN LeROY
   *Broadway Cast reiss: COLUMBIA (SM): CK 64419 (CD)*
8. CARLTON SHOWS COLLECTION *w:* MARIA KESSELMAN-JOHN DU
   LIEU *CARLTON (CHE): 30362 0032-2 (CD) -4 (MC)*
WHAT A FEELING! (ORIG LONDON CAST 1997) Music from
   Various Musicals *feat* LUKE GOSS-SINITTA-SONIA
   *MCI (THE-Disc): MCCD 287 (CD)*
WHAT I HAVE WRITTEN (1996) Music: JOHN PHILLIPS-DAVID
   BRIDIE -S/T- *ICON (Pinn.Imports): ICON 19963 (CD)*
WHAT THE PAPERS SAY (BBC2 23/3/90 previous C4-Granada)
   theme "English Dance No.5" from 'Eight English Danc
   es' (Malcolm ARNOLD) Philharmonic Orch (Thompson)
   *CHANDOS: CHAN 8867 (CD)*
WHATEVER HAPPENED TO THE LIKELY LADS (BBC2 orig 9/1/73)
   theme mus "Whatever Happened To You" (Mike Hugg-Ian
   La Frenais) by HIGHLY LIKELY *see COLLECTIONS 2,4*
WHAT'S MY LINE (BBC 1951) *see COLLECTIONS 163,381*
WHAT'S UP, TIGER LILY (1966) Music: JOHN SEBASTIAN The
   LOVIN' SPOONFUL -S/T-with 'You're A Big Boy Now' on
   *SEQUEL KNIGHT: NEXTCD 176 (CD)*
WHEN A MAN LOVES A WOMAN (94) Music score: ZBIGNIEW PRI
   ESNER Songs by Various Artists incl: PERCY SLEDGE-
   LOS LOBOS-RICKIE LEE JONES etc. -S/T-
   *HOLLYWOOD (Sil.Screen): HR 61606-2 (CD)*
WHEN DINOSAURS RULED THE EARTH *see* ONE MILLION YEARS BC
WHEN SATURDAY COMES (1995) Music sco: ANNE DUDLEY -S/T-
   Various Arts *POLYGRAM TV: 532 307-2 (CD) -4(MC)*
WHEN THE BOAT COMES IN (BBC1 4/1/76)
   theme "Dance To Your Daddy" (trad.arr: David Fansha
   we) sung by ALEX GLASGOW *see COLLECTIONS 2,5*
WHEN THE WIND BLOWS (Cartoon 1987) Music score by ROGER
   WATERS Title song sung by DAVID BOWIE / songs by
   Genesis-Hugh Cornwell-Squeeze-Paul Hardcastle -S/T-
   *VIRGIN (EMI): CDVIP 132 (CD) TCVIP 132 (MC)*
WHEN WE WERE KINGS -S/T- *MERCURY (Poly): 534 462-2 (CD)*
   *-4 (MC)*
WHEN WORLDS COLLIDE (1951) Music sco: LEITH STEVENS
   -S/T- *reissue with* 'WAR OF THE WORLDS'
   *TSUNAMI Impt (Silva Screen): TCI 0612 (CD)*
WHERE EAGLES DARE (1968) Music score: RON GOODWIN theme
   *see COLLECTIONS 35,63,127,238,383*
WHERE THE ACTION IS (USA TV) *see COLLECTION 343*
WHERE THE HEART IS (ITV 6/4/97) theme "Home Is Where
   The Heart Is" by PADDY McALOON on 'Prisoner Of The
   Past' PREFAB SPROUT *COLUMBIA-KITCHENWARE (Sony):*
   *SKCD 70 (CDs) SKMC 70 (MC)*

WHICKER'S WORLD (BBC 60s) theme "West End" by LAURIE
    JOHNSON *see COLLECTIONS 6,372*
WHILE I LIVE (1947) Music score: CHARLES WILLIAMS incl
    *'The Dream Of Olwen' see COLLECTION 387*
WHILE YOU WERE SLEEPING (1995) Music: RANDY EDELMAN
    -S/T- *VARESE (Pinn): VSD 5627 (CD)*
WHISKY GALORE! (1949) *see COLLECTION 225*
WHISTLE DOWN THE WIND (1961) Music sco: MALCOLM ARNOLD
    LONDON Symphony Orchestra (Richard HICOX) *on coll*
    'Film Music' *CHANDOS: CHAN 9100 (CD)*
WHISTLE TEST (BBC2 29/4/86 final ser) Theme 'Sure Beats
    Workin'(Dave Stewart) BEATS WORKIN' *LONDON FFR(X)8
    (7"/12"s deleted) see also* 'OLD GREY WHISTLE TEST'
WHITBREAD ROUND T.WORLD YACHT RACE see SAIL THE WORLD
WHITE MISCHIEF (1988) Music score: GEORGE FENTON
    -S/T- *TER (Disc): CD(ZC)TER 1153 (CD/MC)*
WHITE NIGHTS (1985) *see COLLECTIONS 73,134*
WHITE ROCK (1976) Mus scored & perf. by RICK WAKEMAN
    *A.& M.(Poly): RWCD 20 (CD Box Set)*
WHITE SANDS (1992) Music score: PATRICK O'HEARN -S/T-
    *MORGAN CREEK (Poly): 002252-2 MCM (CD)*
WHITE SQUALL (1995) Music score: JEFF RONA-HANS ZIMMER
    -S/T- *HOLLYWOOD (Poly): 162 040-2 (CD)*
WHO FRAMED ROGER RABBIT (1988) *see COLLECTION 71*
WHO PAYS THE FERRYMAN (UKGold 24/4/93 orig BBC1 1977)
    music: YANNIS MARKOPOULOS *see COLLECTION 168*
WHO PLAYS WINS (ORIG LONDON CAST 1985) comp/performed
    by PETER SKELLERN-RICHARD STILGOE *re-issued on
    FIRST NIGHT (Pinn): OCRCD 6037 (CD)*
WHODUNNIT *see COLLECTION 357*
WHO'S AFRAID OF VIRGINIA WOOLF (1966) Music score: ALEX
    NORTH new score recording by NATIONAL PHILHARMONIC
    ORCH (Jerry Goldsmith,cond) *VARESE (Pinn): VSD 5800
    (CD) also w.dialogue highlights Tsumani: TSU 0112 CD*
WHO'S THAT GIRL (1987) Music: STEPHEN BRAY -S/T- incl
    MADONNA-SCRITTI POLITTI-CLUB NOUVEAU-COATI MUNDI
    -S/T- *SIRE (WEA): WX 102C (MC) 7599 25611-2 (CD)*
WHO'S THE BOSS (USA TV) *see COLLECTION 344*
WHOSE LINE IS IT ANYWAY (C4/Hat Trick 23/9/88-1997)
    theme music: PHILIP POPE *unavailable*
WILD AT HEART (1990) Music score: ANGELO BADALAMENTI
    V.Arts + CHRIS ISAAK 'Wicked Game' -S/T- *SPECTRUM
    (Poly): 551 318-2 (CD) see also COLLECTIONS 260,361*
WILD HOUSE The (BBC1 8/1/97) o.music: STEVE MARSHALL.*NA*
WILD IS THE WIND (1957) Music sc: DIMITRI TIOMKIN theme
    *UNICORN KANCHANA (H.Mundi): DKPCD 9047 (CD) also*
    -S/T- *TSUNAMI Germ (Silva Screen): TSU 0110 (CD)
    see also COLLECTION 365*
WILD ISLANDS (C4 28/7/97) orig mus: STEVE MARSHALL..*NA*
WILD RELATIONS (C4 13/1/97) m: TOM FITZGERALD *unavail.*
WILD ROVERS (1) & 'THE FIRST GREAT TRAIN ROBBERY' 1978
    Music scores: JERRY GOLDSMITH 2 -S/T-
    *MEMOIR (Castle-BMG): CDMOIR 601 (CD)*

WILD WEST The (USA/C4 14/5/95) original music: BRIAN
    KEANE -S/T- *SHANACHIE (Koch): SHCD 6013 (2CD)*
WILD WILD WEST (USA TV) *see COLLECTION 339*
WILDE (1997) Music score: DEBBIE WISEMAN -S/T- on
    *MCI (THE-DISC-Pinn): MPRCD 001 (CD)*
WILLIAM TELL (The Adventures Of)(ITV-1958) title theme
    sung by DAVID WHITFIELD on 'Sings Stage And Screen
    Favourites' *CARLTON: PWK 096 (CD) SDTO 2004*
WILLIAM'S WISH WELLINGTONS (BBC1 25/10/94) KICK PROD
    *see COLLECTION 60*
WILLOW (1988) Music score: JAMES HORNER -S/T-
    *VIRGIN (EMI): CDV 2538 (CD) see COLLECTION 332*
WIMBLEDON (BBC1/2)
    opening theme 1974-98 "Light & Tuneful" by KEITH
    MANSFIELD *see COLLECTION 6*
    Closing theme "Sporting Occasion" by ARNOLD STECK
    'More Famous Themes' *GRASMERE (TC)GRALP 20 deleted*
WIMBLEDON POISONER The (BBC1 11/12/94) music composed
    by RICHARD HARVEY *see COLLECTION 181*
WIND AND THE LION The (1975) Music sco: JERRY GOLDSMITH
    -S/T- *INTRADA (Silva Screen): MAF 7005D (CD)*
WIND IN THE WILLOWS (1996) "Toad's Song" (Jones-DuPrez-
    Jacquemin-Howman) perf by TERRY JONES *Coll '100%
    KIDS PARTY' TELSTAR (WEA): TCD(STAC) 2874 deleted*
WINDS OF WAR The (ITV 9/1983 & 5/1985) Mus: BOB COBERT
    -S/T- Nurnberg Symp.Orch *TER Koch: ZCTER 1070 (MC)*
    *see* WAR AND REMEMBRANCE *and COLLECTIONS 35,353,380*
WINGLESS BIRD The (Catherine Cookson's) (ITV 12/1/97)
    Orig music composed and performed by COLIN TOWNS.*NA*
WINGS (C4 14/1/97) music: MUSIC SCULPTORS *unavailable*
WINGS OF COURAGE (1995) Music sco: GABRIEL YARED -S/T-
    *Imprt COLUMBIA (Silva Screen): SK 68350 (CD)*
WINNER The (1997) Music score: DANIEL LICHT -S/T- on
    *RYKODISC (Vital-ADA): RCD 10392 (CD)*
WINNIE THE POOH Music from WALT DISNEY FILMS on 'The
    Many Songs of WINNIE THE POOH'
    *DISNEY (Carlton-Polyg): WD 11564-2 (CD) -4 (MC)*
    see also WALT DISNEY FILM INDEX p.343
WINTER OLYMPIC GAMES 1992 (BBC1 8/2/92)theme "Pop Looks
    Bach" (Sam FONTEYN) also "Chorus Of Hebrew Slaves"
    from 'Nabucco' (VERDI) *see COLLECTION 155*
WISDOM (1986) Music score: DANNY ELFMAN -S/T- on
    *VARESE (Pinn): VSD 5209 (CD)*
WISH ME LUCK (LWT 8/1/89) theme music: JIM PARKER
    *see COLLECTIONS 5,138,175*
WISH YOU WERE HERE (Thames/Central) theme music
    'Carnival" by GORDON GILTRAP *MUNCHKIN (Grapevine-
    Poly): GRCD 1 (CD)* link music "The Long Road" by
    MARK KNOPFLER -S/T- 'CAL' *VERTIGO Poly: 822 769-2
    (CD) VERHC 17 (MC)*
WITCHCRAFT (BBC 1992) Music score: JOHN SCOTT -S/T- on
    *JOHN SCOTT Rec. (Silva Screen): JSCD 121 (CD)*
WITCHES OF EASTWICK The (1987) Music sc: JOHN WILLIAMS
    -S/T- *WB deleted / see COLLECT 70,171,258,276,277*

WITHNAIL AND I (1987) Mus sco: DAVID DUNDAS-RICK WENT
   WORTH -S/T- *FILMTRAX (deleted)* selection on *SILVA*
   *SCREEN (Koch): FILMCD 041 (CD) see also COLL 110*
WITNESS (1985) Music score: MAURICE JARRE -S/T-
   *VARESE (Pinn): VCD 47227 (CD) CST 8003SMC (MC)*
   *als on TER (Disc): CDTER 1098 (CD) ZCTER 1098 (MC)*
   *see also COLLECTIONS 63,120,212214,363*
WIZARD OF OZ The- songs: Harold Arlen & E.Yip Harburg
  1.FILM MUSICAL 1939 *with:* JUDY GARLAND-RAY BOLGER-
    JACK HALEY-BERT LAHR-FRANK MORGAN -S/T- *reissue*
    *EMI PREMIER (EMI): CDODEON 7 (CD)*
  2.ROYAL SHAKESPEARE COMPANY CAST 1988 (Barbican)
    <u>Highlights</u>: *SHOWTIME (MCI-THE): SHOW(CD)(MC) 003*
    <u>Complete</u>: *IER (Disc): (CD)(ZC)TER 1165 (CD/MC)*
WKRP IN CINCINNATI (USA TV) *see COLLECTION 341*
WOGAN'S ISLAND (BBC1 28/6/95) theme mus "The Celts" by
   ENYA on *WEA (WEA): 4509 91167-2 (CD) WX 498C (MC)*
   *see COLLECTION 213*
WOKENWELL (ITV 18/5/97) mus: ILONA SEKACZ *unavailable*
WOLF MAN The (1940) Music: HANS SALTER-FRANK SKINNER
   *new recording* MOSCOW SYMPHONY ORCHEST (STROMBERG)
   *MARCO POLO (Select): 8.223748 (CD) also includes*
   INVISIBLE MAN RETURNS-SON OF FRANKENSTEIN
WOLVES OF WILLOUGHBY CHASE (1989) Music: COLIN TOWNS
   -S/T- *TER (Disc): CDTER(ZCTER) 1162 (CD/MC)*
   'Story Album' (Michael HORDERN) *TER:ZCVIR 8311(MC)*
WOMAN IN RED The (1984) Songs: STEVIE WONDER featur:
   STEVIE WONDER-DIONNE WARWICK -S/T-
   *MOTOWN (Poly): 530 030-2 (CD) 530 030-4 (MC)*
WOMAN OF SUBSTANCE A (C4 2/1/85) theme: NIGEL HESS
   *see COLLECTIONS 138,192*
WOMAN OF THE YEAR songs: John Kander and Fred Ebb
   ORIG BROADWAY CAST 1981 with LAUREN BACALL-HARRY
   GUARDINO-RODERICK COOK-MARILYN COOPER-EIVIND HARUM
   *RAZOR & TIE (Koch): RE 21462 (CD)*
WOMBLES The (BBC1 73) theme and songs: MIKE BATT all
   on 'Wombling Hits' THE WOMBLES (prod by Mike BATT)
   *CBS SONY: 466118-2 (CD) -4(MC) see COLLECTION 168*
WONDER WOMAN (USA TV) *see COLLECTIONS 341,360*
WONDERFUL COUNTRY (1949) Music score: ALEX NORTH
   *TSUNAMI (Silva Screen): TSU 0118 (CD)*
WONDERFUL TOWN - songs: Leonard Bernstein-Betty Comden
   and Adolph Green
  1.ORIG LONDON CAST 1986 *w* MAUREEN LIPMAN-JOHN CASSADY
    NICHOLAS COLICOS-DANIEL COLL-ROY DURBIN-RAY LONNEN
    *FIRST NIGHT (Pinn) OCRCD 6011 (CD)*
  2.ORIG BROADWAY CAST 1953 *w:* ROSALIND RUSSELL-SYDNEY
    CHAPLIN *SONY BROADWAY: SK 48021 (CD)*
WONDERWALL (1968) Music score: GEORGE HARRISON *Re-iss:*
   *EMI-APPLE: CDSAPCOR 1 (CD) (TC)SAPCOR 1 (MC/LP)*
WOODLANDERS The (1996) Mus score: GEORGE FENTON -S/T-
   *DEBONAIR (Pinn): CDDEB 1007 (CD)*
WOODSTOCK 1969 Woodstock Music Festival *with:* JOAN BAEZ
   JOE COCKER-RICHIE HAVENS-COUNTRY JOE & FISH-CROSBY

**WOODSTOCK 1969** Woodstock Music Festival *with:* JOAN BAEZ
   JOE COCKER-RICHIE HAVENS-COUNTRY JOE & FISH-CROSBY
   NASH & NEIL YOUNG-ARLO GUTHRIE-JIMI HENDRIX-SANTANA
   ShaNaNa-JOHN SEBASTIAN-SLY & FAMILY STONE-TEN YEARS
   AFTER-WHO -S/T- 'BEST OF WOODSTOCK'
   *WEA: 7567 82618-2 (CD) -4 (MC) -S/T- reissue*
   *WEA: (1) 7567 80593-2 (2CD) / (2) 7567 80594-2 (2CD)*
**WOODSTOCK II** (1970) Woodstock festival 69 feat V.Arts
   -S/T- re-issue: *ATLANTIC (WEA): 7567 81991-2 (CD)*
**WOODSTOCK DIARY** The (BBC2 22/7/94) Var.Artists -S/T-
   *WB (WEA): 7567 82634-2 (CD)*
**WOODSTOCK: THREE DAYS OF PEACE & MUSIC** Various Artists
   *WB (WEA): 7567 82636-2 (4CDs)*
**WOODY WOODPECKER** (USA TV) *see COLLECTION 339*
**WOOF!** (Carlton 18/2/89) theme music: PAUL LEWIS
   *see COLLECTION 5*
**WORKING GIRL** (1988) Music score: ROB MOUNCEY songs by
   CARLY SIMON -S/T- *featur:* CARLY SIMON-SONNY ROLLINS
   POINTER SISTERS *reissue: ARISTA (BMG): 259 767 (CD)*
   *see also COLLECTION 17*
**WORKING TITLES** (BBC1 23/10/90) theme mus "Lord's Seat"
   composed and performed by GORDON GILTRAP *see Coll.*
   'MUSIC FOR THE SMALL SCREEN'
**WORLD AT WAR** The (BBC2 5/9/94 orig ITV 31/10/73) music
   CARL DAVIS *see COLLECTION 182*
**WORLD BOWLS** (BBC2) "Brutus" by GORDON GILTRAP
   *see COLLECTION 153*
**WORLD CHESS CHAMPIONSHIPS** (The Times) 1993 from 7/9/93
   BBC theme music: 'Symphony No.12 in D.minor Op.112'
   (SHOSTAKOVICH) by THE ROYAL CONCERTGEBOUW ORCHESTRA
   (Bernard Haitink) *DECCA (Poly): 417 392-2 (2CDs)*
   C4 theme music: original music by PAUL MARDLE....*NA*
**WORLD CHESS** (BBC2 8/1986) theme "Montagues & Capulets"
   from 'Suite No.2 Romeo & Juliet' (Sergei PROKOFIEV)
**WORLD CUP 1994** (BBC trailer & theme) "America" (Leonard
   Bernstein) from 'West Side Story' *POLYDOR (Poly)*
   *USACD 1 (CDsingle USAMC 1 (MC) deleted*
**WORLD CUP 1994** (ITV trail.& theme) "Gloryland" (Charlie
   Skarbek-Rick Blacksey) SOUNDS OF BLACKNESS & DARYL
   HALL *MERCURY (Poly): 522 384-2(CD) -4(MC) deleted*
**WORLD CUP 1990** *see COLLECTION 138,155*
**WORLD CUP RUGBY 1995** - see 'RUGBY WORLD CUP 1995'
**WORLD CUP RUGBY 1991** *see COLLECTION 155*
**WORLD DARTS** (BBC) Theme music "Cranes" by DOUGLAS WOOD
   *see under entry* 'DARTS'
**WORLD FIGURE SKATING CHAMPIONSHIPS** (BBC) theme music
   "Mornings At Seven" (J.Last) JAMES LAST ORCH on
   'By Request' *POLYDOR (Poly): 831 786-2 (CD)*
**WORLD IN ACTION** (Granada 64-92) Theme "Jam For World In
   Action" by JONATHAN WESTON *deleted*
**WORLD OF PETER RABBIT AND FRIENDS** (BBC1 9/4/93) music
   COLIN TOWNS theme "Perfect Day" sung by MIRIAM
   STOCKLEY on 'Beatrix Potter Music Collection' on
   *Carlton: PWKS 4200 (CD) / see also COLLECTION 60*

WORLD OF SPORT (ITV) *see COLLECTIONS 5,167,360*
WORLD SNOOKER (Embassy World Championship) theme music
   "Drag Racer" (D.Wood) DOUGLAS WOOD GROUP
   *see COLLECTION 167*
   Shot Of The Championship "Wicked Game" CHRIS ISAAK
   *Lond: LON(X)(CD)(MC)279*
WORLD OF TIM FRAZER The (BBC 1960) theme "Willow Waltz"
   by CYRIL WATTERS *see COLLECTIONS 6,182*
WRESTLING ERNEST HEMINGWAY (1993) Music score: MICHAEL
   CONVERTINO -S/T- *Imp (Silva Screen): 517 897-2 (CD)*
WRONG TROUSERS,The (Wallace & Gromit)(1993) Mus: JULIAN
   NOTT v/o PETER SALLIS -S/T- incl: 'A Grand Day Out'
   *BBC (Pinn): ZBBC 1947 (MC) / BBC Video: BBCV 5201*
   (Wrong Trousers) *BBCV 5155* (A Grand Day Out) *(VHS)*
WUTHERING HEIGHTS (STUDIO REC.1991) Songs: BERNARD J.
   TAYLOR *with* DAVE WILLETTS-LESLEY GARRETT & Company
   *SILVA SCREEN (Koch): SONG(CD)(C) 904 (CD/MC)*
WUTHERING HEIGHTS (FILM 1991) Music: RYUICHI SAKAMOTO
   *VIRGIN Classics (EMI): VC 759276-2 (CD)*
WYATT EARP (Life and Legend of) (USA TV/ITV 1955-61)
   theme (Adamson-Warren) *see COLLECTIONS 176,342*
WYATT EARP (1993) Music score: JAMES NEWTON HOWARD
   -S/T- *WB (WEA): 9362 445660-2 (CD) -4 (MC)*
WYCLIFFE (ITV 7/8/93) theme music by NIGEL HESS
   *see COLLECTIONS 5,33,192*
WYRD SISTERS (C4 18/5/97) m: KEITH HOPWOOD-PHIL BUSH
   *see under* 'SOUL MUSIC' *and* 'DISCWORLD'
**X**-FILES (BBC2 96) theme by MARK SNOW -S/T-"Songs In The
   Key Of X" with MARK SNOW-SHERYL CROW-FOO FIGHTERS-
   NICK CAVE-ELVIS COSTELLO & BRIAN ENO and others on
   *WEA: 9362 46079-2 (CD) -4(MC)* MARK SNOW single ver
   sion on *WB (WEA): W.0341CD (CDs) W.0341C (MC)*
   "The Truth And The Light" X files theme song MARK
   SNOW on *WEA (WEA): 9362 46279-2 (CD) -4 (MC)*
   *see also COLLECTIONS 59,109,267,273,301,404,405*
X-CARS (BBC1 02/09/96) title music composed and
   performed by DAVID FERGUSON *unavailable*
X-MEN (USA 94/C4 21/4/96) m: SHUKI LEVY-KUSSA MAHCHI on
   '100% KIDS PARTY' *TELSTAR: TCD(STAC) 2874 deleted*
X-RAY (1980) - *see under* 'DEATH WISH'
X-THE UNKNOWN (1956) Music sc: JAMES BERNARD *see Coll*
   'DEVIL RIDES OUT' *SILVA SCREEN: FILMCD 174 (CD)*
XENA: WARRIOR PRINCESS (SKY2 8/9/96) mus.theme & score
   JOSEPH LoDUCA / song "Burial" sung by LUCY LAWLESS
   -S/T- *VARESE (Pinn): VSD 5750 (CD) (Volume 1)*
   -S/T- *VARESE (Pinn): VSD 5883 (CD) (Volume 2)*
   *see also COLLECTIONS 110,302*
**Y**AKSA (1985) *Music by* Nancy Wilson-Toots Thielmans-
   Masahiko Satoh -S/T- *DENON: C38-7556 (CD)*
YEAR IN PROVENCE, A (BBC1 28/2/93) music by CARL DAVIS
   accord:Jack Emblow -S/T- *S.Scr (Con): FILMCD 131 CD*
   *(deleted)* SPOKEN WORD 4 MC: *BBC (Pinn): ZBBC 4006*
YEAR OF LIVING DANGEROUSLY (1981) Music: MAURICE JARRE
   *see COLLECTION 80*

YEAR WITH FRED (BBC2 9/2/87) theme "Carnival Of Venice"
(Briccialdi) by JAMES GALWAY *RCA: (PD)(PK)PL 70260*
YELLOW SUBMARINE (1967) Songs: J.LENNON-P.McCARTNEY
*PARLOPHONE-EMI:CDP 746445-2 (CD) TCPCS 7070 (MC)*
YENTL (1983) Music: MICHEL LEGRAND Songs (M.LEGRAND-
Alan & Marilyn BERGMAN) *sung by* BARBRA STREISAND
-S/T- *SONY EUROPE (Discovery): CD 86302 (CD)*
*see COLLECTION 353*
YEOMAN OF THE GUARD (operetta) songs by W.S.Gilbert &
A.Sullivan
  1. PRO-ARTE ORCHEST (Malcolm Sargent) and GLYNDEBOURNE
  FESTIVAL CHOIR Soloists: ALEX YOUNG-DENIS DOWLING-
  RICHARD LEWIS-JOHN CAMERON *EMI:CMS 764415-2 (2CDs)*
  2. D'OYLY CARTE OPERA COMPANY *also inc* 'TRIAL BY JURY'
  *LONDON (Poly): 417 358-2 (2CD)*
  3. D'OYLY CARTE OPERA COMPANY *feat:* DAVID FIELDSEND-FE
  NTON GRAY-DONALD MAXWELL / MD: JOHN OWEN EDWARDS
  *TER (Disc): CDTER2 1195 (2CD) ZCTED 1195 (MC)*
YOGI BEAR (USA TV) *see COLLECTIONS 339,370*
YOU BET! (LWT 10/9/93) theme mus: JONATHAN SORRELL by
BOOM! Prod *see COLLECTION 33*
YOU CAN'T HAVE EVERYTHING 1937 *fea* ALICE FAY-DON AMECHE
-S/T- select.including songs from 'MELODY FOR TWO'
'GO INTO YOUR DANCE'/'YOU'LL NEVER GET RICH' on
*GREAT MOVIE THEMES (Target-BMG): CD 60014 (CD)*
YOU DECIDE (BBC1 11/7/95) mus: DAVID ARNOLD *unavailable*
YOU GOTTA WALK IT LIKE YOU TALK IT (1971) Music score:
Walter BECKER-Donald FAGEN (from STEELY DAN) -S/T-
*SEE FOR MILES (Pinn): SEECD 357 (CD)*
YOU MUST REMEMBER THIS (BBC1 8/5/95) VE Day Special
Various Wartime Artists (original recordings) on
*HAPPY DAYS (BMG-Con): UCD 252 (CD)*
YOU ONLY LIVE TWICE (1967) Music score: JOHN BARRY
t.song (John BARRY-L.BRICUSSE) by NANCY SINATRA
-S/T- *reissue EMI PREMIER: CZ 559 (CD) see also*
*COLLECTIONS 25,26,305 see* JAMES BOND FILM INDEX
YOU'LL NEVER GET RICH (1941) Film Musical: COLE PORTER
*feat:* FRED ASTAIRE-RITA HAYWORTH -S/T- including
songs from 'MELODY FOR TWO'/'YOU CAN'T HAVE
EVERYTHING'/'GO INTO YOUR DANCE'
*GREAT MOVIE THEMES (Target-BMG): CD 60014 (CD)*
YOUNG AMERICANS The (1993) Music: DAVID ARNOLD songs:
DAVID ARNOLD-NINE INCH NAILS-SHEEP ON DRUGS-STEREO
MCs-DISPOSABLE HEROES OF HIPHOPRISY-KEITH LE BLANC
-S/T- *ISLAND MAST (Poly): IMCD 220 (CD) ICT 8019*
YOUNG AND THE RESTLESS The (US soap 73)'Nadia's theme'
(H.MANCINI) JAMES GALWAY *RCA (BMG): 09026 61178-2*
*(CD) -4 (MC) - see COLLECTION 379*
YOUNG BESS (1953) Music score: MIKLOS ROZSA -S/T-
*Import PROMETHEUS (Silva Screen): PCD 133 (CD)*
YOUNG DOCTORS The (Australian TV/ITV 80's) theme mus
(King-Ollman) *see COLLECTION 367*
YOUNG EINSTEIN (1988) Music sco: WILLIAM MOTZING -S/T-
*IMS (Poly): E.393 929-2 (CD)*

YOUNG GIRLS OF ROCHEFORT The (1968) Music sco: MICHEL
   LEGRAND -S/T- *POLY-EURO (Discov): 834 140-2 (CD)*
YOUNG GUARD (1948) Music: D.SHOSTAKOVICH *see* ZOYA
YOUNG INDIANA JONES CHRONICLES (BBC1 20/11/94) mus:
   LAURENCE ROSENTHAL -S/T- *VARESE (Pinn): VSD 5381*
   *Vol.1 VSD 5391 (2) VSD 5401 (3) VSD 5421 (4) CDs*
YOUNG LIONS The (1958) Music sco: HUGO FRIEDHOFER -S/T-
   *with* THIS EARTH IS MINE *VARESE (Pinn): VSD 5403 CD*
YOUNG MAN OLDER WOMAN (O.CAST ALBUM) feat: REYNALDO REY
   *ICHIBAN (Koch): ICHO 1159-2 (CD) -4 (MC)*
YOUNG ONES The (1962) CLIFF RICHARD & SHADOWS -S/T-
   *MFP (EMI): CDMFP 6020 (CD) see also Coll*
   'CLIFF RICHARD AT THE MOVIES' *see also COLLECT 344*
YOUNG POISONERS HANDBOOK The (1994) Music sco: ROBERT
   LANE and FRANK STROBEL -S/T- feat Various Artists
   *DERAM-LONDON (Polygram): 844 429-2 (CD) -4 (MC)*
YOUNG RIDERS The (USA 90/ITV 5/91) theme: JOHN DEBNEY
   *see COLLECTION 12*
YOU'RE A BIG BOY NOW (1967) Music: JOHN SEBASTIAN The
   LOVIN' SPOONFUL -S/T- with 'What's Up,Tiger Lily'
   *SEQUEL-CASTLE (BMG): NEXTCD 176 (CD)*
YOU'RE UNDER ARREST (Japan 1995) Animated MANGA Film
   -S/T- *ANIMANGA-New Note (Pinn): AM 5 (2CD)*
Z (1969) Mus: MIKIS THEODORAKIS Suite on
   *DRG (Pinn): 32901-4 (2MC)*
Z CARS (BBC1 began 2/1/62) theme "Johnny Todd" (Trad.)
   arr.Bridget Fry JOHNNY KEATING AND THE 'Z' MEN
   *see COLLECTIONS 2,3,100,364,368,372*
ZABRISKIE POINT (1969) Music: PINK FLOYD-KALEIDOSCOPE
   GRATEFUL DEAD-PATTI PAGE-YOUNGBLOODS-JERRY GARCIA-
   ROSCOE HOLCOMB-JOHN FAHEY -S/T- *reissue with extra*
   *prev.unreleased items EMI S/TRACKS: 823 364-2 (2CD)*
ZACHARIAH (1971) V.Arts: COUNTRY JOE & FISH-JAMES GANG
   ELVIN JONES -S/T- *SEE FOR MILES: SEEK 91 (MC)*
ZED AND TWO NOUGHTS A (1985) Music sco: MICHAEL NYMAN
   -S/T- *VIRGIN (EMI): CDVE 54 (CD) TCVE 54 (MC)*
ZERO PATIENCE (1993) Music sc: GLEN SCHELLENBERG *feat:*
   POISON-SWOON + oth -S/T- *MILAN (BMG): 287971 (CD)*
ZIEGFELD FOLLIES (1944) *featur* FRED ASTAIRE-GENE KELLY
   LUCILLE BALL -S/T- *reiss EMI PREM: CDODEON 3 (CD)*
ZIGGY STARDUST (THE MOTION PICTURE) (1982) *featuring*
   DAVID BOWIF -S/T- *EMI: CDEMD 1037 (CD)*
ZOO WATCH LIVE (BBC1 28/8/95) theme music 'Overture'
   from "Carnival Of The Animals" (SAINT-SAENS)
ZORBA THE GREEK (1964) Music composed and performed by
   MIKIS THEODORAKIS *INTUITION (Pinn): INT 31032 (CD)*
   *see COLLECTIONS 63,90*
ZOYA (1944) Music score: DIMITRI SHOSTAKOVICH
   Byelorussian Radio & TV Symphony Orch (Mnatsakanov)
   & Minsk Cha Cho *feat score from* 'THE YOUNG GUARD'
   *RUSSIAN DISC (Koch): RDCD 10002 (CD)*
ZULU (1964) Music sco: JOHN BARRY -S/T- +J.Bond themes
   *SILVA SCREEN (Koch): FILMCD 022 (CD) see also*
   *COLLECTIONS 21,25,63,132,201*

*1.*40 YEARS OF BBC TV THEMES - Norrie Paramor & M.R.O.
*EMPORIO-MCI (Disc-THE) EMPRCD 633 (CD)* * 1996*
1.TELEVISION MARCH 2.DIXON OF DOCK GREEN *(AN ORDINA
RY COPPER)* 3.DOCTOR FINLAY'S CASEBOOK *(MARCH FROM A
LITTLE SUITE)* 4.TONIGHT *(TODAY'S TONIGHT)* 5.MAIGRET
6.THE SECRET GARDEN *(WATERMILL)* 7.TOP OF THE FORM
*(MARCHING STRINGS)* 8.GAUMONT BRITISH NEWS *(MUSIC
FROM THE MOVIES)* 9.JACQUES COUSTEAU *(CALYPSO)* 10.
CALL MY BLUFF *(CICCOLINO)* 11.QUITE CONTRARY *(MOONLI
GHT AND ROSES)* 12.MELISSA *(SNOWDROPS AND RAINDROPS)*
13.LAST OF THE SUMMER WINE 14.COME DANCING THEME
*MRO=Midland Radio Orch * orig BBC: REB 238 LP 1976*
*2.*50 CLASSIC TV THEMES - Bruce Baxter Orchestra
*HALLMARK (Carlt): 33043-2 (CD) (orig 2LP 1977) 1997*
IRONSIDE-KOJAK-COLUMBO-ONEDIN LINE-POLDARK-LIVER
BIRDS (On A Mountain Stands A Lady)-PALLISERS-NO HO
NESTLY-WHATEVER HAPPENED TO THE LIKELY LADS-SEVEN
FACES OF WOMAN (She)-BROTHERS-PROTECTORS (Avenues
and Alleyways)-COLDITZ-DAD'S ARMY (Who Do You Think
You Are Kidding Mr.Hitler)-BONANZA-WAGON TRAIN-MISS
ION IMPOSSIBLE-ALIAS SMITH AND JONES-ANGELS-JOHNNY
STACCATO-EMERGENCY WARD 10-THE SAINT-THE PERSUADERS
DEPARTMENT S-VIRGINIAN-DEPUTY-RAWHIDE-HAWAII FIVE-O
McCLOUD-CORONATION STREET-CROSSROADS-DR.KILDARE (3
Stars Will Shine Tonight)-OWEN MD (Sleepy Shores)-
DR.FINLAY'S CASEBOOK (A Little Suite No.2)-TODAY
(Windy)-ON THE MOVE-NATIONWIDE (Good Word)-SWEENEY
THUNDERBIRDS-STAR TREK-SOFTLY SOFTLY-DIXON OF DOCK
GREEN (An Ordinary Copper)-Z CARS-UPSTAIRS DOWNSTAI
RS (The Edwardians)-THE DUCHESS OF DUKE STREET-WHEN
THE BOAT CAME IN (Dance To Your Daddy)-THE AVENGERS
CALLAN-VAN DER VALK (Eye Level)
*3.*A-Z OF BRITISH TV THEMES FROM THE 60's and 70's
*PLAY IT AGAIN (S.Screen-Koch): PLAY 004 (CD)  1993*
AVENGERS-CAPTAIN SCARLET & MYSTERONS-CATWEAZLE-THE
CHAMPIONS-CROSSROADS-DAD'S ARMY-DANGER MAN-DEPT.S
DOCTOR IN THE HOUSE-DR.WHO-EMMERDALE FARM-FIREBALL
XL5-FORSYTE SAGA-HADLEIGH-HANCOCK-MAIGRET-MAN ALIVE
MAN IN A SUITCASE-NO HIDING PLACE-PLEASE SIR-POWER
GAME-RETURN OF THE SAINT-THE SAINT-SPORTSNIGHT-STEP
TOE AND SON-STINGRAY-THANK YOUR LUCKY STARS-THUNDER
BIRDS-TOP SECRET-Z CARS *incl: 21 original versions*
*4.*A-Z OF BRITISH TV THEMES VOLUME 2 - Various Artists
*PLAY IT AGAIN (S.Screen-Koch): PLAY 006 (CD)  1994*
ADVENTURES OF BLACK BEAUTY-ALL CREATURES GREAT AND
SMALL-ANGELS-ANIMAL MAGIC-AUF WIEDERSEHEN PET-BBC
CRICKET-BERGERAC-BREAD-BUDGIE-DANGER MAN-DOCTOR WHO
THE FENN STREETGANG-FOUR FEATHER FALLS-FREEWHEELERS
GRANDSTAND-HERE'S HARRY-HUMAN JUNGLE-JUKE BOX JURY-
LIVER BIRDS-MAN ABOUT THE HOUSE-THE NEW AVENGERS-
OWEN MD-THE PERSUADERS-RUGBY SPECIAL-SUPERCAR-TALES
OF THE UNEXPECTED-UPSTAIRS DOWNSTAIRS-VAN DER VALK-
VISION ON-WHATEVER HAPPENED TO THE LIKELY LADS

5. <u>A-Z OF BRITISH TV THEMES VOLUME 3</u> - Various Artists
*PLAY IT AGAIN (S.Screen-Koch): PLAY 010 (CD)* 1996
THE BEIDERBECKE CONNECTION *(CRYIN' ALL DAY)* Frank
Ricotti All Stars BLAKE'S 7 Dudley Simpson BLOTT ON
THE LANDSCAPE Dave MacKay DANGERFIELD Nigel Hess
DEMPSEY AND MAKEPEACE South Bank Or DOCTOR FINLAY'S
CASEBOOK *(MARCH FROM A LITTLE SUITE)* Trevor Duncan
EMERGENCY WARD 10 *(SILKS AND SATINS)* Peter Yorke
HETTY WAINTHROPP INVESTIGATES Nigel Hess INTERNATIO
NAL DETECTIVE Edwin Astley JUST WILLIAM Nigel Hess
LOVEJOY Denis King MIDWEEK /NATIONWIDE *(Good Word)*
John Scott THE NEWCOMERS *(FANCY DANCE)* John Barry
THE ONE GAME *(SAYLON DOLAN)* Nigel Hess / Chameleon
POIROT Christopher Gunning THE PROFESSIONALS South
Bank Orch RUTH RENDELL MYSTERIES Brian Bennett
SEXTON BLAKE Vic Flick Snd SHOESTRING George Fenton
SKI SUNDAY *(POP LOOKS BACH)* Sam Fonteyn THE SWEENEY
Harry South TERRY & JUNE *(BELL HOP)*John Shakespeare
THIS IS YOUR LIFE *(GALA PERFORMANCE)* Laurie Johnson
TRIALS OF LIFE George Fenton WHEN THE BOAT COMES IN
*(DANCE TI THI DADDY)* Alex Glasgow WISH ME LUCK Jim
Parker WOOF! Paul Lewis Woof Band WORLD OF SPORT
*(W.OF SPORT MARCH)* Don Jackson WYCLIFFE Nigel Hess

6. <u>A-Z OF BRITISH TV THEMES VOLUME 4</u> - Various Artists
*PLAY IT AGAIN (S.Screen-Koch): PLAY 009 (CD)* 1996
1.ADVENTURES OF NICHOLAS NICKELBY Stephen Oliver 2.
ASK THE FAMILY *SUNRIDE* John Leach 3.AUF WIEDERSEHEN
PET *BACK WITH THE BOYS* Joe Fagin 4.BBC WIMBLEDON
*LIGHT & TUNEFUL* Keith Mansfield 5.BIG DEAL Bobby G.
6.BIG MATCH *LA SOIREE* David Ordini 7.BIRD OF PREY
Dave Greenslade8.CAMPION Nigel Hess 9.CRIMEWATCH UK
*EMERGENCY* John Cameron 10.DID YOU SEE Francis Monkm
an 11.FOLLYFOOT *THE LIGHTNING TREE* The Settlers 12.
GRANDSTAND (1950's-60's) *NEWSCOOP* Len Stevens 13.
HOLIDAY *HEARTSONG* Gordon Giltrap 14.JAMAICA INN
Francis Shaw 15.KINSEY Dave Greenslade 16.MAIGRET
(1990s) Nigel Hess 17.MASTERMIND *APPROACHING MENACE*
Neil Richardson 18.ON THE BUSES Sam Fonteyn 19.
ORANGES ARE NOT THE ONLY FRUIT Rachel Portman
20.PEOPLE IN LONDON *SPANISH ARMADA* Les Reed 21.
PORTERHOUSE BLUE Flying Picketts 22.QUATFRMASS II
*MARS (G.HOLST)* 23.RANDALL AND HOPKIRK DECEASED
Edwin Astley 24.RESORT TO MURDER Bill Connor 25.
SHADOW OF THE NOOSE Duncan Browne 26.SPORTSVIEW
*SATURDAY SPORTS* Wilfred Burns 27.TINKER TAILOR
SOLDIER SPY Lesley Garrett 28.TRAVELLING MAN
Duncan Browne 29.WHICKER'S WORLD Laurie Johnson
30.WORLD OF TIM FRAZER Cyril Watters

7. <u>A-Z OF BRITISH TV THEMES - THE RON GRAINER YEARS</u>
*PLAY IT AGAIN (S.Screen-Koch): PLAY 008 (CD)* 1994
Ron Grainer themes and recordings
A TOUCH OF VELVET A STING OF BRASS *(M.Wirtz)(Disco)*
ALONG THE BOULEVARDS *(from 'MAIGRET')*-ANDORRA *(from
'Andorra' and 'Danger Island')*-ASSASSINATION TROT

'Andorra' and 'Danger Island')-ASSASSINATION TROT
('*Assassination Bureau*')-BORN AND BRED-BOY MEETS GI
RL-HAPPY JOE ('*Comedy Playhouse*')-DETECTIVE-DR.WHO
(*orig*) - DR.WHO (*disco*)- BUTTERED CRUMPET ('*Fanny
Craddock*')-JAZZ AGE-JOHNNY'S TUNE ('*Sunday Break*' &
'*Some People*') -LOVE THEME FROM 'ONLY WHEN I LARF'-
MAIGRET-MALICE AFORETHOUGHT-MAN IN A SUITCASE-ILLIC
IT CARGO ('*Man In The News*')-OLIVER TWIST *performed*
by *The Eagles* - PAUL TEMPLE-THE PRISONER (*original*)
THE PRISONER (*orch*)- REBECCA-SOUTH RIDING-TALES OF
THE UNEXPECTED (*orig*)-TALES OF T.UNEXPECTED (*disco*)
OLD NED ('*Steptoe & Son*')-TRAIN NOW STANDING (*Green
Pastures*)-TROUBLE WITH YOU LILIAN ('*Counting The Co
ster*')-WHEN LOVES GROWS COLD (*Edward & Mrs.Simpson*)
**8.**<u>ACTION THEMES</u> -   Mike Timoney, music associate
*EMPORIO (Disc-THE): EMPRCD 691*                    *1996*
1.SUPERMAN 2.RAIDERS OF THE LOST ARK 3.EYE OF THE
TIGER *ROCKY III* 4.BACK TO THE FUTURE 5.RAMBO: FIRST
BLOOD 6.THE TERMINATOR 7.TOP GUN 8.TOWERING INFERNO
9.THE MORNING AFTER *POSEIDON ADVENTURE* 10.AIRPORT
11.GONNA FLY NOW *ROCKY* 12.BACKDRAFT 13.PREDATOR 14.
ROBOCOP 15.SPEED 16.DIRTY HARRY *Gordon Lorenz Prod.*
--- <u>ADDINSELL Richard</u> - *see COLLECTIONS 41 and 386*
**9.**<u>ADIEMUS: SONGS OF SANCTUARY</u> - London Philharm.Orch
(Karl Jenkins) with Miriam Stockley / Mike Ratledge
*VIRGIN (EMI): CD(TC)VE 925*                         *1995*
ADIEMUS (*DELTA AIRLINES AD / TESTAMENT:THE BIBLE IN
ANIMATION BBC2*) + 8 all composed by KARL JENKINS
<u>ADIEMUS 2: CANTATA MUNDI</u> *Virg: CD(TC)VE(X) 932 1997*
SONG OF TEARS (*CHELTENHAM & GLOUCESTER AD*) + others
*see also COLLECTION 267*
**10.**<u>AFTER THE BREAK</u> - Music from TV ADS - Var.Artists
*SONY MUSIC TV: SONYTV 30CD (CD) 30MC (MC)*          *1997*
1.KEEP ON MOVIN'Soul II Soul & Caron Wheeler  (*RENA
ULT CLIO*) 2.YOU DON'T LOVE ME (NO NO NO) Dawn Penn
(*NISSAN MICRA*) 3.SUMMER BREEZE Isley Bros (*SOLTAN*)
4.I CAN SEE CLEARLY NOW Johnny Nash (*DOLLAND & AITC
ISON*) 5.LEAN ON ME Bill Withers (*ROYAL LIVER ASSUR*)
6.CALIFORNIA DREAMIN' Mamas & Papas (*CARLING PREM*)
7.AIR THAT I BREATHE Hollies (*COMFORT*) 8.SPIRIT IN
THE SKY Norman Greenbaum (*KELLOGG'S BRAN FLAKES*) 9.
LOW RIDER War (*MARMITE*) 10.SPIRITUAL HIGH (STATE OF
INDEPENDENCE) Moodswings w.Chryssie Hynde (*CHANEL
ALLURE*) 11.DREAM A LITTLE DREAM OF ME Mama Cass
(*PEUGEOT 406*) 12.CAN'T TAKE MY EYES OFF YOU Andy
Williams (*PEUGEOT 306*) 13.FEVER Peggy Lee (*CADBURYS
DARKNESS*) 14.LOVE LETTERS Ketty Lester (*ROYAL MAIL*)
15.LET'S FACE THE MUSIC AND DANCE Nat King Cole
(*ALLIED DUNBAR*) 16.MEMORIES ARE MADE OF THIS Dean
Martin (*KODAK*) 17.STORY OF MY LIFE Michael Holliday
(*GUINNESS*) 18.WHEN YOU'RE SMILING Louis Armstrong
(*ELECTRICITY COUNCIL*) 19.I WANNA BE LOVED BY YOU
Marilyn Monroe (*CHANEL # 5*) 20.HOOTS MON! Lord Rock
inghams XI (*MAYNARDS WINE GUMS*)

11. <u>ALIEN TRILOGY</u> - The Royal Scottish National Orch
*VARESE (Pinn): VSD 5753 (CD)* Mus by JERRY GOLDSMITH
JAMES HORNER (ALIENS) ELLIOT GOLDENTHAL (ALIEN 3)

12. <u>AMERICAN TELEVISION'S GREATEST HITS</u> - Daniel Caine
*SILVA SCREEN (Koch): TVPMCD 804 (2CD)*            *1994*
A.TEAM-AIRWOLF-BARNABY JONES-BATTLESTAR GALACTICA-
BAYWATCH-BEVERLY HILLS 90210-BUCK ROGERS IN T.25TH
CENTURY-CAGNEY & LACEY-CHEERS-COSBY SHOW-DOOGIE HOW
SER MD-EERIE INDIANA-EQUALIZER-EVENING SHADE-FALCON
CREST-FREDDY'S NIGHTMARES-HARDCASTLE AND McCORMICK-
HIGHWAY TO HEAVEN-HILL ST.BLUES-HUNTER-INCREDIBLE
HULK-KNIGHT RIDER-L.A.LAW-LITTLE HOUSE ON T.PRAIRIE
LOU GRANT-MacGYVER-MAGNUM,P.I.-MAN FROM U.N.C.L.E.-
MELROSE PLACE-MIDNIGHT CALLER-MORK & MINDY-MUNSTERS
MURDER SHE WROTE-NIGHT COURT-NORTH & SOUTH-NORTHERN
EXPOSURE-POLICE STORY-PURSUIT-QUANTUM LEAP-ROCKFORD
FILES-REMINGTON STEELE-ROSEANNE-SLEDGEHAMMER-STAR
TREK: NEXT GENERATION-SPENSER FOR HIRE-ST.ELSEWHERE
STREETHAWK-TAXI-21 JUMP STREET-TWIN PEAKS-V:THE SER
IES-WALTONS-YOUNG RIDERS   *Daniel Caine, conductor*

--- <u>ANDERSON Gerry</u> *see COLLECTION 135*

13. <u>ANDERSON Leroy</u> - The Typewriter & Other Favorites *
*RCA VICTOR Red Seal (BMG): 09026 68048-2 (CD)*    *1995*
BELLE OF THE BALL-PHANTOM REGIMENT-THE FIRST DAY OF
SPRING-SLEIGH RIDE-PLINK PLANK PLUNK!-BLUE TANGO-
FORGOTTEN DREAMS-BUGLER'S HOLIDAY-THE PENNY WHISTLE
SONG-CLARINET CANDY-HORSE AND BUGGY-A TRUMPETER'S
LULLABY-FIDDLE FADDLE-JAZZ PIZZICATO-JAZZ LEGATO-
SYNCOPATED CLOCK-SANDPAPER BALLET-THE TYPEWRITER-
THE WALTZING CAT-PROMENADE-SARABAND-SERENATA-
BALLADETTE-ARIETTA-HOME STRETCH
* Saint Louis Symphony Orchestra (Leonard Slatkin)

--- <u>ARNOLD David</u> - *see COLLECTION 305*

14. <u>ARNOLD Malcolm</u> - Film Music Of (London Symph.Orch*)
*CHANDOS (Chandos): CHAN 9100 (CD)*
THE BRIDGE ON THE RIVER KWAI (Suite For Large Orch
feat 'Colonel Bogey' (Kenneth Alford)-WHISTLE DOWN
THE WIND (Small Suite For Small Orchest)-THE SOUND
BARRIER (A Rhapsody For Orchestra Op.38)-HOBSON'S
CHOICE (Orchestral Suite)-THE INN OF THE SIXTH HAPP
INESS (Orchestral Suite) *Conductor: *RICHARD HICKUX*

15. <u>ASTAIRE Fred</u> - At MGM - A Soundtrack Anthology
*EMI SOUNDTRACKS (EM): 821 975-2 (2CDs)*          *1997*
CD1 HEIGH HO!-GANG'S ALL HERE-PLEASE DON'T MONKEY
WITH BROADWAY-I'VE GOT MY EYES ON YOU-HERE'S TO THE
GIRLS-THIS HEART OF MINE-IF SWING GOES I GO TOO
YOLANDA-STEPPIN' OUT WITH MY BABY-IT ONLY HAPPENS
WHEN I DANCE WITH YOU-A COUPLE OF SWELLS-YOU'D BE
HARD TO REPLACE-SHOES WITH WINGS ON-WEEKEND IN THE
COUNTRY-THEY CAN'T TAKE THAT AWAY FROM ME-MANHATTAN
DOWNBEAT-WHERE DID YOU GET THAT GIRL-SO LONG OOLONG
HOW LONG YOU GONNA BE-NEVERTHELESS I'M IN LOVE WITH
YOU *Medley:* MY SUNNY TENNESSEE/WHO'S SORRY NOW/SO
LONG OOLONG/THINKING OF YOU/THREE LITTLE WORDS

CD2 EVERY NIGHT AT SEVEN-HOW COULD YOU BELIEVE ME
WHEN I SAID I LOVE YOU WHEN YOU KNOW I'VE BEEN A
LIAR ALL MY LIFE-YOU'RE ALL THE WORLD TO ME-
I LEFT MY HAT IN HAITI-BACHELOR DINNER SONG-OOPS!-
SEEING'S BELIEVING-BABY DOLL-I WANNA BE A DANCIN'
MAN-BY MYSELF-A SHINE ON YOUR SHOES-THAT'S ENTERT.
GOT A BRAN' NEW SUIT-TRIPLETS-I GUESS I'LL HAVE TO
CHANGE MY PLAN-PARIS LOVES LOVERS-ALL OF YOU-FATED
TO BE MATED-THE RITZ ROLL AND ROCK

16. ASTAIRE Fred - Songs From The Movies (Orig Tracks)
*PAST PERFECT (THE): PPCD 78115*               *1994*
Top Hat (35): NO STRINGS-ISN'T THIS A LOVELY DAY-
TOP HAT WHITE TIE & TAILS-CHEEK TO CHEEK-PICCOLINO
Follow The Fleet (36): WE SAW THE SEA-LET YOURSELF
GO-I'D RATHER LEAD A BAND-I'M PUTTING ALL MY EGGS
IN ONE BASKET-LET'S FACE THE MUSIC AND DANCE
Swing Time (36): PICK YOURSELF UP-THE WAY YOU LOOK
TONIGHT-A FINE ROMANCE-BOJANGLES OF HARLEM-NEVER
GONNA DANCE / Shall We Dance (37): BEGINNER'S LUCK
SLAP THAT BASS-THEY ALL LAUGHED-LET'S CALL THE
WHOLE THING OFF-THEY CAN'T TAKE THAT AWAY FROM ME
SHALL WE DANCE / A Damsel In Distress (37): I CAN'T
BE BOTHERED NOW-THINGS ARE LOOKING UP-A FOGGY DAY-
NICE WORK IF YOU CAN GET IT

17. AT THE MOVIES - Various Artists
*RCA (BMG): 74321 41273-2*                     *1997*
1.SOMEDAY I'M COMING BACK *BODYGUARD* Lisa Stansfield
2.THIS CITY NEVER SLEEPS *9½ WEEKS* Eurythmics 3.YOU
DON'T OWN ME *DIRTY DANCING* Blow Monkeys 4.CRASH 95
MIX *DUMB & DUMBER* Primitives 5.GET TOGETHER *FORREST
GUMP* Youngbloods 6.GHOSTBUSTERS Ray Parker Junior 7
NOTHING'S GONNA STOP US NOW *MANNEQUIN* Starship 8.
EVERYBODY'S TALKIN' *MIDNIGHT COWBOY* Nilsson 9.THEME
HARRY'S GAME *PATRIOT GAMES* Clannad 10.NATURAL THING
*PRET-A-PORTER* M.People 11.ROADHOUSE BLUES *ROADHOUSE*
Jeff Healey Band 12.I WILL ALWAYS LOVE YOU *BEST LIT
TLE WHOREHOUSE..* Dolly Parton 13.JUMPING JACK FLASH
Aretha Franklin 14.NEUTRON DANCE *B.H.COP* Pointer
Sisters 15.LET THE RIVER RUN *WORKING GIRL* Carly Sim
on 16.SENTIMENTAL JOURNEY *FOUR ROOMS* Esquivel Orch
17.I'VE HAD THE TIME OF MY LIFE *DIRTY DANCING* Bill
Medley and Jennifer Warnes

18. BACHELOR IN PARADISE - COCKTAIL CLASSICS FROM MGM
*EMI SOUNDTRACKS (EMI) 821 963-2 (CD) Var.Arts. 1997*
BACHELOR IN PARADISE *(MAIN TITLE)*-BOSSA NOVA BESSIE
*(GLASS BOTTOM BOAT)*-OVER THE RAINBOW *(WIZARD OF OZ)*
SUNDAY IN NEW YORK *(TITLE)*-OL'MAN RIVER *(SHOW BOAT)*
HOW ABOUT YOU*(BACHELOR IN PARIS)*-LOVE IS OH SO EASY
*(KALUGA)(HONEYMOON HOTEL)*-ARUBA LIBERACE *(WHEN THE
BOYS MEET THE GIRLS)*-I'VE GOT YOU UNDER MY SKIN*(THE
MATING GAME)*-I GOT RHYTHM *(GIRL CRAZY)*-TEMPTATION
*(GOING HOLLYWOOD)*-GIRL FROM IPANEMA *(GET YOURSELF A
COLLEGE GIRL)*-FASHION SHOW *(NORTH BY NORTHWEST)*-THE
WONDERFUL WORLD OF THE BROTHERS GRIMM *(TITLE THEME)*

APPRECIATION *(VIVA LAS VEGAS)*-DANCING IN THE DARK
*(BAND WAGON)*-COFFEE TIME *(SUBTERRANEANS)*-BACHELOR
IN PARADISE *(END TITLE) Various Original Artists*

19. <u>BALL Michael</u>  - The Musicals
*POLYGRAM TV (Poly): 533 892-2 (CD) -4 (MC)*        *1996*
1.ALL I ASK OF YOU *PHANTOM OF T.OPERA* 2.SOMETHING'S
COMING *WEST SIDE STORY* 3.LOSING MY MIND *FOLLIES* 4.
MEMORY *CATS* 5.DON'T RAIN ON MY PARADE *FUNNY GIRL* 6.
WITH ONE LOOK *SUNSET BOULEVARD* 7.SHOW ME *MY FAIR
LADY* 8.I DREAMED A DREAM *LES MISERABLES* 9.YOU'LL
NEVER WALK ALONE *CAROUSEL* 10.EASY TERMS *BLOOD BROTH
ERS* 11.LAST NIGHT OF THE WORLD*MISS SAIGON* 12.LOVING
YOU *PASSION* 13.ANTHEM *CHESS* 14.LOVE CHANGES EVERYTH
ING *ASPECTS OF LOVE* 15.WITH ONE LOOK (OUTRO) *SUNSET
BOULEVARD*

20. <u>BARRY John</u> - The Best Of (Film and TV Themes)
*POLYDOR: 849 095-2 (CD) 849 095-4 (MC)*        *1991*
GOLDFINGER-SAIL THE SUMMER WINDS *(The Dove)*-LOVE AM
ONG THE RUINS-LOLITA-A DOLL'S HOUSE-FOLLOW FOLLOW
*(Follow Me)*-DIAMONDS ARE FOREVER-BOOM-MIDNIGHT COWB
OY-THIS WAY MARY *(Mary Queen Of Scots)*-THE GLASS ME
NAGERIE-THUNDERBALL-007-PLAY IT AGAIN *(The Tamarind
Seed)*-ORSON WELLES GREAT MYSTERIES-WE HAVE ALL THE
TIME IN THE WORLD *(On Her Majesty's Secret Service)*
THE WHISPERERS-CURIOUSER AND CURIOUSER *(Alice's Adv
entures In Wonderland)*-BILLY-THE GOOD TIMES ARE COM
ING *(Monte Walsh)*-WALKABOUT-THE ADVENTURER

21. <u>BARRY John</u> The Classic John Barry - City Of Prague
Symphony Orch (Nicholas Raine) Suites and Themes
*SILVA SCREEN (Koch): FILMCD 141 (CD)*        *1993*
ZULU-OUT OF AFRICA-BODY HEAT-MIDNIGHT COWBOY-THE
LAST VALLEY-BORN FREE-CHAPLIN-ELEANOR AND FRANKLIN-
DANCES WITH WOLVES-INDECENT PROPOSAL-THE PERSUADERS
ROBIN AND MARIAN-SOMEWHERE IN TIME-THE LION IN WINT
ER-HANOVER STREET-RAISE THE TITANIC

22. <u>BARRY John</u> Classic John Barry Vol.2 -City Of Prague
Symphony Orch (Nicholas Raine) Suites and Themes
*SILVA SCREEN (Koch): FILMCD 169 (CD)*        *1996*
HIGH ROAD TO CHINA-THE WRONG BOX-THE IPCRESS FILE-
THE BLACK HOLE-THE APPOINTMENT-THE SCARLET LETTER-
MONTE WALSH-THE KNACK-CRY THE BELOVED COUNTRY-THE
DOVE-WALKABOUT-MARY QUEEN OF SCOTS-THE QUILLER MEMO
RANDUM-DEADFALL
see also 'EMBER YEARS'

23. <u>BARRY John</u> - Hit and Miss
*MFP (EMI): CDMFP 6392 (CD) TCMFP 6292 (MC)*        *1997*
HIDEAWAY-WHEN THE SAINTS GO MARCHING IN-LONG JOHN-
TWELFTH STREET RAG-HIT AND MISS-BEAT FOR BEATNIKS-
BLUEBERRY HILL-NEVER LET GO-WALK DON'T RUN-BLACK
STOCKINGS-MAGNIFICENT SEVEN-IT DOESN'T MATTER ANY
MORE-SPANISH HARLEM-JAMES BOND THEME-CUTTY SARK-
CHERRY PINK & APPLE BLOSSOM WHITE-UNCHAINED MELODY-
UNCHAINED MELODY-I'LL BE WITH YOU IN APPLE BLOSSOM
TIME-VOLARE-THAT FATAL KISS

24. BARRY John - Moviola
    *EPIC (SONY: 472490-2 (CD)*                                    *1992*
    OUT OF AFRICA-MIDNIGHT COWBOY-BODY HEAT-SOMEWHERE
    IN TIME-MARY QUEEN OF SCOTS-BORN FREE-DANCES WITH
    WOLVES-CHAPLIN-COTTON CLUB-WALKABOUT-FRANCES-ON HER
    MAJESTY'S S.SERVICE (WE HAVE ALL THE TIME)-MOVIOLA
25. BARRY John - Moviola 2: Action and Adventure
    *EPIC (Sony): 478 601-2 (CD) -4 (MC)*                          *1995*
    GOLDFINGER-JAMES BOND THEME-FROM RUSSIA WITH LOVE-
    THUNDERBALL-007-YOU ONLY LIVE TWICE-ON HER MAJESTY'
    S SECRET SERVICE- DIAMONDS ARE FOREVER-ALL TIME HIGH
    (OCTPOUSSY)-UNTIL SEPTEMBER-KING KONG-ZULU
26. BARRY John - Soundscape: The Best of JOHN BARRY
    *COLUMBIA (Sony): 488582-2 (CD)*                               *1997*
    1.PERSUADERS THEME 2.MIDNIGHT COWBOY 3.IPCRESS FILE
    4.THE KNACK 5.WEDNESDAY'S CHILD 6.SPACE MARCH (CAPS
    ULE IN SPACE) 7.THE GIRL WITH THE SUN IN HER HAIR
    (SUNSILK 70's AD) 8.VENDETTA 9.DANNY SCIPIO THEME
    10.JAMES BOND THEME 11.GOLDFINGER 12.DIAMONDS ARE
    FOREVER 13.FROM RUSSIA WITH LOVE 14.YOU ONLY LIVE
    TWICE 15.THUNDERBALL 16.ON HER MAJESTY'S SECRET SER
    VICE 17.007 18.WALK DON'T RUN 19.BEAT FOR BEATNIKS
    20.HIT AND MISS 21.BORN FREE 22.I HAD A FARM IN
    AFRICA 23.JOHN DUNBAR THEME (DANCES WITH WOLVES)
27. BARRY John - The Hits and Misses
    *PLAY IT AGAIN (Koch-S.Screen): PLAY 007 (2CD)  1998*
    Tracks inc: JAMES BOND THEME-DAYS OF WINE AND ROSES
    Johnny De Little  UNCHAINED MELODY Johnny De Little
    GOLDFINGER Shirley Bassey HIT AND MISS-PEPE Russ
    Conway ROCCO'S THEME (ROCKO AND HIS BROTHERS) CUTTY
    SARK (DATELINE LONDON) and many others
28. BASSEY Shirley - Sings The Movies (1)
    *POLYGRAM TV (Poly): 529 399-2 (CD) -4 (MC)*                   *1995*
    GOLDFINGER / CRAZY *COALMINER'S DAUGHTER* / THE BEST
    THAT YOU CAN DO (ARTHUR'S THEME) *ARTHUR* / LOVE ON
    THE ROCKS *JAZZ SINGER* / ELEANOR RIGBY *YELLOW SUBMA
    RINE* / LET'S STAY TOGETHER *PULP FICTION* / THE ROSE
    *THE ROSE* / DO YOU KNOW WHERE YOU'RE GOING TO *MAHOG
    GANY* / WE DON'T NEED ANOTHER HERO *MAD MAX BEYOND
    THUNDERDOME* / IT MUST HAVE BEEN LOVE *PRETTY WOMAN*
    TRY A LITTLE TENDERNESS *COMMITTMENTS* / HOPELESSLY
    DEVOTED TO YOU *GREASE* / MAKIN' WHOOPEE *SLEEPLESS
    IN SEATTLE* / WHO WANTS TO LIVE FOREVER *HIGHLANDER*
29. BASSEY Shirley - Sings The Movies (2)
    *MFP (EMI): CD(TC)MFP 6205 (CD/MC)*                            *1995*
    GOLDFINGER / WHERE DO I BEGIN *LOVE STORY* / TONIGHT
    *WEST SIDE STORY* / BIG SPENDER *SWEET CHARITY* / AS
    LONG AS HE NEED ME *OLIVER* / DIAMONDS ARE FOREVER /
    LADY IS A TRAMP *PAL JOEY* / AS TIME GOES BY *CASABLAN
    CA* / YOU'LL NEVER WALK ALONE *CAROUSEL* / CLIMB EVERY
    MOUNTAIN *SOUND OF MUSIC* / MOON RIVER *BREAKFAST AT
    TIFFANY'S* / FUNNY GIRL / JUST ONE OF THOSE THINGS
    *NIGHT AND DAY* / S'WONDERFUL *AN AMERICAN IN PARIS* /
    YOU'LL NEVER KNOW *HELLO FRISCO HELLO* / MORE *MONDO*

CANE / LIQUIDATOR / I DON'T KNOW HOW TO LOVE HIM

30.BATMAN TRILOGY JOEL McNEELY & ROYAL SCOTTISH N.ORCH
VARESE (Pinn): VSD 5766 (CD)                           1997
featuring music from 'BATMAN' and 'BATMAN RETURNS'
(DANNY ELFMAN) 'BATMAN FOREVER' (ELLIOT GOLDENTHAL)
'BATMAN' TV THEME (NEAL HEFTI/NELSON RIDDLE) and
'BATMAN AND ROBIN' (ELLIOT GOLDENTHAL)

--- BAXTER Bruce see COLLECTION 2

31.BBC RADIO TOP TUNES Midland Radio Or.Norrie Paramor
EMPORIO-MCI (Disc-THE): EMPRCD 660 (CD)              *1996
1.SWEET AND GENTLE-2.SKY AT NIGHT-3.ARCHERS:BARWICK
GREEN 4.OWEN MD: SLEEPY SHORES 5.MIDWEEK 6.MEDLEY:
FAMILY FAVOURITES: WITH A SONG IN MY HEART / TOP OF
THE FORM: MARCHING STRINGS / SING SOMETHING SIMPLE
DESERT ISLAND DISCS:BY THE SLEEPY LAGOON 7.ONEDIN
LINE 8.FILM 74-87: I WISH I KNEW HOW IT WOULD FEEL
TO BE FREE 9.FORSYTE SAGA: ELIZABETH TUDOR 10.THE
LOTUS EATERS 11.SOFTLY SOFTLY 12.MEDLEY PEBBLE MILL
AT ONE:AS YOU PLEASE / DAD'S ARMY: WHO DO YOU THINK
YOU ARE KIDDING MR.HITLER / TOMORROW'S WORLD /
MATCH OF THE DAY   * originally BBC: REB 171 LP 1974

32.BEAUTIFUL HOLLYWOOD Cincinnati Pops Orch (E.Kunzel)
TELARC-Conifer (BMG): CD 80440 (CD)                  1997
FOREST GUMP-THE RIVER RUNS THROUGH IT-ROB ROY-JERRY
MAGUIRE-LEGENDS OF THE FALL-EVITA-THE BRIDGES OF
MADISON COUNTY-POCAHONTAS-THE MISSION-FREE WILLY-
FOREVER YOUNG-CINEMA PARADISO-RUDY-CHAPLIN-GRUMPIER
OLD MEN-BUGSY-SCHINDLER'S LIST-GETTYSBURG

--- BERKELEY Busby - see COLLECTION 240
--- BERNARD James - see COLLECTION 119

33.BEST OF BRITISH TELEVISION (24 GREAT TV THEMES)
MCI (THE): MCCD 225 (CD) MCTC 225 (MC)               1995
CASUALTY-PLAY YOUR CARDS RIGHT-HEART OF THE MATTER
BOTTOM-LITTLEJOHN (House Of Fun)-YOU BET-JOHNNY AND
THE DEAD-YOU ARE THE NUMBER ONE-SCHOFIELD'S QUEST-
T.BILL-HEARTBEAT-HETTY WAINTHROP INVESTIGATES-GMTV
WYCLIFFE-BLIND DATE-DIAL MIDNIGHT-GLADIATORS-GIRL
FRIDAY-DANGERFIELD-THIS IS YOUR LIFE-JUST WILLIAM-
EMMERDALE FARM-NEW AVENGERS-CORONATION STREET

34.BIG PICTURE The - Cincinnati Pops Orch Erich Kunzel
TELARC (Con-BMG): CD 80437 (CD)                      1997
SYMPHONIC SUITES & THEMES from: MISSION IMPOSSIBLE-
BATMAN FOREVER-APOLLO 13-CRIMSON TIDE-FIGHTER SQUAD
RON-INDEPENDENCE DAY-BRAVEHEART-CUTTHROAT ISLAND-
TWISTER-LAST OF THE MOHICANS-DRAGONHEART-EXECUTIVE
DECISION-STARGATE-GETTYSBURG-JUMANJI-SPEED

---.BIG SCREEN ADVENTURE - see COLLECTION 48

35.BIG WAR THEMES - Geoff LOVE Orchestra
MFP Compacts (EMI): CC 211 (CD) HR 8140 (MC)   1988
BRIDGE ON THE RIVER KWAI-LAWRENCE OF ARABIA-GUNS OF
NAVARONE-BATTLE OF BRITAIN-LONGEST DAY WHERE EAGLES
DARE-DAM BUSTERS-633 SQUADRON-GREAT ESCAPE-GREEN BE
RETS-DEER HUNTER-COLDITZ-VICTORYAT SEA-SINK THEBISM
ARCK-WINDS OF WAR-REACH FOR THESKY-WE'LL MEET AGAIN

--- BINGE Ronald - *see COLLECTION 42*
36. BLACK Don - The Don Black Songbook   Various Artists
*PLAY IT AGAIN (S.Screen-Koch): PLAY 005 (CD)     1993*
BORN FREE *(MATT MONRO)*- TO SIR WITH LOVE *(Lulu)* THE
GIRL WITH THE SUN IN HER HAIR *(Davy Clinton)* TRUE
GRIT *(Danny Street)* ON DAYS LIKE THESE *(Matt Monro)*
WISH NOW WAS THEN *(Matt Monro)* CURIOUSER AND CURIOU
SER *(Matt Monro)* THE ME I NEVER KNEW *(Matt Monro)*
BILLY *(Lena Martell)* THE LADY FROM L.A. *(Michael Cr
awford)*I MISSED THE LAST RAINBOW *(Michael Crawford)*
PLAY IT AGAIN *(Wilma Reading)* I'LL PUT YOU TOGETHER
AGAIN *(Hot Chocolate)* TELL ME ON A SUNDAY *(Marti We
bb)* THE LAST MAN IN MY LIFE *(Marti Webb)* ANYONE CAN
FALL IN LOVE *(Marti Webb)* ALWAYS THERE *(Marti Webb)*
THERE IS LOVE AND THERE IS LOVE *(Adam Faith)* IN ONE
OF MY WEAKER MOMENTS *(Anita Dobson)* ANYTHING BUT LO
NELY / LOVE CHANGES EVERYTHING *(both by Marti Webb)*
--- BLACK Stanley - *see COLLECTION 140*
37. BLADE RUNNER: Synthesizer Soundtracks   Various Arts
*SILVA SCREEN (Koch): SILVAD 3008 (CD)          1994*
THE HITCHER: HEADLIGHTS *(Mark Isham)* HEART OF MIDNI
GHT: OVERTURE CAROL'S THEME *(Yanni)* BIG TROUBLE IN
LITTLE CHINA: MAIN TITLE *(John Carpenter)* HAUNTED
SUMMER: NIGHT WAS MADE FOR LOVING *Christopher Young*
DAS BOOT The Boat: THEME *(Klaus Doldinger)* REVENGE:
LOVE THEME *(Jack Nitzsche)* LOCK UP: BREAKING POINT
*(Bill Conti)* TURTLE BEACH: HOMECOMING *(Chris Neal)*
THE PARK IS MINE: HELICOPTER ATTACK *Tangerine Dream*
I LOVE YOU PERFECT: OPENING CREDIT*S Yanni* HALLOWEEN
MAIN TITLE *(John Carpenter)* NEAR DARK: BUS STATION
*(Tangerine Dream)* DEADLOCK: WE KNOW YOU'RE IN THERE
*(Richard Gibbs)* OVER THE TOP: THE FIGHT *(Giorgio Mo
roder)* BLADE RUNNER: END TITLES *(Vangelis)*
*tracks 3,11 performed by Daniel Caine tracks 5,7,14*
*15 Mark Ayres all others performed by the composer*
38. BLUE MOVIES: SCORING FOR THE STUDIOS - Various Arts
*BLUE NOTE (EMI): CDP 857748-2 (CD)             1997*
1.I WISH I KNEW *(FILM 97)* Billy Taylor 2.JAMES BOND
THEME Leroy Holmes 3.KOJAK Willie Bobo 4.BULLITT
Wilton Felder 5.FROM RUSSIA WITH LOVE Count Basie 6
SHADOW OF YOUR SMITH *(SANDPIPER)* Lou Donaldson 7.
DOWN HERE ON THE GROUND *(COOL HAND LUKE)*Grant Green
Dianne Reeves 8.BLOW UP Bobby Hutherson 9.STAR TREK
The Three Sounds 10.MISSION IMPOSSIBLE Billy May 11
ALFIE John Patton 12.MIDNIGHT COWBOY Lee Morgan 13.
LAST TANGO IN PARIS Marlena Shaw 14.MOON RIVER *BREA
KFAST AT TIFFANY'S* Nancy Wilson 15.LOVE STORY THEME
Richard Groove Holmes 16.MASH Bobby Hutcherson 17.
WINDMILLS OF YOUR MIND *THOM.CROWN AFFAIR* Bud Shank
--- BOGART Humphrey - *see COLLECTION 54*
39. BORN ON THE 4TH OF JULY: FILMS OF TOM CRUISE- MUSIC
*SILVA SCREEN (Koch): FILMCD 152 (CD)           1994*
*New Digit.Recordings*Based On The Orig Film Scores*
Born On The 4th Of July: END CREDITS *John Williams*

Risky Business: LOVE ONA REAL TRAIN *Tangerine Dream*
Days Of Thunder:MAIN TITLE/CAR BUILDING *Hans Zimmer*
Color Of Money: MAIN TITLE *(R.Robertson-Gil Evans)*
The Outsiders: STAY GOLD *(Carmine Coppola-S.Wonder)*
Legend: THE UNICORNS *(Jerry Goldsmith)* OPENING/THE
UNICORN THEME *(Tangerine Dream)* Top Gun: TOP GUN AN
THEM *(Harold Faltermeyer)* TAKE MY BREATH AWAY *(Gior
gio Moroder-Tom Whitlock)* Rain Man: LAS VEGAS/END
CREDITS *(Hans Zimmer)* Cocktail: JORDAN *(J.Peter Rob
inson)* The Firm: MAIN TITLE*(Dave Grusin)* A Few Good
Men: CODE RED/FACTS & FIGURES/HONOR *(Marc Shaiman)*
Far And Away: BOOK OF DAYS*(Enya-N.Ryan)* END CREDITS
*(John Williams)*        * City Of Prageu Philharmonic

40.BRIDESHEAD REVISITED: TV Scores Of Geoffrey BURGON
   *SILVA SCREEN (Koch): FILMCD 117 (CD)*            *1992*
   THE CHRONICLES OF NARNIA-BLEAK HOUSE-TESTAMENT OF
   YOUTH-BRIDESHEAD REVISITED (Suite)-NUNC DIMITTIS fr
   om TINKER TAILOR SOLDIER SPY sung by *LESLEY GARRETT
   Philharmonia Orchestra conducted by Geoffrey Burgon*

41.BRITISH LIGHT MUSIC: RICHARD ADDINSELL  BBC Concert
   Orch (Kenneth Alwyn) +Philip Martin & Roderick Elms
   *MARCO POLO (Select): 8.223732 (CD)*            *1995*
   GOODBYE MR.CHIPS (1939) THE PRINCE AND THE SHOWGIRL
   (1957) TOM BROWN'S SCHOOLDAYS (1951) A TALE OF TWO
   CITIES (58) FIRE OVER ENGLAND (1937) + other music

42.BRITISH LIGHT MUSIC: RONALD BINGE with the Slovak
   Radio Symphony Orchestra (Ernest Tomlinson)
   *MARCO POLO (Select): 8.223515 (CD)*            *1994*
   ELIZABETHAN SERENADE *(BBC: MUSIC TAPESTRY Theme)*
   SCOTTISH RHAPSODY-MISS MELANIE *(ITV:JOAN AND LESLIE
   Theme)* LAS CASTANUELAS-MADRUGADU (DAYBREAK)-THE RED
   SOMBRERO-TRADE WINDS-FAIRE FROU FOU-STRING SONG *BBC
   STRING SONG Theme)* CONCERTO FOR SAXOPHONE (3 M/M)
   THE WATERMILL *(BBC THE SECRET GARDEN Theme)* SCHERZO
   THE DANCE OF THE SNOWFLAKES-HIGH STEPPER *(ITV: THE
   ADVENTURES OF AGGIE Theme)* PRELUDE: THE WHISPERING
   VALLEY-VENETIAN CARNIVAL-SAILING BY *(DOCUMENTARY:
   INTERNAT.BALLOON RACE & BBC RADIO4 CLOSEDOWN THEME)*

43.BRITISH LIGHT MUSIC: TREVOR DUNCAN with the Slovak
   Radio Symphony Orchestra (Andrew Penny)
   *MARCO POLO (Select): 8.223517 (CD)*            *1997*
   1.20TH CENTURY EXPRESS 2-5.LITTLE SUITE: MARCH/LULL
   ABY/JOGTROT/HIGH HEELS 6-8 CHILDREN IN THE PARK:
   DANCING FOR JOY/AT THE POOL/HIDE AND SEEK 9.MAESTRO
   VARIATIONS 10.THE GIRL FROM CORSICA 11.MEADOW MIST
   12.VALSE MIGNONETTE 13.WINE FESTIVAL 14.SIXPENNY
   RIDE 15.ENCHANTED APRIL 16.ST.BONIFACE DOWN 17.LA
   TORRIDA 18.VISIONARIES GRAND MARCH 20.LITTLE DEBBIE

--- BRITISH LIGHT MUSIC - *see also COLLECTIONS 130,158*
                 *'ELIZABETH SERENADE' and 'RON GOODWIN'*

44.BRITISH LIGHT MUSIC CLASSICS - NEW LONDON ORCHEST *
   *HYPERION Records (Select): CDA 66868 (CD)*      *1996*
   1.CALLING ALL WORKERS *(Eric Coates/BBC:MUSIC WHILE
   YOU WORK)* 2.HAUNTED BALLROOM *(Geoffrey Toye/BALLET)*

**44.** <u>BRITISH LIGHT MUSIC CLASSICS</u> - NEW LONDON ORCHEST *
*HYPERION Records (Select): CDA 66868 (CD)*     *1996*
1.CALLING ALL WORKERS *(Eric Coates/BBC:MUSIC WHILE
YOU WORK)* 2.HAUNTED BALLROOM *(Geoffrey Toye/BALLET)*
3.VANITY FAIR *(Anthony Collins)* 4.JUMPING BEAN *(Rob
ert Farnon)* 5.DESTINY *(Sydney Baynes/WALTZ)* 6.THE
BOULEVARDIER *(Frederic Curzon)* 7.PAS DE QUATRE *(W.
Meyer Lutz/FAUST UP TO DATE)* 8.THE WATERMILL*(Ronald
Binge/BBC:THE SECRET GARDEN)* 9.THE DEVIL'S GALLOP
*(Charles Williams/BBC:DICK BARTON)* 10.DUSK *(Armstro
ng Gibbs/FANCY DRESS)* 11.PUFFIN'BILLY*(Edward White/
BBC:CHILDREN'S FAVOURIT.)*12.BELLS ACROSS THE MEADOW
*(Albert Ketelby)* 13.THE OLD CLOCKMAKER *(Charles Wil
liams/BBC:JENNING'S AT SCHOOL)* 14.DREAMING *(Archiba
ld Joyce/WALTZ)* 15.ELIZABETHAN SERENADE *(Ronald Bin
ge/BBC)* 16.CORONATION SCOTT *(Vivian Ellis/BBC: PAUL
TEMPLE)* 17.NIGHTS OF GLADNESS *(Charles Ancliffe/WAL
TZ)* * *NEW LONDON ORCHESTRA conducted by RONALD CORP*

**45.** <u>BRITISH LIGHT MUSIC CLASSICS 2</u> - NEW LONDON ORCHES*
*HYPERION (Select): CDA 66968 (CD)* *Ronald Corp 1997
1.KNIGHTSBRIDGE *(Eric Coates/BBC:IN TOWN TONIGHT)*
2.BAL MASQUE *(Percy Fletcher/WALTZ)* 3.GRASSHOPPER'S
DANCE *(Ernest Bucalossi/MILK TV AD)* 4.BARWICK GREEN
*(Arthur Wood/ARCHERS THEME)* 5.ROUGE ET NOIR *(Fred
Hartley)* 6.PEANUT POLKA *(Robert Farnon)* 7.CARRIAGE
AND PAIR *(Benjamin Frankel/SO LONG AT THE FAIR)* 8.
HORSE GUARDS WHITEHALL *(Haydn Wood/BBC:DOWN YOUR
WAY)* 9.MARCH FROM A LITTLE SUITE *(Trevor Duncan/BBC
DR.FINLAY'S CASEBOOK)* 10.SAILING BY *(Ronald Binge/
BBC: RADIO 4 CLOSING MUSIC)* 11.PORTUGESE PARTY *(Gil
bert Vinter)* 12.BEACHCOMBER *(Clive Richardson)* 13.
IN THE SHADOWS *(Herman Finck)* 14.TABARINAGE *(Robert
Docker)* 15.SANCTUARY OF THE HEART *(Albert Ketelbey)*
16.WESTMINSTER WALTZ *(Robert Farnon/BBC:IN TOWN TON
IGHT PROGAMME LINK MUS)* 17.CARISSIMA *(Edward Elgar)*
18.GIRLS IN GREY *(Charles Willliams/BBC: TELEVISION
NEWSREEL)* 19.RUNAWAY ROCKING HORSE *(Edward White)*
20.MARCH OF THE BOWMEN *(Fr.Curzon/ROBIN HOOD SUITE)*

**46.** <u>BROADWAY KIDS</u> - AT THE MOVIES
*LIGHTYEAR (Pinn Imp): 54183-2 (CD)*     *1997*
1.TALK TO THE ANIMALS *(DR.DOLITTLE)* 2.CAN YOU FEEL
THE LOVE TONIGHT *(LION KING)* 3.THE GHOSTBUSTERS 4.
YOU'VE GOT A FRIEND IN ME *(TOY STORY)* 5.SWINGING ON
A STAR *(GOING MY WAY)* 6.BEN 7.WIZARD OF OZ MEDLEY
8.HIGH HOPES*(HOLE IN THE HEAD)* 9.DON'T GO HOLLYWOOD
ON US *(orig song)* 10.PART OF YOUR WORLD *(THE LITTLE
MERMAID)* 11.FAME 12.FEED THE BIRDS *(MARY POPPINS)*
13.KING OF NEW YORK *(NEWSIES)*

**47.** <u>BROADWAY KIDS</u> - SING BROADWAY
*LIGHTYEAR (Pinn Imp): 541742 (CD 1994)*     *1997*
1.BROADWAY KIDS THEME SONG 2.IT'S A HARD KNOCK LIFE
/MAYBE TOMORROW *(ANNIE)* 3.THE KITE *(YOU'RE A GOOD
MAN CHARLIE BROWN)*4.CASTLE ON A CLOUD/LITTLE PEOPLE
*(LES MISERAB)* 5.WHY AM I ME *(SHENANDOAH)* 6.MAMA A

RAINBOW *(MINNIE'S BOYS)* 7.NEWSBOYS *(GYPSY)* BORN TO
ENTERTAIN *(RUTHLESS)* 8.GIRL I MEANT TO BE *(SECRET
GARDEN)* 9.FOOD GLORIOUS FOOD/WHO WILL BUY/WHERE IS
LOVE/CONSIDER YOURSELF *(OLIVER!)* 10.I ALWAYS KNEW
*(ANNIE WARBUCKS)* 11.BIG TIME *(WILL ROGERS FOLLIES)*
12.MY BEST GIRL *(MAME)* MY PA *(THE YEARLING)* 13.THE
SOUND OF MUSIC/GETTING TO KNOW YOU *(KING & I)* with
Petula Clark OTHER GENERATION *(FLOWER DRUM SONG)*
SO LONG FAREWELL/DO RE MI *(SOUND OF MUSIC)* 14.GARY
INDIANA *(MUSIC MAN)* 15.I WON'T GROW UP *(PETER PAN)*
16.LET KIDS RULE THE LAND *(LITTLE LORD FAUNTLEROY)*
17.HAPPINESS *(YOU'RE A GOOD MAN CHARLIE BROWN)*

--- <u>BROOKS Paul</u> - *see COLLECTION 100 'COPS'*

48.<u>BUDD Roy</u> - Big Screen Adventure: London Symph.Orch
*EMPORIO (Disc): EMPRCD 708 (CD)* *1992 reiss 1997*
(1) RAIDERS OF THE LOST ARK / INDIANA JONES SUITE
(2) E.T.SUITE / (3) SUPERMAN SUITE: March Of The
Villains - Can You Read My Mind (Love Theme) - Main
Theme (4) STAR WARS TRILOGY:EMPIRE + RETURN OF:Main
Theme-Princess Leia's Theme-Imperial March-Yoda's
Theme-Han Solo & The Princess-Parade Of The Ewoks

49.<u>BUDD Roy</u> - Rebirth Of The Budd
*SEQUEL (Castle-BMG): NEMCD 927 (CD)* *1997*
1.FEAR IS THE KEY 2.BIRTH OF THE BUDD 3.GET CARTER
4.SOLDIER BLUE 5.THEME TO MR.ROSE 6.ARANJUEZ MON
AMOR 7.JESUS CHRIST SUPERSTAR 8.WHIZZ BALL 9.IN MY
HOLE 10.TOO MUCH ATTENTION 11.LEAD ON 12.ZEPPELIN
13.THE CAREY TREATMENT 14.ENVY GREED AND GLUTTONY
15.GIRL TALK 16.PAVANE 17.CALL ME 18.PLAYTHING 19.
BARQUINHO (LITTLE BOAT) 20.SO NICE 21.HOW WONDERFUL
LIFE IS 22.FIELDS OF GREEN SKY OF BLUE 23.LUST 24.
HURRY TO ME 25.THE HOSTAGE ESCAPES

50.<u>BUGS BUNNY ON BROADWAY</u> - Warner Bros Symphony Orch
*WARNER USA (Silv.Screen): 926494-2(CD)-4(MC)* *1991*
Music by Carl Stalling and Milt Franklyn feat the
voice talents of Mel Blanc *see also* 'STALLING Carl'

--- BURGON Geoffrey - *see COLLECTION 40*

51.<u>CAGNEY AND LACEY AND OTHER AMERICAN TV THEMES</u>
*SILVA SCREEN (Koch): FILMCD 704 (CD)* re-issued 1990
CAGNEY & LACEY-MIKE HAMMER-LOU GRANT-ST.ELSEWHERE-
MAGNUM, P.I.-TAXI-SIMON AND SIMON-HILL STREET BLUES
*m.dir:* Derek Wadsworth / *cond:* Daniel Caine *1985*

52.<u>CALLAS Maria</u> : Diva - The Ultimate Collection
*EMI: CDEMTVD 113 (2CD) TCEMTVD 113 (2MC)* *1996*
Arias from various operas used in films and tv
TOSCA-MADAMA BUTTERFLY-MANON LESCAUT-LA BOHEME-GIAN
NI SCHICCHI-TURANDOT *(PUCCINI)* ANDREA CHENIER *(GIOR
DANO)* BARBER OF SEVILLE *(ROSSINI)* LA VESTALE *(SPONT
INI)* LA SONNAMBULA-NORMA*(BELLINI)* RIGOLETTO-MACBETH
AIDA-OTELLO *(VERDI)* LA WALLY *(CATALANI)* DINORAH *(ME
YERBEER)* CARMEN *(BIZET)* SAMSON & DELILAH *(SAINT-SAE
NS)* ROMEO & JULIET *(GOUNOD)* MANON *(MASSENET)* ORFEO
& EURIDICE *(GLUCK)* MARRIAGE OF FIGARO*(MOZART)* LUCIA
DI LAMMERMOOR *(DONIZETTI)* LA GIOCONDA *(PONCHIELLI*

53. CAREY Tristram see 'QUATERMASS AND THE PIT'
--- CARL STALLING PROJECT - see COLLECTIONS 325,326
--- CARPENTER John - see COLLECTION 178 'HALLOWEEN'
54. CASABLANCA - Classic Film Scores For HUMPHREY BOGART
    *RCA VICTOR (BMG): GD 80422 (CD)*                    *1990*
    CASABLANCA-PASSAGE TO MARSEILLE-TREASURE OF THE SIE
    RRA MADRE-BIG SLEEP-CAINE MUTINY-TO HAVE & HAVE NOT
    TWO MRS.CARROLLS-SABRINA-LEFT HAND OF GOD-SAHARA-VI
    VIRGINIA CITY-KEY LARGO *N.Phil.Or.Charles Gerhardt*
55. CHARIOTS OF FIRE : Synthonic 2000 / Synthesizer Hits
    *RCA INT (BMG): RCA(CD)(MC) 208 (2CD/2MC)*           *1997*
    CD1 OXYGENE IV-THEME FROM ANTARCTICA-TWIN PEAKS-
    L'OPERA SAUVAGE-CROCKETT'S THEME-CHARIOTS OF FIRE-
    SADNESS PART 1-TUBULAR BELLS-AUTOBAHN-DANCES WITH
    WOLVES-ROTATIONS LOGIC-LOVE THEME FROM RAIN MAN-
    EQUINOXE PT.5-FANFARE FOR THE COMMON MAN-MIAMI VICE
    EVE OF THE WAR-MAMMAGAMMA-THE BLACK HOLE
    CD2 CHINA-THE BOAT (DAS BOOT)-BATTLESTAR GALACTICA-
    L'APOCALPYSE DES ANIMAUX-CONQUEST OF PARADISE-MAGIC
    FLY-ROCKIT-TO THE UNKNOWN MAN-AURORA-LUCIFER-TUBBS
    AND VALERIE-VIENNA-THE OMEN-MIDNIGHT EXPRESS-BLADE
    RUNNER-CHI MAI-NAGNETIC FIELDS PART 2-TERMINATOR 2
56. CHAPLIN Charlie : CHARLIE - Chaplin's Film Music
    Munich Symphony Orchestra conducted by FRANCIS SHAW
    *SILVA SCREEN (Koch): FILMCD 711 (CD)*               *1994*
    Suites from: LIMELIGHT-A KING IN NEW YORK-THE GREAT
    DICTATOR-CITY LIGHTS-MODERN TIMES-MONSIEUR VERDOUX
    A COUNTESS FROM HONG KONG conducted by *Francis Shaw*
57. CHAPLIN Charlie : Film Music - MICHEL VILLARD ORCH
    *RCA (BMG): 74321 14145-2 (CD)*              *reissue 1996*
    MODERN TIMES-CITY LIGHTS-A DOG'S LIFE-THE GOLD RUSH
    KING IN NEW YORK-GREAT DICTATOR-LIMELIGHT-COUNTESS
    FROM HONG KONG etc.*see also* FILM MUSIC OF C.CHAPLIN
58. CHAPLIN Charles - Film Music Of CHARLES CHAPLIN
    Brandenburg Symph.Orch, Berlin conduct: CARL DAVIS
    *RCA (BMG): 09026 68271-2 (CD)*                      *1996*
    Music scores: THE KID / THE GOLD RUSH / THE CIRCUS
    CITY LIGHTS / MODERN TIMES
    *see also* 'CHARLIE CHAPLIN THE MUSIC OF HIS FILMS'
59. CHERTOCK Michael - Palace Of The Wind (Piano At..*)
    *TELARC (Conifer-BMG): CD 80477 (CD)*               *1997*
    1.FEATHER THEME *FORREST GUMP* 2.HEAVEN'S LIGHT *HUNCH
    BACK OF NOTRE DAME* 3.ASHOKAN FAREWELL *CIVIL WAR* 4.
    WITH GOD'S HELP *SHINE* 5.PRELUDE IN C.SHARP MIN.OP.3
    (RACHMANINOV) *SHINE* 6.PIANO CONC.NO.3 (RACHMANINOV)
    *SHINE* 7.PRELUDE 15 (CHOPIN) *SHINE* 8.ROUND MIDNIGHT
    9.IL POSTINO THEME 10.BODYGUARD THEME 11.A RETREAT/
    READ ME TO SLEEP/PALACE OF WINDS *ENGLISH PATIENT*
    12.FUR ELISE/PIANO SONATA 14 (BEETHOVEN) *IMMORTAL
    BELOVED* 13.DOE EYES *BRIDGES OF MADISON COUNTY* 14.
    DON'T CRY FOR ME ARGENTINA *EVITA* 15.X-FILES THEME
    16.CLAUDIA'S THEME *THE UNFORGIVEN* 17.SUMMER OF 42
    THEME * Piano At The Movies

**60.** CHILDREN'S BBC THEME TUNES - Various Artists
   BBC (Pinn): ZBBC 1761 (MC)                          1995
   NODDY-POSTMAN PAT-SPOT-FUNNY BONES-PINGU-FIREMAN
   SAM-WILLIAM'S WISH WELLINGTONS-ANIMALS OF FARTHING
   WOOD-LIZZIE'S SONG from PLAYDAYS-JOSHUA JONES from
   PLAYDAYS-JESS THE CAT from POSTMAN PAT-OAKIE DOKE-
   THE WORLD OF BEATRIX POTTER-NODDY SAYS GOODNIGHT

**61.** CHILLER - Cincinnati Pops Orchestra - Erich Kunzel
   TELARC USA (BMG-Conif): CD 80189 (CD)               1989
   PHANTOM OF THE OPERA-NIGHT ON BALD MOUNTAIN-DANSE M
   ACABRE-MARCH TO THE SCAFFOLD-PANDEMONIUM DAMNATION
   OF FAUST-IN THE HALL OF THEMOUNTAIN KING-Theme From
   TWILIGHT ZONE-BRIDE OF FRANKENSTEIN-THE DEVIL & DAN
   IEL WEBSTER-PSYCHO-SLEUTH-POLTERGEIST-WITHOUTA CLUE
   FUNERAL MARCH OF A MARIONETTE:Alfred Hitchock Theme

**---** CINCINNATI POPS see COLLECT.32,34,61,203,231,380

**62.** CINEMA 100: THE OFFICIAL CINEMA 100 ALBUM - Var.Arts
   EMI PREMIER: PRDFCD 1 (72438 37843-2) (2CD)    1996
   THINGS TO COME (1936 A.Bliss) GONE WITH THE WIND
   (39 M.Steiner) CASABLANCA (42 M.Steiner/H.Hupfeld)
   BRIEF ENCOUNTER (45 S.Rachmaninov) SPELLBOUND (1945
   M.Rozsa) THIRD MAN (49 A.Karas) THE GLASS MOUNTAIN
   (49 N.Rota) HIGH NOON (52 D.Tiomkin/P.F.Webster)
   SINGIN'IN THE RAIN (52 A.Freed/N.H.Brown) BEN HUR
   (59 M.Rozsa) BREAKFAST AT TIFFANY'S (61 H.Mancini)
   MAGNIFICENT SEVEN (60 E.Bernstein) LAWRENCE OF ARA
   BIA (62 M.Jarre) DR.NO (62 M.Norman arr:J.Barry)
   THE GREAT ESCAPE (63 E.Bernstein) SHOT IN THE DARK
   (64 H.Mancini) 633 SQUADRON (64 R.Goodwin) DOCTOR
   ZHIVAGO (65 M.Jarre) BORN FREE (66 J.Barry) THE
   GOOD THE BAD & THE UGLY (66 E.Morricone) GRAND PRIX
   (66 M.Jarre) 2001: A SPACE ODYSSEY (68 R.Strauss)
   THOMAS CROWN AFFAIR (68 M.Legrand) MIDNIGHT COWBOY
   (69 J.Barry) LOVE STORY (70 F.Lai) THE STING (70 S.
   Joplin) MURDER ON THE ORIENT EXPRESS (74 R.Bennett)
   DEATH ON THE NILE (78 Rota) E.T.(82 J.Williams)
   OUT OF AFRICA (85 J.Barry) THE MISSION (86 E.Morric
   one) REMAINS OF THE DAY (93 R.Robbins) THE PIANO
   (93 M.Nyman) STARGATE (95 D.Arnold)

**63.** CINEMA CENTURY - Various Artists and Orchestras
   SILVA SCREEN (Koch): FILMCD 180 (3CDs)         1996
   20TH CENTURY FOX FANFARE (A.NEWMAN) CITY LIGHTS (C.
   CHAPLIN) BRIDE OF FRANKENSTEIN (F.WAXMAN) GONE WITH
   THE WIND (M.STEINER) STAGECOACH (R.HAGEMAN +others)
   CITIZEN KANE (B.HERRMANN) CASABLANCA (M.STEINER)
   OLIVER TWIST (A.BAX) QUO VADIS (M.ROZSA) THE QUIET
   MAN (V.YOUNG) THE HIGH AND THE MIGHTY (D.TIOMKIN)
   THE SEARCHERS (M.STEINER) BRIDGE ON THE RIVER KWAI
   (K.J.ALFORD) THE BIG COUNTRY (J.MOROSS) NORTH BY NO
   RTHWEST (B.HERRMANN) BEN HUR (M.ROZSA) PSYCHO (B.
   HERRMANN) LA DOLCE VITA (N.ROTA) MAGNIFICENT SEVEN
   (E.BERNSTEIN) Disc 2 THE ALAMO (D.TIOMKIN) THE PINK
   PANTHER (H.MANCINI) LAWRENCE OF ARABIA(M.JARRE) THE
   GREAT ESCAPE (E.BERNSTEIN) 633 SQUADRON (R.GOODWIN)

Continued next page...

CINEMA CENTURY ...*Continued from previous page*

ZULU *(J.BARRY)* ZORBA THE GREEK *(M.THEODORAKIS)* DOCT
OR ZHIVAGO *(M.JARRE)* BORN FREE *(J.BARRY)*THE LION IN
WINTER *(J.BARRY)* ONCE UPON A TIME IN THE WEST *(E.
MORRICONE)* WHERE EAGLES DARE *(R.GOODWIN)* MIDNIGHT
COWBOY *(J.BARRY)* THE WILD BUNCH *(J.FIELDING)* THE
GODFATHER *(N.ROTA)* JAWS *(J.WILLIAMS)* ROCKY*(B.CONT|)*
TAXI DRIVER *(B.HERRMANN)* STAR WARS*(J.WILLIAMS)* DIVA
'La Wally' sung by **Lesley Garrett** *(CATALINI)* Disc 3
RAIDERS OF T.LOST ARK *(J.WILLIAMS)* CHARIOTS OF FIRE
*(VANGELIS)* CONAN THE BARBARIAN *(B.POLEDOURIS)* E.T.
*(J.WILLIAMS)* ONCE UPON A TIME IN AMERICA *(E.MORRICO
NE)* THE TERMINATOR *(B.FIEDEL)* WITNESS *(M.JARRE)* OUT
OF AFRICA *(J.BARRY)* A PASSAGE TO INDIA*(M.JARRE)* THE
MISSION *(E.MORRICONE)* A ROOM WITH A VIEW 'O Mio Bab
bino Caro' *(PUCCINI)* sung by **Lesley Garrett** CINEMA
PARADISO *(E.MORRICONE)* GHOST *(M.JARRE)* DANCES WITH
WOLVES *(J.BARRY)* 1492:CONQUEST OF PARADISE *VANGELIS*
UNFORGIVEN *(L.NIEHAUS-CLINT EASTWOOD)* THE FUGITIVE
*JN.HOWARD* JURASSIC PARK-SCHINDLER'S LIST *J.WILLIAMS*
64.CINEMA CHORAL CLASSICS - City Of Prague Philh.Orch*
*SILVA SCREEN (Koch): SILK(D)(C) 6015 (CD/MC)      1997*
EXCALIBUR-SCARLET LETTER-JESUS OF NAZARETH-KING OF
KINGS-LION IN WINTER-MISSION-CONAN THE BARBARIAN-
ABYSS-FIRST KNIGHT-1492 CONQUEST OF PARADISE-HENRY
V-OMEN-VIKINGS *Nic Raine conducting The* Crouch End
Festival Chorus *(David Temple)*
65.CINEMA CLASSICS (EMI) 1 Collection - Var.Artists
*EMI CLASSICS: CD(TC)EMTVD 106 (2CD/2MC)      1995*
THE PIANO: *The Heart asks Pleaure First/The Promise
(Nyman)* SHADOWLANDS:*theme (Fenton)* SCHINDLER'S LIST
*theme (Williams)* REMAINS OF THE DAY: *A Portrait Ret
urns/Darlington Hall (Robbins)* PHILADELPHIA: *La
Mamma Morta (Giordano)* DIVA: *Eben Neandro Lontana
(Catalini)* APOCALPYSE NOW: *Ride Of The Valkyries
(Wagner)* PLATOON: *Adagio For Strings (Barber)* MY
LEFT FOOT:*Un'aura Amorosa (Mozart)* FATAL ATTRACTION
*Un Bel Di Vedremo (Puccini)* A ROOM WITH A VIEW: *O
Mio Babbino Caro (Puccini)* IMMORTAL BELOVED: *Piano
Sonata 'Moonlight' (Beethoven)* JEFFERSON IN PARIS:
*Violin Sonata (La Follia) (Corelli)* SLEEPING WITH
THE ENEMY: *Symphonic Fantastique/Dream Of A Witches
Sabbath (Berlioz)* THE MADNESS OF KING GEORGE: *Zadok
The Priest (Handel)* OUT OF AFRICA: *Adagio (Clarinet
Concerto) (Mozart)* DRIVING MISS DAISY: *Song To The
Moon from (Rusalka)(Dvorak)* RAGING BULL: *Intermezzo
Cavalleria Rusticana (Mascagni)* UNTOUCHABLES: *Vesti
La Giubba (Leoncavallo)* GALLIPOLI:*Adagio (Albinoni)*
AMADEUS: *Introitus/Requiem Aeternam (Mozart)* PRETTY
WOMAN: *Dammi Tu Forza (Violetta's Farewell) (Verdi)*
BRIEF ENCOUNTER: *Piano Concerto No.2 (Rachmaninov)*
MOONSTRUCK:*Che Gelida Manina (Puccini)* TRUE ROMANCE
*Flower Duet from Lakme (Delibes)* CHILDREN OF A LESS

ER GOD: *Double Violin Concerto (Bach)* DEAD POET'S
SOCIETY:*Symphony No.9 Choral Ode To Joy (Beethoven)*
66.CINEMA CLASSICS (EMI) 2 Collection - Var.Artists
*EMI Classics: CMS 566647-2 (2CD)* 1997
CD1: 1.SHINE: *1st m/m PIANO CON.NO.3 Rachmaninov* 3.
ENGLISH PATIENT: *I'LL ALWAYS GO BACK TO THAT CHURCH
Yared* 3.BABE: *PIZZICATO from SYLVIA Delibes* 4.ROMEO
& JULIET: *OST VOL.2* 5.HEAVENLY CREATURES: *E LUCEVAN
LE STELLE Puccini* 6.COURAGE UNDER FIRE *Horner* 7.
SEVEN: *AIR ON THE G STRING FROM SUITE 3 Bach* 8.LAST
ACTION HERO: *LE NOZZE DI FIGARO OVERTURE Mozart* 9.
HOWARDS END: *MOCK MORRIS Grainger* 10.THE FRENCH
LIEUTENANT'S WOMAN: *PIANO SONATA IN D.K576 Mozart*
11.SHAWSHANK REDEMPTION: *SULL'ARIA: FIGARO Mozart*
12.PRINCE OF TIDES: *SYMPHONY NO.104 'LONDON' Haydn*
13.PORTRAIT OF A LADY: *IMPROMPTU A.FLAT NO.4 D899
Schubert* 14.DANGEROUS LIAISONS:*CUCKOO & NIGHTINGALE
ORGAN CONCERTO Handel* 15.MRS.DOUBTFIRE: *LARGO AL FA
FACTOTUM:BARBER OF SEVILLE Rossini* 16.FOUR WEDDINGS
AND A FUNERAL: *THE WEDDING MARCH Mendelssohn* 17.
SLEEPING WITH THE ENEMY: *WITCHES'SABBATH Berlioz.*
CD2 MANHATTAN: *RHAPSODY IN BLUE Gershwin* 2.FANTASIA
*SORCERER'S APPRENTICE Dukas* 3.BRIDGES OF MADISON
COUNTY: *MON COEUR S'OUVRE A TA VOIX: Saint Saens* 4.
EVENING STAR: *-S/T- Ross* 5.UN COUER EN HIVER: *PIANO
TRIO Ravel* 6.HANNAH AND HER SISTERS: *HARPSICHORD
CONC.NO.5 Bach* 7.THE SAINT: *LOVE THEME Revell* 8.THE
FIFTH ELEMENT: *LUCIA DI LAMMERMOOR Donizetti* 9.JFK:
*HORN CON.NO.2 Mozart* 10.SOMEWHERE IN TIME: *18th VAR
IATION ON THEME OF PAGANINI Rachmaninov* 11.LOOKING
FOR RICHARD: *-S/T- Shore* 12.HENRY V *-S/T- Doyle* 13.
KILLING FIELDS: *NESSUN DORMA Puccini* 14.MY DINNER
WITH ANDRE: *GYMNOPEDIE NO.1 Satie* 15.SILENCE OF THE
LAMBS: *GOLDBERG VAR.ARIA Bach* 16.AMADEUS: *EINE KLEI
KLEINE NACHT MUSIK Mozart* 17.JEAN DE FLORETTE/MANON
DES SOURCES: *LA FORZA DEL DESTINO OVERTURE Verdi*
67.CINEMA CLASSICS (NAXOS) 1997 - Various Artists
*NAXOS (Select): 8.551181 (CD)* 1997
1.THE PEOPLE VS.LARRY FLYNT *POLONAISE FROM RUSALKA
(DVORAK)* 2.THE PEOPLE VS.LARRY FLYNT *MAZURKA NO.47
IN A.MINOR OP.68 NO.2 (CHOPIN)* 3.BREAKING THE WAVES
*SONATA IN E.FLAT MAJOR BWV 1031.SICILIANA (BACH)* 4.
THE ENGLISH PATIENT *ARIA FROM 'GOLDBERG VARIATIONS'
BWV 988 (BACH)* 5.TIN CUP *WINTER FROM FOUR SEASONS
SUITE Allegro Non Molto(VIVALDI)* 6.ROMEO AND JULIET
*SYMPHONY NO.25 IN G.MINOR K.183 Allegro Con Brio
(MOZART)* 7.THE PORTRAIT OF A LADY *STRING QUARTET NO
14 IN D.MINOR D.810 Death and The Maiden (SCHUBERT)*
8.PRIMAL FEAR *REQUIEM: LACRYMOSA (MOZART)* 9.SHINE
*POLONAISE 6 A.FLAT MAJ.OP53 (CHOPIN)* 10.SHINE *PIANO
CONC.3 IN D.MIN.OP30 Allegro Ma Non..( RACHMANINOV)*
68.CINEMA CLASSICS (NAXOS) 1 - Various Artists
*NAXOS (Select): 8.551151 (CD)* 1992
1.2001 A SPACE ODYSSEY: *ALSO SPRACH ZARATHUSTRA (R.*

Strauss) 2.A ROOM WITH A VIEW: *O MIO BABBINO CARO-GIANNI SCHICCHI (Puccini)* 3.DEATH IN VENICE: *ADAGIE TTO FROM SYMPHONY NO.5 (Mahler)* 4.MONA LISA: *LOVE DUET FR.MADAME BUTTERFLY-VOGLIATEMI BENE (Puccini)* 5.PLATOON / THE ELEPHANT MAN: *ADAGIO FOR STRINGS (Barber)* 6.HANNAH AND HER SISTERS: *LARGO FROM PIANO CONCERTO NO.5 (J.S.Bach)* 7.HEAT AND DUST:*TALES FROM THE VIENNA WOODS (J.Strauss)* 8.OUT OF AFRICA:*ADAGIO CLARINET CONCERTO IN A.MAJOR (Mozart)* 9.APOCALYPSE NOW: *RIDE OF THE VALKYRIES-DIE WALKURE (Wagner)*

69.CINEMA CLASSICS (NAXOS) 2 - Various Artists
*NAXOS (Select): 8.551152 (CD)*                    1992
1.CLOCKWORK ORANGE: *WILLIAM TELL OVERTURE (Rossini)* 2.DIVA: *EBBEN NE ANDRO MONTANA LA WALLY (Catalini)* 3.ORDINARY PEOPLE: *CANON (Pachelbel)* 4.AMADEUS: *SYM PHONY NO.25-ALLEGRO CON BRIO (Mozart)* 5.SEVEN YEAR ITCH / BRIEF ENCOUNTER: *PIANO CONCERTO NO.2 (Rachma ninov)* 6.GALLIPOLI: *ADAGIO IN G (Albinoni)* 7.SUNDAY BLOODY SUNDAY: *SOAVE SIA IL VENTO FROM COSI FAN TUTTE (Mozart)* 8.DIE HARD 2: *FINLANDIA (Sibelius)*

70.CINEMA CLASSICS (NAXOS) 3 - Various Artists
*NAXOS (Select): 8.551153 (CD)*                    1992
1.AMADEUS: *EINE KLEINE NACHT MUSIK ALLEGRO (Mozart)* 2.HOT TO TROT:*PREMIERE SUITE DE SYMPHONIES (Mouret)* 3.WITCHES OF EASTWICK: *NESSUN DORMA FROM TURANDOT (Puccini)* 4.MANHATTAN: *RHAPSODY IN BLUE (Gershwin)* 5.RAGING BULL / GODFATHER III: *CAVALLERIA RUSTICANA INTERMEZZO (Mascagni)* 6.BARRY LYNDON: *SARABANDE-SUI TE NO.11 IN D.MIN(Handel)* 7.EXCALIBUR: *EXCERPT FROM CARMINA BURANA (Orff)* 8.ELVIRA MADIGAN: *PIANO CONCE RTO NO.21-ANDANTE K.467 (Mozart)* 9.WALL STREET: *QUE STA O QUELLA-RIGOLETTO (Verdi)* 10.CLOCKWORK ORANGE ODE TO JOY FROM SYMPHONY NO.9 (Beethoven)*

71.CINEMA CLASSICS (NAXOS) 4 - Various Artists
*NAXOS (Select): 8.551154 (CD)*                    1992
1.CLOCKWORK ORANGE:*POMP AND CIRCUMSTANCE MARCH No.1 (Elgar)* 2.AMADEUS: *SYMPHONY No.29 ALLEGRO MODERATO (Mozart)* 3.A ROOM WITH A VIEW: *IL SOGNO DI DORETTA from LA RONDINE (Puccini)* 4.SLEEPING WITH THE ENEMY SYMPHONIE FANTASIQUE (Berlioz)* 5.SOMEWHERE IN TIME: *18TH PAGANINI VARIATION (Rachmaninov)* 6.WHO FRAMED ROGER RABBIT:*HUNGARIAN RHAPSODY NO 2.IN D.m (Listz)* 7.MOONSTRUCK: *CHE GELIDA MANINA-LA BOHEME (Puccini)* 8.FRENCH LIEUTENANT'S WOMAN: *PIANO SON.No.17 K.576 (Mozart)* 9.10: *BOLERO (Ravel)*

72.CINEMA CLASSICS (NAXOS) 5 - Various Artists
*NAXOS (Select): 8.551155 (CD)*                    1992
1.MY GEISHA: *UN BEL DI VEDREMO 'MADAME BUTTERFLY' (Puccini)* 2.PRIZZI'S HONOR: *OVERTURE TO BARBER OF SEVILLE (Rossini)* 3-6.AMADEUS: *4 EXCERPTS FROM THE REQUIEM* 7.PIANO CONCERTO *No.20 K.466 (Mozart)* 8. ROLLERBALL: *TOCCATA AND FUGUE IN D.MINOR BWV 565 (Bach)* 9.MOONSTRUCK: *O SOAVE FANCIULLA 'LA BOHEME' (Puccini)* 10.THE UNRTOUCHABLES: *RECITAR VESTI LA*

GIUBBA'I PAGLIACCI' (Leoncavallo) 11.HANNAH AND HER SISTERS: *SOLA PERDUTA ABBANDONATA 'MANON LESCAUT' (Puccini)* 12.CHILDREN OF A LESSER GOD: *DOUBLE CONCE RTO D.MIN,LARGO MA NAN TANTO (Bach)* 13.MY LEFT FOOT *UN AURA AMAROSA FROM 'COSI FAN TUTTE' (Verdi)* 14. BREAKING AWAY: *'ITALIAN SYMPHONY' (Mendelssohn)*

73.CINEMA CLASSICS (NAXOS) 6 - Various Artists
   *NAXOS (Select): 8.551156 (CD)* 1994
   1.EXCALIBUR: *PRELUDE TO TRISTAN AND ISOLDE (Wagner)*
   2.AMADEUS:*SERENADE NO.10 B.FLAT.K361 ADAGIO(Mozart)*
   3.MIDSUMMER NIGHT'S SEX COMEDY: *SCHERZO 'MIDSUMMER NIGHTS DREAM' OP.61 (Mendelssohn)* 4.TOUS LE MATINS DU MONDE *TOMBEAU "LES REGRETS" (Sainte-Colombe)* 5. FIVE EASY PIECES: *PRELUDE NO.4 OP.28 (Chopin)* 6. WHITE NIGHTS: *PASSCAGLIA IN C.MINTO FROM BWV 582 (Bach)* 7.ROOM WITH A VIEW: *FIRENZE E COME UN ALBERO FIORITO 'GIANNI SCHICCHI' (Puccini)* 8.GOODBYE AGAIN *SYMPHONY NO.3 IN F.MAJ.OP.90 POCO ALLEGRETO(Brahms)* 9.SLAUGHTERHOUSE FIVE: *BRANDENBURG CONCERTO NO.4 IN G.MAJOR BWV 1049 PRESTO (Bach)* 10.THE MUSIC LOVERS: *1812 OVERTURE OP.49 (Tchaikovsky)*

74.CINEMA CLASSICS (NAXOS) 7 - Various Artists
   *NAXOS (Select): 8.551157 (CD)* 1994
   JEAN DE FLORETTE: *OVERTURE-FORCE OF DESTINY (Verdi)* FANTASIA: *WALTZ OF THE FLOWERS - 'NUTCRACKER SUITE' (Tchaikovsky)* MADAME SOUSATZKA: *ALLEGRO VIVACE FROM PIANO CONCERTO IN A.MINOR OP.54 (Schumann)* ANONIMO VENEZIANO: *ADAGIO FROM OBOE CONCERTO IN D.MINOR (A. arcello)* EXPOSED:*ADAGIO VIVACISSIMO-VIOLIN CONCERTO IN D.MAJ.OP.35 (Tchaikovsky)* PRETTY WOMAN: *DAMMI TU FORZA-LA TRAVIATA (Verdi)* THE LADYKILLERS: *MINUETTO FROM STRING QUARTET IN E.MAJOR G.275 (Boccherini)* LORENZO'S OIL: *AVE VERUM CORPUS K.618 (Mozart)* SWING KIDS: *ALLEGRO MODERATO-PIANO TRIO IN B.FLAT MAJOR 'ARCHDUKE' OP.97 (Beethoven)*

75.CINEMA CLASSICS (NAXOS) 8 - Various Artists
   *NAXOS (Select): 8.551158 (CD)* 1994
   MEETING VENUS: *OVERTURE TO TANNHAUSER (Wagner)* MAN TROUBLE: *NOCTURNE NO.2,E.FLAT MAJ.OP.9 (Chopin)* DANGEROUS LIAISONS: *LARGO FROM SERSE (Handel)* MY DINNER WITH ANDRE: *GYMNOPEDIE NO.1 (Erik Satie)* SNEAKERS: *ALLEGRO VIVO-APPASSIONATO FROM STRING QUA RTET NO.1 IN E.MIN.(Smetana)* AU REVOIR LES ENFANTS: *MOMENT MUSICAL NO.2 (Schubert)* CHARIOTS OF FIRE: *MISERE (Allegri)* A MIDSUMMER NIGHT'S SEX COMEDY: *ADAGIO FR.PIANO CONC.NO.2,D.MIN.OP.40 (Mendelssohn)* FANTASIA: *SORCERER'S APPRECTICE (Dukas)*

76.CINEMA CLASSICS (NAXOS) 9 - Various Artists
   *NAXOS (Select): 8.551159 (CD)* 1994
   TRADING PLACES: *OVERTURE:- MARRIAGE OF FIGARO K.492 (Mozart)* SNEAKERS: *WALTZ NO.15 IN E.MINOR (Chopin)* MUSIC LOVERS: *ANDANTINO SEMPLICE-PRESTISSIMO PIANO CONCERTO NO.1 IN B.FLAT MIN.OP.23 (Tchaikovsky)* EXCALIBUR: *SIEGFRIED'S DEATH AND FUNERAL MARCH FROM*

GOTTERDAMMERUNG (Wagner) NIGHT AT THE OPERA: *ANVIL CHORUS FROM IL TROVATORE (Verdi)* MADAME SOUSATZSKA: *ALLEGRO ASSAI - PIANO SONATA NO.23 IN F.MINOR OP.57 (APPASSIONATA) (Beethoven)* DEAD POETS SOCIETY: *ALLE GRO-ANDANTE: WATER MUSIC (Handel)* UN COEUR EN HIVER *BLUES (MODERATO) FROM VIOLIN SONATA (Ravel)* EXPOSED *COURANTE FROM PARTITA NO.4 IN D.MAJ.BWV 828 (Bach)* PICNIC AT HANGING ROCK:*ANDANTE UN POCO MOSSO (PIANO CONC.NO.5 IN E.FLAT MAJ OP.73 (EMPEROR) (Beethoven)* FANTASIA:*DANCE OF THE HOURS LA GIOCONDA(Ponchielli)*

77.<u>CINEMA CLASSICS (NAXOS) 10</u> - Various Artists
*NAXOS (Select): 8.551160 (CD)* 1994
HEARTBURN: *ARRIVAL OF THE QUEEN OF SHEBA (SOLOMON) (Handel)* BARRY LYNDON: *ANDANTE CON MOTO FROM PIANO TRIO NO.2 IN E.FLAT MAJOR D.929 (Schubert)* A MONTH IN THE COUNTRY: *ANDANTE ALLEGRO NON TROPPO FROM VIO LIN CONCERTO IN E.MINOR OP.64 (Mendelssohn)* TOUS LE MATINS DU MONDE: *SONNERIE DE SAINTE GENEVIEVE DU MONT DE PARIS (Marais)* DANEROUS LIAISONS: *ALLEGRO FROM ORGAN CONC.NO.13 IN F.MAJ (Handel)* GREYSTOKE: THE LEGEND OF TARZAN, LORD OF THE APES: *ANDANTE NOB ILMENTE E SEMPLICE FROM SYMPHONY NO.1 IN A.FLAT MAJ (Elgar)* AUTUMN SONATA: *PRELUDE NO.2 IN A.MIN.OP.28 (Chopin)* MAN TROUBLE: *ET RESURREXIT (MASS IN B.MIN) BWV 232 (Bach)* LOVE AND DEATH: *TROIKA FROM LIEUTENA NT KIJE (Prokofiev)* KIND HEARTS AND CORONETS:*IL MIO TESORO FROM DON GIOVANNI K.527 (Mozart)* FANTASIA: *NIGHT ON BARE MOUNTAIN (Mussorgsky)*

78.<u>CINEMA CLASSICS (NAXOS) 11</u> - Various Artists
*NAXOS (Select): 8.551171 (CD)* 1995
PETER'S FRIENDS: *CAN-CAN FROM ORPHEUS IN THE UNDERW ORLD (Offenbach)* SPY WHO LOVED ME: *AIR FROM SUITE 3 IN D BWV 1068 (Bach)* JFK: *RONDO ALLEGRO FROM HORN CONCERTO NO.2 IN E.FLAT MAJ.K.417 (Mozart)* SERPICO: *E LUCEVAN LE STELLE FROM TOSCA (Pucchini)* FORBIDDEN GAMES: *ROMANCE D'AMOUR (Anon)* SOMEONE TO WATCH OVER ME:*VIENS MALLIKA..DOME EPAIS LA JASMIN (FLOWER DUET FROM LAKME)(Delibes)* HARD TARGET: *FINALE FROM PIANO SONATA 23 IN F.M.OP.57 (Beethoven)* HENRY V: *BAILERO FROM CHANTS D'AUVERGNE (Canteloube)* FOUR WEDDINGS & A FUNERAL: *WEDDING MARCH FROM A MID-SUMMER NIGHTS DREAM (Mendelssohn)* PHILADELPHA:*LA MAMMA MORTA FROM ANDREA CHENIER (Giordano)* AUTUMN SONATA: *SARABANDE FROM CELLO SUITE NO.4 IN E.FLAT MAJ.BWV 1010 (Bach)* MEETING VENUS: *PILGRIMS' CHORUS-TANNHAUSER (Wagner)*

79.<u>CINEMA CLASSICS (NAXOS) 12</u> - Various Artists
*NAXOS (Select): 8.551172 (CD)* 1995
LIVING DAYLIGHTS: *MOLTO ALLEGRO FROM SYMPHONY NO.40 IN G.MINOR K.550 (Mozart)* ACE VENTURA PET DETECTIVE *ROMANCE FROM EINE KLEINE NACHT MUSIK K.525 (Mozart)* FANTASIA:*AVE MARIA D.839 (Schubert)* ROSEMARY'S BABY *BAGATELLE IN A M. (Beethoven)* DEER HUNTER *CAVATINA (Myers)* THE GREY FOX: *M'APPARI TUTT' AMOR FROM MARTHA (Flotow)* AGE OF INNOCENCE: *ADAGIO CANTA*

BILE FROM PIANO SONATA NO 8 IN C MINOR, OP.13 'PATH
ETIQUE' (Beethoven) MY LEFT FOOT: *ANDANTINO THEME
FROM PIANO QUINTET IN A.MAJ,D.667 (TROUT)(Schubert)*
DRIVING MISS DAISY: *SONG TO THE MOON FROM RUSALKA
OP.114 (Dvorak)* CRIES AND WHISPERS: *SARABANDE FROM
CELLO SUITE NO.5 IN C.MIN, BWV 1011 (Bach)* TURNING
POINT:*BALCONY SCENE FROM ROMEO & JULIET (Prokofiev)*
ROLLERBALL:*SYMPH NO.5 IN D.MINOR OP.47 Shostakovich*

80. CINEMA DU MONDE - Various Artists
    *MCI (THE): MCCD(MCTC) 127 (CD/MC)* 1993
    CARPE DIEM *(Dead Poets Society)*-GENERIQUE *(Fort Sag
    ne)*-UNCHAINED MELODY *(Ghost)*-GENERIQUE ET FIN *(Jean
    De Florette)*-ALMA EST PARTIE *(La Pirate)*-SERENADE
    FUR KLARA *(Klara)*-THEME DE CAMILLE *(Le Mepris)*- AU
    MOULIN *Apres La Guerre)*-UNCLE ARVIDSSON'S DREAM *(My
    Life As A Dog)*-L'AMOUR D'UGOLIN *(Manon Des Sources)*
    DREAM IN A BLUE NIGHT *(Concert For Alice)*-KWAN'S SA
    CRIFICE*(Year Of Living Dangerously)*-PELLE EROBREREN
    *(Pelle The Conqueror)*-L'ORAGE *(Jean De Florette)*-
    LOUIS ET MARTINE *(Le Grand Chemin)*-PASTORALE MODERA
    TP *(Babette's Feast)*-HABANERA*(Benvenuta)*-THEME FROM
    MY LIFE AS A DOG *(My Life As A Dog)*

81. CINEMA SOUNDTRACK CLASSICS - Various Artists
    *VARESE (Pinn): VSD 5710 (CD)* 1996
    1.MAGNIFICENT SEVEN a *E.BERNSTEIN* 2.CASABLANCA a
    *MAX STEINER* 3.SPARTACUS a *A.NORTH* 4.CHINATOWN b *J.
    GOLDSMITH* 5.GONE WITH THE WIND a *STEINER* 6.RAIDERS
    OF THE LOST ARK a *J.WILLIAMS* 7.TAXI DRIVER b *B.HER
    RMANN* 8.BEN HUR c *M.ROZSA* 9.OUT OF AFRICA a *J.BAR
    RY* 10.DOCTOR ZHIVAGO a *M.JARRE* 11.NORTH BY NORTHWE
    ST d *B.HERRMANN* 12.PAPILLON a *J.GOLDSMITH* 13.JUNGLE
    BOOK e *M.ROZSA* 14.STREETCAR NAMED DESIRE f *A.NORTH*
    15.DIVA b *V.COSMA* 16.HIGH NOON a *D.TIOMKIN)* 17.ONCE
    UPON A TIME IN THE WEST a *E.MORRICONE / a: Richard
    Kaufman & Nurnberger Symphoniker b: Lanny Meyers &
    Top Design Musicians c: Elmer Bernstein and Nurnber
    ger Symphoniker d: Cliff Eidelman & Seattle S.O.
    e: Hanspeter Seibel and Nurnberger Symphoniker f:
    Jerry Goldsmith & National Philharmonic Orchestra*

82. CINEMA SOUNDTRACK HITS - Various Artists
    *VARESE (Pinn): VSD 5709 (CD)* 1996
    1.BATMAN FOREVER a *E.GOLDENTHAL* 2.FIRST KNIGHT a
    *J.GOLDSMITH* 3.BRAVEHEART a *J.HORNER* 4.UNDER SIEGE 2
    b *B.POLEDOURIS* 5.TIMECOP c *M.ISHAM* 6.JUNIOR d *J.N.
    HOWARD* 7.FORREST GUMP e *A.SILVESTRI* 8.CASPER a *J.HO
    RNER* 9.RICHIE RICH f *A.SILVESTRI* 10.OUTBREAK d *J.N.
    HOWARD* 11.THE CROW g *G.REVELL* 12.WATERWORLD a *J.N.
    HOWARD* 13.APOLLO 13 a *J.HORNER* 14.JURASSIC PARK e
    *J.WILLIAMS* 15.THE AGE OF INNOCENCE e *E.BERNSTEIN* 16
    WHILE YOU WERE SLEEPING h *R.EDELMAN* 17.JUDGE DREDD
    a *A.SILVESTRI*
    *a:Joel McNeely & Royal Scottish Nation.Orch b:Basil
    Poledouris & score orch c:Mark Isham & Paramount St
    udio Orch d:Artie Kane & score orc e:Joel McNeely &*

*Seattle Symphony Orch f:Alan Silvestri & score orch g:Tim Simonet & Crow Orc h:Randy Edelman score orch*

83. CLASSIC ADS - Various Artists and Orchestras
*EMI: CDZ 568116-2 (CD) LZ 568116-4 (MC del.97) 1994*
*Citroen ZX:* OVERTURE (Marriage Of Figaro) *(Mozart)*
*Philips DCC:* Sorcerer's Apprentice *(Dukas)* *Nescafe:*
ADAGIO (Spartacus)*(Khachaturuan)* *Tixylix:* DANCE OF
THE SUGAR PLUM FAIRY (Nutcracker Suite)*Tchaikovsky)*
*British Airways:* FLOWER DUET(Lakme)*(Delibes)* *Maxell
Tapes:* A NIGHT ON BARE MOUNTAIN *(Mussorgsky)* *Bio Sp
eed Weed:* CAN CAN (Orpheus) *(Offenbach)* *Philips DCC*
O MIO BABBINO CARO (Gianni Schicci) *(Puccini)* *Hovis*
LARGO (New World Symph.No.9) *(Dvorak)* *TSB:* MORNING
PAPERS WALTZ *(J.Strauss II)* *Ragu Pasta Sauce:* ANVIL
CHORUS (Il Trovatore) *(Verdi)* *AEG:* MORNING (Peer Gy
nt Suite)*(Grieg)* *Woolworths:*ARRIVAL OF THE QUEEN OF
SHEBA (Solomon) *(Handel)* *Ragu Pasta S:* LA DONNA E.
MOBILE (Rigoletto)*(Verdi)* *Jus-Rol:* WALTZ (Coppelia)
*(Delibes)* *Alton Towers:* IN THE HALL OF THE MOUNTAIN
KING (Peer Gynt) *(Grieg)* *Stella Artois:* OVERTURE La
Forza Del Destino *(Verdi)* *Comfort Fabric Softener:*
WHAT IS LIFE TO ME WITHOUT THEE (Orpheo & Eurydice)
*(Gluck)* *Baci Choc:* INTERMEZZO Cavalleria Rusticana)
*(Mascagni)* *Peugeot 605:* The Moldau (Ma Vlast) *(Smet
ana)* *Thresher Wines:* CANON IN D *(Pachelbel)* *Lloyds
Bank:* SLEEPERS AWAKE (Cantata No.140) *(J.S.Bach)*

84. CLASSIC ADS Volume 2 - Various Artists & Orchs
*EMI: CDM 565721-2 (CD) EG 565721-4 (MC)          1995*
*Baileys Irish Cream:* BARCAROLLE (Tales Of Hoffman)
*(Offenbach)* *British Airways:* VA PENSIERO (Chorus Of
The Hebrew Slaves from Nabucco) *(Verdi)* *Kingsmill
Bread:* SPRING (1st m/m Four Seasons Suite)*(Vivaldi)*
*Batchelor Slimmer Soups:* DANCE OF THE LITTLE SWANS
(Swan Lake) *(Tchaikovsky)* *Lurpak:* FLIGHT OF THE BUM
BLEBEE (Tsar Sultan) *(Rimsky Korsakov)* *Panasonic:*
RONDO (Eine Kleine Nacht Musik) *(Mozart)* *Cadbury's
Choc Break:* TRAUMERI (Kinderszenen) *(Schumann)* *Save
& Prosper Building S:* MINUET *(Boccherini)* *Cadbury's
Fruit & Nut:* DANCE OF THE MIRLITONS (Nutcracker Su)
*(Tchaikovsky)* *Timex Indiglo:* DANCE OF THE HOURS (La
Gioconda) *(Ponchielli)* *Hamlet Cigars:* AIR (Suite No
3) *(Bach)* *Boursin Cheese:* CLAIR DE LUNE *(Debussy)*
*Terry's Nutcracker:* CHINESE DANCE(Nutcracker Suite)
*(Tchaikovsky)* *Old Spice:* O FORTUNA (Carmina Burana)
*(Orff)* *Tesco:* FOSSILES (Carnival Of The Animals)
*(Saint-Saens)* *IBM Computers:* FUR ELISE *(Beethoven)*
*Royal Bank Of Scotland:* PLAYFUL PIZZICATO (Silly Sy
mph.)*(Britten)* *ST.Bruno:* NIMROD (Enigma Variations)
*(Elgar)* *Today Newspaper:* DIES IRAE (Requiem)*(Verdi)*
*Buxton Mineral Water:* ADAGIO (1st mm Cello Concerto
in E.Min) *(Elgar)* *Clark's Shoes:* PETER AND THE WOLF
*(Prokofiev)* *Chanel L'Egoiste:* DANCE OF THE KNIGHTS
(Romeo & Juliet) *(Prokofiev)* *Dulux Weathershield:*
JUPITER (Planet's Suite) *(Holst)*

85. CLASSIC BRITISH FILM MUSIC  Philharmonia Orch* 1990
*SILVA SCREEN (Koch): FILMCD 713 (CD) *Kenneth Alwyn*
Coastal Command (42-R.V.Williams)-Conquest Of The
Air (38-Arthur Bliss)-Red Shoes (48-Brian Easdale)

86. CLASSIC EXPERIENCE Various Artists & Orchestras
*EMI PREMIER: CD(TC)CLEXP 1(2CD/2MC) 1988 reiss 1996*
Collect of Popular Classics used extensively in TV
Commercials, Films and Television Programmes
ARRIVAL OF QUEEN OF SHEBA *(Handel)*-INTERMEZZO KAREL
IA SUITE *(Sibelius)*-BOLERO *(Ravel)*-AIR *(J.S.Bach)*-
ADAGIO from SPARTACUS *(Khachaturian)*-RHAPSODY IN BL
UE *(Gershwin)*-DANCE OF THE REED FLUTE-*(Tchaikovsky)*
SUGAR PLUM FAIRY Coda & Pas De Deux *(Tchaikovsky)*-
MORNING (PEER GYNT)*(Grieg)*-SPRING (FOUR SEASONS) *Vi
valdi)*-RHAPSODY ON A THEME OF PAGANINI*(Rachmaninov)*
LARGO (NEW WORLD SYMPH) *(Dvorak)*-NIMROD from ENIGMA
VARIATIONS *(Elgar)* MEDITATION from THAIS *(Massenet)*
FANTASIA GREENSLEEVES *(V.Williams)*-Canon in D *(Pach
elbel)*-FANFARE FOR COMMON MAN*(Copland)*-WILLIAM TELL
OVERTURE *(Rossini)*-RIDE OF THE VALKYRIES *(Wagner)*-
MONTAGUES & CAPULETS *(Prokofiev)*-NIGHT ON THE BARE
MOUNTAIN *(Mussorgsky)*-MARS from THE PLANETS *(Holst)*
RADETZKY MARCH *(Strauss)*-1812 OVERTURE*(Tchaikovsky)*
TROIKA *(Prokofiev)*-BLUE DANUBE *(Strauss)*-MINUET by
*(Boccherini)*-TURKISH RONDO *(Mozart)*-BARCAROLLE from
The TALES OF HOFFMANN *(Offenbach)*-SLEEPING BEAUTY
WALTZ and DANCE OF THE LITTLE SWANS *(Tchaikovsky)*
INTERMEZZO from CAVALLERIA RUSTICANA *(Mascagni)*-
POMP and CIRCUMSTANCE MARCH NO.1 *(Elgar)*

87. CLASSIC EXPERIENCE 2 - Various Artists & Orchestras
*EMI PREMIER: CD(TC)CLEXP 2(2CD/2MC) 1990 reiss 1996*
O FORTUNA (CARMINA BURANA) *(Orff)*-SWAN LAKE ACT 2
*(Tchaikovsky)*-FLOWER DUET (LAKME) *(Delibes)*-IN THE
HALL OF THE MOUNTAIN KING (PEER GYNT) *(Greig)*-OVERT
URE (CARMEN)/CHANSON BOHEME (CARMEN Act 2) *(Bizet)*-
RONDO SERENADE NO.13 IN GM (EINE KLEINE NACHTMUSIK)
*(Mozart)*-LARGO AL FACTOTEM DELLA CITTA (BARBER OF
SEVILLE)*(Rossini)*-RONDO (HORN CONCERTO NO.4 K.495)-
*(Mozart)*-ADAGIO IN G.MINOR *(Albinoni)*-WALTZ OF THE
FLOWERS (NUTCRACKER SUITE) *(Tchaikovsky)*-FUR ELISE
(BAGATELLE IN A.MINOR OP.173) *(Beethoven)*-CELLO CON
CERTO IN E.MINOR OP.85 *(Elgar)*-PAVANE Op.50 *(Faure)*
PIZZICATI (SYLVIA) *(Delibes)*-GYMNOPEDIE N.1 *(Satie)*
NESSUN DORMA (TURANDOT)*(Puccini)*-ADAGIO FOR STRINGS
*(Barber)*-O MIO BABBINO CARO (GIANNI SCHICCHI) *(Pucc
ini)*-ADAGIO FOR STRINGS *(Barber)*-WATER MUSIC *Handel*
SUMMER (FOUR SEASONS SUITE)*(Vivaldi)*-SLEEPERS AWAKE
(CANTATA 140)*(Bach)*-SHERPHERD'S HYMN PASTORAL SYMPH
*(Beethoven)*-SKATER'S WALTZ *(Waldteufel)*-BADINERIE
(SUITE NO.2) *(Bach)*-LA DONNA E MOBILE (RIGOLETTO)
*(Verdi)*-RONDO (A MUSICAL JOKE *(Mozart)*-DAYBREAK fr.
DAPHNIS & CHLOE *(Ravel)*-1ST M/M SYMPH.NO.6 *(Vaughan
Williams)*-SUNRISE(ALSO SPRACH ZARATHUSTRA)*(Strauss)*
PRELUDE ACT III (LOHENGRIN) *(R.Wagner)*-JUPITER (PLA

NET'S SUITE) *(Holst)*-ROMEO AND JULIET *(Tchaikovsky)*
THIEVING MAGPIE *(Rossini)*-EXCERPTS from MANFRED and
PATHETIQUE SYMPH.*(Tchaikovsky)*-FINLANDIA *(Sibelius)*
88.CLASS EXPERIENCE 3 - Various Artists & Orchestras
*EMI PREMIER: CD(TC)CLEXP 3(2CD/2MC) 1991 reiss 1996*
SYMPH.NO.9 *(Dvorak)*-MY COUNTRY *(Smetana)*-BARBER OF
SEVILLE *(Rossini)*-BRINDISI from LA TRAVIATA *(Verdi)*
OVERTURE to DIE FLEDERMAUS *(Strauss)* SYMPHONY NO.4
ITALIAN *(Mendelssohn)*-CHINESE DANCE from NUTCRACKER
*(Tchaikovsky)*-WALTZ NO 6.(MINUTE WALTZ *(Chopin)*-
SYMPHONY NO.40 IN G.MAJOR *(Mozart)*-CHANSON DE MATIN
Op.15 NO.2 *(Elgar)*-ADAGIO GUITAR CONCER.DE ARANJUEZ
*(Rodrigo)*-SYMPHONY NO.1 IN A.FLAT MAJ.Op.55 *(Elgar)*
ARIA CANTILENA-BACHIANAS BRASILEIROS *(Villa-Lobos)*-
IN THE DEPTHS OF THE TEMPLE (PEARL FISHERS)*(Bizet)*-
CLAIR DE LUNE *(Debussy)*-VESTI LA GIUBBA I PAGLIACCI
*(Leoncavallo)*-VA PEINSERO CHORUS OF HEBREW SLAVES
NABUCCO *(Verdi)*-SHEEP MAY SAFELY GRAZE *(BACH)*-PIANO
CONCERTO NO.5 EMPEROR *(Beethoven)*-OVERTURE HEBRIDES
*(Mendelssohn)*-SCHEHERAZADE YOUNG PRINCE & PRINCESS
*(Rimsky-Korsakov)*-FARANDOLE *(Bizet)*-PETER AND THE
WOLF *(Tchaikovsky)*-RUSSIAN DANCE fromThe NUTCRACKER
*(Tchaikovsky)*-BALLET EGYPTIEN *(Luigeni)*-THE FLIGHT
OF THE BUMBLEBEE *(Rimsky-Korsakov)*-THE DANCE OF THE
HOURS *(Ponchielli)*-SABRE DANCE *(Khachaturian)*-THE
SORCERER'S APPRENTICE *(Dukas)*-THE RITE OF SPRING
*(Stravinsky)*-ESPANA *(Chabrier)*-ITALIAN CAPRICE
SYMPHONY NO.9 (CHORAL) *(Beethoven)*
89.CLASSIC EXPERIENCE 4 - Various Artists & Ocrhestras
*EMI PREMIER: CD(TC)CLEXP 4(2CD/2MC) 1993 reiss 1996*
RUSSLAN & LUDMILLA *(Glinka)*-HOLBERG SUITE *(Grieg)*-
O SOLE MIO *(DiCapua)*-AQUARIUM from CARNIVAL OF THE
ANIMALS *(Saint-Saens)*-DANSE MACABRE *(Saint-Saens)*-
TRIUMPHAL MARCH AIDA *(Verdi)*-LULLABY from DOLLY *(Fa
ure)*-FANTASIA ON A THEME OF THOMAS TALLIS *(Vaughan
Williams)*-LIGHT CAVALRY OVERTURE *(Suppe)*-THE SWAN
CARNIVAL OF THE ANIMALS *(Saint-Saens)*-NOCTURNE from
SPRING QUARTET No.2 *(Borodin)*-MOONLIGHT SONATA *(Bee
thoven)*-BAILERO from SONGS OF THE AUVERGNE *(Cantelo
ube)*-THE STARS SHINE BRIGHTLY from TOSCA *(Puccini)*-
MEMORIES OF THE ALHAMBRA *(Tarrega)*-STRING QUARTET
*(Ravel)*-RECUERDOS DE LA ALHAMBRA*(Tarrega)*-YOUR TINY
HAND IS FROZEN:LA BOHEME *(Puccini)*-NEPTUNE from the
PLANETS SUITE *(Holst)*-VIOLIN CONCERTO IN D.MAJ.Op35
*(Tchaikovsky)*-MARCH from KARELIA SUITE *(Sibelius)*-
ANVIL CHORUS: IL TROVATORE *(Verdi)*-HUNGARIAN MARCH
DAMNATION OF FAUST *(Berlioz)*-CLASSICAL SYMPHONY FIN
ALE *(Prokofiev)*-WALTZ:COPPELIA *(Delibes)*-I SHALL GO
FAR AWAY:LA WALLY *(Catalani)*-HUNGARIAN RHAPSODY NO.
2 *(Liszt)*-PIANO CONCERTO IN A.MINOR *(Greig)*-TURKISH
MARCH: RUINS OF ATHENS *(Beethoven)*-FLYING DUTCHMAN
OVERTURE *(Wagner)*-DANCE OF THE COMEDIANS: BARTERED
BRIDE *(Smetana)*-FORCE OF DESTINY *(Verdi)* YOUNG PERS
ONS GUIDE TO T.ORCHESTRA *(Britten)*- PROMENADE/GREAT

GATE OF KIEV:PICTURES AT AN EXHIBITION *(Mussorgsky)*
--- CLASSIC FANTASY FILM SCORES - see *COLLECTION 186*
90.CLASSIC GREEK FILM MUSIC - City Of Prague Philharm*
*SILVA SCREEN (Koch): FILMCD(C) 165 (CD/MC)* 1995
ZORBA THE GREEK-TOPKAPI-NEVER ON SUNDAY-CHARIOTS OF
FIRE-1492 CONQUEST OF PARADISE-Z-PHAEDRA-HONEYMOON-
STATE SIEGE-BLUE-SERPICO-MISSING-SHIRLEY VALENTINE
* *cond: Nic Raine + Martin Kershaw Bouziki Ensemble*
91.CLASSIC ITALIAN SPAGHETTI WESTERNS VOL.1 - Var.Arts
*DRG (Pinn): DRGCD 32905 (2CD)* 1995
COMPOSERS: Ennio Morricone-Pino Donaggio-Riz Ortola
ni-Francesco De Masi-Carlo Rusticelli-Angelo France
sco Lavagnina-Franco Bixia VOCALS: Katina Ranieri-
Vittorio Bezzi and others
67 SELECTIONS FROM 28 SPAGHETTI WESTERNS (1966-81)
92.CLASSIC ITALIAN SPAGHETTI WESTERNS VOL.2 - Var.Arts
*DRG (Pinn): DRGCD 32909 (2CD)* 1995
COMPOSERS: Ennio Morricone-Bruno Nicolai-Carlo Savi
na-Francesco De Masi-Luis Bacalov-Piero Piccioni-
Riz Ortolani-Armando Trovaioli and others
SPAGHETTI WESTERN MUSIC FROM THE LIBRARY OF ITALY'S
GENERAL MUSIC / MAIN TITLES-VOCALS-RARE TRACKS etc.
93.CLASSIC OPERA EXPERIENCE - Var.Artists & Orchestras
*EMI PREMIER: CD(TC)CLEXP 5(2CD/2MC)* 1996
BRINDISI (LA TRAVIATA-*Verdi*) NON PIU ABDRAI/VOI CHE
SAPETE(MARRIAGE OF FIGARO-*Mozart*) LARGO AL FACTOTEM
(BARBER OF SEVILLE-*Rossini*) SERENADE (DON GIOVANNI-
*Mozart*) HABANERA/TOREADOR'S SONG (CARMEN-*Bizet*) THE
TEMPLE DUET (PEARLFISHERS-*Bizet*) BARCAROLLE (TALES
OF HOFFMANN-*Offenbach*) OMBRA MAI FU (Largo)(XERXES-
*Handel*) O MIO BABBINO CARO(GIANNI SCHICCHI-*Puccini*)
ACH SO FROMM (M'Appari)(MARTHA-*Flowtow*) FLOWER DUET
(LAKME-*Delibes*) IL MIO TESSORO(DON GIOVANNI-*Mozart*)
PORGI AMOR (MARRIAGE OF FIGARO-*Mozart*) CHE GELIDA
MANINA/SI MI CHIAMINO MIMI (LA BOHEME-*Puccini*) THE
HUMMING CHORUS (MADAM BUTTERFLY-*Puccini*) SIGNORE AS
COLTA/NESSUN DORMA (TURANDOT-*Puccini*) BIRDCATCHER'S
SONG/DER HOLLE RASCH(MAGIC FLUTE-*Mozart*) LA DONNA E
MOBILE(RIGOLETTO-*Verdi*) ANVIL CHORUS (IL TROVATORE-
*Verdi*) CELESTE AIDA (AIDA-*Verdi*) SOFTLY AWAKES MY
HEART (SAMSON AND DFITIAH-*Saint-Saons*) SONG TO TIIE
MOON(RUSALKA-*Dvorak*) LA MAMMA MORTA (ANDREA CHENIER
*Giordano*) VESTI LA GIUBBA (PAGLIACCI-*Leoncavallo*)
ONE FINE DAY(MADAM BUTTERFLY-*Puccini*) CHORUS OF THE
HEBREW SLAVES(NABUCCO-*Verdi*) EBBEN NE ANDRO LONTANA
(LA WALLY-*Catalni*) RECONDITA ARMONIA/VISSI D'ARTE
(TOSCA-*Puccini*) PUR TI MIRO (CORONATION OF POPPEA-
*Monteverdi*) CHI IL BEL SOGNO DI DORETTA (LA RONDINE
*Puccini*) EASTER HYMN(CAVALERRIA RUSTICANA-*Mascagni*)
94.CLASSIC PAN PIPES - Classical Music from TV ADS
*CARLTON SOUNDS (CHE): 30360 00682 (CD) -4 (MC)* 1996
1.FLOWER DUET, LAKME *(DELIBES)* Br.Airways 2.MORNING
PEER GYNT *(GRIEG)* AEG 3.SPRING, 4 SEASONS *(VIVALDI)*
Kingsmill Bread 5.CHINESE DANCE, NUTCRACKER SUITE

*(TCHAIKOVSKY)* Terry's Choc 6.RONDO, EINE KLEINE NAC
HT MUSIK *(MOZART)* Panasonic 7.FUR ELISE *(BEETHOVEN)*
IBM 8.AIR ON A G.STRING *(BACH)* Hamlet 9.IN THE HALL
OF THE MOUNTAIN KING,PEER GYNT *(GREIG)* Alton Towers
10.LA DONNA E MOBILE. RIGOLETTO *(VERDI)* Ragu 11.THE
MOLDAU, MA VLAST *(SMETANA)* Peugeot 605 12.LARGO,NEW
WORLD SYMPHONY *(DVORAK)* Hovis 13.PETER AND THE WOLF
*(PRKOFIEV)* Clark's 14.KANON IN D *(PACHELBEL)* Thresh
er Wines 15.BARCAROLLE,TALES OF HOFFMAN *(OFFENBACH)*
Bailey's 16.DANCE OF THE SUGAR PLUM FAIRY, NUTCRACK
ER *(TCHAIKOVSKY)* Tixylix 17.DANCE OF THE HOURS from
LA GIOCONDA*(PONCHIELLI)*Timex 18.DANCE OF THE LITTLE
SWANS, SWAN LAKE *(TCHAIKOVSKY)* Batchelor Soups 19.O
MIO BABBINO CARO, GIANNI SCHICCHI *(PUCCINI)* Philips
20.ADAGIO, SPARTACUS BALLET *(KHACHATURIAN)* Nescafe
21.CLAIR DE LUNE *(DEBUSSY)* Boursin Cheese

**95.** CLASS<u>IC SPORTING ANTHEMS</u> - Various Artists
*CFP (EMI): CDCFP 5000 (CD) TCCFP 5000 (MC)*     *1996*
THE BRITISH GRENADIERS-COLONEL BOGEY-LIBERTY BELL-
ABIDE WITH ME-NATIONAL ANTHEM-NIMROD-JUPITER-RULE
BRITANNIA-JERUSALEM-YOU'LL NEVER WALK ALONE-POMP
AND CIRCUMSTANCE 1-LA DONNA E MOBILE-NESSUN DORMA

**96.** <u>CLASSIC THEMES FROM TV AND RADIO</u> - Var.Artists *1996*
*HAPPY DAYS (Conif-BMG): 75605 52271-2 (CD) -4 (MC)*
1.BARWICK GREEN *(THE ARCHERS)* New Concert Orchestra
2.WON'T YOU GET OFF IT PLEASE *(Tate & Lyle Sugar)*
Fats Waller 3.BY A SLEEPY LAGOON *(DESERT ISLAND DIS
CS)* Eric Coates Symphony Orchestra 4.DEVIL'S GALLOP
*(DICK BARTON)* Charles Williams Queens Hall Light Or
5.NESSUN DORMA fr.Turandot (Puccini) Jussi Bjorling
6.TROUT QUINTET(Schubert)*(WAITING FOR GOD)* Pro-Arte
Quart.Artur Schnabel 7.CORONATION SCOT *(PAUL TEMPLE
DULUX AD)* Queen's Hall Light Orch 8.AS TIME GOES BY
Turner Layton 9.AIR ON A G.STRING (Bach)*(HAMLET CIG
ARS AD)* L.S.O.10.GRASSHOPPER'S DANCE *(MILK AD)* Jack
Hylton Orch 11.SOMEONE TO WATCH OVER ME *(PPP HEALTH
CARE)* Frances Langford 12.DANCE OF THE FLUTES from
'NUTCRACKER SUITE' Tchaikovsky *(CADBURY'S FRUIT AND
NUT)* Philadelphia Orch. 13.I WANNA BE LOVED BY YOU
*(CHANEL NO.5)* Helen Kane 14.RONDO ALLA TURCA Mozart
*(FORD MOTORS)* Symph.Orch 15.OH WHAT A BEAUTIFUL MOR
NIN'*(KELLOGG'S CORNFLAKES)* Glenn Miller Army Air Fo
rces Training Command Orch. 16.ORIENTAL SHUFFLE *(RA
DIO TIMES AD)* Django Reinhardt & Hot Club Of France
17.ITMA SIGNATURE TUNE BBC Variety Orch 18.MY SHIP
*(GALAXY AD)* Gertrude Lawrence 19.TEA FOR TWO *(NEXT
OF KIN)* Raie Da Costa 20.MAKIN' WHOOPEE *(NATIONWIDE
BUILDING SOC)* Eddie Cantor 21.LIBERTY BELL MARCH
*(MONTY PYTHON'S FLYING CIRCUS)* Famous Cresswell Col
liery Band 22.LARGO (NEW WORLD SYMPHONY (Dvorak)
*(HOVIS)* Czech Harmonic Orch 23.ROSES FROM THE SOUTH
(J.Strauss II)*(GRAND HOTEL/YARDLEY LIPSTICK)* Albert
Sandler Palm Court Orch.24.LET'S FALL IN LOVE *(HALI
FAX BUILDING SOC)* Annette Hanshaw 25.WITH A SONG IN

MY HEART *(TWO-WAY FAMILY FAVOURITES)* Andre Kostelan
etz Orch 26.GOODNIGHT SWEETHEART *(GOODNIGHT SWEETHE
ART)* Al Bowlly & New Mayfair Dance Orch (Ray Noble)
97.CLASSICAL FILM THEMES - Various Artists
  *RCA INT (BMG): RCA(CD)(MC) 221 (2CD/2MC)*        *1997*
  2001 A SPACE ODYSSEY 2:INDECENT PROPOSAL 3:AMADEUS
  4:GROUNDHOG DAY 5:HOWARDS END 6:ELVIRA MADIGAN 7:
  APOCALYPSE NOW 8:DIVA 9:SILENCE OF THE LAMBS 10:
  BRIEF ENCOUNTER 11:DIE HARD 2 12:WAYNE'S WORLD 13:
  MANHATTAN 14:PLATOON 15:PRETTY WOMAN CD 2: 1:DOORS
  2:10 3:GODFATHER III 4:FATHER OF THE BRIDE 5:FIRM
  6:DIE HARD 7:THE LAST EMPEROR 8:DEATH IN VENICE (1)
  9:ROLLERBALL 10:HONEYMOON IN VEGAS 11:CROSSING DELA
  NCEY 12:DEATH IN VENCICE (2) 13:OUT OF AFRICA 14:
  LOVE AND DEATH 15:MRS.DOUBTFIRE
98.CLIFFHANGERS: Music from Classic REPUBLIC Serials
  *VARESE (Pinn): VSD 5658 (CD)*                    *1996*
  ADVENTURES OF CAPTAIN MARVEL-ADVENTURES OF RED STRY
  KER-DICK TRACY'S G.MEN-DRUMS OF FU MANCHU-FIGHTING
  DEVIL DOGS-HAWK OF THE WILDERNESS-THE PERILS OF NYO
  KA-ZORRO'S FIGHTING LEGION etc. Cinema Sound Orches
  tra (James King, conductor) *see also 'SHOOT'EM UPS'*
--- COASTAL COMMAND - *see COLLECTION 85*
--- COMMANDER DALGLEISH -*see COLLECTION 181 'SHROUD FOR
                                      A NIGHTINGALE'*
99.COODER Ry - Ry Cooder Film Soundtrack Music
  *WB (WEA): 9362 45987-2 (CD x 2)*                 *1995*
  Long Riders (1980) Southern Comfort (1981) Border
  (1982) Paris Texas (1984) Streets Of Fire (1984)
  Alamo Bay (1985) Blue City (1986) Crossroads (1986)
  Johnny Handsome (1989) Trespass (92) Geronimo (93)
100.COPS - PAUL BROOKS
  *K-TEL (K-Tel): ECD 3369 (CD) EMC 2369 (MC)*      *1997*
  Medley: HAWAII 5-0/CAGNEY & LACEY/HILL STREET BLUES
  Z.CARS/DRAGNET/MIAMI VICE - INSPECTOR MORSE-MISSION
  IMPOSSIBLE-AVENGERS-MISS MARPLE-KOJAK-THE SWEENEY-
  A.TEAM-ROCKFORD FILES-CHARLIE'S ANGELS-MAGNUM P.I;-
  PERRY MASON-MAN FROM UNCLE. Medley: THE BILL/JULIET
  BRAVO/BERGERAC/NO HIDING PLACE/POLICE WOMAN/STREETS
  OF SAN FRANCISCO/MAIGRET/HEARTBEAT
101.COPS ON THE BOX: USA - Various Artists
  *EMPORIO-MCI (THE): EMPRCD 711 (CD)*              *1997*
  1.HAWAII 5-0 2.STARSKY AND HUTCH 'Gotcha' 3.STREETS
  OF SAN FRANCISCO 4.KOJAK 5.NYPD BLUE 6.MIAMI VICE 7
  .COLUMBO 8.CAGNEY & LACEY 9.DRAGNET 10.POLICE WOMAN
  11.DUE SOUTH 12.PERRY MASON 13.MAN CALLED IRONSIDE
  14.TJ HOOKER 15.HIGHWAY PATROL 16.HILL STREET.BLUES
--- COULTER Phil - *see COLLECTION 144 'GALWAY James'*
102.COWARD Noel - Noel: Classic Recordings 1928-1938
  *HAPPY DAYS (BMG-Con): CHCD(MHCD) 168 (CD/MC)*    *1990*
  POOR LITTLE RICH GIRL-ZIGEUNER-DEAR LITTLE CAFE-TOK
  AY-CALL OF LIFE-WORLD WEARY-CABALLERO-I'LL SEE YOU
  AGAIN-GREEN CARNATIONS-STATELY HOMES OF ENGLAND-LOV
  ER OF MY DREAMS-MAD DOGS & ENGLISHMEN-WE WERE SO YO

UNG-GYPSY MELODY-MRS.WORTHINGTON-DANCE LITTLE LADY-
JUST LET ME LOOK AT YOU-SOMETHING TO DO WITH SPRING
DEAREST LOVE-FARE THEE WELL-A ROOM WITH A VIEW-HALF
CASTE WOMAN-WHERE ARE THE SONGS-PLAY ORCHESTRA PLAY

103. COWARD Noel - Songs Of Noel COWARD
FLAPPER-PAVILION (Pinn): PASTCD 7080                1996
1.MRS.WORTHINGTON 2.PARISIAN PIERROT 3.THERE'S LIFE
IN THE OLD GIRL YET 4.POOR LITTLE RICH GIRL 5.I'LL
SEE YOU AGAIN 6.IF LOVE WERE ALL 7.ZIEGUENER 8.A
ROOM WITH A VIEW 9.DANCE LITTLE LADY 10.I'LL FOLLOW
MY SECRET HEART 11.REGENCY RAKES 12.THERE'S ALWAYS
SOMETHING FISHY ABOUT THE FRENCH13.HAS ANYBODY SEEN
OUR SHIP 14.YOU WERE THERE 15.SOMEDAY I'LL FIND YOU
16.DEAREST LOVE 17.THE STATELY HOMES OF ENGLAND 18.
LONDON PRIDE19.ANY LITTLE FISH 20.MAD ABOUT THE BOY
21.MAD DOGS AND ENGLISHMEN 22.THE PARTY'S OVER NOW

104. COWARD Noel : The Masters Voice - HMV RECORDINGS
1928-1953 (Complete) on EMI COWARD 1 (4CD SET) 1992

105. CRAWFORD Michael - Love Songs Album
TELSTAR (WEA): TCD 2748 (CD) STAC 2748 (MC)      1994
MUSIC OF THE NIGHT-POWER OF LOVE-UNEXPECTED SONG-
PAPA CAN YOU HEAR ME-ALL I ASK OF YOU (duet with
BARBARA BONNEY)-WHEN I FALL IN LOVE-YOU'LL NEVER
WALK ALONE-PHANTOM OF THE OPERA (duet: BARBARA BONN
EY)-WEST SIDE STORY (song medley)-STORY OF MY LIFE
BRING HIM HOME-TELL ME ON A SUNDAY-SINCE YOU STAYED
HERE-EVERYTIME WE SAY GOODBYE-FOR ALL WE KNOW KNOW

106. CRAWFORD Michael - Performs Andrew Lloyd Webber
TELSTAR (WEA): TCD 2544 (CD) STAC 2544 (MC)      1991
TELL ME ON A SUNDAY-ALL I ASK OFYOU:Phantom-WISHING
YOU WERE SOMEHOW HERE AGAIN:Phantom-ANY DREAM WILL
DO:Joseph & A.T.D.-AND THE MONEY KEEPS ROLLING IN:
Evita-NOTHING LIKE YOU'VE EVER KNOWN:Song & Dance-
PHANTOM OF THE OPERA-MUSIC OF THE NIGHT:Phantom
MEMORY:Cats-ONLY YOU:Starlight Express-GETHSEMANE:
Jesus C.Superstar-OTHER PLEASURES/FIRST MAN YOU
REMEMBER/LOVE CHANGES EVERYTHING:Aspects Of Love

107. CRAWFORD Michael - Songs From The Stage and Screen
MICHAEL CRAWFORD with London Symphony Orch.      1987
RONCO-TELSTAR (WEA): CDSR 060 (CD) TCSR 060 (MC)
WEST SIDE STORY-WHAT'LL I DO-UNEXPECTED SONG-IF I
LOVED YOU-BEFORE THE PARADE PASSES BY-WHEN YOU WISH
UPON A STAR-IN THE STILL OF THE NIGHT-MEMORY-NOT A
DAY GOES BY-BRING HIM HOME-YOU'LL NEVER WALK ALONE

108. CRIME SCENE The - Var.Artists (Ultra Lounge series)
CAPITOL-EMI Premier (EMI): CDEMS 1594 (CD)       1996
1.DRAGNET/ROOM 43 Ray Anthony 2.I-SPY Earle Hagen 3
THINKING OF BABY Elmer Bernstein 4.FROM RUSSIA WITH
LOVE Count Basie 5.BIG TOWN Laurindo Almeida 6.THE
MAN WITH THE GOLDEN ARMBilly May 7.THE UNTOUCHABLES
Nelson Riddle 8.JAMES BOND THEME Leroy Holmes 9.
MISSION IMPOSSIBLE Billy May 10.HARLEM NOCTURNE Spi
ke Jones New Band 11.WALK ON THE WILD SIDE Si Zentn
er 12.MISTER KISS KISS BANG BANG Elliott Fisher 13.

WILD ONES Lou Busch 14.STACCATO'S THEME Elmer Berns
tein 15.SEARCH FOR VULCANLeroy Holmes 16.PETER GUNN
SUITE Ray Anthony 17.SILENCERS Vicki Carr 18.MUSIC
TO BE MURDERED BY Jeff Alexander w.Alfred Hitchcock

--- CRUISE Tom - see COLLECTION 39

--- CULT FICTION - see COLLECTIONS 356,357,360,361

109.CULT FILES The - Royal Philharm.Concert Orch (Mike
Townsend) + City Of Prague Philharmonic (Nic Raine)
SILVA SCREEN (Koch): FILMX(CD)(C)184 (2CD/2MC) 1996
CD1: THE X.FILES-THE PRISONER-THE SAINT-DANGERMAN-
RANDALL & HOPKIRK DECEASED-THE AVENGERS-JASON KING-
THE PERSUADERS-BLAKE'S 7-RED DWARF-DOCTOR WHO-THE
ADVENT.OF ROBINSON CRUSOE-ALFRED HITCHCOCK PRESENTS
HAWAII 5.0.-PERRY MASON-A MAN CALLED IRONSIDE-KOJAK
MISSION IMOSSIBLE-STAR TREK-SEAQUEST DSV-BABYLON 5
CD2:2001-EXCALIBUR-ALIEN-MAD MAX:BEYOND THUNDERDOME
BODY HEAT-THE OMEN-HALLOWEEN-ASSAULT ON PRECINCT 13
BLADERUNNER-BATMAN-SUPERMAN-THE SHADOW-ROCKETEER
HEAVEN'S GATE-LEGEND-SOMEWHERE IN TIME-TAXI DRIVER-
PINK PANTHER-THE BLUES BROTHERS

110.CULT FILES: RE-OPENED Royal Phil.Concert Orch (Mike
Townsend) + City Of Prague Philharmonic (Nic Raine)
Silv.Screen (Koch): FILMX(CD)(C)191 (2CD/2MC) 1997
CD1: XENA THE WARRIOR PRINCESS-BATTLESTAR GALACTICA
HITCHHIKERS GUIDE TO THE GALAXY-SPACE: ABOVE AND
BEYOND-TWILIGHT ZONE-THE OUTER LIMITS-THUNDERBIRDS-
FIREBALL XL5:ZERO G-FIREBALL XL5:FIREBALL-STINGRAY
vocal-STINGRAY:MARCH OF THE OYSTERS-CAPTAIN SCARLET
JOE 90-UFO-SPACE 1999:1st series-SPACE 1999:2nd ser
BATMAN-THE TIME TUNNEL-LOST IN SPACE-VOYAGE TO THE
BOTTOM OF THE SEA-LAND OF THE GIANTS-HERCULES-
STINGRAY:Orch.version CD2: POLICE SQUAD-BURKE'S LAW
FUGITIVE-KOJAK-MIAMI VICE-STREETS OF SAN FRANCISCO-
BEAUTY & THE BEAST TV-SUPERMAN-EDWARD SCISSORHANDS-
BEETLEJUICE-YOUNG FRANKENSTEIN-MIDNIGHT EXPRESS-
SUSPIRIA-MERRY CHRISTMAS MR.LAWRENCE-WITHNAIL AND I
A CLOCKWORK ORANGE-THE WILD WILD WEST-ADDAMS FAMILY
MASH-MONTY PYTHON'S FLYING CIRCUS

111.CURSE OF THE CAT PEOPLE The Film Music Of ROY WEBB
CLOUD NINE (Silva Screen): CNS 5008 (CD) 1995
BUILD MY GALLOWS HIGH-CROSSFIRE-BEDLAM-NOTORIOUS-
SINBAD THE SAILOR-THE GHOST SHIP-MIGHTY JOE YOUNG-
CORNERED-LOCKET-DICK TRACY-CURSE OF THE CAT PEOPLE

112.DANNA Mychael - Music From The Films Of Atom Egoyan
VARESE (Pinn): VSD 5674 (CD) 1996
EXOTICA (93) FAMILY VIEWING (87) THE ADJUSTER (91)
SPEAKING PARTS (89) and others

113.DAVIS Bette - Classic Scores From Her Films *N.P.O.
RCA VICTOR (BMG): GD(GK) 80183 (CD/MC) reiss.1989
NOW VOYAGER-DARK VICTORY-A STOLEN LIFE-THE PRIVATE
LIVES OF ELIZABETH AND ESSEX-MR.SKEFFINGTON-IN THIS
OUR LIFE-ALL ABOUT EVE-JEZEBEL-BEYOND THE FOREST-JU
UREZ-THE LETTER-ALL THIS & HEAVEN TOO / * National
Philharmonic Orchestra conductor: Charles Gerhardt

114. DAY Doris - Daydreaming: The Very Best Of DORIS DAY
*COLUMBIA (Sony Music): 487 361-2 (CD)* 1997
MOVE OVER DARLING-SECRET LOVE-WHATEVER WILL BE WILL
BE (QUE SERA SERA)-LULLABY OF BROADWAY-LOVE ME OR
LEAVE ME-IT'S MAGIC-EVERYBODY LOVES A LOVER-PILLOW
TALK-DREAM A LITTLE DREAM OF ME-CHEEK TO CHEEK-
FLY ME TO THE MOON-CLOSE YUOUR EYES-QUIET NIGHT OF
QUIET STARS-NIGHT AND DAY-LET'S FACE THE MUSIC AND
DANCE-PENNIES FROM HEAVEN-OVER THE RAINBOW-I'LL NEV
ER STOP LOVING YOU-IF I GIVE MY HEART TO YOU-A VERY
PRECIOUS LOVE-BEWITCHED-THE BLACK HILLS OD DAKOTA-
TEACHER'S PET-MAKIN' WHOOPEE-READY WILLING AND ABLE
SENTIMENTAL JOURNEY

115. DELERUE Georges - Francois Truffaut Film Music
London Sinfonietta conducted by Hugo WOLFF
*NONESUCH (WEA): 7559 79405-2 (CD)* 1997
JULES ET JIM-LE DERNIER METRO-LA VALSE DE FRANCOIS
T-SHOOT THE PIANO PLAYER and others

116. DELERUE Georges - The London Sessions (1)
*VARESE USA (Pinn): VSD 5241 (CD)* 1990
*Music (Suites and Themes) by Georges Delerue from*
*his scores for* PLATOON-RICH AND FAMOUS-HER ALIBI-
BEACHES-EXPOSED-BILOXI BLUES-CRIMES OF THE HEART

117. DELERUE Georges - The London Sessions (2)
*VARESE USA (Pinn): VSD 5245 (CD)* 1990
*Music (Suites and Themes) by Georges Delerue from*
*his scores for* STEEL MAGNOLIAS-INTERLUDE-THE ESCAPE
ARTIST-SALVADOR and 'HOMMAGE TO FRANCOIS TRUFFAUT'

118. DELERUE Georges - The London Sessions (3)
*VARESE USA (Pinn): VSD 5256 (CD)* 1992
SOMETHING WICKED THIS WAY COMES-THE HOUSE ON CAROLL
STREET-A LITTLE SEX-MAID TO ORDER-MAN WOMAN AND CHI
LD-MEMORIES OF ME-AGNES OF GOD-TRUE CONFESSIONS

119. DEVIL RIDES OUT The - Film Music of JAMES BERNARD
*SILVA SCREEN (Koch): FILMCD 174 (CD)* 1996
THE DEVIL RIDES OUT-KISS OF THE VAMPIRE-SHE-SCARS
OF DRACULA-FRANKENSTEIN CREATED WOMAN-QUATERMASS EX
PERIMENT-X THE UNKNOWN-QUATERMASS II *Westminster Ph
ilharmonic Orch, City Of Prague Philharmonic, cond:
Kenneth Alwyn, Paul Bateman and Nic Raine*

--- DIAL M FOR MURDER - *see COLLECTION 194*
--- DISNEY'S HIT SINGLES - *see COLLECTION 406*

120. DOCTOR ZHIVAGO: Classic Film Music of MAURICE JARRE
City Of Prague Philharmon.Orchestra (Paul Bateman)
*SILVA SCREEN (Koch): FILMCD 158 (CD)* 1995
DOCTOR ZHIVAGO-A PASSAGE TO INDIA-RYAN'S DAUGHTER-
LAWRENCE OF ARABIA-GHOST-WITNESS-IS PARIS BURNING-
THE NIGHT OF THE GENERALS-THE MAN WHO WOULD BE KING
FATAL ATTRACTION-VILLA RIDES-THE FIXER-EL CONDOR-
suite from JESUS OF NAZARETH

121. DRACULA: Classic Scores from Hammer Horror *
*SILVA SCREEN (Koch): FILMCD 714 (CD)* 1992
DRACULA (58 James Bernard) DRACULA HAS RISEN FROM
THE GRAVE (68 James Bernard)TASTE THE BLOOD OF DRAC

ULA (70 James Bernard) VAMPIRE CIRCUS (71 David Whi
taker) HANDS OF THE RIPPER (71 Christopher Gunning)
* *Philharmonia Orchestra conductor Neil Richardson*
--- DURBIN Trevor - *see COLLECTION 43'*
122. DURBIN Deanna - Can't Help Singing
*LIVING ERA-ASV (Koch): CDAJA 5149 (CD)*        1995
ANNIE LAURIE-AVE MARIA (Bach-Gounod)-IL BACHIO (The
Kiss)-BECAUSE-BENEATH THE LIGHTS OF HOME-CAN'T HELP
SINGING (with Robert Paige)-ESTRELLITA (Ponce)-GOD
BLESS AMERICA-HOME SWEET HOME-IT'S RAINING SUNBEAMS
IT'S FOOLISH BUT IT'S FUN-KISS ME AGAIN-LAST ROSE
OF SUMMER-LOCH LOMOND-LOVE IS ALL-LOVE'S OLD SWEFT
SONG-MAIDS OF CADIZ-MUSETTA'S WALTZ SONG(La Boheme)
MY HERO MY OWN-ONE FINE DAY (from Madame Butterfly)
PERHAPS-POOR BUTTERFLY-SPRING IN MY HEART-WALTZING
IN THE CLOUDS-WHEN APRIL SINGS
123. DURBIN Deanna - Deanna Durbin Orig Film Soundtracks
*MOVIE STARS (BMG-Con): CMSCD 013 (CD) CMSC 013 (MC)*
LIBIAMO (Drinking Song) *(from 100 MEN AND A GIRL)*
JE VEUX VIVRE*(That Certain Age)* MY HEART IS SINGING
*(THREE SMART GIRLS)* IT'S RAINING SUNBEAMS / A HEART
THAT'S FREE *(100 MEN AND A GIRL)* CHAPEL BELLS / I
LOVE TO WHISTLE / SERENADE TO THE STARS *(MAD ABOUT
MUSIC)* YOUR'E AS PRETTY AS A PICTURE / MY OWN *(THAT
CERTAIN AGE)* LAST ROSE OF SUMMER *(THREE SMART GIRLS
GROW UP)* LOVE IS ALL /LOCH LOMOND / AVE MARIA *(IT'S
A DATE)* WHEN APRIL SINGS*(SPRING PARADE)* WHEN I SING
/ GOIN' HOME *(IT STARTED WITH EVE)* MIGHTY LIKE A RO
SE *(AMAZING MRS.HOLLIDAY)* BEGIN THE BEGUINE / SAY A
PRAYER FOR THE BOYS OVER THERE/ KASHMIRI SONG *(HERS
TO HOLD)* IN THE SPIRIT OF THE MOMENT / WHEN YOU'RE
AWAY / RUSSIAN MELODY / NONE SHALL SLEEP (Nessun Do
rma) *(HIS BUTLER'S SISTER)*
124. DURBIN Deanna - The Fan Club
*FLAPPER-PAVILION (Pinn): PASTCD 9781 (CD)*        1992
AMAPOLA-BECAUSE-WHEN APRIL SINGS-WALTZING IN THE CL
OUDS-MY OWN-BRINDISI-BENEATH THE LIGHTS OF HOME-SPR
ING IN MY HEART-IT'S RAINING SUNBEAMS-MUSETTA'S WAL
TZ SONG-LOVE IS ALL-PERHAPS-ONE FINE DAY-HOME SWEET
HOME-LAST ROSE OF SUMMER-IL BACIO-AVE MARIA-LOCH LO
MONS-ALLELULIA-AVE MARIA    *DEANNA DURBIN Film Songs*
125. DURBIN Deanna - The Golden Voice Of
*HALLMARK (Carlton): 30818-2 (CD) -4 (MC)*        1997
CAN'T HELP SINGING-MORE AND MORE-SPRING IN MY HEART
CALIFORN...-ALWAYS-ONE FINE DAY-LE FILLES DE CADIZ-
AVE MARIA-LOVE IS ALL-HOME SWEET HOME-BENEATH THE
LIGHTS OF HOME-ANY MOMENT NOW-MY OWN-LAST ROSE OF
SUMMER-SPRING WILL BE A LITTLE LATE THIS...-SOMEONE
TO CARE FOR ME-IT'S FOOLISH BUT IT'S FUN-WALTZING
IN THE CLOUDS-ANNIE LAURIE-LOVE'S OLD SWEET SONG
126. EASTWOOD Clint - Movie Themes - Various Artists *
*K-TEL (K-Tel): ECD 3319 (CD) EMC 2319 (MC) 1997*
1.GOOD THE BAD AND THE UGLY 2.EVERY WHICH WAY BUT
LOOSE 3.FISTFUL OF DOLLARS 4.FOR A FEW DOLLARS MORE

5.MISTY (Play Misty For Me) 6.SUDDEN IMPACT 7.ANY
WHICH WAY YOU CAN 8.CLAUDIA'S THEME(The Unforgiven)
9.DEAD POOL 10.DOE EYES (Bridges Of Madison County)
11.TWO MULES FOR SISTER SARA 12.HIGH PLAINS DRIFTER
13.HANG 'EM HIGH 14.OUTLAW JOSEY WALES 15.JOE KIDD
16.PALE RIDER 17.ENFORCER 18.TIGHTROPE 19.MAGNUM
FORCE 20.CITY HEAT * Paul Brooks / Starsound Orch.

127.EASTWOOD Clint - Music From His Films: City Of
Prague Symphony Orchestra (cond: Derek Wadsworth)
*SILVA SCREEN (Koch): FILMCD(C) 138 (CD/MC)*     *1993*
THE UNFORGIVEN-THE GOOD THE BAD AND THE UGLY-A FIST
FUL OF DOLLARS-FOR A FEW DOLLARS MORE-HANG 'EM HIGH
WHERE EAGLES DARE-PLAY MISTY FOR ME-OUTLAW JOSEY WA
LES-RAWHIDE-DIRTY HARRY-SUDDEN IMPACT-MAGNUM FORCE-
TWO MULES FOR SISTER SARA-IN THE LINE OF FIRE

--- EGOYAN Atom - *see COLLECTION 112 'DANNA Mychael'*
--- EIDELMAN Cliff - *see COLLECTION 293*

128.ELFMAN Danny - Music For A Darkened Theatre  -
MCA (S.Screen): MCAD 11550 (2CD)     *1996*
EDWARD SCISSORHANDS-DOLORES CLAIBORNE-TO DIE FOR-
BLACK BEAUTY-BATMAN RETURNS-MISSION IMPOSSIBLE-SOMM
ERSBY-NIGHTMARE BEFORE CHRISTMAS-DEAD PRESIDENTS-
FREEWAY-AMAZING STORIES and other tracks

129.ELFMAN Danny - Music For A Darkened Theatre
MCA USA (Silva Screen): MCAD 10065 (CD)     *1990*
DICK TRACY-BATMAN-NIGHTBREED-BEETLEJUICE-MIDNIGHT
RUN-DARK MAN-SCROOGED-THE SIMPSONS (TV)-PEE WEE'S
BIG ADVENTURE-BACK TO SCHOOL-WISDOM-TALES FROM THE
CRYPT-ALFRED HITCHCOCK PRESENTS THE JAR-HOT TO TROT
FORBIDDEN ZONE-BIG TOP PEE WEE-BEETLEJUICE CARTOON

130.ELIZABETHAN SERENADE - Best Of BRITISH Light Music
*NAXOS (Select): 8.553515 (CD)*     *1996*
1.BY THE SLEEPY LAGOON *(E.COATES)* 2.MARCH OF THE BO
WMAN 'Robin Hood Suite' *(F.CURZON)* 3.BELLS ACROSS
THE MEADOWS *(A.KETELBEY)* 4.CORONATION SCOT *V.ELLIS)*
5.SKETCH OF A DANDY *(H.WOOD)* 6.WESTMINSTER WALTZ
*(R.FARNON)* 7.MARCH FROM A LITTLE SUITE *(T.DUNCAN)*
8.SAILING BY *(R.BINGE)* 9.JAMAICAN RHUMBA *A.BENJAMIN*
10.KNIGHTSBRIDGE MARCH from 'London Suite' *E.COATES*
11.IN A MONASTERY GARDEN *(A.KETELBEY)* 12.LITTLE SER
ENADE *(E.TOMLINSON)* 13.ROSES OF PICARDY *(H.WOOD)* 14
PUFFIN' BILLY *(E.WHITE)* 15.ELIZABETHAN SERENADE *(R.*
*BINGE)* 16.TOM JONES WALTZ *(E.GERMAN)* 17.VANITY FAIR
*(A.COLLINS)* 18.MARIGOLD *(B.MAYERL)* 19.IN A PERSIAN
MARKET *(A.KETELBEY)* 20.DAM BUSTERS MARCH *(E.COATES)*

131.EMBER YEARS 1:JOHN BARRY/ELIZABETH TAYLOR In London
*PLAY IT AGAIN (S.Screen-Koch): PLAY 002 (CD)*     *1992*
JOHN BARRY: -S/T- to 'Four In The Morning' (65) and
ELIZABETH TAYLOR IN LONDON (63) Music by JOHN BARRY

132.EMBER YEARS 2: JOHN BARRY / ANNIE ROSS
*PLAY IT AGAIN (S.Screen-Koch): PLAY 003 (CD)*     *1992*
JOHN BARRY: FROM RUSSIA WITH LOVE-HIGH GRASS-KINKY-
ZULU STAMP-LONELINESS OF AUTUMN-NGENZENI-BIG SHIELD
ALIKI-TETHA LEYANTO-TROUBADOR-MONKEY FEATHERS-007

ANNIE ROSS:RHYTHM OF THE WORLD-A LOT OF LIVIN'TO DO
LET ME LOVE YOU-ALL THE THINGS YOU ARE-I'M GONNA GO
FISHIN-LIKE SOMEONE IN LOVE-LIMEHOUSE BLUES-HANDFUL
OF SONGS-ALL OF YOU-NATURE BOY-WHAT'S NEW & others
133.ENYA  VARIOUS MUSIC USED IN FILM AND TV taken from
'The Celts' WEA: 4509 91167-2(CD) WX 498C(MC) 1987
'Watermark' WEA: 243875-2 (CD) -4 (MC)        1988
'Shepherd Moons' WEA: 9031 75572-2(CD) -4(MC) 1991
'Memory Of Trees' WEA: 06301287-2 (CD) -4(MC) 1995
'Paint The Sky With Stars' WEA: 3984 20895-2  1997
134.ESSEX David - A NIGHT AT THE MOVIES
POLYGRAM TV: 537 608-2 (CD) -4 (MC)           1997
1.GIRL YOU'LL BE A WOMAN SOON (PULP FICTION) 2.CAN
YOU FEEL THE LOVE TONIGHT (LION KING) 3.CRYING GAME
4.THE WIND BENEATH MY WINGS (BEACHES) 5.STARDUST 6.
TOGETHER IN ELECTRIC DREAMS 7.OH WHAT A CIRCUS (EVI
TA) 8.SEPERATE LIVES WHITE NIGHTS 9.ST.ELMO'S FIRE
10.KISS FROM A ROSE BATMAN FOREVER 11.SOMEWHERE OUT
THERE AN AMERICAN TALE) 12.SILVER DREAM MACHINE 13.
SEA OF LOVE 14.IF I HAD WORDS (ANTHEM) (CHESS)
135.F.A.B.-THUNDERBIRDS - Music world of GERRY ANDERSON
SILVA SCREEN (Koch): FILMCD 124 (CD) FILMC 124 (MC)
ROYAL PHILHARMONIC ORCHESTRA New Digital Recordings
Themes and Suites from STINGRAY-SPACE 1999-JOE 90-
U.F.O.-CAPTAIN SCARLET + 30 min.suite THUNDERBIRDS
MUSIC COMPOSED BY BARRY GRAY and DEREK WADSWORTH
136.FAITH Percy - Summer Place - Percy Faith Orchestra
HALLMARK (Carlton): 30484-2 (CD) -4 (MC)      1996
THEME FROM A SUMMER PLACE-MOON RIVER from BREAKFAST
AT TIFFANY'S)-SOME ENCHANTED EVENING(SOUTH PACIFIC)
WINDMILLS OF YOUR MIND (THOMAS CROWN AFFAIR)-THE
SUMMER OF '42-SUNRISE SUNSET (FIDDLER ON THE ROOF)-
SHADOW OF YOUR SMILE(THE SANDPIPER)-MAYBE SEPTEMBER
(THE OSCAR)-HELLO DOLLY-I COULD HAVE DANCED ALL.(MY
FAIR LADY)-OSCAR-MARIA (WEST SIDE STORY)-TARA'S THE
ME (GONE WITH THE WIND)-NEVER ON SUNDAY-LAURA-MANHA
DE CARNAVAL (BLACK ORPHEUS/ORPHE NEGRO)
137.FAMOUS THEMES (1): Remember These? - Var.Artists
GRASMERE (BMG): GRCD 10 (CD) GRTC 10 (MC)     1986
PUFFIN' BILLY (Childrens Fav)-MUSIC EVERYWHERE (Red
iffusion)-CORONATION SCOT (Paul Temple)-ON A SPRING
NOTE (Pathe Gazette)-RHYTHM ON RAILS Morning Mus-BY
THE SLEEPY LAGOON(Desert Island Discs) HORSE GUARDS
WHITEHALL (Down Your Way)-DEVIL'S GALLOP (Dick Bart
on)-DESTRUCTION BY FIRE (Pathe News)-ALL SPORTS MAR
CH (Pathe News)-SPORTSMASTER (Peter Styvestant)-ALP
INE PASTURES (My Word)-CAVALCADE OF YOUTH (Barlowes
Of Beddington)-DRUM MAJORETTE (Match Of The Day)
ELIZABETHAN SERENADE (Music in Miniature)-MELDOY ON
THE MOVE/YOUNG BALLERINA (The Potter's Wheel)-GIRLS
IN GREY (BBC TV News)-WILLO THE WISP/PORTRAIT OF A
FLIRT/JUMPING BEAN (In Town Tonight)-HORSE FEATHERS
Meet The Huggetts)-JOURNEY INTO MELODY/SAPPHIRES &
SABLES/INVITATION WALTZ (Ring Around The Moon)

--- <u>FARNON Robert</u> - *see COLLECTION 220*
--- <u>FASTBINDER Rainer Werner</u> - *see COLLECTION 289*
--- <u>FAVOURITE THEMES FROM BBC TV & RADIO</u> - *see COLL.402*
138. <u>FAVOURITE TV THEMES</u> - Various Artists
    *MCI (Disc-THE): MCCD 069 (CD) MCTC 069 (MC)*    *1992*
    INSPECTOR MORSE-RUTH RENDELL MYSTERIES-SEVEN FACES
    OF WOMAN-UPSTAIRS DOWNSTAIRS-AGATHA CHRISTIE'S POIR
    OT-A WOMAN OF SUBSTANCE-TALES OF THE UNEXPECTED-THE
    PROFESSIONALS-THE MATCH-THE AVENGERS-FOREVER GREEN-
    NEW ADVENTURES OF BLACK BEAUTY-CHIMERA-LONDON'S BUR
    NING-DR.WHO-THE ONE GAME-WORLD CUP 90-ON THE LINE-
    A HUNDRED ACRES-WISH ME LUCK-SUMMER'S LEASE-ITV ATH
    LETICS-THE GOOD GUYS-CLASSIC ADVENTURE
--- <u>FELLINI Federico</u> - *see COLLECTION 295 'ROTA Nino'*
139. <u>FILM MUSIC VOLUME 2: MUSIQUES DE FILMS</u>  Var.Artists
    *EMI CLASSICS: CZS 569314-2 (2CD)*        *1996*
    JEAN DE FLORETTE: *LA FORZA DEL DESTINO (Verdi)* THE
    HORSEMAN ON THE ROOF: *INTERMEZZO OP.117 No.3 Brahms*
    THE PIANO: *THE HEART ASKS PLEASURE FIRST (M.Nyman)*
    PHILADELPHIA: *ANDREA CHENIER: LA MAMMA MORTA (Giord*
    *ano)* OUT OF AFRICA: *CONCERTOS FOR CLARINET & ORCHES*
    *K.622: (Mozart)* PRETTY WOMAN: *LA TRAVIATA: DAMMI TU*
    *FORZA,O CIELO (Verdi)* BEETHOVEN: *PIANO SONATA NO.14*
    *OP.27 NO.2 (Beethoven)* A ROOM WITH A VIEW: *GIANNI*
    *SCHICCHI: O MIO BABBINO CARO (Puccini)* AMADEUS: *REQ*
    *UIEM AETERNAM (Mozart)* PLATOON: *ADAGIO FOR STRINGS*
    *(Barber)* JEFFERSON IN PARIS: *VIOLIN SONATA NO.12 OP*
    *5: LA FOLLIA (Corelli)* SCHINDLER'S LIST: *MAIN THEME*
    *(Williams)* JEUX INTERDITS: *ROMANCE (-)* DEAD POET'S
    SOCIETY: *ODE TO JOY (SYMPHONY NO.9) (Beethoven)*
    BLUE: *FUNERAL MUSIC (Preisner)* LA GRANDE VADROUILLE
    *DAMNATION OF FAUST: MARCH HONGROISE (Berlioz)* THE
    BEAR: *THE SEASONS: BARCAROLLE (Tchaikovsky)* THE
    MADNESS OF KING GEORGE: *ZADOK THE PRIEST (Handel)*
    THE INCORRUPTIBLES: *RECITAR! VESTI LA GIUBBA from I*
    *PAGLIACCI (Leoncavallo)* LE COLONEL CHABERT: *PIANO*
    *SONATA IN B$^b$ D.960 (Schubert)* FATAL ATTRACTION: *UN*
    *BEL DI VEDREMO (MADAME BUTTERFLY)(Puccini)* LA CRISE
    *TRIO PIANO,VIOLIN,CELLO OP.11 ADGAIO (Beethoven)*
    L'ACCOMPAGNATRICE: *DER HIRT AUF DAM FELSEN D.965*
    *(Schubert)* THE PREDATOR: *FLOWER DUET (LAKME)Delibes*
    BRIDGES OF MADISON COUNTY: *CASTA DIVA from NORMA*
    *(Bellini)* LA MENTEUSE: *CONCERTO FOR PIANO AND ORCHE*
    *STRA NO.3 ALLEGRO CON BRIO (Beethoven)*
140. <u>FILM SPECTACULAR!</u> - Stanley Black & His Orch.  *1997*
    *DERAM (Poly): 844 763-2 (2CD) (Decca Phase 4 reiss)*
    JAMES BOND MEDLEY-GREAT ESCAPE-MAGNIFICENT SEVEN-
    GUNS OF NAVARONE-633 SQUADRON-ON THE WATERFRONT-THE
    LONGEST DAY-SPELLBOUND-BEN HUR-THE ALAMO(DE GUELLO)
    GREEN LEAVES OF SUMMER-STAGECOACH-2001 A SPACE ODYS
    SEY-LAWRENCE OF ARABIA-WEST SIDE STORY-MY FAIR LADY
    CLEOPATRA-GONE WITH THE WIND-SOUND OF MUSIC-CHARADE
    CHIM CHIM CHEREE-LOVE STORY-A LOVE LIKE THIS-SAMSON
    AND DELILAH-LARA'S THEME (DR ZHIVAGO)-CASABLANCA

--- <u>FORD Harrison</u> - *see COLLECTION 212 'INDIANA JONES'*

141. <u>FORMBY George</u> - At The Flicks
*PRESIDENT (BMG): PLCD 554 (CD)* *1996*
1.I COULD MAKE A GOOD LIVING AT THAT 2.BABY *(BOOTS BOOTS)* 3.IT'S IN THE AIR 4.THEY CAN'T FOOL ME *(IT'S IN THE AIR)* 5.GOODNIGHT LITTLE FELLOW GOODNIGHT 6. PARDON ME 7.I'M MAKING HEADWAY NOW 8.I COULDN'T LET THE STABLE DOWN *(COME ON GEORGE)* 9.I WISH I WAS BACK ON THE FARM *(SPARE A COPPER)* 10.COUNT YOUR BLESSINGS AND SMILE 11.OH DON'T THE WIND BLOW COLD *(LET GEORGE DO IT)* 12.THE EMPEROR OF LANCASHIRE 13. YOU'RE EVERYTHING TO ME 14.YOU CAN'TGO WRONG IN THESF *(TURNED OUT NICE AGAIN)* 15.I PLAYED ON MY SPA NISH GUITAR 16.I'D DO IT WITH A SMILE 17.BARMAID AT THE ROSE AND CROWN *(SOUTH AMERICAN GEORGE)* 18.WHEN THE LADS OF THE VILLAGE GET CRACKIN' 19.HOME GUARD BLUES *(GET CRACKIN')* 20.BELL BOTTOM GEORGE 21.IT SERVES YOU RIGHT *(BELL BOTTOM GEORGE)* 22.GOT TO GET YOUR PHOTO IN THE PRESS 23.HILL BILLY WILLY 24. UNCONDITIONAL SURRENDER *(SHE SNOOPS TO CONQUER)*

142. <u>FORMBY George</u> - Very Best Of George FORMBY
*SOUND WAVES (BMG): SWNCD 017 (CD) SWN 017 (MC) 1997*
LEANING ON A LAMP POST-RIDING IN THE TT RACES-AUNTIE MAGGIE'S REMEDY-WHEN I'M CLEANING WINDOWS-WITH MY LITTLE STICK OF BLACKPOOL ROCK-WINDOW CLEAN ER-I'M THE UKELELE MAN-THE LANCASHIRE TOREADOR-SITTING ON THE TOP OF BLACKPOOL TOWER-I DON'T LIKE-BLESS 'EM ALL-MOTHER WHAT'LL I DO NOW-IT'S TURNED OUT NICE AGAIN-FRIGID AIR FANNY-GRANDAD'S FLANELETT NIGHTSHIRT-HI TIDDLEY HI TI ISLAND-MR WU'S A WINDOW CLEANER NOW-WINDOW CLEANER NO.2-OH DON'T THE WIND BLOW COLD-THE EMPEROR OF LANCASHIRE-IN MY LITTLE SNAPSHOT ALBUM-HOME GUARD BLUES

143. <u>FORMBY George</u> - When I'm Cleaning Windows
*PRESIDENT (BMG): PLCD 538 (CD)* *1995*
SITTING ON THE ICE IN THE ICE RINK -WHY DON'T WOMEN LIKE ME *(from BOOTS BOOTS)* / DO DE OH DOH-CHINESE LAUNDRY BLUES-YOU CAN'T STOP ME FROM DREAMING / PLEASURE CRUISE *(ZIP GOES A MILLION)* / KEEP FIT *(KEEP FIT)* / RIDING IN THE TT RACES *(NO LIMIT)* / HINDOO MAN-IT AIN'T NOBODY'S BIZ'NESS WHAT I DO/ GOODY GOODY/I LIKE BANANAS-THE LANCASHIRE TOREADOR A FARMER'S BOY-YOU CAN'T KEEP A GROWING LAD DOWN YOU'RE A LI-A-TY/ WITH MY LITTLE STICK OF BLACKPOOL ROCK-TRAILING AROUND IN A TRAILER-DARE DEVIL DICK-SOMEBODY'S WEDDING DAY-SITTING ON THE SANDS ALL NIG HT-MADAME MOSCOVITCH/WITH MY LITTLE UKELELE IN MY HAND *(OFF THE DOLE)* FANLIGHT FANNY*(TROUBLE BREWING)* WHEN I'M CLEANING WINDOWS *(KEEP YOUR SEATS PLEASE)* LEANING ON A LAMP POST *(FEATHER YOUR NEST)*

--- <u>FROM WARSAW TO HOLLYWOOD</u> - *see COLLECTION 223 KILAR*

144. <u>GALWAY James</u> and PHIL COULTER - Legends
*RCA Victor (BMG): 09026 68776-2 (2CD) -4 (2MC) 1997*
RIVERDANCE-HARRY'S GAME-BELIEVE ME IF ALL THOSE END

EARING YOUNG CHARMS-THE GENTLE MAIDEN-WOMEN OF IREL
AND (Mna Na Ehireann)-THE BATTLE OF KINSDALE (THE
VALLEY OF TEARS)-THE THORNBIRDS-LANNIGAN'S BALL-
KERRY DANCES-DANNY BOY-MUSIC FOR A FOUND HARMONIUM-
LAMENT FOR THE WILD GEESE-MY LAGAN LOVE-NATASHA (An
Cailin Fionn)-ASHOKAN FAREWELL (theme from the TV
series 'The CIVIL WAR')-HOEDOWN

145. GARLAND Judy - Collector's Gems From The MGM Films
*EMI ODEON: CDODEON 22 (7243 854533-2) (CD)       1997*
WALTZ WITH A SWING/AMERICANA-OPERA V.JAZZ-EVERYBODY
SING-YOURS AND MINE-YOUR BROADWAY AND MY BROADWAY-
GOT A PAIR OF NEW SHOES-SUN SHOWERS-DOWN ON MELODY
FARM-WHY BECAUSE-EVER SINCE THE WORLD BEGAN/SHALL I
SING A MELODY-IN BETWEEN-IT NEVER RAINS BUT WHAT IT
POURS-BEI MIR BIST DU SCHOEN-MEET THE BEAT OF MY HE
ART-ZING WENT THE STRINGS OF MY HEART-ON THE BUMPY
ROAD TO LOVE-TEN PINS IN THE SKY-I'M NOBODY'S BABY-
ALL I DO IS DREAM OF YOU-ALONE-IT'S A GREAT DAY FOR
THE IRISH-DANNY BOY-A PRETTY GIRL MILKING HER COW-
SINGIN' IN THE RAIN-EASY TO LOVE-WE MUST HAVE MUSIC
I'M ALWAYS CHASING RAINBOWS-MINNIE FROM TRINIDAD-
EVERY LITTLE MOMENT HAS A MEANING OF IT'S OWN-TOM
TOM THE PIPER'S SON-WHEN I LOOK AT YOU-PAGING MR.GR
EENBACK-WHERE THERE'S MUSIC-JOINT IS REALLY JUMPIN'
DOWN AT CARNEGIE HALL-D'YA LOVE ME-MACK THE BLACK-
LOVE OF MY LIFE-VOODOO-YOU CAN'T GET A MAN WITH A
GUN-THERE'S NO BUSINESS LIKE SHOW BUSINESS-THEY SAY
IT'S WONDERFUL-THE GIRL THAT I MARRY-I'VE GOT THE
SUN IN THE MORNING-LET'S GO WEST AGAIN-ANYTHING YOU
CAN DO-THERE'S NO BUSINESS LIKE SHOW BUSINESS

146. GARRETT Lesley - DIVA! - A Soprano At The Movies
*SILVA SCREEN (Koch): SONG(CD)(C)903 (CD/MC)       1991*
La Boheme (MOONSTRUCK)-Gianni Schicchi (A ROOM WITH
A VIEW)-Rusalka(DRIVING MISS DAISY)-The Marriage Of
Figaro (THE MODERNS)-Carmen (CARMEN JONES)-La Wally
(DIVA)-Lakme Flower Duet (THE HUNGER) *PHILHARMONIA
ORCHESTA (Andrew Greenwood) LESLEY GARRETT Soprano*

147. GARRETT Lesley - Soprano In Hollywood / BBC Concert
Orch conducted/orchestrated by PAUL BATEMAN     *1996*
*SILVA SCREEN (Koch): SILKTVCD 2 (CD) SILKTVC 2 (MC)*
1.WITH A SONG IN MY HEART   2.WHEN YOU'RE AWAY
3.LOVER   4.DANNY BOY   5.LOVE IS WHERE YOU FIND IT
6.ONE NIGHT OF LOVE   7.*GERSHWIN IN HOLLYWOOD Medley*
LOVE WALKED IN/THE MAN I LOVE/LOVE IS HERE TO STAY
8.BEYOND THE BLUE HORIZON 9.SMOKE GETS IN YOUR EYES
10.YESTERDAYS 11.JEALOUSY   12.LONG AGO AND FAR AWAY
13.ONE KISS   14.SO IN LOVE   15.SAILIN' THROUGH

148. GARRETT Lesley - Soprano In Red / Royal Phil.Orches
*SILVA CLASS (Koch): SILKTVCD (SILKTVMC) 1       1995*
WALTZ OF MY HEART / IF LOVE WERE ALL *(BITTER SWEET)*
VILJA *(MERRY WIDOW)* /SOFTLY AS IN A MORNING SUNRISE
WHY DID YOU KISS MY HEART AWAKE/WE'LL GATHER LILACS
*(PERCHANCE TO DREAM)* ROMANCE /LOVER COME BACK TO ME
NUN'S CHORUS / LAURA'S SONG / FINAL ARIA / CAN-CAN

149. GERSHWIN George   George & Ira Gershwin in Hollywood
*EMI SOUNDTRACKS: CDODEON 29 (2CDs)*                *1997*
OVERT.Medley:- SWANEE/SOMEBODY LOVES ME/FASCINATING
RHYTHM/EMBRACEABLE YOU/OH LADY BE GOOD/MAN I LOVE/
I GOT RHYTHM/LIZA/RHAPSODY IN BLUE/STRIKE UP THE
BAND *(from Rhapsody In Blue -S/T-)* SWANEE Al Jolson
SOMEBODY LOVES ME Lena Horne / I CAN'T BE BOTHERED
NOW Fred Astaire /I'LL BUILD A STAIRWAY TO PARADISE
Georges Guetary / THEY CAN'T TAKE THAT AWAY FROM ME
Fred Astaire / FASCINATING RHYTHM Tommy Dorsey Orch
LOVE IS HERE TO STAY Gene Kelly / THEY ALL LAUGHED
Ginger Rogers / EMBRACEABLE YOU Judy Garland /135TH
STREET BLUES John B.Hughes / SUMMERTIME Anne Brown
LET'S CALL THE WHOLE THING OFF Fred Astaire-Ginger
Rogers / BUT NOT FOR ME Ella Fitzgerald / NICE WORK
IF YOU CA GET IT Fred Astaire / LIZA Avon Long /
I'VE GOT A CRUSH ON YOU Gene Kelly / THIRD PRELUDE
RHAPSODY IN BLUE Oscar Levant / STRIKE UP THE BAND
Judy Garland-Mickey Rooney / BOY WHAT LOVE HAS DONE
TO ME Tommy Dorsey Or / SLAP THAT BASS Fred Astaire
AREN'T YOU KIND OF GLAD WE DID Dick Haymes & Betty
Grable / MAN I LOVE Peg La Centra / TREAT ME ROUGH
June Allyson-M.Rooney / A FOGGY DAY Fred Astaire /
YOU'VE GOT WHAT GETS ME *fr:* Girl Crazy / OH LADY BE
GOOD Artie Shaw / HE LOVES AND SHE LOVES F.Astaire
I WAS DOING ALL RIGHT Ella Logan / LOVE WALKED IN
Virginia Verrell / PROMENADE (WALKING THE DOG) *from*
Shall We Dance / BEGINNER'S LUCK Fred Astaire /
S'WONDERFUL Gene Kelly-Georges Guetary / THINGS ARE
LOOKING UP Fred Astaire & The Stafford Sisters /
DELISHIOUS Sally Sweetland / SHALL WE DANCE Fred
Astaire / I GOT RHYTHM Judy Garland / YOU'D BE HARD
TO REPLACE Fred Astaire / IN OUR UNITED STATE Bob
FOSSE / FOR YOU FOR ME FOR EVERYONE Dick Haymes
and Betty Grable
150. GERSHWIN George - Gershwin feat: Daniel Wayenberg-
Cristina Ortiz-Paris Conservatoire Orch (G.Pretre)-
London SO (A.Previn) Hollywood Bowl SO (F.Slatkin)
*EMI CLASSICS: CZS 569 308-2 (2CD)*                *1996*
RHAPSODY IN BLUE-AN AMERICAN IN PARIS-PIANO CONCERT
RHAPSODY NO.2-THREE PRELUDES FOR PIANO-SIX SONGS-
PORGY AND BESS Symphonic Tableau-CUBAN OVERTURE
151. GERSHWIN George Musical Overtures Boston Pops Orch*
*DECCA PHASE 4 (Poly): 443 900-2 (CD)*             *1996*
FUNNY FACE (OVERTURE) / GIRL CRAZY (MUSICAL SUITE)
LET 'EM EAT CAKE (OVERTURE) / OF THEE I SING (OVERT
URE) / OH KAY (OVERTURE) / PRELUDES FOR PIANO (Nos.
1 and 3) / RHAPSODIE FOR PIANO AND ORCHESTRA (No.3)
* conducted by Arthur Fiedler
152. GILBERT & SULLIVAN - Best Of ARIAS and DUETS 1995
*SHOWTIME-MCI (THE): SHOWCD 017(CD) SHOWMC 01/(MC)*
*Featur:* Leslie Garrett-Marilyn Hill Smith-Eric Idle
D'Oyly Carte Opera-Gordon Sandison-Felicity Palmer

*153.* GILTRAP Gordon - Music For The Small Screen
*MUNCHKIN (Grapevine/Polyg): MRCD 1 (CD)*       *1995*
HEARTSONG *(Holiday theme BBC1 1980-85)* THE LAST OF
ENGLAND *(BBC Screen 2 'Will You Love Me Tomorrow')*
SHADY TALES *(Mike Mansfield/Thames - unissued)*
THE LORD'S SEAT *('Working Titles' BBC1 1990)*
HOLIDAY ROMANCE *('Holiday' theme BBC1 1991-1993)*
UNBROKEN PROMISE *(BBC Scr.2 'Close Relations')*
BRUTUS *('World Bowls' theme BBC2 sports series)*
THE CARNIVAL *('Wish You Were Here' Theme, Thames TV)*
HOLD THE BACK PAGE *(BBC1 1985 drama ser)* SUNBURST-
REVELATION HIGHWAY-INDOMITABLE / IN UNISON-LUCKY
*(theme & incid.mus.for YTV's 'Benny On The Common')*
--- GIRL THE DOLL THE MUSIC  - *see COLLECTIONS 349,350*
*154.* GODFATHER SUITE - The Milan Philharmonic Orchestra
*SILVA SCREEN (Koch): FILM(C)(CD) 077*       *1991*
CARMINE COPPOLA conducts the Milan Philharmonic Orc
hestra in selections of music featured in all three
of THE GODFATHER Films (Music: NINI ROTA-C.COPPOLA)
*155.* GOLD 18 Epic Sporting Themes - V.Arts *92 reiss.1994*
*RONCO-TELSTAR (WEA): CDSR 042 (CD) TCSR 042 (MC)*
NESSUN DORMA *(WORLD CUP)*-POP GOES BACH *(SKI SUNDAY-
WINTER OLYMPICS)*-GOLD-BARCELONA *(OLYMPIC GAMES 92)*-
WORLD IN UNION *(WORLD CUP RUGBY91)*-CHARIOTS OF FIRE
*(ATHLETICS)*-GONNA FLY NOW *(BOXING)*-BEETHOVEN'S 9TH
*(OLYMPICS 92)*-VA PENSIERO *(WINTER GAMES92)*-GRANDSTA
ND-TOUR DE FRANCE *CYCLING (1)*-SOUL LIMBO *(CRICKET)*-
THE CHAIN *(MOTOR RACING)*-TUTTI AL MONDO-WORLD IN MO
TION *(FOOTBALL)*-BOLERO *(ICE SKATING)*-QUESTION OF SP
ORT-CHASE SIDE SHOOT UP*(GOLF)*-ATHLETICS-SPORTSNIGHT
*156.* GOLDSMITH Jerry - FRONTIERS Royal Scottish Nat.Orch
*VARESE (Pinn): VSD 5871 (CD)*       *1997*
STAR TREK: THE MOTION PICTURE-ALIEN-LOGAN'S RUN-
TOTAL RECALL-TWILIGHT ZONE: THE MOVIE-STAR TREK:
VOYAGER-STAR TREK: FIRST CONTACT-CAPRICORN ONE-
DAMNATION ALLEY-THE ILLUSTRATED MAN
*157.* GONE WITH THE WIND - The Classic MAX STEINER
*SILVA SCREEN (Koch): FILMCD 144 (CD)*       *1994*
Westminster Philharmonic Orchestra (Kenneth Alwyn)
CASABLANCA-THE CAINE MUTINY-TREASURE OF THE SIERRA
MADRE-A SUMMER PLACE-HELEN OF TROY-DISTANT TRUMPET-
THE ADVENTURES OF MARK TWAIN-GONE WITH THE WIND
*158.* GOODWIN Ron - British Light Music-New Zealand Symph
*MARCO POLO (Select): 8.223518 (CD) |* Orchestra *1996*
633 SQUADRON Main Theme-DRAKE 400 Suite-PUPPET SERE
NADE-NEW ZEALAND SUITE Premier-ARABIAN CELEBRATION-
THE VENUS WALTZ-PRISONERS OF WAR MARCH: The Kriegle
MINUET IN BLUE-THE TRAP Main Theme (London Marathon
Theme)-LANCELOT & GUINEVERE Main Theme-GIRL WITH A
DREAM (all composed and conducted by Ron Goodwin)
*159.* GOODWIN Ron - Conducts Film and TV Themes
*FLYBACK (Chandos): FBCD 2004 (CD)*       *1997*
LONDON MARATHON (Theme from 'The TRAP')-HERE WHERE
YOU ARE-*MEDLEY*: KOJAK/HILL STREET BLUES/STAR TREK/

DYNASTY/DALLAS-HERE'S THAT RAINY DAY- *TRIBUTE TO MIKLOS ROZSA:* BEN HUR main theme/PARADE OF THE CHAR IOTEERS/LOVE THEME/THE RED HOUSE/THE FOUR FEATHERS TROLLEY SONG- *DISNEYTIME SELECT:* ZIP A DEE DOO DAH/ SOMEDAY MY PRINCE WILL COME/I WANNA BE LIKE YOU/ LITTLE APRIL SHOWERS/WHEN YOU WISH UPON A STAR- CARAVAN-GIRL FROM CORSICA- *STEPHEN FOSTER SUITE:* OH SUSANNAH/SWANEE RIVER/BEAUTIFUL DREAMER/CAMPTOWN RACES-BEAUTY AND THE BEAST-FESTIVAL TIME-CANDLESHOE FORCE TEN FROM NAVARONE-MINUET IN BLUE-SPACEMAN AND KING ARTHUR-GIRL WITH THE MISTY EYES-AMAZING GRACE

160. GOODWIN Ron - Golden Sound Of Ron Goodwin
*DISKY (THE-DISC):* GS 86365-2 (CD)                    *1996*
ELIZABETHAN SERENADE-WHERE THE GENTLE AVON FLOWS- THEME FROM LIMELIGHT-BLUE STAR (THE MEDIC THEME)- SCARBOROUGH FAIR-WHERE DO I BEGIN (LOVE STORY)- TARA'S THEME FROM GONE WITH THE WIND-LEGEND OF THE GLASS MOUNTAIN-LONG AGO AND FAR AWAY-GALLOPING HOME THEME FROM ADVENTURES OF BLACK BEAUTY-THE BATTLE OF BRITAIN THEME-MISS MARPLE'S THEME-DANGEROUS MOONLIG HT THEME-ROMEO AND JULIET LOVE THEME-633 SQUADRON- BRAHMS LULLABY-THEME FROM 2001 A SPACE ODYSSEY
see also 'BRITISH LIGHT MUSIC'

161. GOODWIN Ron - Miss Marple Films - Odense Symph.Orch
*LEGEND Impt (Silva Screen):* LXE 706 (CD)           *1993*
New Digital Recordings Of Suites from The Miss Marp le Films and other scores composed by Ron Goodwin MURDER SHE SAID-MURDER AT THE GALLOP-MURDER MOST FO UL-MURDER AHOY-FORCE TEN FROM NAVARONE-LANCELOT AND GUINEVERE. *Ron Goodwin and The ODENSE Symphony Orch*

--- GRAINER Ron - *see COLLECTION 7*

162. GRAY Barry - No Strings Attached BARRY GRAY Orch
*CASTLE CLASS (BMG):* CLACD 204 (CD) 1981 Re-Iss.1990
*The original themes from the ATV 1960's TV series* THUNDERBIRDS-CAPTAIN SCARLETT-STINGRAY-AQUA MARINA WELL DONE PARKER-JOE 90-MYSTERONS Theme / *see also (TV Section)* THUNDERBIRDS-STINGRAY-CAPTAIN SCARLETT

163. GREAT BRITISH EXPERIENCE The - Various Artists
*EMI CLASSICS: CDGB 50 (2CD) TCGB 50 (2MC)*          *1997*
1.DEVIL'S GALLOP *(DICK BARTON)* Charles Williams 2.CALLING ALL WORKERS *(MUSIC WHILE YOU WORK)* Eric Coates 3.WESTMINSTER WALTZ Robert Farnon 4.PUFFIN' BILLY *(CHILDREN'S FAV.)* Edward White 5.HORSE GUARDS WHITEHALL *DOWN YOUR WAY* Haydn Wood 6.IN PARTY MOOD *(HOUSEWIVES CHOICE)* Jack Strachey 7.BY THE SLEEPY LAGOON *(DESERT ISLAND DISCS)* Eric Coates 8.GIRLS IN GREY *(BBC TV NEWSREEL)* Charles Williams 9.SILKS AND SATINS *(EMERGENCY WARD 10 Closing mus)* Peter Yorke 10.MARCH FROM A LITTLE SUITE *(DR.FINLAY'S CASEBOOK)* Trevor Duncan 11.BARWICK GREEN *(THE ARCHERS)* Arthur Wood 12.THE RUNAWAY ROCKING HORSE Edward White 13. GIRL FROM CORSICA Trevor Duncan 14.NON STOP *(ITN NEWS 60's-70's)* John Malcolm 15.SKYSCRAPER FANTASY
*Continued next page...*

GREET BRITISH EXPERIENCE The ...*Continued*

   Donald Phillips 16.HEADLESS HORSEMAN Ron Goodwin 17
ON A SPRING NOTE Sidney Torch 18.SEA SONGS *(BILLY*
*BUNTER OF GREYFRIARS SCHOOL)* Vaughan Williams 19.
CHANGING MOODS *(PC 49 THEME 'ADVENTURES OF PC 49)*
Ronald Hanmer20.A CANADIAN IN MAYFAIR Angela Morley
21.DANCER AT THE FAIR John Fortis 22.LAS VEGAS
*ANIMAL MAGIC* Laurie Johnson 23.STARLIGHT ROOF WALTZ
George Melachrino 24.EVENSONG Easthope Martin 25.
KNIGHTSBRIDGE MARCH *(IN TOWN TONIGHT)* Eric Coates
CD2: MARCHING STRINGS *(TOP OF TGHE FORM)* Ray Martin
2.CORONATION SCOTT *(PAUL TEMPLE)* Vivian Ellis 3.
JUMPING BEAN *SEND FOR SHINER* Robert Farnon 4.SOUND
AND VISION *(ATV OPENING MARCH)* Eric Coates 5.YOUNG
BALLERINA *(TV INTERLUDE:THE POTTER'S WHEEL)* Charles
Williams 6.PARISIAN MODE *(WHAT'S MY LINE)* Wolfe
Phillips 7.HORSE FEATHERS *(MEET THE HUGGETS)* Philip
Green 8.PORTRAIT OF A FLIRT *(IN TOWN TONIGHT. LINK)*
Robert Farnon 9.CAVALCADE OF YOUTH *(THE BARLOWS OF*
*BEDDINGTON)* Jack Beaver 10.RUNNING OFF THE RAIL
Clive Richardson 11.SAILING BY *(RADIO 4 LATE NIGHT*
*SHIPPING FORECAST)* Ronald Binge 12.WINTER SUNSHINE
George Melachrino 13.PARAKEETS AND PEACOCKS Jack
Coles 14.MELODY ON THE MOVE Clive Richardson 15.
HIGH HEELS Trevor Duncan 16.THE HAUNTED BALLROOM
Geoffrey Toye 17.ALL STRINGS AND FANCY FREE Sidney
Torch 18.SAPPHIRES AND SABLES Peter Yorke 19.DANCE
OF AN OSTRACISED IMP Frederic Curzon 20.SMILE OF A
LATIN Trevor Duncan 21.BEACHCOMBER Clive Richardson
22.DREAMING Archibald Joyce 23.CONCERT JIG Ernest
Tomlinson 24.A QUIET STROLL *(TV FARMING)* Charles
Williams 25.MARCH FROM LITTLE SUITE Malcolm Arnold
164.GREAT BRITISH FILM MUSIC - NATIONAL PHILH.ORCH *
*DECCA PHASE 4 (Poly): 448 954-2 (CD)      reiss.1996*
1.RICHARD III *(by WILLIAM WALTON)* 2-5.ANNA KARENINA
*(by CONSTANT LAMBERT)* 6-7 OLIVER TWIST *(ARNOLD BAX)*
8-9.AN IDEAL HUSBAND *(ARTHUR BENJAMIN)*10.ESCAPE ME
NEVER*(ERICH WOLFGANG KORNGOLD)* 11.49TH PARALLEL *(R.*
*VAUGHAN WILIAMS)* 12-16.THINGS TO COME*(ARTHUR BLISS)*
* conducted by BERNARD HERRMANN
165.GREAT FILM MUSIC - NATIONAL PHILHARMONIC ORCHEST *
*DECCA PHASE 4 (Poly): 443 899-2 (CD)          1996*
JOURNEY TO THE CENTRE OF T.EARTH-SEVENTH VOYAGE OF
SINBAD-THE DAY THE EARTH STOOD STILL-FAHRENHEIT 451
THREE WORLDS OF GULLIVER *conduct: Bernard Herrmann
166.GREAT FILM SONGS (You Must Remember This) Var.Arts
*HAPPY DAYS-Conifer (BMG): 75605 52283-2 (CD) -4(MC)*
1.AM I BLUE *(ON WITH THE SHOW-1929)* Ethel Waters
2.FALLING IN LOVE AGAIN *(BLUE ANGEL-1930)* Marlene
Dietrich 3.A BENCH IN THE PARK *(KING OF JAZZ-1930)*
Paul Whiteman Orchestra 4.GOODNIGHT VIENNA *(1932)*
Jack Buchanan 5.MEDLEY: TINKLE TINKLE TINKLE/OVER
MY SHOULDER *(EVERGREEN-1934)* Jessie Matthews 6.ONE

MY SHOULDER *(EVERGREEN-1934)* Jessie Matthews 6.ONE
NIGHT OF LOVE *(1934)* Grace Moore 7.OKAY TOOTS *(KID
MILLIONS-1934)* Eddie Cantor 8.SMOKE GETS IN YOUR
EYES *(ROBERTA-1935)* Irene Dunne 9.LULLABY OF BROAD
WAY *(GOLD DIGGERS OF 1935)* Winifred Shaw 10.LOVE IS
EVERYWHERE *(LOOK UP AND LAUGH-1935)* Gracie & Tommy
Fields 11.TOP HAT WHITE TIE & TAILS *(TOP HAT-1935)*
Fred Astaire 12.ISN'T THIS A LOVELY DAY *(TOP HAT-
1935)* Ginger Rogers 13.I'VE GOT A FEELIN' YOU'RE
FOOLIN' *(BROADWAY MELODY OF 1946)* Eleanor Powell
14.WHEN DID YOU LEAVE HEAVEN *SING BABY SING-1936)*
Tony Martin 15.THIS YEAR'S KISSES *(ON THE AVENUE-19
37)* Alice Faye 16.I'VE GOT MY LOVE TO KEEP ME WARM
*(ON THE AVENUE-1937)* Dick Powell 17.WILL YOU REMEMB
ER *(MAYTIME 1937)* Jeanette McDonald and Nelson Eddy
18.JEEPERS CREEPERS *(GOING PLACES-1938)* Louis Armst
rong) 19.I GO FOR THAT*(ST.LOUIS BLUES-1938)* Dorothy
Lamour 20.IT'S FOOLISH BUT IT'S FUN *(SPRING PARADE-
1940)* Deanna Durbin 21.CHATTANOOGA CHOO CHOO *(SUN
VALLEY SEREANDE-1941)* Glenn Miller & His Orchestra
22.I YI YI YI YI (LIKE YOU VERY MUCH)*(THAT NIGHT IN
RIO-1941)* Carmen Miranda 23.MOONLIGHT BECOMES YOU
*(ROAD TO MOROCCO-1942)* Bing Crosby 24.TROLLEY SONG
*(MEET ME IN ST.LOUIS-1944)* Judy Garland 25.THE MORE
I SEE YOU *(DIAMOND HORSEHOE-1945)* Dick Haymes 26.
OUT OF NOWHERE*(YOU CAME ALONG-1945)* Helen Forrest
167.GREAT SPORTS THEMES - London Theatre Orchestra
*EMPORIO (DISC-THE): EMPRCD 715 (CD)* 1997
MATCH OF THE DAY-BBC CRICKET-BBC GRANDSTAND-BBC
GRAND PRIX-5 LIVE SPORTS REPORT-BBC GOLF-POT BLACK-
WIMBLEDON-ITV THE BIG MATCH-RUGBY SPECIAL-HORSE OF
THE YEAR-ITV WORLD OF SPORT-SKI SUNDAY-SPORTSNIGHT-
BBC SNOOKER-A QUESTION OF SPORT
168.GREAT TV THEMES 4 CDs Of 80 Classic TV Themes 1991
*TRING INT (Target): TFP 029 (4CDs) MCTPF 029 (4MC)*
*VOL 1* MIAMI VICE-CHEERS-HAPPY DAYS-QUINCY-CHARLIE'S
ANGELS-CROSSROADS-LITTLE HOUSE ON T.PRAIRIE-OWEN MD
NIGHT COURT-MUPPET SHOW-BONANZA-UPSTAIRS DOWNSTAIRS
MASH-FAME-DUKES OF HAZZARD-MINDER-KIDNAPPED-HUNTER-
STAR TREK / *VOL 2* DALLAS-MOONLIGHTING-CHIPS-HAWAII
5.0-AGAINST THE WIND-HARRY'S GAME-THIS IS YOUR LIFE
HIGH CHAPARRAL-SESAME ST.-RICH MAN POOR MAN-THORNBI
RDS-DOCTOR AT LARGE-BARETTA-THOSE WERE THE DAYS-SUP
ERMAN-MIAMI VICE-SIMON & SIMON-VEGAS-SOAP-VIRGINIAN
*VOL 3* L.A.LAW-DYNASTY-ALL CREATURES GREAT AND SMALL
EASTENDERS-EMMERDALE FARM-STARSKY AND HUTCH-VAN DER
VALK-ROCKFORD FILES-COVER UP-HOWARD'S WAY-MAGNUM-IN
CREDIBLE HULK-MAN FROM THE MOUNTAINS-KUNG FU-WHO PA
YS THE FERRYMAN-KOJAK-MARTIN EDEN-KNIGHT RIDER-9TO5
ALIAS SMITH AND JONES / *VOL 4* HILL ST.BLUES-A.TEAM
MATCH OF THE DAY-NO HONESTLY-ODD COUPLE PAUL TEMPLE
MAN FROM UNCLE-PERSUADERS-REILLY ACE OF SPIES-THE
WOMBLES-SAILING-RAGAMUFFIN-SMURFS-TAXI-THIRTYSOMETH
ING-WHEELS-PETER GUNN-DAD'S ARMY-PEYTON PLACE

169. <u>GREAT WAR MOVIE THEMES</u> - Silver Screen Orchestra
*DISKY (THE-Disc): DC 88069-2 (CD)* 1997
DAS BOOT-PLATOON-BRIDGE ON T.RIVER KWAI-APOCALYPSE
NOW-BALLAD OF THE GREEN BERETS-GUNS OF NAVARONE-
KELLY'S HEROES-THE LONGEST DAY-IS PARIS BURNING-THE
DEER HUNTER-SCHINDLER'S LIST-LAWRENCE OF ARABIA-
A BRIDGE TOO FAR-DEATH OF A SOLDIER
170. <u>GREAT WESTERN THEMES</u> - GEOFF LOVE Orchestra
*MFP (EMI): CC 204 (CD)* 1988
BIG COUNTRY (Another Day Another Sunset)-FISTFUL OF
DOLLARS-SHANE (Call Of The Far-Away Hills)-HOW THE
WEST WAS WON-ALAMO (Green Leaves Of Summer)-MAGNIFI
CENT7-FOR A FEW DOLLARS MORE-WILD BUNCH Song-BALLAD
OF CAT BALLOU-MAVERICK-TheVIRGINIAN-LEGEND OF JESSE
JAMES-HIGH NOON (Do Not Forsake Me)-GOOD THE BAD &
THE UGLY-GUNFIGHT AT OK CORRAL-TRUE GRIT-ONCE UPON
A TIME IN THE WEST-MAN WHO SHOT LIBERTY VALANCE-LAR
AMIE-HOMBRE-BIG VALLEY-RAWHIDE-GUN LAW-WAGON TRAIN
171. <u>GREATEST CLASSICAL MOVIE ALBUM</u> - Various Artists
*TELSTAR (WEA): TCD 2880 (2CD) STAC 2880 (MC)* 1997
1.ZADOK THE PRIEST (Handel) *MADNESS OF KING GEORGE*
Consort Of London 2.RIDE OF THE VALKYRIES (Wagner)
*APOCALYPSE NOW* Philharmonic 3.LA MAMMA MORTA (Giord
ano) *PHILADELPHIA* Lila Larinova 4.THEME (Williams)
*SCHINDLER'S LIST* Tamsin Little 5.THE HEART ASKS PLE
ASURE FIRST/THE PROMISE (NYMAN) *THE PIANO* Johannes
Erdbeer 6.ARIA (Bach) *SILENCE OF THE LAMBS* Chen Pi-
Hsien 7.ADAGIO (Mozart) *OUT OF AFRICA* Emma Johnson
8.FLOWER DUET (Delibes) *TRUE ROMANCE* Mary O'Hara
9.THEME (Mitchell) *TENANT OF WILDFELL HALL* Richard
G.Mitchell 10.ADAGIO FOR STRINGS (Barber) *ELEPHANT
MAN/PLATOON* L.S.O. 12.THEME (Burgon) *BRIDESHEAD REV
ISITED* Geoffrey Burgon 13.MODERATO PIANO CONC.NO.2
(Rachmaninov) *BRIEF ENCOUNTER* Grand State Symph Orc
14.O MIO BABBINO CAR (Puccini) *A ROOM WITH A VIEW*
Royal Phil.Orch 15.DAMMI TU FORZA O CIELO (Verdi)
*PRETTY WOMAN* Czecho-Slovak Radio S.O. 16.CAN-CAN
(Offenbach) *PETER'S FRIENDS* R.P.O. <u>*DISC2:*</u> 1.SPIRIT
OF MAN (R.Strauss) *2001 A SPACE ODYSSEY* L.S.O. 2.
WEDDING MARCH (Mendelssohn) *FOUR WEDDINGS AND A FUN
ERAL* Royal Scottish Orch 3.NESSUN DORMA (Puccini)
*WITCHES OF EASTWICK* Orchestra of the Bolshoi State
Academy Theatre 4.ALLEGRO (Handel) *DEAD POET'S SOCI
ETY* L.S.O. 5.ADAGIO (Bach) *TRULY MADLY DEEPLY* Paolo
Pandolfo-Rinaldo Alessandrini 6.REVERIES-PASSIONS
(Berlioz) *SLEEPING WITH THE ENEMY* Czecho-Slovak Rad
io Symph.Orch 7.EBBEN DE ANDRO LONTANA (Catalini)
*DIVA* Miriam Gauci 8.ANDANTE (Mozart) *ELVIRA MADIGAN*
Howard Shelley 9.ADAGIO (Marcello) *THE FIRM* Derek
Wickens 10.THEME (Morricone) *THE MISSION* Richard
Harvey-Richard Morgan 11.AIR ON A G.STRING (Bach)
*SEVEN* R.P.Orch 12.INTERMEZZO (Mascagni) *GODFATHER 3*
L.S.O. 13.TARA'S THEME (Steiner) *GONE WITH THE WIND*
R.P.Orc 14.ALLEGRO (Handel) *DANGEROUS LIAISONS* Paul

Nicholson 15.UN BEL DI VEDREMO (Puccini) *FATAL ATTR ACTION* Czecho-Slovak Radio S.O. 16.REQUIEM AETERNAM (Mozart) *AMADEUS* Magdelena Hajossyova, Slovak S.Orc

172.GREATEST HITS OF THE MUSICALS - Various Artists
*EMI TV: CDEMTVD 119 (2CD) TCEMTVD 119 (2MC)* 1996
TONIGHT Natalie Wood MUSIC OF THE NIGHT Michael Cra wford I COULD HAVE DANCED ALL NIGHT Audrey Hepburn SINGIN' IN THE RAIN Gene Kelly BLESS YORE BEAUTIFUL HIDE Howard Keel LUCK BE A LADY Dave Willets IF I WERE A RICH MAN Topol HAPPY TALK South Pacific Cast HELLO DOLLY Louis Armstrong CABARET Liza Minnelli FOR ME AND MY GAL Judy Garland & Gene Kelly ALMOST LIKE BEING IN LOVE Gene Kelly SECRET LOVE Doris Day ON A CLEAR DAY YOU CAN SEE FOREVER Shirley Bassey I'VE GROWN ACCUSTOMED TO HER..Rex Harrison CAMELOT Richard Harris BIG SPENDER Shirley MacLaine TELL ME IT'S NOT TRUE Barbara Dickson OH WHAT A BEAUTIFUL MORNING O.B.Cast ANYTHING YOU CAN DO Ethel Merman & Ray Middleton FOOD GLORIOUS FOOD O.L.Cast THAT'S EN TERTAINMENT Fred Astaire DON'T CRY FOR ME ARGENTINA Julie Covington MEMORY Elaine Paige SOME ENCHANTED EVENING South Pacific Cast SUMMERTIME Sarah Vaughan DAY BY DAY Robin Lamont LOSING MY MIND Julia McKenz ie 76 TROMBONES O.B.Cast IF I RULED THE WORLD Harry Secombe S'WONDERFUL Gene Kelly MAKE BELIEVE Kathryn Grayson-Howard Keel TOO DARN HOT Ann Miller I DON'T KNOW HOW TO LOVE Yvonne Elliman A COUPLE OF SWELLS Fred Astaire-Judy Garland HOW LONG HAS THIS BEEN GOING ON Audrey Hepburn ONE Ensemble SEND IN THE CL OWNS Judy Collins NEW YORK NEW YORK OBC IMPOSSIBLE DREAM Gordon MacRae I KNOW HIM SO WELL Elaine Paige Barbara Dickson ANY DREAM WILL DO O.C.R. OVER THE RAINBOW Judy Garland

173.GREATEST MOVIE THEMES London Philharmonic Orch & *
*MFP-EMI Gold: CD(TC)MFP 6236 (CD/MC)* 1996
1.JAWS 2.THE DEERHUNTER ('CAVATINA') 3.STAR WARS 4. GONE WITH THE WIND ('TARA'S THEME') 5.LAWRENCE OF ARABIA 6.APOCALYPSE NOW ('RIDE OF THE VALKYRIES') 7.RAIDERS OF THE LOST ARK 8*THE MAGNIFICENT SEVEN 9.THE LONGEST DAY 10.A BRIDGE TOO FAR 11.GOOD THE BAD AND THE UGLY 12.ET 13.CLOSE ENCOUNTERS OF THE THIRD KIND 14.10 ('BOLERO') 15.LOVE STORY 16.DOCTOR ZHIVAGO 17*BUTCH CASSIDY & SUNDANCE KID ('RAINDROPS KEEP FALLING ON MY HEAD') *Cinema Sound Stage Orch.

174.GREATEST SHOW THEMES Broadway Theatre Orch.& Chorus
*MFP-EMI Gold: CD(TC)MFP 6235 (CD/MC)* 1996
1.CATS: OVERTURE/MEMORIES 2.OLIVER: OLIVER/WHERE IS LOVEI'D DO ANYTHING/AS LONG AS HE NEEDS ME/CONSIDER YOURSELF 3.WEST SIDE STORY: I FEEL PRETTY/MARIA/TON IGHT/AMERICA 4.OKLAHOMA: THE FARMER AND THE COWMAN/ OKLAHOMA/PEOPLE WILL SAY WE'RE IN LOVE/OUT OF MY DR EAMS/OH WHAT A BEAUTIFUL MORNING/POOR JUD IS DEAD/ SURREY WITH THE FRINGE ON TOP/MANY A NEW DAY/KANSAS CITY/I CAN'T SAY NO 5.EVITA: BUENOS AIRES/DON'T CRY

CITY/I CAN'T SAY NO 5.EVITA: BUENOS AIRES/DON'T CRY
FOR ME ARGENTINA/HIGH FLYING ADORED/SHE ISA DIAMOND
ANOTHER SUITCASE IN ANOTHER HALL  6.MY FAIR LADY:
I COULD HAVE DANCED ALL NIGHT/ON THE STREET WHERE
YOU LIVE/WOULDN'T IT BE LOVELY/SHOW ME/THE EMBASSY
WALTZ/GET ME TO THE CHURCH ON TIME/I'VE GROWN ACCUS
TOMED TO HER FACE/WITH A LITTLE BIT OF LUCK 7.THE
SOUND OF MUSIC: SOUND OF MUSIC/HOW CAN LOVE SURVIVE
LONELY GOATHERD/MY FAVOURITE THINGS/SIXTEEN GOING
ON SEVENTEEN/SO LONG FAREWELL/EDELWEISS/AN ORDINARY
COUPLE/NO WAY TO STOP IT/CLIMB EVERY MOUNTAIN

175. GREATEST TV THEMES (LWT themes) - South Bank Orch
  MFP-EMI Gold: CD(TC)MFP 6234 (CD/MC)            1996
  1.LONDON'S BURNING 2.FOREVER GREEN 3.PROFESSIONALS
  4.AGATHA CHRISTIE'S POIROT 5.TO HAVE AND TO HOLD 6.
  UPSTAIRS DOWNSTAIRS 7.THOMAS AND SARAH 8.THE GOOD
  GUYS 9.THE GENTLE TOUCH 10.BOUQUET OF BARBED WIRE
  11.PARTNERS IN CRIME 12.BUDGIE ('THE LONER') 13.
  WISH ME LUCK 14.LOVE FOR LYDIA 15.LILLIE 16.NEW ADV
  ENTURES OF BLACK BEAUTY 17.DEMPSEY AND MAKEPEACE

176. GREATEST WESTERN MOVIE & TV SOUNDTRACKS VOL.2 V.Art
  BEAR FAMILY (Rollercoaster): BCD 15983 (2CD)    1997
  BALLAD OF CAT BALLOU Nat King Cole and Stubby Kaye
  HIGH CHAPPARAL David Rose Orch THE MAN FROM LARAMIE
  Al Martino LONELY MANTennessee Ernie Ford EL DORADO
  George Alexander & Mellowmen THE MAN WITH TRUE GRIT
  Glen Campbell FURY Prairie Chief WICHITA Tex Ritter
  OLD TURKEY BUZZARD Jose Feliciano BRONCO J.Gregory
  LOVE IN THE COUNTRY Limelighters SUGARFOOT Sons Of
  The Pioneers STAGEVOACH TO CHEYENNE Wayne Newton
  GREEN LEAVES OF SUMMER Brothers Four MARMALADE MOLA
  SSES & HONEY Andy Williams CIMARRON CITY Hollywood
  S.O. SHERIFF OF COCHISE Prairie Chiefs WAGON TRAIN
  Johnny O'Neill LEGEND OF WYATT EARP Shorty Long 26
  MEN Lee Adrian WIND THE WIND Dean Martin BUTTONS
  AND BOWS Bob Hope MAN WITH TRUE GRIT Glen Campbell

--- GREENAWAY Peter - see COLLECTION 275 NYMAN Michael
--- GREGORY John - see COLLECTION 246

177. GRUSIN Dave - Two For The Road with HENRY MANCINI
  GRP-MCA (BMG): GRP 9865-2 (CD) 1997       PETER GUNN-
  DREAMSVILLE-MR.LUCKY-MOMENT TO MOMENT-BABY ELEPHANT
  WALK-TWO FOR THE ROAD-DAYS OF WINE AND ROSES-HATARI
  WHISTLING AWAY THE DARK-SOLDIER IN THE RAIN

178. HALLOWEEN: Film Music Of JOHN CARPENTER        1993
  SILVA SCREEN (Koch): FILMCD 113 (CD) / DARK STAR
  HALLOWEEN-THE FOG-ESCAPE FROM NEW YORK-BIG TROUBLE
  IN LITTLE CHINA-CHRISTINE-STARMAN-THE THING-PRINCE
  OF DARKNESS-THEY LIVE-ASSAULT ON PRECINCT 13

179. HAMMER Jan - Escape From Television
  MCA (BMG): MCLD 19133 (CD)                     1987
  CROCKETT'S THEME-THERESA-COLOMBIA-RM CAY-THE TRIAL
  AND THE SEARCH-TUBBS AND VALERIE-FOREVER TONI-LAST
  FLIGHT-RICO'S BLUES-BEFORE THE STORM-NIGHT TALK-
  MIAMI VICE MAIN THEME-FOREVER TONIGHT Extended Mix

180. HAMPSON Thomas - Best Of Broadway: Leading Man
EMI CLASS: CDC 555 249-2(CD) EL 555 249-4(MC) 1996
LEADING MAN *(BEST OF BROADWAY)* ALL THE THINGS YOU
ARE *(VERY WARM FOR MAY)* BRING HIM HOME *(LES MISERAB
LES)* MUSIC OF THE NIGHT *(THE PHANTOM OF THE OPERA)*
SOLILOQUY *(CAROUSEL)* GIGI *(GIGI)* HEY THERE *(PAJAMA
GAME)* UNUSUAL WAY *(NINE)* NOT A DAY GOES BY *(MERRILY
WE ROLL ALONG)* HOW COULD I EVER KNOW *(THE SECRET
GARDEN)* IF I CAN'T LOVE HER *(BEAUTY AND THE BEAST)*
IF EVER I WOULD LEAVE YOU *(CAMELOT)*

--- HANNA-BARBERA - *see COLLECTION 370*
--- HARLE John - *see COLLECTION 407*

181. HARVEY Richard - Shroud For A Nightingale:
The Film and Television Music of Richard HARVEY
SILVA SCREEN *(Koch)*: FILMCD 172 (CD) 1996
GAME SET AND MATCH-GBH-A SMALL DANCE-ASSAM GARDEN-
DEADLY ADVICE-DEFENCE OF THE REALM-DOCTOR FINLAY-
THE WIMBLEDON POISONER-HOSTAGES-SHAPE OF THE WORLD
TO EACH HIS OWN-DANCING WITH THE DEAD-JAKE'S PROGRE
SS-DOOMSDAY GUN also including music theme 'Elegy'
from the P.D.JAMES THRILLERS 'DEVICES AND DESIRES'/
'SHROUD FOR A NIGHTINGALE'/'COVER HER FACE'

182. HATCH Tony & His Orchestra - The Best of Tony Hatch
SEQUEL-CASTLE *(BMG)*: NEMCD 920 (CD) 1996
1.NAKED CITY THEME *(May)* 2.JOANNA *(Hatch-Trent)* 3.
DICK POWELL THEATRE THEME *(Gilbert)* 4.SOUL COAXING
*Polnareff)* 5.MONDO KANE THEME (MORE) *(Ortolani-Oliv
iero-Newell)* 6.MUSIC TO WATCH GIRLS BY *Velona-Ramin*
7.CROSSROADS THEME *(Hatch)* 8.DOWNTOWN *(Hatch)* 9.MAN
ALIVE THEME *(Hatch)* 10.THE DOCTORS THEME *(Hatch)* 11
SPORTSNIGHT THEME *(Hatch)*12.SOUNDS OF THE SEVENTIES
*(Hatch)* 13.MEMORIES OF SUMMER (LOVE STORY THEME-TV)
*(Hatch)* 14.AN OCCASIONAL MAN *(Martin-Blane)* 15.THE
CHAMPIONS THEME *(Hatch)* 16.CALL ME *(Hatch)* 17.EMMER
DALE THEME *(Hatch)* 18.BIRDS *(Hatch)* 19.HADLEIGH *(Ha
tch)* 20.MAORI *(Hatch)* 21.MR.& MRS. (BE NICE TO EACH
OTHER) *(Hatch-Trent)* Jackie Trent 22.WHILE THE CITY
SLEEPS *(Hatch-Trent)* 23.WILLOW WALTZ (TIM FRAZER'S
THEME) *(Watters)* 24.BEST IN FOOTBALL *(Hatch)* 25.
DEVIL'S HERD *Anthony (Hatch)* 26.THE SURREY WITH THE
FRINGE ON THE TOP*(Rodgers-Hammerstein)* 27.LA PALOMA
*Yradier(Hatch)* 28.THE WORLD AT WAR *(Davis)* 29.A MAN
AND A WOMAN*(Lai-Barouh)* 30.OUT OF THIS WORLD*(Siday)*

--- HELLO CHILDREN EVERYWHERE: - *see COLLECTION 408*

183. HENDRICKS Barbara - When You Wish Upon A Star *
EMI CLASS: CDC 556177-2 (CD) EL 556177-4 (MC) 1996
SOME DAY MY PRINCE WILL COME-WHENH YOU WISH UPON A
STAR-BIBBIDI BOBBIDI BOO-IN THE GOLDEN AFTERNOON-
PART OF YOUR WORLD-WITH A SMILE AND A SONG-BELLA
NOTTE-VERY GOOD ADVICE-ZIP A DEE DOO DAH-CRUELLA DE
VILLE-A DREAM IS A WISH YOUR HEART MAKES-I'M LATE-
CIRCLE OF LIFE-FEED THE BIRDS-CHIM CHIM CHER-EE
BEAUTY AND THE BEAST-WHISTLE WHILE YOU WORK
* songs arranged & conducted by Jonathan Tunick

184. HEROES OF THE AIR - Central Band Of Royal Air Force
CFP (EMI): CDCFP 4666 (CD) TCCFP 4666 (MC)        1992
BATTLE OF BRITAIN SUITE (William Walton)-SPITFIRE
PRELUDE AND FUGUE (William Walton)-CONQUEST OF THE
AIR (Arthur Bliss)-BATTLE OF BRITAIN SUITE (Wilfred
Josephs)-COASTAL COMMAND (Vaughan Williams) reis 95

185. HERRMANN Bernard - Citizen Kane: The Classic Film
                      Scores Of Bernard Herrmann
RCA Victor (BMG): GD 80707 (CD)        Re-issued 1991
ON DANGEROUS GROUND:The Death Hunt-CITIZEN KANE:Pre
lude-Xanadu-Snow Picture-Themes and Variations-Aria
from Salammbo (with Kiri Te Kanawa)-Rosebud-Finale
BENEATH THE 12-MILE REEF:The Sea-Lagoon-Descending-
The Octopuss-Homecoming-HANGOVER SQUARE:Concerto Ma
cabre for Piano & Orchestra-WHITE WITCH DOCTOR:Talk
ing Drums-Prelude-The Riverboat-Petticoat Dance-The
Safari-Tarantula-The Lion-Nocturne-Abduction Of The
BakubaBoy-The Skulls-Lonni Bound By Ropes-Departure

186. HERRMANN Bernard - Classic Fantasy Film Scores
CLOUD NINE (BMG-Conif): ACN 7014 (CD only)        1989
Symphonic Suites From 4 Films (All Music by Bernard
Herrmann): THREE WORLDS OF GULLIVER-MYSTERIOUS ISLA
ND-SEVENTH VOYAGE OF SINBAD-JASON AND THE ARGONAUTS

187. HERRMANN Bernard - Film Scores - Los Angeles P.O.
SONY CLASSICS: SK 62700 (CD)        1996
1.THE MAN WHO KNEW TOO MUCH PRELUDE 2.PSYCHO SUITE
SUITE FOR STRINGS 3.MARNIE SUITE 4.NORTH BY NORTHWE
ST OVERURE 5.VERTIGO SUITE 6.TORN CURTAIN MAINTHEME
7.FAHRENHEIT 451 SUITE 8.TAXI DRIVER MAIN THEME

188. HERRMANN Bernard - Music From Great Film Classics *
DECCA PHASE 4 (Poly): 448 948-2 (CD)        reiss:1996
1-4.CITIZEN KANE   5.JANE EYRE   6-7.DEVIL AND DANIEL
WEBSTER   8-9.SNOWS OF KILIMANJARO   10-14.MYSTERIOUS
ISLAND   15-18.JASON AND THE ARGONAUTS
*National Philharmonic Orchestra (Bernard Herrmann)

189. HERRMANN Bernard - Partnership In Terror: HITCHCOCK
City Of Prague Philharmonic conduct: Paul Bateman
SILVA SCREEN (Koch): SILVAD 3010 (CD)        1996
digital recordings of themes & suites from ALFRED
HITCHCOCK films scored by BERNARD HERRMANN
PSYCHO / NORTH BY NORTHWEST / MARNIE / THE MAN WHO
KNEW TOO MUCH / THE TROUBLE WITH HARRY / VERTIGO
TORN CURTAIN (rejected score)

190. HERRMANN Bernard - Torn Curtain: Classic Film Music
SILVA SCREEN (Koch): FILMCD 162 (CD)        1995
CAPE FEAR-CITIZEN KANE-PSYCHO-GHOST AND MRS.MUIR-
OBSESSION-SNOWS OF KILIMANJARO-VERTIGO-TAXI DRIVER-
ON DANGEROUS GROUND plus suite from fantasy films:-
THREE WORLDS OF GULLIVER/THE 7TH VOYAGE OF SINBAD/
MYSTERIOUS ISLAND/JASON AND THE ARGONAUTS +rejected
score TORN CURTAIN (replaced by JOHN ADDISON score)

191. HESS Nigel -Maigret & Other TV Themes by Nigel HESS
FLY (FLY Direct) FLY(CD)(MC) 104        1992
MAIGRET-CLASSIC ADVENTURES-PERFECT SCOUNDRELS-A HUN

DRED ACRES-CHIMERA (Rosheen Du)-MAIGRET (Paris)-GRO
WING PAINS-ARDEN OF FAVERSHAM-FOR TONIGHT(Atlantis)
US GIRLS-TITMUSS REGAINED-HENRY VIII (Stage)

192. HESS Nigel -Screen Notes: Nigel HESS + Chameleon +
London Film Orch + Royal Shakespeare Comp.Ensemble
*FLY-AIR EDEL (FLY Direct): MYRACD 101 (CD)* *1997*
1.THE ONE GAME 2.WYCLIFFE 3.HETTY WAINTHROP INVESTI
GATES 4.SUMMER'S LEASE 5.DANGERFIELD 6.JUST WILLIAM
7.CHIMERA 8.PERFECT SCOUNDRELS 9.ANNA OF THE FIVE
TOWNS 10.MAIGRET (1992) 11.A WOMAN OF SUBSTANCE
12.CAMPION 13.CLASSIC ADVENTURE 14.UNAY GARM
15.ALL PASSION SPENT 16.TESTAMENT 17.VANITY FAIR
18.MUCH ADO ABOUT NOTHING 19.CYRANO DE BERGERAC
20.HENRY VIII 21.NEW YORK

193. HILL SMITH Marilyn - Sings IVOR NOVELLO - Chandos
Concert Orchestra conducted by Stuart Barry *1993*
*CHANDOS (Chandos): CHAN 9142 (CD)*
SOMEDAY MY HEART WILL AWAKE *(KINGS RHAPSODY)*-PRIMRO
SE *(DANCING YEARS)*-LOVE IS MY REASON *(PERCHANCE TO
DREAM)*-DARK MUSIC *(ARC DE TRIOMPHE)*-THE LITTLE DAMO
ZEL-WHEN THE GYPSY PLAYED *(GLAMOROUS NIGHT)*-ON SUCH
A NIGHT AS THIS *(GAY'S THE WORD)*-FLY HOME LITTLE HE
ART *(KINGS RHAPSODY)*-KEEP THE HOME FIRES BURNING-
MUSIC IN MAY *(CARELESS RAPTURE)*-A VIOLIN BEGAN TO
PLAY *(KINGS RHAPSODY)*-SPRING OF THE YEAR-MY DEAREST
DEAR *(DANCING YEARS)*-FINDER PLEASE RETURN*(GAY'S THE
WORD)*-LOOK IN MY HEART *(VALLEY OF SONG)*-WHEN I CURT
SIED TO THE KING *(PERCHANCE TO DREAM)*-WE'LL GATHER
LILACS *PERCHANCE TO DREAM)*-FAIRY LAUGHTER-GLAMOROUS
NIGHT-WHY IS THERE EVER GOODBYE *(CARELESS RAPTURE)*

194. HITCHCOCK Alfred - Dial M For Murder
Czech Symphony Orchestra conducted by Paul Bateman
*SILVA SCREEN (Koch): FILMCD 137 (CD)* *1993*
New Digital Recordings Of Suites From A.H.Films
DIAL M FOR MURDER *(composed by DIMITRI TIOMKIN)*
UNDER CAPRICORN *(RICHARD ADDINSELL)* TOPAZ *(MAURICE
JARRE)* REBECCA and SUSPICION *(FRANZ WAXMAN)* SPELLB
OUND *(MIKLOS ROZSA)* VERTIGO-NORTH BY NORTHWEST-MAR
NIE-PSYCHO *(BERNARD HERRMANN)* FRENZY *(RON GOODWIN)*

195. HITCHCOCK Alfred - Master Of Mayhem
San Diego Symphony Orch.conducted by Lalo Schifrin
*SION (Direct): SION 18170 (CD)* *1997*
1.INVISIBLE THIRD:Overture 2.ALFRED HITCHCOCK THEME
3.VERTIGO:Suite 4.MARNIE:Suite 5.PSYCHO:Intro/The
Murder/City) 6.REBECCA:Suite 7.REAR WINDOW:Intro/
Rhumba/The Ballet/The Finale 8.ROLLERCOASTER:Theme
9.BULLITT 10.MANNIX:Theme 11.DIRTY HARRY:Suite 12.
MISSION IMPOSSIBLE: Plot/Theme * cond Lalo Schifrin

196. HITCHCOCK Alfred - Movie Thrillers
London Philharmonic Orchestra cond.Bernard Herrmann
*DECCA PHASE 4 (Poly): 443 895-2 (CD)* *reissued 1996*
Suites from: PSYCHO / MARNIE / NORTH BY NORTHWEST
VERTIGO / 'A Portrait Of Hitch' : NIGHTMARE / THE
TROUBLE WITH HARRY * conducted by Bernard Herrmann

197.HITCHCOCK Alfred - To Catch A Thief: A History Of
Hitchcock Vol.2 City Of Prague P.O. (Paul Bateman)
*SILVA SCREEN (Koch): FILMCD 159 (CD)* 1995
THE 39 STEPS (1935 vers)-THE LADY VANISHES-LIFEBOAT
ROPE-STAGE FRIGHT-TO CATCH A THIEF-STRANGERS ON A
TRAIN-REAR WINDOW-THE TROUBLE WITH HARRY-VERTIGO-
NORTH BY NORTHWEST-TORN CURTAIN-FAMILY PLOT

--- HITCHOCK Alfred - *see COLLECTION 189*

198.HITS FROM THE MOVIES - Various Original Artists
MFP (EMI): CDMFP 6138 (CD) TCMFP 6138 (MC) 1995
CRYING GAME *Boy George* HEAT IS ON *(Beverly Hills
Cop) Glenn Frey* AXEL F *(Beverly Hills Cop) Harold
Faltermeyer* THE POWER OF LOVE *(Back To The Future)
Huey Lewis & News* NOTHING HAS BEEN PROVED *(Scandal)
Dusty Springfield & Pet Shop Boys* MORE THAN A WOMAN
*(Saturday Night Fever) Tavares* CALL ME *(American Gi
golo) Blondie* BORN TO BE WILD *(Easy Rider) Steppenw
olf* SISTERS ARE DOIN'IT FOR THEMSELVES *(Just Like A
Woman) Annie Lennox-Aretha Franklin* EVERYBODY'S TAL
KIN' *Nilsson* MIDNIGHT COWBOY *John Barry* JOY TO THE
WORLD *(Big Chill) Three Dog Night* WARMTH OF THE SUN
*Good Morning Vietnam) Beach Boys* WOODSTOCK *Matthews
Southern Comfort* GONNA FLY NOW *(Rocky) Bill Conti*

199.HOLLYWOOD - San Diego Symph.Orch cond:Lalo Schifrin
*SION (Direct): SION 18150 (CD)* 1997
1.SUPERMAN:March 2.RAIDERS OF THE LOST ARK:March 3.
BRIDGE OVER THE RIVER KWAI:March 4.CAPTAIN FROM CAS
TILLE:Conquest March 5.GREAT ESCAPE:March 6.PATTON:
March 7.RETURN OF THE JEDI:Parade Of The Ewoks/Impe
ial March 8.MUSIC MAN:76 Trombones 9.WHAT DID YOU
DO IN THE WAR DADDY: Statue Of Liberty March 10:
APOCALYPSE NOW: Ride Of The Valkyries 11.ARMED FORC
ES Medley 12.HUNT FOR RED OCTOBER:Hymn Of The Red
Army13.CINERAMA MARCH 14.DIRTY DOZEN:March 15.GREAT
WALDO PEPPER:March 16.JOHN PHILIP SOUSA STORY:Stars
and Stripes Forever/Liberty Bell/Washington Post/
Manhattan Beach/El Captain/Stars & Stripes Forever

200.HOLLYWOOD DIRECTORS: Music From The Films Of STEVEN
SPIELBERG - City Of Prague Philharm. (Paul Bateman)
*SILVA SCREEN Treasury (Koch): SILVAD 3505 (CD)* 1997
1:JAWS 2:SCHINDLER'S LIST 3:RAIDERS OF THE LOST ARK
4:INDIANA JONES AND THE TEMPLE OF DOOM 5:INDIANA
JONES AND THE LAST CRUSADE 6:1941 March 7:E.T. 8:
HOOK 9:JURASSIC PARK 10:SCHINDLER'S LIST piano vers
11:and 12: CLOSE ENCOUNTERS OF THE THIRD KIND
*all music composed by JOHN WILLIAMS* tpt: 53.55

201.HOLLYWOOD HEROES - City Of Prague Philharmonic Orch
(Paul Bateman/Nic Raine/Kenn.Alwyn/Derek Wadsworth)
*SILVA SCREEN Treasury (Koch): SILVAD 3501 (CD)* 1997
1:GREAT ESCAPE *(E.BERNSTEIN)* 2:DANCES WITH WOLVES
*(J.BARRY)* 3:RAIDERS OF THE LOST ARK *(J.WILLIAMS)* 4:
HIGH ROAD TO CHINA *(J.BARRY)* 5:MAD MAX III BEYOND
THUNDERDOME *(M.JARRE)* 6:THE ALAMO *(D.TIOMKIN)* 7:
BORN ON THE 4TH OF JULY *(J.WILLIAMS)* 8:EL CID *(M.*

ROZSA) 9:ZULU *(J.BARRY)* 10:OUT OF AFRICA *(J.BARRY)*
11:OUTLAW JOSEY WALES *(J.FIELDING)* 12:TORN CURTAIN
*(J.ADDISON)* 13:ROBIN AND MARIAN *(JOHN BARRY)* 14:
CLIFFHANGER *(T.JONES)*                          *tpt: 58.44*

202. HOLLYWOOD TOUGH GUYS - City Of Prague Philharmonic
(Paul Bateman/Nic Raine) / London Screen Orchestra
(Mike Townend) / Mark Ayres / Daniel Caine
*SILVA SCREEN Treasury (Koch): SILVAD 3506 (CD) 1997*
1:TERMINATOR *(B.FIEDEL* 2:BLADE RUNNER *(VANGELIS)* 3:
BIG TROUBLE IN LITTLE CHINA *J.CARPENTER* 4:SPARTACUS
*(A.NORTH)* 5:ROCKY 2 *(B.CONTI)* 6:SUPERMAN *J.WILLIAMS*
7:VILLA RIDES *(M.JARRE)* 8:CAPE FEAR *(B.HERRMANN)* 9:
MONTE WALSH *(J.BARRY)* 10: ONCE UPON A IIME IN THE
WEST *(E.MORRICONE)* 11:PROFESSIONALS *(M.JARRE)* 12:
TARAS BULBA *(F.WAXMAN)* 13:LICENCE TO KILL *(J.BARRY)*
14:SERPICO *(M.THEODORAKIS)*                     *tpt: 57.36*

203. HOLLYWOOD'S GREATEST HITS VOL.1 ERICH KUNZEL cond:
Cincinnati Pops Orchestra with William Tritt, piano
*TELARC (BMG-Con): CD 80168 (CD)                    1987*
20TH CENTURY FOX FANFARE-OVERTURE fromCAPTAIN BLOOD
TARA'S THEME from GONE WITH THE WIND-PARADE OF THE
CHARIOTEERS from BEN HUR-Theme from EXODUS-LARA'S
THEME from DOCTOR ZHIVAGO-THEME from LAWRENCE OF AR
ABIA-LOVE THEME from ROMEO AND JULIET-GOLDFINGER-
THEME from LOVE STORY-THEME from A SUMMER PLACE-THE
ME from JAWS-THEME from THE SUMMER OF'42-THEME from
ROCKY-THEME from TERMS OF ENDEARMENT-MAIN THEMEfrom
OUT OF AFRICA-THEME from CHARIOTS OF FIRE

204. HOORAY FOR HOLLYWOOD! - Various Artists
*MCI (Disc-THE): MCCD 266 (CD) MCTC 266 (MC)    1996*
1.I WISH I WERE IN LOVE AGAIN Judy Garland 2.WITH A
SONG IN MY HEART Perry Como 3.BOYS IN THE BACKROOM
Marlene Dietrich 4.HAPPY TIMESDanny Kaye 5.TENEMENT
SYMPHONY Tony Martin 6.MOONGLOW (THEME FROM PICNIC)
Morris Stoloff 7.SUNSHINE CAKE Bing Crosby 8.JOHNNY
GUITAR Peggy Lee 9.BEAT OUT DAT RHYTHM ON A DRUM
Pearl Bailey 10.SOMETHING'S GOTTA GIVE Fred Astaire
11.HIGH AND THE MIGHTY Dimitri Tiomkin 12.FRIENDLY
PERSUASION Pat Boone 13.WORRY ABOUT TOMORROW Eddie
Fisher 14.LULLABY IN BLUE Eddie Fisher & Debbie Rey
olds 15.ON THE SUNNY SIDE OF THE STRFFT Gogi Grant
16.COME DANCE WITH ME Mario Lanza 17.PINK PANTHER
Henry Mancini 18.THE RHYTHM OF LIFE Sammy Davis Jnr

205. HORNE Lena - At MGM: 'Ain't It The Truth'
*EMI SOUNDTRACKS: CDODEON 32 (CD)                   1997*
JUST ONE OF THOSE THING-SPRING-AIN'T IT THE TRUTH-
LIFE'S FULL OF CONSEQUENCES-HONEY IN THE HONEYCOMB
HONEYSUCKLE ROSE-YOU'RE SO INDIFF'RENT-JERICHO-
BRAZILIAN BOOGIE-SOMEBODY LOVES ME-TETE A TETE AT
TEA TIME-SOLID POTATO SALAD-PAPER DOLL-TREMBLING
LEAF-LOVE-CAN'T HELP LOVIN' DAT MAN-WHY WAS I BORN
BILL-WIIERE OR WHEN-LADY IS A TRAMP-BABY COME OUT OF
THE CLOUDS-IF YOU CAN DREAM-YOU GOT LOOKS

206.HORROR! - Monsters Witches and Vampires / Var.Orch
SILVA SCREEN Treasury (Koch): SILVAD 3507 (CD) 1997
1:OMEN (J.GOLDSMITH) 2:BRIDE OF FRANKENSTEIN (Franz
WAXMAN) 3:DRACULA (J.BERNARD) 4:TASTE THE BLOOD OF
DRACULA (J.BERNARD) 5:DRACULA HAS RISEN FROM THE
GRAVE (J.BERNARD) 6:HORRORS OF THE BLACK MUSEUM (G.
SCHURMANN) 7:HALLOWEEN (J.CARPENTER) 8:PRINCE OF DA
RKNESS (J.CARPENTER) 9:THEY LIVE(CARPENTER-HOWARTH)
10:WITCHFINDER GENERAL (P.FERRIS) 11:DEVIL RIDES
OUT (J.BERNARD) 12:HUNGER (Flower Duet from Lakme)
(DELIBES, sung by Lesley Garrett) 13:CURSE OF THE
WEREWOLF (B.FRANKEL) 14:VAMPIRE CIRCUS (D.WHITAKER)
207.HORROR! - Westminster Philharm.Orch (Kenneth Alwyn)
SILVA SCREEN (Koch): FILMCD 175 (CD)        1996
HORRORS OF THE BLACK MUSEUM (GERARD SCHURMANN 1959)
THE HAUNTING HUMPHREY SEARLE 63) CORRIDORS OF BLOOD
(BUXTON ORR 62) NIGHT OF THE DEMON (CLIFTON PARKER
1957) ABOMINABLE SNOWMAN (HUMPHREY SEARLE 1957) THE
WITCHFINDER GENERAL (PAUL FERRIS 1968) CURSE OF THE
MUMMY'S TOMB (CARLO MARTELLI 64) KONGA (GERARD SCHU
RMANN 1961) FIEND WITHOUT A FACE (BUXTON ORR 1957)
THE DEVIL RIDES OUT (JAMES BERNARD 1968)  THE CURSE
OF THE WEREWOLF (BENJAMIN FRANKEL 1961)
208.HORROR FILM COLLECTION  Classic Italian Soundtracks
DRG (Pinn): DRGCD 32903 (CD)                1995
DARIO'S THEME (musical tribute to Dario Argento)
(Marco Werba) IL TRONO DI FUOCO (THRONE OF THE FIRE
1970 Bruno Nicolai) /LA NOTTE DEI DIAVLOI (NIGHT OF
THE DEVILS 72 Giorgio Caslini) / 7 NOTE IN NERO (7
NOTES IN BLACK 1977 Vince Tempera) / LA CRIPTA E L'
INCUBO (NIGHTMARE CRYPT 64 Carlo Savina) / PROFONDO
ROSSO (DEEP RED 1975 special suite(Giorgio Caslini)
L'ISOLA MISTERIOSA E IL CAPITANO NEMO (MYSTERIOUS
ISLAND OF CAPTAIN NEMO 73 Gianni Ferrio) /IN MONACO
(THE MONK 72 Pierro Piccione) / TERRORE NELLO SPAAZ
IO (PLANET OF THE VAMPIRES 1965 Gino Martinuzzi Jr)
PASSI DI MORTE PER DUTI NEL BUIO (DEADLY STEPS LOST
IN THE DARK 1976 Riz Ortolani)
209.HORROR OF DRACULA The - Music from Hammer Movies
SILVA SCREEN (Koch) FILMCD 708 (CD)         1992
THE HORROR OF DRACULA (58)-DRACULA: PRINCE OF DARKN
ESS (66)-TASTE THE BLOOD OF DRACULA (70) All Music
scored by James Bernard. Narrator: Christopher Lee
Recording includes sound effects & symphonic score
210.HORROR THEMES - Various Artists           1997
SUMMIT (Sound & Media): SUMCD 4122 (CD) THE FLY-THE
THING-THE FOG-CARRIE-PSYCHO-POLTERGEIST 3-EXORCIST-
HELLRAISER-HALLOWEEN-AMITYVILLE HORROR-FRIDAY THE
13TH-VERTIGO-SILENCE OF THE LAMBS-ROSEMARY'S BABY
211.HOW THE WEST WAS WON: CLASSIC WESTERN FILM SCORES 1
City Of Prague Philharmonic Orchestra (Nic Raine)
SILVA SCREEN (Koch): FILMCD 173 (CD)        1996
THE MAGNIFICENT SEVEN (ELMER BERNSTEIN) HIGH PLAINS
DRIFTER (DEE BARTON) GETTYSBURG SUITE RANDY EDELMAN

THE PROFESSIONALS *(MAURICE JARRE)* BUFFALO GIRLS *LEE HOLDRIDGE* THE WILD BUNCH *(JERRY FIELDING)* THE WILD ROVERS *(JERRY GOLDSMITH)* HOW THE WEST WAS WON Suite *(ALFRED NEWMAN)*

212. INDIANA JONES Music From The Films Of HARRISON FORD
*SILVA SCREEN (Koch): FILMCD 154 (CD)*                    *1994*
PATRIOT GAMES-WITNESS-REGARDING HENRY-PRESUMED INNO
CENT-FUGITIVE-STAR WARS-RETURN OF THE JEDI-EMPIRE
STRIKES BACK-MOSQUITO COAST-HANOVER STREET-BLADE
RUNNER-RAIDERS O.T.LOST ARK-INDIANA JONES & TEMPLE
OF DOOM-INDIANA JONES & LAST CRUSADE-FORCE 10 FROM
NAVARONE *City Of Prague Philharm.Orch:-Paul Bateman*

213. INSTRUMENTAL MOODS - Various Original Artists
*VIRGIN (EMI): VTCD 65 (CD) VTMC 65 (MC)*                *1995*
RIVERDANCE John Anderson Concert Orch / CACHARPAYA
Incantation /RETURN TO INNOCENCE Enigma / YEHA-NOHA
Sacred Spirit / THE CELTS *(WOGAN'S ISLAND)* Enya /
SENTINEL Mike Oldfield / SAMBA PA TI Santana /
ALBATROSS Fleetwood Mac /LOVE'S THEME FROM MIDNIGHT
EXPRESS Giorgio Moroder / ADIEMUS *(DELTA AIRWAYS)*
Adiemus / SONGBIRD Kenny G / CAVATINA John Williams
DON'T CRY FOR ME ARGENTINA Shadows /INSPECTOR MORSE
THEME Barrington Pheloung / BRIDEHEAD REVISITED THE
ME *(VOLKSWAGEN)* Geoffrey Burgon / SOLDIER SOLDIER
Jim Parker / CHI-MAI Ennio Morricone / STRANGER ON
THE SHORE *(VOLKSWAGEN)* Acker Bilk /PEOPLE'S CENTURY
People's Century Orchestra / PANIS ANGELICUS from
THE CHOIR Anthony Way

214. JARRE Maurice - Film Music By MAURICE JARRE
*MCI (Disc-THE): MCCD(MCTC) 277 (CD/MC)*                *1996*
Themes and Suites 1.DOCTOR ZHIVAGO SUITE 2.BUILDING
THE BARN *WITNESS* 3.CARPE DIEM *DEAD POETS SOCIETY* 4.
BOMBAY MARCH *PASSAGE TO INDIA* 5.VICTORIA 6.JACOB'S
LADDER 7.RYAN'S DAUGHTER SUITE 8.GORILLAS IN THE
MIST 9.GHOST 10.TO THE TOP OF THE WORLD 11.FATAL
ATTRACTION 12.LAWRENCE OF ARABIA SUITE

215. JARRE Maurice - Lean By Jarre Tribute To DAVID LEAN
*MILAN (BMG): 10131-2 (CD) 10131-4 (MC)*                *1992*
ROYAL PHILHARMONIC ORCH (Maurice Jarre) live record
ing at The Barbican 1992 - REMEMBRANCE-OFFERING-and
Suites from David Lean's: RYAN'S DAUGHTER-A PASSAGE
TO INDIA-DOCTOR ZHIVAGO-LAWRENCE OF ARABIA
see also 'DOCTOR ZHIVAGO'

216. JAZZ AT THE CINEMA - Various Artists
*SONY JAZZ: 487 460-2 (CD)*                             *1997*
1.DON'T CRY FOR ME ARGENTINA *EVITA* Stan Getz 2.
AUTUMN LEAVES *LES PORTES DE LA NUIT* Chet Baker 3.
LAURA Ray Bryant 4.SOMETHING'S COMING *WEST SIDE
STORY* HI-LOS 5.IT AIN'T NECESSARILY SO *PORGY & BESS*
Aretha Franklin 6.GET ME TO THE CHURCH ON TIME *MY
FAIR LADY* Andre Previn 7.AS TIME GOES BY *CASABLANCA*
Supersax & L.A.Voices 8.BLUES DE LA PLUME *MILOU EN
MAI* Stephane Grappelli 9.EXODUS SONG *EXODUS* Marion
Williams 10.TONIGHT *WEST SIDE STORY* Ray Bryant

--- JOHNSON Laurie - *see COLLECTIONS 294,409*

217. JOLSON, Al - Al Jolson At Warner Bros 1926-1936
*EMI ODEON: CDODEON 24 (7243 854537-2) (CD)* 1997
APRIL SHOWERS-ROCK A BYE YOUR BABY WITH A DIXIE MEL
ODY-DIRTY HANDS DIRTY FACE-TOOT TOOT TOOTSIE-BLUE
SKIES-MOTHER OF MINE-I STILL HAVE YOU-MY MAMMY-IT
ALL DEPENDS ON YOU-I'M SITTING ON TOP OF THE WORLD
SPANIARD THAT BLIGHTED MY LIFE-THERE'S A RAINBOW RO
UND MY SHOULDER-GOLDEN GATE-SONNY BOY-BACK IN YOUR
OWN BACK YARD-USED TO YOU-I'M IN SEVENTH HEAVEN-LET
ME SING AND I'M HAPPY-ACROSS THE BREAKFAST TABLE
LOOKING AT YOU-WHY DO THEY ALL TAKE THE NIGHT BOAT
TO ALBANY-LIZA LEE-LITTLE SUNSHINE-ABOUT A QUARTER
TO NINE-I LOVE TO SING

218. JONES Salena - In Hollywood: Making Love
*TER VIP (MCI-THE): CDVIR 8328 (CD)* 1997
1.MAKING LOVE 2.FASCINATION *(LOVE IN THE AFTERNOON)*
3.AN AFFAIR TO REMEMBER 4.THE WIND BENEATH MY WINGS
*BEACHES)* 5.DAYS OF WINE AND ROSES 6.NEARNESS OF YOU
7.I WILL ALWAYS LOVE YOU *(THE BODYGUARD)* 8.LONG AGO
AND FAR AWAY*(COVER GIRL)* 9.THE SHADOW OF YOUR SMILE
*(SANDPIPER)* 10.MOONGLOW *(PICNIC)* 11.THE SONG IS YOU
*(MUSIC IN THE AIR)* 12.MY FOOLISH HEART 13.UNCHAINED
MELODY *(GHOST)* 14.TRUE LOVE *(HIGH SOCIETY)* 15.
PRETEND 16.LOVE WALKED IN *(THE GOLDWYN FOLLIES)*

219. JOPLIN Scott King Of Ragtime Richard Zimmerman,pno
*LASERLIGHT-DELTA (Targ-BMG): 55 542 (3CD Set)* 1994
CD1.MAPLE LEAF RAG-HARMONY CLUB WALTZ-AUGUSTAN CLUB
WALTZ-PEACHTREE RAG-SWIPESY CAKE WALK-ORIGINAL RAGS
GREAT CRUSH COLLISION MARCH-EASY WINNERS-STRENUOUS
LIFE-RAGTIME DANCE-ELITE SYNCOPATIONS-LITTLE BLACK
BABY-PALM LEAF RAG-THE FAVORITE-THE CASCADES-SARAH
SARAH DEAR-ROSEBUD MARCH-BINKS WALTZ-ROSE LEAF RAG
WHEN YOUR HAIR IS LIKE THE SNOW CD2.THE ENTERTAINER
MARCH MAJESTIC-WEEPING WILLOW-THE SYCAMORE-COUNTRY
CLUB-SCHOOL OF RAGTIME-SOMETHING DOING-STOPTIME RAG
EUPHONIC SOUNDS-FELICITY RAG-FIG LEAF RAG-SCOTT JOP
LIN'S NEW RAG-WALL STREET RAG-PARAGON RAG-PINEAPPLE
RAG-ANTOINETTE-SNORING SAMPSON-GLADIOLUS RAG-SEARCH
LIGHT RAG-THE NONPAREIL CD3.SENSATION-FROLIC OF THE
BEARS-KISMET RAG-SILVER SWAN RAG-LILY QUEEN-HIGHLIG
HTS FROM TREEMONISHA-REAL SLOW DRAG-PRELUDE TO ACT3
THE CHRYSANTHEMUM-BREEZE FROM ALABAMA-I AM THINKING
OF MY PICKANINNY DAYS-LOVIN' BABE-PLEASANT MOMENTS-
A PICTURE OF HER FACE-CLEOPHA-LEOLA

220. JOURNEY INTO MELODY - Robert FARNON
*HAPPY DAYS-Conifer (BMG): 75605 52269-2 (2CD)* 1996
CD1 1.JOURNEY INTO MELODY 2.STATE OCCASION 3.STRING
TIME 4.HOW BEAUTIFUL IS NIGHT 5.JUMPING BEAN 6. A
STAR IS BORN 7.PORTRAIT OF A FLIRT 8.ALL SPORTS
MARCH *(BIG NIGHT OUT)* 9.THE COMIC MYSTIC *(JUST WILL
IAM'S LUCK)* 10-12.THREE IMPRESSIONS SUITE: HIGH STR
EET / IN A CALM / MANHATTAN PLAYBOY 13.MELODY FAIR
14.RUSH HOUR 15.HUCKLE BUCKLE 16.THE PEANUT POLKA

17.PROMENADE OVERTURE 18.HALL OF FAME 19.PINCE-NEZ
AND ASPIDISTRAS 20.SEVENTH HEAVEN 21.POW WOW 22.
ROYAL OCCASION 23.PLAYTIME 24.WORLD SERIES 25.
ALMOST LULLABY 26.POODLE PARADE 27.JOANNE 28.ALCAN
HIGHWAY 29.OPENINGS AND ENDINGS *(PANORAMA 1950's)*
30.PROSCENIUM *(ARMCHAIR THEATRE)* CD2 1.WESTMINSTER
WALTZ 2.DERBY DAY 3.MID OCEAN 4.SWING HOE 5.MALAGA
6.PROMISE OF SPRING 7.EN ROUTE 8.TO A YOUNG LADY 9.
OUT OF TOWN MARCH 10.SUMMER LOVE 11.MOOMIN 12.LAZY
DAY 13-15.THREE MORE IMPRESSIONS SUITE: MR.PUNCH /
FIRST WALTZ / DOMINION DAY 16.SCENIC GRANDEUR 17.
FRONTIERSMAN 18.STARDOM 19.JOCKEY ON THE CAROUSEL
*(MAINLY FOR WOMEN)* 20.LA CASITA MIA 21.OPEN SKIES
22.BIRD CHALMER 23.HOLIDAY FLIGHT 24.NEW HORIZONS
25.LITTLE MISS MOLLY 26.HYMN TO THE COMMONWEALTH
27.HEADLAND COUNTRY 28.CITY STREETS

221.JOURNEY TO NEXT - B.Carter-D.Gillespie-Q.Jones
*LIGHTYEAR ENT (Pinn.Imports): 54168-2 (CD)* 1997
*MUSIC FOR JOHN & FAITH HUBLEY'S ANIMATED CLASSICS*
1.COSMIC EYE (1985) Benny Carter 2.URBANISSIMO 1966
Benny Carter 3.VOYAGE TO NEXT(1973) Dizzy Gillespie
4.HARLEM WEDNESDAY (1956) Benny Carter 5.PEOPLE PEO
PLE PEOPLE (74) Benny Carter 6.ADVENTURES OF AN *56
Benny Carter 7.OF MEN AND DEMONS (69) Quincy Jones

222.KHACHATURIAN FILM SUITES - Armenian Philharm.Orch.*
*ASV (Koch): CDDCA 966 (CD)* 1997
ADMIRAL USHAKOV (1953)-PEPO (1934)-PRISONER NUMBER
217 (1945)-SECRET MISSION (1950) UNDYING FLAME
(1956) *conducted by L.Tjeknavorian & recorded 1995

223.KILAR Wojciech - FROM WARSAW TO HOLLYWOOD
*MILAN (BMG): 74321 45972-2 (CD)* 1997 BRAM STOKER'S
DRACULA-DEATH AND THE MAIDEN-LA LIGNE D'OMBRE-CHRON
IQUE DES EVENEMENTS AMORREUX-LA TERRE DE LA GRANDE
PROMESSE-FULL GALLOP-BILAN TRIMESTRIEL-CONTRACT-L'A
NNEE DU SOLEIL CALME-WHEREVER YOU ARE-FATHER KOLBE-
LIFE FOR LIFE-HASARD-JALOUSIE ET MEDECINE-LEPREUSE

224.KORNGOLD Erich Wolfgang - The Warner Bros Years
*EMI ODEON: CDODEON 13* 1996
CAPTAIN BLOOD-GREEN PASTURES-ANTHONY ADVERSE-PRINCE
AND THE PAUPER-ADVENTURES OF ROBIN HOOD-JAUREZ-THE
PRIVATE LIVES OF ELIZABETH & ESSEX-SEA HAWK-THE SEA
WOLF KINGS ROW-CONSTANT NYMPH-DEVOTION-BETWEEN TWO
WORLDS-OF HUMAN BONDAGE-ESCAPE ME NEVER-DECEPTION

--- KUNZEL Erich - see CINCINNATI POPS

225.LADYKILLERS The - Music From Glorious EALING Films
Royal Ballet Sinfonia conducted by Kenneth Alwyn
*SILVA SCREEN (Koch): FILMCD 177 (CD)* 1997
THE MAN IN THE WHITE SUIT *(1951-BENJAMIN FRANKEL)*
PASSPORT TO PIMLICO *(1949-GEORGES AURIC)*
THE TITFIELD THUNDERBOLT *(1952-GEORGES AURIC)*
THE LAVENDER HILL MOB *(1951-GEORGES AURIC)* THE
CRUEL SEA *(1953-ALAN RAWSTHORNE)* THE CAPTIVE HEART
*(1946-ALAN RAWSTHORNE)* SARABAND FOR DEAD LOVERS
*(1948-ALAN RAWSTHORNE)* WHISKY GALORE *(1949-ERNEST*

LADYKILLERS The ...*Continued*
*(1948-ALAN RAWSTHORNE)* WHISKY GALORE *(1949-ERNEST IRVING)* KIND HEARTS AND CORONETS *(1949-MOZART)* THE MAN IN THE SKY *(1956-GERARD SCHURMANN)* THE LADYKILLERS *(1955-TRISTRAM CARY)* THE OVERLANDERS *(1946-JOHN IRELAND)*

226. LAI Francis - A MAN AND A WOMAN / The Very Best Of
*HALLMARK (Carlton): 305562 (CD) 305564 (MC)*        *1996*
BILITIS-LOVE STORY-THE BLUE ROSE-EMOTION-HAPPY NEW YEAR-LOVE IN THE RAIN-SEDUCTION-IMTIMATE MOMENTS-PAR LE SANG DES AUTRES-A MAN AND A WOMAN-LIVE FOR LIFE-AFRICAN SUMMER-SUR NOTRE ETOILE-LA RONDE-LES UNES ET LES AUTRES-SMIC SMAC-SOLITUDE-WHITECHAPEL

227. LANZA Mario - The Ultimate Collection - Mario Lanza
*RCA VICTOR (BMG): 74321 18574-2 (CD) -4 (MC)*        *1994*
BE MY LOVE-DRINK DRINK DRINK-LA DONNA E MOBILE-AVE MARIA-DANNY BOY-GRANADA-BECAUSE YOU'RE MINE-THE LOV ELIEST NIGHT OF THE YEAR-VALENCIA-SONG OF INDIA-THE DONKEY SERENADE-BECAUSE-O SOLE MIO-VESTI LA GIUBBA-SERENADE-FUNICULI FUNICULA-GOLDEN DAYS-ARRIVERDERCI ROMA-YOU'LL NEVER WALK ALONE-BELOVED-COME PRIMA-E LUCEVAN LE STELLE-SANTA LUCIA-I'LL WALK WITH GOD

--- LEAN David - *see COLLECTION 215 'JARRE Maurice'*

228. LEGRAND Michel - Windmills Of Your Mind: Very Best
*HALLMARK (Carlton): 30557-2 (CD) -4 (MC)*        *1996*
THE SUMMER OF 42-WHERE LOVE BEGINS-THEY SIMPLY FADE AWAY-STREET WHERE THEY LIVED-OLD LOVERS NEVER DIE-ON THE ROAD-THE WINDMILLS OF YOUR MIND-CONCERTO FOR CABS-DO YOU COME HERE OFTEN-IN LOVE IN NORMANDY-PARIS WAS MADE FOR LOVERS-PAVANNE FOR PEOPLE-WHERE LOVE ENDS-SEA AND SKY *(vocal by Dusty Springfield)*-A PLACE IN PARIS *(vocal by Matt Monro)*-I STILL SEE YOU (from The GO-BETWEEN)

229. LET'S HAVE A LAUGH! 18 Great British Comedy Themes
London Studio Orchestra
*EMPORIO (DISC): EMPRCD 750 (CD)*        *1997*
HANCOCK'S HALF HOUR-ON THE BUSES (Happy Harry)-MAN ABOUT THE HOUSE (Up To Date)-MEN BEHAVING BADLY 2.4 CHILDREN-MONTY PYTHON'S FLYING CIRCUS (Liberty Bell)-SOME MOTHERS DO 'AVE 'EM-FAWLTY TOWERS-BLACKADDER-PORRIDGE-RISING DAMP-DICK EMERY SHOW-STEPTOE AND SON (Old Ned)-TERRY AND JUNE (Bell Hop) GOOD LIFE-DOCTOR IN THE HOUSE (Bond Street Parade)

230. LEVY Louis & Gaumont British Orchestra: Movie Music
*EMPRESS (Koch): RAJCD 884 (CD)*        *1996*
1. *STRIKE UP THE BAND* a)2. *IT'S LOVE AGAIN:* IT'S LOVE b)-TONY'S IN TOWN 3.GOT TO DANCE MY WAY TO HEAVEN-I NEARLY LET LOVE GO SLIPPING THROUGH MY FINGERS b) 4. *SWING TIME:* WALTZ IN SPRINGTIME-A FINE ROMANCE b) 5.NEVER GONNA DANCE-THE WAY YOU LOOK TONIGHT 6. *BROADWAY MELODY OF 1938:* YOUR BROADWAY AND MY BROAD WAY a)-I'M FEELING LIKE A MILLION 7.EVERYBODY SING-YOURS AND MINE 8. *GANGWAY:* GANGWAY b)-LORD AND LADY WHOOZLS 9.WHEN YOU GOTTA SING-MOON OR NO MOON 10.

*PENNIES FROM HEAVEN:* SO DO I-BUTTON YOUR SHOE 11.
PENNIES FROM HEAVEN c)-LET'S CALL A HEART A HEART
12.*GONE WITH THE WIND:* BATTLE HYMN OF THE REPUBLIC-
OLD KENTUCKY HOME-MARCHING THROUGH GEORGIA-MASSA'S
IN THE COLD COLD GROUND 13.CAMPTOWN RACES-OLD FOLKS
AT HOME-WHEN JOHNNY COMES MARCHING HOME-DIXIE 14.
*PINOCCHIO:* GIVE A LITTLE WHISTLE d)-TURN ON THE OLD
MUSIC BOX 15.LITTLE WOODEN HEAD-WHEN YOU WISH UPON
A STAR e) 16.*ALEXANDER'S RAGTIME BAND:* ALEXANDER'S
RAGTIME BAND-WHEN THE MIDNIGHT CHOO CHOO LEAVES FOR
ALABAM-BLUE SKIES f)-EVERYBODY'S DOING IT 17.EASTER
PARADE-NOW IT CAN BE TOLD g)-ALEXANDER'S RAGTIME BA
ND 18.*LIMELIGHT:* FAREWELL SWEET SENORITA-WHISTLING
WALTZ 19.STAY AWHILE-CELEBRATIN' 20.*SHALL WE DANCE:*
SHALL WE DANCE-LET'S CALL THE WHOLE THING OFF-THEY
ALL LAUGHED 21.THEY CAN'T TAKE THAT AWAY FROM ME a)
22.WHAT'S GOOD ABOUTGOODNIGHT-YOU COULDN'T BE CUTER
h)23.MUSIC FROM THE MOVIES MARCH a:Gerry Fitzgerald
b:Janet Lind  c:Arthur Tracy  e:Sam Browne  f:Hazel
Jean  g:uncredited  h:Eve Becke

231.<u>LLOYD WEBBER Andrew</u> - Cincinnati Pops  Erich Kunzel
*TELARC (BMG): CD 80405*                          *1996*
PHANTOM OF THE OPERA-MUSIC OF THE NIGHT-HERE AGAIN-
ALL I ASK OF YOU-ANGEL OF MUSIC-AS IF WE NEVER SAID
GOODBYE-MEMORY-I DON'T KNOW-DON'T CRY FOR ME ARGENT
INA-STARLIGHT EXPRESS-ANY DREAM WILL DO

232.<u>LLOYD WEBBER Andrew</u> - Greatest Songs - Var.Artists
*SILVA SCREEN (Koch): SONG(CD)(C) 911 (2CD/2MC) 1994*
Leslie Garrett-Royal Philharmon.Orch-R.P.Pops Orch-
Royal Philharmonic Concert Orchestra (Paul Bateman)
*From:* JOSEPH AND THE AMAZING TECHNICOLOR DREAMCOAT-
JESUS CHRIST SUPERSTAR-EVITA-TELL ME ON A SUNDAY-
SONG AND DANCE-CATS-STARLIGHT EXPRESS-REQUIEM-
PHANTOM OF T.OPERA-ASPECTS OF LOVE-SUNSET BOULEVARD

233.<u>LLOYD WEBBER Andrew</u> - Love Songs 1: Royal Phil.Orch
with Lesley Garrett-Chris Corcoran-Sharon Campbell-
and Dave Willetts / RPO conductor: Paul Bateman
*SILVA SCREEN (Koch): SONG(CD)(C)908 (CD/MC)    1993*
ALL I ASK OF YOU-I DON'T KNOW HOW TO LOVE HIM-LOVE
CHANGES EVERYTHING-WISHING YOU WERE SOMEHOW HERE-
DON'T CRY FOR ME ARGENTINA-ONLY YOU-PHANTOM OF THE
OPERA-MUSIC OFTHE NIGHT-ANOTHER SUITCASE IN ANOTHER
HALL-MEMORY-TELL ME ON A SUNDAY-THINK OF ME

234.<u>LLOYD WEBBER Andrew</u> - Love Songs 2: Various Artists
*FIRST NIGHT (Pinn): OCRCD 6044 (CD)            1996*
1.JELLICLE BALL a) 2.MUSIC OF T.NIGHT b) 3.LOVE CHA
NGES EVERYTHING c) 4.DON'T CRY FOR ME ARGENTINA d)
5.HIGH FLYING ADORED b) 6.ANYTHING BUT LONELY c) 7.
MEMORY d) 8.CLOSE EVERY DOOR b) 9.TELL ME ON A SUND
AY c) 10.I DON'T KNOW HOW TO LOVE HIM d) 11.ALL I
ASK OF YOU b) 12.THE LAST MAN IN MY LIFE c) 13.TAKE
THAT LOOK OFF YOUR FACE d) 14.ONLY HE c) 15.JESUS
CHRIST SUPERSTAR b) a:Royal Philharm.Orch. b:Paul
Nicholas  c:Marti Webb  d:Stephanie Lawrence

235. LLOYD WEBBER Andrew - Premiere Collection - Best Of
POLYDOR: ALWTC 1 (MC) 837282-2 (CD) -5 (DCC)    1988
PHANTOM OF THE OPERA (Steve Harley-Sarah Brightman)
TAKE THAT LOOK OF YOUR FACE (Marti Webb)-ALL I ASK
OF YOU (C.Richard-Sarah Brightman)-DON'T CRY FOR ME
ARGENTINA (Julie Covington)-MAGICAL MR.MISTOFFELEES
(Paul Nicholas)-VARIATIONS (Julian Lloyd Webber)-SU
PERSTAR (Murray Head)-MEMORY (E.Paige)-STARLIGHT EX
PRESS (Ray Shell)-TELL ME ON A SUNDAY (Marti Webb)
MUSIC OF THE NIGHT (Michael Crawford)-ANOTHER SUITC
ASE IN ANOTHER HALL (Barbara Dickson)-I DON'T KNOW
HOW TO LOVE HIM (Y.Elliman)-PIE JESU (S.Brightman)

236. LLOYD WEBBER Andrew - Premiere Collection: Encore
POLYDOR: 517 336-2 (CD) -4 (MC) -5 (DCC)    1988
MEMORY (Barbra Streisand) LOVE CHANGES EVERYTHING
(Michael Ball) AMIGOS PARA SIEMPRE (Jose Carreras-
Sarah Brightman) ANY DREAM WILL DO (Jason Donovan)
CLOSE EVERY DOOR Phillip Schofield) OH WHAT A CIRC
US (David Essex) POINT OF NO RETURN (Sarah Brightm
an-Michael Crawford) + I AM THE STARLIGHT-WISHING
YOU WERE SOMEHOW HERE AGAIN-ARGENTINE MELODY-SEEING
IS BELIEVING-JELLICLE BALL- EVERYTHING'S ALRIGHT-
FIRST MAN YOU REMEMBER-ANYTHING BUT LONELY-HOSANNA

237. LONESOME DOVE: Classic Western Film Scores 2
City Of Prague Philharmonic Orchestra (Nic Raine)
SILVA SCREEN (Koch): FILMCD 176 (CD)    1996
LONESOME DOVE (comp:BASIL POLEDOURIS) HEAVEN'S GATE
(DAVID MANSFIELD) SHE WORE A YELLOW RIBBON (RICHARD
HAGEMAN) RED RIVER DIMITRI TIOMKIN) OLD GRINGO (LEE
HOLDRIDGE) HANG 'EM HIGH(DOMINIC FRONTIERE) RED SUN
(MAURICE JARRE) THE PROUD REBEL (JEROME MOROSS) THE
OUTLAW JOSEY WALES (JERRY FIELDING) SONS OF KATIE
ELDER (ELMER BERNSTEIN) and others

238. LONGEST DAY The: Classic War Film Scores
SILVA SCREEN (Koch): FILM(CD)(C) 151    1994
633 SQUADRON-BATTLE OF BRITAIN-FORCE TEN FROM NAVAR
ONE-WHERE EAGLES DARE (Ron Goodwin) BRIDGE ON THE
RIVER KWAI (Kenneth Alford) THE DAM BUSTERS (Eric
Coates) THE GREAT ESCAPE-THE BRIDGE AT REMAGEN (E.
Bernstein) THE GUNS OF NAVARONE (Dimitri Tiomkin)
SINK THE BISMARCK (Clifton Parker) A BRIDGE TOO FAR
(John Addison) BATTLE OF THE BULGE Benjamin Frankel
IS PARIS BURNING-THE NIGHT OF THE GENERALS (Maurice
Jarre) PATTON-MacARTHUR-IN HARMS WAY (Jerry Goldsmi
th) THE LONGEST DAY (Paul Anka) MIDWAY-1941 (John
Williams) DAS BOOT (THE BOAT) Klaus Doldinger
City Of Prague Philharmonic Orchestra-Paul Bateman

239. LOST IN BOSTON IV - Various Artists
VARESE (Pinn): VSD 5768 (CD)    1997
Songs composed by Alan Menken-Howard Ashman/Alan &
Marilyn Bergman/Jule Styne/Stephen Schwartz etc.
Incl: THIRTY WEEKS OF HEAVEN (from BY THE BEAUTIFUL
SEA) MARKING TIME (from PIPPIN) I'M NAIVE (SUGAR)
PRETTY IS (110 IN THE SHADE) THE JOB APPLICATION

*(from BALLROOM)* NOAH *(JAMAICA)* SUDDENLY THERE'S YOU
*(BALLROOM)* BAD *(LITTLE SHOP OF HORRORS)*+ songs from
BIG/ BEST LITTLE WHOREHOUSE IN TEXAS/ SWEET CHARITY
DRAT! THE CAT!/GOLDILOCKS/WORKING

--- LOVE Geoff - *see COLLECTIONS 35,170,329*

240. LULLABY OF BROADWAY - Best Of Busby Berkeley at WB
*EMI PREMIER (EMI): CDODEON 8 (2CDs)* 1996
42 STREET: YOUNG AND HEALTHY-SHUFFLE OFF TO BUFFALO
42ND STR. GOLD DIGGERS OF 1933: WE'RE IN THE MONEY-
I'VE GOT TO SING A TORCH SONG-THE SHADOW WALTZ-REME
MBER MY FORGOTTEN MAN FOOTLIGHT PARADE: HONEYMOON
HOTEL-BY A WATERFALL-SHANGHAI LIL **WUNDERBAR:** DON'T
SAY GOODNIGHT-FASHIONS OF 1934-SPIN A LITTLE WEB OF
DREAMS **DAMES:** THE GIRL AT THE IRONING BOARD-I ONLY
HAVE EYES FOR YOU-DAMES **GOLD DIGGERS OF 1937:** WORDS
ARE IN MY HEART-LULLABY OF BROADWAY-ALL'S FAIR IN
LOVE AND WAR **IN CALIENTE:** THE LADY IN RED **HOLLYWOOD
HOTEL:** HOORAY FOR HOLLYWOOD

--- McKEY Clarence - *see COLLECTION 333*

--- McNEELY Joel - *see COLLECTION 30*

241. MAGIC OF THE MUSICALS - MARTI WEBB and MARK RATTRAY
*MCI (Disc-THE): MCCD 149 (CD) MCTC 149 (MC)* 1992
IT AIN'T NESESSARLY SO-PLENTY OF NOTHIN'-THERE'S A
BOAT-PORGY I'S YOUR WOMAN NOW-LULLABY OF BROADWAY-
I GOT RHYTHM-I GET A KICK OUT OF YOU-SUMMERTIME-LOS
ING MY MIND-BLOW GABRIEL BLOW-NOT WHILE I'M AROUND-
SEND IN THE CLOWNS-DO YOU HEAR THE PEOPLE SING-I DR
AMED A DREAM-EMPTY CHAIR AT EMPTY TABLES-LAST NIGHT
OF THE WORLD-BUI.DOI-DON'T CRY FOR ME ARGENTINA-JES
US CHRIST SUPERSTAR-MAMA-TAKE THAT LOOK OFF YOUR FA
CE-IN ONE OF MY WEAKER MOMENTS-ANTHEM-TELL ME IT'S
NOT TRUE-YOU AND I-ONLY HE-LOVE CHANGES EVERYTHING-
THE MUSIC OF THE NIGHT-MEMORY

242. MAGNUM,P.I. THE AMERICAN TV HITS ALBUM
*SILVA SCREEN (Koch): FILMCD 703 (CD)* re-iss 1990
MAGNUM,P.I-AIRWOLF-COSBY SHOW-MIKE HAMMER-LOU GRANT
CHEERS-HILL STREET BLUES-HOLLYWOOD WIVES-CAGNEY and
LACEY-ST.ELSEWHERE-A TOUCH OF SCANDLE-TAXI-SIMON &
SIMON-ROCKFORD FILES *conducted by Daniel Caine 1986*

--- MAIGRET & OTHER TV THEMES - *see COLLECTION 191*

243. MANCINI Henry - In The Pink:- Ultimate Collection
*RCA VICTOR (BMG): 14321 24283-2 (CD) -4 (MC)* 1995
PINK PANTHER THEME-MOON RIVER-DAYS OF WINE & ROSES
CHARADE-PETER GUNN-TWO FOR THE ROAD-THE THORN BIRDS
LOVE STORY THEME-MR.LUCKY-EXPERIMENT IN TERROR-SHOT
IN THE DARK-BLUE SATIN-BABY ELEPHANT WALK-HATARI-
PENNYWHISTLE JIG-PIE IN THE FACE POLKA-MOMENT TO
MOMENT-MOONLIGHT SONATA-DEAR HEART-SHADOW OF YOUR
SMILE-MOLLY MAGUIRE'S THEME-SUMMER OF 42-LOVE THEME
FROM ROMEO AND JULIET-AS TIME GOES BY-MISTY-TENDER
IS THE NIGHT-EVERYTHING I DO (I DO ITFOR YOU)-THEME
fr.MOMMIE DEARESI-RAIDROPS KEEP FALLING ON MY HEAD-
CRAZY WORLD-MONA LISA-UNCHAINED MELODY-WINDMILLS OF

*Continued next page...*

YOUR MIND-TILL THERE WAS YOU-SPEEDY GONZALES-DREAM
A LITTLE DREAM OF ME-THE SWEETHEART TREE-LONESOME-
LOVE IS A MANY SPLENDORED THING-BY THE TIME I GET
TO PHOENIX-ONE FOR MY BABY-BREAKFAST AT TIFFANY'S-
THAT OLD BLACK MAGIC-EVERGREEN-MIDNIGHT COWBOY
see also 'GRUSIN Dave'

244.MANCINI Henry - Romantic Movie Themes
*RCA CAMDEN (BMG): 74321 40060-2 (CD)* *1996*
ROMEO AND JULIET LOVE THEME-BREAKFAST AT TIFFANY'S
*(w.AMES GALWAY)*-CINEMA PARADISO-THORN BIRDS THEME
*(w.JAMES GALWAY)*-GODFATHER THEME-MIDNIGHT COWBOY-
LOVE STORY-MISTY-THE WINDMILLS OF YOUR MIND-THEME:
THE ADVENTURERS-EVERGREEN-THE SHADOW OF YOUR SMILE
*MEDLEY:* DAYS OF WINE AND ROSES/MOON RIVER/CHARADE/
CAMEO FOR FLUTE-RAINDROPS KEEP FALLING ON MY HEAD-
SECRET LOVE-ONCE UPON A TIME IN AMERICA-SWEETHEART
TREE-THE MISSION-AS TIME GOES BY-THE UNTOUCHABLES

245.MEYER Russ Orig Soundtracks Volume 4 - Various Arts
*POP BIZ (Cargo-Greyhound): LP 014 (LP only)* *1997*
GOOD MORNING AND GOODBYE (1967) / CHERRY HARRY AND
RAQUEL (1969) / MONDO TOPLESS (1966)

246.MISSION IMPOSSIBLE & Other TV Themes
John Gregory Orchestra
*MERCURY (Poly): 532 986-2 (CD)* *1996*
1.MISSION IMPOSSIBLE *(L.Schifrin)* 2.ROCKFORD FILES
*(M.Post-P.Carpenter)* 3.CANNON *(J.Parker)* 4.SOFTLY
SOFTLY *(B.Fry)* 5.COLUMBO *(B.Goldenberg)* 6.M.SQUAD
*(C.Basie)* 7.A MAN CALLED IRONSIDE *(Q.Jones)* 8.GRIFF
*(E.Kaplan)* 9.THE UNTOUCHABLES *(N.Riddle)* 10.MANNIX
*(L.Schifrin)* 11.ROUTE 66 *(N.Riddle)* 12.McMILLAN AND
WIFE *(J.Fielding)* 13.HARRY-O *(R.Hazard)* 14.STREETS
OF SAN FRANCISCO *(P.Williams)* 15.SIX MILLION DOLLAR
MAN*(O.Nelson)* 16.HAWAII 5-O *(M.Stevens)* 17.IT TAKES
A THIEF *(Grusin/Laurence/Berger)* 18.S.W.A.T.THEME
*(B.DeVorzon/J.Barry)* 19.I-SPY *(E.Hagen)* 20.McCLOUD
*(D.Shire)* 21.PERRY MASON *(F.Steiner)* 22.NAME OF THE
GAME *(D.Grusin)* 23.BANACEK *(B.Goldenberg)* 24.JOHNNY
STACATO *(E.Bernstein)* 25.POLICE WOMAN *(M.Stevens)*
26.THE SWEENEY*(H.South)* 27.THE AVENGERS *(L.Johnson)*
28.KOJAK *(B.Goldenberg)*

--- MISSION The - *see COLLECTION 252 'MORRICONE Ennio'*

247.MONROE Marilyn KISS + Jane Russell-Frankie Vaughan
*CAMEO-TARGET (BMG): CD 3555 (CD)* *1995*
YOU'D BE SURPRISED-THE RIVER OF NO RETURN *(RIVER OF
NO RETURN)* I WANNA BE LOVED BY YOU-WHEN IF FALL IN
LOVE *(ONE MINUTE TO ZERO)* BYE BYE BABY-DIAMONDS ARE
A GIRL'S BEST FRIEND *(GENTLEMEN PREFER BLONDES)* ONE
SILVERDOLLAR-I'M GONNA FILE MY CLAIM-WHEN LOVE GOES
WRONG NOTHING GOES RIGHT *(GENTLEMEN PREFER BLONDES)*
AFTER YOU GET WHAT YOU WANT YOU DON'T WANT IT-MY
HEART BELONGS TO DADDY-SPECIALISATION-RUNNIN' WILD-
TWO LITTLE GIRLS FROM LITTLE ROCK-HEATWAVE *(THERE'S
NO BUSINESS LIKE SHOW BUSINESS)* KISS *(NIAGARA)*

248. MONRO Matt - Hollywood and Broadway
*MFP GOLD (EMI): CD(TC)MFP 6137 (CD/MC)*          *1994*
LOOK FOR SMALL PLEASURES-STRANGER IN PARADISE-THE
IMPOSSIBLE DREAM-APPLE TREE-I'LL ONLY MISS HER WHEN
I THINK OF HER-COME BACK TO ME-HELLO DOLLY-SUNRISE
SUNSET-WALKING HAPPY-IF SHE WALKED INTO MY LIFE-PUT
ON A HAPPY FACE-TILL THE END OF TIME-CHARADE-GREEN
LEAVES OF SUMMER-THE SECOND TIME AROUND-EVERYBODY'S
TALKIN'-SHADOW OF YOUR SMILE-I'VE GROWN ACCUSTOMED
TO HER FACE-CHATTANOOGA CHOO CHOO-PRETTY POLLY

--- MOROSS Jerome - *see COLLECTION 377*

249. MORRICONE Ennio - Film Hits
*RCA (BMG): ND 70091 (CD) NK 70091 (MC) reissue 1990*
ONCE UPON A TIME IN THE WEST-FOR A FEW DOLLARS MORE
MOSES THEME-BYE BYE COLONEL-A FISTFUL OF DOLLARS-A
GUN FOR RINGO-BALLAD OF SACCO & VENZETTI-HERE'S TO
YOU-VICE OF KILLING-PAYINGOFF SCORES-THE ADVENTURER
WHAT HAVE YOU DONE TO SOLANGE-VIOLENT CITY-METELLO

250. MORRICONE Ennio - Spaghetti Western Collection
*RCA ITAly (BMG): 74321 26495-2 (CD)*          *1995*
Spaghetti Western MUSIC of 1960's: A GUN FOR RINGO
AT TIMES LIFE IS VERY HARD,ISN'T THAT FATE-GUNS FOR
THE McGREGORS-GUNFIGHT AT RED SANDS-BULLETS DON'T
ARGUE-7 WOMEN FOR THE McGREGORS-DEATH RIDES A HORSE
WE'LL BE BACK,ISN'T THAT FATE-THE RETURN OF RINGO

251. MORRICONE Ennio The Film Music Of Ennio Morricone
*VIRGIN VIP (EMI): CDVIP 123 (CD) TCVIP 123 (MC)*
THE GOOD THE BAD AND THE UGLY-THE SICILIAN CLAN-CHI
MAI (Life And Times Of David Lloyd George)-THE MAN
WITH THE HARMONICA (Once Upon A Time In The West)-
LA CALIFFA (Lady Caliph)-GABRIEL'S OBOE (Mission)-
A FISTFUL OF DYNAMITE-ONCE UPON A TIME IN THE WEST-
COCKEYE'S THEME (Once Upon A Time In America)-THE
MISSION remix-COME MADDELENA (Madelena)--MOSES THEME
(Moses The Lawgiver)-THE FALLS (The Mission)-
MY NAME IS NOBODY-LE VENT LE CRI (The Professional)
DEBOAH'S THEME (Once Upon A Time In America)

252. MORRICONE Ennio - The Mission: Classic Film Music
City Of Prague Philharmonic Orchestra conducted by
Paul Bateman and Derek Wadsworth
*SILVA SCREEN (Koch): FILMCD 171 (CD)*          *1996*
THE MISSION (Suite for Orch & Choir): *The Mission/*
*Gabriel's Oboe/Ave Maria (Guarini)/On Earth As It*
*Is In Heaven/Epilogue: The Falls)* -THE UNTOUCHABLES
*(Theme)*-ONCE UPON A TIME IN AMERICA *Deborah's Theme*
1900 *(Romanza)*-CASUALTIES OF WAR *(Elegy For Brown)*-
TWO MULES FOR SISTER SARA-IN THE LINE OF FIRE-THE
THING-CHI MAI-MARCO POLO-ONCE UPON A TIME IN THE
WEST *(Man With The Harmonica)*-GOOD THE BAD AND THE
UGLY-A FISTFUL OF DOLLARS-FOR A FEW DOLLARS MORE-
ONCE UPON A TIME IN THE WEST-THE GOOD THE BAD AND
THE UGLY *(Ecstasy Of Gold)*-CINEMA PARADISO

253. MORRICONE Ennio - Mondo Morricone: Ennio Morricone
Orchestra featuring Edda Dell'Orsos (vocals)

253. MORRICONE Ennio - Mondo Morricone: Ennio Morricone
     Orchestra featuring Edda Dell'Orsos (vocals)
     *COLOSSEUM (Pinn): CST 8057 (CD)*                    *1996*
     Themes from great Italian Movies of the 60s and 70s
     16 track compilation of film themes that fit neatly
     into the currently hot 'Easy Listening' vogue
254. MORRICONE Ennio Movie Classics: Hugo MONTENEGRO Orc
     *RCA CAMDEN (BMG): 74321 44679-2 (CD)*               *1997*
     SIXTY SECONDS TO WHAT-GOOD THE BAD AND THE UGLY-A
     FISTFUL OF DOLLARS-BATTLE OF ALGIERS-SACCO AND VENZ
     ETTI-THE VICE OF KILLING-BYE BYE COLONEL-FOR A FEW
     DOLLARS MORE-PAYING OFF SLOKEY-THE ADVENTURER-ONCE
     UPON A TIME IN THE WEST-A GUN FOR RINGO
255. MORRICONE Ennio - Time Of Adventure
     *RCA (BMG): 74321 31551-2 (CD)*                      *1995*
     1.ONCE UPON A TIME IN THE WEST-2.ANGER AND TARANTEL
     LA *(ALLONSANFAN)* 3.SHIP HUNTERS 4.SPACE 1999
     5.GRAND SLAM 6.ADVENTURER(Pt3) 7.PEIROL FORCES ROAD
     BLOCK 8.A MAN IN SPACE 9.STELLAR ECSTASY *(HUMANOID)*
     10.ADONAI 11.PROPERTY IS NO LONGER A STEAL *(GARDEN
     OF PLEASURE)*12.MYTH AND THE ADVENTURE *SECRET OF THE
     SAHARA)* 13.LARYNX MANIA *(WHERE ARE YOU GOING ON VAC
     ATION)* 14.IT'S BETTER TO DIE THAN TO STAY HERE *(AN
     INTERESTING STATE)* 15.A FISTFUL OF DOLLARS
256. MORRICONE Ennio - Very Best Of Ennio Morricone
     *MCI (THE): MCCD(MCTC) 056 (CD/MC)*                  *1992*
     HERE'S TO YOU-BALLAD OF SACCO &VANZETTI-FAREWELL TO
     CHEYENNE-MAN WITH T.HARMONICA-THE MAN-DEATH RATTLE-
     FINALE ONCE UPON A TIME IN THE WEST-GOOD THE BAD &
     THE UGLY-A FISTFUL OF DOLLARS-BATTLE OF ALGIERS-PAY
     ING OFF SCORES-VICE OF KILLING-FISTFUL OF DOLLARS 2
     ADVENTURER-FOR A FEW DOLLARS MORE-GUN FOR RINGO-MET
     ELLO-TITOLI-BYE BYE COLONEL
257. MORRICONE Ennio - With Love
     *DRG (Pinn): DRGCD 32913 (CD)*                       *1995*
     MAIN TITLES AND RARE TRACKS FROM 21 ROMANTIC FILM
     SCORES COMPOSED AND CONDUCTED BY MORRICONE BETWEEN
     1960 AND 1990. Films inc. CINEMA PARADISO-BLUEBEARD
     NIGHT FLIGHT FROM MOSCOW-MACHINE GUN McCAIN-RUFFIAN
     TWO SEASONS OF LIFE-LADY CALIPH-THIS KIND OF LOVE-
     ALIBI-DEVIL IN THE BRAIN-BLOOD IN THE STREET-SECRET
258. MOVIE CLASSICS - Various Artists
     *EMI LASER Class (MFP): CDZ 122 (CD) LZ 122(MC) 1994*
     2001 A Space Odyssey: ALSO SPRACH ZARATHUSTRA *(R.St
     auss)* Platoon / The Elephant Man:ADAGIO FOR STRINGS
     Op.11 *(Barber)* My Left Foot: UN AURA AMAROSA ACT 1:
     COSI FAN TUTTE *(Mozart)* Die Hard 2: FINLANDIA Op.26
     *(Sibelius)* Witches Of Eastwick: NESSUN DORMA Act 3:
     TURANDOT *(Puccini)* Alien: SYMPHONY NO.2 'ROMANTIC':
     Andante Con Tenerezza *(Hanson)* Death In Venice: SYM
     PHONY NO.5 IN C.MINOR *(Mahler)* Diva: LA WALLY:EBBEN
     NE ANDRO LONTANA *(Catalini)* Apocalypse Now: RIDE OF
     THE VALKYRIES: DIE WALKURE*(Wagner)* Fatal Attraction
     UN BEL DI VEDREMO ACT 2: MADAMA BUTTERFLY *(Puccini)*

Elvira Madigan: PIANO CONCERTO 21 IN C.K467(*Mozart*)
Gallipoli: ADAGIO IN G.MINOR (*Albinoni*) Excalibur:
FORTUNA IMPERATRIX MUNDI: CARMINA BURANA (*Orff*)
259.MOVIE KILLERS - Various Artists
*TELSTAR (WEA): TCD 2836 (CD) STAC 2836 (MC)    1996*
1.MISERLOU (*PULP FICTION*) Dick Dale & His Deltones
2.LITTLE GREEN BAG (*RESERVOIR DOGS*) George Baker Se
lection 3.GREEN ONIONS (*GET SHORTY*) Booker T.& MG's
4.FEELING GOOD (*ASSASSIN*) Nina Simone 5.I'LL TAKE
YOU THERE(*CASINO*) Staple Singers 6.PLAY DEAD (*YOUNG
AMERICANS*) Bjork and David Arnold 7.LAURA'S THEME
(*TWIN PEAKS*) Angelo Badalamenti 8.SON OF A PREACHER
MAN (*PULP FICTION*) Dusty Springfield 9.THE IN-CROWD
(*CASINO*) Ramsey Lewis 10.OYE COMO VA *CARLITO'S WAY*)
Santana 11.STUCK IN THE MIDDLE WITH YOU (*RESERVOIR
DOGS*) Stealers Wheel 12.TROUBLE MAN (*SEVEN*) Marvin
Gaye 13.LET'S STAY TOGETHER (*PULP FICTION*) Al Green
14.BLUE VELVET Bobby Vinton 15.(LOVE IS) THE TENDER
TRAP (*TRUE ROMANCE*) Robert Palmer 16.MISSION IMPOSS
IBLE Lalo Schifrin 17.MANISH BOY (*GOODFELLAS*) Muddy
Waters 18.JUNGLE BOOGIE (*PULP FICTION*) Kool & Gang
19.SHALLOW GRAVE Leftfield 20.FOR WHAT YOU DREAM OF
(*TRAINSPOTTING*) Bedrock featuring KYO
260.MOVIE LOVERS - Various Artists
*TELSTAR (WEA): TCD 2876 (CD) STAC 2876 (MC)    1996*
1.BROWN EYED GIRL *SLEEPING WITH THE ENEMY* Van Morri
son 2.PERFECT DAY *TRAINSPOTTING* Lou Reed 3.GIRL YOU
'LL BE A WOMAN SOON *PULP FICTION* Urge Overkill 4.IN
DREAMS *BLUE VELVET* Roy Orbison 5.BLUE SPANISH SKY
*WILD AT HEART* Chris Isaak 6.VENUS AS A BOY *LEON* Bjo
rk 7.LOVE SONG FOR A VAMPIRE *DRACULA* Annie Lennox 8
I'VE NEVER BEEN TO ME *PRISCILLA:QUEEN OF THE DESERT*
Charlene 9.SEA OF LOVE Marty Wilde 10.LOVE LETTERS
*BLUE VELVET* Ketty Lester 11.EVERYBODY'S TALKIN' *MID
NIGHT COWBOY* Nilsson 12.WHEN A MAN LOVES A WOMAN
Percy Sledge 13.YOU'VE REALLY GOT A HOLD ON ME
*STRIPTEASE* Smokey Robinson Miracles 14.SOUL ON FIRE
*ANGEL HEART* LaVern Baker15.GIMME YOUR LOVE *SUPERFLY*
Curtis Mayfield16.BABY I LOVE YOU *GOODFELLAS* Aretha
Franklin 17.FALLING *TWIN PEAKS* Julee Cruise 18.LOVE
AND HAPPINESS *9½ WEEKS* Al Green 19.TELL IT LIKE IT
IS *BIG EASY* Aaron Neville 20.FA-FA-FA-FA (SAD SONG)
*CASINO* Otis Redding
261.MOVIE MADNESS - Film Music of Dimitri SHOSTAKOVICH
*CAPRICCIO-TARGET (BMG): 10 822 (CD)    1997*
Score extracts from USSR films incl: HAMLET (1964,
op.116) FIVE DAYS, FIVE NIGHTS (-) GOLDEN MOUNTAINS
(1931,opus 30a) THE FALL OF BERLIN (1949,opus 82)
262.MOVIES GREATEST LOVE SONGS - Var. Original Artists
*POLYGRAM TV (Poly): 516 651-2 (CD) -4 (MC)    1994*
PLAY DEAD (*Young Americans*) Bjork & David Arnold /
LOVE SONG FOR A VAMPIRE (*B.Stoker's Dracula*) Annie
*Lennox* / NO ORDINARY LOVE (*Indecent Proposal*) Sade
                    *Continued next page...*

MOVIES GREATEST LOVE SONGS...*Continued*
UNCHAINED MELODY *(Ghost) Righteous Bros* / LICENCED
TO KILL *Gladys Knight* / SHOW ME HEAVEN *(Days Of Hea
ven) Maria McKee* /FALLING *(Twin Peaks) Julee Cruise*
FORBIDDEN COLOURS *(Merry Xmas Mr.Lawrence)D.Sylvian
-Ryuichi Sakamoto* / GOING HOME *(Local Hero) Mark Kn
opfler* / BOOK OF DAYS *(Far And Away) Enya* / TAKE MY
BREATH AWAY *(Top Gun) Berlin* /GLORY OF LOVE *(Karate
Kid 2) Peter Cetera* /UP WHERE WE BELONG *(An Officer
& A Gentleman) Jennifer Warnes-Joe Cocker* / NOTHING
HAS BEEN PROVED*(Scandal) Dusty Springfield* /I GUESS
THAT'S WHY THEY CALL IT THE BLUES *(Peter's Friends)
Elton John* / BEST THAT I CAN DO (ARTHUR'S THEME)
*Christopher Cross* / LOVE IS IN THE AIR *(Strictly Ba
llroom) John Paul Young* / MY GIRL *Temptations* / Try
A LITTLE TENDERNESS *Commitments* / BROWN EYED GIRL
*(Sleeping With The Enemy) Van Morrison*
--- <u>MOVIOLA</u> - *see COLLECTION 24*
--- <u>MOZART TV</u> - *see COLLECTION 405*
263.<u>MUSIC FROM GREAT AUSTRALIAN FILMS</u> - Various Artists
*DRG (Pinn): CDSBL 12582 (CD)*                    *1982*
NEWSFRONT-GALLIPOLI-MY BRILLIANT CAREER-TALLTIMBERS
CATHY'S CHILD-ELIZA FRASER-BREAKER MORANT-CHANT OF
JIMMIE BLACKSMITH-THE PICTURE SHOW MAN-PICNIC AT HA
NGING ROCK-DIMBOOLA-CADDIE-THE MANGO TREE
264.<u>MUSIC FROM THE ORIENT</u> - Various -S/T- Artists
*MILAN (BMG): 4321 32031-2 (CD)*                  *1996*
CYCLO (1995) Music score: TON-THAT TIET & featuring
RADIOHEAD and The ROLLINS BAND
LITTLE BUDDAH (1992) Music score: RYUICHI SAKAMOTO
RAISE THE RED LANTERN (91) Music score: ZHAO JIPING
265.<u>MY RIFLE MY PONY AND ME</u>: Film Western Songs - V.Art
*BEAR FAMILY (Rollercoast/Swift):BCD 15625 (CD) 1993*
MY RIFLE MY PONY AND ME:Dean Martin-Ricky Nelson fr
om *RIO BRAVO (59)* / LEGEND OF SHENANDOAH: James Ste
wart *SHENANDOAH (65)* / MONTANA *MONTANA (50)* THE SEA
RCHERS *THE SEARCHERS (56)* WAGON'S WEST/SONG OF THE
WAGONMASTER *WAGONMASTER(50)* All sung by Sons Of The
PIONEERS / NEVADA SMITH: Merle Kilgore *NEVADA SMITH
(56)* / BALLAD OF THE ALAMO: Marty Robbins *THE ALAMO
(60)* / THE HANGING TREE: Marty Robbins *THE HANGING
TREE (59)* / BALLAD OF PALADIN: Johnny Western *HAVE
GUN WILL TRAVEL (TV 57)* / THE SONS OF KATIE ELDER:
Johnny Cash *THE SONS OF KATIE ELDER (65)*/ THE REBEL
JOHNNY YUMA: Johnny Cash / RAWHIDE: Frankie Laine
*RAWHIDE (TV 58)* / GUNFIGHT AT OK CORRALL: Frankie
Laine *GUNFIGHT AT OK CORRALL (57)* / BALLAD OF DAVY
CROCKETT: Fess Parker *DAVY CROCKETT (55)* /RIO BRAVO
Dean Martin *RIO BRAVO (59)* / I'M A RUNAWAY: Tab Hun
ter / BONANZA: Lorne Greene *BONANZA (TV 59)* / NORTH
TO ALASKA: Johnny Horton *NORTH TO ALASKA (59)* /HIGH
NOON: Tex Ritter *HIGH NOON (52)* / AND THE MOON GREW
Kirk Douglas *MAN WITHOUT A STAR (55)* / PECOS BILL:
Roy Rogers & Sons Of The Pioneers / YELLOW ROSE OF

TEXAS/ROLL ON TEXAS MOON: Roy Rogers / DON'T FENCE ME IN: Roy Rogers *HOLLYWOOD CANTEEN (44)* / COWBOY: Dickson Hall

--- **MYSTERY MAGIC AND MADNESS** - *see COLLECTION 312*

266. **NASCIMBENE Mario** - Anthology cond: Mario Nascimbene
*DRG (Pinn): DRGCD 32960 (2CD)*                    *1996*
A FAREWELL TO ARMS-THE QUIET AMERICAN-ONE MILLION YEARS BC-FRANCIS OF ASSISI-WHEN DINOSAURS RULED THE EARTH-ALEXANDER THE GREAT-WHERE THE SPIES ARE-THE BAREFOOT CONTESSA-ROMANOFF AND JULIET-ROOM AT THE TOP-SOLOMON AND SHEBA-VIKINGS-CREATURES THE WORLD FORGOT-SIEGE OF LENINGRAD-SCENT OF MYSTERY-SONS AND LOVERS-LIGHT IN THE PIAZZA-BARABBAS-DOCTOR FAUSTUS-JOSEPH AND HIS BRETHREN-VENGEANCE OF SHE-JESSICA

267. **NEW PURE MOODS** - Various Artists
*VIRGIN (EMI): VTDCD 158 (2CD)*                    *1997*
1.CACHARPAYA Incantation 2.WILD MOUNTIN THYME *(SCOTTISH TOURIST BOARD)* Silencers 3.LILY WAS HERE David A.Stewart feat Candy Dulfer 4.CHILDREN Robert Miles 5.HARRY'S GAME Clannad 6.CAVATINA *DEER HUNTER* John Williams 7.BRIDESHEAD REVISTED *(KELLOGG'S CORN FLAKES/VW GOLF)* Geoffrey Burgon 8.DON'T CRY FOR ME ARGENTINA Shadows 9.THEME FROM SCHINDLER'S LIST Tamsin Little 10.RIVERDANCE John Anderson Concert 11.MERRY CHRISTMAS MR.LAWRENCE Ryuichi Sakamoto 12.LITTLE FLUFFY CLOUDS The Orb 13.PLAY DEAD *(VAUXHALL VECTRA)* Bjork w.David Arnold 14.SONG FOR GUY Elton John 15.SWEET LULLABY Deep Forest 16.ONLY YOU *(FIAT TEMPRA)*Praise 17.ALBATROSS Fleetwood Mac 18.OXYGENE IV Jean Michel Jarre 19.CROCKETT'S THEME Jan Hammer 20.YEHA NOHA Sacred Spirit. CD2: ADIEMUS *(DELTA AIR WAYS)* Adiemus 2.CANTUS SONG OF TEARS *(CHELTENHAM & GLOUCESTER B.SOC)* Adiemus 3.TUBULAR BELLS PART ONE Mike Oldfield 4.INSPECTOR MORSE Barrington Pheloung 5.ANOTHER GREEN WORLD *(ARENA)* Brian Eno 6.ANCIENT PERSON OF MY HEART Divine Works 7.PROTECTION*(MAZDA)* Massive Attack feat Tracy 8.THE MISSION E.Morricone 9.HEART ASK PLEASURE FIRST/THE PROMISE *(THE PIANO)* Michael Nyman 10.ARIA ON AIR *(B.AIRWAYS)* Malcolm McLaren 11.RETURN TO INNOCENCE Enigma 12.SADNESS Enigma 13.CHI MAI *(LIFE AND TIMES OF DAVID LLOYD GEORGE)* Ennio Morricone 14.BLOW THE WIND/PIE JESU *(ORANGE)* Jocelyn Pook 15.WOODBROOK Micheal O'Suill eabhain 16.LAST EMPEROR David Byrne 17.PRELUDE *(B.AIRWAYS)* Yanni 18.TWIN PEAKS-FIRE WALK WITH ME Angelo Badalamenti 19.SUN RISING *(ALPEN)* Beloved 20.THEME FROM THE X-FILES DJ Dado

--- **NEWMAN Alfred** - *see COLLECTION 403*

268. **NEXT GENERATIONS**: The Very Best Of Science Fiction
Czech Symphony Orch conducted by William Motzing
*EDELTON (Pinn): 002720-2EDL (2CD)*                    *1997*
1.TERMINATOR *(82 B.FIEDEL)* 2.COCOON *(85 J.HORNER)* 3 STAR TREK II: THE WRATH OF KHAN *(82 HORNER)* 4.ALIEN

*Continued next page...*

NEXT GENERATIONS...*Continued*

*(1979 J.GOLDSMITH)* 5.MAC AND ME *(88 A.SILVESTRI)* 6.
BILL AND TED'S EXCELLENT ADVENTURE *(88 D.NEWMAN)* 7.
GHOSTBUSTERS *(84 E.BERNSTEIN)* 8.STAR TREK: THE NEXT
GENERATION *(94 R.JONES)* 9.INNERSPACE *(87 GOLDSMITH)*
10.STAR TREK *(66 A.COURAGE)* 11.THE PHILADELPHIA EXP
RIMENT *(84 WANNBERG)* 12.V FOR VICTORY*(84 J.HARNELL)*
13.MAD MAX 2 *(82 B.MAY)* 14.FLASH GORDON SUITE *(80
QUEEN/HOWARD BLAKE)* 15.METEOR *(79 L.ROSENTHAL)* 16.
BATMAN *(89 D.ELFMAN)* 17.2010 *(84 D.SHIRE)* 18.STAR
TREK VI: UNDISCOVERED COUNTRY *(91 C.EIDELMAN)* 19.
TOTAL RECALL *(90 J.GOLDSMITH)* CD2: 1.SUPERMAN *(77
J.WILLIAMS)* 2.INVADERS FROM MARS *(86 C.YOUNG)* 3.
STAR TREK: THE MOTION PICTURE *(79 J.GOLDSMITH)* 4.
COUNTDOWN *(68 L.ROSENMAN)* 5.RETURN OF THE JEDI *(83
J.WILLIAMS)* 6.STAR TREK: THE NEXT GENERATION *(90
D.McCARTHY)* 7.MY STEPMOTHER IS AN ALIEN *(88 A.SILVE
STRI)* 8.STAR TREK: DEEP SPACE 9 *(93 D.McCARTHY)* 9.
EXPLORERS *(85 J.GOLDSMITH)* 10.SECONDS *(J.GOLDSMITH)*
11.STAR TREK IV: THE VOYAGE HOME *(86 L.ROSENMAN)* 12
GREMLINS 2: NEW BATCH *(90 J.GOLDSMITH)* 13.FANTASTIC
VOYAGE *(66 L.ROSENMAN)* 14.DEAD ZONE *(83 M.KAMEN)* 15
RETURN OF CAPTAIN INVINCIBLE *(83 W.MOTZING)* 16.THE
FORTRESS *(93 F.TALGORN)* 17.BATTLE FOR THE PLANET OF
THE APES *(73 L.ROSENMAN)* 18.ILLUSTRATED MAN *(69 J.
GOLDSMITH)* 19.STAR WARS *(77 J.WILLIAMS)*

*269.*<u>NO BUSINESS LIKE SHOW BUSINESS</u> - Various Artists
*RCA (BMG): 74321 47966-2 (CD) -4 (MC)*          *1997*
THERE'S NO BUSINESS LIKE SHOW BUSINESS *(ANNIE GET
YOUR GUN)*-IF I WERE A RICH MAN *(FIDDLER ON T.ROOF)*-
WE'RE IN THE MONEY *(42ND STREET)*-SEND IN THE CLOWNS
*(A LITTLE NIGHT MUSIC)*-A BOY LIKE THAT *(WEST SIDE
STORY)* GUYS AND DOLLS-I KNOW HIM SO WELL *(CHESS)*-
HELLO DOLLY-FOOD GLORIOUS FOOD/YOU'VE GOT TO PICK A
A POCKET OR TWO *(OLIVER)* PINBALL WIZARD/SEE ME FEEL
ME *(TOMMY)*-AGE OF AQUARIUS *(HAIR)*-I'M GONNA WASH TH
AT MAN RIGHT OUT OF MY HAIR/SOME ENCHANTED EVENING/
THERE AIN'T NOTHING LIKE A DAME *(SOUTH PACIFIC)*-
WANDERIN' STAR *(PAINT YOUR WAGON)*-DO RE MI/PRELUDE/
SOUND OF MUSIC *(SOUND OF MUSIC)*-GREASED LIGHTNING/
WE GO TOGETHER *(GREASE)*-SUMMER HOLIDAY Megamix

--- <u>NO STRINGS ATTACHED</u> - *see COLLECTION 162*

*270.*<u>NORTH Alex</u> - FILM MUSIC
*NONESUCH (WEA): 7559 79446-2 (CD)*          *1997*
THE BAD SEED (1956)-THE MISFITS (1961)-SPARTACUS
(1960)-A STREETCAR NAMED DESIRE (1951)-VIVA ZAPATA
(1952) London Symphony Orch (E.Stern) concert rec.

*271.*<u>NOT OF THIS EARTH!</u> - The Film Music Of RONALD STEIN
*VARESE (Pinn): VSD 5634 (CD)*          *1995*
NOT OF THIS EARTH (57) ATTACK OF THE 50 FOOT WOMAN
(58) THE TERROR (63) ATTACK OF THE CRAB MONSTERS
(56) SPIDER BABY (64) *featuring* LON CHANEY JNR etc.

--- <u>NOVELLO Ivor</u> - *see COLLECTION 193*

272.<u>NOW VOYAGER</u> - Classic Film Scores Of Max STEINER*
*RCA VICTOR (BMG): GD 80136 (CD) GK 80136 (MC)   1990*
NOW VOYAGER-KING KONG-SARATOGA TRUNK-CHARGE OF THE
LIGHT BRIGADE-FOUR WIVES-THE BIG SLEEP-JOHNNY BELIN
DA-SINCE YOUWENT AWAY-THE INFORMER-THE FOUNTAINHEAD
*\*National Philharmonic Orchestra (Charles Gerhardt)*

273.<u>NUMBER ONE SCI-FI ALBUM</u> - Various Artists
*POLYGRAM TV (Poly): 553 360-2 (CD) -4 (MC)      1997*
CD1: MOVIES
1.STAR WARS 2.INDEPENDENCE DAY 3.ABYSS 4.EMPIRE STR
IKES BACK (Imperial March) 5.SUPERMAN (March) 6.ET
(Flying) 7.BLADE RUNNER 8.RETURN OF THE JEDI (Luke
and Leia) 9.APOLLO 13 10.EVE OF THE WAR (War Of The
Worlds) 14.CLOSE ENCOUNTERS OF THE THIRD KIND 15.
JURASSIC PARK 16.BATMAN THE MOVIE 17.DUNE Prophecy
18.DARK STAR 19.CAPRICORN ONE 20.ALIEN 21.THE BLACK
HOLE 22.2001-A SPACE ODYSSEY
CD2:
TV THEMES 1.THE X FILES 2.STAR TREK NEXT GENERATION
3.DARK SKIES 4.BUCK ROGERS IN THE 25TH CENTURY 5.
BATTLESTAR GALACTICA 6.TWILIGHT ZONE Theme & Variat
ions 7.STAR TREK: VOYAGER 8.BABYLON 5 9.DOCTOR WHO
10.RED DWARF 11.HITCH-HIKERS GUIDE TO THE GALAXY 12
THUNDERBIRDS 13.STING RAY 14.FIREBALL XL-5 15.CAPTA
IN SCARLET 16.JOE 90 17.BLAKE'S 7 18.LOST IN SPACE
1 & 2 19.THE TIME TUNNEL 20.BATMAN 21.STAR TREK TV

274.<u>NUMBER ONE MOVIES ALBUM</u>: 36 Classic Tracks Orig.Art
*POLYGRAM TV: 525 962-2 (2CD) -4 (2MC)           1995*
LOVE IS ALL AROUND *(4 WEDDINGS & A FUNERAL)* Wet Wet
Wet KISS FROM A ROSE *(BATMAN FOREVER)* Seal  IT MUST
HAVE BEEN LOVE *(PRETTY WOMAN)* Roxette LOVE SONG FOR
A VAMPIRE *(DRACULA)* Annie Lennox  WE DON'T NEED ANO
THER HERO *(MAD MAX BEYOND THUNDERDOME)* Tina Turner
SHOW ME HEAVEN *(DAYS OF THUNDER)* Maria McKee  PLAY
DEAD *(YOUNG AMERICANS)*Bjork & David Arnold UP WHERE
WE BELONG *(AN OFFICER & A GENTLEMAN)* Joe Cocker and
Jennifer Warnes  NOTHING HAS BEEN PROVED *(Scandal)*
Dusty Springfield UNCHAINED MELODY*(Ghost)* Righteous
Brothers CRYING GAME Boy George  HOW DEEP IS YOUR
LOVE *(SATURDAY NIGHT FEVER)* The Bee Gees  WILL YOU
*(BREAKING GLASS)* Hazel O'Connor  FOR YOUR EYES ONLY
Sheena Easton  LICENCE TO KILL Gladys Knight
FLASHDANCE 95 Irene Cara  ABSOLUTE BEGINNERS David
Bowie TRY A LITTLE TENDERNESS *(The Committments)*
The Committments WE HAVE ALL THE TIME IN THE WORLD
*ON HER MAJESTY'S SECRET SERVICE)* Louis Armstrong
LIVING DAYLIGHT A-HA  HOLD ME THRILL ME KISS ME
KILL ME *(BATMAN FOREVER)* U2  YOU COULD BE MINE
*(TERMINATOR 2* Guns n'Roses  BLAZE OF GLORY *(YOUNG
GUNS 2)* Jon Bon Jovi  DON'T YOU (FORGET ABOUT ME)
*(BREAKFAST CLUB)* Simple Minds  A VIEW TO A KILL
Duran Duran  DOUBLEBACK *(BACK TO THE FUTURE III)*
ZZ Top  NOTHING'S GONNA STOP US NOW *(MANNEQUIN)*
Starship  EYE OF THE TIGER *(ROCKY 3)* Survivor

*Continued next page...*

**NUMBER ONE MOVIES ALBUM**...*Continued*

HOLDING OUT FOR A HERO *(FOOTLOOSE)* Bonnie Tyler
KIDS ARE ALRIGHT *(QUADROPHENIA)* Who  PINBALL WIZARD
*(TOMMY)* Elton John   PRETTY IN PINK Psychedelic Furs
CALL ME *(AMERICAN GIGOLO)* Blondie   THE HEAT IS ON
*(BEVERLY HILLS COP)* Glenn Frey   THE POWER OF LOVE
*(BACK TO THE FUTURE)* Huey Lewis and The News BROWN
EYED GIRL *(SLEEPING WITH THE ENEMY)* Van Morrison
STUCK IN THE MIDDLE WITH YOU *(RESERVOIR DOGS)* Steal
ers Wheel   TUBULAR BELLS *THE EXORCIST* Mike Oldfield

275. <u>NYMAN Michael</u> - Mucis From Peter GREENAWAY Films
Michael Nyman and Essential Michael Nyman Band
*ARGO/DECCA (Polyg): 436 820-2 (CD) -4 (MC)      1992*
CHASING SHEEP IS BEST LEFT TO SHEPHERDS/AN EYE FOR
OPTICAL THEORY/THE GARDEN IS BECOMING A ROBE ROOM
*(all: The Draughtsman's Contract)* PRAWN WATCHING/TI
ME LAPSE *(A Zed & Two Noughts)* FISH BEACH/WHEELBARR
OW WALK/KNOWING THE ROPES *(Drowning By Numbers)*
MISERERE PARAPHRASE/MEMORIAL*(The Cook The Thief His
Wife And Her Lover)* STROKING/SYNCHRONISING *(Water
Dances)* MIRANDA   *(Prospero's Books)*

276. <u>OPERA AT THE MOVIES</u> - Various Artists
NAXOS (Select): 8.551164 (CD)                    1995
TRADING PLACES: *Overture To The Marriage Of Figaro
(Mozart)* MY LEFT FOOT: *Un'aura amorosa from Cosi
Fan Tutti (Mozart)* SUNDAY BLOODY SUNDAY: *Soave sia
il vento from Cosi Fan Tutti (Mozart)* DRIVING MISS
DAISY: *Song To The Moon from Rusalka (Dvorak)* FANTA
SIA: *Dance Of The Hours from La Gioconda* Ponchielli
SOMEONE TO WATCH OVER ME *Flower Duet from Lakme
(Delibes)* PETER'S FRIENDS *Can-Can from Orpheus In
The Underworld (Offenbach)* THE UNTOUCHABLES *Recitar
Vesti La Giubba - I Pagliacci* Leoncavallo EXCALIBUR
*Siegfried's Death and Funeral March from Gotterdamm
erung (Wagner)* WITCHES OF EASTWICK *Nessun Dorma fr.
Turandot (Puccini)* A ROOM WITH A VIEW *O Mio Babbino
Caro from Gianni Scicchi (Puccini)* MOONSTRUCK *O Soa
ve fanciulla from La Boheme (Puccini)* RAGING BULL /
GODFATHER III *Intermezzo from Cavalleria Rusticana*
Mascagni   DIVA *Ebben Ne Andro Lontana from La Wally
(Catalini)* A NIGHT AT THE OPERA *Anvil Chorus from
Il Trovatore (Verdi)* PHILADELPHIA *La Mamma Morta fr
om Andrea Chenier (Giordano)* APOCALYPSE NOW *Ride Of
The Valkyries from Die Walkure (Wagner)*

277. <u>OPERA GOES TO THE MOVIES</u> - Boston Pops (A.Fiedler)
*RCA VICTOR (BMG): GD 60841 (CD)*
FATAL ATTRACTION:*(Puccini: "Un Bel Di" MADAMA BUTTE
RFLY, Act.2)* WITCHES OF EASTWICK:*(Puccini: "Nessun
Dorma" TURANDOT,Act 3)* MOONSTRUCK:*(Puccini: "Quando
M'en Vo" LA BOHEME, Act 2)* *(Puccini: "Don de Lieta
Usci" LA BOHEME,Act 3)* DARK EYES:*(Rossini:"Una Voce
Poco Fa" BARBER OF SEVILLE, Act 1)* APOCALYPSE NOW:
*(Wagner: "Ride Of The Valkyries" DIE WALKURE,Act 2)*

JEAN DE FLORETTE: *(Verdi: "Overture" LA FORZA DEL DESTINO)* PRIZZI'S HONOR: *(Rossini:"Overture" BARBER OF SEVILLE)* **A ROOM WITH A VIEW:** *(Puccini: "Firenze E Coome Un Albero Fiorito" and "O Mio Babino Caro" GIANNI SCHICCHI) and "Chi Il Bel Sogno Di Doretta" LA RONDINE)* **GODFATHER III:** *(Mascagni:"Intermezzo" CAVALLERIA RUSTICANA)* UNTOUCHABLES: *(Leoncavallo: "Vesti La Giubba" PAGLIACCI, Act 1)*

278.ORIGINALS - The Levi Jeans Ad Collection - Var.Arts
COLUMBIA (SONY: MOOD(C)(CD) 29          1993
WONDERFUL WORLD: Sam Cooke-I HEARD IT THROUGH THE GRAPEVINE: Marvin Gaye-STAND BY ME: Ben E.King-WHEN A MAN LOVES A WOMAN: Percy Sledge-C'MON EVERYBODY: Eddie Cochran-MANNISH BOY:Muddy Waters-AIN'T NOBODY HOME: B.B.King-CAN'T GET ENOUGH: Bad Company-THE JO KER: Steve Miller Band-SHOULD I STAY OR SHOULD I GO The Clash-20TH CENTURY BOY: T.Rex-MAD ABOUT THE BOY Dinah Washington-PIECE OF MY HEART: (Erma Franklin) HEART ATTACK AND VINE: Screamin' Jay Hawkins

279.ORIGINALS - Volume 2 - Various Artists
COLUMBIA (SONY): MOOCD 31 (CD) MOODC 31 (MC)    1994
UP ON THE ROOF *(Drifters)* IT TAKES TWO *(Marvin Gaye & Kim Weston)* SITTIN' ON THE DOCK OF THE BAY *(Otis Redding)* THE IN CROWD *(Dobie Gray)* LA BAMBA *(Los Lobos)* ALL RIGHT NOW *(Free)* MOVE ON UP *(Curtis Mayfield)* I GET THE SWEETEST FEELING *(Jackie Wilson)* HEY JOE*(Jimi Hendrix)* PAPA'S GOT A BRAND NEW BAG *(James Brown)* NO PARTICULAR PLACE TO GO *(Chuck Berry)* LOVE IS LIKE A HEATWAVE *(Martha & Vandellas)* BAD MOON RI SING *(Creedence Clearw.Revival)* LET'S WORK TOGETHER Canned Heat)* THE WANDERER*(Dion)* MY BABY JUST CARES FOR ME *(Nina Simone)* STELLA MAE *(John Lee Hooker)*

280.PAIGE Elaine - Cinema
WEA (WEA): 2292 40511-2 (CD)          1989
WINDMILLS OF YOUR MIND-OUT HERE ON MY OWN-PRISONER-SOMETIMES-MAHOGANY-UP WHERE WE BELONG-UNCHAINED MEL ODY-BRIGHT EYES-ALFIE-MISSING-WAY WE WERE-THE ROSE

281.PAIGE Elaine - Encore
WEA: 0603 10476-2 (CD) 0603 10476-4 (MC)     1995
AS IF WE NEVER SAID GOODBYE - PERFECT YEAR *Sunset Boulevard* MEMORY *Cats* I KNOW HIM SO WELL *Chess* ANOTHER SUITCASE IN ANOTHER HALL *Evita* I DON'T KNOW HOW TO LOVE HIM *Jesus Christ S.* ON MY OWN-I DREAMED A DREAM *Les Miserables* MON DIEU - HYMNE AL'AMOUR-NON JE NE REGRETTE RIEN *Piaf* WITH ONE LOOK *Sunset Boulevard* DON'T CRY FOR ME ARGENTINA (live) *Evita*

282.PAIGE Elaine - Performance
RCA CAMDEN (BMG): 74321 44680-2(CD) -4(MC) re: 1997
1.I HAVE DREAMED *KING AND I* 2.ANYTHING GOES 3.HEART DON'T CHANGE MY MIND 4.ANOTHER SUITCASE IN ANOTHER HALL *EVITA* 5.THE ROSE 6.LOVE HURTS 7.WHAT'LL I DO / WHO 8.1 ONLY HAVE EYES FOR YOU 9.HE'S OUT OF MY LIF LIFE 10.I KNOW HIM SO WELL *CHESS* 11.DON'T CRY FOR ME ARGENTINA *EVITA* 12.MEMORY *CATS* 13. MEMORY Repr.

283. PAIGE Elaine  Stages *WEA: 240 228-2 (CD) -4MC  1983*
MEMORY-BE ON YOUR OWN-ANOTHER SUITCASE-SEND IN THE
CLOWNS-RUNNIN BACK FOR MORE-GOOD MORNING STARSHINE
DON'T CRY FOR ME ARGENTINA-WHAT I DID FOR LOVE-I DO
N'T KNOW HOW TO LOVE HIM-ONE NIGHT ONLY-LOSING MY
MIND-TOMORROW

--- PALACE OF THE WIND - *see COLLECTION 59*
--- PARAMOR Norrie - *see COLLECTIONS 1,31*

284. PEARSON Johnny - Sleepy Shores - The Best of JP
*MUSIC CLUB (DISC-THE): MCCD 304 (CD)            1997*
SLEEPY SHORES-ALL CREATURES GREAT AND SMALL-ONE DAY
IN YOUR LIFE-MISTY SUNSET-CHI MAI-SING-IF-FOR YOUR
EYES ONLY-WHAT'S ANOTHER YEAR-SORRY SEEMS TO BE THE
HARDEST WORD-CONCERTO DI ARANJUEZ-LOVE STORY-PEOPLE
2001 A SPACE ODYSSEY-YOU NEEDED ME-WINNER TAKES IT
ALL-I HONESTLY LOVE YOU-DON'T CRY FOR ME ARGENTINA

285. PEARSON Johnny - Themes and Dreams
*PRESIDENT (BMG): PRCD 132 (CD) TCPRCV 132 (MC) 1989*
THE GODFATHER-ALL CREATURES GREAT AND SMALL-CHI MAI
TRIANGLE Theme/Intro-SEDUCTION from AMERICAN GIGOLO
LOVE DREAMER-FILM 72 Theme-HOUSE OF CARADUS Theme-
LOVE DREAM-FIRST LOVE-CHARIOTS OF FIRE-YOU ARE THE
ONE-CAVATINA from THE DEER HUNTER-LOVE STORY Theme

286. PLAY SAM PLAY...AS TIME GOES BY - Original Artists
*GREAT MOVIE THEMES (Target-BMG): CD 60018 (CD) 1997*
1.AS TIME GOES BY *CASABLANCA* Ingrid Bergman-Dooley
Wilson 2.I CAN'T GIVE YOU ANYTHING BUT LOVE *JAM SES
SION* Louis Armstrong 3.STORMY WEATHER Lena Horne 4.
HONG KONG BLUES *TO HAVE AND HAVE...*Hoagy Carmichael
5.FALLING IN LOVE AGAIN *BLUE ANGEL* Marlene Dietrich
6.INKAM DINKA DOO *PALOOKA* Jimmy Durante 7.OVER THE
RAINBOW *WIZARD OF OZ* Judy Garland 8.THANKS FOR THE
MEMORY *BIG BROADCAST OF 1938* Bob Hope-Shirley Ross
9.CHICA CHICA BOOM *THAT NIGHT IN RIO* Carmen Miranda
10.NIGHT AND DAY *GAY DIVORCEE* Fred Astaire 11.MOON
OF MANAKOORA *HURRICANE* Dorothy Lamour 12.TEMPTATION
*GOING HOLLYWOOD* Bing Crosby 13.RHUMBOOGIE *ARGENTINE
NIGHTS* Andrews Sisters 14.LOBBY NUMBERS *UP IN ARMS*
Danny Kaye 15.SONG IS YOU *TIL THE CLOUDS ROLL BY*
Johnnie Johnstone-Kathryn Grayson 16.FOR ME AND MY
GAL J.Garland-G.Kelly-G.Murphy 17.I'LL SEE YOU IN
MY DREAMS *ROSE OF WASHINGTON SQUARE* Alice Faye 18.
DINAH *BIG BROADCAST* Bing & The Mills Brothers 19.
LET YOURSELF GO *FOLLOW THE FLEET* Ginger Rogers 20.
HOORAY FOR HOLLYWOOD *HOLLYWOOD HOTEL* Var.Artists

287. PRIME TIME MUSICALS - Various Artists
*VARESE (Pinn): VSD 5858 (CD)                    1997*
COPACABANA *(BARRY MANILOW)* ALADDIN *(COLE PORTER)*-
ANDROCLES AND THE LION *(RICHARD RODGERS)*-THE
CANTERVILLE GHOST *(J.BOCK-HARNICK)*-ON THE FLIP SIDE
*(B.BACHARACH-H.DAVID)*-OUR TOWN*(S.CAHN-J.VAN HUESEN)*
HIGH TOR *(A.SCHWARTZ-M.ANDERSON)* Charles Kimbrough-
Beth Howland-Jason Graae-Gregory Jbara-Michelle Nic
astro-Christiane Noll-Jennifer Peich-Sally Mayes...

288. **QUATERMASS AND THE PIT:** Film Music of Tristram CARY
*CLOUD NINE (Silva Screen): CNS 5009* *1996*
Orchestral Suites from: QUATERMASS AND THE PIT (67)
THE FLESH IS WEAK (1957) A TWIST OF SAND (1968)
SAMMY GOING SOUTH (1963) TREAD SOFTLY STRANGER (58)

289. **RABEN Peer** - Rainer Werner Fassbinder Film Music
*MILAN (BMG): 74321 45058-2 (CD) -4 (MC)* *1997*
BERLIN ALEXANDERPLATZ-THE MARRIAGE OF MARIA BRAUN-
MOTHER KUSTER'S TRIP TO HEAVEN-THE NIKLASHAUSER JOU
RNEY-THE STATIONMASTER'S WIFE-FOX AND HIS FRIENDS-
DESPAIR-THE THIRD GENERATION-SATAN'S BREW-CHINESE
ROULETTE-FEAR EATS THE SOUL-MERCHANT OF 4 SEASONS-
GODS OF THF PLAGUE-I ONLY WANT YOU TO LOVE ME-LILI
MARLENE-QUERELLE-IN A YEAR WITH 13 MOONS

--- **RATTRAY Mark** - *see COLLECTION 241*

--- **RED SHOES The** - see 'CLASSIC BRITISH FILM MUSIC'

290. **RICE Tim** - The Tim Rice Collection
*CARLTON SOUNDS: 30362 0027-2 (CD) -4 (MC)* *1996*
1.I KNOW HIM SO WELL Claire Moore and Gemma Craven
2.ONE NIGHT IN BANGKOK Carl Wayne 3.RAINBOW HIGH
Marti Webb 4.A WINTER'S TALE Peter Skellern 5.
I DON'T KNOW HOW TO LOVE HIM Claire Moore 6.ON THIS
NIGHT OF A THOUSAND STARS CarL Wayne 7.CLOSE EVERY
DOOR Dave Willetts 8.EVERYTHING'S ALRIGHT Fiona Hen
dry and Paul Jones 9.ANY DREAM WILL DO Jess Conrad
10.BUENOS AIRES Marti Webb 11.ANTHEM Ensemble 12.
ANOTHER SUITCASE IN ANOTHER HALL Stephanie Lawrence
13.GETHSAMANE Dave Willetts 14.DON'T CRY FOR ME
ARGENTINA Marti Webb 15.JESUS CHRIST SUPERSTAR Carl
Wayne 16.ONE MORE ANGEL IN HEAVEN Jess Conrad 17.
I'D BE SURPRISINGLY GOOD FOR YOU MartI Webb & Carl
Wayne 18.CIRCLE OF LIFE Carl Wayne 19.A WHOLE NEW
WORLD Stephanie Lawrence and Monroe Kent III 20.
CAN YOU FEEL THE LOVE TONIGHT Peter Skellern

291. **RICHARD Cliff** - At The Movies 1959-1974 *1996*
*EMI UK: CDEMD 1096 (2CD) TCEMD 1096 (MC delet.1997)*
Serious Charge (1959): NO TURNING BACK-LIVING DOLL-
MAD ABOUT YOU Expresso Bongo (1959):LOVE-A VOICE IN
THE WILDERNESS*(EP version)*-THE SHRINE ON THE SECOND
FLOOR The Young Ones (1961): FRIDAY NIGHT-GOT A FUN
NY FEELING *(alternate take)*-NOTHING IS IMPOSSIBLE-
THE YOUNG ONES*(original undubbed master)*-LESSONS IN
LOVE-WHEN THE GIRL IN YOUR ARMS-WE SAY YEAH-IT'S
WONDERFUL TO BE YOUNG *(alternate take 24)*-OUTSIDER
Summer Holiday(1963) SEVEN DAYS TO A HOLIDAY-SUMMER
HOLIDAY-LET US TAKE YOU FOR A RIDE-STRANGER IN TOWN
BACHELOR BOY-A SWINGIN' AFFAIR-DANCIN' SHOES-THE
NEXT TIME-BIG NEWS Wonderful Life (1964): WONDERFUL
LIFE-A GIRL IN EVERY PORT-A LITTLE IMAGINATION *(edi
ted vers.)*-ON THE BEACH-DO YOU REMEMBER-LOOK DON'T
TOUCH *(prev.unreleased)*-TN THE STARS-WIIAT'VE I GOI
IU DO-A MATTER OF MOMENTS-WONDERFUL LIFE *(alternate
take 18)* Thunderbirds Are Go (1967): SHOOTING STAR
Continued next page...

**RICHARD Cliff...**_Continued_

Finders Keepers (1966): FINDERS KEEPERS-TIME DRAGS
BY-WASHERWOMAN-LA LA LA SONG-OH SENORITA _(ext.vers)_
THIS DAY-PAELLA Two A Penny (1967): TWO A PENNY-
TWIST & SHOUT-I'LL LOVE YOU FOREVER TODAY-QUESTIONS
_(film version)_ Take Me High (1973): IT'S ONLY MONEY
MIDNIGHT BLUE-THE GAME-BRUMBURGER DUET-TAKE ME HIGH
THE ANTI BROTHERHOOD OF MAN-WINNING bonus tracks:-
YOUNG ONES _(film vers)_-LESSONS IN LOVE _ed.film vers_
BACHELOR BOY _(film v)_-SUMMER HOLIDAY _end title film_

292. ROMANCING THE FILM Rochester Pops Or: Lalo Schifrin
_SION (Direct): SION 18210 (CD)_                    1997
1.GONE WITH THE WIND:Tara's Theme 2.WIZARD OF OZ:
Over The Rainbow 3.CASABLANCA:As Time Goes By 4.
BREAKFAST AT TIFFANY'S:Moon River 5.LAWRENCE OF
ARABIA 6.DR ZHIVAGO:Lara's Theme 7.COOL HAND LUKE:
Symphonic Sketches 8.GODFATHER:Love Theme 9.SPACE
_MEDLEY:_2001 A SPACE ODYSSEY/STAR WARS 10.DIRTY DAN
CING:I've Had The Time Of My Life" 11._MEDLEY:_The
LITTLE MERMAID/AROUND THE WORLD IN 80 DAYS

293. ROMEO AND JULIET - Royal Scottish National Orchest
conducted by Cliff Eidelman
_VARESE (Pinn): VSD 5752 (CD)_                    1997
_FEAT.MUSIC FROM_ ROMEO AND JULIET-HAMLET-HENRY V-
MUCH ADO ABOUT NOTHING-RICHARD III / _COMPOSERS:-_
Sergei Prokofiev-Dimitri Shostakovich-Miklos Rosza
Patrick Doyle-Nino Rota-Alex North-Cliff Eidelman

294. ROSE AND THE GUN - The Music Of Laurie JOHNSON *
_FLY-U.Kanch (H.Mundi-FLY Dir): FLYCD 103_        1992
LADY AND THE HIGHWAYMAN (TVM 89)-A HAZARD OF HEARTS
(TVM 87)-A DUEL OF HEARTS (TVM 88)-A GHOST IN MONTE
CARLO (TVM 90)-THE AVENGERS (Theme/Tag)-THE NEW AVE
NGERS-TIGER BAY THEME-WHEN THE KISSING HAD TO STOP
CAESAR SMITH/THERE IS ANOTHER SONG/THIS TIME (from:
Hot Millions)-SHIRLEY'S THEME/RICKSHAW RIDE (from:
Shirley's World)-I AIM AT THE STARS Theme-THIS IS
YOUR LIFE (Gala Performance)-JASON KING theme-ROMAN
CE (The First Men In The Moon)-THE PROFESSIONALS
*_LONDON STUDIO SYMPHONY ORCHESTRA (Laurie Johnson)_

295. ROTA Nino - Symphonic FELLINI Czech Symphony Orch *
_SILVA SCREEN (Koch): FILMCD 129 (CD)_            1991
_Music Of NINO ROTA For The FEDERICO FELLINI Films_
LA DOLCE VITA-LA STRADA-IL BIDONE-THE WHITE SHEIKH
ROMA-SATYRICON-CASANOVA-ORCHESTRA REHEARSAL-NIGHTS
OF CABIRIA-THE CLOWNS-I VITELLONI-AMARCORD-BOCCACC
IO 70-JULIET OF THE SPIRITS * Derek Wadsworth cond

296. ROZSA Miklos - Epic Film Music - City Of Prague
Philharmonic Orchestra conducted by Kenneth Alwyn
_SILVA SCREEN (Koch): FILMCD 170 (CD)_            1996
Symphonic Suites and Themes from Original Scores:
GOLDEN VOYAGE OF SINBAD _Prelude/Sinbad Battles Kali
/Finale)_-KING OF KINGS _(Prelude)_-EL CID _(Overture/
Love Scene)_-SODOM AND GOMORRAH _Overture_-QUO VADIS

*(Prelude/Arabesque/Romanza/Ave Caesar*-KING OF KINGS
*(The Lord's Prayer)*-BEAU BRUMMELL *Prelude/King's Vi
sit and Farewell)*-BEN HUR *Prelude/Love Theme/Parade
Of The Charioteers)*-ALL THE BROTHERS WERE VALIANT
*(Main Title/Finale)*-MADAME BOVARY *(Waltz/Bonus trk)*
KING OF KINGS *(Orchestral theme version)*

297. SAX AT THE MOVIES - State Of The Heart (Dave Lewis
sax, Taj Wyzgowski gtr) Love Themes from the Movies
*VIRGIN (EMI): CDVIP 181 (CD) (re-numbered)*    *1996*
1.UNCHAINED MELODY 2.LOVE IS ALL AROUND 3.SHOW ME
HEAVEN 4.BECAUSE YOU LOVED ME 5.HOW DEEP IS YOUR LO
VE 6.KISS FROM A ROSE 7.CAN YOU FEEL THE LOVE TONIG
HT 8.SOMEWHERE OUT THERE 9.EVERYTHING I DO (I DO IT
FOR YOU) 10.GLORY OF LOVE 11.THE BEST THAT YOU CAN
DO (ARTHUR'S THEME) 12.I'VE HAD THE TIME OF MY LIFE
13.UP WHERE WE BELONG 14.WHEN A MAN LOVES A WOMAN
15.MY FUNNY VALENTINE 16.I WILL ALWAYS LOVE YOU
17.TAKE MY BREATH AWAY 18.IT MUST HAVE BEEN LOVE
19.WAITING FOR A STAR TO FALL 20.GANGSTA'S PARADISE

--- SCHIFRIN Lalo - *see COLLECTIONS 195,199,292*

298. SCHINDLER'S LIST Classic Film Music: JOHN WILLIAMS
City Of Prague Philharmonic Orchest. (Paul Bateman)
*SILVA SCREEN (Koch): FILMCD 160 (CD)*    *1995*
SCHINDLER'S LIST-JAWS-FAR AND AWAY-THE COWBOYS-THE
STAR WARS TRILOGY-INDIANA JONES TRILOGY-BORN ON THE
4TH JULY-PRESUMED INNOCENT-JURASSIC PARK etc.

299. SCHWARZENEGGER Arnold - Greatest Film Themes
*SILVA SCREEN (Koch): FILMCD (C) 164 (CD/MC)*    *1995*
CONAN THE BARBARIAN/THE DESTROYER-TOTAL RECALL-THE
TERMINATOR-TERMINATOR 2-RED HEAT-RAW DEAL-COMMANDO-
JUNIOR-TWINS-KINDERGARTEN COP-PREDATOR-TRUE LIES

300. SCI-FI : City Of Prague Philharmonic (Paul Bateman/
Nic Raine) / Daniel Caine
*SILVA SCREEN Treasury (Koch): SILVAD 3508 (CD) 1997*
1:STAR WARS 2: EMPIRE STRIKES BACK 3:RETURN OF THE
JEDI *(J.WILLIAMS)* 4:TOTAL RECALL *(J.GOLDSMITH)* 5:
PREDATOR *(A.SILVESTRI)* 6:DARK STAR *(J.CARPENTER)* 7:
STARMAN *(J.NITZSCHE)* 8:GREMLINS II *(J.GOLDSMITH)* 9:
TERMINATOR II *(B.FIEDEL)* 10:THE THING *(E.MORRICONE)*
11:APOLLO 13 *(J.HORNER)* 12:STAR TREK-THE MOTION PIC
TURE *(Jerry GOLDSMITH)* 13:STAR TREK-DEEP SPACE 9 /
14:STAR TREK-GENERATIONS *(D.McCARTHY)*    *tpt: 61.48*

301. SCI-FI THEMES - London Theatre Orchestra
*EMPORIO (DISC-THE): EMPRCD(EMPRMC) 655 (CD/MC) 1996*
STAR WARS-THE X.FILES-CLOSE ENCOUNTERS OF THE THIRD
KIND-2001 A SPACE ODYSSEY-STAR TREK-BATTLESTAR GALA
CTICA-SPACE 1999-BLAKE'S 7-DUNE-STARGATE-BLADE RUNN
ER-TOTAL RECALL-WAR OF THE WORLDS-TOMORROW PEOPLE-
DOCTOR WHO-E.T.

302. SCIENCE FICTION AND FANTASY: TV SOUND TREK Various
*VARESE (Pinn): VSD 5865 (CD)*    *1997*
BABYLON 5-SEAQUEST-XENA WARRIOR PRINCESS-HERCULES-
LEXX TTHE DARK ZONE STORIES-CAPTAIN FUTURE-MISSION
IMPOSSIBLE-STAR TREK and PERRY RHODAN SCI-FI NOVELS

*303.* SENSES - 20 Contemporary Moods And Themes - V.Arts
*POLYGRAM TV: 516 627-2 (CD) -4 (MC)* *1994*
PLAY DEAD *(Young Americans) Bjork and David Arnold*
ROBIN THE HOODED MAN *Clannad* BLADERUNNER LOVE THEME
*Vangelis* BETWEEN THE LINES *Hal Lindes* COCKEY'S SONG
*Once Upon A Time In America) Ennio Morricone* LOVE'S
THEME *(Midnight Express) Giorgio Moroder* ROBINSON
CRUSOE*Art Of Noise* NOMADS OF THE WIND *Brian Bennett*
THEME FROM THE FIRM *Marcello* GYMNOPEDIE1 *Erik Satie*
EQUINOXE PART 4 *Jean Michel Jarre* EVE OF THE WAR
*Jeff Wayne* CACHARPAYA *Incantation* COISICH A RUIN
*(Prince Among Islands) Capercaillie* ROWENA'S THEME
*(Captive) The Edge* CAVATINA *(Deerhunter) John Willi
ams* THE SNOWMAN *Howard Blake* RODRIGO'S GUITAR CONC.
*Nicolas de Angelis* OXYGENE PART 4 *Hank Marvin* GOING
HOME *(Local Hero) Mark Knopfler*

*304.* SERRA Eric - The BEST OF ERIC SERRA
*VIRGIN (EMI): CDVIR 56 (CD)* *1997*
THE BIG BLUE OVERTURE-LA RAYA-LET THEM TRY-MY LADY
BLUE-ALCOOL-RUINES 2-MASQUERADE-IT'S ONLY MYSTERY-
PROCESSION IN THE SHAKUASHI TEMPLE-EDGE OF MADNESS-
RICO'S GANG-SUICIDE-THE FREE SIDE-DARK SIDE OF TIME
THE SNAKE-TIME TO GET YOU LOVIN'-NOON-HEY LITTLE
ANGEL-THAT'S WHAT KEEPS YOU ALONE-THE EXPERIENCE

*305.* SHAKEN AND STIRRED: A JAMES BOND Film Songs Collect
produced and masterminded by DAVID ARNOLD *1997*
*EAST WEST (WEA): 3984 20738-2 (CD) -4 (MC)*
1.DIAMONDS ARE FOREVER *DIAMONDS ARE FOREVER* David
McAlmont 2.JAMES BOND THEME *(M.Norman)* LTJ Buckem 3
NOBODY DOES IT BETTER *SPY WHO LOVED ME* Aimee Mann 4
ALL TIME HIGH *OCTOPUSSY* Pulp 5.SPACE MARCH *YOU ONLY
LIVE TWICE* Leftfield 6.LIVE AND LET DIE Chryssie
Hynde 7.MOONRAKER Shara Nelson 8.THUNDERBALL ABC 9.
FROM RUSSIA WITH LOVE Natasha Atlas 10.YOU ONLY
LIVE TWICE Candi Staton 11.ON HER MAJESTY'S SECRET
SERVICE Propellorheads 12.WE HAVE ALL THE TIME IN
THE WORLD *ON HER MAJESTY'S SECRET SERVICE* Iggy Pop
*see also* JAMES BOND FILM INDEX p.346

*306.* SHAKESPEARE FILM MUSIC - Nat.Philharmonic Orch *
*DECCA (Poly): 455 156-2 (CD)* *1997*
HAMLET (1948, William Walton) RICHARD III (1955,
William Walton) JULIUS CAESAR (1953, Miklos Rozsa)
HENRY V (1944, William Walton) Orchestral Suites
* conducted by Bernard Herrmann *(prev. 421 268-4)*

*307.* SHANE: A TRIBUTE TO VICTOR YOUNG - New Zealand SO*
*KOCH INTernational (Koch): 3-7365-2H1 (CD)* *1996*
SHANE *(1952)* FOR WHOM THE BELL TOLLS *(1943)* AROUND
THE WORLD IN EIGHTY DAYS *(1956)* THE QUIET MAN*(1952)*
SAMSON AND DELILAH *(1949)* *cond.by Richard Kaufman

*308.* SHERLOCK HOLMES: Classic Themes from 221 Baker Str.
*VARESE (Pinn): VSD 5692* *1996*
221B BAKER STREET/THE RED CIRCLE *(Patrick Gowers)*
SHERLOCK HOLMES (Granada TV). SUITE *(John Addison)*
7 PER CENT SOLUTION. MAIN TITLE/MORIATY:GENIUS OF

EVIL/MORIATY:THE GAME IS A FOOT/MORIATY:ELEMENTARY
*(Cyril Mockridge)* ADVENTURES OF SHERLOCK HOLMES.
A STUDY IN TERROR *(John Scott)* A STUDY IN TERROR.
THE UNIVERSAL HOLMES *(Frank Skinner)* various films
THE RIDDLE SOLVED *(Bruce Broughton)* YOUNG SHERLOCK
HOLMES. I NEVER DO ANYTHING TWICE*Stephen Sondheim*
7 PER CENT SOLUTION. THE MASKS OF DEATH *(Malcolm
Williamson)* (Tyburn/C4). MAIN TITLE/THE LEGEND OF
THE HOUND*(James Bernard)* HOUND OF THE BASKERVILLES
MUSIC BOX *(Frank Skinner)* DRESSED TO KILL. SUITE
*(Miklos Rozsa)* PRIVATE LIFE OF SHERLOCK HOLMES.
END TITLE *(Henry Mancini)* WITHOUT A CLUE
*Orchestra cond: LANNY MEYERS / * sung by Judy Kaye*
309. SHOOT 'EM UPS - Classic REPUBLIC Westerns
*VARESE (Pinn):* VSD 5666 *(CD)* 1996
THE LONE RANGER-THE PAINTED STALLION-THE THREE MESQ
ITEERS-UNDER WESTERN SKIES etc. Cinema Sound Orches
tra (James King, conductor) *see also 'CLIFFHANGERS'*
--- SHOSTAKOVICH Dimitri - *see COLLECTION 261*
310. SILENCE - Various Artists
*SONY MUSIC TV:* SONYTV35*(CD)(MC)* (2CD/MC) 1997
1.ADAGIO FOR STRINGS *BARBER* 2.GREENSLEEVES *VAUGHAN
WILLIAMS* 3.PIE JESU FROM REQUIEM *FAURE* 4.CONCERTO
DE ARANJUEZ *RODRIGO* 5.INTERMEZZO FROM CAVALLERIA
RUSTICANA *MASCAGNI* 6.PIANO CONCERTO NO.21 (ELVIRA
MADIGAN THEME) *MOZART* 7.NIMROD (ENIGMA VAR.) *ELGAR*
8.IN TRUTINA(CARMINA BURANA) *ORFF* 9.ADAGIO *ALBINONI*
10.CAVATINA *MYERS* 11.PAVANE *FAURE* 12.ADAGIETTO FROM
SYMPHONY NO.5 *MAHLER* 13.ACT II SCENE FROM SWAN LAKE
*TCHAIKOVSKY* CD2: BAILERO (CHANTS D'AUVERGNE) *CANTEL
OUBE* 2.LARGO NEW WORLD SYMPH.9 *DVORAK* 3.CANON IN D.
*PACHELBEL* 4.LARGO (XERXES) *HANDEL* 5.HUMMING CHORUS
(MADAM BUTTERFLY) *PUCCINI* 6.VALSE TRISTE *SIBELIUS*
7.JESU JOY OF MAN'S DESIRING *BACH* 8.CLAIR DE LUNE
*DEBUSSY* 9.FLUTE CONCERTO K299 (part only) *MOZART*
10.DANCE OF THE BLESSED SPIRITS (ORFEO & EURIDICE)
*GLUCK* 11.MORNING (PEER GYNT) *GREIG* 12.ALLELUIA
(SONG FOR ATHENA) *TAVERNER*
--- SILENCIUM (John Harle) - *see COLLECTION 407*
311. SIMON Carly - Film Noir
*ARISTA (BMG):* 07822 18984-2 *(CD)* -4 *(MC)* 1997
YOU WON'T FORGET ME-EV'RY TIME WE SAY GOODBYE-LILI
MARLENE-LAST NIGHT WHEN WE WERE YOUNG *(Duet with
JIMMY WEBB)*-SPRING WILL BE A LITTLE LATE THIS YEAR-
FILM NOIR-LAURA-I'M A FOOL TO WANT YOU-FOOLS CODA-
TWO SLEEPY PEOPLE *(Duet with JOHN TRAVOLTA)*-DON'T
SMOKE IN BED-SOMEWHERE IN THE NIGHT
312. SIMONETTI PROJECT The: 'Mystery Magic And Madness'
Film and other music of CLAUDIO SIMONETTI
*PRESIDENT (BMG):* PCOM 1137 *(CD)* 1994
PROFONDO ROSSO (Deep Red 1977)-TENEBRAE (82)-PHENOM
MENA (Creepers 84)-SUSPIRIA (77) OPERA (87) CROWS +
I'LL TAKE THE NIGHT-SEARCHING-ALBINONI IN ROCK (Ada
gio)-CARMINA BURANA's THEME-DAYS OF CONFUS

*313.* <u>SINATRA Frank</u> - Screen Sinatra
*MFP (EMI): CDMFP 6052 (CD)*                        *1988*
FROM HERE TO ETERNITY-YOUNG AT HEART-SOMEONE TO WAT
CH OVER ME-TENDER TRAP-ALL THE WAY-MONIQUE-TO LOVE
AND BE LOVED-ALL MY TOMORROWS-C'EST MAGNIFIQUE-JUST
ONE OF THOSE THINGS-THREE COINS IN THE FOUNTAIN-NOT
AS A STRANGER-JOHNNY CONCHO THEME-CHICAGO-THEY CAME
TO CORDURA-HIGH HOPES-IT'S ALL RIGHT WITH ME-DREAM

*314.* <u>SINTRA Frank</u> - Remembers The Movies 1943-1946
*GREAT MOVIE THEMES (Target-BMG): CD 60016 (CD) 1997*
THREE LITTLE WORDS-WHERE OR WHEN-THAT OLD BLACK
MAGIC-IF I HAD MY WAY-MY IDEAL-TILL THE END OF TIME
MAKE BELIEVE-I ONLY HAVE EYES FOR YOU-EMPTY SADDLES
SOMEBODY LOVES ME-THAT'S FOR ME-IT'S BEEN A LONG LO
NG TIME-WHITE CHRISTMAS-YOU'LL NEVER KNOW-AS TIME
GOES BY-EASY TO LOVE-I'VE GOT YOU UNDER MY SKIN-
ON THE ATCHINSON TOPEKA & SANTA FE-PEOPLE WILL SAY
WE'RE IN LOVE-DON'T FENCE ME IN-WITH A SONG IN MY
HEART-A HOT TIME IN THE OLD TOWN OF BERLIN-
I'LL REMEMBER APRIL-THERE GOES THAT SONG AGAIN

*315.* <u>SLICE OF PYE</u> - Orig British Cast MUSICALS - V.Arts
*DRG (New Note-Pinn): DRGCD 13114 (CD)*              *1996*
Musicals: ANNIE-FUNNY GIRL-BAR MITZVAH BOY-BARNARDO
THE CARD-CARRY ON LONDON-CHARLIE GIRL-MR.BURKE MP-
SONGBOOK-THE TIME OF YOUR LIFE Artists include: JOE
BROWN-LISA SHANE-ROSA MICHELLE-BARRY ANGEL-GEORGE
MITCHELL SINGERS-TONY HATCH-JACKIE TRENT-WALLY WHYT
ONS VIPERS-DIANE LANGTON-SIDNEY JAMES-GEORGE FORMBY

*316.* <u>SONDHEIM Stephen</u>: A Celebration at Carnegie Hall
*RCA VICTOR (BMG): 09026 61484-2 (2CDs) Complete*
SWEENEY TODD-FOLLIES-COMPANY-FUNNY THING HAPPENED..
DICK TRACY-MERRILY WE ROLL ALONG-INTO THE WOODS-SIN
GING OUT LOUD-PACIFIC OVERTURES-ASSASSINS-SEVEN %
SOLUTION-ANYONE CAN WHISTLE-A LITTLE NIGHT MUSIC-
SUNDAY IN THE PARK.... *see also 'TURNER Geraldine'*

*317.* <u>SOUND GALLERY</u> - Various Artists
*EMI STUDIO 2: CDTWO 2001 / 7243 832280-2 (CD)  1995*
OH CALCUTTA:Dave Pell Singers BLACK RITE:Mandingo-
PUNCH BOWL:Alan Parker NIGHT RIDER *(Cadbury's Milk
Tray)*:Alan Hawkshaw RIVIERA AFFAIR:Neil Richardson
JET STREAM:John Gregory HALF FORGOTTEN DAYDREAMS
John Cameron JAGUAR:John Gregory LIFE OF LEISURE
Keith Mansfield GIRL IN A SPORTSCAR:Alan Hawkshaw-
YOUNG SCENE *(ITV BIG MATCH)*:Keith Mansfield
IT'S ALL AT THE CO-OP NOW *(Co-op ad)*:Alan Hawkshaw
FUNKY FEVER:Alan Moorehouse & Bond Street Parade
SHOUT ABOUT PEPSI *(Pepsi)*:Denny Wright & Hustlers
THE HEADHUNTER:Mandingo BLARNEY'S STONED *Dave Allen
Theme)*: Alan Hawkshaw THE EARTHMEN:Paddy Kingsland
I FEEL THE EARTH MOVE:John Keating THE PENTHOUSE
SUITE:Syd Dale THE SNAKE PIT:Mandingo BOOGIE JUICE
Brian Bennett THE DETECTIVES *(Two Ronnies 'Charlie
Farley & Piggy Malone'theme)*:Alan Tew JESUS CHRIST
SUPERSTAR:John Keating MUSIC TO DRIVE BY:Joe Loss

318. SOUND GALLERY 2 - Various Artists
     *EMI STUDIO 2: CDTWO 2002 / 7243 852990-2 (CD) 1996*
     1.JASON KING THEME Laurie Johnson 2.POWERHOUSE POP
     Keith Mansfield 3.THE GOOD WORD *(NATIONWIDE THEME)*
     Scotsmen 4.TWO LANE BLACKTOP James Clarke 5.ZODIAC
     David Lindup 6.THAT'S NICE Alan Moorehouse 7.I CAN
     SEE FOR MILES Lord Sitar 8.ACCROCHE TOI CAROLINE
     *(VISION ON/TAKE HART)* Paris Studio Group 9.MARSEILL
     AISE GENERIQUE Francis Lai 10.FRANCAIS FRANCAIS Fra
     nck Pourcel 11.LEFT BANK 2 *(VISION ON 'PICTURE GALL
     ERY')* The Noveltones 12.LIGHT MY FIRE John Andrews
     Tartaglia 13.AVENGERS TAG *(AVENGERS)* Laurie Johnson
     14.OPEN HOUSE *(OPEN HOUSE BBC RADIO 2)* Brian Fahey
     Orch 15.MAMA ELEPHANT E.Cap 16.INTERNATIONAL FLIGHT
     David Snell 17.UP TO DATE *MAN ABOUT THE HOUSE THEME*
     Simon Park 18.ON THE BRINK Mike Vickers 19.SPORTS
     CAR SPECIAL Johnny Pearson 20.COUNTDOWN Brian Fahey
     21.MISS WORLD Syd Dale 22.ENTER THE DRAGON Jack Par
     nell 23.BREAKAWAY Steve Karman 24.CAESAR SMITH Laur
     ie Johnson 25.RAT CATCHERS Johnny Pearson 26.AT THE
     SIGN OF THE SWINGIN'CYMBAL*(PICK OF THE POPS)* Brian
     Fahey 27.THEME ONE *(RADIO 1 THEME 67)* George Martin

319. SOUND OF HOLLYWOOD Hollywood Bowl Orch John Mauceri
     *PHILIPS (Poly): 446 499-2 (CD)* 1995
     SELZNICK FANFARE *Newman* GONE WITH THE WIND *Steiner*
     KING KONG *Steiner* SHALL WE DANCE *George Gershwin*
     MGM FANFARE *and* WIZARD OF OZ *Stothart* GIGI *and* CHEZ
     MAXIMS WALTZ *Loewe* VERTIGO *Herrmann* ADVENTURES OF
     ROBIN HOOD *Korngold* SOUND OF MUSIC *Rodgers* JURASSIC
     PARK *and* E.T. *Williams* DANCES WITH WOLVES *Barry*
     20TH CENTURY FOX FANFARE *Newman* STAR WARS *Williams*

320. SOUND SPECTRUM - Various Artists
     *WHEN! (CASTLE-BMG): WENDC(WENMC)(WENLP) 005* 1995
     GET CARTER / LOVE IS A FOUR LETTER WORD / GETTING
     NOWHERE IN A HURRY / PLAYTHING all by Roy Budd
     GROW YOUR OWN John Schroeder Orch A TOUCH OF VELVET
     AND ASTING OF BRASS City Of Westminster String Band
     STILETTO Chico Rey and the Jet Band HEAVY WATER
     Ray Davies Button Down Brass HURRY TO ME Roy Budd
     SPEAKIN'OF SPOKEN Lovin'Spoonful SUPERSHINE NUMBER9
     Sister Gosling & Ducklings HEADBAND John Schroeder
     THE LONER (BUDGIE) Milton Hunter Orc BUSY BOY from
     CATWEAZLE Ted Dicks BIRDS Tony Hatch Orc MACH 1 Ray
     Davies Button Down Brass 2001 Cecil Holmes Soulful
     Sound PEGASUS Mike Vickers HOT WHEELS (THE CHASE)
     Badder Than Evil SPLIT LEVEL City Of W.String Band

321. SOUNDS ORCHESTRAL - SOUNDS RARE
     *SEQUEL (BMG): NEMCD 992 (CD) 1997* 1.HAVE FAITH
     IN YOUR LOVE 2.SOUNDS LIKE JACQUES 3.GO HOME GIRL
     4.DO NOTHING TILL YOU HEAR FROM ME 5.PORCELAIN 6.
     AIN'T THAT PECULIAR 7.BOY AND A GIRL 8.FIFTH AVENUE
     WALKDOWN 9.OUR LOVE STORY:TVTHEME 10.FROM NASHVILLE
     WITH LOVE 11.IMA 12.GLORIA GLORIA 13.BLUE TANGO 14.
     BLUE BOLERO 15.WEST OF CARNABY 16.THE HOPPING DANCE

SOUNDS ORCHESTRAL ...*Continued*

17.BLACK IS BLACK 18.I COULDN'T LIVE WITHOUT YOUR
LOVE 19.MAS QUE NADA 20.BAUBLES BANGLES AND BEADS
322.SPACE AND BEYOND City Of Prague Philh.Orc.Nic Raine
*SILVA SCREEN (Koch): FILMX(CD)(C) 185 (2CD/MC) 1997*
2001:A SPACE ODYSSEY *(68-RICHARD STRAUSS)*-SPECIES
*(94-CHRISTOPHER YOUNG)*-CAPRICORN ONE *(78-JERRY GOLD
SMITH)*-APOLLO 13 *(94-JAMES HORNER)*-THE RIGHT STUFF
*(83-BILL CONTI)*-ALIEN*(79-JERRY GOLDSMITH)*-THE BLACK
HOLE *(79-JOHN BARRY)*-COCOON *(85-JAMES HORNER)*-THE
EMPIRE STRIKES BACK *(80)* STAR WARS *(77-J.WILLIAMS)*
ENEMY MINE *(85-MAURICE JARRE)*-LIFEFORCE *(85-HENRY
MANCINI)*-CLOSE ENCOUNTERS OF THE THIRD KIND *(77-JW)*
STAR TREK I/II/IV/V/VI/DEEPSPACE NINE/NEXT GENERATI
ON/VOYAGER/GENERATIONS/HEAVY METAL *(ALEX.COURAGE/
JERRY GOLDSMITH/DENNIS McCARTHY/J.HORNER/LEONARD
ROSENMAN/CLIFF EIDELMAN)*
323.SPIELBERG Steven - SPIELBERG Connection Fantasia
*HALLMARK (Carlton): 30763-2 (CD) -4 (MC)        1997*
JAWS-ARACHNOPHOBIA-BACK TO THE FUTURE-INDIANA JONES
AND THE TEMPLE OF DOOM-ALWAYS-CLOSE ENCOUNTERS OF
THE THIRD KIND-HOOK-SCHINDLER'S LIST-RAIDERS OF THE
LOST ARK-COLOR PURPLE-CASPER-E.T.-EMPIRE OF THE SUN
1941-INDIANA JONES & THE LAST CRUSADE-JURASSIC PARK
see also 'HOLLYWOOD DIRECTORS'
324.SPIRITS OF NATURE - Various Original Artists
*VIRGIN (EMI): VTCD 87 (CD) VTMC 87 (MC)        1996*
1.YE-HA NO-HA (WISHES OF HAPPINESS AND PROSPERITY)
Sacred Spirit 2.SWEET LULLABY Deep Forest 3.LITTLE
FLUFFY CLOUDS The Orb 4.THE SUN RISING The Beloved
5.X-FILES (DJ DADO PARANORMAL ACTIVITY MIX) DJ Dado
6.RETURN TO INNOCENCE Enigma 7.STARS (MOTHER DUB)
Dubstar 8.THE WAY IT IS Chameleon 9.PLAY DEAD Bjork
& David Arnold 10.ARIA ON AIR *BRITISH AIRWAYS AD*
Malcolm McLaren 11.ADIEMUS *DELTA AIRWAYS AD* Adiemus
12.ONLY YOU *FIAT TEMPRA* Praise 13.FALLING*TWIN PEAKS*
Julee Cruise 14.MAD ALICE LANE: A GHOST STORY *LAND
ROVER DISCOVERY* Peter Lawlor 15.SENTINEL Mike Oldfi
eld 16.THEME FROM THE MISSION Ennio Morricone 17.
THE HEART ASKS PLEASURE FIRST/THE PROMISE from THE
PIANO Michael Nyman 18.FASHION SHOW II from THREE
COLOURS RED Zbigbniew Preisner 19.CHARIOTS OF FIRE
325.STALLING Carl - CARL STALLING PROJECT - Warner Bros
Cartoons 1936-1958 / Various Artists
*WARNER USA (Silv.Screen): 926027-2 (CD)-4 (MC) 1990*
*Music from WB 'Merrie Melodies' cartoons:* HILLBILLY
HARE-DAFFY DOC-BEANSTALK BUNNY-SPEEDY GONZALES etc.
326.STALLING Carl - CARL STALLING PROJECT Vol.2  W.Bros
Cartoons 1939-1959 / Various Artists
*WARNER USA (Silv.Screen): 945430-2 (CD)        1995*
see also 'BUGS BUNNY ON BROADWAY'
327.STALLONE Sylvester - Music From The Films Of
*SILVA SCREEN (Koch): FILMCD 139 (CD)           1993*

Music from: ROCKY (76-Bill Conti)-ROCKY 2 (79-Bill
Conti)-ROCKY 3 (82-Bill Conti)-ROCKY 4 (85-Bill Con
ti)-FIRST BLOOD (82-Jerry Goldsmith) RAMBO FIRST BL
OOD 2 (85-J.Goldsmith)-RAMBO 3 (88-Giorgio Moroder)
COBRA (86-Sylvester Levay)-LOCK UP (89-Bill Conti)-
NIGHTHAWKS (81-Keith Emerson)-PARADISE ALLEY (78-Bi
ll Conti)-OVER THE TOP (87-Giorgio Moroder)-F.I.S.T
(78-Bill Conti)-CLIFFHANGER (93-Trevor Jones)

328. STAND BY ME - Love Songs From The TV Commercials
MUSKETEER-START (S.Gold): MU 3013 (CD)        1995
STAND BY ME Ben E.King (Levi) ONLY YOU The Platters
Hellmans Mayonnaise/Network Q DRIFT AWAY Dobie Gray
Cadbury's Drifter  WILL YOU STILL LOVE ME TOMORROW
Shirelles Real Fires/Lunn Poly  WHEN A MAN LOVES A
WOMAN Percy Sledge (Levi)  RESCUE ME Fontella Bass
National Breakdown  GAMES PEOPLE PLAY Joe South
Eversun Lotion  I'M INTO SOMETHING GOOD Herman's He
mits Typhoo Tea/Kellogg's Special K  MY BLUE HEAVEN
Fats Domino Peugeot 106 WALKIN'THE DOG Rufus Thomas
Hush Puppies  I GOT YOU (I FEEL GOOD) James Brown
Clairol / Old Spice  BE-BOP A LULA Gene Vincent
Farley's Rusks  UP ON THE ROOF Drifters British Air
ways  LEADER OF THE PACK Shangri-las Lurpak I PUT A
SPELL ON YOU Screamin' Jay Hawkins Perrier WARM AND
TENDER LOVE Percy Sledge Lea & Perrins  BUT I DO
Clarence Frogman Henry Fiat Cinquecento  VENUS Fran
kie Avalon Cusson's Pearl  RUNAWAY Del Shannon Vaux
hall Club  GOODNIGHT SWEETHEART, WELL IT'S TIME TO
GO The Spaniels  Lemsip

329. STAR WARS / CLOSE ENCOUNTERS - Geoff Love Orchestra
MFP (EMI): CD(TC)MFP 6395 (CD/MC) or 7243 857687-2
(70's albums reissued now on 1 CD first time 1997)
STAR WARS-U.F.O.-STAR TREK-BARBARELLA-SPACE 1999-
2001 A SPACE ODYSSEY-MARCH FROM THINGS TO COME-PRIN
CESS LEIA'S THEME FROM STAR WARS-DOCTOR WHO-MARS
BRINGER OF WAR FROM PLANETS SUITE-CLOSE ENCOUNTERS
OF THE THIRD KIND-LOGAN'S RUN-THE TIME MACHINE-MAIN
TITLE & 'CANTINA BAND' FROM STAR WARS-BLAKE'S SEVEN
THEMES FROM THE OMEGA MAN

330. STAR WARS TRILOGY Orig Soundtrack Anthology    1994
ARISTA (BMG): 07822 11012-2 (4CD box set) FEATURING
'Star Wars'/'The Empire Strikes Back' + previously
unavailable expanded score 'Return Of The Jedi' and
special outtakes + unreleased mus + 50 page booklet

--- STEIN Ronald - see COLLECTION 271
--- STEINER Max - see COLLECTIONS 157,272

331. STREISAND Barbra - The Broadway Album
COLUMBIA (Sony M): CD 86322 (CD) 40-86322 (MC)
1.PUTTING IT TOGETHER SUNDAY IN T.PARK WITH GEORGE
2.IF I LOVED YOU CAROUSEL 3.SOMETHING'S COMING WEST
SIDE STORY 4.NOT WHIlF I'M AROUND SWEENEY TODD 5.
BEING ALIVE COMPANY 6.I HAVE DREAMED THE KING AND I
7.SOMETHING WONDERFUL KING & I 8.SEND IN THE CLOWNS

                    Continued next page...

STREISAND Barbra...*Continued*

*A LITTLE NIGHT MUSIC* 9.PRETTY WOMEN *SWEENEY TODD* 10
LADIES WHO LUNCH *COMPANY* 11.CAN'T HELP LOVIN' DAT
MAN *SHOW BOAT* 12.I LOVES YOU PORGY *PORGY & BESS* 13.
PORGY I'S YOUR WOMAN NOW *PORGY & BESS* 14.SOMEWHERE
*WEST SIDE STORY*

--- SUNSET BOULEVARD - *see COLLECTION 393*

*332.* SWASHBUCKLERS - City Of Prague Philhar.Paul Bateman
*SILVA SCREEN (Koch): FILMXCD 188 (2CD)* *1997*
CD1: Suites & themes 1.CAPTAIN BLOOD *(E.W.KORNGOLD)*
2.PRIVATE LIVES OF ELIZABETH & ESSEX *(E.W.KORNGOLD)*
3.HOOK *(J.WILLIAMS)* 4.THE CRIMSON PIRATE *(W.ALWYN)*
5.WILLOW *(J.HORNER)* 6.ROBIN HOOD *(G.BURGON)* 7.ROBIN
HOOD PRINCE OF THIEVES *(M.KAMEN)* 8.ROBIN AND MARIAN
*(J.BARRY)* 9/10.ADVENTURES OF ROBIN HOOD *(KORNGOLD)*
CD2: Suites & themes 1.THE SEA HAWK *(E.W.KORNGOLD)*
2.MARK OF ZORRO *(A.NEWMAN-H.FRIEDHOFER)* 3/4/5/6 THE
DUELLISTS *(H.BLAKE)* 7.THE BUCCANEER*(E.BERNSTEIN)* 8.
ADVENTURES OF DON JUAN *(M.STEINER)* 9.MONTY PYTHON'S
THE MEANING OF LIFE *(J.DUPREZ)* 10.SEVENTH VOYAGE OF
SINBAD *(B.HERRMANN)* 11.GOLDEN VOYAGE OF SINBAD *(M.
ROZSA)* 12.SWORDSMAN OF SIENNA *(M.NASCIMBENE)* 13.
CUTTHROAT ISLAND *(J.DEBNEY)*

*333.* SYNTHESIZER HITS Digital Music - Clarence McKEY
*MUSIC DIGITAL-DELTA (Target-BMG): 55 137 (3CD) 1995*
CD1.CONQUEST OF PARADISE-CHARIOTS OF FIRE-TWIN PEAK
S THEME-MAID OF ORLEANS (JOAN OF ARC)-I'LL FIND MY
WAY HOME-MAGIC FLY-EQUINOXE PART 5-AUTOBAHN-PULSTAR
ELECTRICA SALSA-LIVING ON VIDEO-AXEL F-MIAMI VICE-
MIDNIGHT EXPRESS-WILL OF THE WIND-PEPPERBOX-L'OPERA
SAUVAGE-MAGENTIC FIELDS CD2. EVE OF THE WAR-THEME
FROM ANTARCTICA-DUNE-LUCIFER-APOCALPYSE DES ANIMAUX
ARRIVAL-POPCORN-MADAME CUTIE-THE ROBOTS-ZOOLOKOLGIE
CAMILLA-THE TAO OF LOVE-OXYGENE IV-BATTLESHIP GALAC
TICA-CROCKETT'S THEME-CHI MAI-ONYX CD3. MAMMAGAMMA
ROTATIONS LOGIC-HYMNE-TOCCATA-TUBULAR BELLS THEME-
TO THE UNKNOWN MAN-TUBBS AND VALERIE-MODEL-TOUR DE
FRANCE-GENETIC ENGINEERING-AURORA-I HEAR YOU NOW-
PAZUZO-FLETCH-THEME-ERIC'S THEME-ITALIAN SONG-FIRST
APPROACH-FOURTH RENDEZVOUS

*334.* TAKE A BREAK! - Various Artists: TV ADS Compilation
*SONY MUSIC TV (Sony): SONYTV20(CD)(MC)* *1996*
1.SEARCH FOR THE HERO *(PEUGEOT 306)* M.People 2.SHOW
ME HEAVEN *(CADBURY)* Maria McKee 3.I JUST WANNA MAKE
LOVE TO YOU *(DIET COKE)* Etta James 4.LET THERE BE
LOVE *BRITISH MEAT* Nat King Cole 5.WHAT A WONDERFUL
WORLD *MICROSOFT* Louis Armstrong 6.SOMEONE TO WATCH
OVER ME *(PPP HEALTHCARE)* Ella Fitzgerald 7.I PUT A
SPELL ON YOU *DIET COKE* Nina Simone 8.FLY ME TO THE
MOON *(FORD PROBE)* Doris Day 9.ANGELINA *(MASTERCARD)*
Louis Prima 10.DON'T WORRY BE HAPPY *AXA* Bobby McFer
rin 11.GUAGLIONE *GUINNESS* Perez Prado 12.REACH OUT
I'LL BE THERE *TETLEY TEA*Four Tops 13.HE AIN'T HEAVY

HE'S MY BROTHER *(PANADOL)* Hollies 14.DAYS *(YELLOW PAGES)* Kinks 15.SEXUAL HEALING *(PEUGEOT 306)* Marvin Gaye 16.WONDERFUL LIFE *(STANDARD LIFE)* Black 17. NOTHING COMPARES 2U *(COW & GATE)* Sinead O'Connor 18 SAVE THE BEST FOR LAST *(BISTO)* Vanessa Williams 19. BREAKOUT *SALON SELECTIVES* Swing Out Sister 20.CARS *CARLING PREMIER* Gary Numan 21.ADDICTED YO LOVE *(HALL'S SOOTHERS)* Robert Palmer 22. THE PROFESSIONALS *(NISSAN ALMERA)* London Studio Symphony Orchestra

335. <u>TANGERINE DREAM</u> - Dream Music
*SILVA SCREEN (Koch): FILMCD 125 (CD) Selection 1993*
THE PARK IS MINE - DEADLY CARE - DEAD SOLID PERFECT *composed and performed by* Tangerine Dream

336. <u>TANGERINE DREAM</u> - Dream Music 2
*SILVA SCREEN (Koch): FILMCD 166 (CD) Selection 1995*
DEAD SOLID PERFECT-LEGEND-HEARTBREAKERS-STREETHAWK-CATCH ME IF YOU CAN-RISKY BUSINESS

337. <u>TASTE OF MUSIC, A</u> - Music from BBC TV Programmes:- Rick Stein's Taste Of The Sea / Antonio Carlucci's Italian Feast / Far Flung Floyd / Floyd On Italy / Floyd on Africa. performed by CROCODILE MUSIC 1997
*BBC WORLDWIDE (Pinn): V.1021 (CD) V/1022 (MC)*

338. <u>TATI Jacques</u> - Music From The Films Of Jacques TATI
*POLYGRAM Fra (Discovery): 836 983-2 (CD) reiss 1995*
1.JOUR DE FETE (1948) Mus: JEAN YATOVE 2.MON ONCLE (1956) Mus: ALAIN ROMAINS 3. MONSIEUR HULOT'S HOLIDAY (1953) Mus: ALAIN ROMAINS-FRANCK BARCELLINI

339. <u>TELEVISION'S GREATEST HITS 1</u> - 65 Orig TV Themes
*TVT-EDEL/CINERAMA (Pinn): 0022702CIN (CD) reiss 96*
CAPTAIN KANGAROO-LITTLE RASCALS-FLINSTONES-WOODY WOODPECKER SHOW-BUGS BUNNY-CASPAR THE FRIENDLY GHOST-FELIX THE CAT-POPEYE-YOGI BEAR-MAGILLA GORILLA-TOP CAT-JETSONS-FIREBALL XL5-HOWDY DOODY-BEVERLY HILLBILLIES-PETTICOAT JUNCTION-GREEN ACRES-MR.ED-MUNSTERS ADDAMS FAMILY-MY THREE SONS-DONNA REEDSHOW-LEAVE IT TO BEAVER-DENNIS THE MENACE-DOBIE GILLIS-PATTY DUKE SHOW-DICK VAN DYKE SHOW-GILLIGAN'S ISLAND-McHALE'S NAVY-I DREAM OF JEANNIE-I LOVE LUCY-ANDY GRIFFITH SHOW-STAR TREK-LOST IN SPACE-TWILIGHT ZONE-SUPERMAN ALFRED HITCHCOCK PRESENTS-BATMAN-FLIPPER-RIFLEMAN-COMBAT-BONANZA-BRANDED-F.TROOP-RIN TIN TIN-WILDWILD WEST DANIEL BOONE-LONE RANGER-HAPPY TRAILS-MISSION IMPOSSIBLE-MAN FROM UNCLE-GET SMART-SECRET AGENTMAN DRAGNET-PERRY MASON-ADAM 12-FBI-HAWAII 50-77 SUNSET STRIP-SURFSIDE 6-IRONSIDE-MANNIX-MOD SQUAD-TONIGHT

340. <u>TELEVISION'S GREATEST HITS 2</u> - 65 Orig TV Themes
*TVT-EDEL/CINERAMA (Pinn): 0022712CIN (CD) reiss 96*
3 STOOGES-MERRIE MELODIES-ROCKY & BULLWINKLE-HUCKLEBERRY HOUND-MIGHTY MOUSE-COURAGEOUS CAT & MINUTE MOUSE-PINK PANTHER-ROAD RUNNER-GEORGE OF THE JUNGLE-JONNY QUEST-SPIDERMAN-UNDERDOG-LOONEY TUNES-PEANUTS THEME-MISTER ROGER'S NEIGHBOURHOOD-ODD COUPLE-COURTSHIP OF EDDIE'S FATHER-MARY TYLER MOORE-GIDGET-THAT GIRL-BEWITCHED-LOVE AMERICAN STYLE-HONEYMOONERS-THE

MONKEES-I MARRIED JOAN-BRADY BUNCH-PARTRIDGE FAMILY
MY MOTHER THE CAR-CAR 54 WHERE ARE YOU-IT'S ABOUT
TIME-MY FAVOURITE MARTIAN-JEOPARDY-HOGAN'S HEROES-
GOMER PYLE-RAT PATROL-TWELVE O'CLOCK HIGH-TIME TUNN
EL-VOYAGE TO THE BOTTOM OF THE SEA-SEA HUNT-DAKTARI
TARZAN-ADVENTURES OF ROBIN HOOD-RAWHIDE-BAT MASTERS
ON-MAVERICK-WAGON TRAIN-HAVE GUN WILL TRAVEL-REBEL-
THE VIRGINIAN-PETER GUNN-ROUTE 66-ISPY-THE AVENGERS
THE SAINT-HAWAIIAN EYE-GREEN HORNET-OUTER LIMITS-
DARK SHADOWS-BEN CASEY-MEDICAL CENTER-MYSTERY MOVIE
ABC'S WIDE WORLD OF SPORTS-JACKIE GLEASON-SMOTHERS
BROTHERS COMEDY HOUR-MONTY PYTHON'S FLYING CIRCUS

*341.* TELEVISION'S GREATEST HITS 3 - 70's and 80's
*TVT-EDEL/CINERAMA (Pinn): 0022722CIN (CD) reiss 97*
SESAME STREET-MUPPET SHOW-ALVIN SHOW-SPEED RACER-MR
MAGOO-INSPECTOR GADGET-THE SMURFS-DASTARDLY& MUTLEY
SCOOBY DOO-FAT ALBERT & CROSBY KIDS-ARCHIES-JOSIE &
PUSSYCATS-DUDLEY DORIGHT-FRACTURED FAIRY TALES-BOB
NEWHART SHOW-CHEERS-GREATEST AMERICAN HERO-WELCOME
BACK KOTTER-ROOM 222-WKRP IN CINCINNATI-TAXI-BARNEY
MILLER-THREE'S COMPANY-HAPPY DAYS-LAVERNE & SHIRLEY
FACTS OF LIFE-GOOD TIMES-ONE DAY AT A TIME-GIMME A
BREAK-MAUDE-JEFFERSONS-ALL INTHE FAMILY-SANFORD AND
SON-DALLAS-DYNASTY-KNOTS LANDING-L.A.LAW-MARCUS WEL
BY MD-ST.ELSEWHERE-MASH-WALTONS-LITTLE HOUSE ON THE
PRAIRIE-HART TO HART-CHARLIE'S ANGELS-WONDER WOMAN-
LOVE BOAT-AMERICAN BANDSTAND-SOLID GOLD-ENTERTAINME
NT TONIGHT-MIAMI VICE-SWAT-BARETTA-STREETS OF SAN
FRANCISCO-BARNABY JONES-STARSKY & HUTCH-ROOKIES-KOJ
AK-A.TEAM-NAME O.T.GAME-QUINCY-HILL ST.BLUES-SIMON
& SIMON-MAGNUM-ROCKFORD FILES-SATURDAY NIGHT LIVE

*342.* TELEVISION'S GREATEST HITS 4 Black & White Classics
*TVT-EDEL/CINERAMA (Pinn): 0022732CIN (CD)*     *1997*
ASTRO BOY-ROGER RAMJET-MIGHTY HERCULES-GUMBY SHOW-
BEANY AND CECIL SHOW-TENNESSEE TUXEDO-QUICK DRAW
McGRAW-WALLY GATOR-KING LEONARDO AND SHORT SUBJECTS
BIG WORLD OF LITTLE ADAM-KUKLA FRAN AND OLLIE-SOUPY
SALES SHOW-CAPTAIN MIDNIGHT-MAKE ROOM FOR DADDY-
FATHER KNOWS BEST-MY LITTLE MARGIE-ADVENTURES OF
OZZIE AND HARRIET-HAZEL-OUR MISS BROOKS-KAREN-THE
REAL McCOYS-LASSIE-LIFE AND LEGEND OF WYATT EARP-
GUNSMOKE-THE LAWMAN-26 MEN-COLT 45-CHEYENNE-BRONCO
LEGEND OF JESSE JAMES-HOPALONG CASSIDY-EVERGLADES-
ADVENTURES IN PARADISE-DR.KILDARE-MEDIC-BURKE'S LAW
HIGHWAY PATROL-M.SQUAD-DETECTIVES-UNTOUCHABLES-THE
FUGITIVE-CHECKMATE-TIGHTROPE-BOURBON STREET BEAT-
PETE KELLY'S BLUES-ASPHALT JUNGLE-MR.BROADWAY-NAKED
CITY-TWENTY FIRST CENTURY-FRENCH CHEF-CANDID CAMERA
YOU BET YOUR LIFE-AMOS 'N' ANDY-ABBOTT AND COSTELLO
SHOW-LAUREL AND HARDY LAUGHTOONS-LAWRENCE WELK SHOW
TED MACK'S ORIGIN.AMATEUR HOUR-MISS AMERICA PAGEANT
RED SKELTON SHOW-BOB HOPE SHOW

*343.* TELEVISION'S GREATEST HITS 5 - In Living Color
*TVT-EDEL/CINERAMA (Pinn): 0022742CIN (CD)*     *1997*

STINGRAY-THUNDERBIRDS-GIGANTOR-COOL McCOOL-GO GO
GOPHERS-WORLD OF COMMANDER McBRAGG-SECRET SQUIRREL-
THE ATOM ANT SHOW-WACKY RACES-HONG KONG PHOOEY-
SUPERCHICKEN-TOM SLICK RACER-H.R.PUFNSTUF-LAND OF
THE LOST-SIGMUND AND THE SEA MONSTERS-BANANA SPLITS
PLEASE DON'T EAT THE DAISIES-THE GHOST AND MRS.MUIR
NANNY AND THE PROFESSOR-HERE COME THE BRIDES-THE
FLYING NUN-FAMILY AFFAIR-DATING GAME-NEWLYWED GAME-
LET'S MAKE A DEAL-ALL MY CHILDREN-GENERAL HOSPITAL-
PEYTON PLACE-MARY HARTMAN MARY HARTMAN-GENTLE BEN-
SKIPPY THE BUSH KANGAROO-LIFE AND TIMES OF GRIZZLY
ADAMS-HIGH CHAPARRAL-THE BIG VALLEY-CIMARRON STRIP
LAREDO-THE MEN FROM SHILOH-IT TAKES A THIEF-THE
MAGICIAN-SWITCH-THE FELONY SQUAD-POLICE WOMAN-MEN-
CANNON-JUDD FOR THE DEFENSE-EMERGENCY!-POLICE STORY
SIX MILLION DOLLAR MAN-BIONIC WOMAN-THE GIRL FROM
U.N.C.L.E.-NIGHT GALLERY-KOLCHAK: THE NIGHT STALKER
THE INVADERS-LAND OF THE GIANTS-LOST IN SPACE-OLYMP
IC FANFARE-MASTERPIECE THEATRE-WHERE THE ACTION IS-
ROWAN AND MARTIN'S LAUGH IN-THE DEAN MARTIN SHOW-
THE CAROL BURNETT SHOW

*344.* TELEVISION'S GREATEST HITS 6 - Remote Control
*TVT-EDEL/CINERAMA (Pinn): 0022752CIN (CD)*          *1997*
FISH-NIGHT COURT-WHAT'S HAPPENING-DIFFERENT STROKES
MR.BELVEDERE-GROWING PAINS-CHARLES IN CHARGE-SILVER
SPOONS-WEBSTER-TOO CLOSE FOR COMFORT-WHO'S THE BOSS
PERFECT STRANGERS-ALICE-IT'S A LIVING-ANGIE-227-THE
GOLDEN GIRLS-ALF-MORK AND MINDY-POLICE SQUAD-BENSON
MOONLIGHTING-SOAP-BENNY HILL SHOW-THE YOUNG ONES-
THE PEOPLE'S COURT-FAMILY FEUD-THE PRICE IS RIGHT-
SISKEL & EBERT-MONDAY NIGHT FOOTBALL-LIFESTYLES OF
THE RICH & FAMOUS-FAME-PAPER CHASE-FANTASY ISLAND-
FALCON CREST-THE COLBY'S-HIGHWAY TO HEAVEN-DUKES OF
HAZZARD-B.J.& THE BEAR-THE FALL GUY-JAMES AT 15-
EIGHT IS ENOUGH-BAA BAA BLACK SHEEP-TRAPPER JOHN MD
CHIPS-VEGAS-MATT HOUSTON-CAGNEY & LACEY-T.J.HOOKER-
HARDCASTLE & McCORMICK-HUNTER-MACGYVER-KNIGHT RIDER
AIRWOLF-THE INCREDIBLE HULK-V THE SERIES-THE NEW
TWILIGHT ZONE-DOCTOR WHO-MYSTERY-HARDY BOYS & NANCY
DREW MYSTERIES-ROOTS-VIETNAM A TELEVISION HISTORY

*345.* TELEVISION'S GREATEST HITS 7 -Cable Ready 80s & 90s
*TVT-EDEL/CINERAMA (Pinn): 0022762CIN (CD)*          *1997*
THE SIMPSONS-REN AND STIMPY-BROTHERS GRUNT-DUCKMAN-
ADVENTURES OF PETE AND PETE-SPACE GHOST COAST TO
COAST-CLARISSA EXPLAINS IT ALL-BARNEY AND FRIENDS-
WHERE IN THE WORLD IS CARMEN SANDIEGO-SAVED BY THE
BELL-MAJOR DAD-MY TWO DADS-BLOSSOM-FULL HOUSE-EMPTY
NEST-FAMILY MATTERS-COSBY SHOW-DIFFERENT WORLD-ROC-
FRESH PRINCE OF BEL AIR-HOME IMPROVEMENT-ROSEANNE-
SEINFELD-MAD ABOUT YOU-IT'S GARRY SHANDLING'S SHOW-
JOHN LARROQUETTE SHOW-HUDSON STREET-THE SINGLE GUY-
DAVIS RULES-MURPHY BROWN-THE NANNY-DESIGNING WOMEN-
DOOGIE HOWSER MD-WINGS-ANYTHING BUT LOVE-SISTERS-
EVENING SHADE-THE DAYS AND NIGHTS OF MOLLY DODD-

TELEVISION'S GREATEST HITS 7...*Continued*

I'LL FLY AWAY-THIRTYSOMETHING-MY SO CALLED LIFE-
BEVERLY HILLS 90210-MELROSE PLACE-HEIGHTS-21 JUMP
STREET-IN THE HEAT OF THE NIGHT-MIDNIGHT CALLER-
AMERICA'S MOST WANTED-UNSOLVED MYSTERIES-SLEDGE
HAMMER-THE EQUALIZER-N.Y.P.D.BLUE-LAW AND ORDER-
TWIN PEAKS-STAR TREK THE NEXT GENERATION-LOIS AND
CLARK THE NEW ADVENTURES OF SUPERMAN-ALIEN NATION-
TALES FROM THE CRYPT-QUANTUM LEAP-MAX HEADROOM-
LIQUID TELEVISION-HBO FEATURE PRESENTATION-THE
TRACEY ULLMAN SHOW-KIDS IN THE HALL-LATE SHOW
WITH DAVID LETTERMAN

*346.*TEMPLE Shirley - America's Sweeteart
    *FLAPPER-PAVILION (Pinn): PASTCD 7097 (CD)*          *1996*
    1.YOU'VE GOTTA SMILE TO B.HAPPY 2.GOODNIGHT MY LOVE
    3.THAT'S WHAT I WANT FOR CHRISTMAS 4.IN OUR LITTLE
    WOODEN SHOES 5.HOLY GOD WE PRAY THY NAME (HYMN) 6.
    SILENT NIGHT 7.BE OPTIMISTIC AND SMILE 8.HOW CAN I
    THANK YOU 9.WE SHOULD BE TOGETHER 10.IF ALL THE WOR
    LD WERE PAPER 11.WHEN YOU WERE SWEET SIXTEEN 12.COU
    RTROOM SCENE: STARS AND STRIPES FOREVER/THANK YOU
    FOR THE USE OF THE HALL/LOCH LOMOND/SWING ME AN OLD
    FASHIONED TUNE/LITTLE MISS BROADWAY 13.AN OLD STRAW
    HAT 14.COME AND GET YOUR HAPPINESS 15.REBECCA'S MED
    LEY:ON THE GOOD SHIP LOLLIPOP/ANIMAL CRACKERS IN MY
    SOUP/WHEN I'M WITH YOU/OH MY GOODNESS/GOODNIGHT MY
    LOVE 16.THE TOY TRUMPET 17.THIS IS A HAPPY LITTLE
    DITTY 18.I LOVE TO WALK IN THE RAIN 19.WOT CHER!
    (KNOCKED 'EM IN THE OLD KENT ROAD) 20.ONE TWO THREE
    21.LADY-DE-O 22.FIFTH AVENUE 23.YOUNG PEOPLE 24.I
    WOULDN'T TAKE A MILLION 25.TRA-LA-LA-LA 26.LEO IS
    ON THE AIR (KATHLEEN AIR TRAILER)

*347.*TEMPLE Shirley - On The Good Ship Lollipop
    *PRESIDENT (BMG): PLCD 541 (CD)*                      *1995*
    ON THE GOOD SHIP LOLLIPOP *(from BRIGHT EYES 1934)*
    BABY TAKE A BOW *(STAND UP AND CHEER 1934)* WHEN I'M
    WITH YOU/BUT DEFINATELY/OH MY GOODNESS *(POOR LITTLE
    RICH GIRL 1936)* LAUGH YOU SON OF A GUN *(LITTLE MISS
    MARKER 1934)* AT THE CODFISH BALL/THE RIGHT SOMEBODY
    TO LOVE/EARLY BIRD *(CAPTAIN JANUARY 1936)* LOVE'S
    YOUNG DREAM/THE TOY TRUMPET *(THE LITTLE COLONEL 36)*
    ON ACCOUNT-A I LOVE YOU *(BABY TAKE A BOW 1934)* GOOD
    NIGHT MY LOVE/THAT'S WHAT I WANT FOR CHRISTMAS/YOU
    GOTTA S.M.I.L.E.TO BE H.A.P.P.Y. *(STOWAWAY 1936)*
    IN OUR LITTLE WOODEN SHOES *(HEIDI 37)* PICTURE ME WI
    THOUT YOU/GET ON BOARD LI'L CHILDREN/HE WAS A DANDY
    HEY WHAT DID THE BLUE JAY SAY/DIXIE-ANNA *(DIMPLES
    1936)* ANIMAL CRACKERS IN MY SOUP/WHEN I GROW UP
    *(CURLY TOP 1935)* BELIEVE ME IF ALL THOSE ENDEARING
    YOUNG CHARMS/POLLY WOLLY DOODLE *(LITTLEST REBEL 35)*
    THE WORLD OWES ME A LIVING *(NOW AND FOREVER 1934)*

*348.*TERFEL Bryn - Something Wonderful
    *DG (Poly): 449 163-2 (CD) -4 (MC)*                    *1996*

SOME ENCHANTED EVENING-OH WHAT A BEAUTIFUL MORNING-
YOU'LL NEVER WALK ALONE-EDELWEISS-A FELLOW NEEDS A
GIRL-WHAT A LOVELY DAY FOR A WEDDING-COME HOME-SO
FAR-NO OTHER LOVE-SURREY WITH THE FRINGE ON TOP-
IF I LOVED YOU-SOLILOQUY-JUNE IS BUSTIN' OUT ALL
OVER-THIS NEARLY WAS MINE-YOUNGER THAN SPRINGTIME-
BALI HAI-THERE IS NOTHING LIKE A DAME-IT MIGHT AS
WELL BE SPRING-I HAVE DREAMED-SOMETHING WONDERFUL

349. TEST CARD CLASSICS: The Girl The Doll The Music
*FLYBACK-CHANDOS (Chandos): FBCD 2000 (CD)*        *1996*
1.INTRODUCTION 2.ROYAL DAFFODIL *(Gordon Langford)*
Stuttgart Studio Orch 3.RIGA ROAD *(R.Egin-Mike Run)*
Westway Novelty Ensemble 4.ANGRY *(D.Mecum-J.Cassard
H.Brunies)* Oscar Brandenburg Or 5.CAPABILITY BROWN
*(Ernest Tomlinson)* Stuttgart Studio Orch 6.WALTZ IN
JAZZTIME *(Syd Dale)* Cavendish Ten 7.BELLA SAMBA *(J.
Finten-R.Von Kessler)* Benito Gonzales Latin Sound
8.HOLIDAY HIGHWAYMAN *(Brian Couzens)* Stuttgart Stud
io Orch 9.CORDOBA *(W.Tautz)* Orchest.Heinz Kiessling
10.MY GUY'S COME BACK *M.Powell-R.McKinley-B.Goodman*
Oscar Brandenburg Orch 11.THE LARK IN THE CLEAR AIR
*(trad.arr Gordon Langford)* Langford Orch 12.PANDORA
*(Ray Davies)* New Dance Orch 13.FIRECRACKER *(Frank
Chacksfield)* Ferdnand Terby Or 14.HEBRIDEAN HOEDOWN
*(Gordon Langford)*Stuttgart Studio Orch 15.HIGH LIFE
*(Otto Sieben)* Gerhard Narholz Orch 16.SAMBA FIESTA
*(Heinz Kiessling)* Orch.Heinz Kiessling 17.STATELY
OCCASION *(Ernest Tomlinson)* Stuttgart Studio Orches
18.CHELSEA CHICK *(Johnny Scott)* Mr.Popcorn's Band
19.GREENLAND SLEIGH DOGS (ALASKA) *(Roger)* Roger Rog
er Orch 20.THESE FOOLISH THINGS *(Jack Strachey)* Cav
endish Ten 21.MARCH FROM THE COLOUR SUITE *(Gordon
Langford)* Stuttgart Studio Orch 22.LONG HOT SUMMER
*(Roger)* Ensemble Roger Roger 23.GOING PLACES *(D.Go
ld-E.Ponticelli-G.Rees)* Oscar Brandenburg 24.440Hz

351. TEST CARD CLASSICS 2: Big Band Width - Various Arts
*FLYBACK-CHANDOS (Chandos): FBCD 2001 (CD)*        *1997*
1.FING AIN'T WOT THEY USED T'BE *(Lionel Bart)* Oscar
Brandenburg Orch 2.SMILING FORTUNE *(Ronald Sekura)*
Orchestra Alexander Martin 3.THE STORY OF MY LOVE
*(Peter Voelkener)*George Winters Orch 4.LUCKY BOUNCE
*(Norman Giedhill)* Skymasters 5.HERE IN A SMOKY ROOM
*(Brian Fahey)*Otto Keller Band 6.WALTZ EXPRESS *(Hans
Ehrlinger)* Orch.Joe Scott 7.SLINKY *Trevor Lyttleton
tleton)*Brasshoppers 8.CARRY ME BACK TO OLD VIRGINNY
*(Hans Conzelmann-Delle Haensch)* Delle Haensch Band
9.BEAT-IN *(Pedro Gonez-Walter Waal)* Frank Pleyer &
His Orch 10.ALAMO *(Henry Mcintire-Olaf Norstad)* Orc
Joe Palmer 11.SMALL TOWN *(William Gardner)* William
Gardner Orch 12.TAKE OFF *(Erich Schneider Reinerez)*
Henry Monza Orch 13.MEET ME ON THE BRIDGE *(Brian
Fahey)* Skymasters 14.HAPPY WALK *(Ralph Heninger)*
Frank Pleyer & His Orch 15.CHARLESTON TIME *(Jimmy
Continued next page...

TEST CARD CLASSICS 2...*Continued*

Thanner-Karl Hans Ahl) Jimmy Thanner Orch 16.APRON
STRINGS *(Ernest Ponticelli)* Hans Hatter Orch 17.
SCOTCH BROTH *(Ernest Ponticelli-Gordon Rees-Neil
Richardson)* Oscar Brandenburg Orch 18.TELE-VISION
*(Hans.Conzelmann-Delle Haensch)* Delle Haensch Band
19.CONCERTO GROSSO 67 *(Ernst Quelle-Rico Mares)*
Eric Landy Orch 20.HIGH BALL *(Bill Geldard)* Otto
Keller Band 21.HALLELUJAH HONEY (aka MICHAEL ROW
THE BOAT ASHORE) *(Trad.arr Frank Valdor)* Orchest
Frank Valdor 22.SOHO SWING *(Charles Kalman)* Walt
Peters & His Orch 23.DAISY *(H.Conzelmann-D.Haensch)*
Delle Haensch Band 24.WALKING ON THE SHORE *(Paul
Termi)* Orch.Franco Taomina 25.HELLO LISSY *(Fred Spa
nnuth)* Orch.Joe Palmer 26.CRAIG HILL SURPRISE *Harry
Leader-Red Budtree)* Otto Keller Band 27.POST HASTE
*(Trevor Lyttleton)* Brasshoppers 28.SWINGING AFFAIR
*(E.Ponticelli-Gordon Rees)* Oscar Brandenburg Orch.
29.JEFF'S SPECIAL *(Jeff Hasky)* Orch.Jeff Hasky 30.
INDIAN BOOTS *(Horst Bredow)* George Winters Orchest

*351.*<u>THAT'S ENTERTAINMENT</u> - Best Of MGM Musicals V.Arts
*EMI PREMIER: CDODEON 21 (CD)*       *1996*
THAT'S ENTERTAINMENT-GET HAPPY-FROM THIS MOMOENT ON
OVER THE RAINBOW-OL' MAN RIVER-SINGIN' IN THE RAIN-
TROLLEY SONG-VARSITY DRAG-EASTER PARADE-ALL OF YOU-
ON THE ATCHINSON TOPEKA AND T.SANTA FE-HONEYSUCKLE
ROSE-I LIKE MYSELF-HALLELUJAH-THERE'S NO BUSINESS
LIKE SHOW BUSINESS *Original MGM -S/T- Recordings*

*352.*<u>THEMES AND INSTRUMENTALS</u> - Various Artists
*RCA INT (BMG): RCA(CD)(MC) 220 (2CD/MC)*     *1997*
CD1 1:ALBATROSS Fleetwood Mac 2:BABY ELEPHANT WALK
Henry Mancini 3:GOOD THE BAD AND THE UGLY Hugo Mont
enegro 4:PETER GUNNHenry Mancini 5:JAMES BOND THEME
John Barry 6:STRANGER ON THE SHORE Acker Bilk 7:THE
ENTERTAINERMarvin Hamlisch 8:LIGHT FLIGHT Pentangle
9:HARRY'S GAME Clannad 10:ROCKET TO THE MOON Jim Br
ickman 11:INSPECTOR MORSE 12:CROCKETT'S THEME 13:
MIAMI VICE Jan Hammer 14:SCARBOROUGH FAYRE Intune
15:LA SERENISSIMA (VENICE IN PERIL) Rondo Veneziano
CD2 1:MON AMOR Frank Thore 2:PETITE FLEUR Chris Bar
ber & Monty Sunshine 3:THEME FROM A SUMMER PLACE
Percy Faith 4:CHERRY PINK AND APPLE BLOSSOM WHITE
Perez Prado 5:PINK PANTHER THEME Henry Mancini 6:
LIGHT MY FIRE Booker T.& MG's 7:BETWEEN THE LINES
Hal Lindes 8:ARIA Acker Bilk 9:SHEPHERD'S LAMENT
Gheorge Zamfir 10:THORN BIRDS THEME Geoffrey Burgon
11:FROM RUSSIA WITH LOVE John Barry 12:SNOWFLAKES
ARE DANCING Tomita 13:WINDMILLS OF YOUR MIND Michel
Legrand 14:MIDNIGHT IN MOSCOW Kenny Ball 15:HANG'EM
HIGH Hugo Montenegro 16:SUKIYAKI Kenny Ball

*353.*<u>THEMES ALBUM The</u> - Various Artists    *reissued 1994*
*EMPORIO (THE): EMPRCD 516 (CD) EMPRBX 008 (4CD Box)*
ARTHUR'S THEME-SHE'S OUT OF MY LIFE-HILL ST.BLUES-

NIGHTS IN WHITE SATIN-BOLERO-WOMAN-ONLY HE HAS THE
POWER TO MOVE ME-CHARIOTS OF FIRE-THORN BIRDS LOVE
THEME-THE WAY HE MAKES ME FEEL (YENTL)-CACHARPAYA-
DERRY AIR-WINDS OF WAR-EDUCATING RITA-COUNTRY DIARY
OF AN EDWARDIAN LADY-JEWEL IN THE CROWN-TERMS OF
ENDEARMENT-GOOD THE BAD AND THE UGLY

354. THEMES FROM CLASSIC SCIENCE FICTION FILMS - V.Arts
*VARESE (Pinn): VSD 5407 (CD)*                    *1993*
THE MOLE PEOPLE-THE CREATURE FROM THE BLACK LAGOON-
THIS ISLAND EARTH-THE INCREDIBLE SHRINKING MAN-IT
CAME FROM OUTER SPACE-THE CREATURE WALKS AMONG US-
HOUSE OF FRANKENSTEIN-HORROR OF DRACULA-TARANTULA-
SON OF DRACULA-REVENGE OF THECREATURE-DEADLY MANTIS

355. THEMES OF HORROR - Mike TIMONEY
*EMPORIO (THE): EMPRCD 628 (CD)*                  *1995*
1.THE FLY *(H.SHORE)* 2.THE THING *(E.MORRICONE)* 3.THE
FOG *(J.CARPENTER)* 4.CARRIE*(P.DONAGGIO)* 5.PSYCHO *(B.
HERRMANN)* 6.POLTERGEIST III *(J.RENZETTI)* 7.THE EXOR
CIST (Tubular Bells) *(M.OLDFIELD)* 8.HELLRAISER *(OSB
OURNE-WYLDE)* 9.HALLOWEEN (a) Mr.Sandman *(P.BALLARD)*
(b)Halloween *(J.CARPENTER)* 10.THE AMITYVILLE HORROR
*(L.SCHIFRIN)* 11.FRIDAY THE 13TH *(H.MANFREDINI)* 12.
VERTIGO *(B.HERRMANN)* 13.THE SILENCE OF THE LAMBS
*(H.SHORE)* 14.ROSEMARY'S BABY *(K.KOMEDA)*

356. THIS IS CULT FICTION - Various Original Artists
*VIRGIN (EMI): VTCD 59 (CD) VTMC 59 (MC)*         *1995*
LITTLE GREEN BAG *(Reservoir Dogs)* George Baker Sel.
MISIRLOU *(Pulp Fiction)* Dick Dale & His Del Tones
MISSION IMPOSSIBLE Lalo Schifrin / SHAFT MAIN THEME
Isaac Hayes / JUNGLE BOOGIE *(Pulp Fiction)* Kool &
The Gang / MAN FROM UNCLE THEME Hugo Montenegro Orc
EVERYBODY'S TALKIN' *(Midnight Cowboy)* Nilsson
STUCK IN THE MIDDLE WITH YOU *(Reservoir Dogs)* Steal
ers Wheel / BLUE VELVET Bobby Vinton /TOUCH OF EVIL
Henry Mancini Orch / WE HAVE ALL THE TIME IN THE WO
RLD *On Her Majesty's Secret Service* Louis Armstrong
JAMES BOND THEME John Barry 7 / JOE 90 THEME Barry
Gray Orch / THE HARDER THEY COME Jimmy Cliff / HERE
COMES THE HOTSTEPPER *(Pret-A-Porter)* Ini Kamoze /
GUAGLIONE *(Guinness / KIKA)* Perez Prado Orchestra
PLAY DEAD *(Young Americans)* Bjork and David Arnold
AVENGERS THEME Laurie Johnson Orch / YOU NEVER CAN
TELL *(Pulp Fiction)* Chuck Berry / THE RUBLE *(Pulp
Fiction)* Link Wray / SAINT THEME Les Reed Brass /
HAWAII 5-0 Ventures / STREETS OF SAN FRANCISCO MAIN
THEME John Gregory Orch / LONG GOOD FRIDAY Francis
Monkman / THE SWEENEY Power Pack Orch / HIGH WIRE
(DANGERMAN) Bob Leaper Orch / TWIN PEAKS THEME /
ALL THE ANIMALS COME OUT AT NIGHT *(Taxi Driver)*

357. THIS IS CULT FICTION ROYALE - Various Artists
*VIRGIN (EMI): VTDCD 151 (2CD)*                   *1997*
1.BULLITT MAIN TITLE Lalo Schifrin 2.THE PERSUADERS
John Barry 3.EVA Jean Jacques Perrey 4.THE PRISONER
Ron Grainer 5.SPACE 1999 Barry Gray 6.DIRTY HARRY

Lalo Schifrin 7.THE SWEENEY Harry South (perform.by Wallace & Brint) 8.MAN IN A SUITCASE Ron Grainer 9. JAMES BOND THEMEMonty Norman 10.GET CARTER Roy Budd 11.WHODUNNIT (PRECINCT) S.Haseley 12.THE CHAMPIONS Tony Hatch 13.JOE 90 Barry Gray 14.PROTECTORS (THE AVENUES AND ALLEYWAYS) Mitch Murray-Peter Callander (performed by Tony Christie) 15.RANDALL AND HOPKIRK DECEASED Edwin Astley 16.VAN DER VALK (EYE LEVEL) Jack Trombey 17.AVENGERS Laurie Johnson 18.SAINT Edwin Astley (perf: Les Reed Brass) 19.DEMPSEY AND MAKEPEACE Alan Parker (perf: South Bank Orch) 20. JASON KING Laurie Johnson 21.SAPPHIRE AND STEEL Cyril Ornadel 22.UFO Barry Gray 23.THE BARON Edwin Astley 24.THE PROFESSIONALS Laurie Johnson (special 12" Blueboy mix) CD2: MISSION IMPOSSIBLE L.Schifrin 2.DEPARTMENT S.Edwin Astley 3.MAN FROM U.N.C.L.E. Jerry Goldsmith (perf: Hugo Montenegro) 4.RETURN OF THE SAINT Martin-Dee (Saint Orch) 5.PROFESSIONALS Laurie Johnson (perf: London Studio SO) 6.STINGRAY Barry Gray 7.DANGER MAN (HIGH WIRE) Edwin Astley (perf: Bob Leaper Orch) 8.007 John Barry 9.ON THE WAY TO SAN MATEO (from BULLITT) Lalo Schifrin 10. FIREBALL XL5 Barry Gray (vocal: Don Spencer) 11. THUNDERBIRDS Barry Gray 12.STRANGE REPORT Roger Webb (perf: Geoff Love) 13.NEW AVENGERS Laurie Johnson 14.CAPTAIN SCARLET Barry Gray 15.SUPERCAR Barry Gray 16.TISWAS Jack Parnell-David Lindup 17. MAGIC ROUNDABOUT Alain LeGrand 18.TALES OF THE UN EXPECTED Ron Grainer 19.AQUA MARINA Barry Gray (v: Gary Miller) 20.CROWN COURT (DISTANT HILLS) Reno-Haseley 21.HILL ST.BLUES Mike Post 22.TWIN PEAKS Angelo Badalamenti 23.BLADE RUNNER BLUES Vangelis
358.THIS IS EASY - Various Artists
*VIRGIN (EMI): VTDCD 80 (2CD) (7243 841534-2) 1996 Disc 1:* 1.BOND STREET*(CASINO ROYALE)* Burt Bacharach 2.CHAMPIONS Tony Hatch 3.SUPERSTARS Johnny Pearson 4.SPANISH FLEA The Mexicans 5.SENTIMENTAL JOURNEY Juan Garcia Esquivel 6.A SWINGIN'SAFARI Bert Kaemp fert 7.LAS VEGAS *(ANIMAL MAGIC)* Laurie Johnson Orch 8.PINK PANTHER THEME Henry Mancini 9.THE BIG MATCH Keith Mansfield 10.UP UP AND AWAY Fifth Dimension 11.STRANGE REPORT Geoff Love Orch 12.THE IN CROWD Percy Faith Orch 13.A TASTE OF HONEY The Mexicans 14. NEW AVENGERS London Studio Symphony Orchestra 15.THE RIVIERA AFFAIR Neil Richardson 16.ASTEROID *(PEARL & DEAN THEME)*Pete Moore Orch 17.AVENUES AND ALLEYWAYS *(THE PROTECTORS)* Tony Christie 18.MAN IN A SUITCASE Ron Grainer Or 19.DO YOU KNOW THE WAY TO SAN JOSE Ron Goodwin Orc 20.MUSIC TO WATCH GIRLS BY Andy Williams 21.1,2,3 Percy Faith Orch 22.MISIRLOU Martin Denny 23.CLASSICAL GAS Mason Williams 24.NEW ADVENTUR.OF BLACK BEAUTY South Bank Orch 25.THERE'S ALWAYS SOMETHING THERE TO REMIND ME Sandy Shaw 26. CROSSROADS Tony Hatch Orch 27.GOOD THE BAD AND THE

UGLY Hugo Montenegro Orch / *Disc 2:* 1.WALK ON BY
Dionne Warwick 2.WINDMILLS OF YOUR MIND *(THOMAS CRO
WN AFFAIR)*Noel Harrison 3.RAINDROPS KEEP FALLING ON
MY HEAD *BUTCH CASSIDY..* B.J.Thomas 4.ANYONE WHO HAD
A HEART Burt Bacharach 5.SUMMER BREEZE Ray Conniff
6.MAN AND A WOMAN Francis Lai 7.GET CARTER Roy Budd
8.I CAN'T LET MAGGIE GO Honeybus 9.LIGHT MY FIRE
Jose Feliciano 10.CLOSE TO YOU Matt Monro 11.AS TEA
RS GO BY Nancy Sinatra 12.GALA PERFORMANCE *(THIS IS
YOUR LIFE)* Laurie Johnson 13.CALL ME Chris Montez
14.CHELSEA MORNING Sergio Mendes 15.IT NEVER RAINS
IN SOUTHERN CALIFORNIARay Conniff 16.WHAT THE WORLD
NEEDS NOW IS LOVE Ron Goodwin 17.AU JOURD'HUI C'EST
TOI Francis Lai 18.A HOUSE IS NOT A HOME Burt Bacha
rach 19.WIVES AND LOVERS Jack Jones 20.GO BETWEEN
Michel Legrand 21.MIDNIGHT COWBOY John Barry 22.I
I SAY A LITTLE PRAYER Aretha Franklin 23.MY UNKNOWN
LOVE Count Indigo 24.LOOK OF LOVE Isaac Hayes

**359.** THIS IS EUROVISION - Various Artists
*VIRGIN (EMI): VTDCD 142 or 724384423520 (2CD) 1997*
1.NE PARTEZ SANS MOI *(SWITZERLAND 1988)* Celine Dion
2.CONGRATULATIONS *(UK 1968)* Cliff Richard 3.MAKING
YOUR MIND UP *(UK 81)* Bucks Fizz 4.SAVE YOUR KISSES
FOR ME *(UK 76)* Brotherhood Of Man 5.WHAT'S ANOTHER
YEAR*(IRELAND 80)* Johnny Logan 6.BEG STEAL OR BORROW
*(UK 72)* New Seekers 7.A LITTLE PEACE *(Germany 1982)*
Nicole 8.APRES TOI*(LUXEMBOURG 72)* Vicky Leandros 9.
TU TE RECONNIATRAS *(LUXEMBOURG 73)* Anne-Marie David
10.WHY ME *(IREL.92)* Linda Martin 11.J'AIME LA VIE
*(BELG.86)* Sandra Kim 12.ROCK'N'ROLL KIDS *(IREL.94)*
Paul Harrington-Charlie McGettigan) 13.HALLELUJAH
*(ISRAEL 1979)* Milk & Honey and Gali Atari 14.LET ME
BE THE ONE *(UK 1973)* Shadows 15.POUPEE DE CIRE POUP
EE DE SON *(LUXEMBOURG 65)* France Gall 16.THE VOICE
*(IRELAND 1996)* Eimear Quinn 17.UN BANC UN ARBE UNE
RUE *(MONACO 71)* Severine 18.LOVE GAMES *(UK 84)*Belle
& The Devotions 19.JACK IN THE BOX *(UK 71)* Clodagh
Rodgers 20.LA LA LA *(SPAIN 68)* Massiel CD2: 1.POWER
TO ALL OUR FRIENDS *(UK 73)* Cliff Richard 2.HOLD ME
NOW *(IREL.87)* Johnny Logan 3.PUPPET ON A STRING *(UK
67)* Sandie Shaw 4.LONG LIVE LOVE *(UK 74)* Olivia New
ton John 5.BOOM BANG-A-BANG *(UK 1969)* Lulu 6.I LOVE
THE LITTLE THINGS *(UK 64)* Matt Monro 7.ALL KINDS OF
EVERYTHING *(IREL.1970)* Dana 8.DING-A-DONG *(HOLLAND
75)* Teach-In 9.A BI NI BI *(ISRAEL 78)* Izhar Cohen &
Alphabeta 10.IN YOUR EYES *(IREL.93)* Niamh Kavanagh
11.BAD OLD DAYS *(UK 78)* Co-Co 12.I BELONG *(UK 1965)*
Kathy Kirby 13.PARLEZ VOUS FRANCAIS*(LUX.78)* Baccara
14.SING LITTLE BIRDIE *(UK 59)* Pearl Carr-Teddy John
son *15.MESSAGE TO YOUR HEART (UK 91)* Samantha Janus
16.L'OISEAU ET L'ENFANT *(FRANCE 77)* Marie Myriam
17.ROCK BOTTOM *(UK 77)* Lynsey De Paul & Mike Moran
18.LONELY SYMPHONY *(UK 1994)* Frances Ruffelle 19.
ONE STEP FURTHER *(UK 1982)* Bardo

360. THIS IS THE RETURN OF CULT FICTION - Various Arts
*VIRGIN (EMI): VTCD 112 (CD)* *1996*
1.PROFESSIONALS London Studio Or 2.ENTER THE DRAGON
Lalo Schifrin 3.STARSKY AND HUTCH *GOTCHA* Tom Scott
4.SIX MILLION DOLLAR MAN John Gregory Orchestra 5.
CHARLIE'S ANGELS theme 6.WONDERWOMAN theme 7.DR WHO
Peter Howell 8.VISION ON *ACROCHE TOI CAROLINE* Paris
Studio Group 9.TWO RONNIES *THE DETECTIVES* Alan Tew
10.MAGNUM P.I.Mike Post 11.GET SMART Ray Conniff Or
12.DAVE ALLEN AT LARGE THEME Alan Hawkshaw 13.KOJAK
14.TALES OF T.UNEXPECTED Ron Grainer 15.TAXI *ANGELA*
Bob James 16.FORD PROBE AD *FLY ME TO THE MOON* Julie
London 17.VISION ON(GALLERY) *LEFT BANK 2* Palais All
Stars 18.LAST TANGO IN PARIS Gato Barbieri 19.HILL
STREET BLUES Mike Post 20.NORTH BY NORTH WEST R.P.O
Elmer Bernstein 21.ONCE UPON A TIME IN AMERICA Enn
io Morricone 22.BUDGIE THEME Nick Harrison 23.TAXI
DRIVER Bernard Herrmann and Tom Scott alto sax 24.
WHITE HORSES Jacky 25.PERRY MASON *PARK AVE.BEAT* Bob
Crane 26.RETURN OF THE SAINT Saint Orch 27.I DREAM
OF JEANNIE 28.MAN ABOUT THE HOUSE *UP TO DATE* Hawksw
orth Big Band 29.ON THE BUSES *HAPPY HARRY* Tony Russ
ell 30.WORLD OF SPORT Don Jackson 31.BEWITCHEDtheme
32.MINDER*I COULD BE SO GOOD FOR YOU* Dennis Waterman
33.PLEASE SIR Sam Fonteyn 34.GRANGE HILL *CHICKEN
MAN* Alan Hawkshaw 35.SKI SUNDAY *POP LOOKS BACH* New
Dance Orch 36.ROOBARB & CUSTARD Johnny Hawksworth

361. THIS IS THE SON OF CULT FICTION - Various Artists
*VIRGIN (EMI): VTCD 114 (2CD) VTMC 114 (2MC)* *1997*
1.REAL ME *QUADROPHENIA* Who 2.WHOLE LOTTA LOVE *TOP
OF THE POPS* CCS 3.ALL RIGHT NOW *WRIGLEY'S GUM* Free
4.LUST FOR LIFE *TRAINSPOTTING* Iggy Pop 5.A TEAM
Mike Post 6.BORN TO BE WILD *EASY RIDER* Steppenwolf
7.SMOKE ON THE WATER *STRONGBOW CIDER* Deep Purple 8.
PEOPLE ARE STRANGE *LOST BOYS* Echo and The Bunnymen
9.WEREWOLVES OF LONDON *COLOR OF MONEY* Warren Zevon
10.THE LIONS AND THE CUCUMBERS *VAMPYROS LESBOS* Vamp
iros Sounds Incorpor. 11.PORPOISE SONG *HEAD* Monkees
12.WHITE RABBIT *PLATOON* Jefferson Airplane 13.VENUS
IN FURS *DUNLOP TYRES* Velvet Underground 14.GIRL YOU
'LL BE A WOMAN SOON *PULP FICTION* Urge Overkill 15.
BE BOP A LULA *WILD AT HEART* Gene Vincent 16.GREEN
ONIONS *GET SHORTY* Booker T.& MG's 17.LOUIE LOUIE
*N.L.ANIMAL HOUSE* Kingsmen 18.BRING DOWN THE BIRDS
*BLOW UP* Herbie Hancock 19.NORTHERN EXPOSURE theme
David Schwartz 20.DUELLING BANJOS *DELIVERANCE* Eric
Weissberg-Steve Mandell 21.SUICIDE IS PAINLESS *MASH*
Jamie Mandel 22.CALLING YOU *BAGDAD CAFE* Jevetta Ste
ele 23.CAVATINA *DEER HUNTER* John Williams

362. THOSE MAGNIFICENT OVERTURES: West End Theatre Orch
*CARLTON SHOWS (CHE): 30362 0035-2 (CD) -4 (MC) 1996
OVERTURES:* JESUS CHRIST SUPERSTAR-GREASE-BUDDY-LES
MISERABLES-STARLIGHT EXPRESS-MISS SAIGON-SUNSET BOU
LEVARD-PHANTOM OF THE OPERA-SHOW BOAT-SOUTH PACIFIC

*363.*THRILLERS! - City Of Prague Philharm.(Paul Bateman/
Nic Raine/Derek Wadsworth) / London Screen Orchest
Royal Philharmonic Concert Orch (Mike Townend) and
Lesley Garrett w.Chamber Orch of London (Nic Raine)
*SILVA SCREEN Treasury (Koch): SILVAD 3504 (CD) 1997*
1:NORTH BY NORTHWEST *(B.HERRMANN)* 2:PATRIOT GAMES
*(J.HORNER)* 3:UNTOUCHABLES *(E.MORRICONE)* 4:FUGITIVE
*(J.NEWTON HOWARD)* 5:QUILLER MEMORANDUM *(J.BARRY)*
6:NIGHTHAWKS *(K.EMERSON)* 7:IN THE LINE OF FIRE *(E.
MORRICONE)* 8:THE FIRM *(D.GRUSIN)* 9:IPCRESS FILE
*(J.BARRY)* 10:MAGNUM FORCE / 11:MISSION IMPOSSIBLE
*(L.SCHIFRIN)* 12:PRESUMED INNOCENT *(J.WILLIAMS)* 13:
INNOCENT SLEEP *(M.AYRES, sung by* Lesley Garrett)
14:WITNESS *(M.JARRE)* *tpt: 50.18*
*364.*THUNDERBIRDS ARE GO: TV THEMES FOR GROWN-UP KIDS
*PULSE (BMG): PLSCD 195 (CD)* *1997*
1.THUNDERBIRDS Barry Gray Orch 2.FIREBALL XL5 Flee-
Rekkers 3.CAPTAIN SCARLET Barry Gray Orch 4.JOE 90
Barry Gray Orch 5.STINGRAY Gary Miller & Barry Gray
Orch 6.AQUA MARINA Gary Miller & Barry Gray Orchest
7.MYSTERONS Barry Gray Orch 8.DOCTOR WHO Eric Winst
one Orc 9.Z-CARS Johnny Keating 10.SPORTSNIGHT Tony
Hatch Orch 11.AVENGERS Laurie Johnson Orch 12.THE
CHAMPIONS Tony Hatch Orch 13.DANGER MAN *HIGH WIRE*
Bob Leaper Orch 14.MAN IN A SUITCASE Ron Grainer Or
15.THE FUGITIVE John Schroeder Orch 16.DEPARTMENT S
Cyril Stapleton Or 17.POWER GAME Cyril Stapleton Or
18.EMMERDALE FARM Tony Hatch Orch 19.RETURN OF THE
SAINT Saint Orch 20.CROSSROADS Tony Hatch 21.THE
FORSYTE SAGA Cyril Stapleton Orch 22.MAIGRET Eagles
*365.*TIOMKIN Dimitri Film Music - R.C.M.O.* *1986*
*UNICORN KANCHANA: DKPCD 9047 (CD) DKPC 9047 (MC)*
ROMAN EMPIRE-PAX ROMANA-GUNS OF NAVARONE-RHAPSODY
OF STEEL-WILD IS THE WIND-PRESIDENT'S COUNTRY Suite
THE ALAMO-RAWHIDE-HIGH NOON *Royal College Of Music
Orchestra (David Willcocks) with David King (organ)
*366.*TIOMKIN Dimitri Western Film World London Studio SO
Laurie Johnson,John McCarthy Sing. *UNICORN KANCHANA*
*(H.Mundi): UKCD 2011 (CD)* Suites: GIANT-RED RIVER-
DUEL IN THE SUN-HIGH NOON-NIGHT PASSAGE-RIO BRAVO
*367.*TOP TV SOAP THEMES - Various Artists
*EMPORIO-MCI (DISC-THE): EMPRCD 662 (CD)* *1996*
EASTENDERS-CORONATION STREET-NEIGHBOURS-HOME & AWAY
PRISONER CELL BLOCK H-SONS AND DAUGHTERS-BROOKSIDE-
WALTONS-EMMERDALE-YOUNG DOCTORS-SOAP-FALCON CREST-
CROSSROADS-PEYTON PLACE-FLYING DOCTORS-SULLIVANS
*368.*TOP TV THEMES - Various Artists
*CASTLE COMM (BMG): MCCD 152 (CD)* *1993*
1.FIREBALL XL5 Flee Rekkers 2.CAPTAIN SCARLET Barry
Gray Orch 3.JOE 90 Barry Gray Orch 4.THUNDERBIRDS
Barry Gray Orch 5.THE AVENGERS Laurie Johnson Orch
6.THE SAINT Les Reed 7.RETURN OF THE SAINT Saint
Orch 8.HIJACKED Barry Gray Orch 9.Z-CARS Johnny

*Continued next page...*

<u>TOP TV THEMES</u> ...*Continued*

8.HIJACKED Barry Gray Orch 9.Z-CARS Johnny Keating
6.THE SAINT Les Reed 7.RETURN OF THE SAINT Saint
Orch 8.HIJACKED Barry Gray Orch 9.Z-CARS Johnny
Keating & Z-Men 10.THE FUGITIVE John Schroeder Orch
11.HANCOCK'S TUNE (ITV) Derek Scott 12.DEPARTMENT S
Cyril Stapleton Orch 13.DOCTOR WHO Eric Winstone Or
14.DANGER MAN *High Wire* Bob Leaper Orch 15.GENERAL
HOSPITAL *Red Alert* Johnny Pearson Orch 16.OUR HOUSE
The Piccadilly 17.CROSSROADS Tony Hatch Orchestra
18.WAGON TRAIN *Roll Along Wagon Train* Robert Horton
369.<u>TRUFFAUT Francois</u> - *see COLLECTION 115*
370.<u>TUNES FROM THE TOONS</u> - The Best Of HANNA-BARBERA
*MCI (MCI-THE): MCCD(MCTC) 279 (CD/MC)*    *1996*
1-2 DASTARDLY & MUTTLEY 3-5 TOP CAT 6-8 YOGI BEAR 9
-12FLINTSTONES 13-14 HUCKLEBERRY HOUND 15-16 PERILS
OF PENELOPE PITSTOP 17-18 SNOOPER & BLABBER 19-21
JETSONS 22-23 HAIR BEAR BUNCH 24.SECRET SQUIRREL 25
HONG KONG PHOOEY 26-27 JOSIE & THE PUSSYCATS 28-29
SCOOBY DOO WHERE ARE YOU 30.NEW SCOOBY DOO 31-32
TOUCHE TURTLE 33-34 WALLY GATOR 35-37 PIXIE & DIXIE
38-40 QUICK DRAW McGRAW 41-42 SNAGGLEPUSS 43.HONEY
WOLF 44.AUGIE DOGGIE 45.YANKY DOODLE 46.LIPPY LION
& HARDY HA HA 47.WACKY RACES 48.BANANA SPLITS THEME
371.<u>TURNER Geraldine</u> - The Stephen SONDHEIM Songbook
*SILVA SCREEN (Koch): SILVAD 3011 (CD)*    *1997*
1.LIKE IT WAS/OLD FRIENDS *(MERRILY WE ROLL ALONG)*
2.LOSING MY MIND *(FOLLIES)* 3.I WISH I COULD FORGET
YOU *(PASSION)* 4.NOT WHILE I'M AROUND *(SWEENEY TODD)*
5.COULD I LEAVE YOU *(FOLLIES)* 6.WITH SO LITTLE TO
BE SURE OF *(ANYONE CAN WHISTLE)* 7.THE MILLER'S SON
*(A LITTLE NIGHT MUSIC)* 8.BUDDY'S BLUES *(FOLLIES)* 9.
I REMEMBER *(EVENING PRIMROSE)* 10.A PARADE IN TOWN/
THERE WON'T BE TRUMPETS *(ANYONE CAN WHISTLED)* 11.
BEING ALIVE *(COMPANY)* 12.ANYONE CAN WHISTLE *(same)*
13.ANOTHER HUNDRED PEOPLE *(COMPANY)* 14.WHAT CAN YOU
LOSE/LOVE I HEAR *(DICK TRACY/A FUNNY THING HAPPENED
ON THE WAY TO THE FORUM)* 15.GOODBYE FOR NOW *(REDS)*
372.<u>TV CLASSICS</u> (Volumes 1-4) - Various Artists
*CASTLE COMM (BMG): MBSCD 412 (4CDBox Set)*    *1993*
(CD1): FIREBALL XL5 *(FLEE REKKERS)* CAPTAIN SCARLET-
JOE 90-PARKER WELL DONE *(BARRY GRAY ORCH)* STINGRAY
*(GARRY MILLER vocal)* MYSTERONS THEME *(BARRY GRAY O)*
THUNDERBIRDS MAIN THEME *(BARRY GRAY ORCH)* AVENGERS
*(LAURIE JOHNSON)* ROBIN HOOD *(GARY MILLER)* THE SAINT
*(LES REED BRASS)* RETURN OF THE SAINT *(SAINT ORCH)*
(CD2): MAIGRET 62 *(EAGLES)* A MAN IN A SUITCASE *(RON
GRAINER ORCH)* AQUA MARINA *(GARRY MILLER vocal)* HIJA
CKED *(BARRY GRAY ORCH)* THE CHAMPIONS *(TONY HATCH O)*
Z CARS *(JOHNNY KEATING & Z.MEN)* THE FUGITIVE *(JOHN
SCHROEDER ORCH)* HANCOCK'S THEME *(DEREK SCOTT MUSIC)*
POWER GAME THEME *(CYRIL STAPLETON ORCH)* THE FORSYTE
SAGA THEME-DEPARTMENT S. *(CYRIL STAPLETON ORCH)* DR.

WHO *(ERIC WINSTONE ORCH)*(**CD3**): MR.ROSE INVESTIGATES
*(ROY BUDD & TONY HATCH ORCH)* WHO DO YOU THINK YOU
ARE KIDDING MR.HITLER *(BUD FLANAGAN)* OLD NED (STEPT
OE AND SON THEME)-HAPPY JOE *(RON GRAINER ORCHESTRA*
HADLEIGH-MAN ALIVE *(TONY HATCH SOUND)* LUNAR WALK
*(JOHNNY HAWKESWORTH ORCH)* THANK YOUR LUCKY STARS
*(PETER KNIGHT & KNIGHTRIDERS)* HIGH WIRE (DANGER MAN
THEME)*(BOB LEAPER ORCH)* RED ALERT (GENERAL HOSPITAL
THEME) *(JOHNNY PEARSON ORCH)* GIRL IN THE WHITE COAT
*(DEREK SCOTT ORCH)* SIR FRANCIS DRAKE-OUR HOUSE *(PIC
CADILLY STRINGS)* (**CD4**): CROSSROADS-EMMERDALE FARM-
SPORTSNIGHT *(TONY HATCH OR)* ROLL ALONG WAGON TRAIN
*(ROBERT HORTON)* THE SHAKE-WEST END (WHICKER'S WORLD
THEME)-NO HIDING PLACE-SUCU SUCU (TOP SECRET THEME)
LATIN QUARTER-ECHO FOUR TWO *(LAURIE JOHNSON ORCHES)*
MR.& MRS.*(JACKIE TRENT & TONY HATCH)* orig PRT rec.

373. TV THEMES AMERICA - Var.Arts    *1989 re-issued 1995*
*EMPORIO (THE): EMPRCD 556 (CD)*
DALLAS-PERFECT STRANGERS-KNOTS LANDING-HEAD OF THE
CLASS-MIDNIGHT CALLER-MISSION IMPOSSIBLE-MACGYVER-
CAGNEY AND LACEY-DYNASTY-ODD COUPLE-HIGH CHAPARRAL
M*A*S*H*-BONANZA-TAXI-ROCKFORD FILES-DOCTOR KILDARE

374. TV TOWN - (Ultra Lounge series) - Various Artists
*EMI: CDEMS  1616 or 7243 8534 092 (CD)*        *1997*
1.BUBBLES IN THE WINE Freddy Martin 2.NAKED CITY Ne
lson Riddle 3.ODD COUPLE Billy May 4.MAN FROM UNCLE
A.Caiola 5.THANKS FOR T.MEMORY Dave Pell 6.MUNSTERS
Jack Marshall 7.THE FUGITIVE Si Zentner 8.DICK VAN
DYKE/ALVIN SHOW Nelson Riddle 9.HUMAN JUNGLE John
Barry 10.BATMAN David McCallum 11.MANNIX Billy May
12.ONE STEP BEYOND (FEAR)/TWILIGHT ZONE Ventures 13
MOD SQUAD Al Caiola 14.MR.LUCKY Si Zentner Orch
15.MY THREE SONS Nelson Riddle 16.BURKE'S LAW Liber
ty ST 17.BEWITCHED Peggy Lee 18.MELANCHOLY SERENADE
Jackie Gleason 19.POWER HOUSE Spike Jones

375. UNSUNG MUSICALS Volume 3 - Various Artists
*VARESE (Pinn): VSD 5769 (CD)*
tracks include: NOTHING TO DO WITH LOVE *(PERSONALS)*
AT THE SAME TIME *(FREAKY FRIDAY)* PENNY BY PENNY *(A
CHRISTMAS CAROL)* WONDERFUL LIFE *(A WONDERFUL LIFE)*
REVEILLE SUN *(HERE'S WHERE I BELONG)* HERO *(BABE)*

376. UPSHAW Dawn - Sings Rodgers and Hart
*NONESUCH (WEA): 7559 79406-2 (CD)*        *1996*
1.HE WAS TOO GOOD TO ME *(SIMPLE SIMON)* 2.MANHATTAN
*(GARRICK GAIETIES 1925)* 3.YOU'RE NEARER 4.I DIDN'T
KNOW WHAT TIME IT WAS *(TOO MANY GIRLS)* 5.SING FOR
YOUR SUPPER *(BOYS FROM SYRACUSE)* 6.NOBODY'S HEART
*(BY JUPITER)* 7.THOU SWELL *(A CONNECTICUT YANKEE)* 8.
TWINKLE IN YOUR EYE *(I MARRIED AN ANGEL)* 9.I COULD
WRITE A BOOK *(PAL JOEY)* 10.WHY CAN'T I *(SPRING IS
HERE)* 11.EVERY SUNDAY MORNING 12.IT NEVER ENTERED
MY MIND *(HIGHER AND HIGHER)* 13.MOUNTAIN GREENERY
*GARRICK GAIETIES 29)* 14.A SHIP WIHOUT A SAIL *(HANDS
UP)* 15.DANCING ON THE CEILING *(EVER GREEN)*

377. <u>VALLEY OF GWANGI</u>  Jerome Moross Classic Film Music*
     *SILVA SCREEN (Koch): FILMCD 161 (CD)*              *1995*
     THE WAR LORD-THE SHARKFIGHTERS-RACHEL RACHEL-THE
     MOUNTAIN ROAD-FIVE FINGER EXCERCISE-ADVENTURES OF
     HUCKLEBERRY FINN-WAGON TRAIN-THE VALLEY OF GWANGI
     * City Of Prague Philharmonic Orch (Paul Bateman)
378. <u>VAMPIRE CIRCUS</u> - Original Horror Movie -S/T-
     *SILVA SCREEN (Koch): FILMCD 127 (CD)*              *1993*
     RETURN OF DRACULA (1958 mus: Gerald Fried)- VAMPIRE
     CIRCUS (71-David Whittaker)- FRIGHT NIGHT (85-Brad
     Fiedel)- TRANSYLVANIA TWIST (91-Chuck Cirino)- VAMP
     (86-Jonathan Elias)- CHILDREN OF THE NIGHT (92-Dani
     el Licht)- THIRST (79-Brian May)-TRANSYLVANIA 65000
     (85-Lee Holdridge)- FOREVER KNIGHT (TV 92-Fred Moll
     in)- TO DIE FOR (89-Cliff Eidelman)-SON OF DARKNESS
     (TO DIE FOR 2) (91-Mark Mackenzie)- THE HUNGER ('Fl
     ower Duet' from LAKME sung by LESLEY GARRETT)- DRAC
     ULA (73-Robert Cobert)- SUNDOWN (89-Richard Stone)
379. <u>VENTURES</u> - Batman and Other TV Themes
     *SEE FOR MILES-C5 (Pinn): C5HCD 653*                *1997*
     BATMAN THEME-ZOCKO-CAPE-GET SMART-MAN FROM UNCLE-
     HOT LINE-JOKER'S WILD-UP UP AND AWAY-GREEN HORNET
     00-711-VAMPCAMP-SECRET AGENT MAN-CHARLIE'S ANGELS-
     MEDICAL CENTRE-STAR TREK-STREETS OF SAN FRANCISCO-
     STARSKY AND HUTCH-BARRETTA'S THEME-HAWAII 5.0-SWAT-
     POLICE STORY-MASH-POLICEWOMAN-NADIA'S THEME FROM
     THE YOUNG AND THE RESTLESS
380. <u>VICTORY AT SEA</u> - Eric KUNZEL & Cincinnati Pops Orch
     *TELARC USA (BMG-Con): CD 80175 (CD only)*          *1989*
     VICTORY AT SEA (5 selections from 1950's TV Series)
     THE WINDS OF WAR/WAR & REMEMBRANCE-CASABLANCA Suite
     COLONEL BOGEY March-WARSAW CONCERTO-VALIANT YEARS-
     Main Title from BATTLE OF BRITAIN-OVER THERE-March
     THE LONGEST DAY-GENERAL'S MARCH-ARMED FORCES Medley
381. <u>VINTAGE THEMES</u> British Radio,Television & Newsreels
     *EMI PREMIER: CDEMS 1554 (CD) (7243 834996-2)*      *1996*
     1.IN TOWN TONIGHT (Celebrity M) *PORTRAIT OF A FLIRT*
     *(R.Farnon)* Queen's Hall Light Orch (S.Torch) 2.ITMA
     *IT'S THAT MAN AGAIN (M.North)* New Century Orchestra
     3.MUSIC IN THE AIR *(B.Lloyd)* Queen's Hall Light Orc
     (S.Torch) 4.DEAR SIR *CITY DESK (R.Hanmer)* New Centu
     ry Orch 5.GRAND HOTEL *ROSES FROM THE SOUTH(Strauss)*
     Norrie Paramor Orch 6.ROUNDABOUT *WINDOWS OF PARIS*
     *(T.Osborne)* Tony Osborne Orch 7.THE NAVY LARK *TRADE*
     *WIND HORNPIPE (J.Moody-T.Reilly)* Tommy Reilly harm.
     8.MUSIC HALL *THE SPICE OF LIFE (J.Kennedy-M.Carr)*
     Charles Shadwell Orch 9.BBC TELEVISION MARCH *(Eric*
     *Coates)* Sidney Torch Orch 10.PICTURE PARADE *(J.Beav*
     *er)* Pinewood Studio Orch 11.BBCTV NEWSREEL *GIRLS IN*
     *GREY (C.Williams)* Charles Williams Orch. 12.WHAT'S
     MY LINE *PARISIAN MODE (W.Phillips)* Woolf Phillips
     Orch 13.THE GROVE FAMILY *FAMILY JOKE (E.Spear)*Tommy
     Reilly harm. 14.EMERGENCY WARD-10 *SILKS AND SATINS*
     *(P.Yorke)* Georges Devereaux Orch 15.ITN NEWS *NON-*

STOP (J.Malcolm) Georges Devereaux Or 16.BLUE PETER
*BARNACLE BILL (A.Hope)* New Century Orch (S.Torch)
17.ANIMAL MAGIC *LAS VEGAS (L.Johnson)* Group 40 Orch
18.THIS IS YOUR LIFE *GALA PERFORMANCE (L.Johnson)*
KPM Mood Music 19.GAUMONT-BRITISH NEWS FANFARE *(Lou
is Levy)* Louis Levy & His Gaumont British Symphony
20-29 *NEWSREEL THEMES* performed by New Century Orch
(Sidney Torch): 20.SPORTS ARENA MARCH *(L.Stevens)*
21.BREAKFAST BUSTLE*(Len Stevens)* 22.SOCIETY WEDDING
*(Clive Richardson)* 23.THE PADDOCK *(Philip Green)*
24.LONDON PLAYHOUSE *(Sidney Torch)* 25.AIRPORT*(Clive
Richardson)* 26.DAGGER IN THE DARK *(Ronald Hamner)*
27.METROPOLIS *(Jack Brown)* 28.PRODUCTION DRIVE *(Fra
nk Cordell)* 29.MANNEQUIN *(Jack Beaver)* 30.GAUMONT
BRITISH NEW MARCH *MUSIC FROM THE MOVIES(Louis Levy)*
Louis Levy and His Gaumont British Symphony
382.<u>VISIONS</u> - Var.Artists  *(1982 K-Tel)  this edit.1994
MCI (Disc-THE): MCCD (MCTC) 190 (CD/MC)*
FLYING *(ET)* LSO HARRY'S GAME *Light Shadows* SUICIDE
IS PAINLESS*(M*A*S*H)* *Eastern Images* HILL STR.BLUES
*Derek Hinde Quartet* CHARIOTS OF FIRE *Masterworks*
BRIDESHEAD REVISITED *SRE Band* BEST THAT YOU CAN DO
(ARTHUR'S THEME) *LSO* I DON'T KNOW HOW TO LOVE HIM
*Jesus Christ Superstar LSO* DON'T CRY FOR ME ARGENTI
NA *(Evita) LSO*  EVE OF THE WAR *(War Of The Worlds)*
*LSO* FAME *LSO* STAR WARS *LSO* FOR YOUR EYES ONLY *LSO*
DALLAS *LSO* SHOESTRING *LSO*  THE CHAIN *(Grand Prix)*
*Nick Glennie Smith* ANGELA *(Taxi) Avenue 4.am* TAKE
TAKE THAT LOOK OFF YOUR FACE *(Song and Dance) LSO*
383.<u>WAR!</u> - City Of Prague Philharmonic (Paul Bateman)
*SILVA SCREEN Treasury (Koch): SILVAD 3502 (CD) 1997*
1:WHERE EAGLES DARE *(RON GOODWIN)* 2:BATTLE OF THE
BULGE *(B.FRANKEL)* 3:CASUALTIES OF WAR *(E.MORRICONE)*
4: 633 SQUADRON *(R.GOODWIN)* 5:SINK THE BISMARCK!
(C.PARKER) 6:BRIDGE AT REMAGEN *(E.BERNSTEIN)* 7:
MACARTHUR / PATTON *(J.GOLDSMITH)* 8:DAS BOOT (BOAT)
*(K.DOLDINGER)* 9:NIGHT OF THE GENERALS *(M.JARRE)* 10:
GUNS OF NAVARONE *(D.TIOMKIN)* 11:LONGEST DAY*(P.ANKA)*
12:BATTLE OF MIDWAY *(J.WILLIAMS)* 13:IN HARM'S WAY
*(GOLDSMITH)* 14:IS PARIS BURNING *(M.JARRE) tpt 54.19*
384.<u>WAR FILM THEMES</u> - Various Artists
*CASTLE COMM (BMG): MCCD 278 (CD)*                    *1995*
1.SCHINDLER'S LIST 2.633 SQUADRON 3.THE RIVER KWAI
MARCH 4.BALLAD OF T.GREEN BERETS 5.GUNS OF NAVARONE
6.APOCALPYSE NOW *(RIDE OF THE VALKYRIES)* 7.BORN ON
THE 4TH OF JULY *(AMERICAN PIE)* 8.PLATOON *(BATTLE
HYMN OF THE REPUBLIC)* 9.PLATOON *(SITTIN'ON THE DOCK
OF THE BAY)* 10.TOP GUN *(DANGER ZONE)* 11.LONGEST DAY
12.DAM BUSTERS MARCH 13.GOOD MORNING VIETNAM *(WHAT
A WONDERFUL WORLD)* 14.GALLIPOLI *(ADAGIO)* 15.TOP GUN
*(TAKE MY BREATH AWAY)*16.A BRIDGE TOO FAR 17.MASH 18
PLATOON *(WHEN A MAN LOVES A WOMAN)* 19.FOR THE BOYS
*(I REMEMBER YOU)* 20.BORN ON THE 4TH... *(MOON RIVER)*
--- <u>WARNER BROS.YEARS</u> - *see COLLECTION 224*

385. WARRIORS OF THE SILVER SCREEN City Of Prague Phil.*
     *SILVA SCREEN (Koch): FILMXCD 187 (2CD)*          *1997*
     Symphonic Suites: BRAVEHEART-THE THIEF OF BAGDAD-
     TARAS BULBA-ANTHONY AND CLEOPATRA-FIRST KNIGHT-
     HENRY V-EL CID-PRINCE VALIANT-BEN HUR-THE VIKINGS
     Themes from: ROB ROY-SPARTACUS-THE 300 SPARTANS-THE
     WAR LORD-THE LAST VALLEY-CONAN THE BARBARIAN-JASON
     AND THE ARGONAUTS
     *City Of Prague Philharmonic Orch cond:Paul Bateman*
     *with The Crouch End Festival Chorus*
386. WARSAW CONCERTO - The Music of Richard ADDINSELL
     Royal Ballet Sinfonia (Kenneth Alwyn) *
     *ASV (Koch): CDWHL 2108 (CD)*          *1997*
     INVOCATION for Piano and Orchestra (1955)-MARCH OF
     THE UNITED NATIONS (1942)-WARSAW CONCERTO (1941)
     BLITHE SPIRIT (1945)-THE DAY WILL DAWN (1942)-THE
     GREENGAGE SUMMER (1961)-HIGHLY DANGEROUS (1950)-THE
     LION HAS WINGS (1939)-OUT OF THE CLOUDS (1954)-
     PASSIONATE FRIENDS (1948)-THE SEA DEVILS (1953)-
     UNDER CAPRICORN (1949) * Concert recorded 1996
387. WARSAW CONCERTO & OTHER FILM THEMES Bournemouth SO*
     *CFP (EMI): CDCFP 9020 (CD) CFP 41 4493-4 (MC)*  *1988*
     WARSAW CONCERTO from 'Dangerous Moonlight'(Film 41)
     (Richard Addinsell)- THE DREAM OF OLWEN from 'While
     I Live' (Film 47) (Charles Williams)-SPELLBOUND CON
     CERTO from 'Spellbound' (Film 45)(Miklos Rozsa)-THE
     CORNISH RHAPSODY from 'Love Story' (Film 44)(Hubert
     Bath) -RHAPSODY IN BLUE (Film 45) (George Gershwin)
     *(K.Alwyn) feat Daniel Adni (Piano) 1980 reiss 1988*
388. WATCHING THE DETECTIVES - Starshine Orchestra
     *HALLMARK (Carlton): 30726-2 (CD) -4 (MC)*          *1997*
     INSPECTOR MORSE-LA LAW-THE BILL-POIROT-THE SWEENEY-
     LAW AND ORDER-BERGERAC-JULIET BRAVO-MAGNUM PI PRIVA
     TE INVESTIGATOR-MISS MARPLE-RUTH RENDELL MYSTERIES-
     STARSKY & HUTCH-TAGGART-HILL STREET BLUES-NYPD BLUE
     -CAGNEY AND LACEY-KOJAK
389. WAXMAN Franz - LEGENDS OF HOLLYWOOD
     *VARESE (Pinn): VSD 5242 (CD)*          *1990*
     *New recordings of Suites from Franz Waxman's scores*
     TASK FORCE-OBJECTIVE BIRMA-PEYTON PLACE-SORRY WRONG
     NUMBER-THE PARADINE CASE-DEMETRIUS & THE GLADIATORS
390. WAXMAN Franz - LEGENDS OF HOLLYWOOD - Volume 2
     *VARESE (Pinn): VSD 5257 (CD)*          *1991*
     BRIDE OF FRANKENSTEIN-MR.ROBERTS-POSSESSED-CAPTAINS
     COURAGEOUS-THE NUN'S STORY-HUCKLEBERRY FINN etc.
391. WAXMAN Franz - LEGENDS OF HOLLYWOOD - Volume 3
     *VARESE (Pinn): VSD 5480 (CD)*          *1994*
     ELEPHANT WALK (6 tracks)-THE FURIES (5)-DESTINATION
     TOKYO (5)-THE SILVER CHALICE (6)-NIGHT AND THE CITY
     NIGHT UNTO NIGHT-HOTEL BERLIN-MR.SKEFFINGTON (2)
392. WAXMAN Franz - LEGENDS OF HOLLYWOOD - Volume 4
     *VARESE (Pinn): VSD 5713 (CD)*          *1996*
     *New recordings of Suites from Franz Waxman's scores*
     *Queensland Symphony Orch.conducted by Richard Mills*

1.UNTAMED (1955) 2/3/4.ON BORROWED TIME (39) 5/6/7.
MY GEISHA (62) 8.DEVIL DOLL (36) 9.MY COUSIN RACHEL
(52) 10/11/12.STORY OF RUTH (60) 13/14/15.DARK CITY
(1950) 16/17/18/19/20.A CHRISTMAS CAROL (1938)

393.WAXMAN Franz - Sunset Boulevard: Classic WAXMAN
*RCA VICTOR (BMG): GD 80708 (CD)*     *Re-iss: 1991*
PRINCE VALIANT:Prelude/King Aguar's Escape/The Fens
First Chase/The Tournament/Sir Brack's Death/Finale
A PLACE IN THE SUN:Suite. THE BRIDE OF FRANKENSTEIN
Creation Of The Female Monster. SUNSET BOULEVARD:
Main Title/Norma Desmond/The Studio Stroll/The Come
back (Norma as Salome). OLD AQUAINTANCE: Elegy For
Strings and Harp. REBECCA: Prelude/After The Ball/
Mrs.Danvers/Confession Scene/Manderley In Flames.
THE PHILADELPHIA STORY: MGM Fanfare/Main Title/The
True Love. TARAS BULBA: The Ride To Dubno.
*NATIONAL PHILHARMONIC ORCHESTRA (CHARLES GERHARDT)*

394.WAYNE John - True Grit: Classic Films Of JOHN WAYNE
City Of Prague Philharmonic cond.by Paul Bateman
*SILVA SCREEN (Koch): FILMCD 153 (CD)*     *1994*
STAGECOACH-SHE WORE A YELLOW RIBBON *Richard Hageman*
THE SEARCHERS *(Max Steiner)* THE HIGH AND THE MIGHTY
THE ALAMO *(Dimitri Tiomkin)* HOW THE WEST WAS WON
*(Alfred Newman)* IN HARM'S WAY *(Jerry Goldsmith)* THE
QUIET MAN *(Victor Young)* THE COWBOYS *John Williams)*

395.WEBB Marti - Performance with Philharmonia Orc.1989
*FIRST NIGHT (Pinn): OCRCD 6033 (CD)*     *reissued 1995*
*Introduction:* I DREAMED A DREAM *Les Miserables* /
ALMOST LIKE BEING IN LOVE *Brigadoon* / MUSIC OF THE
NIGHT *Phantom* /LOSING MY MIND *Follies* /ANYTHING BUT
LONELY *Aspects Of Love* / ONLY HE *Starlight Express*
MEMORY *Cats* / LOVE CHANGES EVERYTHING *Aspects*/ ONCE
YOU LOSE YOUR HEART *Me and My Girl* /LAST MAN IN MY
Life *Tell Me On A Sunday*/BLOW GABRIEL *Anything Goes*
see also 'MAGIC OF THE MUSICALS'

--- WEBB Roy - *see COLLECTION 111*

396.WEST Mae Orig Commercial Recordings and Film -S/T-
*JASMINE (BMG-Con): JASCD 102 (CD)*     *1996*
I LIKE A GUY WHAT TAKES HIS TIME-EASY RIDER-I FOUND
A NEW WAY TO GO TO TOWN-I'M NO ANGEL-THEY CALL ME
SISTER HONKY TONK-I WANT YOU I NEED YOU-WILLIE OF
THE VALLEY-FRANKIE AND JOHNNY-THAT DALLAS MAN-WHEN
A ST.LOUIS WOMAN COMES DOWN TO NEW ORLEANS-MY OLD
FLAME-MEMPHIS BLUES-TROUBLED WATERS-HE'S A BAD BAD
MAN-MON COEUR S'OUVRE A TA VOIUX (SOFTLY AWAKES MY
HEART)-I'M AN OCCIDENTAL WOMAN IN AN ORIENTAL MOOD
FOR LOVE-MISTER DEEP BLUE SEA-LITTLE BAR BUTTERFLY
ON A TYPICAL TROPICAL NIGHT-I WAS SAYING TO THE
MOON-NOW I'M A LADY

397.WESTERNS! - City Of Prague Philharm.(Paul Bateman/
Nic Raine/Derek Wadsworth) Philharmonia Orch. (Tony
Bremner) / Westminster Philh.Orch (Kenneth Alwyn)
*SILVA SCREEN Treasury (Koch): SILVAD 3503 (CD) 1997*
*Continued next page...*

WESTERNS! ...*Continued*
1:BIG COUNTRY *(J.MOROSS)* 2:WILD ROVERS*(J.GOLDSMITH)*
3:UNFORGIVEN *(C.EASTWOOD)* 4: A DISTANT TRUMPET *(Max STEINER)* 5: and 6:ONCE UPON A TIME IN THE WEST *(E. MORRICONE)* 7:HOW THE WEST WAS WON *(Alfred NEWMAN)*
8:DANCES WITH WOLVES *(J.BARRY)* 9: MAGNIFICENT SEVEN *(E.BERNSTEIN)* 10:FISTFUL OF DOLLARS *(E.MORRICONE)*
11:STAGECOACH *(arr,TOWNEND)* 12:TRUE GRIT *(E.BERNSTE IN)* 13:TWO MULES FOR SISTER SARA *(E.MORRICONE)* 14: SONS OF KATIE ELDER *(E.BERNSTEIN)*          *tpt 57.44*

398. WILD BUNCH The: Best Of The West - Var.Themes with Czech Symphony Orchestra conduct by William Motzing
*SILVA SCREEN (Koch): FILMCD 136 (CD)*          1993
DANCES WITH WOLVES-THE ALAMO-THE MAGNIFICENT SEVEN- THE SONS OF KATIE ELDER-THE BIG VALLEY-RAWHIDE-THE BIG COUNTRY-RETURN OF A MAN CALLED HORSE-RIO LOBO- BALLAD OF CABLE HOGUE-BLUE AND THE GREY-SILVERADO- GUNFIGHT AT THE O.K.CORRAL-ONCE UPON A TIME IN THE WEST-A FISTFUL OF DYNAMITE-YOUNG GUNS 2-WILD BUNCH

399. WILLETTS Dave - On and Off Stage - Dave Willetts &*
*SILVA SCREEN (Koch): SONG(CD)(C) 902 (CD/MC)*     1990
*Songs from:* PHANTOM OF THe OPERA-LES MISERABLES-LA CAGE AUX FOLLES-NINE-GUYS & DOLLS-PENNY MILLIONAIRE *plus the following songs:* TI AMO-NIGHTS ARE FOREVER THE ROSE-HELLO AGAIN *etc.* / *Philharmonia Orchestra

400. WILLIAMS John (UK,guitar) Plays The Movies
*SONY CLASSICS: S2K 62784 (2CD) S2T 62784 (2MC) 1996*
CD1: KISS FROM A ROSE-EVERYTHING I DO-UNCHAINED MEL ODY-LOVE IS ALL AROUND-GODFATHER THEME-MOON RIVER- SOMEWHERE OVER THE RAINBOW-THE MISSION-CAVATINA-THE UMBRELLAS OF CHERBOURG-IT HAD TO BE YOU-BAGDAD CAFE THE ENTERTAINER-IL POSTINO-ONCE UPON A TIME IN AMER ICA-ONCE UPON A TIME IN THE WEST-SCHINDLER'S LIST
CD2: Various Guitar Music from album 'WORLD OF JOHN WILLIAMS' including CONCIERTO DE ARANJUAZ *(Rodrigo)* STREETS OF LONDON *(McTell)* CATARI CATARI *(Trad)* etc

401. WISDOM Norman - The Wisdom Of A Fool
*SEE FOR MILES (Pinn): SEECD 377*          1997
DON'T LAUGH AT ME-WISDOM OF A FOOL-DREAM FOR SALE- UP IN THE WORLD-NARCISSUS *(with JOYCE GRENFELL)*- BEWARE-ME AND MY IMAGINATION-SKYLARK-WHO CAN I TURN TO-BOY MEETS GIRL *(with RUBY MURRAY)*-YOU MUST HAVE BEEN A BEAUTIFUL BABY-HEART OF A CLOWN-I DON'T 'ARF LOVE YOU *(w.JOYCE GRENFELL)*-BY THE FIRESIDE-JOKER- IMPOSSIBLE-YOU'RE GETTING TO BE A HABIT WITH ME- HAPPY ENDING-MAKE A MIRACLE *(with PIP HINTON)*-ONCE IN LOVE WITH AMY-MY DARLING MY DARLING-LEANING ON A LAMPOST-FOR ME AND MY GIRL-LAMBETH WALK

402. WORLD OF SOUND: FAVOURITE THEMES FROM BBCTV & RADIO
*KOCH UK (Koch): 33635-2 (CD)*          1997
1.999 Roger Bolton 2.SOMEBODY STOLE MY GAL *(BILLY COTTON BAND SHOW)* Billy Cotton Band 3.CASUALTY Ken Freeman 4.CHILDREN'S HOSPITAL Debbie Wiseman 5.BY THE SLEEPY LAGOON *(DESERT ISLAND DISCS)* Eric Coates

6.DOCTOR WHO Ron Grainer 7.EASTENDERS Simon May 8.
FAWLTY TOWERS Dennis Wilson 9.I WISH I KNEW HOW IT
FEELS TO BE FREE *(FILM 98)* Billy Taylor Trio 10.
GOING STRAIGHT Ronnie Barker 11.HAVE I GOT NEWS FOR
YOU Big George Webley 12.HETTY WAINTHROP Nigel Hess
13.IN PARTY MOOD *(HOUSEWIVE'S CHOICE)* Jack Strachey
14.HOWARDS' WAY Simon May 15.KNIGHTSBRIDGE MARCH
*(IN TOWN TOWN TONIGHT)* Eric Coates 16.HIT AND MISS
*(JUKE BOX JURY)* John Barry 7+4 17.BRING ME SUNSHINE
*(MORECAMBE & WISE SHOW)* Morecambe & Wise 18.MUCH
BINDING IN THE MARSH BBC Rad.19.CALLING ALL WORKERS
*(MUSIC WHILE YOU WORK)* E.Coates 20.MICHAEL'S THEME
*(PARKINSON)* Harry Stoneham 5 21.AT THE SIGN OF THE
SWINGIN' CYMBAL *(PICK OF THE POPS)* Brian Fahey 22.
MARS (PLANET'S SUITE, HOLST)*(QUATERMASS)* Various A.
23.IMPERIAL ECHOES *(RADIO NEWSREEL)* Band Of The RAF
24.RHODES Alan Parker 25.SAILING BY *(R4 SHIPPING FO
RECAST)* John Scott 26.SIX-FIVE SPECIAL Don Lang 27.
ON A MOUNTAIN STANDS A LADY *(LIVER BIRDS)* Scaffold
28.MARCHING STRINGS *(TOP OF THE FORM)* Ray Martin Or

403.<u>WUTHERING HEIGHTS</u>: A Tribute To Alfred NEWMAN
    New Zealand Symphony Orch cond: Richard Kaufman
    *KOCH INT.CLASSICS: 37376-2 (CD)*      *1997*
    WUTHERING HEIGHTS (1939) - PRINCE OF FOXES (1949)
    DAVID AND BATHSHEBA (1951) - DRAGONWYCK (1946)
    PRISONER OF ZENDA (1937) - BRIGHAM YOUNG (1940)

404.<u>X-THEMES</u> The: Songs From The Unknown - Various Arts
    *DISKY (THE-Disc): DC 87718-2 (CD)*     *1997*
    1.X-FILES THEME Unidentified Flying Orch 2.TUBULAR
    BELLS Mike Oldfield 3.BLADE RUNNER London Phil.Orch
    4.BASIC INSTINCT THEME as 1 5.PSYCHO SUITE Lalo Sch
    ifrin & San Diego S.O. 6.FULL CIRCLE Colin Towns 7.
    DRACULA THEME as 1 7.TWILIGHT ZONE MAIN THEME as 1
    8.BATTLE OF THE PLANETS London Phil.Orc 9.CAPE FEAR
    as 1 10.VERTIGO SUITE as 5 11.I ROBOT Andrew Powell
    12.TWIN PEAKS as 1 13.DANCE OF THE SUGAR PLUM FAIRY
    as 3 14.TALES OF THE UNEXPECTED Ron Grainer Orchest

--- <u>YOUNG</u> Victor - *see COLLECTION 307*
--- <u>ZIMMERMAN</u> Richard - *see COLLECTION 219*

405.<u>MOZART TV</u> Favourite TV Tunes In The Style Of The
          Great Classical Composers - Various Arts.
    *DELOS IISA (Nimbus): DE 3222 (CD) CS 3222 (MC)*  *1997*
    1.I'LL BE THERE FOR YOU *(FRIENDS)* (Vivaldi) 2.HILL
    ST.BLUES-3.MASH-4.BRADY BUNCH (Mozart) 5.BEWITCHED
    (Debussy) 6.X-FILES (Hovhaness) 7.ANGELA *TAXI*(Villa
    -Lobos) 8.GREEN ACRES (Joplin) 9.LOVE IS ALL AROUND
    *MARY TYLER MOORE* Satie 10.MR.ED Rodrigo 11.JEOPARDY
    (Handel) 12.JETSONS (B.Britten) 13.WHERE EVERYBODY
    KNOWS YOUR NAME *(CHEERS)* (J.Ireland) 14.I LOVE LUCY
    (H.Purcell) 15.STAR TREK VOYAGER (R.Strauss)

406.<u>DISNEY HIT SINGLES AND MORE!</u> - Various Orig Artists
    *WALT DISNEY (Poly): WD 11563-2 (CD) -4 (MC)*   *1997*
    1.CIRCLE OF LIFE *(LION KING)* Elton John 2.SHOOTING
                        *Continued next page...*

DISNEY HIT SINGLES AND MORE! ...*Continued*

STAR *(HERCULES)* **Boyzone** 3.SOMEDAY *(HUNCHBACK OF NOT RE DAME)* **Eternal** 4.BEAUTY AND THE BEAST **Celine Dion & Peabo Bryson** 5.COLOURS OF THE WIND *(POCAHONTAS)* **Vanessa Williams** 6.YOU'VE GOT A FRIEND IN ME *(TOY STORY)* **Randy Newman** 7.CRUELLA DE VILLE *(101 DALMAT IONS)* **Dr.John** 8.HE'S A TRAMP *(LADY AND THE TRAMP)* **Peggy Lee** 9.BIBBIDI BOBBIDI BOO *(CINDERELLA)* **Louis Armstrong** 10.EVERYBODY WANTS TO BE A CAT *ARISTOCATS* **O.Cast** 11.ZIP A DEE DOO DAH *(SONG OF THE SOUTH)* **Or. Cast** 12.CHIM CHIM CHEREE *(MARY POPPINS)* **O.Cast** 13. JUNGLE BOOK GROOVE: I WANNA BE LIKE YOU + BARE NECE SSITIES **Master Upbeat Mix** 14.WHISTLE WHILE YOU WORK *(SNOW WHITE)* **O.Cast** 15.HAKUNA MATATA *(LION KING)* **OC** 16.A STAR IS BORN *HERCULES* **Jocelyn Brown** 17.PART OF YOUR WORLD *LITTLE MERMAID* **Olivia Newton John** 18.A WHOLE NEW WORLD *(ALADDIN)* **P.Bryson-Regina Belle** 19. CAN YOU FEEL THE LOVE TONIGHT *LION KING* **Elton John** 20.WHEN YOU WISH UPON A STAR *PINOCCHIO* **L.Armstrong**

407.SILENCIUM: SONGS OF THE SPIRIT - JOHN HARLE
*ARGO-DECCA (Poly): 458 356-2 (CD)* 1997
1.MORNING PRAYER 2.SPIRITU *(BABY IT'S YOU,C4)* 3.AIR AND ANGELS 4.FAMILY OF LOVE 5.LACRIMOSAM *(BUTTERFLY KISS)* 6.ASTREA *(NISSAN AD)* 7.SCHOOL OF MYSTERIES *(DEFENCE OF THE REALM,BBC1)* 8.LIGHT *(HMS BRILLIANT, BBC1)* 9.HYMN TO THE SUN 10.VICES & VIRTUES 11.NIGHT FLIGHT 12.SILENCIUM *(SILENT WITNESS theme, BBC1)* **John Harle** composer/solo saxoph. Silencium Ensemble **Catherine Bott-Sarah Leonard-Nicole Tibbels** (sop's) **Alexander Balanescu** (viola) **Paul Clarvis** (perc) and Choristers Worcester Cathedral,Academy of St.Martin in The Fields, Children from New Brighton PS.Wirral

408.HELLO CHILDREN EVERYWHERE: TOP BBC CHILDREN'S TUNES
*KOCH UK (Koch): 33636-2 (CD)* 1997
1.BERTHA 2.BARNACLE BILL *BLUE PETER* 3.CAMBERWICK GREEN 4.CHIGLEY 5.PUFFIN' BILLY *CHILDREN'S CHOICE* 6 FIREMAN SAM 7.HEADS & TAILS 8.HENRY'S CAT 9.JIM'LL FIX IT 10.ACROBAT *JONNY BRIGGS* 11.MAGIC ROUNDABOUT 12.MOPP AND SMIFF 13.PLAY AWAY 14.POSTMAN PAT 15. RAGTIME 16.RECORD BREAKERS 17.ROOBARB AND CUSTARD 18.RUBOVIA 19.SUPERTED 20.SWAP SHOP 21.PARADE OF TIN SOLDIERS *TOYTOWN* 22.TRUMPTON 23.WILLO THE WISP

409.JOHNSON, Laurie...With A Vengeance
*SEQUEL-CASTLE (BMG): NEMCD 935 (CD) 1997* 1.AVENGERS 2.TOP SECRET 3.DR.STRANGELOVE 4.NO HIDING PLACE 5. BEAUTY JUNGLE 6.DOIN'THE RACOON 7.ECHO FOUR-TWO 8. M1 (M-ONE) 9.SOLO 10.CITY 11.LIMEHOUSE 12.WEST END 13.LATIN QUARTER 14.GRAND CENTRAL 15.TIMES SQUARE 16.SOUTH BEACH 17.SEVENTH AVANUE 18.STICK OR TWIST 19.DRUM CRAZY 20.MINOR BOSSA NOVA 21.DEAR FRIEND 22 HEATWAVE 23.TWANGO 24.WINTER WONDERLAND 25.HOE DOWN 26.THE DEPUTY 27.DONKEY SERENADE-28.SPRING SPRING SPRING 29.CHAKA 30.SABRE DANCE

SOUNDTRACKS AND VIDEOS
*Some Disney Videos Are Available For A Ltd Period Only*

A WALT DISNEY CHRISTMAS  -S/T- *not available*
              VHS Video: *Buena Vista: D.200922*
ALADDIN (1993) Music and songs: ALAN MENKEN-HOWARD ASHM
    AN-TIM RICE  -S/T- *feat* "A Whole New World" sung by
    PEABO BRYSON-REGINA BELLE *Walt Disney: DISCD 470 CD
    DISMC 470 (MC) & PDC 310 (MC)*  VHS Video: *D.216622*
ALICE IN WONDERLAND (1951)  Music score: OLIVER WALLACE
    -S/T- *deleted*      VHS Video: *Buena Vista: D.200362*
ARISTOCATS The (1970) Songs: RICHARD and ROBERT SHERMAN
    -S/T- *Walt Disney Rec: DSMCD 473(CD) DSMMC 473 (MC)*
              VHS Video: *Buena Vista: D.241902*
BAMBI (1943) Songs: FRANK CHURCHILL-E.PLUMB-LARRY MOREY
    -S/T- *deleted Children's Coll.Spoken Word and Songs
              on Walt Disney: PDC 304 (MC)*
              VHS Video: *Buena Vista: D.209422*
BASIL THE GREAT MOUSE DETECTIVE (1986) Music: HENRY MAN
    CINI *-S/T- (-)*     VHS Video: *Buena Vista: D.213602*
BEAUTY AND THE BEAST (92)  Mus score: ALAN MENKEN Songs
    ALAN MENKEN-HOWARD ASHMAN Songs"Beauty & The Beast"
    "Belle"/"Be Our Guest" sung by CELINE DION-PEABO BR
    YSON   *Walt Disney: WD 71360-2 (CD) WD 71360-4 (MC)
    Coll: PDC 309(CD)*   VHS Video: *B.Vista: D.213252*
BEDKNOBS AND BROOMSTICKS (1971)  Songs by R.& R.SHERMAN
    -S/T- *deleted*      VHS Video: *Buena Vista: D.200162*
BLACK HOLE The (1979)           Music Score: JOHN BARRY
    -S/T- *deleted*      VHS Video: *Buena Vista: D.200112*
BLACKBEARD'S GHOST (1967)   Music score: ROBERT BRUNNER
    -S/T- *deleted*      VHS Video: *Buena Vista: D.200622*
CINDERELLA (50)    Music and songs: OLIVER WALLACE-PAUL
    J.SMITH-MAC DAVID-AL HOFFMANN and JERRY LIVINGSTON
    -S/T- *deleted Collection  Walt Disney: PDC 300 (MC)*
              VHS Video: *Buena Vista: D.204102*
DUCKTAILS THE MOVIE (91)        Music score: DAVID NEWMAN
    -S/T- *N/A*          VHS Video: *Buena Vista: D.210822*
DUMBO (1941)  Music: F.CHURCHILL-O.WALLACE-N.WASHINGTON
    -S/T- *deleted*      VHS Video: *Buena Vista: D.202472*
FANTASIA (Disney 40) featur: The Philadelphia Orchestra
    (Leopold Stowkowski) -S/T- (dig.remastered in 1990)
    *Disney-R.Vista:  DSTCD 452D (2CD) DSTMC 452MC (2MC)*
              VHS Video: *Buena Vista: D.211322 (deleted)*
FOX AND THE HOUND The (1981) Songs: RICHARD & R.SHERMAN
    -S/T- *deleted*      VHS Video: *Buena Vista: D.220412*
GOOFY MOVIE The (1995) Music: DON DAVIS + V.Artsists
    -S/T- *W.DISNEY (B.Vista): WD 76400-2 (CD) -4 (MC)*
HERCULES (1997)             Music score: ALAN MENKEN
    -S/T- *DISNEY (Carlton/Poly): WD 60864-2 (CD) -4(MC)*
              VHS Video: *Buena Vista: D.*
HUNCHBACK OF NOTRE DAME The (1996)   Music: ALAN MENKEN
    Lyr STEPHEN SCHWARTZ song "Someday" sung by ETERNAL
    -S/T- *W.Disney (Technicol): WD 77190-2 (CD) -4 (MC)*
              VHS Video: *D.610058 (VHS)*

JAMES AND THE GIANT PEACH (1995) M/Songs: RANDY NEWMAN
-S/T- *W.DISNEY (B.Vista): WD 68120-2 (CD) -4 (MC)*
JUNGLE BOOK (67) Songs: RICHARD and ROBERT SHERMAN sung
by LOUIS PRIMA-PHIL HARRIS-STERLING HOLLOWAY   etc.
-S/T- *Walt Disney Records: WD 70400-2 (CD) -4 (MC)*
*Children's Coll on Walt Disney (Pinn): PDC 305 (MC)*
VHS Video: *Buena Vista: D.211222*
LADY AND THE TRAMP The (1956)  Songs: PEGGY LEE-J.BURKE
Mus: OLIVER WALLACE sung by Peggy Lee -S/T- *deleted*
*Spoken Word & Songs Coll Walt Disney:  PDC 301 (MC)*
VHS Video:*Buena Vista D.205822 (ltd)*
LION KING The (1994) Music sco: HANZ ZIMMER) songs incl
"Circle Of Life" (TIM RICE-ELTON JOHN) ELTON JOHN
*Walt Dsiney Rec: DSMCD 477(CD) DSMMC 477 (MC)*
*Rocket (Polyg): 522690-2 (CD) 522690-4 (MC)*
VHS Video: *Buena Vista: D.229772*
LITTLE MERMAID The (1990) Songs: ALAN MENKEN-HOWARD ASH
MAN   -S/T- *W.Disney: DSTCD 451 (CD) DSTMC 451 (MC)*
*ALSO ON Walt Disney Collection: PDC 307 (CD)*
VHS Video: *Buena Vista: D.209132 (ltd)*
MARY POPPINS (64)  Songs: RICHARD & ROBERT SHERMAN sung
by JULIE ANDREWS-DICK VAN DYKE-DAVID TOMLINSON etc.
-S/T- *Walt Disney Records DSMCD (DSMMC) 459 (CD/MC)*
VHS Video: *Buena Vista: D.200232*
MICKEY'S CHRISTMAS CAROL (1983) -S/T-  *W.Disney Records*
*PDC 312 (MC)*       VHS Video: *Buena Vista: D.201882*
NIGHTMARE BEFORE CHRISTMAS The (93) Music: DANNY ELFMAN
-S/T- *Walt Disney Records: DSTCD(DSTMC) 478 (CD/MC)*
VHS Video: *Buena Vista: D.241932*
OLIVER AND COMPANY (1989)  Music score by J.A.C.REDFORD
-S/T-   *Walt Disney Records:  PCD (PWK) 450 (CD/MC)*
VHS Video: *not available*
101 DALMATIONS (1961)  Songs: MEL LEVIN m: BRUNS/DUNHAM
-S/T- *deleted*     VHS Video: *Buena Vista: D.212632*
PETER AND THE WOLF     VHS Video: *Buena Vista: D.211872*
PETER PAN (1953) Songs by OLIVER WALLACE & PAUL J.SMITH
-S/T-  *Walt Disney Records: DSMCD (DSMMC) 466 (CD/MC)*
*Children's Collect: Walt Disney Records: PDC 306 (MC)*
VHS Video: *Buena Vista: D.202452*
PETE'S DRAGON (77)  Music dir: IRWIN KOSTAL with V.Arts
-S/T- *deleted*     VHS Video: *Buena Vista: D.200102*
PINOCCHIO (1939) Mus:LEIGH HARLINE-P.SMITH-N.WASHINGTON
*reissue: Walt Disney: DSMCD 461 (CD) DSCC 461 (MC)*
*Spoken Word and Songs Coll WaltD isney PDC 302 (MC)*
VHS Video: *Buena Vista: D.202392*
POCAHONTAS (1995) Music score: ALAN MENKEN Songs: ALAN
MENKEN-STEPHEN SCHWARTZ inc "Colours Of The Wind"
sung by VANESSA WILLIAMS -S/T- *Disney: WDR 75462-2*
*(CD) -4 (MC) / Sing-A-Long: Disney: DISCD(MC)*
*481 (CD/MC) /  Story and Song: Disney: PDC 316 (CD)*
VHS Video: *Buena Vista: D.274522*
RELUCTANT DRAGON The        VHS Video: *Disney: D.205332*
RESCUERS The (1976) 'Story Of The Rescuers' -S/T- *delet*
VHS Video: *Buena Vista: D.240642*

RESCUERS DOWN UNDER The (90) Mus score: BRUCE BROUGHTON
-S/T- *Imp (Silva Screen): 60613-2 (CD) -4(MC)*
*ALSO ON Walt Disney Collection: PDC 308 (CD)*
VHS Video: *Buena Vista: D.211422*
RETURN OF JAFAR (1994) VHS Video: *Buena Vista: D.222372*
ROBIN HOOD (1973)  Songs: GEORGE BRUNS-FLOYD HUDDLESTON
with ROGER MILLER-PHIL HARRIS-TERRY THOMAS-P.USTINOV
-S/T- *deleted* VHS Video: *Buena Vista: D.202282*
SLEEPING BEAUTY (1959) Mus: GEORGE BRUNS  -S/T- *DISNEY:*
*WDR 75622-2 (CD)*   VHS Video: *Buena Vista: D.204762*
SNOW WHITE & THE SEVEN DWARFS (37) Songs: FRANK CHURCHI
LL-LEIGH HARLINE-PAUL SMITH feat: ADRIANA CASELOTTI
-S/T- *Walt Disney Records: WD 74540-2 (CD) -4 (MC)*
*Children's Coll on Walt Disney Records PDC 303 (MC)*
VHS Video: *Buena Vista: D.215242*
SONG OF THE SOUTH (1946)  Music by: DANIEL AMFITHEATROF
CHARLES WOLCOTT-PAUL SMITH-ALLIE WRUBEL-RAY GILBERT
-S/T- *not available* VHS Video: *Buena Vista:D.201022*
SUMMER MAGIC (1963)    Songs: RICHARD and ROBERT SHERMAN
w:BURL IVES-HAYLEY MILLS -S/T- *del VHS:Buena Vista*
SWORD IN THE STONE (1963) Songs: RICHARD/ROBERT SHERMAN
-S/T- *not available* VHS Video:*Buena Vista: D.202292*
THREE CABALLEROS The (1945) Music: CHARLES WOLCOTT-PAUL
J.SMITH-EDWARD PLUMB   VHS Video: *B.Vista: D.200912*
TOY STORY (96) Music & songs RANDY NEWMAN "You've Got A
Friend In Me" (R.Newman) sung by RANDY NEWMAN -S/T-
*W.Disney (Technicol): WD 77130-2(CD) WD 77130-4(MC)*
VHS Video - *Disney: D.272142*
WIND IN THE WILLOWS The    VHS Video - *Disney: D.204272*
WINNIE THE POOH Music from WALT DISNEY FILMS on 'The
Many Songs of WINNIE THE POOH'
*DISNEY (Carlton-Polyg): WD 11564-2 (CD) -4 (MC)*
WINNIE THE POOH AND A DAY FOR EEYORE   (-) Music & Songs
RICHARD & ROBERT SHERMAN  *featur:* STERLING HOLLOWAY
-S/T- *not avail.*   VHS Video: *Buena Vista: D.205322*
WINNIE THE POOH AND CHRISTMAS TOO / -S/T- *not available*
VHS Video: *Buena Vista: D.241232*
WINNIE THE POOH AND THE BLUSTERY DAY (1968)    Songs by
RICHARD & ROBERT SHERMAN  *featur:* STERLING HOLLOWAY
-S/T- *deleted*     VHS Video: *Buena Vista: D.200632*
WINNIE THE POOH AND THE HONEY TREE (1966)    Songs by
RICHARD & ROBERT SHERMAN  *featur:* STERLING HOLLOWAY
-S/T- *deleted*     VHS Video: *Buena Vista: D.200492*
WINNIE THE POOH AND TIGGER TOO (64)  Songs: RICHARD and
ROBERT SHERMAN *feat:* STERLING HOLLOWAY-PAUL WINCHEL
-S/T- *not avail.*   VHS Video: *Buena Vista: D.200642*
WINNIE THE POOH: THE GREAT RIVER RESCUE (New Adventures
Of)    VHS Video: *Buena Vista: D.241032*

## *MUSIC COLLECTION*

DISNEY'S HIT SINGLES AND MORE! - Various Orig Artists
*WALT DISNEY (Poly): WD 11563-2 (CD)*          *1997*
For Track Listing - SEE COLLECTION 406

## A CHRONOLOGICAL FILM INDEX OF THE JAMES BOND MOVIES

1) **DOCTOR NO** 1962 / *Sean Connery* / *Ursula Andress*
*Bernard Lee-Lois Maxwell-Jack Lord-Joseph Wiseman*
Title theme 'The James Bond Theme' (MONTY NORMAN)
-S/T- *reissue: EMI Premier: CZ 558 (CD)*

2) **FROM RUSSIA WITH LOVE** 1963 / *Sean Connery* / *Daniela*
*Bianchi-Robert Shaw-Pedro Armendariz-Lottie Lenya*
"From Russia With Love" (Lionel Bart) MATT MONRO
-S/T- *reissue: EMI Premier: CZ 550 (CD)*

3) **GOLDFINGER** 1964 / *Sean Connery* /*Honor Blackman-Gert*
*Frobe-Shirley Eaton-Harold Sakata-B.Lee-L.Maxwell*
Title song "Goldfinger" (John Barry-Leslie Bricusse
Anthony Newley) sung by SHIRLEY BASSEY
-S/T- *reissue: EMI Premier: CZ 557 (CD)*

4) **THUNDERBALL** 1965 / *Sean Connery* / *Claudine Auger*
*Adolfo Celi-Luciana Paluzzi-Rick Van Nutter-Martine*
*Beswick* "Thunderball" (J.Barry-Don Black) TOM JONES
-S/T- *reissue: EMI Premier: CZ 556 (CD)*

5) **YOU ONLY LIVE TWICE** 1967 / *Sean Connery* / *Tetsuro*
*Tamba-Akiko Wakabayashi-Mie Hama-Karin Dor-Bern.Lee*
Title song (J.Barry-Leslie Bricusse) NANCY SINATRA
-S/T- *reissue: EMI Premier: CZ 559 (CD)*

6) **ON HER MAJESTY'S SECRET SERVICE** 1969 *George Lazenby*
*Diana Rigg-TellY Savalas-Ilse Steppat-Gabr.Ferzetti*
Title song "We Have All The Time In The World"(Hal
David-John Barry) sung by LOUIS ARMSTRONG
-S/T- *reissue: EMI Premier: CZ 549 (CD)*

7) **DIAMONDS ARE FOREVER** 1971 / *Sean Connery* / *Jill St.*
*John-Charles Gray-Lana Wood-Jimmy Dean-Bruce Cabot*
Title song (John Barry-Don Black) by SHIRLEY BASSEY
-S/T- *reissue: EMI Premier: CZ 554 (CD)*

8) **LIVE AND LET DIE** 1973 / *Roger Moore* / *Jane Seymour-*
*Yaphet Kotto-Clifton James-David Hedison-BernardLee*
Title song (Paul & Linda McCartney) PAUL McCARTNEY
-S/T- *reissue: EMI Premier: CZ 553 (CD)*

9) **THE MAN WITH THE GOLDEN GUN** 1974 *Roger Moore* /*Britt*
*Ekland-Christopher Lee-Maud Adams-Herve Villechaize*
Title song (Don Black-John Barry) sung by LULU
-S/T- *reissue: EMI Premier: CZ 552 (CD)*

10) **THE SPY WHO LOVED ME** 1977 / *Roger Moore* / *Barbara*
*Bach-Curt Jurgens-Richard Kiel-Caroline Munro*
"Nobody Does It Better" (Carol Bayer Sager-Marvin
Hamlisch) sung by CARLY SIMON -S/T-
-S/T- *reissue: EMI Premier: CZ 555 (CD)*

11) **MOONRAKER** 1979 / *Roger Moore* / *Lois Chiles-Michael*
*Lonsdale-Richard Kiel-Geoffrey Keen-Bernard Lee*
"Moonraker" (John Barry-Hal David) SHIRLEY BASSEY
-S/T- *reissue: EMI Premier: CZ 551 (CD)*

12) **FOR YOUR EYES ONLY** 1981 *Roger Moore-Carole Bouquet*
*Topol-Lynn HollyJohnson-Julian Glover-Jill Bennett*
Title song "For Your Eyes Only" (Michael Leeson-
Bill Conti) by SHEENA EASTON -S/T-      *DELETED*

13)   OCTOPUSSY 1983 / *Roger Moore* /*Maud Adams-Louis Jor
      dan-Kristina Wayborn-Kabir Bedi-Desmond Llewellwyn*
      Title "All Time High" (John Barry-Tim Rice) - RITA
      COOLIDGE -S/T- *RYKODISC (Vital): RCD 10705 (CD)*

13a)  **NEVER SAY NEVER AGAIN** 1983 *Sean Connery* / *Barbara
      Carrera-Kim Basinger-Klaus M.Branduaer-Max V.Sydow*
      Title song "Never Say Never Again" (Michel Legrand
      -Alan and Marilyn Bergman) and sung by LANI HALL
      -S/T- *Silva Screen: (Conifer): FILMCD 145 (CD)*

14)   A VIEW TO A KILL 1985 / *Roger Moore* /*Tanya Roberts
      Christopher Walken-Grace Jones-Patrick Macnee*
      Title song "A View To A Kill" (That Fatal Kiss) by
      DURAN DURAN -S/T- *EMI: CDP 746159-2 (CD)*   DELETED

15)   THE LIVING DAYLIGHTS 1987   *Timothy Dalton* / *Maryam
      D'Abo-Jeroen Krabbe-Joe Don Baker-John Rhys Davies*
      Title song "The Living Daylights"(John Barry-A.HA)
      -S/T- *W.Bros: WX 111C (Cass) 925616-2 (CD) DELETED*

16)   LICENCE TO KILL 1989 *Timothy Dalton* / *Carey Lowell
      Robert Davi-Talisa Soto-Anthony Zerbe* / Title Song
      "Licence To Kill" (Walden-Cohen-Afansieff) GLADYS
      KNIGHT / M: MICHAEL KAMEN -S/T- *MCA: MCGC 6051(MC)*

17)   GOLDENEYE 1995 *Pierce Brosnan* / *Samantha Bond-Robb
      ie Coltrane-Desmond LLewellyn-Judi Dench-Sean Bean*
      Music score by ERIC SERRA / Title song "Goldeneye"
      (Bono-The Edge) by TINA TURNER *Parlophone (EMI):*
      -S/T- *Virgin US (EMI): CDVUSX 100 (CD)*

18)   TOMORROW NEVER DIES 1997 *Pierce Brosnan* / *Jonathan
      Pryce-Michelle Yeoh-Samantha Bond-Judi Dench*
      Music score by DAVID ARNOLD / Title song by
      SHERYL CROW / closing song vocal by k.d.lang
      -S/T- *A.& M.(Poly): 540 830-2 (CD) -4 (MC)*

---

## B O N D    C O L L E C T I O N S

BEST OF JAMES BOND (30th Anniv.Coll) Orig Artists
      *EMI: CDBOND 007 (CD) TCBOND 007 (MC)*            *1992*
      JAMES BOND THEME-GOLDFINGER-NOBODY DOES IT BETTER-A
      VIEW TO A KILL-MR KISS KISS BANG BANG-FOR YOUR EYES
      ONLY-WE HAVE ALL THE TIME IN THE WORLD-LIVE AND LET
      DIE-ALL TIME HIGH-LIVING DAYLIGHTS-FROM RUSSIA WITH
      LOVE-LICENCE TOKILL-THUNDERBALL-YOU ONLY LIVE TWICE
      MOONRAKER-ON HER MAJESTY'S SECRET SERVICE-MAN WITH
      THE GOLDEN GUN-DIAMONDS ARE FOREVER-007

ESSENTIAL JAMES BOND The - City Of Prague Symphony Orch
      estra conducted by Nicholas Raine            *1993*
      *Silva Screen (Con):FILMCD 007 (CD) FILMC 007 (Cass)*
      DR.NO-FROM RUSSIA WITH LOVE-007-GOLDFINGER-THUNDERB
      ALL-YOU ONLY LIVE TWICE-ON HER MAJESTY'S SECRET SER
      VICE-DIAMONDS ARE FOREVER-MAN WITH T.GOLDEN GUN-SPY
      WHO LOVED ME-MOONRAKER-FOR YOUR EYES ONLY OCTOPUSSY
      THE LIVING DAYLIGHTS-VIEW TO A KILL-LICENCE TO KILL

*see COLLECTIONS 23,25,26,27,38,108,140,305,352,356,357*

```
 1)  LOVE ME TENDER          video: FOX 1172    5 songs-1956
 2)  LOVING YOU           video  unavailable    7 songs-1957
 3)  JAILHOUSE ROCK       vid: WHV PES 50011     7 songs-1957
 4)  KING CREOLE          vid: POLYG 6343723    12 songs-1958
 5)  G.I.BLUES            vid: POLYG 6343583    10 songs-1960
 6)  FLAMING STAR            vid: FOX 1173       6 songs-1961
 7)  WILD IN THE COUNTRY     vid: FOX 1174       6 songs-1961
 8)  BLUE HAWAII          vid: POLYG 6343703    16 songs-1961
 9)  FOLLOW THAT DREAM    vid: WHV PES 99460     6 songs-1962
10)  KID GALAHAD          vid: WHV PES 99335     6 songs-1962
11)  GIRLS GIRLS GIRLS    vid: POLYG 6343663    14 songs-1962
12)  IT HAPPENED AT THE WORLD'S FAIR vid:-  10 songs-1963
13)  FUN IN ACAPULCO      vid: POLYG 6343643    11 songs-1963
14)  KISSIN' COUSINS      vid: WHV PES 51148     9 songs-1964
15)  VIVA LAS VEGAS Love In L.Vegas   vid:-     9 songs-1964
16)  ROUSTABOUT           vid: POLYG 6343623    11 songs-1964
17)  TICKLE ME            vid: POLYG 0858423     9 songs-1965
18)  GIRL HAPPY           vid: WHV PES 51487    11 songs-1965
19)  HARUM SCARUM Holiday v: WHV PES 50486       9 songs-1965
20)  PARADISE HAWAIIAN STYLE v:POL 6343683      10 songs-1965
21)  FRANKIE AND JOHNNY   vid: WHV PES 99666    13 songs-1966
22)  SPINOUT California Holiday v:PES51489       9 songs-1966
23)  EASY COME EASY GO    vid: POLYG 6347603     7 songs-1966
24)  DOUBLE TROUBLE       vid: WHV PES 50485     8 songs-1967
25)  CLAMBAKE             vid: WHV PES 99667     7 songs-1967
26)  STAY AWAY JOE        vid: WHV PES 50525     5 songs-1968
27)  SPEEDWAY             vid: WHV PES 50476     9 songs-1968
28)  LIVE A LITTLE LOVE...WHV SO 35767 +26       4 songs-1968
29)  CHARRO!              vid: not available     2 songs-1969
30)  CHANGE OF HABIT      vid: POLYG 6347583     5 songs-1969
31)  TROUBLE WITH GIRLS  v: WHV SO 35629 +3      7 songs-1969
32)  ELVIS - NBC TV SPECIAL v: BMG 74321 106623    -1968
33)  ELVIS - THAT'S THE WAY IT IS WHV PES 50373   -1970
34)  ELVIS - ON TOUR        video: WHV PES 50153   -1972
35)  THIS IS ELVIS Compil. video: WHV  SO 11173   -1981
```

---

```
BLUE HAWAII            SOUNDTRACK INFO     07863 66959-2 (CD)
CHANGE OF HABIT       + 28 & 29 & 31       07863 66559-2 (CD)
CHARRO!               + 28 & 30 & 31       07863 66559-2 (CD)
CLAMBAKE                   + 14 & 26       07863 66362-2 (CD)
DOUBLE TROUBLE                 + 22        07863 66361-2 (CD)
EASY COME EASY GO              + 27        07863 6655-8  (CD)
ELVIS-NBC TV SPECIAL 1968                     ND 83894 (CD)
FLAMING STAR              + 7 & 9          07863 66557-2 (CD)
FOLLOW THAT DREAM        + 6 & 7           07863 66557-2 (CD)
FRANKIE & JOHNNY              + 20         07863 66360-2 (CD)
FUN IN ACAPULCO              + 12          74321 13431-2 (CD)
G.I.BLUES                                  07863 66960-2 (CD)
GIRL HAPPY                   + 19          74321 13433-2 (CD)
GIRLS GIRLS GIRLS            + 10          74321 13430-2 (CD)
HARUM SCARUM                + 18           74321 13433-2 (CD)
IT HAPPENED AT THE WORLD'S.. + 13          74321 13431-2 (CD)
JAILHOUSE ROCK                             07863 67453-2 (CD)
KID GALAHAD                 + 11           74321 13430-2 (CD)
```

```
KING CREOLE                              07863 67454-2 (CD)
KISSIN'COUSINS               + 25 & 26   07863 66362-2 (CD)
LIVE A LITTLE LOVE..+ 29 & 30 & 31       07863 66559-2 (CD)
LOVE ME TENDER          4 songs on Coll 'Essential Elvis'
LOVING YOU                               07863 67452-2 (CD)
PARADISE HAWAIIAN STYLE           + 21   07863 66360-2 (CD)
ROUSTABOUT                        + 15   74321 13432-2 (CD)
SPEEDWAY                          + 23   07863 66558-2 (CD)
SPINOUT                           + 24   07863 66361-2 (CD)
STAY AWAY JOE                + 14 & 25   07863 66362-2 (CD)
TROUBLE WITH GIRLS   + 28 & 29 & 30      07863 66558-2 (CD)
VIVA LAS VEGAS                    + 16   74321 13432-2 (CD)
WILD IN THE COUNTRY           + 6 & 9    07863 66557-2 (CD)
```

ELVIS COMMAND PERFORMANCES: Essential 60's Masters II
   *RCA (BMG): 07863 66601-2 (2CD)*                    *1995*
   Songs from Elvis Presley Movie Musicals / disc one:
   G.I.BLUES-WOODEN HEART-SHOPPIN'AROUND-DOIN'THE BEST
   I CAN-FLAMING STAR-WILD IN THE COUNTRY-LONELY MAN-
   BLUE HAWAII-ROCK A HULA BABY-CAN'T HELF FALLING IN
   LOVE-BEACH BOY BLUES-HAWAIIAN WEDDING SONG-FOLLOW
   THAT DREAM-ANGEL-KING OF THE WHOLE WIDE WORLD-I GOT
   LUCKY-GIRLS GIRLS GIRLS-BECAUSE OF LOVE-RETURN TO
   SENDER-ONE BROKEN HEART FOR SALE-I'M FALLING IN
   LOVE TONIGHT-THEY REMIND ME TOO MUCH OF YOU-FUN IN
   ACAPULCO-BOSSA NOVA BABY-MARGUERITA-MEXICO-KISSIN'
   COUSINS-ONE BOY TWO LTTLE GIRLS-ONCE IS ENOUGH-VIVA
   LAS VEGAS-WHAT'D I SAY disc two: ROUSTABOUT-POISON
   IVY LEAGUE-LITTLE EGYPT-THERE'S A BRAND NEW DAY ON
   THE HORIZON-GIRL HAPPY-PUPPET ON A STRING-DO THE CL
   AM-HAREM HOLIDAY-SO CLOSE YET SO FAR-FRANKIE & JOHN
   NY-PLEASE DON'T STOP LOVING ME-PARADISE HAWAIAAN ST
   YLE-THIS IS MY HEAVEN-SPINOUT-ALL THAT I AM-I'LL BE
   BACK-EASY COME EASY GO-DOUBLE TROUBLE-LONG LEGGED
   GIRL-CLAMBAKE-YOU DON'T KNOW ME-STAY AWAY JOE-SPEED
   WAY-YOUR TIME HASN'T COME YET BABY-LET YOURSELF GO-
   ALMOST IN LOVE-A LITTLE LESS CONVERSATION-EDGE OF
   REALITY-CHARRO!-CLEAN UP YOU OWN BACKYARD
ESSENTIAL ELVIS (Film Soundtracks) *RCA: PD 89980 (CD)*
   LOVE ME TENDER (2)-LET ME-POOR BOY-WE'RE GONNA MOVE
   LOVING YOU (3)-PARTY-HOT DOG-TEDDY BEAR-MEAN WOMAN
   BLUES-GOT A LOT O'LIVIN' TO DO (2)-LONESOME COWBOY
   JAILHOUSE ROCK (2)-TREAT ME NICE-YOUNG & BEAUTIFUL
   DON'T LEAVE ME NOW-I WANT TO BE FREE-BABY I DON'T
   CARE-MEAN WOMAN BLUES-LOVING YOU-TREAT ME NICE
COLLECTOR'S GOLD - *RCA (BMG): PD(PK) 90574 (3CD/3MC)*
   (1) Hollywood Album: GI BLUES-POCKETFUL OF RAINBOWS
   BIG BOOTS-BLACK STAR-SUMER KISSES WINTER TEARS-I SL
   IPPED I STUMBLED I FELL-LONELY MAN-WHAT A WONDERFUL
   LIFE-AWHISTLING TUNE-BEYOND THE BEND-ONE BROKEN HEA
   RT FORSALE-YOU'RE THE BOSS-ROUSTABOUT-GIRL HAPPY-SO
   CLOSE YET SO FAR-STOP LOOK & LISTEN-AM I READY-HOW
   CAN YOU LOSE WHATYOU NEVER HAD (2) Nashville Album
   (15 Tracks) (3) Live In Las Vegas 1969 (20 Tracks)

BRITISH SONG CONTEST (SONG FOR EUROPE) 1997
*BBC Television Centre 09 March 1997 / Terry Wogan*
Winning Order / Song Title / Performing Artist / Points
```
------------------------------------------------------------
1 - LOVE SHINE A LIGHT - KATRINA AND THE WAVES -  69830
2 - YODEL IN THE CANYON OF LOVE      - DO RE MI -  58696
3 - YOU STAYED AWAY TOO LONG      - JOANNE MAY -   51584
4 - FOR THE LIFE YOU DON'T YET KNOW - SAM BLUE
5 - CRYING                        - PAUL VARNEY
6 - HEART OF STONE-
7 - LIGHTEN UP                          - BEYOND
8 - ROOM FOR CHANGE               - LAURA PALLAS
```

"LOVE SHINE A LIGHT" composed by Kimberley Rew and
performed by KATRINA AND THE WAVES then went on to
represent the UK in The 42nd..


## EUROVISION SONG CONTEST 1997

*1997 Eurovision Song Contest Held In Ireland on 4th May
1997 and Transmitted By BBC1 TV and BBC Radio 2*

Final Position / Country / Song / Artist / Points
```
------------------------------------------------------------
1. U.K.        "Love Shine A Light" KATRINA & WAVES -227
2. IRELAND     "Mysterious Woman         MARC ROBERTS -157
3. TURKEY      "Dinle"    SEBNEM PAKER 7 GRUP ETNIK -121
4. ITALY       "Fiume Di Parole"            JALISSE -114
5. CYPRUS      "Mana Mou"        HARA and ANDREAS -  98
6. SPAIN       "Sin Rencor"        MARCOS LLUNAS -  96
7. FRANCE      "Sentimentes Songes"          FANNY -  95
8. ESTONIA     "Keelatud Maa"      MAARJA-LIIS LLUS -  82
9. MALTA       "Let Me Fly"        DEBBIE SCERRI -  66
10.SLOVENIA    "Zbudi Se"             TANJA RIBIC -  60
11.POLAND      "Ale Jestem"     ANNA MARIA JOPEK -  54
12.GREECE      "Horepse"          MARIANNA ZORBA -  39
12.HUNGARY     "Miert Kell Hogy Eimenj"         VIP -  39
14.SWEDEN      "Bara Hon Aiskar Mej"         BLOND -  36
15.RUSSIA      "Primadonna"      ALLA PUGACHEVA -  33
16.DENMARK     "Stemmen I Mit Liv"  THOMAS LAEGARD -  25
17.CROATIA     "Probudi Me"                   ENI -  24
18.BOSNIA-HERZEGOVINA "Goodbye"     ALMA CARDZIC -  22
18.GERMANY     "Zeit"           BIANCA SHOMBURG -  22
20.ICELAND     "Minn Hinsti Dans"      PAUL OSCAR -  18
21.AUSTRIA     "One Step"        BETTINA SORIAT -  12
22.NETHERLANDS "Niemand Heeft NogTijd "MRS.EINSTEIN -   5
22.SWITZERLAND "Dentro Di Me"      BARBARA BERTA -   5
24.NORWAY      "San Francisco"      TOR ENDRESEN -   0
24.PORTUGAL    "Celia Lawson"       ANTES DO ADEUS -   0
```

*see also EUROVISION SONG CONTEST 1985-97 pages 106-107*

## SUBSCRIPTIONS
## TO TELE - TUNES
## 1998

THE TELE-TUNES REFERENCE BOOK IS UPDATED WITH QUARTERLY
CUMULATIVE SUPPLEMENTS PUBLISHED APRIL, JULY, OCTOBER
THE MAIN BOOK IS PUBLISHED ANNUALLY IN JANUARY
IN ADDITION TO THIS, MIKE PRESTON MUSIC ALSO OPERATES A
TELEPHONE DATABASE INFORMATION SERVICE WHICH CAN BE
CONTACTED MONDAY TO FRIDAY FROM 09.30am - 16.30pm.
SUBSCRIBERS TO THE FULL TELE-TUNES SERVICE HAVE ACCESS
TO THIS DATABASE. THIS SERVICE PROVIDES EXTREMELY FAST
ANSWERS TO THE VERY LATEST QUERIES ON TV AND FILM MUSIC

*PLEASE NOTE HOWEVER THE TELEPHONE DATABASE INFORMATION
LINE IS FOR SUBSCRIBERS TO THE FULL SERVICE ONLY.
IF YOU HAVE A MUSIC QUERY BUT DO NOT SUBSCRIBE PLEASE
WRITE ENCLOSING A STAMPED ADDRESSED ENVELOPE.*

BACK ISSUES: FOR FULL DETAILS OF AVAILABLE ISSUES SEE
NEXT PAGE. SUPPLEMENT BACK ISSUES ARE NOT AVAILABLE.

*SUBSCRIPTION SERVICE DETAILS FROM:-*
SUBSCRIPTION DEPT. MIKE PRESTON MUSIC THE GLENGARRY
3 THORNTON GROVE MORECAMBE LANCASHIRE LA4 5PU U.K.

*TELEPHONE / FAX : 01524 - 421172*

## * T E L E - T U N E S   B A C K   I S S U E S *

Some Of The Following BACK-ISSUES Are Available Direct From *MIKE PRESTON MUSIC,THE GLENGARRY, 3 THORNTON GROVE MORECAMBE, LANCASHIRE LA4 5PU U.K.* Cheques Payable To:- 'MIKE PRESTON MUSIC'. (Prices Include Postage & Packing)

Tele-Tunes 1998 Current Ed: ISBN 0 906655 15 3...£16.50

```
Tele-Tunes 1997 Completely Revised Edit (352p)...£15.95
Tele-Tunes 1996 ..........................Out Of Print
Tele-Tunes 1995 New Revised Ref Book Ed (368p)...£13.95
Tele-Tunes 1994 New Revised Ref Book Ed (344p)...£13.50
Tele-Tunes 1993 ..........................Out Of Print
Tele-Tunes 1992 New Revised Ref Book Ed (304p)...£12.50
Tele-Tunes 1991 ..........................Out Of Print
Tele-Tunes 1990 New Revised Ref Book Ed (264p)...£12.50
Tele-Tunes 1988-89........................Out Of Print
Tele-Tunes 1987-88 Annual Book (208p)..(Ltd Ed)..£12.50
Tele-Tunes 1986-87 Annual Book (192p)..(Ltd Ed)..£12.50
Tele-Tunes 1985-86 Annual Book (160p)..(Ltd Ed)..£12.50
Tele-Tunes 1981-84........................Out Of Print
Tele-Tunes 1978-80 Second Revised (152p).........£12.50
Tele-Tunes 1978-79 First Edition...........Out Of Print
```

Tele-Tunes Supplements 1984-1997..........Out Of Print
Tele-Tunes Supplements 1998  Subscribers only see p.351

## S U P P L E M E N T S   1 9 9 8

JANUARY TO MARCH 1998     —     Published     APRIL 1998

JANUARY TO JUNE  1998     —     Published     JULY 1998

JANUARY TO SEPT. 1998     —     Published   OCTOBER 1998

E.& O.E.